363.2 McClure, James,
MCC   1939—

     Spike Island

DATE			

DISCARD

SPIKE ISLAND

By the same author
The Steam Pig
The Caterpillar Cop
The Gooseberry Fool
Snake
Killers
Rogue Eagle
The Sunday Hangman

SPIKE ISLAND

PORTRAIT OF A BRITISH POLICE DIVISION

JAMES MC CLURE

Pantheon Books, New York

HO,806

Library of Congress Cataloging in Publication Data

McClure, James, 1939–
  Spike Island: portrait of a British police division.

    1. Liverpool—Police—Case studies. I. Title.
HV8196.L5M3   363.2′09427′53   80-7701
ISBN 0-394-42446-8

For Lorly and our three children,
James, Alistair and Kirsten,
who spent two years marooned in
a sea of recorded sound,
but kept faith
and the flag flying

CONTENTS

AUTHOR'S NOTE

Small liberties have to be taken with clock and calendar in a book of this kind, and some superficial detail has been altered in the interests of the public who became involved. All names have been either changed or omitted, except where they belong to sundry outsiders, such as public figures and novelists, who are mentioned in passing.

This means that I am unable to list here those police officers who deserve a special vote of thanks for assisting me in my research, giving so generously of their time and of their trust. Neither am I able to apologise to the few who did all this only for their tapes to prove impossible to transcribe, which left me to salvage vital fragments from my notes. Yet nobody who chanced to fall within these pages sought to be singled out, and it is equally true that everyone serving in 'A' Division at the time contributed something to this portrait, however indirectly. So perhaps it is most fitting that I should simply say a heartfelt 'thank you' to one and all.

Aside from those whose anonymity must be respected, I am particularly grateful to Duncan Campbell, Steve Morrison and Gail Broughall for the parts they played in the initial stages of this study, and to Messrs G. J. Fellows, E. F. Bazley and G. V. Thomas, without whose help I could not have undertaken it. Three Liverpudlians – Laurie Marlow, Mary Jones and Tony McIver – must be remembered for their splendid Northern hospitality, and I am greatly indebted to my agent and publishers – Pat Kavanagh, Lord Hardinge of Penshurst and André Schiffrin, and to Sonny Mehta – for their steadfast encouragement.

But above all, perhaps, I should express my gratitude to the person who made this book possible in the first place: Mr K. G. Oxford, Q.P.M., the Chief Constable of the Merseyside Police. It took a remarkable chief officer to allow a 'warts and all' study to be made of a division under his command (to use his own expression), and to accept the result as he has done. I can only hope that I have made the most of this singular opportunity so far as my ability will allow.

Oxford, 9 October 1979   J.McC.

PREFACE

James McClure is to be congratulated on producing a most readable book out of the day-to-day work of the police officers of 'A' Division. While he was with us there were none of the over-dramatised incidents so beloved by the media, which when supplemented by a diet of the exaggerated exploits of fictional policemen give a false public impression of the real nature of police duty – although drama in real life is ever just beneath the surface, as I refer to later. Nevertheless, by painstaking observation over long weary hours he has pieced together a tapestry which shows the police officer as he has never been shown before.

Above all else the book shows that policemen are human beings. It drives home the fact that the British Policeman is of the people, with strengths and weaknesses in equal proportion to the rest of the community. It also highlights the dedication of many police officers, striving towards the ideal of selfless public service in the face of many and varied difficulties.

The Police Service is one of the few groups where the art of story-telling has survived the advance of electronic entertainment. This force, and the Police Service, abounds in raconteurs who love nothing better than a fresh audience to regale with stories of their exploits, real or imagined. Several of the stories related in the book come within this category and need to be well salted before digestion; they are still good tales for all that – I first heard them many years ago and a long way from Merseyside.

The views expressed by police officers are their own and must not be seen as representing official policy. Like most people, policemen enjoy a grumble from time to time and will speak their feelings, as so many do in these pages. It must be remembered that what they say is not always representative of the Force as a whole and that many of their colleagues would be prepared, as I would be, to give them an argument over these views.

Liverpool is a rumbustious, vital city where the population are renowned for their independence, their ready wit and their intolerance of faceless authority. Crime and disorder are ever present and have always been so throughout the turbulent history of the city. There are reasons enough why this should be so but this is not the place for a discourse on causation. Suffice it to say that Liverpool is a tough city and that toughness is nowhere more apparent than in the city centre at night. This is where Mr McClure saw the police in action and he faithfully portrays the frequently hectic, often dangerous task of policing 'A' Division.

It must be remembered, however, that this is a concentrated problem. There are many parts of Liverpool and Merseyside in general where life goes on more placidly, where people are law-abiding and where crime is well below the national average. Merseyside frequently suffers at the hands of the media, which will seize upon isolated incidents on the shop floor, the football terraces and the streets and then give the impression that the whole area suffers from some fatal malaise. Nothing could be further from the truth. Merseyside, and Liverpool in particular, has a proud history of civilised achievement.

During 1978 there was a substantial decrease in crime on Merseyside, and since the Force was formed in 1974 the average annual rate of increase has been much lower than the national rate. Whether these figures indicate that the peak crime rate has been passed is still a matter for conjecture, but there is hope.

This improvement has not been brought about by mere chance. A great deal of effort has been expended by officers like those depicted by Mr McClure and a constant review of strategy has resulted in more effective deployment of resources. I am optimistic that these measures will continue to bring improvement and will encourage all those in local government, commerce, industry and many other walks of life who are striving to change the accepted image of Merseyside.

K. G. Oxford, Q.P.M.
Chief Constable,
Merseyside Police

10

INTRODUCTION

The force-area of the Merseyside Police covers some 250 square miles and is divided into eleven largely independent territories, each with its own headquarters, personnel, equipment and budget.

'A' Division, the smallest of these territories, is superimposed upon innermost Liverpool, and has been described by one of its officers as 'a sort of Band Aid stuck over where they ripped the heart out'. There you have it, many of his colleagues would say, in a nutshell: the shape, the background, and the kind of service we give, chiefly because of a lack of manpower and money. Every police division is, however, essentially an abstraction, and all would want to add their own qualifications for, to paraphrase another officer, a division is 'an island of the mind', and consequently open to any number of interpretations.

This much may be said without fear of contradiction: that the size and character of a division are determined by the nature of the place and the people over which it extends, and so, before 'A' Division itself is considered in any detail, these should both be reviewed briefly.

Liverpool lies aged beyond its years on the north-east bank of the great Mersey estuary. Its umbilical cord was a small stream which once ran down that long, uneven slope of Triassic sandstone to feed a pool at the water's edge, creating there a harbour for the first longboats to come knifing in out of the Irish Sea. There were Viking colonies on both sides of the estuary during the eighth century, and Liverpool may in fact derive its curious name from the Norse *hlithar-pollr*, 'the pool of the slopes'.

It grew slowly for almost a millennium. On the eve of its adolescence, Liverpool was still only a stripling port of some 5000 inhabitants and seventy-odd vessels, carrying on a modest trade in wool and fish with France, Spain and Ireland. Then, in 1700, the *Liverpool Merchant* set sail for West Africa to pick

11

up 200 slaves, a novel cargo destined for Barbados, and left behind it a wake that destroyed the flat calm of the pool for ever.

And as ripples of commercial excitement widened, work was begun on a wet dock which, when its floodgates were opened in 1709, signalled the start of nearly a century of swashbuckling untroubled delinquency. Liverpool shot up into a town of 77,000 people, took control of five-sixths of the African slave trade, invested in privateering, developed its import interests, and brought back rum, tobacco and sugar in its slave-holds at the end of each triangular voyage. It had made about 5000 of these voyages, and was transporting something like 49,000 slaves a year across the Atlantic, when the trade was abolished in 1807.

This was not the blow it might have been. Hard on the heels of abolition came the advent of the steamship and a sudden upsurge in trade with North America, and soon Liverpool had established itself as the greatest cotton-port in the world. This was, however, possibly its last piece of luck, for since then it seems to have been visited only by a succession of cruel ironies.

Continuing prosperity brought staggering increases in the number eager to have some share in it, and the sweet smell of success was rapidly all but overwhelmed by an appalling stench of poverty. Slums grew overnight like germ mould on a culture, clumping disease and misery around the town's fine centre, and spilling virulence into every street until nobody was immune to it. Then the potato famine in Ireland, a country once garrisoned by troopships sailing from Liverpool, brought an influx of more than 300,000 refugees in just the first six months of 1847 alone, and that is to say nothing of those who arrived before and after. And, although most of the refugees used the port simply as a stepping-stone, a vast number – greater than its total population in 1800 – stayed on. Such were the conditions of squalor that European visitors, long accustomed to thinking their slums were far worse than any in England, stood aghast and said they had never seen anything quite like it.

Liverpool, now under the guidance of a reformed council

12

after a succession of mayors engaged in the slave trade, responded with new-found idealism by appointing the first medical officer of health ever to take office in Great Britain. It followed this up with the nation's first borough engineer, district nurse, slum-clearance scheme and public wash-house; while in the private sector it introduced, again for the first time, societies for the prevention of cruelty to both children and animals. Neither was it easily daunted by the size of a task. In 1904, when it owned one in every seven registered ships at sea, a start was made on the most gigantic Anglican cathedral in England, and in 1934 it opened one of the world's largest road-tunnels, linking it to Birkenhead under the Merscy.

Yet the inner-city area of Liverpool is today one of the most wretched in Western Europe, just as it was more than a century ago. In 1977 its infant-mortality rate was at the average level for 1930, and its general living-standards were judged to be those of the forties. It had Europe's worst teenage-unemployment problem, and an over-all jobless figure of about 12 per cent, rising to an estimated 80 per cent in certain parts, including several in 'A' Division.

It was also said to have the country's worst law-and-order problem in a year when the number of recorded crimes on Merseyside went up by 11,246 or $10\frac{1}{2}$ per cent to 118,753 (of which the inner-city divisions' share was one third), crimes involving violence rose by 20.8 per cent, and the detection rate dropped by 4.6 per cent to 39.4 per cent. 'A' Division took the brunt of the increase in violence and disorder, and the Chief Constable warned that, if things did not improve considerably, the city centre might need 'an army of occupation' by 1980.

What went wrong does not fall within the compass of this book, except where police officers themselves choose to speculate and to reflect on how their work has been affected. It could be suggested, however, that the decline of this prodigious and prodigal city owes a great deal to its youthful vigour and best of intentions – virtues which, by their very nature, tend to be at odds with such notions as mature consideration. It might also help to review one or two factors that will be mentioned obliquely.

As a port of crucial importance to the Allies, Liverpool suffered heavily during the bombing raids in 1940 and 1941, which destroyed 6500 homes and severely damaged 125,000 others. This left it with huge areas of war rubble to clear and an immense housing problem that had to wait until 1952 before any major work could begin. But when Liverpool really got going in the sixties, with grand plans for the city centre and some idyllic rural notions, it could hardly be seen for brickdust. In what has been described by some as an act of 'self-inflicted civic vandalism', and by others as a compelling urge to make a completely fresh start, it bulldozed down 30,000 homes in less than a decade, and sent the occupants out to new towns like Kirkby and expanded old towns like Runcorn, promising not only grass but that it would indeed be greener – which, more often than not, it wasn't.

The city's population plunged from 850,000 to 560,000, losing many of its most enterprising people; giant wastelands appeared, laying bare 12,000 acres of the inner core, rate revenues dropped, and a planning blight was brought about by a scheme to build an inner motorway serving the docks. Flats built on bomb-sites in the northern half of 'A' Division were demolished to make way for this highway, and £8.5 million was spent on compensation and land purchases before, for want of any use for it, the motorway scheme was abandoned. By the seventies, the fourteen or so miles of docks were no more than a shadow of their former selves, largely because of mechanisation.

Liverpool, several times bitten but never shy, seems determined to proceed more cautiously into the eighties, well aware that its straitened circumstances allow it little leeway. Whenever in need of a crumb of comfort, however, it can always point to the fine job it made of modernising the city's main shopping-area. This lies not far from where the pool, long since filled in and tucked away as neat as a navel, once reflected the return of the first slave-ship.

The people of Liverpool tend to regard themselves as a race apart. This is fairly true of all Northerners, and in his engross-

14

ing work *The North Country* (1967) Graham Turner makes this arresting point: 'The industrial north is a relatively new society . . . just about as old, in fact, as the United States.' In such a context, Liverpudlians are probably right to feel unique, just as New Yorkers believe they're unique, and for much the same reasons.

Although other Northern cities have institutions and streets that bear foreign-sounding names to support a claim to cosmopolitan beginnings, none had the variety of nationalities that a boom-port would attract – including Spaniards and Egyptians – and neither did their immigrants arrive as early. The black population of Liverpool, for instance, which started to become properly established after the turn of the century, actually dates back to 1780. Then again, because of being a major port, Liverpool has also been constantly enriched by new words and ideas its seafarers have brought back from around the world. 'Scouse', the name given to the Liverpudlian dialect, is itself of foreign origin, having started off as *labskaus*, the Norwegian for a simple and inexpensive stew.

Not that most Liverpudlians need utter a word to be instantly identified. Their speech is very fast, rather cold-in-the-nose, and they sometimes drop their aitches although, hunlike some, they never use them where they do not belong. In fact, a chest consultant at the Liverpool Royal Infirmary, Dr Colin Ogilvie, said in 1977: 'The Liverpool accent reflects the constant nasal and bronchial catarrh which people here take for granted.' Bearing in mind what those slave-ships brought back with them, it could be another of those cruel ironies that one in four Liverpudlians dies of disease associated with smoking, that their lung-cancer rate is twice the national average, and that they have an enormous alcoholism problem.

The latter undoubtedly has something to do with another major characteristic: an astonishing propensity for gratuitous violence. 'I was appalled by the amount and the extent of it when I first came to work on Merseyside over two years ago,' the Chief Constable, Mr K. G. Oxford, formerly of the Metropolitan Police, said in the *Liverpool Daily Post* on 18 April 1977. 'Mythology has it – and I exclude nobody from this –

15

that the area is tough. It has the unfortunate effect that people feel they must react to this and *be* tough.' So perhaps this is why the cheeky Cockney sparrow has been able to over-shadow a people whose wit, friendliness toward strangers, and sheer vitality could not be matched anywhere – provided the time and the place are right, which seems a great pity.

Yet this evil streak, as some down-to-earth people call it, when they tire of apologetics in the face of dreadful injuries in-flicted far in excess of any need, may also have its positive side in the wickedly sharp sense of humour that Liverpudlians possess. 'If you live in Liverpool,' some Scouser once said, 'then you must either laugh yourself sick or burst into tears' – and the list of top-ranking comedians it has produced is pro-hibitively long. Even longer, though, is the list of those whose gifts will never be discovered, but Tom O'Connor, who specialises in indigenous material, acts as their comic mediator on television and in cabaret to brilliant effect:

Well, there's three of 'em, comin' 'ome in this car that they have found. Bombin' along the street, knocked a bobby off his bike. The bobby shouted after the driver, 'Didn't yer see me?' He says, 'I knocked yer down, didn't I?'

'A' Division to a T, according to the bobbies who delight in this parable. Yet another vehicle taken and driven away with-out the owner's consent, yet another attack on a police officer, and just the sort of remark one would expect from a typical Liverpool 'buck', with his breathtaking contempt for authority. And they usually retell it with flair because, if there is one sweeping generalisation to be made about these police officers, then it is the fact that most of them are accomplished mimics with a sharp ear for nuance.

Their persistent use of the word 'buck' may in fact convey at a stroke something distinctive about their own attitudes. Like 'bridewell', the term they use for what in most other forces would be a charge office and cells, and which is derived from St Bride's Well, a house of correction in nineteenth-century London, 'buck' is another abbreviated legacy from the past. An imported one, too, for although Ireland still has its dashing

16

young 'buckos' the word has almost disappeared from every-day use in Liverpool. There is a curious ambivalence about it, for it can convey, depending upon circumstances, everything from utter loathing to avuncular indulgence, with a hint of pride by association. 'Bucks' are, the implication seems to be, something special.

Just as the officers of 'A' Division tend to see themselves as somewhat out of the ordinary, chiefly because their problems are unparalleled elsewhere in the force area.

'It only consists of 1417 acres,' says a very senior officer, 'so if you relate that to the size of the others it's a small little patch. But, of course, it's the busiest by far, having the main shopping, commercial and banking centres. And although the residential population is only 22,500, which is buttons really, on a weekday afternoon, with people working, shopping and being entertained, you've got at least a quarter of a million here.

'In the evening, most of these people go home out of the city – but a lot of them come back later on because, in this very small division, we've got about 500 licensed premises. By licensed premises, I mean public houses, restaurants and clubs. In fact, "A" Division alone has 119 clubs, and seventy-one of them have "special hours" certificates. These allow them to sell drink until 2 a.m., with half an hour's drinking-up time. So at 2.30 a.m. you get the contents of some seventy-one clubs – that's several thousand people – disgorging into the city centre to "pinch our cars and bust our windows and break into our shops!" which is, of course, what my fellas and girls are out there for.'

'A' Division forms an oblong roughly two miles across by a mile and a half deep, divided again down the middle into two crude squares known as the North and South sub-divisions. It is a shape easily pictured if this open book is taken to repre-sent the whole area, and these opposing pages the two 'subs', with the bottom of a bookmark protruding slightly from the foot of the left-hand page, to take in the Pier Head at the centre crease.

Each sub-division is further divided into two 'sections' – the

17

upper and lower half of each page – and each section into five or six 'foot beats', making a total of twenty-one beats in all. These beats average out at 67.5 acres each, but their actual sizes vary enormously, depending on the type of district.

The division has five blue lamps, as it were. There is a police station in St Anne Street in the top half of the North Sub-division, where it occupies part of the divisional head-quarters building, and another in the South Sub-division at Copperas Hill. Each sub-division also has an enquiry office – North's at the Pier Head, South's at force headquarters in Hope Street – and then there is the Main Bridewell, or central lock-up, off Dale Street.

The divisional commander is a chief superintendent, and he has four superintendents – sharing the same twenty-four-hour responsibility – to assist him. Two are part of the divisional command; one is his deputy, and the other, a detective super-intendent, is also responsible to the detective chief superinten-dent in charge of the force's Criminal Investigation Department. The two remaining superintendents act as sub-divisional commanders, each with a chief inspector (the next rank down) as his deputy. One is based at St Anne Street and the other at Copperas Hill.

Chief inspectors and above are administrators in the main, so most of them wear civilian clothes in the ordinary course of events, and keep roughly to a nine-to-five day, with some split shifts and special supervisory duties. Uniformed inspectors, on the other hand, are very much in the public eye, being directly in charge of the three-shift system worked by the 'beat bobbies', and of the four mobile patrols, popularly known as panda cars. Also in their charge are the Day and Evening Patrol sections, which cover fourteen beats, chiefly along main roads and in troublesome areas. Days and EPs operate from 10 a.m. to 6 p.m., and from 6 p.m. until 2 a.m., with frequent overtime until about 4 a.m. on account of disorder associated with clubs.

Further assistance is given by the Traffic Department, which superimposes its own patrols and has its own radio channel (the department's 'jam butty' cars are distinguished by the red

18

stripe across their sides, and its officers by the white covers on their caps), and by the Dog Section, which works on much the same basis. Neither has the divisional commander any direct responsibility for the patrols from the Operational Support Division (OSD), which covers the city centre on a semi-permanent basis at his invitation.

To return to 'A' Division's uniformed branch, some of its officers work out of uniform in the Car Squad and in the Plain Clothes Section – or 'vice squad' – on shifts arranged to meet the demands of these more specialised duties.

Detectives, as distinct from Plain Clothes officers, belong to the CID branch, which is about one sixth the size of the uniformed establishment. It follows much the same organisational pattern; the detective superintendent has a detective chief inspector as his deputy, and two detective inspectors have sub-divisional commands. The sub-divisions differ somewhat, however, in that the 'North Sub CID' crosses over into the South Sub-division to take in much of its shopping and entertainment area.

As for the total strength of 'A' Division during the period covered by this book, it stood at 445 police officers (34 below establishment), 41 traffic wardens, and 60 or so civilians, including typists, clerks, porters, cleaners and canteen workers.

Those are the dry bones of the matter. This veteran officer is very much his own man, and speaks rather softly.

I've always had this idea that 'A' Division headquarters is a sort of defensive redoubt in the middle of an island. (*Smiles*) Policemen tend to think of their division as an island, you know. It exists first and foremost as a territorial entity, and it's administered like one, inside this precise physical perimeter. So most of its bobbies never cross over into a neighbouring division, or take themselves further afield, unless they've got some special reason. Nor are they expected, in the ordinary hurly-burly, to even think much beyond this invisible shoreline.

Oh, it's a very territorial thing, a division; very insular. Strenuous efforts are made through force headquarters to get uniform policies, but you'll find administrative differences and

19

operational differences from one division to another – it's as bad as going to another force at times. Like Christianity, the Merseyside Police General Manual of Instructions lies like a veneer over the more primitive tribal customs of different divisions. It's partly historical, especially here in Merseyside where you used to have the old borough forces before amalgamation.

And there's something else about divisions as a whole. Things get accentuated in bobbies' minds to the point where they think the people in their division are unique – *uniquely bad*, quite often! Or take what they mean by a 'woolly back' here. That means a county bobby, but the implication is he's had a soft life; it doesn't matter if he's fought for five years on the outskirts of Manchester or Kirkby, he's still a woolly back. They wear these divisional letters like battle honours.

But the point is they tend to identify the islanders, if you like, as being separate – and I mean separate! – to the people who live in other divisions. And they attribute to them all sorts of qualities and defects, until they get in this semi-boasting situation where they say, 'All the hayseeds are out in "F" Division and the county bobbies are in "J" Division.' *They* don't have to put up with what *we* have to put up with, y'know! It's as if as soon as you step over the line on the boundary street the actual race of people changes.

This tendency is probably stronger here in 'A' Division than in most others, because so few of the bobbies are islanders themselves – hardly a handful actually reside here. They come from all round, miles away some of them, and then there are the ones who live over the water, y'know, on the Wirral. I suppose 'A' Division's an off-shore island to them! Although they'd most of them use the tunnel and come out the Mousehole over there. That's a thought, all the same: the ferry. Come across from Birkenhead on that, and you could be going to land on an island really. There's even a bit of 'A' Division jutting out through the docks like a sort of jetty to the Pier Head. You could get off, y'know, walk up through the city centre, up to St Anne Street, do your eight hours and go home again, without ever setting foot outside the North Sub, never mind anything else.

And you can imagine a young bobby doing this, one who's new to the job, and letting his imagination roam a bit; seeing this island drawn on one of those old charts, if you like, with spouting whales and kiddies with wind and that. To his left, the North Sub, and it's a bit of a desert island that side. All those cliff-

20

dwellers in the high-rise flats; the bucks running wild and a few buckesses too; all the old warehouses stuffed with copper and whisky like sort of Ben Gunn's caves, mostly empty now, along the dock road; and above it all, the Great Pyramid of Tate & Lyle's sugar refinery. Then straight in front of him, the market place: all that glitters, merchants and money-lenders, beggars and meths-drinkers lying about legless! Sort of fanning out behind the Royal Liver building. Then, to his right, the South Sub: the jungle noises and even more jungle behaviour of club-land; then yellow-people country, Chinatown; then, up in the right-hand top corner, black-people country, Upper Parliament Street, a bit of Liverpool 8 – not forgetting 'Paddy's Wigwam', of course, the Catholic cathedral at one end of Hope Street. Then, if he's coming on Nights, he'll probably see five sort of stockades with campfires burning; places he can get in out of the cold and be safe from a hiding for a while, or being asked how long the next train to Portsmouth takes.

Only this wouldn't happen in true life, because a new recruit gets posted to one sub or the other, the desert or the tourists' side, and doesn't get to know much about what lies on the other side of the Great Divide, if you like – not to begin with, anyway. He'd – or she'd – just have to put 'unexplored' on their maps and leave the edges on that side a bit smudgy and ragged. It's different for the old bobbies who have spent most of their lives here, and can remember when it was Rose Hill police station and not St Anne Street. In fact they'd tell you that in those days the people round here – some of them probably still do – used to call the area Spike Island.

21

PART ONE: OUTLINES

I

The game is on, down in the city centre. It's all a game, police officers often say with a shrug, a bloody great game, and that's all there is to it. But this particular game, played right in among its spectators on a bright bustling Saturday morning, is at least one of the less harmful, and today will see the home side spring a nasty surprise on the visitors in Adidas running-shoes.

These itinerants form a small team of street hawkers, led by a strapping young man in blue denims and a pretty plastic pinafore – just one of a dozen or so that he has for sale at give-away prices. His colleagues, who share an equal lack of self-consciousness, include a fat man with sagging trousers, selling belts from a shiny three-legged stand, and a thin un-shaven man, selling Wilkinson's Sword razor blades. The others are as nondescript as the crockery, soft goods and ornaments which fill their cheap suitcases, while even more unremarkable are those who simply keep watch.

The vigilance of these lookouts is twofold. They have to report any encroachment on the Church Street pedestrian precinct by hawkers not belonging to their team, so that these interlopers can be instantly warned off by the minder. More importantly, however, they have to spot approaching police officers in time for everything to be packed away before a caution can be given or, if cautioned already, an arrest is made on a charge of wilfully, and without reasonable excuse, ob-structing the free passage of the highway. They are assisted in their task by virtue of the fact that the British police helmet was partly designed, for rather different reasons, to be seen above the densest crowd. With a minimum height requirement of 5 feet 8 inches for male officers in the Mersey-side Police – which means the shortest man is no shorter than the average Englishman – this brings them all up to at least 6 feet, and many are very much taller than that.

A helmet, no more than a distant black blob with a sparkle in its centre, appears at the top end of Church Street. In under

25

thirty seconds, not a street hawker as such can be seen – apart from an elderly woman selling flowers in a side street, but she belongs to a tradition that has granted her, in the words of one senior officer, a sort of common-law right to be there. This flower seller displays her wares on a collection of upturned milk-crates; the very same kind of plastic crates that nearly all the other hawkers carry about with them, as though making a claim to similar respectability. Even the man with the razor blades, who can slip his entire stock into his pockets, has a crate at his feet as he lounges, in all innocence, watching the helmet grow nearer.

Then the helmet moves left and enters one of the big stores a good hundred yards away. A couple of minutes pass before out come the suitcases again, and the belt man leaves an alleyway to continue a brisk business, setting up shop with all the aplomb of a first violin setting up his music-stand. The minder emerges apronless with something new to sell, which he carries in two heavy cardboard boxes. He chooses a new pitch, farther out in the mainstream of shoppers, and begins to bark the virtues of a photograph album that requires no glue or gummy corners, while keeping his own sharp watch for the Law. Being a tall man himself, he is able to see easily over the heads, hats and cloth caps bobbing about him.

Church Street, a wide thoroughfare paved from one side to the other, and set about with benches, trees and raised flowerbeds, reverts to normal for about the twentieth time since the start of the morning. Passers-by, many with muted signs of poverty, typified by weary mothers wearing raincoats on a warm day to half-hide a shabby dress, begin to gather around the hawkers, damming the flow past the windows of the big stores. Swirls appear in the cross-currents set up, as others hurry around people who trouble them in some way. An old man with a tobacco-tin in one hand, who begins to sing very loudly but, it would seem, to no one there, is allowed his private stretch of pavement. Two large derelicts, arguing over a bottle of cider, clear enough space to swing a tiger in, and a black child, weeping bitterly, walks blind without bumping into anyone. Some pause, however, for a sweet-faced girl in

26

peasant clothing, who is handing out leaflets that call for 'active opposition to attacks on women's lives', and for equal pay for equal work. One man who stops, possibly out of old-fashioned courtesy, looks a trifle sheepish as he reads the invitation to join the Women's Action Group any Thursday night; realising, perhaps, his support may not have been sought after all, but that, in turn, the girl had just been too polite to say so. A sandwich-board evangelist divides a downward rush of football supporters, his text warning of terrible things to come, and a cocky kid in team colours calls out: 'Oh aye, got yer lot panickin', 'ave we, pop ?'

Then it happens. The album seller is caught in the act by a sweet-faced girl, only a little over the minimum height requirement of 5 feet 4 inches for a female officer in the Merseyside Police, who has appeared suddenly in full uniform out of the press around him. For an instant, he stands like a man torpedoed, then attempts to pack away his wares. But she reaches out to lay a hand on his arm – the gesture necessary to make an arrest a fact – and the protests begin, with him towering over her.

The rest of the team, having ditched their own goods, edge in to see what the outcome will be, plainly amused by this turn of events. The belt specialist leans against the brick surround of a nearby raised flowerbed, and says, 'Don't know what 'e's resistin' for; she's a right little cracker, that one!' 'Aye, there's quite a few these days,' concurs his companion, empirically aware, presumably, that women now accounted for about a quarter of the force's intake of recruits, many being attracted by equal pay for equal work and the promise of no discrimination. 'But will 'e take it from a lass, with every boogger starin' ?' And a lot of people are staring, enjoying the conflict and the chance to eye a trim official figure without compromise. Faces, as distant as the flower seller and the leafleteer beside her, have turned and are showing a lively interest. A few smiles break out.

Abruptly, the confrontation ends. The album seller, who has picked up one of his boxes, throws it up into the air without warning, and then takes to his heels. The constable jumps

27

back, snatches off her cap and sprints after him, going as fast as her skirt will allow her. Nobody in his path moves to impede his flight, neither does anyone join in the chase, as it swings past the flower seller and disappears down the side street. 'Bloody hell!' says the belt man, laughing. His companion grunts, 'I said it, didn't I? But 'e was daft to. Jesus, look at the busies!' Police officers are appearing from nowhere, and vanishing behind the row of stores.

A uniformed inspector and his sergeant, carrying the long polished sticks issued to their ranks and above, and which lend them an air of sauntering elegance, arrive on the scene to have a quiet word with the hawkers. One thing is obvious: business is going to be suspended for quite some time, perhaps even into the afternoon, and the belt man is plainly no longer lost in awed admiration. The constable returns breathless and trying not to show it, but the personal radio clipped to her lapel heaves like a trawler. 'I think he went in the back of C. & A.'s, sir,' she reports to the inspector. 'They sometimes—'

'Never mind, lass,' he interrupts kindly. 'He'll come again.'

That, too, was part of the game; this one and every other.

2

Church Street is a good example of the sort of area given extra cover by the Days and EPs (Day and Evening Patrol sections). These are generally made up of the division's more experienced officers, although this, in the late seventies, can now mean virtually anyone, including a recruit near the end of his or her two-year probationary period. Days and EPs is the only 'status' posting available to the constable who wants to remain in uniform and walking a beat, rather than to specialise in any way, even as a driver. Many deny that it has, in fact, any status – except in a probationer's eyes, perhaps – and spend their time on Days and EPs waiting for something else to suggest itself. Others, like this constable in his mid-twenties, with a misleadingly dour air about him, and a strong Lancastrian accent, can't be bothered with such talk.

28

I try not to think of 'them' at all, the ones we're supposed to be up against. They're just *there*. I don't feel I'm up against a villain, y'know. Crime's one of the things of society which is going to happen whether I lock up or not. I lock 'em up, but I get no enjoyment out of it. I get more enjoyment out of speakin' to old women on the street.

I like helping people, and possibly being a bobby is the best way you can do it and remain anonymous at the same time. You're not a social worker who says, 'And *we* did this!' My job is lockin' people up, so I don't have to say, 'Well, just look at this! Isn't it great?' I think it's me nature; I love helping people, watchin' them – studyin' 'em really, I suppose. And I suppose some of them like studying me.

It's amazing what you see 'em do. Things they'd never admit to in a million years! And that's apart from the sex aspect – y'know, other men's wives in different cars, eyes straight forward and you've not seen a bloody thing. Take a certain councillor in this city. He's walkin' down Church Street and it's election time and somebody's stuck a Tory poster up. He looks all about him, there's nobody in the street – bar me, actually, who's up in one of the archways where I get a better view – and he gives it the two fingers. That's *fantastic*, y'know! You wouldn't believe it – man of intelligence. Then I compared m'self and I thought: Well, it's one of those things you fancy doing. You walk past a thing you hate and (*two-finger gesture*)!

You get a man and a woman together, and ninety per cent of the time he's tryin' to please her – she's never tryin' to please him. What I like is you get a lot of women who are definitely boss – y'know the bosses' type – and they're lost. They come up to ask you a question, and some *silly* bloody question, and the husband's standing there in the background going, with his face, 'It's not me, officer, it's not me!' (*Laughs*) You get this quite a lot.

It's basically you can be nosy. A lot of people won't admit this, but you can be nosy without being called nosy. It's yer job to be. Apart from the rubbish pay and rubbish conditions, I enjoy it. It offers – it's very hard to explain – the unusual? You were the man at the scene, you were there, everybody's lookin' at you.

That's one thing about the uniform, it gives you confidence. You tend to notice a bird and think: Oh, that's beautiful! I'd never have done this in plain clothes, I don't think, but once I followed her for about two hundred yards, three hundred, and eventually I stopped her. 'Hi!' – y'know. And I'm engaged to

29

her at the present time. Now, if I hadn't done that in uniform, she's probably have said, 'On yer bike!' There's respectability in uniform, but mainly it's the extra confidence. You can deal with a fight single-handed, whereas, out of uniform, you'd be thinking, well, this is *me*, y'know!

I suppose I'm really the old-fashioned bobby. I tend to stop and chat to people, and I've had quite a lot of information from them. Oh aye, I know a lot of people down on my beat; a hell of a lot. It's the only way of workin' the job. You're also the happier kind of bobby, because you're always one of them, the people. Whether they act as commoner or high class, people tend to look on you as an equal in many respects. You get the fellow in the Rolls-Royce: 'Oh, I *am* sorry, officer, I didn't mean to do that. . . .' You also get the fella in the clapped-out Cortina: 'OK officer, you're one of us, son!' It's amazing how equal you become, and you're just accepted. Of course, there are always the ones who're too good for you; the fella who's rich, who's made it in the world, but generally a person who had no money as a kid. You can understand it.

In the police force itself, there's a hell of a lot of different classes. I mean I'm the lowest of the low, and not because I'm a constable. It's because I'm not flash, because I'm not trying for the CID. I couldn't care less about the CID. Others try and look down on yer, and think: Christ Almighty, he must be thick, y'know.

3

The helmet has emerged again from the big store up at the top end of the pedestrian precinct. A teenaged boy, his ashen face flushed in blotches, is being escorted to a van waiting at the kerb to take him to St Anne Street police station. The back of the van is difficult to open, and the constable on the foot-wide padded seat beside him has to hold on to the doors to ensure they stay closed. The van, a Ford transit model, has done more than 125,000 miles and, like most of the division's small fleet of vehicles, is badly in need of replacement.

The city centre is so compact that within barely two minutes, heading north past Lime Street station, the van reaches a set of traffic lights on the edge of the fan-shaped

30

entertainment and commercial area. This is where the council flats begin, and now, high on a desolate slope, cut off from its surroundings by wide carriageways, wasteland and a glittering nestle of parked cars, the police station itself comes into view. Some street signs still stand in the long grass and the weeds and the rubble below it, and a few small cobbled roads, used as short-cuts into the one-way system, skirt a mound which was part of the aborted inner-ring motorway. The sky is blue and huge, but somehow this only compounds a feeling of arid emptiness.

'A' Division headquarters, which incorporates St Anne Street police station, mainly on its first two floors, is a grey brick of a building banded by glass. There is a POLICE sign the length of a bus above its main entrance – anything smaller would be difficult to make out from the nearest thoroughfare – and its front steps lead down to a rough pathway going nowhere in particular, other than towards the improvised car-park. Many people, in fact, aren't aware that this is the main entrance, and tend to use the back way instead, coming straight off St Anne Street into a narrow yard crowded with vehicles.

The van comes to a stop there, in a walled bay outside the blank door to the bridewell.

The buzzer makes a sound like an electric hair-clipper pressed against the bone behind one's ear. This is the only half-way unpleasant feature of an area which, in its pastel colours, rubber-tile flooring, utility furniture and specialised accommodation, somewhat resembles the casualty department of a small hospital.

The bridewell sergeant and his assistant, a constable styled the bridewell patrol or 'BP', leave the large office and its general-enquiries window to go into the room behind it. Here the sergeant, a lean reserved man nearing forty, stops behind a high counter and waits for the BP to open the far door. This is always an instant of heightened interest, but the teenaged boy is just another knot in an endless string.

'Any chance of a cuppa?' asks the van driver.

'We've got one male for the Main,' the sergeant reminds

31

him, smoothing out a Form 3 charge sheet as big as a blotter. 'Give you till ten past, all right?'

'Ta, boss.'

The BP and the van driver retire into the medical room behind the counter, where the kettle and teapot are kept. The sergeant beckons and the constable steps forward with his prisoner to make the charge.

'I've just arrested this lad for theft. The circumstances are that at eleven-thirty I went to Cuthbert's store, Church Street, where I saw the witness Perrett. He told me that at ten forty-five he had been on duty in his employer's store and he saw this boy standing in the record department, select an LP from the stand, put it in this carrier bag and leave the department through a pay-point, making no attempt to pay for it. He went down the escalator to the ground floor, where he was stopped and escorted back to the office. I asked him if he'd heard and understood what was being said, and he said, "Yes." I said, "Have you any explanation?" And he said, "No." I told him he was being arrested for theft, cautioned him, and brought him here.'

The sergeant turns his attention to the boy, who is flicking at the zip tag on his old windcheater. 'You heard and understood what's been said? Is that correct?'

'Yes, sir.'

'Let's see the bag. A pair of new jeans and a new jersey—'

'He's paid for those,' says the constable, handing over a typewritten sheet of paper.

'This is the statement of the store detective?'

'Yuh.'

The sergeant reads it through, noting the title of the record; for the sake of expediency, goods in shoplifting cases are nowadays retained by the retailer – putting an end to the horror stories told by bridewell staff faced with a pile of perishables and no means of refrigerating them.

'*Close to the Edge*, eh? What kind of music is that?'

The boy shrugs. 'I 'eard 'em once.'

'Not worth getting arrested for, is it?'

'Pardon?'

32

Implicitly, the sergeant has now accepted the charge, so he clicks his regulation black ballpen and prepares to write. 'What's your full name?'

'Richard John Swithin.'

'What's your address, Richard?'

'Kirkby.'

'What street?'

The list of particulars includes the boy's form at school, his mother's maiden name and his place and date of birth. Some prisoners give false names but neglect to change their birthdays, which often allows the routine check with Mercro – the Merseyside Criminal Records Office – to reveal any deception on the part of a known offender.

'Just put all your property on the counter, Richard. Have you got a receipt for these?'

'That's for the jumper; that's for the jeans.'

The sergeant examines the receipts and looks over the scatter of bus tickets, chewing-gum wrappers and pound notes placed on a fat paperback. 'Have you put something back in your pocket there?'

'It's just a bit of chewy.'

'You keep it out here until you're finished.' The sergeant goes round and searches him – a job normally done by the BP – and adds a ballpen to the other items. 'Got a medallion around your neck?'

'No.'

'And your mother's given you this money, has she?'

'That's for a jumper for school, and that's for fruit.'

As the sergeant returns behind the counter he notices the boy place an elbow on the edge of it, then quickly straighten up. 'Been in trouble before, Richard?' Prisoners are never permitted to lean on a charge-office counter, for it shows disrespect.

'I got released for disorderly. Bound over, see? They dropped the case.'

'You've not been in trouble for anything else?'

'No, the record was me first.'

Now the money has to be carefully counted and placed,

33

together with the rest of the boy's possessions, in a sealed envelope. 'Where do you buy this from?' the sergeant asks, as he adds the paperback to a list on the charge sheet which the prisoner will endorse.

'I bought it last week from Lewis's. I've got three of 'is books; I was readin' it on the way down.'

'Forty-three, sixty, ninety – four pound ninety pence. Sign here, Richard. You'll get it back when you leave.' The formalities are over for the present, as a juvenile cannot be charged unless he has a parent or guardian with him. 'What's the story about?'

'It's a war story,' the boy replies with enthusiasm, then looks wary. 'I can name all the characters in the story so far, if you happen to 'ave read it, y'know. I've got me place in the book.'

The sergeant smiles very slightly; his quiet impersonal tone never varies, probably making this sort of misunderstanding occur quite often. 'All right, Richard, come with me and sit here till your dad comes.'

The juvenile detention room is only a step or two behind the counter, next to the medical room, and has a large pane of glass in its door so that frequent checks can be made on its occupants. For once on a Saturday morning, the room, with its table, ash-tray, two chairs and big barred window, is empty.

'One male, yer say, boss?' enquires the van driver, adjusting his flat cap.

The sergeant points to the 'Remarks' section on the prisoner's Form 3: *A runner*. 'He's been picked up on warrant for armed robbery in Wales. Want a con to go with you?' Nobody is ever called a PC in the Merseyside Police, which can sound strange at first, particularly as 'con' has such different associations for most people.

'Could be handy. Ta.'

'Got cuffs?'

The driver nods and waits while the sergeant goes alone down the short passageway into the cell wing, to return with a rangy wild-looking youth loping behind him. The prisoner is evidently amused by being handcuffed, as though it represents official recognition of the fact he's no ordinary villain –

34

which, in a sense, is right enough, for prisoners on Merseyside are very seldom manacled.

'Any good at running?' the BP asks the probationer he has found to act as escort down to the Main Bridewell, or central lock-up, in the city.

'Sorry?'

Everyone has a laugh, and the van party is let out into the yard. The sergeant glances in at the shoplifter, and sees him leaning back in a chair, with his hands around his throat, and his face suffused with blood. He taps on the glass, making the boy start and look round.

'Looks like we've got one here with suicidal tendencies,' he murmurs to the BP. 'Any of that tea left?'

A bridewell sergeant can also refuse a charge, which may happen around half a dozen times a month. This does not mean, however, that the arrest was necessarily unlawful, or that no prosecution will follow. Here another bridewell sergeant, a droll well-read former wages clerk in his thirties, gives some idea of this aspect of his work.

A lot of people come to the counter and they clam up, refuse to say anything – apart from wanting to see a solicitor and all that. I must admit I don't do it for everyone, but with those I think it's worth bothering with I'll turn round and explain to them it hasn't reached the final stage yet.

A young bloke gets brought in here from Mothercare, and with him were two toddlers, one in a push-chair. His wife was in hospital having their third, and was due out on the Monday – this is Saturday afternoon – and he's gone into Mothercare to get a new mattress for the cot, plus some other bits and pieces. By the way, this was before, when Lord Street and Church Street were just ordinary roads.

He'd just been looking at something on the shelves – he had the one in the push-chair outside, and the other one just standing by him – when a van goes past the doorway, and the youngster with him is away. He had this mattress tucked under one arm, so he just ran out, stopped his toddler at the edge of the pavement, and attached him to the push-chair. He says, 'Stay there a minute' – and walks back into the shop to get lifted for

35

shoplifting. He'd gone out past the till and, as far as the store detective was concerned, that was it.

So when he came in here with his kiddies and told me this story there was no doubt in my mind he was telling me the truth. I refused the charge and he went on his way.

The thing is, you see, the advent of the store detective. A lot of firms don't have their own, but use these outside security firms and, I suppose, they measure things on results. And, of course, they don't have the discretion to exercise the way we do. Oh aye, people have been surprised when they realise we're still human.

4

As a token of very basic humanity, the 3 is missing from the third-floor button inside the lift at St Anne Street. It doesn't take a detective to figure out why. The short answer is wear and tear. Or, just press the button, and within a matter of seconds, the lift door will open at the level given over entirely to canteens, bars and recreation areas.

The probationer, back from his trip down to the Main Bridewell, is taking his refreshments, as they are officially termed, in the large canteen for sergeants and constables; in common parlance, he's having his scoff – one of those Afrikaans words brought back from the South African war. Cheese salad and chips, jam tart and custard, and a pint of milk in a carton.

He is joined by another recruit and her 'tutor con', or mentor for the first month on the streets. Three other officers, friends of the tutor con on the South Sub-division, where no meals are provided, also come across with their trays. And inevitably, almost, the conversation becomes another lament about the Land-Rovers once used in the city centre, but now rusticated to the outer divisions on account of their 'aggressive' image. The bucks had called them 'battle taxis', and the bobbies just 'jeeps'.

'I mean, that was the point, wasn't it?' mutters a big fella, buttering his roll. 'Non-aggressive policing? The guy who thought that one up has obviously, never in his life, seen the

36

town centre of Liverpool on a Saturday night. We have to be aggressive to a certain extent – it's the only way we can deal with the situation. And we have to be *more* aggressive now, much more.'

His contemporaries murmur agreement.

'There's a certain pub in Casey Street – you'll get to know it – where, without fail, every Friday and Saturday night there's a large-scale disturbance. We used to expect it between ten to half-ten, and all the jeeps in the division used to just drive down there and come in either end of the street. By the time they met in the middle! Well, there wasn't a bastid left in the street, because they didn't like the jeeps. They seemed to impart an aura of fear – of terror! – because they didn't know how many big hairy bobbies were in the back of it. But last time I was there four pandas arrived, and they all kept fightin' – they ignored us completely. See what I mean? When we had the jeeps, their presence was quite sufficient.'

A slightly built constable, probably around twenty-three, looks up. 'We were in this mobile only two days old – a brand-spanking-new police car – when there's this report of a disturbance at this pub over on the South Sub. We parked the car round the back and walked round the front. As I walked through the door, there were bottles flyin' – oh, bottles, tables, chairs, the lot! I turned round to Bob and said, "*No* way. We're not goin' in here." We walked out into the street and got on the radio: "Con requires assistance, large-scale disturbance, the Green Turtle." Y'know, "Mayday!" The wireless operator was shoutin' for assistance, and no one was comin'.'

'We were comin' from the south dock road!' chips in the big fella.

'Aye, that was the nearest. In the end, I said, "Get 'E' Division and 'B' Division; we need help badly." And, next thing, we hear a bangin' noise from round the back of the pub, and this is while we're waiting for assistance to come. So we both run round the back of the pub, and there's this buck wellying shite out of the wings of the car! We grab hold of him.'

The big fella says: 'This is when I arrive.'

37

'Bob's got hold of him around the waist, and I've got—'

'I turned up at the front.'

'He turned up at the wrong place, y'see! Thought Bob and me were in the pub gettin' murdered!'

'Yes,' says his would-be rescuer, 'so we all piled in the pub. "In 'ere, lads!" And we're all in the pub fightin', lookin' for the bodies!'

'Meanwhile, there's a small row of double-decker houses round the back of the pub, and these families saw us with this lad.'

Someone groans in anticipation.

'They set on us. Well, there was me, the buck and then Bob, and we were hangin' on for grim death. I was on the—'

'Ten or twelve bobbies in the pub fightin'! We didn't know where they fokkin' were!'

'And I was on me wireless, screamin' for help, and there was this dozen families on top of us. A hand come over from nowhere, grabbed me wireless out of me hand and it just went *phhhhhhit!* Oh, over the top somewhere.'

'Hell,' says the probationer, his mouth too full to say more.

'The next thing this dog van turns up. But, just before that, Bob and I were lookin' at each other, and all me past years were flashin' in front of me eyes – I thought I'd 'ad it!'

'Aye.'

'Eventually, when we got back to the station, our uniforms were in ribbons.'

'In *ribbons*,' the big fella repeats with special emphasis.

5

Clothes brushes large enough to scrub a deck are scattered all over St Anne Street police station. Just as a well-groomed cat may absently give its coat a couple of licks, the brushes are not infrequently used on almost immaculate uniforms. One 'A' Division inspector, who is writing an MSc thesis on patrol abandonment – or the tendency to quit street policing for a speciality as quickly as possible – suggests that this could be a

38

response to the 'tainting', both physical and mental, to which a police officer is exposed during an eight-hour shift. A sergeant nearing his retirement is of the opinion: 'Smartness is essential to help you do your job; it gives members of the public something to respect right from the start, and it, well, sets you apart like from the scruffs.' In a different context altogether, while describing what it was like to have grown up in 'buck territory', this young officer touches on much the same topic.

You either ran or you fought. I was a good runner, whereas me father was a boxer and didn't like me runnin' – thought I was a bit of a coward, y'know. But I was a *pretty* coward! (*Laughs*) Me face wasn't marked. Anyway, when I put the uniform on as cadet, he instilled it into me – and so did the job, the instructors at trainin' school – that you were wearing the cloth and you couldn't run. Because, once you ran, the bucks would think everyone would do the same – you're carryin' everybody round with you, type of thing. So I'm comin' home and I jump off the bus and I walk smack-bang into four of 'em, and they all 'ave a go. There's not even words exchanged. It's just into each other and a straight battle. Anyway, this time I frightened the life out of 'em, because I put three on the floor. I thought: I'm doin' great 'ere! And I look round for the fourth. He must have planted me with a bit of four-by-two on the back of me head, because it was just like grey. I can remember hittin' the floor and the grey, and I *knew* what was comin'. I'm shakin' me head, tryin' to clear it, when this black thing come in. I tried to cover me face, but it was too late. Anyway, the boot connected and smashed me nose.

6

The *Close to the Edge* lad has quite a bit of company by now, including a youngster caught stoning a bread van. The BP comes out of the juvenile detention room and says to the bridewell sergeant, 'This fly little bugger has given us another set of false particulars, so, in a fit of pique, I've put him back in there until I can restrain m'self from stranglin' 'im.'

39

The buzzer goes. Two young detectives bring in a grey-haired, rather shabby man wearing built-up heels that do nothing to make him more impressive. His eyes are frantic to please.

'I've arrested this man for indecent assault,' the taller of the two detectives states. 'The circumstances are that at one-fifteen today I went to. . . .'

The prisoner is alleged to have persuaded a group of young children to come to his bathroom in a block of flats, and to have masturbated in front of them, before bringing himself to orgasm while lying on a six-year-old as she lay, fully dressed, on his bed. He had not actually attempted intercourse.

'What is your name?' asks the sergeant in the same quiet voice he always uses. The only difference in his manner, as he fills in the details on the charge sheet, is that he doesn't call the man anything, whereas most prisoners are immediately addressed by their first name. Each question is answered with an earnest politeness, while the man twists his cloth cap in hands with nails long bitten to the quick.

He flinches at the start of the body search by the BP, and keeps his eyes fixed on the two detectives, as if imploring them not to hurt him. Perhaps the fact that nothing has happened so far is what is so unnerving. With chill clinical detachment – suggesting, in fact, something being handled with rubber gloves rather than velvet ones – the rest of the procedure is completed, and the charge put to him.

'Have you anything to say?'

He looks down and shakes his head.

'No reply. Right, sign here for your property.'

'Sir, are you going to— ?'

'I think', says the sergeant, 'that this party's going to have to be locked up for his own safety?' The irony he allows himself is acknowledged by a wink from the arresting officer. 'Come,' he says, taking out his cell keys.

The prisoner hesitates, seeing the sergeant walk off down the short corridor. Then he realises he is simply meant to follow him and, with a final glance at the detectives, who have turned away to fill in a form, he hastens to catch up.

40

The cell block is painted pale blue and forms a rough T, with two female cells to the right of the down stroke, and eight cells for males arranged across the top. Each cell is about eight feet square, and has a lavatory in a recess, which is flushed by a handle outside in the corridor. There are no barred windows; instead, the far wall has a section of thick glass bricks, and at night illumination is provided by a protected lamp in the ceiling. There is no furniture as such, but a wide bench of varnished wood is built over the ventilation and heating unit beneath the window bricks; in the safety cell, designed for housing unconscious drunks, this bench is only a few inches above floor level, and there is a restraining ring set in the wall behind it. Very rarely, however, are drunks lodged anywhere but at the Main Bridewell, so the cell wing has no strong odours of any sort, and is as clean as one would expect a place to be which seldom has anyone in it for more than a matter of hours.

The cell into which the prisoner is shown bears almost no trace of its former occupants, apart from LEGALIZE CANNABIS scratched beside the bell-push. He slips in obediently and turns, wanting to say something but remaining tongue-tied. The inch-thick steel door, with an eye-level judas hole, swings toward him – cell doors are hung the wrong way round, so to speak, to prevent prisoners springing violent surprises – and bangs shut.

The buzzer is sounding again. This time there is a striking contrast between the fresh downy-cheeked features of the arresting officer and the boy who, although six years his junior at thirteen, has a hard adult face and very old eyes. With them are two members of the Car Squad, both red with exertion. The prisoner, they say, broke into a car in the city centre and drove off in it. They gave chase on foot – the squad has no vehicle assigned to it – and saw him crash into another vehicle. The occupants of this second car, a mother and the daughter who was taking her home after an operation, were both back in hospital, their injuries unconfirmed as yet.

'Weren't fokkin' me,' says the boy.

'Denies he had anything to do with it,' the uniformed con-

41

stable sighs, placing one half of a pair of scissors on the counter. 'He had this in his hand, used it on the ignition.'

'I tell yer, it—'

'Quiet, son, unless you want to make trouble for yourself. You didn't get him in the car, then?'

'No, boss,' one of the Car Squad breaks in, 'but he had a receipt on him for goods we found under the front seat. Six-eighty's worth of gear – we've got it here, see? Blue pully, boxer shorts, jeans from Owen Owen.'

'Are these yours, then?'

'Never 'ad dem in no motor wid me! Dese fokkers dey grabbed us when I was just walkin''—'

'That's enough,' says the sergeant. 'Gary, isn't it?'

And so Saturday afternoon gathers its customary momentum, with the bridewell sergeant permitting himself virtually no personal comment except to ask, 'Wasn't worth gettin' yourself arrested for, was it?' – or, more often, 'Why steal a thing like that?' At a quarter to three, a poorly dressed, dumpy girl of sixteen is brought in to be charged with shoplifting. He looks at a description of the bottle of expensive perfume found in her possession, looks at her trembling hare-lip, and says nothing.

I suppose there are some police officers who, like anybody else, are a bit more highly strung, but I always keep a low profile. You just can't let it get at you; you have to contain yourself. If they speak well to me, I speak well to them, and vice versa. I must say, I've been very lucky. I've not been assaulted once in eighteen years. You'll probably find most men of my height – I'm six one and a half – haven't been assaulted often. Personally, I'm not abrupt with people, I try and explain things before I start shoutin', but I would say it's mainly your physical bearing. And I've never used my truncheon, either. Luck again, because I've never had any call to – although I've dealt with enough violent drunks and other violent prisoners in my time.

I joined from the Irish Guards because the work appealed to me, not so much because I didn't like criminals. I was six years on the beat, then another six in Mounted – three of them as sergeant – before I transferred out in order to gain promotion. I've passed my inspector's exam, so I'm just waitin' for the gods to look upon me. (*Shrugs*) I don't particularly like it much in the

42

bridewell. I prefer to be outside, getting about and meeting people. I meet plenty of people in here all right, but there's a lot of routine to it and, when it's quiet, you can be very bored. You could come on and have no prisoners at all, but generally on this station I'd say the average was about eight a shift, although – like today – it can go up to fifteen or twenty, juveniles mostly.

The most difficult side of the job is deciding if there is enough evidence to bring the prisoner before the court. If the evidence isn't sufficient, but you know there's a case to answer, then we'll delay the charge by bailing him under the provisions of Section 38 (2) to return to this station when enquiries into the matter are complete – or it could be voided in the meantime by letter. You refuse a charge maybe once a week. A car could be outstanding on our stolen list, and this in fact is the owner! That happens quite often. The amount of bail is at our discretion. Usually it's about fifty pound, but for minor offences, drunkenness, ten, twenty pound, payable if the person fails to answer. We call for sureties if we're not happy about him turning up in court. The courts also give bail. You're amazed that some of these prisoners can come back in a couple of weeks three or four times, for different offences, and still be out. I mean, they used to have fewer opportunities to commit crime, and some of them were deterred from crime, too. They had families themselves and thought better of it.

Over the past six or seven years, there seems to have been a trend for kids between eleven and sixteen to come in regular now. Probably too much is taken for granted in society today; people are too greedy, and there's not enough discipline, of course. The parents are to blame for this, not the schools. I exercise discipline with my two daughters, who are six and ten. No physical chastisement, but I certainly wouldn't let them do what they like. They tend to think: Why can't I do this? Why can't I do that? Then this spoiled child will go too far, and they'll come up to you and say, 'Hey, Dad, isn't so-and-so naughty?' They realise then.

7

The mood of the bridewell changes as the droll sergeant takes over a few minutes before 3.30 p.m., when those on Afternoons

43

until 11.30 p.m. come on. 'Sorry, luv, but don't shout at us. So far as shoplifting's concerned, we're just piggy in the middle.'

'Oh, very dry,' murmurs his bespectacled BP, a man of some whimsy himself.

The whole station is changing mood now, as the rest of their watch prepares to go on parade, and it isn't simply a matter of the refreshed replacing the weary, giving the place a bit of an uplift. Each watch working the three-shift system, whether it be Red, Green or Blue Group, has its own corporate disposition. 'Aye, aye, 'ere come the Ghurkas! You know why, don't yer, son? Take no prisoners. . . .' A favourite expression of rivalry that becomes pointed when directed at a lazy 'foot-man', given to leaving his beat untidy with those causing annoyance or distress to the general public. Much depends on the inspector in charge, and on the leadership provided by the section sergeants, but they cannot exercise the same degree of influence on the group as a whole. Then again, mood is affected by the hour, by the day and by the season.

On a Saturday in autumn, with nightfall on its way and the weather staying warm and dry, there is an air of quiet expectancy in the cons' room off the long passage running the full length of the building. At a glance, it could be a press room at the rear of a grandstand somewhere: battered typewriters, wooden tables, fanlights rather than windows, cream walls and hardly a thing on them, apart from information sheets and a cryptic SAVE ENERGY poster.

A probationer is seated in the corner opposite the doorway, lighting a last-minute cigarette with the nine-carat gold lighter he received on his twenty-first birthday just a short while ago. He has an alert pleasant face with a wide mouth and upturned nose, reminiscent of the illustrations in boy's adventure books of the twenties. His speech is staccato, very positive, yet not wholly self-assured.

I haven't been to court yet – I'm in my sixth month. I've been to the coroner's court; that's when I had to take someone out

44

of the river. A body, a suicide job. It was the first dead body I'd ever seen, but I didn't have time for a reaction.*

I worked in a bank for three years, saw no future in it. Thought there was a better chance of promotion in this job. It was a thing I'd always wanted to do for the variety and that. This division is the best; this is where the action is! I put in for it.

I've made five arrests for crime; the rest all summonses. My first arrest was for theft. I thought: Well, this is a start. It's all luck, no skill involved. My luckiest was for assault [on] police. I came out from the Main Bridewell, after lockin' up three drunks, and saw a fight goin' on and people being hit. Do you call that luck? (*Laughs*) Then a burglary, a betting office – just drivin' past and they'd just come out the door.

I've been afraid once, that time I was assaulted. A bunch of blokes, really big, y'know. But I think if we started getting firearms it would be a shame. Firearms are a bad thing; we wouldn't be able to keep our reputation as the finest police force in the world. I've just come back from holiday in France actually, and the French police . . . oh, my God! They walk around in fours and fives! (*Grins*) They'd be lost here. You've got your radio, and I say they'd be there in nigh on thirty seconds. It's great at night; it keeps you company. If you get bored, change channel to another division! But that never happens; it's all in our division. And you've got your baton. It's a bloody nuisance. If you don't tie it up properly, it bangs against the back of your leg; mine's aching just there.

Nobody in my family's in the police. I've got a cousin who's a Special in Wales. You don't lose friends; they forget I'm a bobby. I'm unique, y'know – I don't look like one when I'm not on duty! They think it's a big novelty. But I suppose I do feel strongly about good and bad, people nicking things. My father's dead, my mother's not well off, we've had our hard times – y'know, chips for Sunday dinner – so I don't see why anyone else should moan. We never claimed any Social Security, never; we would rather have gone without food. I remember once, when I was nine, I stole a bar of chocolate and took it home. Never touched it. And my conscience was that bad I took it and

*He and his colleague received rewards from the Liverpool Shipwreck and Humane Society 'for the rescue of a woman, later found to be dead, who had committed suicide by jumping into the River Mersey'.

45

put it back in its place. I don't want to say I'm an angel – I've pissed in shop doorways as well! Me brother's a mechanical engineer for Burmah Oil, my one sister's a captain in the Army, and my other sister and her husband have a farm in Wales. My mum's quite happy now, settled down.

The constable seated two tables away, going over a crime report to be submitted to his sergeant, is also twenty-one, but a panda driver with two-and-a-half years' service, not counting the time he spent as a police cadet. He is 5 feet 11 inches, on the light side, and wears glasses in the regulation gilt frames. His fiancée quite likes the idea of joining the police herself, a notion which he opposes vigorously because 'the days have gone by when you could say fellas don't hit a woman – they do'. When he has time, he plays badminton and table tennis, but has to expend most of his energy working towards setting up a home. An elderly person in distress would find him most reassuring, and might well describe him as 'studious looking, ever so quietly spoken and grown up for his age'. The question of age is one he often finds troublesome, especially when telling a motorist twice his years to stop being ridiculous and behave, and this is a problem shared by a great number of his fellow officers, many of whom have just gone nineteen. A problem that can become acute when, for example, one teenager is duty bound to make another teenager comply with 'adult' standards of behaviour outside a drinking club at 2 a.m.

I hated school. I was never one for studyin', and didn't want a job that was nine-to-five, so I joined the cadets. I wouldn't recommend them to anybody; you're just a glorified tea boy. Although, when you go to Bruche for your ten weeks' initial training, for the first two weeks they teach you what a divisional office does, what the collator does, and you're all right there, because you've worked in them. The rest of what they taught you was pretty good, but obviously differed slightly from what happens in the street. When you first come back, you're with your tutor con for four weeks, and hopefully he shows you what to do.

After me first four weeks, when I saw how various bobbies dealt with people, I thought I'd go out and be as friendly as I

46

can with the bucks. I'll try it a little bit different: I'll go up to them and have a game of football with them, if they'll let me, or I'll talk to them and find out just why it is they hang around street corners. Why not do somethin' else? It didn't work, though. I spoke to them and they thought it was great – y'know, a bobby speakin' to them and kickin' their football and that. But as soon as you got round the corner, that was it. They'd forgotten the next time, and they threw stones at you like they threw them at anyone else. (*Smiles and shrugs*) I think they're just bored.

And I don't blame the kids, not the younger ones. If someone's born in that block of flats over there, they don't stand a chance from the word 'go'. They're born criminals by virtue of the fact their brothers have probably been inside, their fathers have been inside, and their mothers just couldn't give two hoots. Funnily enough, it's the youngest ones who give the most trouble. Oh, the youngest ones give you all the cheek in the world, but most of the bobbies can't be bothered lockin' up a twelve-year-old anyway.

The worst side of the job is sudden deaths, fatal accidents. My first accident was a fatal; when people look at you, they don't know you've been on the job only four weeks. The best side is that I think we can help people, just little things. Like a fella we found locked in an office one day, and he couldn't get to a telephone. I said, 'OK, we'll get the keyholder for you,' and, as an extra thought – I knew what it'd be like if I was late home – I said to him, 'Would you like me to ring yer wife?' So I felt I'd done something, rather than just get him out.

Personally, I don't think Uniform is boring. Even if you arrested seven shoplifters in a week, each one would have something different about them. I flinch in a way, when it's an elderly person or they look poor. I remember I locked two people up once who looked really poor, so I felt a bit uptight about it at the time, y'know. The woman looked about sixty, and she was only about thirty-four; the man – his clothes were that tatty – had pinched a 24p piece of cheese. When they were searched in the bridewell, the gentleman had £1128 in cash on him which he'd saved through the years, never bothered with a building society or a bank. So, you see, I could have let them off there, if I didn't have me job to do!

That's the way it goes. I get frightened; I suppose every bobby must at some stage. I went to this report of a fight last night,

47

when they said there were twenty or thirty lads fightin'. I was singly manned in the car, which made me feel a bit on me own, I suppose, although I hurried to get there. I'm gettin' paid for goin' there, so I get there. I'm on every day, trying to save for this house, y'see.

Just before the parade, which is held at the far end of the corridor in a large sunny room, partially filled by an overflow of tall steel lockers from the changing-rooms next door, the group has to absorb a good deal of information. The procedure is, in part, rather like skimming through a de-sensationalised tabloid, starting at the editorial page. Chief Constable's Orders deal with new policies and regulations, outlining what is expected, and give notice of promotions and postings; Chief Superintendent's Orders do much the same thing at divisional level, warn of coming major events and add snippets of sporting and social interest. Then there are the crime bulletins, both local and general, larded by portraits of unamused people, and filled with figures, trends and other items of intelligence. Two books have also to be consulted: one warns of any court appearances due shortly, and the other gives the results of cases already heard, because, unless their written statements are contested, police officers don't in fact have to go to court for run-of-the-mill matters. Loud groans of total disbelief are not infrequent in this corner.

The parade itself is conducted with the minimum of ceremony. Nobody is asked to 'produce their appointments'; women officers aren't issued with truncheons anyway, and nobody gets a pair of handcuffs, although they are allowed to carry their own inconspicuously. Truncheons, too, must remain out of sight in the special trouser pocket designed for them, lest they cause an officer to appear threatening or merely unapproachable.

'There are one or two little tricks a few of them get up to, though,' an astute inspector points out. 'Little things to boost their confidence a bit, specially on Nights. There's what you could call the "black glove syndrome" – wearing their gloves

48

on a nice warm evening. Like the gunfighter in *Shane*, y'know! Then you get the posers who will leave just the end of their [baton] strap showing. "Sorry, sir! Didn't notice!" '

'There's also the fella', adds an eavesdropper, 'who buys himself a five-cell torch for the weight of it, makes him feel happier really. Still, we've come a long way since bobbies used to *carry* their gloves because they had marbles stuck down the fingers. Imagine a smack over the ear with one of those! The corner of a wet cape was another favourite, I'm told.'

'Pa-rade, shun.' The group, divided into its three sections – west, east and mobiles – takes up a fraction of the floor space. 'At ease.'

A sergeant begins reading out duties. 'Four-five-eight-five, you're on Three Beat, first refreshments. Five-one-six-one, you're on Four Beat, second refreshments – keep your eye on Kwiksave in Great Homer Street, which has been damaged by vandals.'

'Sir!'

It doesn't take long.

Then the inspector issues some further instructions, and double-checks to see if certain points have been properly noted before the parade. 'And a complaint of robbery at the Green Garter public house in Dale Street, where—'

'Aware of that, ma'am!' says the officer on that beat, coming to attention momentarily.

'The Victoria Hotel, Great Howard Street. The licensee will be away for a fortnight.'

'Aware of that, ma'am!'

'A black and silver fountain pen, found in the locker room, is in the bridewell. And that's all. Parade, atten-tion.'

For just an instant longer, the loudest sound in the room is the ritual carefree whistling coming from members of the watch they have relieved. Then the single file breaks rank to collect their personal radios, fit fresh batteries, and go out into the 700 acres now in their keeping.

49

8

The van driver's first job is to call at Copperas Hill on the South Sub-division and pick up a couple of prisoners for the Main Bridewell. But on strolling out into the vehicle-yard he finds one of the blue-and-white pandas still there, blocking his line of exit.

'Havin' second thoughts, lads?'

'Fokkin' Keystone Kops,' grumbles the constable in the front passenger's seat, removing his large frame with difficulty from the Mini. 'Give us a hand, will yer?'

Together, they push-start the panda, and the constable repeats his struggle with the door to slump low in his seat like the driver, for otherwise their flat caps would press against the car's roof. Fifteen minutes in that position, and getting off to a fast sprint is out of the question.

The van driver is in luck: his engine starts at a twist of the key, and he leaves the yard, turning right at the lights into St Anne Street. From here, it's only a short journey down through the dip, across London Road and up to an intersection that looks, what with its boarded-up shops (one or two still carrying on 'business as usual'), holed rooftops, yawning gaps and heaps of rubble, something like the crossroads in a shell-torn village. His first stopping-point is now barely a hundred yards or so away to the left.

'The Cottage', as it is affectionately known by some officers, hasn't the appearance of the busiest police station in England, outside of West End Central in London, but such is its reputation. No larger than the average suburban bank, constructed in warm materials and designed to seem not uninviting, Copperas Hill is embedded in the community on a busy corner opposite St Andrew's Gardens, an oval tenement block better known – and far better described – as the Bullring. In fact, the police station faces directly into the 'arena' through a vast archway, almost as high as its own two floors, which penetrates the full width of the five-storey building.

The Bullring has long been associated with an ungiving and

50

hostile attitude towards the police, upon whom its residents are said to have rained everything from abuse to chamber-pots and armchairs. Things are far less daunting these days, the old hands insist, now that the council has put in some students and all. Nevertheless, even an experienced officer still has to have his wits about him.

I was draggin' a fella out of the Bullring one day – for screwin' a car, y'see – and this lot was about to set on me. It was only fifty yards to the police station, and I thought: Shall I start runnin' and make a fool of m'self? *Leave 'im alone!* they're all shoutin', and some are holdin' on to him as well. So I said to them, 'How old are your children? You wouldn't be sayin' that if it was *your* kids he'd been takin' into empty houses, would yer?' They all started gettin' hold of this fella then: *Right, yer bastid!* And they brought this fella into the police station for me.

After checking with the bridewell sergeant, the van driver leaves the cheery enquiry office – it has yellow wallpaper with an orange stripe – and goes on up the stairs, passing a flourishing pot-plant on the landing, to see one of four officers in the section that has just come in off the streets. Cosy colour schemes and other homely touches help to make Copperas Hill feel so different from functional St Anne Street, but its 'cottage' qualities probably owe as much, if not more, to the enforced intimacy of its small rooms, several of which are seriously overcrowded. Simply finding enough locker space for roughly 150 people is a problem, and the 'rest' area has been reduced to the cook-it-yourself canteen kitchen, where a pair of easy chairs, squeezed in beside the sink, face a television set on the worktop.

'Oh, no,' sighs the probationer filling the kettle.

'Oh, aye,' says the van driver. 'Sarge wants a word about this male what bit the Foreign Legionary fella on the arm.'

And so the teamaking is left to two other probationers and a woman police officer just 'out of her time'.

HELEN: I've not done a lot today. There were the automatic alarms – people setting them off when they got to work – and shoplifters later on. We had to take reports of the burglaries that happened during the night, but for the first part of the shift I did reports.

51

JOHN: I did reports for a while, then scoff, then relieved the security man guarding the vehicle-yard at Hope Street.

ALLAN: I was on London Road. I did a summons and a lock-up for D-and-I [drunk and incapable] at one-thirty. I didn't have any trouble with him, he was singin' and that – oh, a good song, y'know! He didn't know the words, though.

HELEN: It's not necessarily what I expected – y'know, dealing with automatic alarms and things like that – but the rest of it is. And people ask you strange questions like 'How long is the train journey from Liverpool to Manchester?' *Huh?* I mean, Pardon?

JOHN: You're increasing your knowledge of the city all the time.

HELEN: I don't come into it as much as I used to; now I usually go to Southport.

JOHN: Yes, I rarely come in of a night now. I just don't want to know any more; it's too risky, just because you're a policeman.

HELEN: (*Laughing*) Well, you meet a lot of people you locked up as well, don't you?

JOHN: That's the embarrassing thing, isn't it?

HELEN: And you go home and all you ever get is 'Now, this fella got booked, and *I* got booked.' Oh God! It's a main topic of conversation, I find.

ALLAN: It dominates, doesn't it? They just go on talking about the police for ages. I don't know why.

JOHN: I can't understand why people don't like the police force. I can understand why the bucks don't like it – that's obvious, because we're always lockin' them up. But the majority of people – like students, y'know – don't like us. It's a biased opinion, isn't it?

HELEN: They dislike it because it reminds them of discipline.

JOHN: Yes, but they're intelligent people! They must realise there's no way you can have no police force. You might never get a perfect police force, but you've got to have some kind.

HELEN: They see us as something restrictive, just another wall to climb over. To the battlements! (*Laughs*) All the time.

JOHN: You can never explain to anyone what it's like to be a policeman.

HELEN: They just don't believe you. But you can never believe what it's like in any job, not unless you do it yourself.

JOHN: It's less dangerous than I expected.

ALLAN: I think it's more.

HELEN: It's dangerous when you go round the Gardens [residential areas], especially if you're on your own and at night. But

52

around the city it doesn't bother me at all. There are so many people there, I don't really think about it.

JOHN: None of us have been beaten up, have we? And I've been in over a year now. I've been hit, a few little punches, bruises, but I've never been beaten up badly. I was surprised, because I thought it goes on all the time. I expected to be beaten up a lot.

HELEN: It's more like scuffles.

JOHN: Yes, you get bags of scuffles, but I expected. . . .

ALLAN: When I came down here, I didn't expect to see these giant fellas, y'know! Absolutely massive fellas – I didn't realise anybody could be that big. They're fightin' and you've got to go and break them up.

JOHN: And you're dealing with people older than yourself, aren't you?

ALLAN: It's frightening for me when you go towards a crowd that's fighting outside a pub, because you look young and they're going to treat you as young. It puts you below them, y'know – people are goin' to treat yer as a kid.

HELEN: You also never know which way a crowd's going to turn. That can be terrifying. You've got to try and weigh it up from the outside before going in – never on your own, even if you've got a staff! Not having one, I've not known what it's like to have one, so it's never bothered me.

JOHN: I've never used mine – never even drawn it.

ALLAN: I haven't.

JOHN: But I think most policemen like being policemen, don't they?

HELEN: Well, once you've got your two years in, it's a very secure job. You've got to do something really drastic to get kicked out. I couldn't take a nine-to-five job.

ALLAN: No, you'd just be another person, wouldn't you? You go out of here as a police officer – you're something different. And there's a fascination in the job.

JOHN: Only I think the appraisal is a ridiculous system. [Probationers are appraised on a 'progress report' every three months.]

ALLAN: But I don't suppose there's another way they can do it, is there?

JOHN: I don't think it's fair having to worry all the time how many jobs you've got in. It's a worry, there's no doubt about it.

HELEN: It's always at the back of your mind; you just can't get rid of it. Oh hell, I've got to do somebody – I've got my progress due.

53

JOHN: It's wrong really.

HELEN: You feel terrible at times, because you'd really rather be after the really big crimes, not summonses.

JOHN: It's not easy doin' somebody for having only one light. You feel awful.

HELEN: Yes, you know it happens to yourself. What I like is locking somebody up.

ALLAN: A good lock-up is a score, isn't it? It's getting one back on them.

JOHN: What I like is the idea you get put on a beat and you just walk anywhere around. You haven't got someone saying, 'Right, walk down there, and walk down there, and walk' – like in offices, y'know, sitting down at such and such a time, typin' away.

ALLAN: I'm the same: being on me own and locking up. You get a good lock-up and it's good for your progress. With a good detection – somebody who's broken into a car – you can feel more comfortable than with six drunks and a couple of shoplifters!

HELEN: Shoplifting's a pain. It wouldn't be so bad if the store detective came back with you, but they just write out a statement and you have to do all their work for them.

JOHN: A good lock-up, and you're laffin'.

HELEN: Sometimes we get an anonymous phone call. There are quite a lot of people who see things, but they just don't want to get involved.

ALLAN: And people just have to stay in their houses around Myrtle Gardens, because if they go off they get broken into. They're frightened to go out! People come to Hope Street GEO [general enquiry office] and ask you to walk them back to Myrtle Street – old ladies who are frightened to go back up. I did one the other day. This old lady came – she was seventy, and her husband was dead – and said some family kept pestering her all the time, so I walked her home.

HELEN: A lot of the trouble we have is the public not understanding why we do things.

ALLAN: (Nods) It's like handcuffing somebody. We had to handcuff this fella; he was goin' mad. He was struggling and he was fightin' – he spat on my leg! – and yet, if we'd taken the handcuffs off him, he'd have gone berserk. And this crowd was gathering round, and I thought they were going to have a go at us.

HELEN: I haven't got any handcuffs.

54

JOHN: I haven't.

ALLAN: I don't use them personally. They're dear. Eleven pound out of a month's wages – that's a lot, isn't it?

JOHN: But I wonder if it might be good to be more violent than we are, because it puts them all off, y'know!

HELEN: If the bucks knew there was only four of us on today, and none of us has more than two years and our oldest is about twenty. (*Laughs*) Madness, isn't it?

JOHN: I was in some place opposite St Anne Street, and we were searching all the houses for stolen cigarettes, and we found a radio that'd been stolen. We took it downstairs and turned it on, and we could hear the radio operator sending all our bobbies to the different places. So the bucks knew all right, and they were off!

9

A film-maker would despair at the sight of 'A' Division's small radio-room, which opens off the main bridewell office at St Anne Street. In visual terms, it contains nothing to suggest moments of high drama, other than those accidentally induced, perhaps, by the excessively large electric fan.

The radio itself is a nondescript metal box, just big enough to bury a cat in, and quite without interesting dials, lights or gadgetry of any sort. The only map is a faded drawing-office print, and the details of 'A' Division's operational status are kept, with the aid of a blue wax pencil, on a home-made board, propped wherever room can be found for it. Neither is the computer console, situated to the operator's right on a small safe, particularly engaging; ordinary offices all over the world have similar aids. Just as they have the same wheel-about circular files for data cards, junior-management swivel chairs and, of course, telephones.

Sound is what makes the radio-room dramatic at times – that, and the most agonising silences.

One by one, the officers now on patrol in 'A' Division establish radio contact.

55

'Four-five-eight-five.'

'Go ahead, Four-five-eight-five.'

'I'm on Three Beat, first refreshments, over.'

'Ah, roger. Alpha standing by.'

The exchanges are as much a formula as 'How do you do?', but the duty operator makes his responses with the lively interest of a host welcoming guests at his door.

I like to get an atmosphere going, to build up a rapport with them. When I come in, I try to get a picture of the day – very briefly – from these log sheets, and then, as the bobbies come on, I fit them into it. I know most of them and their capabilities, which differ of course. Some I'd think twice about sending to a civil matter [a dispute over the size of a garage repair bill, for example] – some have only done a few weeks on the street, and they've very little experience of life. I make a point of talking to these recruits to get to know them, and if there's one who makes a lot of mistakes, I usually ask them to call in here and see me. I say, 'If you're ever in doubt about anything, don't be afraid to ask questions over the air – I'm the only one who can hear you, and I'll phrase my replies discreetly!' I was a young con myself once, and there was nobody I could ask.

A foot sergeant comes through, requesting a vehicle check. The operator punches the registration number on the console keyboard and, within seconds, is able to read back the owner's name, his address and the vehicle's description; adding that there is no record of it having been stolen.

'Can you get the keyholder, please?' asks the next caller, who has found an automatic alarm ringing in an office building; there is, however, no sign of any break-in.

The keyholder's name and telephone number are on one of the cards in the circular file. The card also describes the property, the nature of its business, and gives advice on the minimum number of officers needed to surround it, plus what positions they should take up. But all that's necessary on this occasion is a quick call.

It's a bit like a game, I suppose, but one played in deadly earnest. You don't want anyone to get hurt. People come before property every time, and our people before any other people. The job

56

doesn't think like this, nor do the courts. Property has an absurd value – take the Great Train Robbery, for instance. For a lot of money, they got big sentences. To me, that isn't important. What is important is that guy they knocked on the head.

The bridewell sergeant looks in, resting his arms on the stable door. 'When are you going to play me request, then?'

'Not your birthday again, is it? "Love to Aunty Mavis, Uncle Willie and all the kids"?'

'Got a paper there? Wanted a look at the—'

'Got the *Guardian*,' the operator replies, tossing it over. 'Just had me two hours in a sauna.'

'Oh aye? Don't worry, son, your secret's safe with me.'

They laugh, and the radio makes its *Shhhhhh* noise. 'Inspector South.'

'Inspector South, go ahead, sir.'

'Leaving Copperas Hill to do a few pegs, over.'

'Ah, roger, sir. Thanks for that.'

'Gone a bit quiet, has it?' the sergeant asks.

'All routine so far.'

The thirty-three-year-old constable now on duty is one of the regular radio operators. The son of an educationalist, whose works are published by Macmillan, he spent most of his early years in Africa, and still has the 'classless' easy-going manner of many colonials. His professionalism is equally marked; he seldom glances up at the map, having in his mind's eye a picture of the whole 'island' so vivid he's often able to anticipate the twists and turns of a chase, as well as where the quarry is most likely to go to ground.

For an ordinary civilian, life in civilisation after being abroad can be very, very dull, and I found this country terribly mundane when I got back.

I wasn't interested in the slightest in grammar school over here. I think my dad wanted me to go to university, but I felt I couldn't sit down to six years' grind – I had to *do* something, and I also liked contact with people. Life's not exciting for me unless the adrenalin's flowing, y'know; I had to get out there and find something that'd make it different. So I left school and went on a wander for a bit, then joined the cadets.

57

I would say the three requirements of a bobby are: a degree of compassion, a modicum of morality and a big quota of common sense.

The men left on the job, when I joined fourteen years ago, were most of them ex-servicemen; they'd fought for this country, and they'd decided what they wanted it to be like when they got back. They were hard men, and anybody who stepped out of line they thought of as 'un-English' – behaving like a lout. They were the men who decided who to lock up, and who to leave out on the streets, and they had a point: they were very, very firm, and they got a lot of respect.

They tried to bring us up the same way but, of course, we didn't have the same motivations. I mean, I was born in an air-raid shelter, y'see – a war baby! And we were expected to emulate these older bobbies, or otherwise we'd be thought soft. In some ways, we did emulate them, although there were a lot of people – that's why I preferred to work on my own – who had a more liberal attitude. We understood, y'see. We'd crawled home drunk. I'd worked on a travelling fairground, and I understood more how he felt. I'd also been brought up in a disciplined family – a kind of self-discipline we were taught – and I thought that was the way: you should go round showing other people they were wrong, not by beating them up and locking them up, but by explaining things to them.

I worked the coloured area as my first beat. They threw me in at the deep end because, although I'm five-eleven, I weighed about nine stone and looked very, very young. I don't know, maybe they thought they might push me off the job (*laughs*) because I was one of the littlest men on parade. Anyway, I got on like a house on fire, because I treated them like the Africans, you see. I shouted at them as much as they shouted at me – I'd been used to seeing their village scene and how they lived. I mean, two West Indians saying goodnight can be a fearful experience for somebody who's not used to it – anyone would believe there's a riot going on! There isn't a colour problem as long as you understand they've got a different cultural background.

Then it slowly changed. These men got old enough not to be on the streets, and they got into soft jobs. A younger type of policeman, perhaps people like myself, came on the job who weren't so physical. Violence had started to die away in the schools as well, corporal punishment and that, and people had

58

begun to object to it. At one time, if a guy spoke out of turn in a police station, he just got a backhander – there were no two ways about it. You'd take a prisoner in, one you'd never had any trouble with, and they'd say, 'Empty yer pockets out.' He'd say, 'Wot?' – and wallop! I don't know, it was a gradual change; some people carried it on for years and years. I can remember it easiest by two incidents that were two years apart. One where I was commended for locking a man up, and the second, about eight years ago, when I ended up at a disciplinary hearing. They were both street fights and I acted in exactly the same manner each time, because it was the manner I was used to acting in: not using violence until the very last moment. This was when I began to think about taking my baton out.

I've been assaulted quite a few times – many, many more times than I've charged people with assault. You must expect a certain amount of knockabout on this job. This nose is broken, but my prisoner wasn't charged because I couldn't remember who had hit me! (*Laughs*) You never remember who butted you in the face, because everything goes black and sparks fly in your eyes and you can't believe it's happened to you! But I've usually found that, if you've got time to stop and say something, most people physically superior to me are mentally inferior, and you can talk them out of it.

You see, it's a mental attitude as well. You can be physically quite big and not able to look after yourself. Some of these women officers would probably be better at handling a man in the street than you would, y'know – a man might just rub him up the wrong way. I think it's great; let's have them all out on the streets! I was as 'anti' as anyone to start off with, when the Sex Discrimination Act went through in '75, but now I can see the value of it. It gives a greater balance. There's a lot you can't do in front of a woman and get away with. You just have to behave in a more gentlemanly way, I think, and it's good for us. If you're in an all-male society, it can get a bit rough.

I was a panda driver when a tanker hit my car and broke my neck. While I was off ill, and there was a chance I might be pensioned on medical grounds, I thought then of going in the social services. I think we could complement one another a lot more than we do. I find that people I've met who are social workers, as we call them, are often very much detached from the realities. When I returned after about nine months I was put on light duties, as the accident had resulted in a series of blackouts,

59

and then I came in here. I think for this job they try to attract men with wide Uniform experience, a good working knowledge of the area, and able to give advice. But I'm not really a typical police officer, because I don't mix with policemen off duty – most of my friends are teachers and musicians. I don't fit into the mould, never have, although I get on great while I'm here. It's just I don't like talking shop.

'Alpha, last caller say again.'

'Three-eight. . . .' The radio chops loudly, turning the voice into blurts of sound that remain unintelligible.

'You're breaking badly – Three-eight-five-nine, is it? I'm still not reading you. Say again, please.'

Somehow the operator picks out the essentials of the message. 'Alpha to all patrols in the vicinity of Elliott Street, theft from the person, youths in white shirts and blue jeans.'

10

Inspector South presses down on the accelerator, making the chips of broken glass beneath his heel grind and squeak; the Escort came back into service only this morning, having had yet another 'bricked' windscreen hurriedly replaced. No klaxon sounds and no blue lights flash, for 'A' Division's six patrol cars have none. On the contrary, they are fitted with miser carburettors, and aren't intended to travel at speed.

Divisional drivers are trained to elementary standard – some, not many, undergo intermediate courses. They're not to be trusted at high speeds, and they're repeatedly told that they're driving a *beat* vehicle – just something to get them around. It's surprising how many cars 'back' into police vehicles! They're told to follow but, if it becomes a chase, they must let them go, because a chase endangers the general public. For the same reason, we're forbidden to put up roadblocks. Where chasing is necessary, then it's left to the Traffic Department, but even then the stated philosophy is that the offender should rather be allowed to get away, to be dealt with another day, than cause any unnecessary accidents.

60

So the Escort, making for a possible escape route to the east of Elliott Street, is moving only as fast as conditions will allow. And yet there is a fairground illusion of speed, of a headlong exhilarating rush down a twisting tunnel of mirrors and bright colours, as a narrowed field of focus loses the detail of display windows and shop signs to concentrate on legs. Hundreds of legs, limbs, skittles, all set on doing something damned silly, just like that. Switch left. Missed. Switch right. Switch left, switch right, left again, straight on, into a bend, rattling over rough ground, switch. Then the nose steadies, breaks clear of the tunnel and swoops up a slope below St John's Centre, fast losing momentum. And there they are: two of them, belting across in their white shirts and blue jeans, heading for where the bus queues stand waiting. They vault the railing along the central reservation, stumble and reach the kerb as the Escort coasts to a halt beside them.

'Lucky for some,' murmurs the inspector, getting out. 'Just a minute, lads, I'd like a word with you.'

The automatic alarm shrills out from the line of barricaded shops.

'Oh, not again!' groans the beat officer, reporting this fact to the radio-room.

'Not *again*,' says the operator, giving a laugh. 'Been logged four times today – you know why, don't you ?'

'I can guess. Give you a result in a minute, over.'

She starts back down the wide littered pavement, threading her way through the Saturday-afternoon throng attracted by the market stalls, and once again enters a small supermarket that never dares to raise its steel shutters. The manager is delighted to see her – and full of apologies. A mistake, he says, a silly mistake and he's terribly sorry for any inconvenience. No, no, of course he wasn't being broken into, not with the shop open! He can't understand how these things happen. She can. A few moments ago, he probably had someone in there who frightened him, and so. . . . 'Set off in error,' she radios back. 'Keyholder on the premises.' Then out again into the fading light, back to the market stalls, where an old

61

man comes up, stammering with shock, and says his wallet has g-g-gone. Never felt a thing, nine pound were in it, n-n-nine pound two and a half new pennies, and me pension-book and me only snap of the missus, God rest 'er, and it's gone. Can you h-h-h-help us, luv?

'Fokkin' busy!' roars the drunken docker, reeling back against the alley wall. 'Fokkin' touch me, and I'll fokkin' *burst* yer!'

The young constable edges nearer, keeping one hip turned toward him lest a kick catches him in the groin.

'I fokkin' will!' the drunk threatens, balling a great fist.

'I told yer, yer locked up,' the constable says.

'Fok that! Never bin fokkin' drunk and fokkin' incapable in me fokkin' life! So you can fok off and—'

'You're not D-and-I now, are you?'

'What's that?'

'And I know yer, don't I?'

The drunk peers at him, blinking to clear his bleary vision. 'Oh aye? You do, do yer? All yer fokkin' busies look—'

'Did you for D-and-D,' the constable lies again, sweat on his forehead.

'Dis-disorderly?'

'Aye, pop, drunk and disorderly. Christ, how many bevvies 'ad you 'ad that time?'

The fist uncurls slightly, and the expression softens as he slurs in reply, 'Fair number, was it?'

'Oh aye!'

The drunk beams and nods, preoccupied with trying to recall this happy occasion.

'A'right, lad?' says the section sergeant, coming into the deep shadow off the busy street, putting away his radio.

'A'right, boss.'

'Thought yer bottle was goin' to go there for a second like!'

The constable returns the sergeant's wink and then sees his prisoner into the van when it arrives, gripping firmly to hide the fact his hands are shaking.

'No need for that,' the docker grumbles. 'Fokkin' police brutality, that is. Got a light?'

*

62

People veer away from the man with blood streaming from his face in Church Street. The beat man immediately makes for him.

'Been assaulted!'

'Where was this, sir?'

'Over there! Just this minute! I bought this hot dog and it was. . . .' The man is white with shock and speaks like someone who has just had a tooth out.

'You're OK, sir?'

'See him? By the hot-dog stand? He—'

'That one? Best you sit down, and I'll get the ambulance.'

A space is willingly provided at the end of a public bench, and people crowd around, unable to get close enough. A Days and EP man comes up, sees his colleague using the radio, and says genially, 'A'right, on yer way now! On yer way, ladies. . . .'

'Bloody cheek,' mutters a lady in an emerald green coat and a red wig. 'I only wanted to see how bad the poor fella was, didn't I?'

'On yer bike.'

Nowhere can seem more forlorn than Love Lane in the gloaming. The foot patrol makes her way along the deserted cobbles, dwarfed by the giant Victorian viaduct of sooty brick on her left, a mere match-head against the dizzy walls of bonded warehouses to the right, alone with the weeds and the litter and the oily rainbow puddles. The scrawny cat is still curled inside the Haig carton, where it was over an hour ago, but it must have woken for a time to press its trousers, which now have nasty licky spikes all over them, ready for a night out. The Embassy filter-tip box is new, probably tossed out of the Expo security patrol van as it made its rounds. Then the same knots in the ropes securing the tarpaulined load on the artic trailer; three months ago it would have seemed unbelievable anyone could remember details like that, and find them almost disappointingly familiar. Because if those knots weren't still the same, then. . . . And into the yard of the warehouse at the end, round the corner and along to the padlocked entrance.

63

All correct, nothing has changed, not a sound, except for the radio.

The beat man on Victoria Street has moved from the outside edge of the pavement, where one remains conspicuous during daylight hours, to follow a new line, now that darkness has come, lost in the shadows. He reaches a shop doorway, glances about, sees no sign of his sergeant, and ducks in for a smoke.

A blank-faced man in a leather jacket wanders by, looking left and looking right. He seems to pause briefly as he passes a parked car, and could be trying the door-handle, but moves on again in the same leisurely fashion. The constable begins to follow him, the cigarette crushed underfoot, forgotten.

When the suspect turns up a side street, he turns up the one before it, runs to the top end, cuts across and looks back down again – the leather jacket has vanished. No, he hasn't: he's with a companion in a yellow Ford Cortina parked only a few paces away, and has just started the engine. Where this second man appeared from is anybody's guess, but the matter is still worth investigating. As the constable shows himself, the Cortina leaps forward and crashes into the rear of the vehicle in front of it. The two men jump out and make for Victoria Street.

The driver gets away, but his companion is grabbed and swung off balance, falling between two parked cars, with the constable on top of him.

'Yer locked up, mate!'

'OK, OK, but get the fok off of me stomick, will yer? Jesus!'

A taxi draws up alongside them.

'A'right, boss?'

'Smashin',' says the constable, his colour high with excitement. It's his first crime arrest.

At the fifth knock, the door to the council flat opens.

'Oh, my God!' gasps the elderly woman at the sight of the uniform, reaching out to steady herself against the wall. 'I knew it!'

The probationer winces and tries to smile cheerfully. 'Mrs Holmes? Don't get—'

'I knew it! Moment I 'eard the knock, I said to our Denis, "It's yer dad they've come about! You go. I can't—"'

'Mr Holmes is fine! Honest! Ready to come home now, so the hos—'

'Wot? Wot did yer say?'

'The hospital just wanted you to know so you'd bring his things in the morning, his shoes and his suitcase like. He's been discharged, see? OK, luv?'

She can't help a loud sob; perhaps it's the relief. A man of about forty, wiping batter crumbs from his mouth with the back of his hand, shuffles into the passage. The probationer hastily explains that there is nothing to get upset about.

'Got me mam in a right state, haven't yer? All that knock, knock, bloody knockin'.'

'Well, nobody answered, so I—'

'Know what I mean?'

'If you heard—'

'Look, copper, sod off, will yer?' the man says, pushing his mother aside and slamming the door.

FEAR THEE NOT, I AM NEAR THEE reads the text stuck to the mirror over the mantelpiece. The sole occupant of the flat, still in her church best, confides in little more than a whisper, 'It affects you; the lady next door has given me two tablets. Through there is where they got in, see? The window, kitchen window. It frightens you like, and I was only gone the two hours. Saturdays we have a bit of a "do" and Pastor Jones likes us to get down there – nothing fancy, a bit o' tea, a bit of a sing-song like. Mrs Braithewaite, the coloured lady across the way, was down there with me, or she would have seen something, I'm sure of it. That's where they come in, through the window. Two tablets she gave me next door. Said they'd settle me nerves like; I don't know. . . .'

How chill the room is. The constable looks around him. Some diced rhubarb lies in a bowl on the parlour table, the cupboards are all closed, everything is neat, and the floor is covered only by a grey underfelt; it was the same in the front room, with its two upturned armchairs, and out in the hallway.

'Was it carpets they took mainly, Mrs Mawling?'

'Just me rent money.'

The constable steps into the kitchen, looking embarrassed by his gaffe. Seventy-year-old Mrs Mawling has, in fact, very little. He opens the kitchen cupboard; inside it is a packet of oatmeal porridge, a coffee-jar half-full of sultanas, a box of salt and a canister of sugar.

'Touch anythin' here, luv? Nothin' gone – have you looked?'

'They had those down.'

'Them biscuits?' He reaches up and carefully brings down the tins in his gloved hands. Both tins are still in their cellophane wrappers, and one bears a card from last Christmas. 'Aye, they probably thought you had your savin's in these, but didn't bother when they saw they were—'

'I was surprised,' she says, 'very surprised they didn't take them. Lovely biscuits, they are – I keep them in case me grandchildren come on a visit, so I'll have something for them. You know the sweet tooth kiddies have.'

She could have one herself, judging by the rhubarb and the sultanas.

'Right, so they bust the window, got down over the sink, had a go at the biscuits, lifted the rent from over there – they didn't touch anything else?'

'They had all me things out.'

'Where was that?'

She leads him back into the parlour. 'Here, all thrown about.'

'You've been doin' a spot of tidyin'?'

Mrs Mawling shudders and has to lift her chin before replying. 'It – it frightened me like. And I couldn't have people coming into me house the way it was. I mean. . . .' Tears brim but she fights them back with frail courage, sitting down at the small table with the rhubarb on it.

The constable eyes her warily, apparently alert to some tension in Mrs Mawling he didn't notice earlier. 'No harm done, luv; nothin' here Scene of Crime could've got prints off.

66

Was it all polished up new when you went to the "do", or did you do that before you— ?'

'Before I told them next door me rent'd been stolen.'

'And you did just in here ?'

'Here and the kitchen.'

'What about the bedroom ?'

She makes no response, and doesn't seem to hear the question when it is repeated. 'Won't be a minute, luv,' the constable says casually, withdrawing into the passage.

The bedroom door must be the one on the right with, contrary to usual practice, a key in its lock on the outside. His nose wrinkles slightly; most places where old folk live tend to smell a bit, so he probably hadn't thought anything of this before, but now the set of his mouth indicates that there was a second, very different conclusion he might have jumped to. He unlocks the door and goes in, halting abruptly. The bed has been stripped and its mattress ripped open. The wardrobe has lost its door, and the bedside locker has been broken in pieces, scattering medicines and air-letters everywhere. Someone has urinated over the carefully patched bed linen, and a human turd lies on the dressing table.

Love Lane looks like a film set now, ideal for a bit of Dickens, or even, with the help of a little studio fog, a scene from *Jack the Ripper*. The cat has gone and the padlock on the whisky store hasn't moved one millimetre. Not that much has happened anywhere on the division over the last few hours, to judge by what has been coming over the radio; the usual routine stuff, D-and-Ds, D-and-Is, a wounding, a breaking and entering, and the inevitable automatic alarm calls, which couldn't be more boring. Then a sudden lift to the spirits: the inspector's white Escort has just turned up Stone Street. 'Thought I'd give you a peg. How's it going ?'

'All correct, ma'am.'

They chat for a while about this, that and the other, before going their separate ways again. Love Lane is only one corner of a large beat, and that beat only a corner of the sub-division.

67

II

Inspector North, as she will be known for these eight hours on the radio, is regarded by some of the older bobbies, male chauvinists to a man, as one of their very best officers.* 'There's only one way a woman could do it, and that's by what I think is leadership. She can't come and start bossin' men around, like a fella who'll threaten to punch yer 'ead in if you don't do what you're told. She's great, a smashin' inspector.' She is also, one suspects, everything an older bobby might wish for in a bonny curly-haired daughter: someone unassuming, competent and womanly – as opposed to 'feminine' – while possessed of a certain girlish charm. It takes another woman to remark, 'Aye, she really is as nice as she seems, only underneath she's *tough*, see? Knows her own mind, and cares what happens to her bobbies.' Inspector North is thirty, helps with a children's club when she can, and has lately discovered that sewing makes an ideal pastime for picking up and putting down. Her husband is also a uniformed inspector.

I've often wondered why I joined. We've got no relatives on the job, so I didn't know what I was letting myself in for! (*Laughs*) There's no doubt about that. But I have never gone through a stage of disillusionment.

I joined and was posted into the CID before my two years' probation was finished – which is unheard of now, but we were the Women's Section then, a slight difference. So I did sixteen months in CID and came back into uniform, and during that time I think I'd been in three divisions, all different areas and different ways of working. Of course, with the men, that's unheard of, too: they're posted to a division and they stay there. I think that's what causes their unrest, to be quite honest. There's no doubt about that. I found 'A' Division very depressing. The longest spell I did here before was a year in CID and sixteen months in uniform, and then I moved out to Marsh Lane and was glad to get away. Y'know, you're always getting abuse of one sort or another from the public – not aimed at you, at the uniform. But, of course, you're in it, so you're getting it, as it were!

*Ordinarily senior officers are addressed as Mr, Mrs or Miss So-and so, and very seldom by their rank.

68

They say this is the most deprived part of Liverpool, but I wouldn't, I must say. We've even had people knocking at the door at home collecting for them – 'You're not on!' Oh aye, they seem to get far more spent on them than anyone. My mum lives in a corporation flat, and I'd say she's been in it as long as the people in the flats at the back of St Anne Street. Now, in all that time the corporation have never been round to her, they've never done anything. The odd bit of paint every five years or so? Never been near. But these people have all been moved out in order to be modernised. Oh aye, they get far more spent on their flats because everybody talks about it: We must do this and do this and do that. They have playgrounds – they're wrecked. But that's not the corporation's fault, it's not our fault. It's the way they treat them. There was nothing like that where I came from. They didn't provide anything at all, no playgrounds, nothing.

You're sort of never getting on top of it really and, when it comes to the young lads and girls on foot, it's most frustrating. You can be very, very conscientious and flog around but, no matter how hard you work, you're only one, aren't you? Let's be honest, you've got quite a big area to cover, and there's no way you can stop things going on. Uniform is very much preventative police work, and you've got to have a lot of men to do it. Today we've got three sergeants on the foot section and five men. (*Laughs*) It's atrocious really. Oh, on paper, they'll say, on paper we've got twenty-odd men here. This is all very well, but you've got sickness, annual leave, rest days, courses – you've got three officers off now, injured on duty. We should really start off with far more, so we end up with a reasonable number – not five! (*Laughs again*) I gather last week we ended up with only a couple; y'know, three sergeants and about two foot-men.*

Most of the divisions cover perhaps an area like this and an area like where I live, where people are pro-police and you come out and help the bobby. But you don't get that relief here. It's always the one sort you're dealing with, and you find that, after a while, the bobbies perhaps don't learn to react to ordinary people. They're used to this lot, so they're immediately on the bounce, and ordinary people don't appreciate that much, the ones you come across in the town centre. Nearly all our foot section are recruits, and all you need with them is one bobby with a lot of service who isn't loath to punch up prisoners, and some seem to think: Ooooo, that's the thing! And they'll do it.

*'Men', in this context, being no indication of gender.

69

I know of ones who are that way inclined, and you've got to watch them like a hawk. But the vast majority of bobbies don't agree with violence and, whereas at one time there was a lot of it going on, it's certainly being weeded out now. It's got to be. We're also taking on people with far more qualifications, so the job itself is improving. They've the sense now to realise *anybody* can fall back on that, while the better ones don't have to.

Touch wood, I've never had any bother with violence in my eleven and a half years. Perhaps it sounds a bit pompous, but all I used to do was act daft! And it's surprising what it gets you away with, because they think: Oh, look at this one – we've *her* kidded soft! I've got away with murder, I have really! (*Laughs*) Afterwards you can look back and think: Oooorgh, that could easily have gone nasty . . . but it hasn't. Perhaps one of these days it will backfire on me and, if it did, it might make me far more apprehensive. But at the moment, of course, I sail on quite happily.

Once I arrested two men for possessing an offensive weapon. At the time I didn't think anything about it, but when I went back to the same division a few years later I had it quoted back at me. I was on my own in a jeep when I stopped and searched them, and they had a cosh the same sort of shape as a bobby's truncheon but far heavier, made of leather sort of stitched. The men were both sort of twenty – I'd just been made sergeant, so I was twenty-three – and they were both big. I said to them, 'What are you doing with it?' 'Ah, we're just taking it down to the police station – we found it.' They hadn't, you know. That was painfully obvious, because it'd been raining and this cosh they'd just found was dry, y'see. So I said to them, 'I'm going down to the police station. Hop in, I'll take you down there.' They were in the back of the jeep and the doors didn't lock, so they could have been out and away. All I did was chatter on about everything and anything until I got them back in the yard – just *cute*, y'see! The bobbies in the bridewell nearly died when I took them in there. 'God,' they said.

The sergeants are also making their rounds. Once nobody thought of becoming a sergeant until he had at least seven years' service, if not ten, but the manpower shortage has changed all that, and many sergeants are themselves almost as young as their sections. Some members of the 'old school'

70

regard this as a lamentable state of affairs, and point to the problems caused by lack of experience and a corresponding lack of authority. That these exist is undeniable, but there would seem to be a positive side to the change as well. Being still as young as they are, the sergeants possibly have a better understanding of their charges, and are able, through a less obvious form of authority, to provide the kind of leadership better suited to the modern recruit. This sergeant is a robust twenty-five-year-old, standing 5 feet 11 inches; essentially a friendly man, and graced by good looks that give him an easy self-confidence, he is married to an air-hostess – they have in fact just returned from a £24 round trip to Bermuda, which accounts for his tropical tan.

I think we expect a lot from these probationers. The first four weeks on the streets can be quite frightening, y'know, so he or she has got to have a bit of a hand behind 'em. Their tutor bobby might say, 'OK, lock 'im up and, if he smacks you, I'll grab 'im.' But after that four weeks they're out on their own, and my job's to go out and supervise them, make sure they're getting the right kind of jobs, and make sure they're in the right places to find them. Every three months I have to do a report on them, see, so it's important to know how they are. I go and walk with them for half a day or something, and see how they are with the public – whether they're mature, over-sympathetic, overbearing or whatever – and I advise them.

With this over-sympathetic behaviour, you'll get a lot of people who will come up to you in the street and tell you a story. You can become too involved in it, become really sorry, and think: Ah, dear. . . . Then you try and do too much. The idea is, y'see, to go and give them the assistance they need, but not to become involved too personally. I remember one time, when I'd just joined the job, there was an old woman whose dog had been run over. She's cryin' her eyes out, and I felt really sorry. There were tears in *my* eyes, y'know! Ah, God, where am I going to get her another dog from? All this, you see – which I don't suppose was a bad idea. The dog had to be removed, and we had a van driver nearby and he came down. He said, 'Now, don't you worry, luv! We'll move the dog for you, we'll give it a nice burial.' and I thought: This *is* a nice bobby, this! Nearby we had a brickworks, so we go down there and I'm still upset about the

71

old lady. We drive into the brickworks and I say, 'What are you doin' this for?' Next thing, he has a word with one of the managers, and the doors of the big oven open. He picks the dog up by the tail, swings it round his head, and in it goes. I thought: You bastid! What did you do that for? But I learned something. Well, perhaps that's not the best example of what I mean. . . . (Shrugs) There are certain times, especially in domestic disputes, when the person you're talking to is just as guilty as the one you might have to lock up, you see.

On the whole, though, I prefer a bobby who's a little over-sympathetic to one who is all-powerful. You get one or two who will go out on the streets the big I AM. Y'know, *I'm* a policeman and *you're* going to do as I say.

That's completely wrong. You might have bobbies who've worked for years on a particular area, a violent area, and they've built up a good relationship, so the people think: Oh, the bobbies aren't *that* bad, y'know. Then you get an idiot of a bobby, one who's all-powerful, and he'll smack a kid in the street or something. Next minute, everything's flyin'! What happens then? He'll shout for assistance, and other bobbies will have to go in and bale him out.

If you're nice to start with, you can always turn nasty later if you have to – that's what I tell these recruits. Because it's the worst thing in the world to go up to somebody and say, 'Hey, on yer bloody way! Move yer arse *now*!' and he says, 'Oh, I'm awfully sorry, I'm going.'

The advice I give to bobbies when they first come to me, is that there's no point in being a hero, especially in the first month or so on the job. When you find an empty premises that has been broken into, never go in on your own – there's no point in going in and being hit over the head or whatever. Always radio for a back-up. Don't shout 'Con requires assistance' because then everybody comes, and it means you're on the floor, getting kicked to hell! (*Laughs*) There's no point, either, in going into a situation where the bucks will obviously know you're new, because they'll automatically use that against you.

It's hard to judge at first. A policewoman, a nice girl, was told to go round the back into the Four Squares the other night, a rough area. She was to go with a message to a house she'd been to before, and the fella that's in there is violent and a plonkie, y'see. It was about three o'clock in the morning, and I was actually in Soho Street and ready to go with her. From the radio,

72

I gathered she was saying, 'Is there anybody else to go with me?' There wasn't, because they were all tied up, so she said, 'Can I wait until it's daylight before I go in?' That's wrong, y'know, but I admire her honesty. I know police officers who'd say, 'Yes, I'm on me way,' not go, and then say, 'Oh, no reply from that house.' I was in Soho Street not because I'm braver than anybody else, but because I know, if a situation arises, I'll either deal with it or radio for assistance. Whereas she would be just that little bit unsure: When do I call for assistance? What if it's not required after all?

You'll see some police officers during their first few months on the job who are very quiet and very reserved, shy even. Nine months later and they're completely different; they can walk anywhere – and that can only be gained by experience.

This North Sub is depressing, I find. When I'm walking out, I look round and see just how rough the people in this area are, how poor they are, how poorly clothed. Even in the shopping-centre, it's very rare you see somebody 'nice'. They *look* poor, they look as though they've only got a few bob in their pockets – which most of them have – and that depresses me. I walk around the derelict buildings, and that depresses me. I walk around the estate, which is full of gobshites – bloody idiots who all they do is hate the police – and that depresses me. There are nice people, too; it's a struggle for them here, and that depresses me.

But then again, some who look poor are sometimes the ones with the money, aren't they? Perhaps they just spend it on different things! Here I am, a sergeant, and I love a pint. But if I go out and have a couple of pints and a cigar I really feel it, y'know. It's eaten me money away. Occasionally you say, 'Well, no, I can't – I'm stayin' in.' But these people I'm talking about, these yobs who hang about the city centre like, whenever you have dealings with them, they always smell of drink. Every day we're locking up 'unemployed' who've been out drinkin', and you can see from the cement on their trousers, mud on their boots, they've been working on building-sites – absolutely pathetic.

You get the feeling you're losing at times over what happens in the courts, but I love being a police officer. It's my life really. I'm always suspicious of people who say they're dedicated to a job, but I am. I left the police force in '74 to work abroad on a millionaire's yacht, and I missed it so much. It wasn't the actual job I missed; being on Nights in the rain getting thumped is not

73

the type of thing you miss. It was the lads, sitting down and having a cup of tea with them, laffin' and jokin' about what had happened the night before. You're in that sort of mood, and then the radio will go – and you're suddenly with that same group in a situation on the street and you're all working together. It's hard to describe in words; I don't think you get it in any other job. We're all in the same boat, you see: we've all got a second-hand car we're tryin' to keep on the road, we're all short of cash, we all go scrappin', we all go suppin' – and you do it all together. It's great.

12

The uniformed officers of 'A' Division show a marked awareness of their physical vulnerability, and clearly most probationers regard the personal radio they carry as their only real defence against getting badly hurt. 'I mean it's like fokkin' *ice hockey* when they get started in a wine lodge, but we don't have none of that paddin' and shin guards and other gear, do we? Not that we'd want it. Christ, can you imagine the bucks?' The nearest thing to protective clothing on general issue is, in fact, a clip-on tie which, like the tail of a lizard, comes away in the hand when roughly grasped.

Given time, however, many of these recruits will probably begin to make the claim so often heard among police officers, 'Me mouth is me major weapon,' and mean something that has nothing to do with calling for help. Here a chief inspector looks back on his early years.

When you shift a crowd from outside a pub, you learn to deal with people. The first time I tried to do it, as a very young bobby, I was challenged by a member of the crowd and I threatened to lock him up. He called my bluff and said, 'Well, go on!' I chickened out and walked away with my tail between my legs – a thoroughly humiliating experience. Some years later, when I'd got a lot more service in, I came across a similar situation in Upper Parliament Street.

It's a crowd outside a pub after closing-time on a summer's evening. People are having to step into the roadway to get past

74

them, so I'm going to have to shift 'em or somebody might get knocked down. I try 'Come on, off home! You've had your drink now. Come on, off!'

And they aren't going to go. Now, they were all people who knew each other. They were in the middle years of their marriage, sort of thing – thirty-, forty-year-olds – and not boys you could bluff. Anything you did to one they would all respond to – and, of course, there was a comedian amongst them. A leader, a loud-mouth, and he started taking the mickey out of me. I'm just not going to shift this lot, no way.

But by now I'm a craftier young man than I was, and so I say, 'Hey, mouth, over 'ere! I want to talk to yer.' He's delighted: 'Oh, Christ, I'm gettin' locked up! Bloody hell! Will yer all come and bail me out?' With that, the crowd are immediately alerted.

So I draw him to one side and I say, 'Listen, mate, you've been in there drinking all night.'

'Nuttin' wrong wid dat!'

'Hang on a minute. I've been walkin' a beat. I haven't 'ad a drink, me mouth's parched. And when I get this lot shifted – *when* I get 'em shifted – I'm in the side-door there for me *one pint this evenin'*. I'm choked. You've 'ad yours. Let me 'ave mine.'

'Oh, sorry, skin! Sorry. Didn't realise. Come on, on yer way! On yer bike!'

They're off – and I don't drink!

Only I didn't mind telling a lie like that because by now I've learned the psychology of the crowd. If I was authority against them, they'd present an impassive face. But if I told them I was going to do something against police rules – well, they'd support me to the hilt on that.

Guile is not always sufficient, though, these same experienced officers are quick to point out. 'I mean, how can you reason with someone when they're not in a reasonable mood – not *capable* of reasoning? And somebody's going to get injured, some innocent person they don't fancy the look of, and they're yelling, " 'Ow would yer like to wake up wid a crowd around yer?" There's a line, see, they go beyond. I'm just sorry for these kids that're coming on the job now. I never had to worry like they do. Society valued me and the innocent bystander

75

more than this ravin' idiot who needs lockin' up till the juices are down, so he can get in his Burton's suit for the magistrate. They're in the front line – that's the important point. CID go round in pairs, the OSD in pairs, all experienced men, older. These kids aren't your hard-knock bobbies anyway, but they're so *exposed*, aren't they? In every direction.'

The senior police surgeon makes an entrance like a small honey bear on a circus ball. Dynamic, jolly and widely popular, chiefly because he scorns professional mystique and puts even the newest recruit at ease, he never wears a white coat in his surgery at the Main Bridewell, but begins every examination by saying, 'I am a qualified medical practitioner.' Once, before he had an opportunity to make this declaration, a patient from his general practice looked up and said, 'Hello, Doc! Have they got you, too?' A story he delights in, just as he relishes the bizarre. In addition to his work for the police and the National Health Service, he has a private forensic practice, specialising in industrial accidents, in Rodney Street – Liverpool's equivalent to Harley Street, and the birthplace of both Gladstone and Nicholas Monsarrat.

I very rarely used to treat injured bobbies, and I've been a police surgeon for twenty-seven, twenty-eight years. Now they're two a penny; in fact, I hardly have to treat prisoners now.

The most common injury the police have here in Liverpool are kicks to the testicles. Very common and very painful; at the time, it's a terrible shock – and they're off work for several weeks. Then you get broken noses, dislocated thumbs, fractured ribs, and some are sliced by bottles. I see lots of women police injured too, and I'm worried about them on the streets. They're just not safe on their own.

People complain against the police for everything now, and the result is the police are afraid to restrain them – and the result is they get injured. In the old, old days, you never got policemen injured, because they'd use their baton. Well, they're issued to protect the police.

I've seen thousands of these injuries, but there has been a marked decline since the Police Act of 1964. A baton wound is a laceration. A bit of blood always makes a mess – I mean a

76

bottle of ink does and that's about as much blood as we're talking about, if that. Good God! What's happened to him? All it is, is a cut over the eyebrow; three or four stitches do the job, no question of hospital. But the blood makes such a mess, and it's so dramatic when you see it on television.

There's no question of the police being brutal – they're marked men if they start that business. They're normal family people and I'm the same as them: you react to a situation as it develops. I deal with a variety of clients in a day; I can be as gentle as a lamb with some, I can be nasty with others, depending on how they treat me. Once a prisoner starts violence, he's going to be arrested come what may! And the more force he's going to use, the more force is going to be applied to him. I very rarely see force in excess of need, as you might say, and then I've made my feelings known in superior quarters. I'm never isolated in this – other people on the job have noticed – and we have got rid of that particular person.

But we know these standard defences. Whenever we get a bobby injured, we know we're going to get a complaint against the police. In fact, whenever I do get a bobby injured, I always examine the defendant as well, to sort of box the job in.

This business of complaints against the police, well. . . . (*Chuckles*) Whenever I deal with a case – especially a drunken driver – I always get accused of being drunk! Or I'm bent or I'm queer! I was even called *ugly* the other night, which is a new one.

13

In just over a minute, the Afternoon shift will have ended. The battered drunk struggles and heaves and tries to lash out at the two uniforms bent over him. 'Mother o' God!' he screams, as the grip on his wrists is tightened. 'Dere killin' me! Help! Jesus an' Mary! Don't! Don't. . . .' He begins to shriek wildly, drumming his heels and rolling the one eye which isn't a pulpy red mess.

'If yer don't shut up, pal, I'll smack yer m'self,' growls the constable holding him down. 'Lie still, will yer? You're only making it harder for—'

'Yer killin' me, yer fokkers! Six! Six o' yer! Just—'

77

'Lie still! And watch yer language! Understand?'

'I'm dyin',' whimpers the drunk, vomiting again.

'Oh, very nice, and on me S-9s, too, this time,' sighs the constable, stamping one leg of his trousers. 'What the hell have you lot been doin' to this fella?'

The nurse on the other side of the casualty trolley giggles. 'We thought it was one of yours like,' she says, cutting away the sodden shirt to reveal a bottle wound in the drunk's side. 'H'm, that's nasty.'

'This? *Mine?* Wouldn't touch it with a bloody barge—' He laughs, struck by how absurd this is, and the nurse, who is splattered with sick and blood herself, laughs with him. 'But seriously, luv, came in by himself, did he?'

'Couple of fellas brought him. Dumped him over there by the door, then before Sister could—'

'Six fellas,' the drunk mumbles.

'Aye, and do you know who they were, pal? Know their names?'

'*Seven* fellas!'

'But do you know any of their names, Mr McKenna?' the nurse coaxes. 'Can you tell us who did this to you?'

'Eight coonts built like brick—'

'Hey! What did I just—?'

'Don't worry,' whispers the nurse. 'I'm used to it, if you aren't!' She draws the drip-stand a little closer. 'Feeling a bit quieter now, are we, luv? Mr McKenna?'

'Wha'? Wha' yer say?'

'Nurse was sayin' you just lie nice and still and we'll fix you up, OK?'

'You're safe in hospital now and—'

'Went in this club, see. . . .' Mr McKenna loses consciousness.

'Aye, aye, we're off. Is the doctor comin'?'

The nurse nods. 'Great. Thanks very much. Here, wipe that with this. Sorry if—'

'Any time I'm passing'! Y'know, if you see something you fancy, just tip us the wink like.' And the constable makes his own wink wickedly suggestive.

78

14

It's a wet windy mid-week morning, going on for nine, and the personal radio in the front office at Copperas Hill has hardly drawn breath for twenty minutes now. Call after call is a report of yet another automatic alarm ringing somewhere in 'A' Division, just like the start of a crime wave on television.

A drenched probationer, about to go out again, holds open the front door for a detective sergeant hurrying in without a raincoat.

'Cheers, lad. All right?' says the DS.

'All right, sir—' He might have been about to add 'for some, that is', but his turn in the CID could come, if he keeps his nose clean.

With a nod to the bridewell sergeant, the DS carries on through the doorway on the left, paying no attention to the radio. At the beginning and end of every working day, for upwards of an hour or so, the strident cacophony of alarms seldom signifies anything more than the carelessness of people either entering or locking up their own premises. Besides which, unless a detective is on Nights, or engaged in a particularly tricky mission, personal radios play no direct part in his life, but remain with the uniformed officers at street level.

Once up the flight of stairs, and past the rubber plant on the landing's window-sill, things are always a lot quieter, although today there seems to be an unnatural hush in the room used by the sub-division's fifteen detective constables. The DS looks in on them, to find another detective sergeant trying to solve a problem with a piece of knotted string. Not a new problem, either, but one that has been pressing for a couple of weeks or so: How does one fit another desk into a room already so overcrowded that, unless care is taken, anyone leaving his chair bumps into the person seated behind him?

'Boss, what if we put the phone on the files and—'

'Tried it,' says the detective sergeant with the string, 'and I've measured this side of the files as well.'

The DS at the door beats a discreet retreat down the wing occupied by the sub-divisional commander, the deputy com-

79

mander, the detective inspector in charge of the CID, and the five detective sergeants, who have an office of their own which is roomy enough for three. There he wedges himself into a corner, behind a desk stacked with papers, and notes the time of his arrival in his duty diary, which has a full page for each day's activities. With any luck, he'll be able to begin by entering a complicated robbery enquiry that still requires several hours' typing, but knows he can't count on doing so. He and his seventeen colleagues each handle an average of 340 cases a year, and this means taking on at least one new job a day, depending on how they fall.

Despite this workload, however, he shows no sign of stress. He is thirty-five, well dressed in the style of middle management, and has a handsome unguarded face that would look just right in an advertisement for family life insurance.

You're thinking ahead in the CID, whereas in Uniform you're mainly reacting to situations. You've got to think ahead; your mind's active, and you're moving from one job to another all the time. This keeps the brain going, keeps alive the interest. I mean, a fourteen-hour day here goes just like that! (*Snaps fingers*) In fact, since I've been here, I've never woken up and thought: Oh God, I've got to go in there again.

I don't think you ever think of the hazards of the job, quite honestly. Every few months or so, you see police officers have been assaulted in the streets, and the same names keep cropping up time and again, y'know. Obviously, it's the approach, I would think. A nice quiet approach is the one I've always adopted – it was shown to me by another detective who taught me the job – and I've never been badly injured. I mean, in this office, I can't recall anybody being assaulted in three and a half years. I think as detectives you develop this as well. You know, you've *got* to be able to get on with people, you've got to be able to talk with people -- and to get through to them, particularly if they don't want you to. I try to treat everybody the same; that's my interpretation of the job. You can't do it all the time, but certainly always with complainants. I'll look after an old lady in Myrtle Gardens who's been robbed just the same as a rich businessman.

I joined the Cheshire police fourteen years ago from the Post Office because a great friend of mine joined, and I thought I'd

80

give it a bash. I was in Uniform for four years, and I've been in divisional CID ever since. I was watching a new programme on television the other night – bloody 'Target', it was. I could never be a character like that bloke. His aggressive attitude. . . . (*Shakes head*) To his own people as well, y'know, and of course they treated the divisional CID like crap. To my mind, the divisional CID are the blokes really involved in the work. Having said that, I'd still like to get on the Regional Crime Squad, Serious Crime Squad, move out a little, y'know. We're all made differently, of course, but on the whole I'd say most detectives I've worked with have been of a similar manner to me. They're not aggressive. I also think a lot of young fellas, if they come off the streets into CID, if they're aggressive, they'll change. They find it doesn't get them anywhere.

After the amalgamation [of police forces] in 1974, I came over here from Cheshire – quite a big change! The people were totally different to the people I'd been dealing with. In Cheshire, I could go out on me own and arrest somebody, and I very often did that. But over there. . . . (*Smiles*) Oh, I tried it once or twice, but I certainly wouldn't do it now. It's a different world here . . . oh, absolutely. I think if you brought my two lads over here and put them in the Bullring, it would break their hearts. I like to think they're going to be pretty strong-minded when they grow up, but put them in this environment and I just don't think they'd exist, quite honestly. Even my wife doesn't realise it's just an existence with a lot of these people – and there are quite a lot of good ones. It's a terrible state to be in really; unemployment, lack of cash, lack of things to do. You can't blame the kids, in many respects.

I suppose we're containing a situation – this is all we're doing really. But in some respects it's out of hand. It's not safe to walk these streets at night, which is a terrible indictment on society. I certainly would never come over to Liverpool with my wife at night; if we go out for an evening, we probably go to Chester, somewhere like that. I wouldn't dream of coming to Liverpool. There's a fear here you will be attacked, and it's a genuine fear.

We're dealing with it all the time, y'know, with innocent people. OK, they're wandering round at night, they've been into a club and they've had a few drinks, but there's nothing bad about that. They come out and they're just picked on and savagely attacked. We deal with some terrible bloody wounding offences, completely unprovoked. You think, y'know: That could have been me! One particular incident I dealt with, this bloke is just hurled through a shop-window; a bloody huge piece of glass went right through his back and pierced his intestines. This was two o'clock in the morning. He'd been out for a drink and was on his way back to the Feathers Hotel. A complete stranger to the city who could have died easily, y'know; he'd lost pints of blood at the scene. Fortunately, as in so many cases, we've got a good ambulance service and they're quick in response.

The majority of these attacks are late at night, and are obviously associated with clubs. This is one of the big problems, I think, with the city: the club situation. The majority of them are poorly run. They're there for the money; get everybody in, get their money and get them out. Obviously, it's been allowed to escalate as well, with the licences being issued to them. There's an awful lot of villains involved in these clubs; even if they can't get the licence, there's always a way round it and they'll put a front man in. Even a lot of the public houses are the same: the husband's got form, so he's the barman, and the wife's the licensee.

There's not very great premeditation in these attacks. There's four or five of them, they've had a drink, they come out of a club and they see someone on their own. It's a quick decision – maybe one goes over, and then the others join in. This is what I deal in, a lot of it.

I try not to get emotionally involved in my work – oh, very much so. It would be a bad thing if I did get involved. My wife was a nurse, y'know, and she would never go back to nursing for that reason: she got too emotionally involved in her work.

Children can be the upsetting part. But, you see, I dealt with an indecency case where there were about seven children involved, and they ranged in age from about nine years to twelve years. . . . (Shrugs) If this was over the water – anywhere else but Liverpool – you would have got this thirty-year-old man approaching the children to render services. On this occasion, it was the children who approached the man and took money off him. Child prostitution, in other words, and this is going on now. It's a terrible thing. The problem with these offences is getting to know them; in this case, one of the girls talked to her elder sister. Certainly I was never emotionally involved in that. Although they were only children, they were the instigators.

Let's face it, with children these days of course they're matur-

82

ing much younger, aren't they? They're reaching puberty at ten and eleven years of age, and obviously they're always experimenting and things like that. With our kids, I think we try to be very, very open. We used to all bath together until very recent years, and they know all about it, let's put it that way One would hope from that they'd develop a healthy attitude to it.

Most of my spare time is spent with the family – I've two boys, eight and ten – and what we do, we sort of do together. When I get home – y'know, on a summer evening – we go out with the children. We've got some nice spots to go to, where I live. We can go down to the river and watch the huge tankers coming by.

The first step towards becoming a detective is to be posted as a CID aide for six months, after which the officer usually goes back into uniform until, provided he or she has shown an aptitude for the work, a vacancy occurs.

Some aides are only too glad to get away from it for good. 'Y'know the old sayin', "Uniform is hours and hours of utter boredom punctuated by seconds of sheer fokkin' terror"? That's not a bad description really, only if it's borin' you've always a good chance of a laff with the lads. But in CID you're always bein' pushed. Not by the bosses so much, y'know – by the job. The pressure's sort of *self-inflicted*, you could say.'

A uniformed sergeant feels: 'CID? Don't want to know it. I tried it as an aide. I hate CID. I like to be in at the kill.' A view echoed by this former aide: 'It's different in Uniform. Usually you see a thing happening – or hear it – and you're in there! The fella's all covered in blood and snot, and you lift the one what done it, feel 'is collar, grab the bastid. You're not sayin' to yerself: Is this the one? Or: I know he bloody did it, only how can I prove it? Black and white, a lot of Uniform work is, not bloody grey like the jacks have to deal with.'*

While another former aide has this to say: 'First thing I learned on the job was that it was a game; some you win, some you lose, you mustn't let it bother yer. Different sorts of game,

*These are the figures for crime arrests during one month at Copperas Hill, excluding prisoners on shoplifting charges: Uniform, 42; Days and EPs, 13; CID, 17; Plain Clothes, 5; Car Squad, 1; OSD, 46.

mind. Uniform is – what? Football? Rugby? Something you do outdoors anyway, but CID's like sort of cards, if you like. A table and lots of bits of paper, and you often don't know who you're fokkin' playin' with, to be honest! You know what I had nightmares about? Paper!'

And then there is that other source of stress. 'If there's a break on your beat, you go along and take a few details for your [Form] 52, tell the old dear that the CID will be along, and that's about all, really. You've done your job. Then the jack goes along and listens to all her troubles, gets a bit involved just to see if she maybe knows somethin' she doesn't realise – or is scared to tell him about. Comes out, both shoulders wringin' wet, knowing she expects him to do something – half the time, there's sod all he can do. It's frustrating, I suppose you'd call it.'

But whether or not an aide takes to CID work, they all seem to experience the same shock to begin with. 'Oh, I knew about the hours – y'know, you work nine to five one day, then nine to eleven the next – so that didn't bother me. It was the paperwork. Christ, I'd noticed if you asked a jack what the job was like, he'd just rabbit on about the paperwork, but I thought it was to – well, put you off like. I learned different, I can tell yer! You can get a file *that* thick (*indicates three inches or so*) and still be bloody at it! Lists of exhibits, copies of statements, all the correspondence with the solicitors you've got to do, criminal injuries compensation. . . . And you've got to watch the spellin' and grammar and all sorts, because a brief's going to be reading your stuff in court and, if there's a mistake, some clever sods never miss the chance of takin' the piss, makin' everyone laff at the bobby.'

A detective constable's desk can have upwards of forty or more Form 52s on it; small booklets in which a uniformed officer enters the brief details of a crime before handing the matter over. This pile has a new addition or two every day, many of which are patently non-starters, such as 'Sneak theft from handbag in ladies' toilet, St John's Centre', although the complainant must still be interviewed. Stacks of wire trays hold cases that have been opened – there could be upwards of

84

twenty of these pending – and then there are the fat cardboard folders filled with partially completed court files, many of which will eventually run to over a hundred documents.

The problem of the extra desk has been shelved again until time permits. Most of the eight men on duty have taken their share of the overnight 'breaks' off the spike, and are already on their way to make preliminary enquiries. The spike was once a real one, and anyone found rearranging the slips, so as to give himself an undemanding selection, was accused of 'spike dancing'; both terms are still in use, although now it's simply a matter of initialling jobs listed in the crime report book.

A face remains at the middle window, epitomising the picture many people have of a young detective. High-cheeked, blond and unblinking, it stares at a corner of the Bullring, never changing expression, never laughing at anyone's jokes, quite unmoved. Every now and then, someone gives its fashionably long wig a twist, or lends it a pair of sunglasses, just for a giggle. How the head of the shop dummy got there, nobody seems to know, but they wouldn't be without it.

Y'know, in every CID office I've been in – and I've been a detective for twenty-two years – life is one big laff all day. This is why the American police on telly aren't so bad, but the ones we do about England are terrible. 'Softly Softly' was outrageous – everybody so rank-conscious! *Sergeant* Snow and all that! All right, a 'sir' is a 'sir' – or just 'boss' – but sergeants and cons are all on first names. We're laffin' and jokin', we talk about what happened the night before. Telling little stories about what *really* happened – y'know, you go to these houses to search them, and the girl has just got out of bed and got nothing on. Some have got no shame, and they just come to the door and say, 'Come in'! Of course we laugh and joke about it! It's a pleasure to come to work.

Now nearing his retirement, after a total of more than thirty years as a policeman in Liverpool, this grey-haired, gentle-faced officer, who could so easily be mistaken for a school-master, is the 'CID clerk' at Copperas Hill and, in effect, combines all three functions in one.

'At your age,' said the boss who introduced me to this job, 'you don't want to go chasing over rooftops.' I didn't want to do it, but there's nobody else and so I'm making the best of it. You miss the hurly-burly, getting out and feeling a few collars, locking up.

But it's essential to have an experienced CID man answering the telephone. Particularly these days, when we get very young policemen who invariably go first to the scene of a crime and, because of the circumstances, may not be able to decide then and there what the offence is. For example, sometimes they can't decide on how bad a wounding is: whether it's a Section 20, lack of intent; a Section 47, no skin broken perhaps, but actual bodily harm; or a Section 18, where there is intent to cause grievous bodily harm, which is the more serious. Sitting here, I can supply complainants with further information, or pour oil on troubled waters if they feel they haven't received the proper attention, and I can deal with solicitors ringing up about various details.

Then I keep our crime book up to date and do general administrating; all the files come through me, and I send them to the boss. I can also give the DCs advice and help with the preparation of these court files, committal evidence, perhaps a DPP's report. It's such a young detective office, and the vast majority who come in now are very naïve.

Some are detectives before they're policemen! (*Laughs*) Once upon a time, you had to be a very experienced policeman before you were even considered for the CID, a very commendable, mature policemen. What I do is judge a man on his attitude towards a prisoner. Some bring them into the office and start saying, 'You're this – and you're that. . . .' It doesn't pay off. If you try to make him look small, I don't think you'll get his co-operation.

I look on it in this light. I could have been born in that building (*points to the Bullring*) – couldn't we all? I was born in West Derby village, where there were green fields and what have you – a working-class area, granted, but not the slums of Liverpool. Half these kids get off to a bad start because it's their *birthright* to be a buck. But there are an awful lot more good kids that come from bad homes than there are bad kids from bad homes, and this is a distinction a lot of young policemen don't make. Certainly, unless a detective realises this, he'll never get to know anybody.

86

Let's face it, ninety per cent of a detective's 'deductions' are the result of having good informants. All right, we have the sciences. The fingerprint and forensic people for bad jobs like rapes, where you collect and collate the evidence like hairs and that. But with the average burglar, apart from prints sometimes, you don't have this. The only way you'll get it is to have a good informer. I've put them away for years, and they've come out and rung me up; I don't even have to give them anything. Why? Only because I haven't sort of – well, degraded them.

The telephone rings. It's a DC calling to say he is back on the spike, and won't be down at the Crown Court all day after all. Just as predicted, the accused in the case of the stolen ash-tray has decided to admit the job, after pleading not guilty at the magistrate's court and electing trial by jury. So much for those hours of extra paperwork. The DC has a couple of people to see in connection with an assault in a Chinese restaurant, then he'll make his way back to the office. The clerk puts down the receiver.

There was definitely less work in the old days. They used to say 'Yes' if they were caught and you had them bang to rights. Yes, they'd make a statement saying they did it. Of course, you had the odd one or two, the hard fellas – y'know, even if you had them on fingerprint evidence, they'd still say, 'It wasn't me!' And with a fella like that there's nothing you can do to change his mind. Although, in those days, we did have one or two little levers – particularly if you got him on a Friday night or Saturday morning, when there was no court, and Liverpool or Everton were playing at home. You'd find out which one he was, and say, 'You're goin' to miss the match tomorrow. If you want your bail, then cough the job.'

All right, it was wrong. In law it was wrong to do that. But it was done. It suited both parties. And you put in a good word for him at court: you'd say he wouldn't do it again, something had upset him and he was very sorry. But, of course, the whole system's changed. There are very few 'guilty' pleas now. Everybody is represented, and the solicitors always tell them, 'It's a "not guilty" plea' – y'know, we'll have a go, and go for another remand.' And so it drags on.

The clerk gathers up some papers and goes off to give them to

87

the detective inspector. Over in the far corner of the room a DS from St Anne Street is delivering a message, and has become side-tracked by an account of the interview he had yesterday with a social worker, while trying to have a much-burgled old man moved to a different neighbourhood. 'Oh aye, then it got personal,' he chortles. ' "You're ostracised from society," this fella said, delousin' the back of 'is 'ead. "The public at large don't like you, the criminals don't like you, *we* don't like you!" Honest, this is true, this is. Wearing sandals in weather like this, because he's more intelligent than us what wear proper shoes. *Superb.*'

The rain has stopped, the wind has dropped, the air smells of wet brick and exhaust fumes. Three complainants remain to be seen, and then the DC, making his rounds on foot, can get back to the work he has planned for the day.

'Where now?' asks the aide at his side.

'Break at some wholesaler's.'

The wholesale firm is off a busy thoroughfare, down a narrow side street leading into a maze of even smaller streets, and its warehouses must have been standing there since the last century. The office is altogether Dickensian, and the manager, summoned by a typist with traces of 'punk' make-up, needs only a quill pen and a pair of whiskers to look the part that imagination has already created for him.

'Not a lot gone, gents. Just a couple of boxes of tins of fruit and one of wine-glasses. This has happened before, of course. Kids from the flats round the back don't miss a thing, do they? They're in like a flash, of course. Sorry to trouble you really, and I've told the insurance people, of course.'

'Can we see where they got in, sir?'

'Of course.'

Back through the office, where surreptitious glances bounce round the room like a ball in a squash court, and then down the splintered staircase, listening to a lament on the decline of public morality. The detectives are shown an empty storeroom with a very inadequate door that has apparently been forced – although, when they examine it themselves, this isn't apparent

88

at all. Neither is it clear why these three boxes should have been left in there all on their own.

'Well?' says the DC, as they start back up the side street.

'Another world,' the aide murmurs with a grin.

'I mean the alleged break.'

'More like a stock control problem, d'you think?'

'What can you prove? Let's try the old fella again.'

This time the great panelled door of the fine Georgian terrace house – now divided into flats – opens to their knock, and a small weathered man, with a widow's peak and tattooed hands, looks out fearfully. His nerves, he explains in the echoing hallway, are still all shook up.

The detectives are led into a high-ceilinged room with a huge sash window and very little else. There are two chairs, one hard and one soft, huddled over a small gas fire in the enormous grate and, just within reach, stands a small table. On the stained red tablecloth are a couple of eggy plates, half a bottle of milk, a packet of sliced bread, two paperbacks – *Teeny Bopper Idol* and *The Billion Dollar Killing* – and a prodigious quantity of carbon scraped from burnt toast. A single empty stout-bottle under the sink in one corner serves to intensify the feeling of palpable loneliness. Both CID men become noticeably subdued, and the DC asks if the old fella was perhaps an ex-seaman. An affirmative answer gives them something in common, and they chat for a minute or so about the shipping lines they once served on.

Then a gnarled shaking hand is extended. 'They pulled a knife out and said they'd cut me finger off for the ring. It were only silver, but it had sentimental value, y'know. And then they—'

'Who was it that—?'

'Three with masks, coloured fellas. They weren't in the chip shop, and when I came out, next thing was – *whoosh!*'

'And where—?'

'I told the other fella, y'know, the bobby at the hospital. I think I've got one – yes, I think I could point him out to you.'

'It's just if we can go over the whole thing again in detail, you see, because—'

89

'I had four pints, right ?'

'Right.'

'I had four pints. I got a meat-and-potato pie and a curry, came out the chip shop and – *whoosh*! Hand over me mouth and dragged me into the garage.'

Slowly, very slowly, the story of the robbery is extended and all the bits and pieces filled in, although, even then, they still don't amount to much. A good twenty minutes go by before the detectives are ready to leave.

'I think I've got one,' says the old sailor, tapping his temple. 'Hard to tell with these coloured fellas, but I think I could point 'im out to you.' If he has said that once, he has said it two dozen times. 'I'm not swearin' to do it. It was that fast, y'see. I came out the chip shop and – *whoosh*!'

'Fine. I'll come back with a book of pictures, then. OK ?'

'Today ?'

'Tomorrow more like – in the evening, OK ?'

'I'm not promisin' nuttin', mind. Three it was, with masks on. I. . . .'

There is something else he wants to say. Perhaps the three staple foods on the table say it for him: he could be buying them all from the milkman, and not setting foot outside the house any longer.

The last call takes hardly five minutes. The proprietor of a tobacconist-cum-novelty shop has had a skateboard stolen from his window display by a group of four boys he has seen before on several occasions. But, as pictures of juveniles cannot be taken and kept, the best the DC can do is to give the man his name and telephone number.

'If you see them in here again, just—'

'You see my problem, don't you, officer ?'

'Aye, the bus stop is—'

'Me being right on a bus stop like, as I say, is half of the trouble. They wait till they see the bus comin', three of them comes up to the counter for penny chews – I've got to count them out, see ? – and the fourth little blighter—'

'Well, sir, we can give it a try, can't we ? OK ?'

'That's the problem.'

90

'I can see that. You'll give us a ring, then?'

'*If* they comes back,' mumbles the proprietor, but he is plainly mollified by having this chance of a good grumble.

It makes a change to drop into an antique shop on the way back, and to browse about while the owner finds something to preoccupy his only customer. The DC introduces the aide, hands over a description of some jewellery stolen two days ago, and slips into a discussion about the engraving on the brass face of the new grandfather clock. He is very partial to grand-father clocks, and has developed an interest in antiques as a whole, tempting him to linger in the dim and delightful clutter. But the aide, as eager as a puppy to explore more of a new and intriguing forest, is already tugging at his lead. 'What's next?' he asks as they reach the pavement. 'That one-o-four still stuck in your typewriter,' the DC reminds him.

15

The detective sergeant who had hoped to get some typing done is actually making headway. So when the bridewell sergeant rings through for a DS during the lunch-hour one of his colleagues volunteers for the job and goes down. There are two girls waiting below, one of whom is in a considerable state of distress; she'd flagged down a police car, saying that a social worker had advised her to see the CID about a problem. The station has no interview-room as such, apart from a cubby hole also used for the uniformed sergeants' lockers, but an office is standing vacant on the floor above, so he takes them up there.

This DS is a spare, solemn and rather reserved man whose recreations are fell walking and birdwatching – a form of 'escapism', he suggests, from the world in which he works. He dresses very quietly.

In the CID here you tend to be the middle-of-the-road, happily married man – children, other pursuits – and completely devoid of interest, really, in anything in town, in anything going on there, like clubs and such.

But when you come on duty, to sort of equip yourself to deal

91

with these scallywags living round here, you do tend to put on this 'overcoat'. Y'know, appear to be very, very sort of tough and hard – as if you've been through all they've been through – to maintain a dialogue.

Perhaps you feel that they've seen so much television that it's as if they *expect* you to be a sort of 'hard man' and, if you're any less than that, it's a sign of weakness! I was born and bred in Liverpool off Scotland Road, one of the toughest areas, but my family were regarded as sort of a 'good' family, a quiet family. All the children were always well cared for and well clothed, and a completely different kettle of fish to the other kids at school, who were always getting into trouble and everything. But when you're dealing with them you don't betray this quietness – that's your own personal thing really. Of course, it's nice to meet decent people of any class, and to be appreciated by people. You tend sometimes to fall over backwards and go out of your way to help them.

So it's not a deliberate thing, this stance, this standing with your hands in your pockets, but I'm aware it can happen. I remember going into a hospital to take a statement once off somebody, and there was somebody in a bed there I knew socially. I found myself talking to him as if he was the suspect – y'know, I was acting differently. A lot of it is defensive really, I suppose; you just keep this deception going, you let on you know everybody in town. But these people who go into clubs . . . it's as if they're chasing something, trying to find something in life that doesn't exist. The myth of being part of the jet set ?

I've suddenly reached a stage in life – y'know, I'm thirty-seven – when you cast your mind back and suddenly realise how much your life has changed. I come from a humble background, and I feel that the police have given me a tremendous amount of my freedom; I'm indebted to the police really. It's difficult to pinpoint. I suppose being in the CID you touch on all sorts of things and, over a period of time, I think you develop what you might call a certain sophistication that you never had before. Only it's a natural type of thing, where you can mix freely and easily into different types of society – you can converse with people. Perhaps, when you're interviewing somebody like a bank manager and you feel in control of the situation, you might not feel so confident if you met them under different circumstances! But I've developed an interest in classical music, for instance.

Now I don't know if I had stayed in that engineering work-shop, whether I would have. I doubt that very much actually.

92

There are more things in life that are available to you: I mean I would never dream of going near a football match now, and I don't feel this from a purely snobbish point of view. I find now that if I'm watching television I'm very, very selective.

There are obviously hazards in the CID, but I don't think there are many, in all honesty. It's not as if we're working in a Chicago-type police situation where in every house you go to there's a danger you'll be shot at. There is a tendency in the job to play things down, to take the heat out of the situation, no matter what. If you go, say, to a bad robbery or incident, you can't try to make something of something that isn't there.

I mean, we're going out tomorrow looking for a fella with a shotgun. I wouldn't *dream* there was any possibility that someone's going to storm in there with a shotgun and start shooting it out. That's the last thought in my head. I suppose, to an outsider, that might seem a silly and illogical point of view to take really. But I think that if you've done this type of thing on so many occasions over the years, and nothing has come of it, then you tend to have this blasé attitude towards it anyway. You get used to it.

I have been angry to the point of violence, I must admit that, on one or two occasions. I think it's in your basic make-up really. I did, in fact, catch two fellas in my house – it's been done twice. Now, I'd always said – it might have been bar-room talk, of course – that if ever I caught anyone in my house I'd break their legs! This type of thing, you see! And yet, when the situation arose – granted they were only sixteen – I didn't feel particularly violent towards them. I felt a sort of feeling of calmness. You would think that, if ever I was going to be violent, that I would be violent then, but I wasn't. (*Laughs*) Possibly some sort of clue to my basic temperament.

Having said that I'm indebted to the police, I can't in all honesty say I regard my job as a wonderful job, though. I sometimes really feel I would have been happier if I had a more mundane type of job, like being a teacher or something like that. I don't know. I personally find the hours we work here very, very tiring, mentally and physically really. By the time you get home at six o'clock if you're on Days, you're not awfully good company for the family, y'know – I've two girls, one's eleven and the other's coming up to nine. You're mentally drained and it usually takes half an hour asleep in your chair before you feel yourself again. (*Pause, a slow smile*) A few years ago, while I was in the Drugs Squad, I read a book by a bloke called Jack

93

Kerouac, and he was always sort of in pursuit of happiness – what's life all about? Sometimes I sort of philosophise: Just what am I after? Of course, you end up going round in circles, and you realise life is about work really. And I look at my father – he's retired, spent all of his life on the docks – and I can see in him what boredom does to you.

This business of early retirement in the police tends, in some instances, to make us sort of wish our lives away. I've been in nineteen years altogether, about six of them in uniform, and I'll still be only forty-four when I retire in six and a half years' time. You tend to think: Ah, when that time comes there'll be this golden opportunity to leave all this aggravation behind! I think a lot of people think that policemen get used to going to search somebody's house – y'know, the children screaming and the people saying, '*You're* not comin' in 'ere!' I don't think we ever get used to it; I don't think it's something you ever get accustomed to.

The interview with the distressed girl begins, a broken murmur against the diesel din of taxi cabs beneath the windows, dogs barking, the shrieks and whoops of Bullring children; bare facts in a bare room, jumbled, slowly settling, falling into place. Dad wants her, engaged, hopes to be married soon, wrists scarred, in hospital for depression, let out again, nothing changes, she was only a kid at the time, engaged, could spoil everything, when mum died she shared a bed with him, kept him warm, doesn't want to cause trouble, but it could spoil everything, he was lonely and sad and it didn't seem bad, not then, engaged, sorry for him really, but you know how it is, must tell someone, out it comes. While the detective sergeant listens with sympathetic detachment, making it easy for her, hearing nothing he hasn't heard before.

'Incest,' he says, returning to the sergeants' office a little after two. 'How's it going, then?'

'Great. Fella rang in for you, ringing back about three.'

16

A detective (*says one notably successful sergeant*) is only as good as his informants really. We haven't got crystal balls – crystal

94

ball balls, that is! – but people think we arrive at something and just do a Sherlock Holmes. If only they knew the ball-aching enquiries involved, and half the time it's tip-offs on stuff. These fellas, y'see, they're half-wits. If they were clever, they wouldn't have to go around thievin'. They've always got to tell someone, either their girl friend, wife, anyone; they will rabbit and talk. One'll see the other with plenty of money, and he'll say, 'How did 'e get that?' Someone always knows.

Most of my informants are people I've locked up. You lock 'em up and treat 'em right and that's it. I mean all this nonsense that some idiots put out – they get 'ammered, the thumbscrews put on 'em, or thirty coppers kickin' 'em – *is* bloody nonsense, y'know. The best informant I ever had was somebody I locked up for housebreaking. He was one of these fellas who had a child suffering from a congenital disease, y'know, and the problem was he wanted to see this child and he was in custody. So I went and picked his wife and his kid up – they couldn't get in to the police station – and they had an hour with him in the bridewell, y'know. And then, when he went in the nick, he used to say to me, 'If you see me wife, tell her this, tell her that.' I did a lot of things for him really. I helped him in a lot of ways. I must admit it was mostly done with an ulterior motive. I thought that here is a fella who was right in amongst them, they know he's a rotten sod, that he gets locked up, they're not going to suss him. When he came out of jail, he said he was going straight, y'see – which they all do – and I got him only a labouring job, but that's all he wanted. I was just chattin' away to him one day – I don't know if he felt he owed me somethin' or what – and he said, 'You know that job last night? The load of antiques – do you want it?' I said, 'Yeah, that'll do,' and he gave me the address of who'd done it.

So I go round there, do a warrant on the house, locked the receiver up and the burglar as well. They never even suspected who'd done it. I got on to the insurance company, and they said, 'Did you get it from an informant?' 'Yeah.' 'OK, we'll give him a hundred and fifty for it' – a good bit over the usual ten per cent. And I took him to the insurance investigator and he gave him the money.

From then on, I was just too much! I told him, 'You've got to turn up results and, if you do, you'll get a good backhander off the police or you'll find an insurance company will want to mug you.' And there's no messin' at all; they don't want to know who

95

he is – only their investigator will mug him, so there's no argy-bargy.

This is it. You've only got to have a few like that, and they're turning over all the time.

Then comes the interrogation, and here a CID officer with twenty years' experience outlines his approach.

The finest type of information is, y'know, Billy Smith screwed Tesco's last week, and the cigarettes are under the bed in his judy's house. But we also pick up who's had a row with so-and-so, who's knockin' a slice off somebody's wife, who's had a row with somebody in prison – that's very important.

Say, for instance, a bobby brings a fella in for a job. 'Definitely 'aven't done this! Bloody carve up, this is! I'm writin' to the 'Ome Secretary!' – the usual bullshit you get. He's not talkin' to anybody. 'Not sayin' nuttin' till I've seen me solicitor!' What I do is check at the record office, find his associates, read his antecedents, and I talk to him as if I know more about him than he realises. This confuses him a bit. But he's not going to cough for the first half-hour, so I leave him in the cells for a bit.

Then I say to him, 'I see you got three years in 1973. Where did you serve it?' 'Walton,' he says. 'Which landing were you on?' 'D,' he says. I know that in 'D' Wing Billy Jones had a fight with Joey Smith because one of their brothers had been knockin' a slice off his wife while he was inside, y'see, and so I chat to this. Now, they love gossip, thieves. He will then gossip a bit about this, and I'll learn a little more. Even if he doesn't cough the job, he'll tell me about the fight they had in the lavatory – and, after a while, I'll have some plane of communication with him.

He knows he's done the job, but unless he's a very clever type of thief he doesn't know quite how much we know. We may have only fifty per cent of the evidence – very rarely will we get an admission where we haven't any evidence at all, y'understand – and you let him think you've got eighty.

If, say, it's a robbery job, then he wasn't the one who did the violence. 'Er, I didn't really want to go on the job. Er, when the other fella 'it the old fella, I dragged 'im off. I didn't want no part of the violence' – bullshit like this. Then you will also throw him some smoothness in, that he'd only done the job because his wife had nerves, his grandmother had swallowed sixpence, his son had fallen downstairs. All bucks have terribly sick and injured relatives, all thieves have excuses like these.

96

You've got a line of patter, almost like a shoe salesman, to sort of get them to talk. There are thieves who've been in lumber before; they know these lines, so you've got to vary them a bit. A tactic with a low thief is to accuse him of a big job he hasn't done, and eventually he'll bargain by coughing his small job.

But I can imagine anybody outside the police service thinking that when a criminal admits an offence he must have been battered to do it. This is very rarely the case – in fact, I'd say hardly ever – because to get an admission off the average hoodlum you'd have to nearly kill him.

He lives by violence, y'see. With these people, their parents are violent, their brothers are violent, violence is nothing to them, from babies they're getting clouted. Say a respectable type of man is walking down London Road tonight and he gets a bit of a hiding and he comes in here: it's a few cuts and bruises maybe, but the effect on that man afterwards. . . . If that happened to a hoodlum, he wouldn't like the hammerin' but it wouldn't affect him a great deal. Same as a copper to a degree; I've had a few hammerings – I don't like a bloody hammering, now I'm forty-five and at the thrombosis age – but I wouldn't be affected the same way. But the man in London Road could be terribly upset over it for some months, y'see, affected nervously, frightened. Give a buck a clout and he could feel a bit of a martyr; you'd have to batter him up so much you'd have to inflict quite bad injuries.

In fact, any form of interrogation that involves beating somebody – well, just a bloody amateur does that. If you *want* to batter somebody, you *might* get an admission to one job. But I'm not interested in one job. I want an admission to twenty jobs.

So it's a line of technique, a sales patter really, and that thief – in many ways – wants to cough. It's like a small Roman Catholic boy going to confession: he feels better when he's coughed, y'see, and all the weight's gone off his mind. A thief is naturally nervous. It takes a degree of courage to do a job, you can imagine this for yourself: going to rob a shop or somebody does take a degree of courage. But the more jobs he does, and the more confidence he gets, there's also this greater awareness he's going to get nicked. He gets cold feet. A cat passes and he thinks it's the police. Or it starts to rain and he's not happy, and he thinks: Oh, fok it – and goes home. In other words, whenever he's lyin' in bed at home and he hears a Ford car pull up outside, he thinks: Jesus, it's the busies! It builds up in him. You pull a thief in, and in many cases the relief pours out; it's like cleansing his soul.

97

Now afterwards (*chuckles*) he's going to go back on this. He's going to say he was tricked into this cough statement. It was forged, he was battered – the usual allegations you get. He'll also be saying this because a thief will be ridiculed by other thieves if they know he's coughed the job to the police. I've had fellas in to me, who've said, 'Well, I'll do a deal with you. I'll tell you the score on the job, everythin' – right? Only my replies to your questions will be denials – *no* chance of *me* makin' a fokkin' cough statement!' And you'll go along with this. He's got his vanity, y'see.

17

WANTED, proclaims the poster in the spacious CID office on the first floor at St Anne Street, *Amorous Al and Luscious Liz of the Notorious Razamataz Twenties Gang* – a pair of chubby, bare-footed four-year-olds, dressed *à la* Chicago and brandishing a booze-bottle. Mural decorations, slogans and quotable quotes abound in this long, otherwise impersonal room, which is shared by sergeants and constables alike, as is the single telephone on the clerk's desk.

The workload on the North Sub-division is comparable to that on the South: an inspector heads a team of eight sergeants and twenty-five constables who deal with around 12,000 crimes a year. This lends a fresh piquancy to the tract . . . *when you're up to your arse in alligators, it's difficult to remind yourself that your initial objective was to drain the swamp.*

Down at the far end of the room, past *Why worry, it may never happen!* and *Those of you/ who think/ you know every-thing/ are annoying/ those of us/ who do,* someone has pasted up beside his desk:

We trained hard . . . but it seemed that every time we were beginning to form up into teams we were reorganised. I was to learn later in life that we tend to meet any new situation by re-organising, and a wonderful method it can be for creating the illusion of progress, while producing confusion, inefficiency and demoralisation, Petronius Arbiter, 210 BC.

'Aye, crackin' that,' enthuses a 'woolly back' who moved to

98

'A' Division after the amalgamation. 'Yours, is it? Know if anyone's got the car?'

'Yuh, it's out.'

'Bloody hell. Another job that'll have to wait till tomorrer.'

Only two of 'A' Division's five CID vehicles are operational today, which is about one less than average. Just to get the job done, many detectives will be using their own cars, but all they can claim in recompense are bus fares.

'Lollipop!' shriek the jeering children, instantly recognising the dilapidated Mini with its LLP number-plates. 'Lolli-lolli-lolli-POP!' Then the light turns to green and they're left in a cloud of exhaust smoke.

'Kids are lovely, aren't they?' says the detective in the front passenger-seat, turning to look back at them. 'Good at tellin' yer things, oh aye. Went to this robbery job at a club, and it was, "No, boss, never seen 'er, boss!" And this kid said, "She were in 'ere yesterday."'

The other detective constable on the rear seat laughs.

'No, I mean it. I feel sorry for them around here, I really do. We were watchin' them the other night, about half a dozen of 'em rippin' away the plywood sheeting the Corporation had so kindly put up over a disused shop. They were havin' immense fun pulling it off and smashin' it to smithereens – then they'd probably go inside and set fire to the joint, y'know, which is right underneath the flats where they live, y'know. And these kids were no older than my eldest who's four.'

In the CID, you're going out at half-eight and coming in at midnight. That's a hell of a gap not to see your family. I mean, you walk in the house and you're being told, 'Oh, Penny's walking, y'know.' When was that? Wednesday. I never knew. It's a fact; I never knew.

Ahead lies a wan watercolour landscape, a wash of drear wasteland, blue haze background, simple shapes, grey tenement blocks, no shadows and no real impression of light. Lifeless. It seems impossible that this is the place of which such stories are told. . . .

99

– Heard about the jack last week? Comin' in in the morning, goin' right by where there's this complainant he's gotta see, so he thinks: Bugger it, why not? Still before nine, y'see. So he stops off, whips up to the second floor – doesn't use the lift, which is reekin' of piss as usual – but they're off to work already. So he comes down again, there's 'is pride and joy, 'is motor, upside down outside the flats – and all 'is wheels gone! Explain *that* to the missus.

– Dead lucky they were, there's no doubt about that. Get this call, see, which turns out to be malicious, but they don't know that. Stop by these flats and, for once, they get straight out. Wallop! A fokkin' breeze block off of the fourth floor – straight down, straight through the panda's roof! Shat theirselves. Who can blame them? Just kids, I reckon.

– I chased two lads in a car they'd stolen – one was twelve, the other thirteen – and they crashed it. My inspector went after the one who was injured, and me, being the fitter and younger bloke by a couple of years, went after the one who was running. I chased him into a place where he ran into flats and tripped over the bottom stairs. I grabbed hold of him, everybody in the flats came out, and I'm trying to get him through this swing door. They got the young lad away, and then, within seconds, women, men, boys and girls were all hammerin' hell out of me, kicking and thumpin' me. Now that really soured me about Liverpool people. I'm not talking about half a dozen, I'm talking about twenty people havin' a go, while all I was doing was me job. This lad that had stolen the car didn't live in the place at all! But, because he was one of them, and I was from the opposing faction, shall I say, I was the lad who got it.

– You get bottled, you get stoned. It's not the personal contact that bothers yer, it's the stuff what comes over the walls and off of the landin'. See that slope down there? They bring the cars there they've stolen, tie down the accelerator and aim it for the wall at the bottom. Boom! If they're lucky, it starts a fire.

. . . and yet such stories are commonplace. That's why the DS at the wheel and his DC have brought along a third man to 'sort of ride shotgun' while they're out of the car.

100

From close up, the picture changes. Here a collage of bus tickets, splintered plywood, glass fragments, twists of wire and bent nails; there a Jackson Pollock dribble and swirl of bright colour, aerosol anarchy over a pebble-textured wall; Campbell soup-tins, old magazine pictures, gay litter juxtaposed; concrete forms compound fractured, poking reinforcing rods from the weed; the marvellously disturbing stuff that modern galleries are made of. While, glimpsed through front windows, hang prints from Woolworth's; forest lakes and golden sunsets, pretty doe-eyed girls in bonnets, cuddly wet-nosed puppies.

The Mini stops in the square courtyard of a four-storey block of flats, the surface of which glitters with a frost of broken glass. The men in front get out and, having glanced round at the balconies, cut across to a brand-new unpainted door. The wooden jamb surrounding it is peppered with nail-holes, its window is boarded over, and there is a three-sided dent just below it, presumably made by a brick.

'Couple in their fifties,' explains the DC left guarding the car. 'They're sort of at the end of their tether. The bloke saw some stolen cars dumped near here on his way home from work, and the lads from St Anne Street came and took them away. The bucks have been giving them hell ever since. Started with just their back windows put in – that's happened six times, even with special glass with wire in it – and rubbish on the doorstep, their bin emptied out. The wife's had a ciggie pushed in her hair, had bikes ridden at her, she's always getting verbal abuse in the street. They got into the house once with iron bars, but the dogs were there – they took it out on one of the dogs afterwards, came crawling in with lacerations to the head and paws. When the special glass was put up, they just heaved scaffolding pipes through, could've killed anyone in the bathroom. She's in and out of the hospital, only existing on tranquillisers, but they can't get the Corpy to move them. He was caught coming home, hammered in the street, nobody came to help him. He asked the caretaker if he could use the phone, ring us at St Anne Street, but he wouldn't allow it, scared of the bucks turning on him next. Still goes to work, mind; wonder if I would! The sarge is trying to get the housing to move them, that's why he wants to see them now, get some

101

more evidence like, see what can be done. You tend to feel responsible even though it isn't your job, not really.'

The DS knocks loudly. Dogs bark furiously, leaping up at the inside of the door, but nobody answers. 'Hope to Christ they're all right,' he mutters, and knocks again.

'Could be out,' the DC suggests. 'Try round the front?'

The three windows facing on to the side street are also protected by boards, making it impossible to see inside. The DS turns about and crosses over to the small row of shops serving the area. The first in line, a greengrocer's, is hidden behind a patchwork of steel plates, each about a yard square and a quarter of an inch thick, that have been welded together to cover the entire frontage. The remainder have replaced their windows with brick walls or metal shutters, save for the butcher, who takes his meat, cash, till and equipment home with him every night. It needs no more than a cursory glance into the dim, electrically lit interiors to confirm the couple aren't there, either.

'We'll come back later when we go to lift that buck,' the DS decides, and they return to the car. 'All right, blue? Any bother?' The detective left on guard shakes his head; apart from having been described in gynaecological terms by a trio of giggling toddlers, his vigil has been uneventful.

Situations such as these are a common source of frustration among CID and uniformed officers alike. After four years of patrolling the North Sub on foot, this constable – an exserviceman – is resigned to a different role from that he had imagined.

You don't feel you get much public support on this job. But, you see, I don't think the public themselves are well protected by the courts.

By that I mean, you get someone round here. . . . (*Begins afresh*) Over there in Soho Street there's a really bad family. One of the lads goes and breaks into one of the flats, and he steals a colour television. Now an old-age pensioner, who lives in the area, sees him do this, and he reports it to us, and he says he's willing to go to court as a witness. Next day I go round because all his windows have been put in.

102

It's a terrible indictment, I think, on society. There's nothing we can do to prove that lad put the windows in, although we know who did it – he was straight out on bail again, of course. And that's why a lot of people have no faith in the Law, no confidence in it, and quite right too.

The Mini makes its way through a maze of dismal streets, moving higher up the slope. 'There could be no drug situation, if you think about it,' says the DS to the man in the back, who is hoping to go into the Drugs Squad. 'If we were to suddenly make all drug-taking legal, scatter it on the ground like bloody Indian corn, then give them all a revolver each. In the morning, them that's still alive, we'll charge 'em with bloody murder!' His companions laugh. 'Seriously, what drug situation could you possibly have? And what could they cry about? They've done what they wanted to do, they've had their big treat – they've murdered everybody in sight, which is basically what they want to do, isn't it? These silly sods, pacificists till they've flipped their jugs.' The car slows down, stopping opposite a terrace of twinkle-bright houses. 'Aye, this must be the place. Won't be a minute.'

The student's face blanches as he opens his front door on the two tall strangers. 'It's all right, lad,' says the DS with a laugh. 'CID, come about the toaster you've had nicked. Who did you think it was?'

A mumble, and they are led into a small cosy room filled with books, records and the little touches to be expected: empty wine-bottles arranged like a still life, a stick of incense in a brass holder, Oxfam artefacts and a map of Tolkien's Middle Earth. The student excuses himself for a moment, having left something boiling on the stove.

'Makes a bit of a change,' says the DC, looking round with interest.

'Reckon they've done a good job on the place,' the DS replies, checking his watch. 'Got to see that brief at half-three. Stuff's worth more than seven grand, they're saying now.'

'Yuh, and I've got that safe job at the hotel.'

The student returns, still very tense, and warily explains the circumstances surrounding the toaster's disappearance.

The bonhomie shown by the detectives, as they examine the porch where it was last seen, does nothing to mitigate his apparent sense of an abyss between them. *WANTED*, says the poster on the kitchen wall, *Amorous Al and Luscious Liz of the Notorious Razamataz Twenties Gang*.

The other CID vehicle, a battered Cortina, is parked behind a row of council flats in Kirkby, discreetly out of sight of the neighbours. The two South Sub detectives in the front seat are gauging the disposition of a very large, yellow-eyed dog that has taken up a defensive position at the gate in the wooden fence. Like postmen, policemen are no strangers to tetanus injections; unlike postmen, however, they cannot rely on the owner calling the animal off.

'I wonder,' says the aide, his tone whimsical, 'if I say, "Shooo!" – if it'll go away?'

'No chance,' scoffs the DC. 'But I'm not sitting here all—' And he opens the driver's door.

'Not goin' to 'it it with yer briefcase, are yer? You did that the last time and he took a piece out.'

'It's looking a bit dozy.'

The dog advances one menacing step, but at that moment a small boy runs out, giving it a pat on his way to the car.

'Is it your dog?'

'Yuh.'

'Is yer mum in like?'

'Yuh.'

'You Shaun, then?'

'Nah.'

The boy watches them circle the dog, and then turns his attention on the detective going through a file on the back seat. 'That fella dere thought I was Shaun. I'm Robbie. He's ten. I'm thirteen.' This information fails to excite any interest; the detective has nothing to do with the case, having just been picked up at Walton Prison. 'I know dem,' the boy says, resting his elbows on the car window-sill, 'all of der police. Yuh, I know dem by sight, I know dem when I see dem.'

'Oh aye?' murmurs the detective, amused and looking up at him. 'Know me too, do you?'

104

'I don't go to rob. But I go wid dem, when dey go to rob. I know all der police. By sight. Even if I've never seen dem before. I won't get nicked 'cos I only go wid dem. If dey caught me, and I'm runnin', dey can't do nuttin' by me. We know all the floorwalkers, some walk round wid trolleys. You know me, I'm not soft. I go in one row, see, and dey folla yer. I'll tell you how you know dem, 'cos dey folla yer. Boots is crowded wid dem, in it? Yer push along the counter and dey come up. "Wot yer doin'?" Then dey rob. I get caught but I got nuttin', that's why I don't get caught. And if we see dem, we just go out the shop and come back.'

'So you don't go to rob, just yer mates?'

'Wot's that?'

'This? A file. Court file.'

'I don't get caught,' says Robbie, beginning another amiable monologue which lasts until the two other detectives return. 'Where's Shaun?' he asks.

'Out. Just told yer mum he's got to come and see us.'

'Oh,' says Robbie, frowning. 'Aren't yer goin' to nick 'im?' he adds, as though the rules of some game need to be re-stated. 'Y'know, when he comes in like?'

'We'll have to wait and see, won't we?'

The Cortina leaves the yard, and the DC at the wheel says, 'Should've met the mother. What a woman – tattoos right up both arms. Fantastic.'

'Oh aye?' The third detective shrugs, as though content with his curious encounter with young Robbie.

It can be borin', all these calls we make – which is what we do mostly, to be honest. You don't get time to be out on the street lookin' for *more* jobs, do yer? (*Laughs*) But at least in the jacks you move around, you're not stuck in the one division all day. Also . . . I don't know, there's always somethin'. Y'know, something that makes you go (*jerks head back in a double-take*)! Things people do, things they come out with, the places they live in and all. You know it must be real, but – bloody hell! Keeps the interest goin'.

Not so much a fascination for the harsh realities, perhaps, as a taste for some form of incidental surrealism. Coming up on the right, a tall block that has great squares of blue sky showing

105

through where entire flats have been devastated. Over on the left, terraces of homes destroyed by young lovers removing roof-tiles to spell out, in gigantic black letters against orange, the names of their sweethearts. And now, on the right again, just as the Cortina leaves this drab, poverty-tarnished 'new town', an enormous mound of earth looms up, part of a costly scheme to give the people an artificial ski-slope.

Back at St Anne Street, the DS hands over the Mini and cadges a lift into town with the OSD, while his partner is delayed by a query from a solicitor who wants further details concerning a serious-wounding charge. He tosses the toaster case on to the pending pile, and takes a file along to the telephone.

Slightly built, restless and quick to laugh, with a style of dress in keeping with a modish Mexican moustache turned down at the corners, he is twenty-nine and – like a surprising number of officers – has joined the police twice.

My father had always wanted to join; he tried to get in but could never make it, y'see; in those days you had to be big and strong and not really have a lot of brains, type of thing. I was in an office and they started an occupational guidance thing in Liverpool – the first one in the country, I think, because it was under-developed and all this kind of caper – and they made me a short list of either repping [commercial salesman], the Customs or the police. There it was again, y'see, so I thought: Bang – and went and joined them.

[He resigned during his probation because he seldom had a chance to see his girlfriend.]

We got married in the July and had this weird and wonderful idea of becoming hippies. So that's what we did: we hippied abroad to France. We got tied up in that 'Rudi the Red' business when they were besieging the Sorbonne, and there were riot police everywhere! (*Laughs*) We went through Paris, down to Versailles, and my lot's goin' clickety-click with their cameras, 'cos to them we were just a bunch of hippies. We went to the Spanish border, and they were floodin' out! Oh aye, the Spanish police were just whackin' 'em! So we came back here and I tried to join again.

106

I went to see the Chief [Constable] on an interview, and he said, 'Well, I think you're a bit immature, and what's to stop you getting a bee in your bonnet a second time? I think you should just settle down and decide what you want to do; you were only with us eleven months.'

So I did all sorts then. I worked as a store detective at Christmas time for five or six weeks, didn't catch *anybody*. Me brother was with the Pru, as an insurance salesman, but the round they offered me was in the Dingle, and I didn't fancy that; I'd dealt with that many people comin' in with bruised heads, y'know, gettin' robbed on their rounds. I went to another company in town for fifteen months. That was interesting in a way, meetin' people and all that. Then I went on the line at Ford's putting wiper motors in Ford Capris. Well, have you ever tried putting a rubber washer down a thread? I weighed it up and I used to sling all the rubber washers. What I didn't know was that these cars were water-tested and it *leaked*. So I left that then, and came back on this type of thing. I went on a four-week refresher course and was posted to 'A' Division on panda cars.

I liked Uniform, a good laff, y'know. Only had one assault on me I ever charged anybody with; it was a bit embarrassing that as well, because my watch had broken and I'd had to borrow one. Me and a guy – who's now an inspector – were standin', mindin' our own business in Duke Street, and this cowboy came down in a big Yankee car. It ends up he gets breathalysed, because he's actually paralytic, y'know, and he's a buck and he wouldn't have it, and his friends wouldn't have it, and they started working out on us. My wife's watch came off – y'know, a little gold chain – and I'm in the bridewell when I remember this, so I shot back to the scene, found it and charged him with damage as well. The bridewell sergeant said, 'Let's look at yer watch.' Oh jeez, can you imagine it? A dainty little watch! Whoooo!

After the pandas, I got a crackin' little job over at Copperas Hill doing the traffic enquiry section, then I was in Plain Clothes, came out into the CID half-way through [as an aide], went back into Plain Clothes, then into Uniform again. I did five, six weeks on the beat, which was soul-destroying because I'd been out of uniform for nearly two years, and on that job you're runnin' round like a mad thing! Goin' out on the beat, people comin' up and asking you directions, there's the radio telling you where to go all the time . . . oh, it was terribly depressing that. Then I

107

just walked in one day and they said, 'Bang, you're going back in the CID permanently.' Made up, I was.

I didn't work with anyone to start with, because they were all paired off, y'see. It's terrible, y'know, when they're all paired off – oh, it really is – especially when you want to go round clubs and that. They get to know you as a team, y'see, and three-handed is heavy. I think it was in the October that Sally and I had done a couple of jobs and I suggested working together, y'know. She's very, very sound, but if you wanted to do anything naughty you couldn't! Then in March '76, in bowls George, y'see; I had a safe job and he started comin' round with me. He's got the same sense of humour and suddenly we clicked, y'see, and I sort of drifted into working with him.

Really, it's a public relations job, and keeping your ears open for little snippets of information. You don't sort of deduct anything – Oh, it *must* be so-and-so – do you? Be honest. You go to a job and you ask who's done it. 'Haven't a clue,' they say. 'That's why we asked you to come down.' Well, where do you go from there, y'know? Fingerprints, photographs, door-to-door, kids in the street, snouts if you have snouts. If you enjoy something, it's not a chore. It's like when you're washin' your new car (*polishing action*) – 'Oh, this is great, isn't it?' – whooo-hoooo, and everybody in the street watchin'. But if you've got an old banger, and your missus is sayin', 'Now you've *got* to wash it!' *Weeergh*, y'know! If you enjoy it, you can have a laff over it.

I don't take all these crimes personally, y'see. That's the way you get through to the bucks. You say to them, 'Listen, pal, I'll be honest with yer, it wasn't my money you took. I'm not going to come down on yer, I'm not goin' to stick yer in Risley for a fortnight, or wait until about four o'clock in the morning and turn yer mother's over' – all this garbage that gets their bottle goin' a bit, y'know. 'On the other hand, if you want to be nasty, yer can be – it's entirely up to you.'

Don't get me wrong. OK, it's a serious game when people get assaulted and things like that, but it's the system – it's pointless taking it personally. I have a laff with the villains; this is the difference, you see. Well, you see, everybody walks round and they're so serious – I could never be like that on a job, and George couldn't, either. You're only here, I think, to enjoy yourself. Like we locked a guy up in Dale Street, and I said, 'Now who's goin' for a ride in a police car, then? You can tell all your friends you've been for a ride in a police car!' Basically, it's taking the piss out of them, because that's what they're doing every day of the week, taking the piss out of us. It's a fact; they're laffin' up their sleeves at us, and it's one opportunity of getting your own back. So I don't sort of rant and rave at the back of the court when a guy gets off. You've caused him this aggravation, you've cost him a few bob – either by locking him up just before the day he was due to go for his dole, or by keeping him in custody, somethin' like that – so there's no point.

Woundings don't really get me goin', because the woundings we get are usually bucks on bucks in clubs and things like that. Although there was one I dealt with last Sunday, when a very respectable fella came back from a football match: nine o'clock at night, he's walkin' down Church Street, and a guy came up with a cut-throat razor and just slashed him right across the face. A deep scar for the rest of his life. If you got hold of that hooligan you would, y'know, want to smack his bottom for him, y'know.

It's a violent city, because I've sort of experienced it bringing my wife into town to the pictures – very, very far and few between those times are, because if there's a gang of bucks rowdy-ing, she sees the hackles rise, y'know. It annoys me: you've got decent people comin' in for a night out, and they're just there to spoil everyone's enjoyment. You know, in this city, if you've got anything nice, whether it's a business, a car or anything, the bucks'll spoil it for yer – because you shouldn't have it, y'see! (*Laughs*)

But, if I had to go all serious like some, I would hate it, I tell yer. There are guys who I just couldn't work with because of their attitude. I've been with guys who've walked into an office and said to this little dolly bird, 'I'M CID! I want to see the boss!' (*imitates a man convinced of his infinite superiority*) The attitude they believe they're the big-time jack, y'know, with everybody – oh, I just don't want to know that. And you find that when you go to speak to somebody in town, in a club or a pub or in an office, that you're not the only detective who's ever been there, so, if you come out with the big-time detective stuff, they'll laff their heads off when you're gone.

18

The dummy in the window at Copperas Hill is now wearing a pair of round-lensed spectacles of the seedier sort associated with Dr Crippen, and has turned away from the darkening sky over the Bullring. The office is crowded with DCs, some about to go home, others with a good five hours or more ahead of them, all looking somewhat harassed. 'So much to —— do, so little —— done,' one of them grumbles, out of deference to the chic brunette engaged on compiling silverware descriptions from an auctioneer's catalogue. 'If it hadn't been for the missus, I'd have been out of this stinkin' rat-hole years ago,' an older detective declares vehemently, throwing down a stack of reports, most of which record, with brutal simplicity, how the poor get poorer. He gets a weary look from a colleague who has spent the afternoon trying to retrieve a watchmaker's set of tools; the man faces ruin without them. Then the lean, quietly spoken detective sergeant drifts in for a moment, finishing off a conversation with a tall broad-shouldered DC who has one hand in a bandage.

'It surprised me,' says the DC, shrugging, 'there was no feelin' at all.' He smiles. 'You know, *Yer dairty bastid!* – didn't feel like that. It was nothing.'

'My feelings are it's not a crime as such,' the DS replies, giving a slight shrug himself. 'It's classed as a crime, but it's more of a social problem. You—'

'What's this?' asks the clerk. 'The incest job?'

The DC nods. 'Yuh, we just locked the father up.'

Everyone turns, ears pricked. 'What'll he get, do you reckon?' someone asks.

'Don't know really. Seven years suspended?'

'Why did she cough, boss?' an aide wants to know.

Even those on Days linger to discuss the case; the general consensus being that, more often than not, this isn't a sexual offence which 'turns you up like', and it shouldn't really be part of police work. Then again, as with a number of 'social problems', only the police are vested with the power to do anything effective about it. 'She didn't realise at first we'd have to charge him and that,' the DS explains. 'Naturally a bit upset about it, but she said she could see there was no alternative.' The discussion broadens. 'If the child's under thirteen,' says the brunette, 'then the father gets life, I think,' and she takes out *Moriarty's Police Law* to read aloud the rele-

110

vant section. As she does so, a wag snatches the spectacles off the dummy, puts them on askew and hunches himself up. 'Go on – more! more!' he urges in a quavering falsetto, licking his lips lasciviously. 'Knickers, knockers! Don't stop!' A good laugh is just what everyone needed.

Soon the office is almost deserted, and the clerk gets up to slip on his jacket. 'How did you get that?' he asks, pointing a half-filled sleeve at the bandaged hand.

'Huh! I was fixin' this bird-table, see, and—'

The telephone rings: Uniform are on their way from the hospital with two victims of a robbery.

The grey-haired couple are badly shaken but determined to appear cheerful. The man is particularly chipper, chuckling after every other sentence, and has a livid bruise down one side of his face. His wife, pale but without a curl out of place, goes off to be interviewed separately by a detective sergeant working Lates.

'Have a seat,' says the DC, offering the shopkeeper the clerk's chair, before perching himself on the corner of a desk. 'You're all right?'

'Not too bad! A bit shaky, y'know, but. . . .' He sits down and glances about him, taking in the calendar girls and other little details which make the office seem – now the silverware detective has gone – very much a masculine preserve. 'Not so bad really!' He squares his shoulders.

'What time was it roughly?'

'Half-past five.'

'And what happened?'

'Well, we've got a deep freeze right opposite the door at the back of the counter. I had me back to it, making a list to go to the wholesaler's, and I heard the door slam.'

'You mean "close"?'

'No! The door was open. The door slammed to and, with that, this darkie jumped over the counter.' He raises a hand to indicate someone taller than himself. 'I would say he was about five foot ten and—'

'We'll get the descriptions after. Go on.'

111

Another detective comes over and joins the interview with a sympathetic nod at the bruise. 'How're you feelin'?'

'Not so bad!' His laugh is very man-to-man. 'Well, he jumped over the counter and, of course, grabbed me and started, er, firin' away – y'know, questioning me – and the other fella comes round and grabs the wife and throws her on the floor and sits on 'er. And, of course, this darkie goes down to the safe, but there's nothin' in the safe.'

'And where', asks the DC, in a slow drawl that counterpoints the flurry of words, 'were you at this time? Had you fallen over?'

'No, I stood on me feet, wrestlin' with him! You know, tryin' to grab him as much as I could.'

'Yuh.'

'He went in the safe, there was nothing there – nothing at that time of night – and, of course, he started punchin' away! Well, when I say "punching", I don't know what he used. The next thing I felt a bloody crack on the head, y'know! And he grabbed the drawer open, grabbed all the notes, jumped on the counter, and the white fella – sittin' on the wife – said to me, "Lay down, yer bastid," he said, "or I'll kill 'er!" I wasn't havin' that!'

'No,' murmurs the other detective. 'So you were lying behind the counter?'

'Yes. Of course, as he jumped, I tried to push him flat on his back over the counter – if I could. And with that he drew the lump hammer on me.'

'Did the other one have anything?' asks the DC.

'I couldn't tell you!'

'H'm. Would you recognise them again?'

'I'd recognise the darkie, because he's been in the shop before. Oh, he's been in a few times, buyin' stuff.'

'What about the white one?'

'Never seen 'im before. He had been in twice before, this white fellow, and asked for late *Echo*s, and we said we hadn't got any.'

'Twice tonight?'

The shopkeeper shakes his head. 'Yes, I couldn't understand that! I said, "We'll get no more tonight." Twice I said it.'

112

'He was looking to see who was in the shop,' explains the DC. 'Now what did they—?'

'Came in twice. "They're all sold out," I said. "We'll get no more tonight." Can't understand that!'

'How much?' the DC asks.

'Couldn't tell you right off, because I haven't checked it properly. But anything from one hundred and twenty to one-fifty.'

'And have you any injuries apart—?'

'No, only this.'

'You were really lucky, weren't you?'

The bruise looks very like one that might have been made by a glancing blow from a lump hammer.

'If he'd 'it me with that hammer, I wouldn't be here!' the shopkeeper replies, shaking with laughter.

An hour passes. The shopkeeper can supply very little in the way of descriptions. Both assailants were about 5 feet 10 inches and in their late teens; the black one had frizzy hair and a long blue raincoat, and the white one wore a blue-checked shirt and slacks.

'Was he blond?'

'I couldn't even tell you. As I say, I didn't take much notice of it at the time, because I was more interested in tryin' to save m'self and the wife.'

The DC nods. 'You can always get more money, can't you?'

'Yes,' he says quietly.

'But this black fella you say grabbed you, what was he? A West Indian? An African? A half-caste?'

'Definitely a half-caste!'

'Did he have a moustache?'

'Now, that I don't know.'

'He didn't,' asks the DC with a smile, 'have two noses, did he?'

The shopkeeper chuckles. 'It's a funny thing, tryin' to give a description when you're fightin' somebody!' He draws on his umpteenth cigarette. 'Y'know, forty years I've been in that area. . . .'

His wife comes through to look at the mug-shot books. 'It's about two years since they last robbed the till,' she says, 'and

113

I said then we were going to sell the shop.' Their eyes meet. 'We might not be so lucky a third time.'

One of those stable-door moments, perhaps, when the whole idea of detection can seem rather pointless.

A couple of Chinese take-away meals are very welcome by seven-twenty. The two DCs carry them through into the canteen kitchen where, besides the two easy chairs, there are four small tables jammed up against a vending machine. Three uniformed constables are just finishing their refreshments.

Peter, the DC with the bandaged hand, has been in the police for five years, and is in his first year as a detective. He is married to a teacher, and his chief interests are reading and cricket, although he now finds he has very little spare time. His colleague, Harry, a gangling affable man of 6 feet 2 inches, has been in the CID for fourteen months of his sixteen years in the force, and is married to a nurse. He reads a good deal, as he's at home on his own for a couple of evenings a week, and has a way with words. He once brought down the house in court by replying, when asked how he had observed the activities in a Chinese brothel, 'Through a chink in the curtain, m'lud.'

The uniformed officers throw away their sandwich papers, wash their cups and wander off, leaving the television set on.

PETER: I think we were better off when we were a mystery. All these police programmes have taken the mystery out of being a policeman, and people think they know what you're doing, but in fact they don't. A lot of the time, all we can do is walk around with an air of efficiency!

HARRY: It is a bit true-to-life when you get a big job, like the armed robbery we had. We had to follow it up piece by piece, and then these two fellas were set up by informers, y'know. We got a call and we had three minutes to get there – they were coming out of this pub, y'see. So we go down to St Anne Street to get the OSD out, get them armed. (*Smile appears*) But by the time they'd finished issuing weapons it would've taken them ten minutes to do it. Sign the book, sign for the ammunition. 'What number's that gun?' 'What number's this?' So, in the end, my mate Keith just went shooting out and we got only the one – one got away, y'see. But we got the other fella on the

114

Saturday.* It varies, you see: you're working right from the bread-and-butter stuff – the sneak thefts – right up to the heavy level. And once you get a big job you've got to leave the bits and pieces, and consequently you get behind.

PETER: I don't think half the Uniform know how we work – they don't know how busy we are. Is it a long way from Starsky and Hutch? Christ, yes! The closest I ever came to that was in Task Force, but even that has changed now. The method of policing has changed a lot in the last two years.

HARRY: I'll tell you when it was; it was when they started asking university students to come.

PETER: The change is in the probationers. Nobody seems to listen to people any more. They've learned at Bruche every situation; you do this, you do that. So they go in with preconceived ideas and it doesn't matter what happens, they will do what they think is right, rather than listen and think. Give a bit, take a bit – they don't seem to do that now. Y'see, unless you treat people differently, you never get anywhere. There are people dotted like – like little gems everywhere, but, unless you're prepared to talk to everybody, you just don't meet 'em.

HARRY: Aye, that's true.

PETER: I find that once you get into their homes they're entirely different. They don't like to be seen talkin' to a policeman outside – the person next door could think they were a copper's nark. But once you get into their homes, and just start talkin' to them, I find they're all right. I like the people around here.

HARRY: I like the people.

PETER: Most of them have a good heart on them, even the dirtiest, filthiest—

HARRY: It's bred into them, y'see. To be seen talking to a bobby is. . . . (Laughs)

PETER: Even with the real baddies, there's something about them – something you can talk to. The relationship doesn't change. They still get locked up. They still – I wouldn't say 'hate' us, that's probably the wrong word. . . . (Shrugs) But you find they may say to another buck, 'Ar, he's not bad, that fella.'

HARRY: It helps, you see.

PETER: They might have some grievance – say, another buck's upset them. And normally, instead of fightin', they think: I'll fokkin' do 'im! So they come in here with information, and we take it from there, y'know.

*He and his partner received commendations for these arrests.

115

19

Down in the Bridewell, the uniformed sergeant leans on his front counter, waiting for the Main Bridewell to call back on the telephone beside him. He is twenty-nine and a brawny barrel of a man with a fine pair of sideboards bracketing his jovial face; gregarious, shrewd and imperturbable, he epitomises much that is the 'ideal British bobby', yet would possibly disconcert those conditioned by myth-makers.

Footsteps clatter down the stairs. 'Dad! Dad! Where we goin' now, Dad?' pleads a CID aide, tugging like a toddler at the detective's coat tails, as they hurry out into the street.

'Definitely a murder job,' the bridewell patrol observes a little sourly, being stuck indoors and in one place for the rest of his shift. 'Round the Rat an' Anchor, d'yer think?'

But the sergeant's smile is indulgent. Not all that long ago, he was an ambitious detective constable himself.

Murders. . . . Well, in my experience of the CID over eight years, I never knew a Christmas when we didn't get a murder. It was always domestics: he'd strangled her, she'd 'it 'im with the fryin'-pan or somethin'! (*Laughs*) You always get a good increase in murders then, because the rest of the year they're out at work or on the ale – Christmas Day being the one day in the year they're both in the house, and you know how they get on one another's nerves!

Sex attackers are the best example of the out-of-the-ordinary murder; most outstanding [unsolved] murders in this country are cases of a fella who'll pick a little girl up. You usually find that he'll indecently assault her, and, by the time he's ejaculated and feels remorse and worry, it comes on him. Y'know, when he can no longer strike a match on his piece of anatomy, and all the passion's gone! That's when he starts thinking cold-bloodedly: Christ, me wife's goin' to comment, and what am I going to do? and the easiest way out – it's ridiculous really – is they kill 'em. Strangle 'em, hit them or do somethin' stupid, then throw them out the car.

A murder enquiry like that is an absolute nightmare. All kids

116

look alike when you describe 'em – it's like those Identikit fellas; they all look alike. You might as well say, 'The usual Identikit picture', mightn't yer? There was one in a blue Morris 1100 – I can't remember exactly, somewhere in the South – and every single solitary owner of a Morris 1100 in this country had to be checked out, all the past owners and that, and the enquiry was four years old. Can you imagine the task in that? It's not as if they can be creative and say a Saab or something, which would cut it down a bit! You might get fifty, a hundred people in this sub alone who own a Morris 1100, and twelve detectives upstairs will get ten each. You end up going to the owners who sold it to a friend who sold it to someone they don't know. He's got the day-to-day rubbish of tryin' to detect burglaries and robberies and GBHs in the city, and he's got this on top, y'know, and you wonder why they feel like slashin' their wrists, y'know!

But with murders they're usually standin' there, waitin' for yer. The one I locked up last year in Bevington – the husband rang me up, in fact. He asked for the CID, came through and said, 'You'd better come round. I've killed me wife.' So I go to the house and he's standin' there, and she's lyin' on the floor, strangled, y'know. He coughed manslaughter and didn't even go to jail.

The longest murder enquiry while I was at Birkenhead took forty minutes. That was the longest one in eight years! (*Laughs*) It took forty minutes from the body being found to the offender being locked up. Fella found with a knife in his stomach, and it was only a case of gettin' hold of the mate he'd been with – that took about twenty minutes – and asking, 'Who did you see him with last?' He told us and we went round to this fella's house and he had bloodstains all over him and we gripped him.

'Yessir, can we help you?'

A weary couple approach the counter, carrying a cheap suitcase and leading a small unhappy boy. 'It's like this, see,' says the father, producing his wallet from under a tar-stained donkey jacket. 'Got this cheque, see; it's a good 'un, signed by me boss, Mr Flynn, see. There, twenty-seven fifty – right? Only it's like this, see. . . .' The long and short of it is they've run out of money, having arrived in Liverpool only to find the people with whom they had expected to stay have been evicted. Now they're stranded more than a hundred miles from home

117

with nowhere to sleep and nothing to give the lad for his tea.

'Can't do nothin' about the cheque,' the sergeant tells them, handing it back, 'but isn't there someone who could put up a bit o' money for yer? You know, someone at home like?'

'Well, there's me brother . . .,' the mother says, stooping to disengage the child from her knees. 'Will yer stop that, Patrick?'

'Then we've got no problem, have we? All your brother's got to do is take it down to his nearest police station and, when we've got confirmation, it can be paid out to you here, OK? Just you give this officer the details.'

'God bless yer, luv.'

It's a while before there's another lull, and the sergeant can settle down with a mug of tea, nodding to the DC and the aide as they go back upstairs.

Once upon a time, fellas used to go in the CID and you'd never ever see them again, and this created the two-force system you have in most places. But this Chief Constable, Mr Oxford, doesn't like this, y'see – he's an ex-detective himself. He believes, whatever department we're in, we're all policemen, and if you're a CID man you're just a uniformed bobby who hasn't got his uniform on. He's trying to breed a better all-round policeman; one who's been in and out of different departments, so anything you ask him about drugs, disorder or crime, say, he'll have a good knowledge of. Which, I suppose, is logical.

The only way the job loses is that you get moved [on promotion to sergeant] from an area you know well to an area you probably don't know where to find at first! And you lose that many informants as well. Of course, some still ring me up: had one only yesterday on the phone to our house, and I passed it on to a mate of mine at Birkenhead. You'll also find a lot of detective constables are getting overtime and expenses and are making a good living, and they say, 'If I get promoted, I'm going to lose money, I'm going back on three shifts,' and they aren't taking exams, or (laughs) aren't passin' 'em. But you got to look at things in the long run, y'know, and I've got twenty years before they kick me out.

When I came back into uniform, I hadn't seen a traffic accident report for eight years – didn't even know what they looked like. Parking tickets? I didn't even know there were such things – apart from when I got them stuck on me car, y'know! You get so

118

insular in the CID, I had to readjust my mind. All I'd been thinking about was burglars and robbers and muggers, and if a person was drunk or riotous I didn't want to know. I was a detective; it wasn't my affair! But then you realise you've got to get your coat off and do the job.

20

A new sound in the night. A wild despairing cry that hollows the stomach.

The constable on duty in the Pier Head enquiry office – a one-man police station in effect, although not a bridewell – looks up casually from his textbook for a listen. Odd noises are commonplace outside the long narrow building fronting the landing-stage, into part of which the enquiry office is squeezed. Most of them originate way back at the end adjacent to the bus terminal, where a cafeteria continues to do business through a hatchway after hours, creating there a focal point for revellers, vagrants and young rowdies. And to begin with, they say, until a station keeper's ear becomes attuned to the nuances, he can find himself rushing out every five minutes or so, expecting the worst of each hoarse shout or burst of savage laughter.

The new sound is repeated. Puzzled rather than alarmed, the bobby gets up, puts on his helmet and goes to investigate, leaving a footman, who'd popped in to use the lavatory, manning the counter. Down near the cafeteria is a freakish sight, made all the more bizarre by the deafening lament that goes with it.

'*Fok-kin' 'ell !*' the old fella bellows, as he paces up and down frantically. 'Fok me!' he cries, causing several old dears, only there for the bus, to cower back aghast and excited. 'Fok . . . kin' . . . 'ell!' he shouts again, spinning on his heel to complete another figure of eight. 'Fok me!' His shirt flaps open to his waist, and sweat pours down his thin, very white chest. 'Fokkin' 'ell, fokkin' 'ell, fokkin' 'ell!'

'Hey, what's up, pop?' the bobby asks in a butter-rich Irish brogue, falling in step with him.

'Oh, fokkin' hell!'

119

'Ya, all right, I know. But calm down and tell us what's goin' on.'

The old fella pauses, glances over one shoulder and confides: 'George'll bloody string me op! He's got the rope waitin' fer me!'

'Who's George?'

'George is me cat.'

'Oh,' says the bobby. Then adds conversationally, 'Is it a tom like?'

'No, George is me cat. *He'll fokkin' string me op!*'

And the old fella's off again, to the delight of a fast-gathering crowd. But he is taken by the elbow and steered firmly into the enquiry office.

'Bloody hell,' says the other bobby behind the counter. 'Who's this, then, Pat?'

'He was goin' at a great rate of bloody knots up and down here, and—'

The old fella pulls toward the glass doorway, is tugged back, turned round and made to sit on the bench which faces the counter. Pat stands arms akimbo, shaking his head.

'What are we going to do with you?' he asks.

'Oh fok, don't keep me 'ere,' implores the old fella. 'George'll get me!'

'Well, where does George live?'

'Eee, Bootle way.'

'And where have you just come from?'

'Dingle.'

'But that's in two opposite directions! So what were you doin' in the Dingle?'

'George was chasin' me.'

And that's all he will say, over and over. Until Pat finally turns away for a few words about something else with his colleague. Hardly two minutes later, however, their conversation is interrupted.

'No problem,' says a serene-looking pensioner, who has buttoned himself up and now appears quite respectable.

The abrupt transformation takes a second or two to sink in. 'Now what the hell', says Pat, 'was goin' on out there?'

120

'I'm sorry if I bothered—'

'No, you tell me! I want to hear.'

'Well, people look at me,' the pensioner explains, edging towards the door. 'When I'm not doin' it, I'm just a no-mark. Y'know, people all look at me and say, "Look at the poor old fella over there!" ' He shrugs. 'I'm sorry to trouble yer, lads. 'Bye!'

And he's off, leaving Pat to sigh over his textbook, 'Oh Jesus, you don't half get 'em' – and the other bobby to return to his beat again.

21

Once out of probation, a constable can take the first steps toward becoming an all-rounder by being posted to either the Car Squad or to the Plain Clothes Section, both of which are based at St Anne Street. This means that after two or more years of spit and polish, black cloth and silver buttons, and having to keep to a designated area, the officer is suddenly able to dress like a civilian again, and to go almost anywhere he or she pleases within the divisional boundaries. Such freedom has its price, though.

'Being in plain clothes,' says the sergeant in charge of the Car Squad, 'they have tremendous opportunities to disappear and things like that. Fair enough, provided they let me know what they're doing, and we haven't a job on, there's no problem. I do a lot of things while I'm at work but, on the other hand, I put in a lot of hours we don't get paid for. I might have been on duty for twelve hours, but if I think there's a job coming off I stay on – it doesn't bother me. Bothers my wife from time to time! Almost invariably I'm working a Late on Thursday, Friday and Saturday; in the eight months I've been in the squad, I think I've had only two weekends off.'

In fact all plain-clothes officers tend to work longer hours – and often a good deal harder – than their uniformed colleagues whose eight-hour shifts are paced by the vagaries of chance, as it were, and can be as uneventful as tea with the vicar.

This gives plain-clothes officers something in common with detectives, but their work is largely self-initiated and there are other differences as well, including the matter of dress. Members of the CID are obliged to retain at least a jacket, collar and tie in the ordinary course of events, never knowing when next they'll have to be presentable, and this is tantamount to wearing a uniform in most hostile circles, which are rather given to informality. Plain-clothes officers, however, need obey only the conventions of the level of society at which they choose to operate.

Not that a chameleon-like anonymity is always to their advantage, as the Car Squad sergeant makes clear. 'Sometimes we're criticised in court. The defence will say, "You didn't identify yourselves as police officers." He's totally wrong. As we've said in court time and again, we do so immediately – for our own protection. If we didn't tell them, they might think that we're bucks, and they might have a go at you with anything.'

But for much of the time this isn't a Catch 22 when it comes to the crunch. 'I'd think there must be fifty of them we know are bang at it,' says the sergeant. 'We know them – and they know us! This is the unfortunate thing about it.' And the officers of the Plain Clothes Section (or 'vice squad') echo the same sentiments; every speciality begets its own intimacies, and only the rank beginner is likely to feel the full weight of its deterrent effect.

22

Car thieves begin early in 'A' Division. Barry can just get his chin above the charge-office counter at St Anne Street. 'That's the one I was goin' to throw m'self over the landin' fer,' says his rolypoly mum with the two front teeth. 'I'm waitin' fer 'im to be put down – give me a bit o' peace and quiet.' And the two detectives now in charge of the case laugh, being obviously on the best of terms with the lady they call Tessie the Terrible. 'It's all gin and oranges to you, isn't it, luv?' one of them remarks gratefully. While his partner, with a hint of avuncular pride, tells the new bridewell patrol, 'Show his brother any car – the one that's inside – and he'll have it away in two seconds!' Barry grins repeatedly; two hours ago, he stole a Cortina – although, so that an intention permanently to deprive the owner won't have to be proved, the actual charge is having taken and driven it away without his consent. 'Write yer name at the bottom,' says the bridewell sergeant, pointing a finger at the list of personal property now being returned to Barry, who has been given bail. 'He said write it, not print it!' scolds Tessie the Terrible. 'At your age!'

Barry is eleven; had he been two years younger, then he couldn't be charged with an offence. 'It's amazing!' says an OSD sergeant who transferred up from Brighton, having never seen anything like 'A' Division before. 'We find kids of eight, nine, ten, driving cars! Nobody believes it; the courts don't believe it. I went to court with one little lad who'd rolled up the carpets and stuck a couple of AA books as well under the seat, which was pushed up as far as it would go. Instead of sitting, all he was doing was standing on the pedals – just steering, of course, no gear changing or anything like that. And the court couldn't believe he could drive a vehicle, so eventually he got away with it. Imagine what they're like at seventeen, eighteen! A right handful, no doubt about it.'

'There were these two who took a huge wagon, a lorry,' another sergeant recalls. 'One stood on the driver's seat and his mate sat on the floor, workin' the pedals – y'know, sort of "captain to engine room" type of thing!'

The threat to life posed by these wholly incompetent drivers is appalling, and as much a part of the violent nature of inner Liverpool as anything else – although, except when someone gets killed, this isn't generally taken into account. Almost as disturbing is the degree of wanton destruction involved: time and again, vehicles are simply 'bricked' and battered into total write-offs, without so much as a licence disc being taken.

Teenagers are by and large more purposeful in their depredations. They'll take a car when the last bus has gone, when they want a proper joyride, when they intend stripping

123

it for parts – or for a combination of these and like reasons. Some will even hope to sell it whole to a 'ringer', and the CID has its own car squad to investigate this side of things, leaving the plain-clothes sergeant and his eight constables to concentrate on prevention.

The Car Squad works out of a tiny office which must have been designed as a stationery storeroom or something, for it has only a fanlight and no proper window. There are a couple of tables, some chairs, a filing cabinet and one or two of the improvisations which give so many areas of police work on Merseyside an air of dogged make-do.

Two constables in jeans and summer shirts are just leaving, one tucking a baton into his waistband and the other wrapping his windcheater round the squad's one item of specialist equipment, a pair of binoculars.

'Going to do obs on top of the ——, boss,' he says, as they reach the door. 'Then, if it gets too cold like, we'll go down to on the stairs – OK ?'

'I'll be along later, lads. I'm just looking through the collator's bulletins.'

The sergeant is a spry wiry man of forty-three, with a narrow ascetic face, a donnish head of grey hair brushed straight back, and the hushed confidential manner of a contented introvert. Before joining the police fifteen years ago, he was an insurance inspector, having started his career as an office boy in the Royal Liver Building, Liverpool's most famous landmark.

Financially I would probably have been better off had I stayed in insurance, but certainly from the point of view of married life I wouldn't have been as happy. It entailed taking charge of district offices all over the country, and when I met my wife I hadn't spent more than about three weeks in Liverpool in five years. Money isn't everything.

I've got a boy of eight and a half and a girl of just over eleven, and I wonder what sort of world they're growing into frequently. It's a thing I'm not too happy about. You wonder if you did right in having children, because the state the country is getting into now is frightening. They're taking a lot of the power away

124

from the police. I wouldn't want to bring my wife into town, purely from the point of view of not wanting her to be attacked. The number of times I've come in when I'm off duty I could count on one hand in the last four or five years. Don't get me wrong; I enjoy working in the city centre, but I've got something positive to do there.

We're responsible really for all car thefts, of and from. We don't always stand much chance of catching people for taking vehicles – not having a car allocated to us – but if we can catch them, that's fine. Very often, when we hear a call go out on the radio, we have an idea of where that car is going to be dumped and so, if we're mobile, we make our way there. I haven't had a full section for three months now, although this week I've only got one away. We have to scrimp and scrounge. (*Laughs quietly*) Actually, I've used my own car on numerous occasions, which is why I leave it in the yard during the evenings – although I'm not supposed to officially – purely because the bucks all know it, and if I left it outside it's very likely to end up with the windows smashed or big scrapes down the side.

By looking at these collator's bulletins, we pick up patterns, the times and places offences are being committed. There's a big increase round the cathedrals in the summer, with foreign visitors to the city. It only takes a matter of seconds for the bucks to get into a car and, in most cases, only seconds for them to steal a car. We had an incident a couple of months ago when the whole thing was done in under a minute.

Normally, it's juveniles and teenagers. With our age group being roughly eleven to twenty-two, it's very difficult for us to pass on our knowledge to the Uniform lads, because there are so many of these youngsters and we can only give descriptions of them – we can't use photographs. It's almost impossible to describe someone so a bobby will recognise him a week later, unless he has something unusual about his clothing or something. Strangely enough, most of them are now pleading 'not guilty'! (*Laughs*) It does happen, a tremendous amount, where the solicitor is making money hand-over-fist by persuading people to plead not guilty and elect trial. It's always a frustration, court; you catch them bang at it and they go to court and get given conditional discharges and things like that. When you get eleven- and twelve-year-olds blatantly breaking into cars, and doing it time and time again, it's not sufficient.

I'm an extremely placid person. I don't agree with people

125

getting knocked about, and there are occasions when I've found it necessary in the past to talk to various constables about it. I wouldn't dream of hitting a prisoner – it just doesn't interest me. But I do think they should be punished.

The thirty-bob lock! You have certain manufacturers who make these cars costing four, five thousand pound, and one would think they'd have some system of securing such a vehicle. From what I understand, there are only about five keys for the whole range of ——, and that's one of the most common of the lot. Another problem is steering-column locks. A lot of people don't bother to set them – they don't set automatically. If the buck can get the engine started, he's away. Setting the lock might make only a minute's difference to the buck, but a minute's a long time and it could save the owner his car. Boot locks. On some cars they're poor. I'm not very keen on boots you just close and they're locked without using a key; I think with a kick in the right place, they just spring open! If you really want to secure your car, then cut-outs are fairly effective; the Regional Crime Squad cars have them. (*Shrugs, implying there is no total safeguard*)

They reckon on about twelve month in the car squad. It's a continuous war. It has a lot of satisfaction as well, from the point of view particularly if we manage to catch someone we know has been at it some time. (*Shrugs again*) I like to change with the times, but it still upsets me to see the calibre of people we're getting in the police force. What I want are good thief catchers, who can be trusted to work without supervision. I thoroughly enjoyed my first three months in this section, where I had eight lads who were prepared to work. Even if it came to two o'clock in the morning, they'd stay on and work through to four and five.

High on a building overlooking an open car-park, and some side streets where there is parking as well, the constable using the binoculars has his eye on two youths in the inevitable white shirts and denims. This is the second 'short cut' they've taken through the car-park in less than five minutes, and they both seem unnaturally interested in the interior of a bottle-green Rover; just the sort of car possibly to have a sheepskin jacket tossed on the back seat, or perhaps even a large expensive-looking parcel. They disappear from view down an alley to his left.

126

The wind up there is blustery and cold, and a cigarette burns nauseously at the rate of a fuse, condemning itself to an early grave in the thick patina of pigeon droppings.

They're back, walking through the car-park along the same diagonal. The constable with the binoculars reaches for his radio, ready to alert his 'runner' on the ground below, who keeps a low profile – and his own radio out of earshot – until the moment comes to break cover. They walk up to the Rover, around it and on to the bus stop, timing everything to perfection by boarding a bus just as it pulls away.

'Shhh-uh!' says the watcher on the rooftop, turning to make a sweep of the side streets.

Below him, pedestrians continue to follow surprisingly intricate patterns, invisible on the ground but restated by their passage, with only the old and the very young showing a tendency to wander. Not quite a case of the straight and narrow, but any deviant is always worth a second look.

Nothing up the side streets, nothing in the—

The 'Go!' is given. In what must have been only a matter of seconds, three youths have reached a car on the far side of the Rover and, having presumably found it secure, are going in through the rear window. With a quick slash, the rubber seal around the glass is parted, the ends gripped and the whole thing pulled away, while the window itself topples silently on to the back seat. Even as he turns to hurl himself down the fire escape, the watcher on the roof sees a pair of running-pumps disappearing over the boot in search of plunder.

But, with any luck, they'll catch at least a couple of them bang at it, for what that's worth. On average, ten cars a day are broken into in 'A' Division, and ten are either stolen or taken and driven away. The Car Squad averages one prisoner.

23

There is only one supervision vehicle roadworthy tonight, so Inspector North has dropped in at Copperas Hill to offer his opposite number a lift across to the officers' canteen at refreshment time. They're gossiping when the bridewell sergeant

127

pokes his head in, flourishing a folded copy of the evening newspaper.

'Quite chuffed with m'self. Eight across: Who wrote *The Cherry Orchard*? And I said Chekhov!'

'Oh, it's not like that on the north side,' their visitor says primly. '*We* discuss case law. Sex, women, football – they're all out. As for crossword puzzles, *well*.'

'Customers,' the bridewell patrol informs the sergeant. 'Van's just come in the yard.'

'Shall we go?' says Inspector North.

'Why not?'

But, before leaving, Inspector South makes a quick check round the station, and comes across an ogle of young cons with a girlie magazine. They have it opened at a double-spread in which a freckle-faced nude sprawls languorously on a freshly made double-bed, her legs apart towards the camera.

'What you might call an open invitation like, sir?'

'Fantastic knockers, boss! Could smother yer!'

'She's got shoulders', grunts Inspector South, 'like a Hungarian gravedigger.' And their laughter brings him beaming into the small charge office, where a tall mop-haired man is being led up to the counter by a Days and EPs constable carrying a crowbar. 'What's this, then?'

Both look as though the crowbar changed hands at some cost to personal dignity.

'London Road, sir. Fella here bein' a bit naughty. You know, walkin' down the middle, shoutin' 'e was goin' to put a stop to the traffic problem.'

The prisoner's scowl gives way to a lopsided grin of embarrassment.

Words like 'naughty' are used fairly extensively in 'A' Division, often when stronger language would be excusable. Perhaps the American theatre critic, Eric Bentley, in discussing the arrogance of Anglo-Saxon understatement, also provides an insight into many bobbies when he says: 'The undramatic is their peculiar drama.'

A BOBBY: The majority of them are decent enough people, but there are some who to me are just pigs – morally and physically,

128

y'know, pigs. It's a strain workin' with them. You read in the papers about three senior police officers in London being involved in these backhanders – to me that's sickening. I'd just throw away the key on people like that. I really would, y'know. They are in a position of trust.

There are times when you think: Christ, there's no need for that! I let him know in no uncertain terms how I feel about it. But it goes that far (*snaps fingers*) because the ripple can become a wave. Some people may call it cowardice, but you've got your own end to protect as well, y'know. Unless, of course, it's somethin' really criminal, somethin' that's really untoward! Then I'd have no compunction about doin' 'im, none whatsoever.

I think there are some people who get a queer pleasure out of violence – and out of talkin' about violence – and that to me is pretty sick. I mean, there's enough violence goin' on outside on the streets, y'know, without it being meted out by us. But it's true to say that in certain circumstances violence has to be used; there's no doubt about that, y'know, because you won't be an effective police officer if you're not prepared to use it at some time – force meetin' force, y'know.

After refreshments, Inspector South borrows the car to do the rounds on his side of the dividing line. He whisks out of the yard, is lucky with the lights at the Islington intersection, and leaves the brooding cementscape of the North Sub behind him.

Then down he goes into the neon-scribble city centre, round Lime Street station and up redbrick Renshaw Street, doubling back down the brief elegance of Bold Street, left into the seedy backstreets of clubland, and over into the paint chart of Chinatown's Nelson Street, passing frontages pink, green, scarlet, sky-blue and turquoise, stopping by the Pearl City on the corner.

The Chinese mostly came over on the Blue Funnel boats; they've been here, I suppose, about ninety years. They're peaceable, law-abiding and very family-minded people. In fact, we had a survey done about fourteen years ago, and found that Chinese and Jewish children had the lowest incidence of trouble with the police. Recently, of course, we've had a bit of trouble with a young arrogant type of Chinaman who is, shall I say, associated with K14, the tong from Hongkong. It was formed by roughly the criminal element in Shanghai as a form of resistance movement against the Japanese and, as with a lot of resistance movements, there isn't a great deal of difference between patriotism and hooliganism, is there? (*Chuckles*) But we've never had much trouble with tongs, because the Liverpool Chinese knows he's here now and hasn't anything to fear from them. We've had the K14 once in the station at Copperas, and we got rid of them out of Liverpool, very, very quickly. They're marvellous people, the Chinese.

There he gives a peg to one of his constables – and lends her a pen, as she's come out without one. On again, glancing down every side-street, homing in on the strident clamour of an automatic alarm system. Another of his foot patrols is standing guard outside the shop, which has a broken plate-glass window.

'Keyholder on the way, Dave?'

'Supposed to be, sir – only he lives in Wigan. Took two hours before he bothered last time.'

'What they get?'

'Dunno, sir. Not much *to* get, if yer know what I mean.'

'I'll send a relief down – second refreshments?'

The bobby nods morosely and Inspector South is on his way again, niggled by having lost one of his scant west section, but enjoying his progress through a square mile or so for which after nearly two decades of close acquaintanceship, he has an almost possessive affection. Several passers-by show signs of recognition; some effusively, some shyly, some by looking away all too casually. Yellow faces, white faces, black and in-between faces; the orange faces of kids of every hue, dancing round an enormous bonfire beside a warehouse. The fire brigade is in attendance.

'All right, lads?' Then the feedline: 'Arson, was it?'

'Arsin' about more like! Load o' little pyromaniacs. . . .'

Fraternal laughter; all the world's a nursery and we are elder brothers.

On up Duke Street. On up Upper Duke Street, the radio murmuring nothing of interest. Fine old buildings on the left, desolation on the right and, against that skyline, the biggest Anglican cathedral in all England, built of sandstone the colour of an old bloodstain. It towers above a long steep slope of weed that

130

drops away down to a row of tawdry council dwellings; too weighty, though, to soar heavenwards, elevating the thoughts of men, it simply dwarfs them with its awesome mass, much as a rusting supertanker in dry dock might do. And it's to be even bigger: seventy-three years after it was begun in the hope of impressing the world with Liverpool's commercial prosperity, workmen are still busy high on the only scaffolding to be seen in this dilapidated area. While, within, the Neo-Gothic kitsch and deliberate gloom, so redolent of mawkish Victorian preoccupations with death, seem at odds with a people renowned for their defiant vitality – although, it is true, three of them used the dark entranceway to advantage last week, when they mugged a couple of tourists.

Inspector South has a tale to hang on many a brass knocker the length of Canning Street beyond, but turns right into Hope Street, travelling between the grave of the first-ever railway casualty and the faded façade of a Georgian crescent. At the far end of the crescent, a youth in tight jeans alters his stance, bringing his hips into line with an assumed air of heterosexual innocence. It's a pinkle-twisters' paradise, this shadowy strip behind the cathedral, but prostitutes – unless encountered flagrante delicto – are the preserve of the Plain Clothes Section really. Inspector South merely makes a note of the face, lest he should come across it in a sack some day, and noses into a side road. Here the houses are Georgian, too, most of them divided up into a number of flats, and the residents range from the unemployable to the wealthy academic, with a leavening of students and other young people. The front doors are the give-away: some shiny with new paint, some left to peel, a single bellpush or a whole row of them. He drives slowly with only his sidelights on, as is the custom, but sees nothing suspicious.

Hard right and hard left into Upper Parliament Street, right on the brink of the division, passing a chemist's shop on one corner that looks like an armoury. Most of the faces are black now. The Somali Club, the Caribbean. . . .

I like Arab Somalis. We've had some crime with them, mainly shooting, but only after provocation when they've been attacked. The original Liverpool coloured person was never involved in crime. Those who are involved tend to be largely Lagos Nigerians and Kingston Jamaicans, although I'd imagine they're the type who would be criminals back in their own country, so that's not all of them. We get West Islanders who're noisy and cause trouble, only mainly among themselves and usually over women. I don't find them a bad type at all; they're hardworking, very happy and cheerful people. The primary schools on our ground have very nearly every race under the sun, and there's very little lack of racial harmony. Our racial integration took place long before anyone made a science of it! My personal view, pessimistic and no doubt coloured by a policeman's bias, is that a lot of problems we're going to have on our ground – we've had very few so far – will be artificially created for political purposes by the fellas empire-building in the Good Guy industry.

Nearing the farthest corner of his territory, Inspector South passes Myrtle Gardens, a grim council tenement block which has the same reputation as the North Sub's notorious Four Squares off Soho Street. Many of its ground-floor windows are smashed, National Front slogans are sprayed on its grey walls, and the play area is jagged with broken bottles. Over the road is a new housing project.

That, I'm firmly convinced, was designed by a major in the Russian School of Infantry; it's impossible to get a vehicle in there. Its young half-caste kids – nine, ten, eleven – are wilder than any kids I know, and I'm anticipating trouble in a few years' time, when these fellas get in there and start stirring things. This is the Liverpool 8 area. Now, Myrtle Gardens, you'll hear young policemen say, is full of thieves and hoodlums. It has a high percentage of them, but the majority are hardworking people of all races, who just want to bring their families up in peace – who strive towards an ambition of getting a house out of the area.

Inspector South begins to make his way back to the gracious streets behind the cathedral. There are very few pedestrians, all of whom seem to be going about their lawful business – although, for a moment, he wonders if the youngsters dashing across one of the dusty open spaces are quite as innocent as their laughter. Then the Georgian façades reappear, and he turns left off Grove Street into a low leafy tunnel. Falkner Square has a lushness that alone makes it something of a

132

novelty in 'A' Division. The small park in the centre, surrounded on three sides by avenues and again by the front gardens of the terrace houses overlooking it, is thick with trees, shrubs and bushes, all growing in uninhibited profusion behind the iron railings.

With headlights blazing, making it impossible for anyone to detect the approach of a marked police vehicle through the dazzle, Inspector South tags on to a slow procession of circling cars, none of which is carrying passengers. Women stand at intervals along the pavements, their hair unkempt, their clothing shoddy; few wear any make-up, and none of them has on tights or stockings.

24

High noon and Falkner Square is bound to be back in business with the lunch-hour trade, those feverish executives and mild-mannered clerks who say they're just popping out for a bit of a whatsit.

'Heard the latest complaint?' asks a panda driver, bored and approaching the square along deserted Canning Street. 'Uniformed policemen are laffin' and jokin' with the cows. Don't smile at them!'

'Oh aye, I had an old lady only last Monday sayin' she was fed up being pestered by the mooshes every time she went out,' his observer replies with some sympathy. 'I mean, she was sixty-seven, y'know – amazin'! The trouble is, y'see, you see them about that much, y'know, and I suppose they get to know you.'

'There's a young one now,' says the driver. 'You wouldn't believe it, would you?'

The adolescent on the corner of Falkner Square is an ungainly figure in a striped cardigan, grubby blouse and an uneven skirt reaching to mid-calf. Her expression is one of double-chinned belligerence.

'A sex appeal limited – as our wise inspector would say – to a middle-aged, half-pissed, three-badge naval stoker, haven't we? Y'know, one who's been at sea for—'

'Shall we chase 'em?'

133

'Yeah.'

The panda driver turns right into the avenue. 'Look at those two horrors on the corner here by the Embassy. . . .' He slows down and calls out, 'Come on, ladies. Off home, then!'

'You'll get haemorrhoids hangin' round these cold pavements, girls!'

The pair pretend an interest in the thin one's cigarette lighter.

'If you said "piles", they'd have understood!' laughs the driver, then points across the street at a diminutive girl in a red-checked shirt, the almost regulation wobbly hemmed blue skirt and wooden sandals; her feet are engrained with dirt to her ankles. 'Look at the boots on that one! Like tank tracks!'

'It's hard on the feet,' murmurs the observer.

'You're well up in this! When did you say your rest day was?'

Grinning, his colleague turns back to the two on the corner. 'You'll get piles on those cold pavements!' Then he shakes his head and sighs, 'Look at the state of them. . . .'

'They're fokkin' horrible, aren't they?'

An Audi saloon ghosts up to the intersection, sees the panda car and turns away suddenly down Sandon Street with clumsy expedition. Scowling, the two girls wander off, while a less observant kerb-crawler, coming up from behind the panda, is so intent on assessing Miss Tank Track that he almost causes a collision. Unabashed, however, he continues his circuit.

'Along there,' says the panda driver, 'in that big Yankee car, looks to me like a livin'-on merchant. We might pipe him.'

'Yeah.'

As the police vehicle approaches, the American sedan takes off abruptly, leaving a trio of women to mouth a few unmentionables. The panda crew follow in its wake, hoping to draw alongside and take a look at the driver. It's hardly a chase, because their quarry sticks strictly to the speed limit, but the Mini's poor acceleration makes it sound a little like one, heightening the excitement. They catch up at the traffic lights at the edge of the division, where – for the duration of the red – there is a window-to-window confrontation. Nothing is said, but the big engine is encouraged to growl menacingly.

'Oh aye, a puddin' eater – must be.'

'Well, we've piped him now,' says the driver, signalling a left turn that will take them back into the South Sub. 'Let him get out of the city, but if he comes back down we'll have a word with 'im.'

What does he do for them? Well, he doesn't break their arm, y'know! That's what it amounts to. He could be a fella with a club, a fella with a taxi business. He'll say to her, 'I know you're cowin' it. I'm goin' to set customers up for yer. I'll mind yer.'

– They like to have a minder in the area, watchin' 'em. He might follow the car when they go with a fella who's gettin' a bit rough with them – a regular like – in case 'e tries to murder 'em. This is sometimes the service they give.

– But usually he'll just say, 'You either pay me or I'll break yer nose and nobody'll go near yer.'

– If this prostitute has got somebody like that, really puttin' the arm on 'er, and she's not makin' a lot of money out of it herself, she's going to turn to somebody she knows on the vice squad and say, 'For Christ sake, get this fella off me back!' If she just gets another fella to beat him up, that'll only shut him up for a while, then he'll be back to beat 'er up! But if she sets the dogs on 'im the vice can get him eighteen months.

25

It's always good for a giggle when a con gets posted to the Plain Clothes Section. Nudge, nudge, they go, along the crowded bar at St Anne Street.

'Aye aye, 'ere 'e comes, lads, the Last of the Virgins! What'll it be, Rich?'

'Cheers, Allan, a lager'd be great.'

'Bloody hell! One day on the job and already the poor fella's stone deaf! Is it right he should be gettin' paid to abuse 'is talents this way?'

'Sorry?' says Rich.

'Fancy an Aston Martin, do yer? Or are yer thinkin' of

startin' off with somethin' a bit more modest like – y'know, a Granada maybe?'

'Oh aye, it's a standin' joke that,' says one of his new colleagues. 'It's best if you've got an old banger to try and get shot of it first before you come on the section. Otherwise, y'see, with all the second-gear work we do up the square, you find you soon need a new motor – and this lot'll be sayin', "Aye aye, who's this takin' the rent now?"'

Not all remarks made out of earshot of the ladylike stewardess and her 'swear bottle' are as good-humoured. 'Wonder who 'e knows?' mutters a sour-faced con, still walking the beat long after probation. 'I mean, that's what it's all about, innit? Load of fokkin' posers. . . .' And he turns to stare coldly at the circle seated beside the social club's dance-floor.

Seven of the section's eleven constables are there, most of them in their early twenties, and one of the two sergeants as well, a middle-aged stalwart drinking Pernod. Although at liberty to dress as they wish, their clothing is none the less conventional enough, and the same could be said of their hair styles. Three in fact favour jackets, collars and ties on this occasion while the rest are in an assortment of inexpensive leisure wear – jeans, open-necked shirts, zippered tops – that provides a range of guises as diverse as the individuals themselves, without any apparent attempt to masquerade 'under cover'. What could rankle, however, is perhaps implicit in this very lack of extremes and in the group's lively self-absorbed camaraderie: every member of the Plain Clothes Section is hand-picked for the job, and those judged more susceptible to corruptive influences excluded.

Even so, constables are not permitted to go into clubs and, as a further precaution, everyone at operational level – including the inspector in charge – serves no more than a year at a time in the 'vice', which falls under the administrative control of the Deputy Divisional Commander.

This Plain Clothes idea we've got here (*says the inspector*) started off as a Liverpool thing. We get all the vice aspects in one basket, and we say to a group of men, 'Come on. You deal with it.' It's interesting that in other forces very few of them had

136

anything like this – y'know, CID used to do it. One of the reasons why nothing like the scandals in the Metropolitan Police have happened here, touch wood! The mistake they made, as I see it, was that vice was thrown in as an extra job on already hard-pressed detectives – well, you're bound to have problems. And I think twelve months is enough. They can come back after a break of, say, two years, but the snag is, of course, by then they're in the CID or in Traffic, so generally speaking you're pretty short of qualified Plain Clothes men. (*Smiles*) Nobody's ever wanted out, but I know one or two we'd like who didn't want back in. It's a harassing job, really.

Not only does the section deal with licensing, gambling, prostitution, pornography and, to a considerable extent, drug-users as well, but its officers are also responsible for absconders from institutions, deserters from the armed forces, young people missing from home (a legacy of the defunct Women's Section), and for making the sort of discreet enquiries which would be impossible in uniform.

We're in a good position, of course (*says one of the sergeants*) because, although we might say we've a load of paperwork, we've only got a load when we've gone out and done a job. In other words, the work we do is of our own making – other than missing-from-homes, which don't have much paper attached to them anyway – a bit like in Uniform. Now, the CID are inundated with paper, and how often can a CID man go out during the day and actually detect offences? Very seldom.

This could make it sound as though the Plain Clothes Section simply enjoyed the best of both worlds, while being spared the less attractive aspects of each of them. But what complicates the issue – and makes that twelve-month limitation seem a sound idea in more ways than one – is the uniquely exposed nature of the work itself, which places every newcomer on the threshold of a third and rather different world. Something of the kind suggested by the stag-night banter round the bar, while veterans of 'the Vice' provide undertones of a tribal initiation, hinting at perils and temptations to be overcome in exchange for wisdom and insight.

'It'll take the blinkers off 'im, won't it, Arthur?'

137

'Put hairs on his chest, no danger.'

'Put years on mine! But seriously, son, remember what we told yer.'

'And take me word for it,' adds Arthur, as Allan intervenes with the pint of lager, 'yer outlook's bound to change. Oh aye, life'll never seem the same after.'

26

Insights are two a penny in police work, as the senior bridewell surgeon might say. 'I've twice been called in to determine sex and, of course, we get transvestites. I've had drunken drivers like that! It's very embarrassing for them.'

Perhaps, for the blushing prisoner involved, it would be some comfort to know that the bobby who arrested him just might, if it's a cold enough night, be wearing a pair of pantihose. 'It gets you in the legs – y'know, walkin' round half the ruddy night when it's freezin' – so some of the lads have the bottom half of tracksuits on underneath, the missus's tights are quite popular, and some get themselves the proper long underwear, only the good stuff's expensive.'

But that isn't an insight of the telling sort, which can be muted yet still produce a moment's reflection. Such insights are common enough in the bridewell: the grown men with just a few coppers to jingle, the married men with a condom in their wallet, the mothers with lucky mascots for bingo, the canny children who carry nothing to identify them, and the unexpecteds, like the punk rocker with a birthday greetings telegram from his granny.

'Aye, that's right, Joe,' the bridewell sergeant tells the spruce bachelor caught shoplifting, 'spread 'em all out so I can list 'em. Pipe, pouch, matches, Parker fountain pen, three Biros, two pencils. What's this key for? Bank of England?'

'Me room, sair.'

'Five, ten, seventeen pence and four pound in notes. That the lot? Just sign underneath here.'

Then the sergeant remembers to unzip the tobacco pouch and take a careful sniff at its contents. He sneezes.

138

This isn't what makes the bridewell patrol stare: she's watching the prisoner struggling to write his own name, one uncertain letter at a time, tongue out just like a child with a crayon.

You get used to it, they say, although all eyes turn every time there's a rattle of personal possessions being emptied out on to the counter. What Plain Clothes does, however, is to provide fresh insights, ranging from the coldly clinical to the sort that thaw society's conventional attitudes.

Whenever Plain Clothes raids licensed premises, about half a dozen people have samples of their drinks taken and sealed in sterilised bottles for analysis. Everyone knows the stuff's lager or gin or vodka, but courts require quibble-proof evidence that alcohol was being consumed, and this is expressed as a bleak figure, usually of between five and seven per cent.

A batch of samples has this morning arrived back from the forensic laboratory at Chorley, and a sergeant is going through the results, starting with the last club they raided. Five per cent, five, five, six, five— He stops.

'Heavens, look at the proof of these!' he says. 'They're both over thirty!'

'The two gorgeous birds who gave us the correct details?' asks a constable drifting over. 'Y'know, sittin' with the three suave fellas in the corner?'

'Right. The barman must've been in on it.'

'Oh aye, and look at this one from the week before. You remember little Rita? With the big eyes and all?'

'Seventeen-point-three. Get 'em stoned, typical.'

The teetotal chief inspector has been most things other than a detective.

While I was in Plain Clothes, Jimmy and I were patrolling around at half-past eleven at night, and we were going in the toilets at the top end of Caledonian Street to check them, when Jimmy says, 'Hey, down there – a couple on the job!' I didn't pay much attention; there are bobbies who can invest a shirt on a chair with the female form divine, y'know. But as we came out and start walking down I realised it was true. That at the

139

side door of the Philharmonic Hall – the orchestra entrance – there's a street-lamp, and under it a couple are clearly copulating! And I also realised it was a prostitute known as Big Fat Agnes.

She was the one who used to say she gave yellow trading stamps, and she'd come up and invite you to ' 'Ave a short time, luv, a bob down and a bob a week?' A terrible bloody creature! Mentally she was quite reasonable to talk to, but physically she was described by our venerable sergeant as a piss-stained reptile. She couldn't talk to you without wetting herself. She used to say, 'Excuse me, luv,' and she'd crouch down and wee – half-way through a conversation with her! But there was no harm in her, none.

Well, she's coupled with a young Jewish lad, and her hands are resting lightly on his shoulders, and he's *bangin'* away like nobody's business. I put *my* hand on the lad's shoulder before they realised we were there! And he whips back and closes his coat.

'It's a'right,' says Agnes. 'It's the Vice.' Meaning: Don't panic – they're policemen. So much for your disguises and everything! And I come out with the policeman's usual expression, 'Well, well, what's goin' on 'ere?' The little Jewish lad says, 'It's all right, officer. We were only talking.' 'Oh aye,' says I. 'Open yer coat.' And there's his John Thomas, standin' to attention, circumcised, a cold night, little wisps of steam coming from it! So I said, 'You're both locked up. Common prostitute behavin' in a riotous or indecent manner, and you can be done for aidin' and abettin'.'

So off we set for the bridewell, and behind me I can hear Jimmy talking to this lad. 'Now, listen, son,' he said. 'This one is poxed to the eyeballs. We'll get you your bail so you can get home, half-fill a jam jar with Dettol and then top up with warm water. Just put yer JT in it, and let it soak for half an hour.' He's worried sick, this lad – had to work in his father's shop next day, and we're going to court. So I said to him, 'Start work in the ordinary way, tell yer dad you've been goin' mad with the toothache, and skip away at half-past nine, sayin' yer goin' to the dentist. Down to the court at ten, a quick guilty plea, time to pay, back in the shop and say, "It feels wonderful now!"'

Agnes got a month and we had to make arrangements for her baby. The lad was fined two pounds and, in fact, didn't ask for time to pay. I saw him afterwards and he said it was fine, his

140

dad hadn't suspected a thing. But I never did find out if he carried out Jimmy's startling prophylactic advice! He's a sadistic bugger, y'know.

The chief inspector has in fact another title, albeit an honorary one today, which can be found painted on the door of a converted cell: GOVERNOR – of the Main Bridewell.

27

The Main Bridewell, central lock-up for the Liverpool Petty Sessions area, stands just a few yards up Cheapside off Dale Street, adjacent to the magistrates' courts, and behind a high wall. An unprepossessing sight from the outside, it is none the less one of the most remarkable structures in the city. Dickensian, in a word, although this hardly explains why men who call it that and themselves 'big hairy bobbies' admit they never spend a minute longer there than they need to. It is, perhaps, a place to be felt rather than seen.

Built in 1861, and so solid that from within it gives the impression of being subterranean, the Main has three floors of barrel-vaulted cells on the Pentonville model, doors and walls as thick as a man's fist and trunk respectively, thrice-locking handmade locks, echoing flags, a ghost and an attic chamber where, until recent renovations, a flutter of pigeons came and went as they pleased. Renovations which unearthed leg-irons, birches, early riot shields and a central heating system which was in its way every bit as good as the one just installed, although primitive to operate.

Like it or not, however, every officer in 'A' Division gets to know the Main well, particularly as it is to here that all drunks are brought directly.

After pressing the bellpush in the porch, the constable waits with his prisoner to be scrutinised through the sliding peephole in the huge brown steel door, and then is admitted to a large room with a barrel-vaulted ceiling supported by cast-iron columns with fluted tops. Immediately to his right is a

141

notice board to which is pinned a child's drawing of a 'black maria', a Transport and General Workers' Union pamphlet, a missing persons notice and another dating back to 1865 which details the diet a prisoner can expect in the New Gaol at Beaumaris on Anglesey Island. There are new glass-walled offices to the right and straight ahead, and on the left, facing the long charge-office counter, is a stout pen of polished wood about four feet high, clamped tightly to four of the fluted columns, and containing a low bench. The three bespectacled middle-aged officers behind the counter – a tall inspector, who accepts the charges, and two constables, one slight in build, the other a big affable-looking man – prepare to receive their forty-third prisoner with practised ease.

'The circumstances are,' says the constable, drawing a deep breath, 'at quarter-past eleven tonight I was on duty in Lime Street when I saw this man standing up in the middle of the road waving this bottle. I went up to him and his breath smelled of drink. His speech was slurred; he was unsteady on his feet. I arrested this man for being drunk and incapable.'

'Well, Davie, what do you say to that?'

'Woorrrrgh.'

The charge is accepted, the prisoner searched – the slight BP makes a joke of it, but keeps his hip turned to ward off anything unexpected – and the particulars are noted down, some of them from memory.

'But what was the date of your birth?' asks the inspector.

'Huh?'

'Come on, when's yer birthday?' one BP prompts.

'He wants to send yer a card, y'see,' says the other.

'Does he?'

'Yeah.'

'Oh dear.'

The inspector taps the counter. 'What year were you born?'

'Fifty-eight.'

'*Thirty*-eight!'

'Fifty-eight,' says the prisoner airily, picking up his watch and trying to read the time on it.

'Go away! You're more than nineteen!' And the inspector

142

fills in the charge sheet with, 'Thirty-eight. Put that back.' As the prisoner drops the watch back into the meagre pile of his possessions, he's handed a copy of the charge.

'Come on,' says the big BP, 'we'll give you a knock in the morning. Come on, Davie, come and get yer head down.'

'I'm mixed up.'

'You want to walk on yer own or—'

'No!' says the prisoner, hastening to catch up as the BP saunters out of the charge office into a low passageway where the light is soft after the harsh glare of the fluorescents.

The BP continues to walk a few paces ahead of him, unlocks a grille, leaves the gate open, and goes down a long corridor with cell doors on either side of it.

'Can I be put in wi' Billy ?' asks the prisoner.

'Billy's in there,' the BP tells him, pointing his keys at a cell he's just approaching, from which all sorts of disjointed sounds are coming, adding to the echoes.

'Orgh.'

The BP pauses at the door, waits for the prisoner to catch up, and then unlocks it. 'Here we are, lads. Davie's come to join yer!'

And just as the massive door closes on him, Davie turns and says, 'Fifty-eight.'

One of the great comforts of having the Main Bridewell, particularly from a young constable's point of view, is that, no matter how violent your prisoner may be, once you've managed to get him there your troubles are over. Even if he happens to be the giant who made a name for himself by bending beer-pump handles flat on pub counters, and is reputed still to take ten bobbies to restrain him, or perhaps a slip of a girl given the strength of five by a mixture of drugs and drink.

Both constables on duty tonight, who have the air of a sucessful tennis doubles team, have worked in the Main Bridewell now for the best part of four years. Stan has twenty years' service, stands 5 feet $9\frac{1}{2}$ inches and is highly regarded for his portraiture in oils; while Dave is a six-footer, writes a fair bit in his spare time, and has been in the police force for twenty-one years.

DAVE: When I walk ahead, that's when I know them. Otherwise, I say to the officer, 'You come with me.'

STAN: You'll find others, you've only got to touch 'em and they're on yer! So, if you give them sort of a position of trust – 'Come with me', y'know, and you walk ahead – then there's no aggro. It's very important for every prisoner to, you know, keep his dignity.

DAVE: Oh aye.

STAN: The company director will be aloof, rather cool and collected; the drunken yob will keep *his* dignity by being abusive and offensive, y'know! (*Both laugh*)

DAVE: The easiest way to control a prisoner – any number of prisoners – is to unbalance them. 'Oh, you want a fag?' 'Yuh.' You give him a light. The next one: 'And you sit down, yer bastid, and behave y'self!' Do you see? Unbalance them; they don't know where they are. I do that myself personally, and I do it consciously: give a fella a fag and come down on the next one – they think *you're* crazy! That's when there's a whole lot of them.

STAN: Drunks.

DAVE: I think all the charge office staff have been assaulted?

STAN: I got kicked in the eye and the knee not long ago. Had me nose broken in me first twelve months as a bobby! Two queers in a public toilet, and I tried to separate them.

DAVE: Oh, we deal with a lot of violent people in here, but we have a major advantage in that we know at least seventy per cent of the prisoners who come through the door – probably more than that. We're on surname terms with at least fifty per cent, and first-name terms with about twenty-five per cent. Of course, people don't come into a police station once in their life – very rarely. They come in more than once and, of course, they know that once they're through the door they must behave themselves.

And they do, more often than not. The shouting and cursing seems to be nipped in the great clang of the door closing, and resignation takes over, frequently sweetened by the small talk that recognises expediency on both sides. From the card-table where the tea is poured, the Main Bridewell is actually almost snug and certainly cosy, being warm, dry and orderly in comparison with many other types of police work, while also – puns apart – enormously secure. Yet Dave and Stan feel somewhat restless. 'I liked it for the last three years,' says Dave, 'but

144

recently I'm not sure. I've always been a bit of a wanderer m'self. A policeman isn't like another worker, of course: when you get into a position that's suitable for you, in the police service that could end at the end of the watch. You could be out, fully operational, which is unsettling in itself.' But the main thing is they believe they'd be better employed 'teaching these young officers to be policemen', although not on three shifts. 'Our experience will never be recovered,' Dave explains. 'You see, when Stan and I joined, we were instructed by fairly senior constables, and then allowed out on our own to make our own decisions on every occurrence that came up. Now then, officers of today are equipped with a radio to start off with and, if they've got a doubt, all most of them do is speak. The job loses out, y'see.'

Theirs is a concern shown by many older officers in 'A' Division: the modern bobby seems to be losing the personal touch, however rough and ready it might once have been.

The manpower shortage must take a large share of the blame, and so perhaps must personal radios (although the thin ranks could not hope to manage without them), but not a few young officers would also blame well-meant legislation which has, in the words of one of them, 'treated a sort of marriage like a divorce'. Possibly his meaning is made clearer by this sergeant in his twenties.

It's becoming very cold. In the old days – which people tell me about – the policeman could give a kid who'd stolen something petty a thick ear. Now he's got to lock him up and put him through all that, because if he hit that kid he'd get complained about.

Since the new complaints procedure, informal ways of dealing with people are increasingly out the window. Your discretion is eroded to quite a degree. I can become very bitter when people don't trust me.

Like you can go to a guy now and try and bollock him for a traffic offence. It becomes a temptation, if you bollock him good style and see him bridling, to do him anyway – or you take the details so you can, if he complains. Say he writes in a letter of complaint and it's sent down to you: what you do is attach it to

145

the prosecution form you've just made out. You say to the boss, 'That's what he got done for; that's what he's complaining about.' Which isn't necessarily right, y'know. You should be in a position to say, 'Yeah, I gave him a bollocking. I called him a coont. I told him he was a twat for driving like that, and if he did it again, I'd lock him up.'

But you can't do that, you can't cough it. You'll go through the formality of denying everything, and say, 'No, I didn't say that.' There's something wrong when it gets to be like that, y'know.

One drawback of the Main Bridewell is that the sublime – all prisoners behind bars, one singing 'Danny Boy' – can so rapidly become ridiculous – three vanloads of prisoners all seated under the child's picture and along the other wall, waxing fractious over any delay.

While BP Dave goes along the line, promising room service if only they'll be patient, the inspector decides to clear the decks a little by bailing the thumb-chewing girl of eighteen who was brought in just before the rush. Her charge sheet reads CPL: common prostitute loitering. 'They complain about that,' he says. 'They say what right have we to call them common!'

'But I didn't go up to any cars,' she says, still indignant over her arrest, and coming back from the door.

'Contrary to Street Offences Act—'

'At least they could've given us a lift back!'

'The police', says the inspector stiffly, 'are under no obligation to give people lifts.'

'Dey usually do.'

'Well, it's not a practice I would subscribe to.'

'Come on, luv,' says Dave, beckoning her to the door, which he is holding ajar. She slops across, making as much noise as she can with her wooden sandals on the brown rubber tiles. 'Tirrah!' Boom goes the door.

'I don't think she's all there,' laughs the pretty mum-to-be, whose pregnancy inflates the neat non-police uniform of a 'lady supervisor' (searching females is her main duty). 'She's been in a couple of times, and she just sits and gawps at you. She's very *dim* for a prostitute really.'

146

28

'There's such a big contrast,' remarks Don, who hasn't been a constable in the Plain Clothes Section for more than a few months. 'On one hand, you realise how lucky you are – y'know, I'm very happy, I go home to a nice wife. But we see the other side of it, and it's a bit sickening at times. Very interesting but very depressing.'

Steve shrugs politely. 'It doesn't touch my life. I don't suppose I ever compare my world to their world. You just forget about it, because you'll never change it, no matter what you do. I just do me job and go home. I'm single, y'see.'

He's also twenty-eight, lean and laconic, and on his second tour of duty as a Plain Clothes constable, having been a CID aide and in the Days and EPs as well since joining the force as a cadet in 1965. 'At the time, it was the only job I could get; it's not I always wanted to be a bobby, but it suits me now. It's good. Could be a lot more money put into it, not just in pay but in equipment and everything. Really, I think we're doing it without anything at all.' And on the personal side: 'I like any form of sport; I play divisional football. Being single, the last few years I've managed to get abroad for my holidays. I don't like horror movies and that, rubbish they are, but a good Western, yuh.' He is dressed in slacks and an open-necked shirt; like most bobbies, uniformed or otherwise, his hair isn't short – neither is it particularly long.

Don is twenty-four, solidly built, and wears a neat collar and tie with his hand-knitted pullover; he has a friendly moustache, smokes a pipe and his wife is a police officer. He spends his free time 'Decorating, of course, and fishing. I read quite a lot, crime books mostly – I'm crime-oriented! Birdwatching. We like to take a drive out into the country, a couple of pints, little walks, meetin' reasonable people – y'know, decent people for a change. I like to get away to the Lakes, Snowdonia; a lot of bobbies want to do that, y'know, get away from it.' He has been in the police for five years. 'I did three years in the Civil Service – National Insurance – but I'd a yen to join the

147

bobbies since about sixteen or so. I suddenly decided the Civil Service wasn't for me. In this job, well, you're looking after people who can't look after themselves really.'

They are joined by a quietly dressed constable called Mark, who is twenty-six.

DON: My wife dreaded the thought of me coming into Plain Clothes! (*All laugh*) Again because she only knows the myths and stories about it, and expected me to roll in rotten drunk every night! But I go home and I talk about it – I can't help it. I sound off. I still live partly with the job at home, y'know. She might be talking about a school-crossing sign or an argy-bargy at work, but she can forget it. It's more to the front of my mind.

STEVE: It's a standin' joke: come into Plain Clothes and they also think you're takin' the rent or something. It doesn't bother me. One of my first reactions is: What does he know?

MARK: You work in twos from the security point of view. If you went in places in Plain Clothes by yourself, people would make complaints about yer – y'know, allegations of money passin' and all sorts. And because of dealin' with females.

STEVE: The unfortunate thing about it is obviously characters are different, and some people can't get on with each other. This can make the job a bit of a misery.

DON: It's make or break.

MARK: We use our own cars, y'know, and claim bus fares. One of these cows shat in one of our lad's cars! Brand new car, only had it about a month, and she shat all over his back seat.

DON: We had one the other night, Susie and I. (*Laughs*) Two of them actually. They both said, 'I'm not a prostitute! I'm not doin' nothin'!' We caught them bang at it. They even approached me – Susie was to my left, and they didn't see her. 'Get in,' I said. One says, 'I'm havin' me period!' Whereupon the other says, 'I'm bloody floodin' 'ere!' Fortunately, it didn't go on the car. (*Laughter*) Which is going back to the time when there's this cow who gets out of me car, and proceeds to hoist her skirt up and put this Tampax in, y'know. (*Shakes head*) Whereupon, at this late stage, she developed a modicum of decency and walked round the corner, still showin' her backside, to lean against the wall and do it. That's really, y'know, a low form of life.

MARK: Some of them stink, too, don't they? They really do!

DON: The stink is just because their standard of living is, y'know,

148

pretty low. They don't wash. There are fleas in the house.

STEVE: A typical buck's house you can tell by the smell – like a dirty toilet. Phil Peters went into one and he was physically ill! The bath was a quarter full – the toilet was flowin' over.

DON: That was a *woman*, y'know, and when I got into bed that night it really plagued me, y'know, because there's this warm back to cuddle up to – it really bugged me, that.

STEVE: You've got to be careful of them droppin' packets of tonkies down your seat. Normally they shove them down the seat so they don't find them when they're searched at the Main, y'know.

MARK: Yeah, if you've got kids, they pick them out and say, 'What the hell's this?' You take your wife and kids out in the same car. It's not very nice.

DON: My wife said, 'You're not putting cows in the back of our car,' but eventually she realised I was in a job where it had to be done.

MARK: We can't complain, because they'd say officially you're not supposed to use your own cars, you're on a disciplinary job or something. But how else can we get the job done?

STEVE: The girls are all right really. When I first came in, you were apprehensive to talk to 'em. Y'know, you didn't know how to speak to 'em because you'd never approached them before, never had any dealings with them before – obviously! (*Laughter*) But after you've been on it a few months you get talking to them in their own language, and some of them you get on well with, you can have a good laff with. Obviously that's better for getting information out of them.

MARK: They're all right; some of them are OK.

STEVE: They get three pound for a play-around – y'know, a wank. Not many of them will do gobbling. They're depraved and all the rest of it, but they've got their limit to what they'll do.

DON: I was just debatin' it with the wife – why they go on the streets – and I said, 'Well, some of them are forced to, y'know. A girl we cautioned, her husband had left her and she's got two kids and she's twenty-two – got no form for anything at all. She was forced into circumstances where she needed the money.' 'What about the Social Services?' my wife said. Well, I know for a fact, from my own experience in the National Insurance, that all of it isn't what it's cracked up to be. You can't go and get a pair of shoes for the kids just like this (*snaps fingers*), and they needed the money. (*Soft laugh*) Even so, it's the mentality.

149

. . . If my wife was in the same position with two kids, she'd be out workin' full-time in a pub or as a waitress maybe, y'know. A lot of it is laziness and greed.

STEVE: They make the money, they drink the money. There are one or two with intelligence who think: I'll make a few bob in this game and get out. There's one I know who progressed from on the streets – gettin' a few bob, savin' it, buyin' some gear – to a job in a sauna, gets a lot more money there, and is away out of it, y'know, into a better environment.

DON: These mooshes are all bent, aren't they? The thing is a lot of them are prominent people. I think it's a bit of an eye-opener for everybody when you first come on this squad, and you go up there and watch what's goin' on, the people in their big cars and all the rest of it. And when you listen to some of the stories the cows tell about them, that's an eye-opener certainly.

STEVE: I won't go wid so-and-so, 'cos he'll want to take us back to 'is shop, and I'll be dere fer *effin' hours*!

DON: (*Grin fading*) You look at these mooshes and you think, What do they *want*? What sort of man is it that can come up to some of the girls there? When I first joined the Plain Clothes, it was such a big shock. And then you get used to it, and now I think I can understand some of these fellas: they've either got problems at home or their wife doesn't want to know or, one way or another, they're going to get something off these girls that they can't get anywhere else – whether they're married or not.

MARK: It's been well publicised that they're not committing any offence, and they're a bit blasé about it – 'Can't do nothin' to me!'

STEVE: That's when you put your hat on, y'know, start threaten-in' them, advisin' them not to come round again, but there's not much you can do anyway. I think the problem is them. If you got the girls in off the street into German-style brothels, you'd probably solve it.

DON: The mooshes' needs are going to still exist, as there are going to be girls willing to sell their bodies, whether there is a law against it or not. If they want it stopping, prosecuting the mooshes is the only way. You can't stop these girls – every time you lock them up, they're back there.

(*The conversation drifts to clubs. . . .*)

DON: I've been to a city-centre club with my wife about three times. I wouldn't now, never.

150

MARK: I wouldn't; never have.
STEVE: Well, there are one or two you can go in and be reasonably safe.
(. . . *and then to pornography.*)
STEVE: But even that caters for a need, doesn't it? These fellas will go in and buy a dirty book, and they'll have a wank over it. If they couldn't get the books, what would they be doin'? They'd be out with young kids.
DON: I think some of this legislation is necessary.
MARK: What annoys me more than anything is kids being used for the production of pornography.
DON: Yes, and actually getting their hands on it – y'know, havin' a flick-through. The penalties can't be too strong for that.
STEVE: That stuff we got from —— catered for everything. We were cataloguing it for a month or more and, quite honestly, it did turn yer stomach.
DON: I'd never seen a pornographic book with a child in it, and that's the kind of thing that'll probably go home with me, and somewhere along the line I'll have to talk about it with the wife, y'know; get it out of me system, because I'll be so sickened by it.
STEVE: Horrible.
DON: One of the sergeants brought in about a dozen 'gay' books and, before they went down to the stipendiary magistrate's, parts had to be pointed out as being what we considered to be obscene. So they were dished out, four each, and I got through one – stickin' in me bits of paper! – but half-way through the second I just couldn't read any more. It put me off right away, and it changed me for a short time about homosexuals – who aren't sick, y'know, they're just somebody with a different attitude to their sex lives. But then again, I realised it was *their* pornography! (*Laughs*)
STEVE: You see. . . .
DON: There are some books I wouldn't say were pornographic now, but – a few months ago – I'd have said they were.
MARK: You've been readin' too many of 'em! (*Laughter*)
DON: I think it's—
MARK: It's the same with everybody, though, isn't it?
DON: (*Nods*) You read the file when it comes back, to see what the other lads think of the stuff, and they say it's not, it's rubbish.
MARK: If you've seen one, to an extent you've seen them all. Even one on bestiality, whether it makes yer sick or not, you've

151

seen it. But if anyone under eighteen sees it, that's different.

STEVE: Good job you do only twelve months on this job, isn't it? Burn yer sex life out, wouldn't yer? (*Roar of laughter*)

MARK: Y'see, we can laff here, and joke at fellas wearin' armour and bloody leather jackets, but it's people's way of life, isn't it?

DON: Or do you think a lot of it's made up, just to sell the contact magazine?

MARK: I think a lot of it is, but there are people like that, no doubt about it.

DON: We're a little bit behind here. In the States, there's kids being killed now for films – the ultimate of the sex kick. I think in every man there's something, y'know, at the back of his mind, or part of his being, that's a bad side. There are some things you do in life that you regret and keep hidden there. There's this black side of everybody, and with pornography they're going further and further down the well into yer mind, and the further you get into your subconscious the dirtier the things you do.

29

The section sergeant shrugs. 'It's a funny thing to describe a division. I'm in Uniform at the moment, and it depends a lot on your job and how you see it. But if you want to sort of look at it as a whole. . . .' He grins. 'Well, Uniform's mostly physical, isn't it? Even standin' round on a corner. So you could call that side "the body" if you like. Obviously CID's more intellectual, unquote, so that's "the mind". Plain Clothes? I suppose that's "the soul", y'know, if it isn't a ridiculous thing to say about a policeman!' Then he turns the handle of his glass beer-tankard to face the other way. 'I personally tend just to think about it in terms of cycles more – y'know, the way it changes according to what shift you're on, who the boss is, who your mates are, if you get a sudden death to do. And it does change, no doubt about it.'

152

PART TWO: CYCLES

ONE

I

The game is on, down in the city centre. It's all a game, police officers often sigh, just a bloody great game with a few variations. At this time of night, for example, when the clubs have long been closed and the taxi ranks stand empty, everyone still abroad tends to see himself as either duty bound or delinquent. Thus the whole basis of Them and Us alters dramatically, leaving nobody simply to watch from the touchlines. Not only that, but increased vigilance on one side, plus the effects of drink and drugs on the other, conspire to distort every confrontation, however fleeting. All this doesn't necessarily mean that the game is any more eventful than most – if anything, it's frequently a lot duller – yet it does take place at an hour when paradox reigns supreme and the strangest things sometimes happen.

On Nights now, the incident with the street hawker and his boxes almost forgotten, she turns into Church Street under a lovers' moon that casts a black shadow. Her reflection slips like a wraith through the carefree crowd lining the big shop-windows, mingling with matrons in twin sets, suave young men-about-town, brides and a pouting prance of teenagers in pretty price-tagged party-dresses. While out on the flagstones, nineteen and uniformed, with the give-away white cover to her cap removed for camouflage in the darkness, she walks quite alone down the pedestrian precinct.

Twelve hours ago it was bustling with shoppers; if she sees anyone carrying a shopping-bag now, the chances are she will stop them. Here is where the old flower-seller sat, among her upturned milk-crates besides Marks & Spencer, and there is the pitch chosen by the sweet-faced girl in peasant clothing, who handed out leaflets about equal pay for equal work and the violence men to do women.

Her passing freezes a cuddle of middle-aged couples in a dim doorway, causing them to giggle as though surprised by a maiden aunt, and this probably makes their evening.

Farther on, a dishevelled man, drunk but capable of getting himself home safely, emerges from a side-street to stop short of the nearest raised flowerbed. 'G'nice, ossifer!' he calls across, waits warily for her smile, then turns clumsy-footed to survey the gentle slope like a skier weighing up a slalom.

Down at the corner with Whitechapel, blood is drying in thick drips on the pavement, marking the spot where a young apprentice, savagely beaten by club doormen, stood earlier and whispered he needed assistance.

Seeing nothing that merits her close attention, she listens to the night, to its far-off wild whoops and shrill whistles, listens hard for the sound of glass breaking. She quite likes the night; it can be exciting.

Gradually she makes her way towards Dale Street. At this hour and in this lighting, the banking area with its classical façades, columns, cornices and polished granite could be a remote corner of Atlantis. Still listening, hearing and seeing very little now, she starts up another deserted street, crunching over a spill of builder's sand. Like a stingray disturbed on the ocean bed, a newspaper lifts and glides before her, scraping its wing-tips.

The silence deepens.

Then from a fissure, erupting from a notorious club that should have shut up shop hours ago, comes a crab-scuttle of brawling young drunks, locked in battle. And as they pour out across the roadway, flailing and cursing, their partners dance about in tipsy attendance, shrieking at them to desist. It's bedlam.

She hesitates, heart pounding, and there's a bit of a mix-up on the radio. Uncertain of what to do next, but aware of the immediate danger to traffic, she starts forward, stops, has a think, then continues. Some of them see her advancing.

'Go home,' she says, dry-mouthed, lapsing into the right idiom and accent. 'Get lost, the lot of yer. . . .'

A slip of a girl rounds on her. 'Fok off, yer busy!' she retorts. 'Yer got no fokkin' right to tell us what to do!'

To them all: 'Go home. Go on, on yer way.'

'Yer not a busy twenty-four hours a day!' shouts the girl,

156

with a ferocity that seems to alarm the others, who have already begun a mocking retreat. 'Yer fokkin' cow!' she screeches. 'Jesus!'

'Get lost, I told yer!'

The girl approaches, shrugging off restraining hands. 'Yer fokkin' cow!' she repeats, then closes the gap to spit out, 'Yer *fokkin' queer!*'

'It's our Pam,' chuckles the driver of the first panda to arrive, which comes to a halt at that instant. 'Looks like she's got 'em sorted all right, boss!'

Indeed it does. The mob is dispersing rapidly, led by a scatter of fleeing girls. But a slim blonde in jeans is still going hammer and tongs at the young probationer, heedless of further police reinforcements or of her friends' entreaties, and she's doing so in a way that appears unusually personal.

'Who's been hittin' you?' demands an inspector, coming up just then. 'Who's been sayin' things to you?'

'I'm locking this one up for D-and-D, sir, and I was just—'

'Yer not a fokkin' busy twenty-four hours a day!' storms the girl, lunging forward. 'So who gives yer—?'

'Right, yer locked up!' snaps the inspector, like a referee sending off a player, and the girl is put into the back of the second panda.

What happens next takes everyone by surprise, for it all seems to be over then and the prisoner's friends have abandoned her, not wishing to be arrested themselves. As the panda driver leans into the two-door Escort to return his upturned seat to its normal position, the girl kicks out suddenly and knocks him off balance. Then she catapults out and throws herself at the probationer; she still seems oblivious to anyone else, and her strength is astonishing. Two policemen, each large enough to cope singlehanded with the average fighting drunk, grab her and have to struggle hard to keep her away from their colleague, who is warned to stand clear on the other side of the vehicle. There is no time to analyse the situation in the heat of the moment, but it's obvious that there is something about the probationer which incenses the girl beyond reason.

Virtually ignoring the men trying to get her back into the

157

car, the girl shouts again and again, 'Yer not a fokkin' busy twenty-four hours a day!' – as though she has some insight that will bring a telling admission. But the probationer says nothing, and finally, with the assistance of two other officers, the girl is manhandled on to the rear seat once again, where she huddles glaring at her captors.

The inspector rubs at his thigh where her knee caught him. 'You'd best', he says, with a little laugh that concedes a degree of awe, 'jump in fast, lad, and make the Main before—'

The girl is already on her way out of the far door, having noticed the probationer approach to get into the front seat. The men hastily interpose themselves and another struggle begins, both inspired and inhibited by some form of chivalry, it seems, for the average fighting drunk would have more than met his match by now. Eventually, after much cursing and many blunt entreaties, they're unable to subdue the girl any other way, and have to use handcuffs.

'My vanity's outraged!' remarks the inspector, with that same little laugh, as the panda prepares to move off.

The sergeant retrieves his watch from their own vehicle, and nods as he refastens the strap. 'Aye, you don't like cuffin' a woman, but with that one you had to!'

'Christ, look at—'

The girl has slumped back on the rear seat of the reversing car and is aiming her feet at the probationer's head. The feet lash out, strike a glancing blow, and the probationer pitches forward into the dashboard. Then she's up, twisting round and punching at the feet, while the driver accelerates away in the direction of the Main Bridewell.

By the time the inspector and the sergeant get there, after an abortive attempt to make the club open its doors to them, the girl is at the counter being charged with drunk-and-disorderly, and appears very much calmer. In fact, now that rage no longer disfigures her face, it's possible to see that she is a good-looking young woman herself, despite the jaded harshness conferred by her mode of living.

The probationer, shaken but not complaining of any injuries, is out of sight, steadying herself with a cigarette in one of the side offices.

158

'You're sure', asks the inspector, in a fatherly fashion, 'you're all right, luv?'

'Sure, sir.'

He plainly has his doubts, but just as plainly the reply pleases him, so he doesn't press the point much further. Instead they have a few laughs over the arrest, and then drift out into the charge office, where about half a dozen uniformed officers are awaiting attention. The probationer attracts glances of the sort that indicate concern among members of a close-knit family, and the girl, isolated in their midst, suddenly becomes aware of her presence.

'Just put your things on the counter,' says the bridewell inspector, tapping the charge sheet.

But the girl has fixed on the probationer with a stare of extraordinary intensity, and once again nobody else seems to matter. For a second or two, they face one another and the contrast between their circumstances is vividly acute, although hardly remarkable in a bridewell. Just what so provokes the girl must lie at a deeper level; something her friends can't have perceived, because they have urged her to be sensible and come away with them. But whatever it is, she sees it again, becoming fiercely bitter before exploding into violence.

The girl glances at the bridewell inspector, drops one of her tawdry valuables, stamps on it and then dangles it before him, claiming that the damage was inflicted during her arrest. As he responds angrily, she turns on the probationer in a fresh outburst of unbridled fury, and has to be dragged off to the cells, fighting every foot of the way.

'Amazin'!' says one of the bridewell staff, on his return to the charge office. 'Tried to bite the inspector, ripped his one epaulette off, kicked our Pam again – the strength of 'er! It's definitely assault now, gotta be.'

Breaking the valuable is what really tipped the balance. If the girl intends to produce it as evidence of a violent assault by police officers, as her brazen act would imply, and if they themselves don't charge her with assault, a barrister is almost bound to ask why. And so the probationer, who is new to the game, must be advised accordingly.

*

159

She is 5 feet 7 inches and has chestnut hair, long lashes and the kind of colouring that doesn't need make-up. She also has a good deal of self-composure, suggestive of a comfortable upbringing, and lives on the Wirral.

I like the whole job. I like walking round in uniform. You've got an identity – you're a policewoman! (*Laughs*) I haven't always wanted to be one. When I was fourteen I was a rebel. I hated the police. I used to hang round with a group of people who used to be in trouble with the police a lot – they hated them, so I hated them. I really did. I ran away from home, and when the police got me back they gave me a telling-off – and I hated them especially for that.

I like . . . I like people coming up – they're really very nice to you. (*Smiles*) I don't like the way they expect you to know everything! I always carry my A-to-Z with me and I say, 'I'll show you where it is and tell you how to get there.' 'Oh, but *you're* supposed to know this, aren't you?' I'm not a map of the district! Loads of people say things like, 'Oh, you're too nice to be a policewoman! You're lovely! We'll meet yer after work!' I don't mind. It's all in good humour and sometimes I'll have a laff with them. I've been out with policewomen who get really annoyed with people who do this, but it doesn't bother me; they're only trying to be friendly. I only dislike the bobbies' protective attitude towards us from their point of view, because it must be a burden to them.

A call went out – it was only on Mornings – that two customers wouldn't pay at a restaurant just round the corner. I go, and the next thing you hear on the radio is: 'Could someone go and back a policewoman up?' And two cars arrived! If that had been a bobby that'd gone, they'd have left him on his own. Or you get prisoners in the bridewell and they start swearing, and the bosses there say, 'You apologise for that!' *I* don't mind; they're just drunk, y'know. Or if you get a prisoner they ask him if he's said anything to you; they handle them roughly if he's a big-looking fella, or if he's drunk and shouting. It annoys me when I can manage on my own, and the situation's under control – there's no need for that. If they get too rough with them, he's going to bang his head and go to hospital, and all of a sudden you've got a charge against you, because you were the arresting officer. I get on with policemen much better than I do with policewomen in general – I get on a lot better with men

160

anyway. I do sometimes wonder why some of the girls on our section joined – I've never asked any of them why they joined. They enjoy certain parts of it, but if there's anything dicey they're away! I think a women's section would suit them better.

When I'm off, I like camping a lot – and walking. I play a bit of badminton. I'm not very sporty or anything. I suppose I'm reasonably intelligent; I was in the top class at school. I hated it. I could pass me exams, but it was just a fluke because I never did any work. I got a good job with the county council, but I didn't really like work – it was a bore. I used to work with people all older than me, all middle-aged women, and it was the same day in and day out. It was a joke me joining the police! (*Laughs*) Nobody thought I would stick it. My boy friend then always said, 'When you join the police, you won't have any time for me.' I thought: The hell with the lot of them. I suppose sometimes this job is boring. The other night was terrible! I thought: What am I doing walking round here? It's freezing cold and nothing's happening. But you never know what will happen.

I don't know what it's like. . . . You want to do it because it's exciting, but you're frightened at the same time. I wanted to go in there, but afterwards you think what might have happened. (*Shrugs*) They were fighting in the middle of the road, so I suppose you have to do something about it. As I got near, I heard a call go out. I said where I was, but they mustn't have heard me, and they put the call out again. I stopped for a moment and thought: Should I go in there? Why not? I didn't hear bottles smashing or anything, and I knew there were people coming anyway.

So I went in. It was mostly lads fightin', although there were some girls screaming, 'Don't 'it 'im! Don't 'it 'im! That lad's me wairld! *I love 'is bones!*' (*Laughs*) I went up and said, 'Go home, get lost, the lot of yer' – and this girl was turning round and swearing at me. I told her she was locked up, waited for the car to come, and grabbed her. I didn't originally want to lay a charge of assault because, although no doubt she'd assaulted me, she'd assaulted a lot of other people, too. Oh, she'd kicked me in the head and it was sore, but it wasn't very, very sore. Me hand was the worst, but I wasn't sure whether that was from her hitting me or me hitting her. I know I called her a cow afterwards, but I suppose I feel sorry for her in a way. You have to feel sorry for everybody, considering the way they're brought up

161

is completely different. She could better herself, I'm sure. Do you know, she's only the same age as me? Born the same year as I was.

2

'It's ridiculous, I feel like a dinosaur!' says a constable on the North Sub, with twenty-six years' service in the division. 'When I joined, if you saw anybody walking the streets after midnight, you used to stop them and ask what they were doing, because people just didn't walk about after midnight. The last tram would go and that was it. Nothing. You'd wander round just seeing papers blowing and alley cats and things like that. When you heard a footstep, ho ho! It could be a welcome relief.'

The focal point of such memories is a rubble-strewn rectangle of sorts on the slope immediately below St Anne Street divisional headquarters.

'Rose Hill police station,' says Old Chalky, who sometimes pauses there on his way up to the social club. 'Started off as a gas mill, would you believe it? Oh aye, North Liverpool Gas Manufacturing Company! Turned into a dairy around 1903, then Liverpool City took it over around 1914. Used to parade down in the basement where they kept the cows once. Y'know, the byre!'

He solemnly regards the chips of brick and mortar as some-one might study the marble debris of a golden age. 'Funny mixture really; common brick with this very bright red Victorian brick. Two storeys, but it had this high-pitched roof that gave it the look of a church or a mission hall. Big double doors comin' in off the street, see? Two sets of 'em. Go through and CID's one side, bridewell's t'other, this flight of steps goin' up the middle.' He waves his stick. 'Over there, iron railings overlookin' the parade-room, like the bridge of a ship. Massive mahogany desks along the wall; lightin'-up times, shippin' tides – you name it. Down the one end, there's this snooker-room partitioned off, sort of a bungalow effect; smoke

162

comin' out of its little windows, bobbies inside playin' crash, yellin' and screamin'! In the middle of the floor like, this ping-pong table – or we'd play battington, sort of our own invention, with the bats and a badminton court we'd got marked out. Come in at nine – y'know, loose collars and studs – and go out shirts dark blue and wringin' with sweat! Of course, in those days, you'd parade in your own time, and you'd march out to yer beat in a line – oh aye, left-right, left-right. That's gone now.'

Chalky flicks aside a rusty tin can. This stick of his is uncommonly like the one he used to carry as a uniformed sergeant, except that it has a curved handle instead of a rounded top and wrist cord. Signalling-sticks, they called them – and still do, as it happens, although the brass ferrule is no longer needed for rapping out nocturnal messages on the pavement. Tak, tak. . . . Several sleeping streets away, the bobby on that beat sighs and draws his truncheon. . . . Tuk, tuk, tuk! On me effin' way, Sarge! And the truncheons they issued then could take it, being fashioned by metal-cutting tools from *lignum vitae*, the same South American hardwood some ships had for their propeller shafts.

'It was different,' says Chalky, breaking his reverie to glance about the blighted slope and then at the modern building behind him. 'Different in an obvious way, of course, but there's somethin' else that's missin'. Know what I mean?'

Not only pensioners like himself, but also dozens of officers in their middle-service know what he means. They say it makes them sorry for the young bobbies of today, and in particular for those on the North Side, who seem to suffer a sense of loss without being able to account for it.

JACK: All around here were these old-fashioned courts of tiny houses opening into paved areas. [He is an inspector now, and his companion a superintendent.]

FRANK: Typical Industrial Revolution streets. You went straight from the street into the living-room, then there was a kitchen behind and two bedrooms upstairs. Very narrow, crowded streets, with a few little workshops here and there, giving employment locally. A lot of the men went to sea, and most of the

163

others worked on the docks – just casual labour in those days. St Anne Street stands where there were artisans' dwellings – that's how they were categorised on the old crime reports! Three storeys with outside landings. There was no shopping-area. Just the odd family corner shop which stayed open until about ten o'clock at night, selling everything from french letters to bread. It was a very close-knit, identifiable community – people went in and out of one another's houses and this type of thing. All more or less obliterated by the new entrances for the Wallasey tunnel in the late sixties.

JACK: Yes, not really so long ago.

FRANK: Those houses running up the hill from here to Netherfield Road, although they were just those small crowded terrace houses, they were jewels as far as cleanliness was concerned. I used to take a great delight in looking at this. Not only did they scrub the house, but it was almost ritualistic to come out and scrub the pavement in front of it – they would holystone the flags! You used to walk up those streets in the daytime, Saturdays and Sundays particularly, and the doors would be standing open, with the radio going inside. But now the people lock up everything because someone will come and steal their purse.

JACK: They were vibrant. All the pubs had a darts team, a football team, bowls teams. But all that side of it, the active energetic types, they've all quit. That's why the area is so flat.

FRANK: There are very few people who sort of strive now.

JACK: I saw a man down here who used to be a petty officer when I was in the Navy. He was embarrassed when I saw him come out of the tenements – he used to look away. Those sort of people were desperately keen to get out of it if they could, and he did move eventually.

FRANK: They were an ameliorating influence between the wars and after. There was also the role the Catholic grammar schools played, which operated the scholarship system. A lot of lads went through it, and they wanted out. There are a lot of people in this city of good standing who had their origins here – and quite a few policemen, even in those days.

JOHN: What I think the trouble is now is that all the opportunities are there for getting out without trying too hard. It was a different atmosphere.

FRANK: Mind you, it was a sergeant's nightmare. Because he had to visit all the pubs on a regular basis, and there was one on every corner with some stuck in between!

164

JOHN: Yes, and I can remember going into some houses where every room was a flat, with a man, his wife and children living in it. In those circumstances, people were obviously very quick to have domestic disputes, and so I think they probably needed the bobby an awful lot.

'What they've done', says the CID sergeant now in charge of the force's Photographic Department, who started out at Rose Hill, 'is they've built flats and they've built maisonettes, but basically what they've done is that they've taken the front door away from people.'

And when he speaks of 'the good old days' the phrase becomes more than a simple expression of nostalgia.

You had no personal radio twenty-odd years ago, just all this money in your pocket to phone in if you got stuck in anything. You were on your own.

One old bobby said to me when I first started, 'If yer call them by their Christian names, they won't 'it yer. Because', he said, 'they're goin' to get locked up – only alternative they have is to kill yer, and there's not many that'll do that to a bobby, 'cos it's a hangin' job. And if they're too big a crowd, don't rush in; remember who they are, and pick 'em off one at a time.' So you had to know the people. You knew every bad family in every street. You also knew every back crack and nook and cranny, and all the short cuts. There were no trees in the division, no grass in the division – oh, there was one tree, in a doctor's garden.

And we could get around the division quicker, I reckon, than they do now! If a policeman was in trouble at the north end of Scotland Road, you'd get a flash of lights from a bus driver – and you'd jump on the next Ribble bus going up! It was a bit like the Keystone Kops! A runnin' board full of bobbies, all goin' to help yer mate who was in trouble! You used to shove your prisoner in the place for luggage under the spiral staircase, and say, 'Be quiet, you! Right, 5 Rose Hill, driver!' And next thing, he'd deviate off his route and stop outside the bridewell.

Bus stories proliferate.

'Rose Hill was on the principal north–south route,' says a superintendent over lunch in the officers' canteen, 'and if a bus had drunks from the city on board, the driver would drive

165

straight up, honking his horn. They had it timed to a T, didn't they? He'd flash his lights, and the bridewell sergeant would just lean over the balcony while the Nights parade was still going on. "There's a Ribble bus outside the window," he'd say. "All right, lads?" And up we'd go!'

'A bit rough and ready at times,' says another veteran of Rose Hill, 'but it was, well, how could you put it? Never cold-blooded, as it tends to be now. They had this word, y'know: "Fair-ation". "That's fair-ation, boss!" they'd say, if you had them bang to rights over something. Or if a bobby got naughty and just smacked 'em, they'd say, "Fair-ation, boss! Dere's no need f'dat!" Oh, things were very warm by today's standards.'

There is certainly always warmth in these recollections, and this makes a decided contrast with the way so many young officers, when asked who lives around St Anne Street, reply dismissively – defensively, perhaps: 'Oh, just a load of bucks and gobshites.'

'Contact was the thing,' a former sergeant in the area believes. 'You used to walk along the streets and they'd all be out on their doorsteps, able to take a good look at yer, get to know what yer looked like – and you'd have yer tea specks. Now tea specks just aren't on these days! I mean, there's no way you can slip in and out of a house on the tenth floor, is there? What's happened, y'see, is they've stacked all the streets one on top of another, and the bobby's left walkin' out in a sort of no-man's-land in between.'

There were 'ale specks', too, of course, and gaps in the curtains through which a bobby could peer, enlivening his vigil with a spot of idle voyeurism, while 'milking' the pad-locks to see if a tug would betray the presence of intruders. He was invited to weddings and christenings, and sometimes to funerals; when he had his helmet knocked off by young lads, he could give them a good belting with full parental approval.

In fact it could be suggested that Rose Hill bobbies had things very much their own way, and that this is what lies behind the sense of loss so often evident at St Anne Street. Yet that would not explain its curiously wistful quality.

*

166

Reflecting on his time at Rose Hill, this former sergeant – now a chief superintendent at force headquarters – smiles suddenly. 'Policemen who are deep thinkers', he says, unfolding his arms, 'always give this impression of being Bulgarian. . . .' Then he laughs and goes on, 'But we did a survey before Athol Street closed – that was another police station in the same division – and I think we came to the conclusion that ninety per cent of the callers had no direct "police connection".'

At Rose Hill, they'd call in and ask the man on duty to phone somebody for them; they couldn't use the phone many of them – they weren't used to it. Or, if it was an official they were phoning, they felt the bobby would do it better. They'd pay the tuppence or whatever, and he'd give them a receipt for it. There was a constant stream of late-night callers to look at the station clock to set their alarms. There was another constant stream for gas shillings, and certain bridewell sergeants would keep a special bag of them for the convenience of these folk. They always referred to it as the 'gas shillin' ', whether it was for the electricity meter or not! 'Have yer gotta shillin' for der gas, sair ?' (Laughs) First aid was another thing: kids falling down and cutting their knees, dog bites, coming in and getting bandaged up. . . . All sorts of things. They would come in to settle arguments – abstract things, nothing to do with the police. Who won the Cup the year before the war ? Questions like that. They used the police as their general information and general assistance centre. You'd also get things we were concerned in, like lost dogs and children missing from home, but the great majority was service really. And of course you locked the same people up on Saturday night, but there wasn't a great deal of animosity about that – they accepted it was part of the way of life.

I used to get enormous pleasure out of doing these simple little things. That's regrettably what has disappeared now, and I think the buildings have a lot to do with it – to do with this business of isolation in the area. St Anne Street's a new building; it's sharp, it's angular, and it's got a lot of glass in it. The old buildings weren't. They all had a sort of warmth, character – they were as dilapidated as the rest of the area! The bobbies were living in the same sort of conditions, if you like, as the people were living in. The rain came through the roof when it was coming through their roofs, and the snow would blow on your shoulders in the toilet. There was a greater sense of – well, affinity in those days.

3

A sense of affinity is very marked in Inspector North, who is out making the rounds on a night that has so far proved singularly uneventful. He seems to have a countryman's feel for the land where he works, and something of a countryman's characteristics, too. There is nothing impetuous about him, nothing flippant or pretentious; his speech and actions are unhurried, deliberate, and his expression is generally grave.

He turns his white Escort down Great Homer Street, travelling north between blank-faced blocks of council flats. A steel fence extends down the left-hand side of this broad lifeless stretch of asphalt, and on the right is a short parade of barricaded shops, plus the odd impersonal brick building.

This used to be a long line of terraced houses. The problem is planners tend to judge everything by middle-class concepts; working-class people like to live in the same street as their mothers and all sorts, to meet in the little ale-house on the corner. They're not particularly interested in gardening; don't forget, they work physically very hard at work, and they've no desire to come home and dig the garden! (*Glances at the tower blocks to his right*) There was a certain amount of social control in a street, y'know. Granny lived there and she kept an eye on the kids – or somebody else did: 'I'll tell yer mother when she comes 'ome!' It affects us mainly, I think, with borderline cases. Families who were maybe having a little difficulty, who were helped out by the neighbours watching and influencing. Put them on the seventh floor and they've got no chance.

He turns off and drives round the back of the shops, where he surprises three youths who are taking an unusual interest in a car parked at the rear of a small bakery. The youths see the police vehicle and run off with such a clatter that the baker, with the flour of tomorrow's loaves on his arms, comes hurrying to the iron grille which guards his property. Inspector North returns to the road again.

I've just finished reading a book by Paul Foot, and one of the

168

things he points out is that policemen spend the major part of their time chasing round after the minor incidents, while millions of pounds are stolen by means of fraud, and that they should spend more of their time looking into that type of thing. Which is basically an oversimplification of it, because what policemen do in fact is keep public order: they enable people to go about their lawful business without being impeded. White-collar crime is very, very seldom reported. A lot of it, you see, isn't a police investigation to begin with; it's an accountant's investigation. So it isn't until they come along and say, 'We're two thousand short,' that the police are able to come in and do something about it.

After leaving school at fourteen, Inspector North worked as a butcher's apprentice at the Co-op, went into the Army, returned to the Co-op for a while, then joined the Liverpool City force. A spell on the docks – an area no longer in the care of the Merseyside Police – bored him into resigning, but he joined up again not long afterwards. As he picks his way through the open maze of dead-end streets leading down to the dock road, many of which are blocked off by concrete bollards where they disappear into the wastelands, he is assisted by vivid memories of how it once was.

I came to Liverpool when I was five, and there were children playin' in the streets in their bare feet. Very often a kid wouldn't come to school because he had no shoes. We lived first in an upper-working-class neighbourhood. You know, we used to play cricket, play football, cops and robbers – nobody wanted to be the robbers much – went to the pictures on Saturday. Then we moved only four tram stops away to a railway house. Completely different. We didn't play cops and robbers much. (Smiles) In fact the game was to go to the local shop, hide in an entry and all run, one after another, to have an apple off the display. I never enjoyed the apples. If ever a policeman had knocked on our door, my arse would've been skinned.

A movement in the shadow of a warehouse sends the Escort hastening forward, but it's only a nightwatchman stepping out for a breath of air and to see if the drizzle's stopped. It hasn't.

Yes, I've lived in the worst areas of Liverpool, really the very, very worst, so consequently, when I first came on the job, I

169

rather resented this word 'bucks'. I thought it a dreadful expression – although I use it myself now – because I knew there were certain working-class people who had far higher moral values than a lot of the middle class, or even the upper classes. And when I see these bucks coming through the Main Bridewell I sympathise with them a bit. I think to myself: The die was cast the day they were conceived – there was little they could do to stop their passage through this building. The other night I was standing at the counter and a man came in. I looked at the sheet, and I looked up and said, 'You'll never learn, will you, Arthur?' He was in my class at school. There he was, standin' there with his son of twenty-one, and they'd pinched a car.

Inspector North drives down to the Pier Head and then up Dale Street, skirting the edge of his territory. A hire car, about to accept a fare illegally, accelerates away. A youth, approaching along the far pavement, throws down whatever he's smoking, obliterates it with his heel, and hurries on.

I was lucky. I came from a home where we had trade union consciousness, a political and educational consciousness, and certainly a consciousness about right and wrong – so I had a religious consciousness as well – and the strap was never far away. But, although Arthur came from a family in a similar income group, their ideas of right and wrong were very loose, very sloppy. I don't feel any conflict between being a socialist and a policeman. As a matter of fact, I would say the average working-class socialist is probably more strict in his interpretation of law and order than 'liberal' people. It's not the left-wing approach that's the soft approach, but the intellectuals who have the soft approach – and probably you've got more intellectuals in the Labour Party than you have in the Conservative Party.

The radio crackles. The van driver is asked to make Lime Street, where transport is required for two males, both D-and-D, and a female, D-and-I. Having done that, would he call at Copperas Hill where a prisoner, arrested for shopbreaking, is awaiting transfer to the Main Bridewell?

When it comes to crime, middle-class people tend to have certain protections; they're able to operate within the orbit of their occupations. They don't have to go out at night with their galoshes on and scale up a wall. They do it while they're working

170

– undercover, as it were – whether it's stealing a few pens, which is almost acceptable to society, or by engaging in fraud like John Stonehouse. When I read these sorts of things, I become annoyed that people should suggest they be let off lightly. A fella who screws a car may be misguided, may be foolish, but they have betrayed a trust through sheer greed, y'know. If they get caught, I treat them exactly the same as anybody else. I think some policemen don't – 'Gosh, this fella's quite well-to-do!' 'Apply the Act to them,' I say, 'that's all you've got to do. We aren't here to moralise.'

Inspector North heads for the heights of Everton Brow, abutting 'B' Division, where a foot-man has just found a five-year-old wandering in search of a public telephone that hasn't been vandalised. The child says his mother's 'terrible sick and that', whereas she is paralytically drunk, and how she managed to get home from her club to the boy and his baby sister is a mystery, especially as there doesn't seem to be a man about. One mobile is dealing with a sudden death – a phrase better understood as 'an unexpected death' – and the other has been called to a domestic dispute.

They all say the man on the beat is the most important man in the force. Yet one wonders, because it seems to be the place everybody wants to spend the least amount of time. One of the big problems is, of course, the expectations of people coming on the job. You've only got to look at the newspaper adverts and never is a fella pounding a lonely beat. It's always a big flashy car and chances of being a detective. If there's any social control being exercised right now, it's certainly not by the CID.

4

A BOBBY: I can remember one time I went to a place two o'clock in the morning – a domestic. Beltin' down with rain. There's this young woman about twenty-eight, quite fit and all – y'know, a good figure – wearing a nightdress, and there's these three kids – the oldest one's about six, got a cardigan round 'im – and they're all in their bare feet on the path, gettin' soaked.
    I pull over in the jeep, which had the heater on full, y'know,

171

and I get them all under cover. So she tells me her husband won't let her in, and he's saying, 'I'll let 'er in', and I'm saying, 'The bloody kids won't come in while you're here!' He'd got a bottle of Aussie whites – Australian white wine; it's lovely stuff to drink, but you tend to get blown on it, y'know.

So I go in. I know what I'm going to do: he's going to go with me when I go. I start – y'know, 'You're not a fokkin' man, you're a fokkin' mouse! Your kids are out there in the rain!' I'm in full steam, y'know.

He stands up – I've got him that far – and I start backing off. I get to the door and he says it: 'If you weren't in uniform, I'd *burst* yer!' So me tunic's off and I'm sayin', 'Come on, then!' I got him straight into the back of the jeep, and I got his wife and kids into the house. So I get him to the police station, charge him with drunk and disorderly, and I find out this guy's got problems. They all have problems, I suppose – why they tell us, I don't know! I've got enough problems of me own! But I listen – you don't know, they might be genuine. I listen and then he says, 'Oh, I want me wallet in the 'ouse; it's still gotta lotta money in it.'

OK, so I go back, knock on the door – it was a good excuse to go back and see if the missus is all right, y'know – and I go in. All the kids have gone to bed except the oldest girl and the mother. She gives me a cuppa tea while I'm sittin' there with me mate, and she said, 'Y'know, he's givin' me ten pound for the week – for the four kids, for meself and for him, y'know – to feed, everything.'

So I said, 'Well, he wants his wallet.' She said, 'Here it is, 'ere – eighty pound in it.' I thought: That's great, isn't it? Gives 'er ten pound a week!

'Ah,' I said, 'there's sixty, isn't there?' She said, 'No, I counted it; there's eighty.' I said, 'There's sixty, isn't there?' I suppose it's a technical theft; never really thought on it. Anyway, as far as I'm concerned, I'm doin' the right thing, y'know. And in the end, she twigged: 'Oh yeah, there's sixty!'

So I took the numbers of the sixty quid, got her to sign it, and she had an extra twenty quid for the week, to see to the kids and herself.

This fella went to court the next day, and this is when I realised that locking domestics up for drunk and disorderly is wrong, because he goes to court and gets fined. Most domestics are caused by money worries or drink, so what have you achieved?

172

What I used to do after that was lock 'em up for breach of the peace, where you can arrest 'em in the house and he gets bound over. Doesn't cost 'im or 'is family a penny – unless he comes back a second time, and if he does that he deserves to go.

In fact the idea of charging with breach of the peace, instead of with drunk and disorderly (which can be done only outside the home, and often requires various subterfuges), is now general practice on Merseyside, and is accredited to the 'county bobbies' who had themselves always used it before amalgamation.

5

Dawn is not far off when Inspector North returns to St Anne Street to complete some paperwork, having had a fairly busy time of it after all, but nothing to write home about. He pushes his way through the double set of twin doors to be confronted in the entrance hall by a hysterical gypsy woman loudly questioning the efficacy of prayer.

'I've been a good wumman, said me prairs every night I'm that religious, and then—'

'This man discharged a firearm?' asks the droll sergeant, having changed groups to return to the street. 'You're sure of that?' And he looks at the other gypsy woman with her.

'What's the story?' says Inspector North.

'These two gypsy women came in, sir, and they first told me this caravan had been damaged. Then, during the course of the conversation, it comes out that a shotgun owned by one of the fellas had possibly been discharged.'

'Oh aye? Well, we'd best get down there, I suppose. How many authorised firearms officers have we got on duty?'

'Two in the Task Force,* meself and one CID man.'

'And me. Yuh, that should be enough.'

The sergeant makes for a telephone to ring the sub-divisional commander at his home. 'Hello, sir? Sergeant McBayne. I want authorisation for the issue of firearms. Briefly. . . .' And

*The OSD replaced Task Force, but the name lingers on.

173

he relates the story again. 'Well, we're going to arrest for criminal damage to the caravan certainly. By all accounts, the people on the site are locked in their caravans and terrified to come out, and there is a suggestion these two fellas may do a bunk tonight. Right, sir, I'll give you a result as soon as possible.'

'Five?' murmurs the bridewell sergeant, running an eye over his small armoury and picking out five .38 revolvers, which are stored in their cardboard boxes. He adds five stiff, austerely functional holsters, and six rounds for each man. Then the book has to be signed and countersigned; it shows that firearms have been issued seventeen times in the last twelve months, mainly to officers escorting bullion shipments.

From the way the firearms are handled, they quickly lose any vestigial glamour and become as mundane as a bus conductor's ticket-punch. Inspector North hides his holster beneath his tunic with a faint air of distaste, much as a man might disguise a hernia. There is tension, though, part discharged in jokes and nervous banter.

The detective is asked, 'Got yer bullet-proof vest?'

That gets a good laugh.

'Apparently,' says the sergeant, 'there are quite wide open spaces around this caravan of his.'

Inspector North smiles. 'Well, if you hear a bang, you'll have to duck!'

At 5.08 a.m., watched by a small crowd of fellow-officers who have appeared from nowhere, the armed men walk out past the staring gypsy women. Then a perfectly modulated voice calls out, in exasperated tones with a curiously familiar ring to them, 'Will everyone with no business in this bridewell *please* leave by that door at once – and that's you, too, sir, if you will!'

'She's a character, that one,' sighs the radio operator. 'Says she's barmy about organic chemistry – actually *reads* the stuff! Gettin' engaged to an advertising exec from the Smoke next week.' The bridewell patrol is blonde, proudly Jewish and a svelte twenty-seven.

174

An air hostess is a *horrible* job. Cleaning dirty loos after people who don't know – well, where they're supposed to – and having to say, 'Yes, sir', 'No, sir', 'Three bags full, sir', to very rude people who've managed to save the fare and think they're *it*. I come from an army background and was first a drama student and then an actress. I taught English in France for a year – I've also lived in Germany and Holland – and was on jumbos for a couple of years. I sold advertising for Pearl & Dean for a while, but I was fed up with a nine-to-five office job. I'm not a women's libber, but I do like a chance to get on. I also applied to do social work and three other jobs, and in one week I got five positive replies. I chose the police force and I'm not sorry I did because, let's face it, if ever I did finish up doing any social work, then those little so-and-so's wouldn't be taking advantage of me the way they do with the social workers! You should see them going to court – all this hard-luck story, and then they come out and *laugh* in the social workers' faces!

I'm enjoying it for the most part. There are *bits* I don't enjoy, like having to stand abuse from really nasty people. They can call me an 'effing pig' as I'm walking down the road, and that's acceptable. Yet I can't even say, 'Damn you!' because I'm a police officer. (*Laughs*) An actress, people say, where's the connection? Every day that I go out on those streets, it's all an act. I'm not from Liverpool, but when I go out and speak to the kids I've got to have a Scouse accent. It's not a brilliant one, but at least they don't think I'm stuck up. The only time I'm afraid is when I have to go down Love Lane by myself on Nights. Because, as far as I'm concerned, any crime that takes place in dockland – where the bonded warehouses are – will be organised crime, and what chance have I got? My family was anxious about me becoming a police officer, but my father is in a way quite pleased; he's a security officer now himself.

It does change your life a bit. With things like drugs and that, a couple of years ago I could tell you, oh, dozens of people who took them and even a few pushers. But now, you see, I don't hear anything anymore. Of course, I live in the city centre and therefore meet a lot of people, desirable and undesirable. The thing is you use your discretion; there are some very, very minor things you can overlook. But I felt on one occasion, while visiting someone's house, that it was too serious – it was *immoral*. So I remembered the details of what this person said, and reported them. Of course, a few people weren't too happy about it,

175

although they still speak to me, but then again. . . . (*Laughs*) Some of my friends have said, 'Katie's a great chick; the only thing wrong with her is she's a busy.'*

The moon is enormous and low over the wastelands, with the sky lightening rapidly behind it. Inspector North, parked about quarter of a mile from the caravan site, is waiting for the Night Superintendent to arrive in his high-powered 'jam-butty' with a Traffic man at the wheel. The Night Super – the responsibility is shared on a rota basis – has to cover the entire force area, and is on his way down from St Helen's, having decided that this incident merits his personal attention. Inspector North will, however, remain in command.

The probationer on the back seat has been in the police for five weeks, after two and a half years as a cadet. 'I love it,' he says, then adds with a laugh, 'I'm a bit worried about this! I wouldn't mind if I had a gun meself!'

'Think the service should be armed?'

'I've never come across arms before, so it's never been in me mind! But no, if we were, it'll only bring the baddies out with their arms.'

'I've carried firearms now about half a dozen times,' says Inspector North, who has been a police officer for more than eighteen years, 'and I've never taken it out of the holster. Don't particularly want to, but it's nice to know, if things do turn nasty, you've got the confidence of being able to answer back.' He checks in his rear-view mirror again, but there is still no sign of the Traffic car. 'It's one of those situations where we have no desire to use guns. I would sooner catch him with his trousers down – in every possible sense of the word! – and grab 'im and that's it. And I'll be more likely to hit him with my stick than shoot him.'

Flick-flack. It's still drizzling and, although the car is stationary, the windscreen wipers are kept going, flick-flack, flick-flack, like a metronome set to steady any flights of fancy.

'He's come, sir!'

'I'll have a quick word. . . .'

*Received commendation in 1977 for 'search of premises on fire'.

176

And it is quick. Inspector North is back in the car only a minute or so later and the convoy divides up, watched by a passing milkman. From here on, the streets are totally deserted, and not another vehicle is seen. 'These are a terrible set of traffic lights,' grumbles Inspector North, as he waits for the green not far from the caravan site.

It is one of those roads running nowhere. Mounds of earth and rubble lie along it to the left, and on the right are misty flatlands backed by a sky the colour of a rain puddle pinked by a flesh wound. A wide, wide sky that continues uninterrupted until a strangely foreign-looking church, standing quite alone with an iron cross out of true atop its pointed façade, appears like the remains of a Mexican mission post.

Inspector North smiles when he sees it. 'Oh aye, it's changed so much around here, I thought I'd come to the wrong place!' There are torch lights in the mist ahead, gathered near a gap in the heaps of rubble. 'You can stay here, young man, by the car,' he says, getting out and closing his door softly. 'If we need you, we'll shout – OK ?'

'OK, sir.' The probationer climbs out and looks about him, taking in the eerie landscape and the huddle of shadowy figures. 'Like a story off the television, this,' he says, with a shiver of cold and excitement.

Not if Inspector North is to have his way. First he checks with his unarmed advance guard, who have been keeping watch. Then, seeing no sign of life outside or inside the small caravan propped up at one end by a piece of wood, and nothing alarming about the lorry parked beside it, the five armed officers move in swiftly over the churn of tyre-tracks. The first suspect, a teenaged boy, is found sleeping with a large dog on the front seat of the lorry, and is quickly and quietly removed from the scene. Inspector North ducks his large frame into the caravan and confronts a man and a woman lying in front of a curtain under a heap of bedding. Something moves between them.

'What's in there ?' he demands.

'Oh, it's the baby.'

And they deny ever having a shotgun.

177

There's a loud crack when a detective sergeant moves to make quite sure of this, pitching him forward. The wooden support has snapped under this last straw and, for a few seconds, the new day is total uproar. About nine other off-spring were asleep behind that curtained partition.

'Time of arrest?' asks the bridewell sergeant, filling in the charge sheets now that the two Night CID men have completed their preliminary interviews with the two prisoners.

'Five forty-five,' the droll sergeant replies, glancing at the bridewell clock and noting it's almost 7.30 a.m. and the end of the shift.

No shotgun has been found, so the affable gypsy and his surly son are being remanded on bail until enquiries have established whether to proceed against them. Somebody certainly inflicted considerable damage to a caravan on another site during the night, but both deny having had any part in it.

'Now, don't be waltzing off,' warns the bridewell sergeant, 'or we'll have to put out a warrant for you, understand?'

'Yes, sir. Oh, she's a bitch of a woman. . . .'

Inspector North, who has been catching up on that paper-work, looks in as the gypsies leave. He has plainly enjoyed this bit of excitement, even though his revolver never left its holster. Equally obvious is the quiet pride he takes in a work-manlike anticlimax.

6

'There's my love,' says the round lady cleaner, winking one of her lovely large eyes at the sergeant with a tan from Bermuda. 'Always got a moment to spare for yer.'

Jemma is waiting with her bucket and mop outside the door to the charge office at St Anne Street. 'I can go in, I can do. But, as I always say about anybody who comes in there and they're gettin' charged, there's nobody guilty until they're proved guilty. So why should I go in? I think that's a bit wrong. Some of them are, I suppose, not guilty. Gotta be.'

She cleans the bridewell twice a day, between 6.30 a.m. and

178

9.30 a.m. (the shift she's on now) and between 5 p.m. and 8 p.m., venturing across from her council flat in notorious Soho Street.

'I've been here just on twelve months. I was scared stiff at the start – thought they were all a shower of you-know-what! But the wairk is smashin'. Some of them are boogers. Seen one of 'em put a ciggie out on the floor, and he said, "If we didn't, *you* wouldn't be 'ere to clean it!" A couple like that: pigs. But, on the whole, good.'

The sergeant passes through the door again, allowing a brief glimpse of three prisoners he's just brought in.

'They're livin' by their wits,' murmurs Jemma, 'but what they do has got nuttin' to do wid me. I don't like to say it, but what can you do when it's all around yer? It maddens yer when you get afraid of comin' 'ome.'

Jemma has to be wary of what pubs she goes into now, all on account of her cleaning job, besides having to put up with abuse from neighbours, most of whom live on the dole. What she enjoys watching – although, she says, it infuriates her – is a flat being emptied of its colour television and other goods she considers luxurious, just before a visit by someone from the Social Services. 'You know what's wrong? Let's face it: the churches – and I'm a Catholic. It's a money-makin' game, isn't it? The bingos, encouraging mothers to go. . . . I've got four kiddies, me eldest's a nursing sister. It's wrong.'

A few minutes later, Jemma is in tears. The pup in the strays' kennel, the one whose puddles she wiped up last night, chatting away to it, telling it about the far worse messes made by humans, is dead.

'Don't worry, luv,' says the bridewell sergeant, 'we'll see it gets a nice burial.'

7

Exasperation provokes a sudden outburst on the CID landing, as three detectives, overladen with jobs off the spike, make for the stairs.

'We've got *x* amount of men,' says one of them, pushing the stairs door open, 'but they're only there on bloody paper! I mean, come Christmas – or the next government inspection – and we'll have twenty-five detectives and seven cardboard replicas stood in the corner, and they'll count heads, y'know. The rest will have been dropped by bloody parachute, clutchin' their *Daily Mirrors*, into some crime-infested area round by Copperas Hill or somethin'! Figures can be made to do anythin', can't they?'

His colleagues grin, hastening to keep up with him.

'Christ,' he says, his bottle beginning to go a bit, 'if the Government decides they're going to reduce crime this year, what do they do? They do like they've done before: they re-classify – they make anything under a pound not a crime, and they immediately lose two million crimes! "Oh, thanks very much, Mr Prime Minister." What a load of rubbish!'

'Aye, it's like—'

'Or, if juvenile crime is becomin' a nightmare, they up the age of criminal responsibility and lose *another* three million crimes! A load of rubbish, isn't it? We *know* it's a load of rubbish! It's a big con job, a big *political* con job on the public.'

'But what can we do about—?'

'There's only one way to stop crime payin',' he says, holding open the ground-floor door, 'and that's to bloody nationalise it. Which is true, isn't it? Because straight away there'll be something wrong with the bloody job, and they'll all be out on bloody strike – won't they?'

Over at Copperas Hill, a detective sergeant is going through the Crime Book, seeing who has taken what off the spike.

What we consider a crime in the CID is an offence which is recordable for statistical purposes. If I come and smash your toilet window in your house, it's not a crime for recordable purposes because it's under twenty pound. If I come and smash your big window, which cost twenty-one pound, it's a crime. But if you're *caught* smashing the toilet window, then it is a crime, because there's a prisoner. (*His finger stops beside a scribbled signature*) A crackin' lad – worked such long hours one week that he collapsed on me in the corridor. Walked down the

180

corridor saying, 'Will you help me?' I thought he was saying, 'Will you help me with a file?' So I said, 'Yeah, what's the problem?' 'No, will you help me?' He bounced off three walls, slumped and I caught him just before he hit the deck.

'I hear', says a DC entering the room, 'that they issued firearms over at St Anne Street this mornin'.'

8

A monogrammed gun-belt – quick-draw holster, thigh thongs and all – hangs between FBI markmanship certificates in a small, jungle-lush office in the basement at St Anne Street. Thirty-eight plants flourish in pots placed on every available flat surface, sweetening the air with exotic blooms, and cascading their greenery down the pale yellow walls. All the room lacks is a humming bird.

'I grow all these,' says the inspector in charge of the Central Property Office to his visitor, 'except for this one, of course, which is a plastic flower. It's to make the other plants feel happier, y'see, to think he's blooming spring, summer, autumn and winter. This one's nicknamed the Wandering Jew. This really big one in the corner is called the Coffin Tree. In its native land, this tree is somewhat sacred; the natives scrape the trunk out and put their dead in it.'

'Must be for the bloody Wanderin' Jew,' mumbles the sergeant in the other corner. 'It's surprisin',' he adds with a grin, nodding at the cluttered window-sill above him, 'how much light comes in when, y'know, you take them down from there!' Then he carries on sorting hundreds of watches and bracelets into small lots for the next quarterly auction.

Multiplicity is the property office's life-blood. 'We get in about fifty thousand items a year,' says the inspector. 'They wait a year before going on sale; the last couple realised about four thousand pounds. That gold watch there was about six hundred in the shops, and should fetch four hundred at least. We sell everything: jewellery, household goods, bicycles – everything except firearms.'

The Python .357 magnum revolver lying before him is not

lost, stolen or strayed, but his own. As are the custom-built gun-belt and the FBI certificates that show his rise from 'Police Marksman' to the zenith of 'Distinguished Expert'. Surprisingly, perhaps, he looks the part, having the same sort of fifties hairstyle, glasses and bland features which typify so many resolute faces in the pages of *Guns and Ammo*.

My father started me off shooting forty-two years ago, and eventually I joined the Grenadier Guards and became a firearms instructor; I was in an armoured division and carried a P38.* In 1950, when I joined the police, the armouries here were a complete shambles. All they had were very old weapons, handed in over many years, and nobody had ever taken a great deal of interest in them. Very few military men who came into the police had ever handled revolvers [not being of commissioned rank], and there was no expertise. It was simply a case of the police never being armed, except on very rare occasions. So when Lord Derby was shot – which was in early 1952, I think – and the butler murdered, both by an under-butler armed with a Schmeisser submachine-gun, such a mess was made of everything it was decided some form of training would take place, and that there'd be a standardisation of firearms. Myself and several other men undertook this.

Now everybody coming into the force has a very basic training – safe handling of firearms, recognition of ammunition – and every divisional commander is allocated so many men who are fully trained in the use of a revolver, or in the use of a combination of revolver, rifle and shotgun. I introduced the FBI course to the force – the one I attended was through the good offices of some sheriffs from America stationed at Burton Wood – and am in a position to qualify people I instruct. There are four different stages, and now we've a number who are pretty highly qualified: about a hundred Marksmen, thirty Sharpshooters, maybe a dozen Experts, and eight – possibly ten – Distinguished Experts. The FBI say the first twelve shots must be fired within twenty-five seconds, and we can put them into an area three inches across in about twenty-one seconds from seven yards away; that's with a reload in between, and starting off with the gun in the holster, fastened down.

The revolvers are the four-inch-barrelled Smith & Wesson

*Semi-automatic pistol.

182

Model X .38 Special, and for detective use we've got the Model 36 Smith & Wesson, also in .38 Special with a two-inch barrel. People always say that a revolver is a close-range weapon, and so it is, but in the hands of a man who is trained you can shoot somebody two hundred yards away with it. The shotgun is an intermediate weapon really. We've got to consider that, when using weapons in a city, we don't want to overshoot, and that, in darkness, the sights on a revolver or a rifle are completely useless. We also want ammunition we can use not particularly to kill the man with, but to immobilise him. The effective range is usually forty yards, but at sixty yards we can be fairly confident that one of those pellets will hit him, putting him out of action. When the light is there, the shotguns we use have rifle-sights which allow us to use them up to a hundred yards fairly accurately, provided we're using rifle-slugs or the CS gas cartridge. The rifle's used when we have extreme ranges – a man sniping from a twenty-two-storey block of flats, or we might be in some of the more rural areas. We have adopted the L39 A1 and its successor, and also have some T4s, a Parker–Hale sniper rifle fitted with a telescopic sight. These are extremely accurate, and the bullet will go through a brick wall.

We've been armed on many occasions and have never had to use them, but the expertise is ready, willing and able, whenever it's needed.

Firearms are my private hobby, as well as an interest in the police. Everything has, in my opinion, an honest or civilised use – in the same breath, everything can be twisted and used evilly. The polythene bag you're going to carry your lunch in; if you put that over a child's head, you suffocate them. So where do you draw the line? I find that an awful lot more people are beginning to take notice of firearms – you've only got to see the mushrooming of clubs all over the country. Now, whether or not some of these people intend to use this skill against society – or against the police – I don't know. I would hope not.

His lunch-break over, the inspector stows away the .357 magnum – which retails at around the £250 mark – and discards some soiled cleaning materials. This enthusiasm for firearms takes him to Clint Eastwood films, and he's just seen *Magnum Force* at the Odeon. 'I notice so many faults', he says, 'that sometimes I say to myself, "This is just *nonsense*." '

*

Across the way, and a few yards up the passage from his office, is the strongroom where valuables, dangerous drugs and, of course, weapons are stored in well-ordered confusion. There are dozens of air rifles, swords, bayonets, shotguns sawn-off and otherwise.

The inspector pushes aside an old Martini Henri rifle and an industrial nailgun, and lifts out a shotgun that has not been tampered with. 'The young man who owned this committed suicide with it, blew his head off. Now the father wants it back, but he isn't the holder of a shotgun certificate, so he's making arrangements to sell it to a man with one. The story is he's going to use the money to buy a headstone for his son's grave.'

On top of a cupboard is a battered food-carton which contains several IRA handguns captured in Liverpool. 'Most the IRA have got are rubbish [like these], you'll find. But last year at Bisley a member of the RUC said to me, "Be very careful," he said. "The IRA have just taken possession of five hundred .357 magnums, all spanking brand-new with consecutive numbers, paid for and sent over by the Americans." ' The inspector handles one of the revolvers as a vet might examine an injured kitten, then replaces it gently. 'They treat 'em, y'know, like dirt. I mean, if I treated my guns like that, I'd shoot myself – deliberately!'

Like so much of 'A' Division's headquarters, the basement is part of the architect's scheme that has gone a-gley. What was originally intended as a car-park is now divided up by *ad hoc* partitions.

At the northern end, a space large enough for about two dozen vehicles now houses instead the bulkier of the annual intake of 50,000 items. An entire household of furniture and effects fills one corner – 'Property donated by a man in prison to his best friend, but he won't come and take it,' explains the inspector. Beside the unwanted gift is a small mountain of stolen blankets, recovered from the home of a woman who claimed she was running a mail-order business. Scores of bicycles, prams and other wheeled conveyances stand in rows or hang from the rafters, half-obscuring the boom in purloined or unclaimed drum-sets. The ubiquitous store-dummies are there, too, standing stark naked just within the doorway like

184

abandoned school-teachers taking the host of papier-mâché, slot-in-the-head spastic children and guide dogs on an excursion. 'We get in touch with the charities,' says the inspector, 'and they say, "Yes, we'll be along for it" – but this goes on for months and months, until the poor things get broken up. We can only store items for so long, y'know, and we haven't the transport.'

At the southern end of the basement, in vast storerooms filled with gigantic pigeonholes, each containing a category of items such as toys, toilet-rolls or false teeth, is ample evidence of why the Central Property Office has a staff of more than a dozen constables and civilians, besides the inspector and the sergeant.

'The idea of the Police Property Act of 1887', explains the inspector, 'was to protect the poor who found a valuable piece of property. If you find something and bring it in, we book it and you can have it back in a month, provided it hasn't been claimed by the owner – and, of course, insurance companies write in. At the end of three months, we have the right to sell the property but, as I say, we wait a year. People don't reward finders as often as they should, y'know.'

It seems reasonably likely that the priestly vestments and Holy Communion kit in the pigeonhole reserved for 'beliefs' will soon attract a claimant, but nobody is taking bets on the full set of witch's regalia, plus ritual devices, lying snug alongside them. And the stuffed crocodile has been around for a while, too.

Medicines enough to stock a pharmacy twice over, prisoners' property, gore-stained exhibits in plastic bags, a box of suicide notes, two hundred bunches of key-rings, devices nobody can imagine a purpose for, a great pile of pornography awaiting an escort to the pulper, and, a few feet away, a pair of large flower-pots in which two dried-up, utterly miserable plants stand at death's door.

The inspector crouches down to examine them. 'If I kept these alive,' he murmurs, 'they'd say I was trying to grow cannabis, so I just allow them to wither. Actually, the sooner we finish off the job the better, as I could do with transferring some of mine.'

9

Unhurriedly, a young constable carries his third cup of coffee this afternoon along a dim corridor and into the brightly illuminated corner office housing the Plain Clothes Section at 'A' Division headquarters. The room is furnished with clinical simplicity, and there is a noticeable absence of pin-ups on its walls. A colleague is going through the latest batch of suspected cannabis back from the forensic laboratory at Chorley, seeing what the tests say. Over on his own desk by the window, two piles of glossy magazines stand a blotter's width apart. One pile is fringed by paper strips inserted to mark certain pages. After preparing a dozen or so fresh strips, and sipping at his coffee, he licks a finger and begins to work his way through the top magazine off the unsampled pile, testing his own reactions. Twice he flicks back for a second glance at an illustration, then he carries on again, blinking through his cigarette smoke. He stops and reaches for a slip. The slack-mouthed girl in the photograph is sprawled unclothed on a tumbled bed, with her legs open towards the camera; an overt invitation to either the large dog in the foreground, or to the small naked boy fondling it, for each clearly has an erection. The slip is positioned, and the paging goes on.

'Oh aye, reports they 'ad on 'im this thick!' grunts a furious young constable on his return from court, stirring his canteen tea in such agitation that he spills some of it. 'Y'know, big as a phone-book! All 'is little upsets and funny ways, which are all down to 'is parents, poor little bastid, so 'e can't 'elp it if 'e gives in to temptation. No reports on the ol' fella! I mean, it's all there, isn't it? Psychological, bloody medical – not a word.'

Reports of a different sort are causing various degrees of anguish in the CID office at St Anne Street as the afternoon fast dwindles away. A Scenes of Crime officer, calling into see if anyone wants a fingerprinting job done, responds with

186

empathy. 'I had this Form 52 once, vague description – oh, I wrote a pile of rubbish. Came back from the inspector with "139 London Road" at the bottom of it. I wondered: Does he know somethin' I don't know? I got out the Kelly's and looked up 139. "Ball's the Jeweller's," it said – so I had to start again!'

10

When Inspector South arrives at Copperas Hill to begin the Afternoon shift (3.30–11.30 p.m.) he dumps a packet of sandwiches and a paperback copy of *A Bridge Too Far* on his locker in the cramped inspectors' office.

I read about six books a week. I go through the *Sunday Times* and the *Observer* book-pages each weekend, and I order the ones that interest me for 10p at the local library. Basically, I like biographies of interesting people, and I'll read anything on crime, provided it's interesting. Y'know, John Wainwright, Maurice Proctor – I think Proctor's far better on the practical policeman. But one gets so many of these books which are like Enid Blyton writing about jungle warfare.

Until his promotion a year ago, Inspector South had spent more than seventeen years out of twenty-two years' service in the CID, where he was the first detective sergeant in Liverpool entrusted to handle a murder case on his own.* The transition back into uniform has left him somewhat wistful and with a number of adjustments to make. 'When I was a section sergeant fourteen years ago, I had a cyclist with fifteen years in, a couple of bobbies with nine or ten, a couple at five or six, two just about out of their probation, and they all taught each other. It was like a family: the older children brought up the younger children. Now one has to cut your cloth according to your means, tailor it to their inexperience.'

*Standards are high. Perhaps the CID's proudest boast is that Liverpool, contrary to common practice in the provinces, has never had to call in Scotland Yard's Murder Squad.

His compromise has been to turn his group into a kind of Swiss Family Robinson, with himself as the father figure, passing down his know-how in specially prepared 'survival' sheets, and even scavenging for cheap steak to enhance the 'do's' held to celebrate a particularly good arrest or simply the group's strong corporate feeling. He is very proud of its morale, and of the fact that its crime-arrest figures are consistently the highest.

Now in his mid-forties with a fifteen-year-old son, Inspector South was himself the only surviving child of an Irish lorry driver. Educated by Jesuits, he won a grammar school scholarship and had just matriculated when his father's failing health forced him to quit the sixth form for a railway clerk's desk. He passed an examination to a teachers' training college while doing his National Service but, after a taste of security work, decided instead to become a policeman. He has a round head, a puckish face and the presence of a medium tank, notwithstanding his innate courtesy, cheerful disposition and ready smile.

Basically, my job is to protect the innocent and the timid. I personally love the police service, but police work isn't a nice thing really, and we've far too many people trying to make it palatable to those who are opposed to any form of law and order. People who will trample on other people for their own selfish ends, and then sort of howl and use any method available to complain if anybody tries to stop them. (*Laughs*) I'm sure most families have got one, y'know! Wherever you are, in a university or in a factory, you'll always get one unpleasant selfish person, who might be selfish in a less dramatic manner, but who will nevertheless walk over people. I'm a firm believer in wickedness and evil; there are influential people in our country today who refuse to accept these things exist. I'm equally of the belief that the vast majority would sooner do someone a good turn than a bad one.

People talk about criminals being 'the victims of society', and that this is their subconscious method of attacking the capitalist system – a theory I have heard expressed by one of the self-appointed protectors of the oppressed, who would be unemployable outside politics or the social services. It's a silly theory

188

that rather annoys me, because the majority of victims are invariably of their own social and economic background, and in the roughest of tenements sixty to seventy per cent of the people are bringing up their families as best they can in the circumstances.

Often these people are not of high intellect, and so are restricted in the type of work they do; they have very menial unpleasant tasks and aren't on high wages. That they do these tasks is a tribute to them in many cases – they could just steal or go on the Social Security – and it's these people who are the real victims. They very rarely complain officially, and who can blame them? They have to live among these others who will trample on anybody for their own selfish ends. (*Smiles at his show of feeling*) Like any job, if you're in the nitty-gritty of it, it's very hard to be dispassionate.

In other words, to view a situation dispassionately can mean you're devoid of passion, compassion – or devoid of a sense of urgency or responsibility. Say, for instance, we have some sort of emergency situation in one of these tenements tonight. I'm not going to regard the sort of people causing a large-scale disturbance as a crowd of bewildered peasants, desperately seeking reformation as victims of an oppressive capitalist system, am I? (*Laughs*) I'm going to regard them as a sort of crowd of dirty-ankled, half-pissed lame brains with a collective IQ of forty-three, who are trying to inflict as much damage as possible on persons and property. I must come in swiftly and draconically in many cases. There are people one could humour; I could be polite and humorous with them, but still intimate that, if they didn't stop it and go away, I'll arrest them. With an awful lot of stern upright policemen the only thing they can do with any degree of success is look stern, isn't it? (*Laughs*) Sternness is often a mask to cover incompetence and inexperience – it's the finest mask. But there are others, natural agitators who have incurred local admiration for their fighting ability, I'd have to go up to and say, 'If yer don't fok aff fast, mister, yer *in*!' These only understand directness because of the way they've been brought up; anything less than directness means you're frightened of them. And if they weren't away in thirty seconds I'd arrest them and have them removed from the scene to stop a further conflagration – they're like a match to paraffin! (*Smile fades*) Basically, as far as I'm concerned, we can afford the Great Train Robbery, we can afford the London Airport job, and the

Dulwich Art Gallery job, but we can't afford forty burglaries in a working-class district.

'All yours,' says the inspector he is relieving, 'and after a Morning like that you're bloody welcome to it.'

II

Not all CID officers back in uniform are able to adjust to their new circumstances with the vigour shown by Inspector South, whose main advantage is, perhaps, that he has always regarded himself first and foremost as a *policeman*.

'Do you know,' says one dyed-in-the-wool uniformed officer, 'there is no such *thing* as a detective constable? There isn't! You show me where it's written down! And there isn't really a detective sergeant, a DI or even a DCS, either. 'Detective' is just, well, sort of a job description stuck on the front, that's all. Not a rank, like most people seem to think. The rank part is sergeant or inspector or whatever.

'And what's a rank mean in the police service anyway? It means you're a boss; it shows who's senior to who, who you have to listen to. But your *office*, that's quite different. You're an independent officer of the Crown appointed in the office of constable – everyone is. So, in a way, rank is just a job description, too, and hence you get constable at the bottom and chief constable on top. People who hold the office of constable are also members of a police force, of course. To make it work, somebody has to be responsible, to give orders, or it'd be a complete shambles.

'But this is where a police officer is quite different to the services – y'know, the Army or the Navy or anything, like hospitals: he stays personally responsible for all his actions. A con can't say, "Well, me boss said I should do that", if what he's done is against the law or isn't right morally, isn't acceptable. That's no excuse! It's all down to him, as it were. That's where we get our discretion from, of course, which bobbies don't have in Toronto, say, where they get a quota of tickets to issue to motorists on Mornings. I could never be on a job like that.'

190

12

Around the corner from Copperas Hill, in a small pub brimming with opening-time business, a detective sergeant is setting up the first round for a few friends whose CID shift ended officially about an hour ago. No amount of cajoling, nor even the barman's bleak withering stare, can make one detective constable change his order from plain tonic water to something alcoholic.

In this area, masculinity seems to be judged on the amount of ale you can drink. I *can* drink. I don't drink a lot. I enjoy what I do have. If I go out with my wife, I might have a vodka and tonic, but I'm not one for shovelling drink down me. I believe in being my own man.

He is thirty-five, ruddy-complexioned and built like a yeoman of old; he has eyebrows with a sharp enquiring lift to them, and a steady piercing gaze, reminding one of an eagle owl; he laughs a good deal, but can look like thunder. His courteous manner seems born of strength and, although his uncompromising nature makes him doubt his popularity, colleagues say there is nobody they'd rather have with them in a tight corner. He enjoys music and reading (he's halfway through *Cromwell* by Antonia Fraser), and he has two children, aged six and ten.

I think there's a lot of herd instinct in this job. They feel obliged to go along with everyone. I believe man is a gregarious animal, not a herd animal. People might take me for being unusual for it, but I've always believed it's my own conscience that dictates to me, not what anyone else dictates to me. If anyone ever said to me, 'Lay off,' I'd want to know why. And if I didn't get a right answer I wouldn't lay off. You see, if one of my superiors said to me, 'Arrest that man,' and I didn't think he should be arrested, I'd say, 'You arrest him.' And I've done this. Well, my father's very quiet in his way, but he always makes up his own mind.

I was never brought up in a city, for a start. My father was a farmer, and we had our own place until I was in my late teens. I was brought up on the land and, if I had the money, that's where I'd be now. I left school at sixteen and a half and went away to sea to have a look round – y'know, at someone else's expense! I stopped with the sea for just over four years. I went away on deck, which was stupid really; I left school with only five O-levels so I could have gone as a midshipman, but I wanted to earn a bit of money as well. The type of fellas I went away with frankly didn't appeal to me. When we went to foreign ports, to Bangkok, I'd go round the temples, see what the place was about. There's lots of people who have gone away to sea, been all over the world, and all they've been is from one bar to another. (*Laughs*) Everyone to his own, but I went away for a reason and, once I'd been around a bit, that was it. My mother's father was a policeman. He was a grand old fella, a fella I admired very much, and he always said, 'Oh, I'd like to see you join the police.' I think it's a worthwhile job. I think that without the law there'd be no freedom – and I believe in freedom; I really do believe in freedom.

I find city dwellers think they know about life. They know very little really. Take these stag do's. I've been to two of them, and they leave me cold. But people think you're strange if you're like me. I get no pleasure or amusement out of seeing people debase themselves; I feel sorry for people like that. I'm not a Puritan! (*Laughs*) Don't get me wrong, but there's a time and a place for everything, and a lot of the bobbies are boys in men's trousers, I call them. They amuse me, to be honest; they're so limited and narrow. Most canteen conversations will be about three topics: sex, football or booze.

In the country, at a very early age, you see sex in the raw and you realise you're part of this. You see, I believe that man's an animal – he's a higher animal, but basically his needs are the same as the beasts of the field really. He's got to have his field, somewhere to shelter from the elements, and he breeds the same, his needs are the same – like you've got to eat to live, not live to eat.

But towns. . . . I think you can blame these blocks of flats for a lot of the crime, I really do. Because I think the frustration must be absolutely fantastic, because there's hundreds of people living on top of you, and hundreds and hundreds living below you. Rats with a space of their own, territory of their own, will get on quite amicably – but put six rats in a shoe box and they'll kill each other. That's what happens, I think, in these cities.

192

So you've got to try and understand why people do things. I like to try and look at things objectively, to take more than one point of view – which, I'm afraid, a lot of my colleagues are sadly, sadly lacking in. If you don't understand *why* – say, you're interviewing someone – you'll get nowhere. Even if you don't agree with the reasons, you've got to understand what could make a person act like that. I'm inquisitive by nature. I always ask, 'Why?' I don't believe in much – I don't believe in a deity or anything like that, although I'm quite well versed in the Bible and can quote chapter and verse.

I remember once I went to Bootle, where it's predominantly Catholic, to go to court there. I got in the box and the clerk said, 'Officer, take the oath.' I said, 'With the greatest respect, I take an oath of affirmation.' The clerk said, 'Kindly explain to the magistrates why you don't take the oath.' So I explained the reason, and there was snorting and huffing from the Bench. Later on, when I came out, there was this superintendent, and he said to me, 'What's this about you?' I said, 'What do you mean?' He said, 'I've had a report you won't take the oath in court.' So I said, 'That's completely wrong for a start. I do take an oath – and I stand by my oath.' He said, 'You affirm, don't you? What are you trying to do? Draw attention to yourself?' So I said, 'With the greatest respect, you must be speaking from ignorance. If you wish, I'll go into an hour's debate on why I don't take the oath.' A cardinal came and this same man, in full uniform, was offered the cardinal's ring and he kissed it. Well, fair enough, y'know, but that's what I mean about narrow-mindedness in the police force.

I think the law is paramount. If I have to carry out the law, as a servant of the law I'll carry it out – even if the law is a bloody stupid law, and the law can be an ass. But the law is there, and the law is supposed to be the voice of the people, so these laws must be what the majority of the people want – and, of course, there is a way a wrong law can be repealed.

It's quite a long day – not that I mind, so long as there's something positive being done. But the women sometimes growl and so do the children. I'm a family man and like to be with them.

193

13

One of the two Plain Clothes sergeants has borrowed his brother's sporty orange Mini for the evening, and is taking an unholy delight in some of the places it may be seen. His first stop is at a cinema club specialising in Super-8 erotica; all seats £1.50 with a cut rate for pensioners.

'What was it yer wanted?' mumbles the blonde cashier in her ticky-tacky box office, confused by the novelty of a fresh-faced man in his mid-thirties who insists upon identifying himself. 'Er, the boss is up the casino like, and I dunno if. . . .'

Whereupon the usher, who closely resembles the sort of old timer often made deputy sheriff in Westerns, pops his grizzled pate out of the auditorium to enquire, 'A'right, boss? Comin' in?'

The sergeant slips into the auditorium and stands beneath the EXIT sign. On his left is the block of forty-eight seats, filled almost to capacity tonight by ageing males, and ahead of him stretches a wide side-aisle. Halfway down the aisle is a round-backed wooden chair in which the usher sits, casually vigilant, facing the audience; one wrong move anywhere beneath those folded overcoats, and he'll let fly with a torch beam.

Up on the small screen a young couple collapse naked on to a motel bed, arouse one another perfunctorily, and then, after several impracticable attempts to spice their lives with variety, resign themselves to the missionary position. Abruptly, the picture becomes as puzzling as any slide shown on 'Ask the Family', when Robert Robinson challenges his contestants to identify common objects seen in extreme close-up and from unusual angles. Well-schooled heads in the audience tip to the right, and the semi-abstract image of pink, brown and purple forms is immediately resolved into a vast Dali-crisp image of coupled genitalia. The camera draws back, hovers, plunges.

The sergeant glances sideways. Lined faces are rapt, lit by a gentle mix of colour as through a chapel window; they appear reverent, awed, yearning; they make the booming grunts of

194

lust from the loudspeakers seem curiously incongruous, if not downright ill-mannered. The sergeant nods to the usher and leaves.

Up zips the Mini, out of the shadows into the bright lights, and a parking-space is found for it near a casino that rivals any James Bond set for sumptuous sophistication. There an impeccable honey-blonde at the reception desk is confused by the novelty of someone in a sports jacket seeking admission; moreover, the law states that only members and their guests can be admitted. Then a severe young man appears, catching the light in the diamond ring on his little finger, and, somewhat distastefully, directs the girl to give this policeman a free membership card. Only then is the sergeant allowed in, much to his amusement.

The owner of the cinema – and a great deal else besides – is seated near a glittering bar, surrounded chiefly by distinguished elderly couples exchanging remarks sotto voce. He greets the sergeant warmly, and orders another drink from a waitress with breasts like marshmallows and eyebrows like liquorice. To set the conversation going, the sergeant makes a jovial remark about the cut-rate for pensioners.

'When I started that,' chuckles the owner, 'it was like Sherwood Forest with all them sticks!'

Casually, the matter of the offending scene is introduced. 'It's got to come out,' says the sergeant, who knows that the owner does his own cutting. 'That wasn't simulated – y'know, the usual Droopy Dora touch! You're getting a bit blasé.'

Amused, the owner starts a debate on the subtle distinctions between what is and what isn't acceptable, and demonstrates his knowledge of the law at some length, being plainly highly intelligent, articulate and witty. None the less, the sergeant's discreet warning has got across, and soon it's time to move on again.

Nowhere he goes tonight – and he has his pick of any and all licensed premises – will his costume be quite appropriate. The effect is subtle but undeniable; it makes wary everyone he encounters, and so serves, unconsciously perhaps, as a warning not to try anything – much as a bouncer's bow tie carries its

195

own stamp of authority, singling him out from among those clad simply for pleasure. This particular sergeant is aware, however, of the need to keep a clear head in this minefield of the unexpected, and takes care to pace his drinks and pick up a snack whenever possible.

Driving up Canning Street to make a quick check on Falkner Square, he comes across another Mini on its way down. They stop at an intersection.

'Don't talk to me, boss!' the constable at the wheel calls across.

'Why?'

'I've had a lousy night. I ended up assisting with this bloody lunatic with a knife, and I lost me car keys in the struggle, didn't I? Had to go home for a new set of keys!'

The sergeant laughs; this is the first he's heard of the incident, not having a personal radio. 'How many have you locked up tonight?'

'None!'

They both laugh, and drive off in opposite directions. The camaraderie is pronounced as they criss-cross the night, meeting up time and again in different parts of the division, and the sergeant obviously delights in it.

Falkner Square is quite dead. He decides to go down to Eric's, which will have closed its iron doors tonight to everyone bar police officers and punk rockers – 'They're good kids, no fightin', no messin' about; they wear outlandish clothing, that's all.' Eric's is directly opposite the filled-in site of the Cavern, so-called birthplace of the Beatles, and once used the name itself, having a vaulted cellar that is practically identical. On the way down into the city centre, a panda car rushes by, followed half a minute later by an ambulance.

14

A BOBBY: I very nearly locked the Beatles up once. Before they were famous, they used to play at a place called the Black Bull, on the north end of Liverpool. I was a local bobby and we used

196

to go up and see the kids comin' out, chase them home, stop fights, etcetera, and these lads had the pavement blocked up with guitars, amplifiers and speakers and whatnot. I said, 'Excuse me, you'll have to move those; you're blocking the footwalk.' One of them said, 'But we're the Beatles!' I said, 'If yer don't fok aff, I'll put me beetle-crushers on you!' And they got most offended, y'know.

15

'Nobody ever called me a slut! I've never been a slut in me life! Oh God, why don't yer listen to me?'

The Main Bridewell inspector looks up from the counter. The long bench against the far wall is filled with prisoners awaiting their turn, all but the most drunken of whom are gazing at a short girl with an astonishingly raucous voice.

'How would you feel if your wife was called a slut?' she bawls across, tears pouring down her cheeks. 'Who's the father of yer baby?'

'Shhhhhhhh!' says the girl next to her. 'Shhhhhh!' say the other prisoners, urgently.

'You're coonts, that's all you are!'

'Sit down, luv,' says the inspector.

The girl slumps on the bench, outraged and sobbing. Her arresting officer moves closer to ensure she stays there.

'What's 'is number?' she demands, leaping up to memorise it. But his mackintosh has no numbers on its epaulettes. 'They won't even be honest, and they're supposed to be the law! *They're* not even the law! Well, how would you like your wife to be called "slut"?'

The officer regards her silently, quite unmoved.

'I just come out the club to *stop* the fight, but *he* wouldn't get my meanin', the coont! He is only a coont – a prick, in my eyes.'

'Shhh, sit down, luv,' begs the girl next to her.

'Shut up!' barks a bridewell constable.

'The twit!' she shouts, grabbing at the officer. 'He isn't even fokkin' 'uman!'

197

'Listen, luv,' says the inspector, still unruffled, 'don't you lay hands on that officer again.'

'I don't care what you are! He shouldn't lay fokkin' hands on me!'

To allow her to see the number on his tunic, the officer unbuttons his mackintosh, imitating the teasing technique of a stripper. But the girl is distracted by what's happening at the counter, where her companion is being charged. She catches something about the complainant having blood streaming from her eyes.

'You liar! You bloody liar!'

'Officer!' snaps the inspector, as the constable in the mackintosh moves angrily towards her, forcing her back on the bench.

'Yes, sir? Sorry. . . .'

The girl is hoarse by the time it comes to the circumstances of her arrest being related, but no less indignant.

'You bloody liar!'

'—was restraining this woman here. This woman was shouting, "I'll kill the fucking twat." '

'You liar! You bloody liar!'

Taking a deep breath, the officer adds, 'I noticed that she was smelling strongly of intoxicants. . . .'

'You bloody liar! I want the number, 'cos nobody's callin' me a fokkin' slut and everything!'

'Just tell me what your name is,' murmurs the inspector, so calmly that the girl's manner alters instantly.

'Doreen Clements,' she says, sniffing.

'Have you any middle names, Doreen?'

'Uh-uh.'

'Doreen Clements. Miss or Mrs?'

'Miss.' Another sniff.

'Where do you live, Doreen?'

She tells him. 'I'm a slut as well, I'd like you to note that.'

'You're at it again, aren't you? How old are you, Doreen?'

'Nineteen.'

'Born in Liverpool?'

'Yeah.'

'Been in here before?'

'No.'

'Then I'll tell you the routine. This lady's going to search you, and see what objects are in your handbag.'

'Before you start, Mr Jailer, he called me "slut"!'

'Come on, luv,' says the female searcher.

16

Down the narrow twisted lane, on the wall of what was once probably a warehouse, is a piece of sculpture that commemorates the Beatles, but looks at first glance more like a Madonna and Three Children – Ringo having fallen out of favour at the time of its execution. Below it is the sporty orange Mini, and below that again is a smoky, vaulted cellar so vibrant with deafening sound that a glass of beer, set down on a ledge, ripples. The sergeant, standing beside the tee-shirted manager, surveys the crowd. It's a collection of young people nobody would look at twice, were it not for the extraordinary way they adorn themselves. Near at hand, an angular youth, sweat streaming down his bared chest, tows himself hither and thither by means of a chain halter.

'What are yer?' enquires a petite figure in silver-sprayed netting, coming coyly up to the sergeant. 'The fuzz?' He smiles. 'Ooooooo!' she exclaims, as though he strikes her as delightfully bizarre. 'Do you like it? Is it *exciting*?' Then off she skips, very well contented.

And the sergeant, satisfied that his nose has detected not a whiff of cannabis, adjourns his discussion about the problems of drug control to the manager's tiny office upstairs.

Crash. There's a sudden commotion in the entrance hall.

'The bastids!' curses a doorman, diving into the lane with his companions. 'Little bastids! Just wait till we catch yer!'

But the gang of marauding youths, who used a plank to smash the illuminated sign above the big iron doors, is waiting for no one. Much relieved to find his brother's car still intact, the sergeant leaves the manager to dial 999, while he makes his way up towards Lime Street, joining in the chase just below St John's Centre.

'It wasn't me that threw it!' protests a panting youth, as he's collared, quite literally. 'It was Kevin!'

199

'Don't worry,' a consoling voice shouts out. 'Yer only sixteen – they can't touch yer!'

'Aaaaaah, you weren't drinkin' at sixteen, were yer?' tut-tuts the sergeant, passing him on to uniformed officers.

'Eh? Me? Never! No, he's tellin' lies! I'm eighteen!' The youth begins to blubber. 'Ma! Yer can't lock us up! Kevin's got me in the shite and I done nothin'!'

Still smiling slightly, the sergeant slips into a small elegant gaming club nearby, where he asks softly to see the cheques book – just a routine check, hardly more than a formality. The dominant sound in the long wood-panelled room is a continuous clicking, rather like an airport information display endlessly revising its departure-times; a strange sound that seems too constant and loud to be made by gaming chips, as they're stacked, scooped up and redistributed. But, then, the members themselves say very little, seldom smile, and respond to the vagaries of fate with grave decorum. He is brought a small cup of coffee on a salver, and wanders with it from table to table, watching the play. His job has made his knowledge of the different games and their rules fairly sophisticated, but his interest seems to lie chiefly in the faces; not only are the Chinese members (Liverpool's most inveterate gamblers) past-masters of the inscrutable.

He has a ham roll in a club for swinging singles, lipreading what the proprietor has to tell him because the disco speakers are turned up so high, and then a half of bitter in another club across the way, where the manager hints darkly at how much he resents his presence. He lingers, making several interesting observations. Two clubs later, and growing mildly weary of the noise, he decides to make another check on Falkner Square, stopping off briefly at the General Enquiry Office in Hope Street while he's about it.

17

There seems to be a fair amount of plain clothes traffic in and out of Hope Street washroom at night, which suggests a certain prejudice towards the amenities provided in the city centre's clubs, pubs and so forth. A lavatory is, after all, one room in which a detective is obliged to stand with his back turned.

We 'ad this fella who was doin' all the snatches off the old ladies. We knew 'e was doin' it, but we couldn't prove it. No evidence against 'im, because these old women were either too shaken or too shocked to identify 'im – or didn't have the eyesight – and this bugger was pickin' 'is mark. He didn't like me, purely because I kept houndin' the bugger, tryin' to get a cough. I kept interviewin' 'im week after week – no joy. And one night we went in this dive and there he was with 'is mates. I'd had a few too many and I went into this toilet, and thought one of the lads – our lads – 'ad followed me in. The two stalls were very close together, shoulder to shoulder, and the next thing I felt was a belt in me back. Not too hard, so I didn't turn round. 'Sod off,' I said – thinking it was me mate. Nothing was said. Next thing I get another belt in the back, and this one *hurt*. I turned round and there was this little git, stoned out of 'is bloody mind on drugs, and 'e starts pickin' a fight, y'know. But that could've been a knife, couldn't it ?

18

Bzzzzzzzzzzzzzzz

The BP opens the yard door to admit a respectable-looking man of about forty. The arresting officer explains that the circumstances are he came across this man helping himself to a length of rope that was among some broken scaffolding on the edge of a building site. The man doesn't deny taking the rope, but claims he thought it was 'rubbish' – which is, of course, no excuse. The bridewell sergeant accepts the charge and begins taking down the particulars.

'Occupation ?'

'Ah God, this is goin' to cost me me job, y'know,' the man says despairingly, turning a shade whiter. 'I mean, I know you fellas have got yer duty to do and all, but – y'know, can't I just put it back like or somethin' ?'

The bridewell sergeant shakes his head. 'No way, Mr Morgan,' he says. 'You took what didn't belong to you, and you've got to go to court, see.'

Mr Morgan winces, awed by the absolutes of the law, and plainly mortified by being caught in an act of dishonesty. 'When, sir?' he asks in a small voice, very respectfully.

'Thursday.'

'It'll be in the papers!'

'This job? Can't see the—'

'But—'

'Look, you get there early, on the dot like, and the reporters won't—'

'I suppose I've got to say?'

'Yuh.'

'I'm – I'm a school caretaker.'

'Clerk,' says the bridewell sergeant, entering the word on the charge sheet.

'Er, sorry – "caretaker" 's what I said,' Mr Morgan corrects him politely. 'Only been in the job three months, see? And if me bosses—'

'Clerk,' says the bridewell sergeant, very firmly.

The last half-hour has been very confusing and upsetting for Mr Morgan, so it takes a few seconds longer for the penny to drop.

'Talkin' of that,' says a bobby, 'what about the recruit that's supposed to have come in the bridewell and said, "Er, when you've got a minute, Sarge, any chance of us seein' a copy of this Ways and Means Act the lads are always on about?" ' And he gets a big roar of laughter.

While that tale may be apocryphal, references both direct and indirect to the Ways and Means Act are far from uncommon. Just what is meant by them depends, as the Act itself does, upon the circumstances, but broadly it covers anything 'naughty' that expedites justice, promotes fairness or simply makes life easier, provided that 'good' can be claimed to come of it.

Mr Morgan's case is an obvious example of the Act's tacit

202

application. Others could include the bobby in the Bullring who was helped to remove a car thief, the teetotaller who lied to clear a pub crowd from the Queen's highway, and the jeep driver who thought the wine drinker's family could do with an extra twenty pounds one week. Guile is usually an essential factor, of course, and the more outrageous at times, the greater the sense of satisfaction.

We were in a jeep one night, and we surprised these two bucks in the doorway of a chemist shop with a brick. You see, they were going to put the door in, and we got there about ten seconds too soon. So we locks these two up and they were real bad men, both armed robbery merchants. So we locks them up for attempt burglary. It's a bit thin, though. Suspected persons loitering? Even thinner. Going equipped to commit damage? What's that – a five-pound fine? This startling officer walks into the bridewell and says, 'I've arrested these two men for gross indecency. The circumstances are they were in the doorway of Jones's chemist shop, masturbating each other and—' They gave a cough statement! 'Oh no, boss! Attempt burglary!' Now that was quick thinking. These were bad men and we weren't going to let them go.

'Ways and Means Act,' murmurs a middle-service bobby, as he recalls having settled an old score over in the Four Squares. 'There was this fella, y'know, had this puppy he'd take for a walk every night, and he used to shout "Coont!" at us, soon as he saw me. He'd sort of hide round the corner, shout "Coont!" – and he'd be off. It went on for months, y'know. Then one night I come up behind him. "Hello, sir! Nice dog, that. How old would he be now?" "Fourteen months," he says, and he's made up I fancy his dog like. "Oh," I said, "so he's over the twelve-month?" "Er, yes, officer, that's true – must've slipped me mind. Tell yer what, first thing to-morrow—" "Here," I said, and I give him this summons, all written out. "I'm doin' yer for no dog licence." '

Others tell of the hard knock who was finally made to cough a bad wounding job by the simplest of ploys. Whenever detectives had a moment to spare, whether at work or at home, they'd give the hard knock a ring and ask, 'Is Bill Riley in?' –

203

insisting this was indeed the number they'd been given. After a week of this, the hard knock – worn out by the mystery of Bill Riley and his innumerable friends – had admitted the assault in some detail.

19

On his way down Canning Street from Falkner Square, where business is picking up now, the sporty orange Mini chances upon the other Plain Clothes Mini at the very same intersection.

'Guess what, boss?'

'You tell me.'

'I've just been in *another* fight! Outside the Hoffenbrau House. Just drivin' past, mindin' our own little business, when a couple of bucks try to play *High Noon* in the middle of Mount Pleasant. So I jumped out and said, "If yer don't eff off, I'll do yer!" Whereupon he says, "Are you from the police?" "Well done!" I said – and they effed off!'

Everyone laughs.

'They're good lads,' chuckles the sergeant, releasing his clutch again.

Discretion is the secret of the game; without it the peace-keeping machine would grind to a halt, choked by an arrest for every offence seen committed, and the streets would be left empty for the predators to take over.

I've got two sergeants and about half a dozen men on tonight. All right, I've got the OSD to assist me, and dogs and that sort of thing, but very, very quickly, if my section decided to go out and just take the first drunks they see, we'd all be standing back at the bridewell! And, all right, a drunk doesn't take very long, but by the time the officer's picked him up, dragged him up the hill, the charge sheet's been made out, and the résumé, probably an hour's gone.

What every uniformed inspector fears, of course, is when his scant resources of manpower have sudden demands made

204

upon them that preclude the use of discretion. Nor is there any need to produce dramatic examples of emergency situations to illustrate this point; four shoplifters arrested late on Wednesday afternoon are enough to bankrupt the South Sub, just when the officers involved should be helping to control several thousand football fans, pouring out of Lime Street station for a mid-week match.

20

'Look at that fella,' grunts Inspector South, nodding ahead of him. 'Got a face like a cobbler's thumb. . . .'

The big genial sergeant with the fine pair of sideboards, back on the streets after his spell of duty in the bridewell at Copperas Hill, eases the panda towards the kerb.

'No, not carryin' anything,' says Inspector South.

'Want a word ?'

'Not really.'

They continue on their way, giving 'pegs' to the nineteen- and twenty-year-olds spread out over the South Sub. Only one constable on duty tonight is out of her probation. They call in at the Hoffenbrau House and go up to the discothèque.

'Bionic men,' says Inspector South, as they enter the dim purple-lit entrance-hall. 'All right, lads ?'

The stocky belligerent-looking doormen lose their icy composure, smile feebly and shuffle their feet. Detective he may have been, but uniform suits Inspector South, who wears it with the flair of a tugboat captain, projecting an image which is at once both benign and as tough as needs be. Beyond the chrome and swinging décor of the discothèque, the manager's office is homely, papered from floor to ceiling by excellent photographs, many of his wife and child. He was once a *Daily Mirror* photographer, and Inspector South, a keen amateur in his youth, lavishes informed praise. Then he enquires about some trouble he's got wind of, something about a well-known bully-boy making a comeback. They gossip.

Then on again, this time to a club run by Chinese. There the

205

tension in the backroom is high; rumour has it that trouble-makers have marked it down for a visit. Everyone chain smokes.

When the proprietor goes out of the room for a minute, the sergeant says, with a shake of his head, 'Have you ever seen a fella in such a state? Clap yer hands and he'll be on his back.'

'Fear,' says Inspector South, 'and these are good people.'

The proprietor would be happy to keep them there all night, but on they go again, making one more stop at a club before returning to the city centre. These visits could be part of the beneficial effect of cross-breeding Uniform and CID attitudes. Inspector South doesn't simply deal with situations as they arise, but tries to foresee events by maintaining close personal contact with those who have a mutual interest in maintaining order on his 'ground'. He also tries to ensure that his group, whose inexperience makes them particularly vulnerable, is aware of where trouble may strike, what form it could take, and of what faces they should be especially wary. Then again, Inspector South simply enjoys this contact, and would be thoroughly miserable if denied it, he says, while the sergeant, an ex-CID man himself, heartily concurs.

In Lord Street, they come across two battered youths, who are being looked after by a foot-man until the ambulance arrives.

'All right, lad?'

'All right, sir. These two have just come out a club.'

'Doormen did that?'

'Aye, they say—'

'No, they didn't do nothin',' one of the youths interrupts. 'I told yer wrong, see?'

The same old story. Again and again casualties are found staggering along the pavements, crying out for vengeance against force used in excess of need, but as soon as they've had time to reconsider their position these victims of clubland have other explanations for the injuries received. They're simply too frightened to make a complaint, and so the statistics for violence on Merseyside, which are based upon reported crime, cannot help but fail to be a true reflection of the amount of actual bloodshed.

206

'Con requires assistance! Corner Lime Street and London Road!' The radio operator's voice is high and urgent.

'Hold on to yer hat!'

Nothing claims priority over 'con requires assistance', a clumsy-sounding expression that is as peremptory as 'Go!' Whether in a vehicle or on foot, everyone makes a dash for the corner.

'It's our Mary!' chortles the sergeant. 'She can fight like a bloody man!'

Two panda cars have arrived just ahead of them, and the Night CID careers up in a Cortina, coming to a screeching halt that would have done Starsky and Hutch proud. The police-woman's two male prisoners immediately give up the struggle, and each is bundled into a panda, while Inspector South checks to see if she's all right. Apart from one or two bumps and a bent thumb, she says she's fine, and accepts their jocular congratulations in high good humour. Over on the other corner, a crowd of the prisoners' friends watch the arrest in silence, obviously impressed by the swift back-up.

'If a man takes a punch on the face, that's all right,' mutters Inspector South, with an air of misgiving, as he gets back into the car, 'but with a woman that could destroy her looks, y'know.'

Car doors slam all round; then the panda crews re-emerge, beckoning. In the heat of the moment, they'd overlooked the fact they had stopped pointing uphill, and had switched off their engines before leaping out. Now they need a push to get started.

Delighted by this spectacle, the crowd on the other corner begins a slow clapping, enlivened by ironic cries of 'We are the cham-pions!' Moments such as these can have an effect on morale that fatter pay packets alone will do little to sweeten.

Approaching the end of his shift, Inspector South pays a quick call at the Main Bridewell, where the two prisoners from the London Road corner have just been charged with being drunk and disorderly. The long bench against the wall is almost empty now, and the female searcher is making a pot of tea. Then the radio chirrups, and he's asked to make Copperas

Hill, where the bridewell sergeant has a problem that needs sorting out by a senior officer. On the way up there, through the city centre, he notices a Days and EPs man, assisted by officers from the OSD, removing a violent man from a Chinese restaurant. A waiter hurries out, bearing one officer's helmet.

This particular sub-division has the highest incidence of assault on police; the Liverpool side of the force has the highest incidence in the country, and 'A' Division's share is the highest of that. These assaults are mainly with the fists and feet – oh, and with motor vehicles.

In many cases, we don't charge with assault. Say it's a reasonable type of person, who suddenly gets drunk and wants to fight people, you just— Take those two: they'd assaulted that girl and pulled her about, but they were only charged with being drunk and disorderly.

I have been a policeman for twenty-three years and I've arrested thousands in my time, but I've only charged with assault five times – and on four of those occasions I ended up in hospital. I take the view that if I'm arresting a violent man for drunk and disorderly I expect him to struggle.

But I would say the attitude of the courts is remarkably irresponsible – almost criminally irresponsible – towards assaults on the police. People assault policemen today knowing nothing is going to happen to them. They get ten-, twenty-pound fines; very few of them go to prison.

I would think that society should worry when policemen *stop* being assaulted. You see, nobody likes to be assaulted, and policemen don't have to be assaulted – a policeman just doesn't do his job and he doesn't get assaulted, does he?

21

The shift changes. The pubs have closed, but the clubs still have a long way to go yet.

'I think the 1962 Licensing Act made a tremendous revolution regarding people's habits,' says the constable who regards himself as a dinosaur. 'I mean before then people didn't go out late at night because there was nowhere *for* them to go – it was

208

as easy as that! Who would want to go out and wander the streets? Their houses were so abysmal, so absolutely dreadful, that the pub was the focus of their enjoyment. At least in a pub there was warmth, light, probably a piano, music.'

The unexpected happens in a smoke-choked warren with an excess of warmth, light and heavy rock music. For five minutes or so, having smelled cannabis on his way in, the Plain Clothes sergeant has been toying with a fruit juice at a rickety table left awash in spilled beer and peanuts. Then, glancing to his left, he studies the hand of cards held by an elderly Chinaman seated at the next table. He indicates which card he would discard, and the old man, delighted he should understand Chinese poker, obliges. Their silent partnership continues until the end of the game, whereupon, quite without warning, the old man's opponent – possibly his grandson – begins to do card tricks. His sleight of hand is astonishing, and the old man cackles gleefully at the stranger's mystification. Five minutes later, refreshed by this unlikely diversion, the sergeant nods his farewells and leaves, having just pulled off something of a card trick himself. Although watched very carefully, he picked out a knave of clubs, as it were, hidden in the shuffle of people whose homes are probably abysmal.

His next call is to a club where people don't so much spend an evening as end an evening, being a favourite retreat of Post Office workers and others on shifts that finish too late for them to unwind in their local. It has linoleum on the floor, American cloth on its tables, charges 15p for a cup of coffee, and displays no interest in up-market pretensions. In keeping with its informal workaday atmosphere the owner wears a tee-shirt and slacks, and appears ready to deal personally with any trouble-makers.

The sergeant finds him behind a hidden door, typing a novel in a tiny office which is overwhelmed by whisky stocks and enormous, strikingly sensitive pencil drawings of his wife suckling their baby. Two completed books lie on the shelf above the typewriter, and several examples of silk-screen surrealism, dense with symbolism touching on such things as

209

nuclear war and the unconscious, stand propped in a corner. The club-owner learned the silk-screen process while serving four years of a seven-year sentence for manslaughter, during which time he won two Arthur Koestler Awards for his creativity.* Stocky, shrewd and likeable for his sheer vitality, he is none the less a man with whom few would feel at ease. The sergeant, totally at his ease, enquires after the progress on the new book, and hopes it will have an ending less harrowing than the last one, which both he and his daughter had enjoyed before reaching the final pages. It's going to be another ungarnished story of life beyond the pale, says the club-owner, and he's making no concessions, being concerned only with the truth and the way things really are. They have a laugh over that, and talk on above the boom of music reaching them through the door.

Where have I been tonight that you can get away from the outside influence of the world? To my mind, the greatest thing the Devil ever invented was the transistor radio! Because it's *there* and you don't stop and think and evaluate yourself, life. Take that fella, he says there's no God. Look at the pictures he's painted! There's no God? (*Laughs*) I caught him out last week. He was talking and he said, 'Ah, he must've bin watchin' over me' – and looked to Heaven. 'At last', I said, 'you admit! You admit there's a guy watchin' over you!' 'Oh, I've done it now,' he said. He's a thinker, and that's what I like about him. He notices things. He doesn't accept things at their face value.

Two hours and several clubs later, the sergeant drops in at St Anne Street, checks on the constables' evening, and then turns the sporty orange Mini towards home. He'll read for a while, and perhaps make a few notes for the Boys' Brigade Bible class he's due to take at 10 a.m. Besides his interest in the Boys' Brigade (he led a local revival of the movement), he teaches canoeing and is active in the force's Christian Association. He is thirty-five, of average build, and has two sons as

---

*A BOBBY: 'He was a doorman. There was a bit of a ruckus between rival club-owners and they went in with shotguns, y'know. He didn't kill anyone – he took the rap for it. He's a nice fella at heart, but trouble comes to him.'

210

well as a daughter. Although he has the air of a man not to be trifled with, his personality is marked by a youthful buoyancy and zest, often expressed in laughter. His experience in the police has been very varied – panda car driver, dog handler, detective – and he has qualified as an inspector. Putting him into Plain Clothes is, he says, a little like 'Daniel walkin' into the lions' den', much as he enjoys it.

Everything I do is done with an ulterior motive, if you like. Paul said, 'I have learned – whatever my lot – to be contented.' Now, that is me. I am content. If they want to put me in the bridewell I'll make a good job of it.

People say I'm naïve. I believe in the Bible from Genesis to Revelations, and when these wonderful people say to me, 'Look, the world has been going for four million years', I say, 'Garbage. It started in the year 4004 BC. If you don't want to believe it, don't believe it – but you cannot prove to me that any one thing in the Bible is wrong.'

I've been in the force sixteen years. I chose it because there was a fella on the allotments at the back of me in the police, and he used to rave about it. My father worked on the docks, and he used to say, 'Ah, the police! That's the job, y'know!' – security was the thing in those days. I thought: Well, it's different. I was going to be a quantity surveyor. I went to Southport Tech and took my GCEs, but my parents were finding it a bit of a struggle, so I joined the cadets. A chap who was in the same class as me got into quantity surveying, and I saw him about ten years later and he'd gone an old man! I thought: I'm glad to be in the police force because – and a lot of bobbies will say the same thing – I feel no different to when I first came on the job. It keeps you young, because every day you have a fresh problem. It's not like going to a factory.

I was saved at the age of nineteen, just when I came on the job. This was my beef: that, although I mixed with a couple of policemen I knew to be Christians, they didn't. . . . (*Trails off*) I don't like swearing on the Bible because, as a Christian, I read the Bible and in there it says, 'You will not swear on my word.' Really, you should affirm. But I'm a policeman as well, and so I think: Oh well, Lord, you must forgive me, but the evidence I will give *shall* be the truth!

He's got religion – *derogatory*! He's religious – *derogatory*! I'm

211

not *religious* at all – that's why I don't belong to the Church of England. How many people does it save? I belong to a Gospel church [United Reformed] because I think you've got to go back to the Gospel when it was preached in the days of the Lord, to when it was powerful. It doesn't stop me drinking. Let's face facts: the first miracle of the Lord was turning water into wine, and we're not talking about non-alcoholic wine here. But I don't like to get drunk, because a Christian shouldn't.

A Christian shouldn't swear. I've never had to speak to the bucks in their own language – as soon as you lower yourself to their level, they have no respect for you. And when a buck loses respect for a policeman it colours his actions. I've never had any trouble doing my job – there's a guardian angel watchin' over me! (*Laughs*)

The greatest thing that ever happened to me was when a hardened bobby apologised to me for swearing in front of me. I thought: Dear heavens! Thanks, Lord. It's showing through at last. I never pull them up; if they want to use language, let them. Never point your finger, or you'll find three fingers pointing back at you! (*Laughs*) Although a Christian, I've not led a pure life. Paul said – Paul of all people! – he said, 'Why is it the things I should not do, I find that I do? And the things I should do, I find I don't do?' When I read Paul's words, I think: Thanks, Lord, for making him write those words in the Bible. It makes me feel a little bit better. . . .

I can't stand a liar. I can understand a thief. Some I like, some I don't. There are some, as soon as you lay hands on them, throw up their hands and it's like a game of tick. It's a game and you must treat it as a game; you mustn't get involved in the sentences. If you miss a prisoner, you say, 'Och, they'll come again' – and they will.

What upsets me are the things I can't do anything about. To see how kids are abused in this city! It's diabolical, and we don't know the beginning of it – left alone the half. Incest's a very common thing; mainly daddy comes home in a drunken state, wifey doesn't want to know him, so he climbs into bed with his daughter – whatever the daughter's age – and, in effect, rapes her. When he's done it once, he does it twice and so on. Many of the girls end up on the game, and very often that's when you get to know what's gone on. Too late! How many fathers are brought to court because they rape their daughters? I dealt with this child who died, a baby of seven or eight months; allegedly pneumonia. You know how things completely unconnected with

212

the job stick in your mind? I had to stand outside this house to make sure no one entered the flat – it was a first-floor flat. And there was a big mama on the ground floor and she was singing over and over again, 'Lea-ning, lea-ning, safe and secure from all our woes. . . .' The chorus of that hymn, y'see.* She sang that all afternoon. When this baby was examined in the hospital, it had some old fractures but they were not provable contributory causes of her death. The doctor, having examined her, was on his way and the Sister grabbed hold of him and said, 'Excuse me, Doctor, I don't think you've done a complete examination.' 'Why?' he said. She said, 'Well, examine her private parts. . . .' The baby was split from front to back. Now, how could we prove that daddy had used this poor baby for his own sexual gratification? What job really sends me cold? That's the job.

Very rarely do I mention Christianity amongst policemen. I look on it this way: if the Lord wants me to talk, I'll get an opportunity. Recently I came on to another [Uniform] section, and immediately they don't know what you're like, how to take yer, and they know you're a Christian. There was a do and I went along to it, because you must have rapport to do the job, and they saw I did drink (*laughs*), although I don't go away legless like some! I never allow myself to get in a position when they say, 'Ah, he's a true Christian, and did yer *see* him? He was *pissed* out of his *mind*.' You try and say afterwards [that] you're a true Christian; oh heavens above, you're wasting your time. They saw I was actually human and that I cracked jokes – albeit not dirty ones – and from that time on, great.

They'd do a lot for me, y'know. I'd say, 'I'm sorry, mate, but I've got to have someone on Great Homer Street; so-and-so's at large' – they don't want to do the job. I mean, who wants to get bricks and bottles thrown at them! No way! Who wants to run the risk of a good hiding? – which is quite likely there. No way! But they did it anyway, because I'd ask them. I never give an order when I can make a request.

I look at it this way: if, as the Bible says, the Master was spat on, mocked and beaten and jeered, why shouldn't his servant be? So no matter what happens to me, it's certainly not going to be as bad as what happened to Him. And heavens above, I'm only here for seventy years! – and I doubt it's that long. I hate to say this, but we're coming to the time when Time will be no more. (*Laughs*)

*'Leaning on Jesus'.

213

TWO

I

'I feel very acutely that one doesn't live for ever,' the OSD chief inspector remarks, looking out over 'A' Division as the sky darkens, 'and certainly this job brings it home to you. God, I wish I had five pounds for every sudden death I've been to. . . .'

Images.

Click-clack goes the slide projector, and the white wall of the surgery in the Main Bridewell is splashed with a vast pool of blood that almost surrounds a docker with his head crushed.

'So much blood,' muses the senior police surgeon, glancing round at his small audience of officers with time to kill. 'It's often difficult to believe, isn't it?' Some nod; others stare, awed.

Click-clack. A young man sprawls on his bedroom floor with a bent javelin behind him and what looks like a third nipple above the heart. 'That was the hole on this side,' says the police surgeon, touching the corpse with the shadow of his forefinger.

'Good shot,' observes a probationer, with an uncertain laugh.

'Well, he held it there, and then he ran at the wall. The other end pushed it through.'

'I don't know how he had the courage to do it!'

'Yeah,' agrees a colleague.

'How instantaneous would it be, Doc?'

'Oh, he died a sudden death. Shock.'

Click-clack. A chest of drawers bulging with canned foodstuffs.

Click-clack. A wardrobe filled with provisions. More supplies stacked on top of it.

'That's his bedroom, by the way.'

'Oh aye. Wasn't this the fella who thought somethin' terrible was goin' to happen? The world comin' to an end like?'

214

'That's the one.'

Click-clack. A middle-aged dumpy woman, naked, curled on her right side in an overflowing bath, as serene as an embryo in uterus. 'Women commit suicide by drugs, men with hanging – it's a general rule. This one took drugs, fell asleep and drowned in the water.'

'They're good pictures, Doc. Take 'em yourself?'

'Oh yes. This is with my wide-angle.'

Click-clack. The unfamiliar perspective makes perception falter for an instant, then the shapes resolve into the interior of a lavatory cubicle, shot from above, with the body of a drug addict jammed hard against the door, swimming in excreta.

Click-clack. Shoes and other small left-overs of an old woman who burned away to virtually nothing in her body fat, having collapsed on an electric heater.

Click-clack. An elderly man sitting upright and murdered on his sofa.

Click.

The projector light is blotted out and the next picture withheld for a moment or two. 'I went to a hanging,' says the police surgeon, 'and I said to the officer, "Where's the body?" He said, "It's upstairs." On my way up, I said "Excuse me" to this fellow on the landing, and then when I got to the top – Blimey! I got the fright of my life! I suddenly realised the fellow was on a rope, and *he* was the body I'd come to see!' Everyone chuckles.

Clack. And there dangles the self-same body; neck stretched, feet just brushing the carpet.

Click-clack. A filthy room waist-deep in broken furniture, cardboard boxes, mattresses, rags, bottles, unintelligible corruption; somewhere in there lie the remains of a young woman who died a natural death, and then her baby died of starvation.

Click-clack, click-clack. Death can be something of an abstraction, even among those expected to risk their lives in the public interest. Click-clack, click-clack. So this sort of thing can be a help to youngsters, forewarning them lest the real thing comes as too much of a shock to the system. Click-clack, click-clack. In time, of course, each will have a personal store of such recollections. Images with a smell and a feel and a

215

sound as well, perhaps, ready to spring to mind, click-clack.

'. . . I'm very conscious life is so short,' continues the OSD inspector, seating himself at the table in the officers' canteen. 'It was my daughter's ninth birthday on Saturday, and my wife said, "It's nine years since you were at Bramshill." Nine years? I thought: That seems a life-time away! How old will I be in nine years? God, I'll be forty-four – y'know, if I get there.

'They're the sort of thoughts that often strike me.'

2

The panda driver out on the North Sub tonight is a hefty cheerful-faced constable of twenty-seven in the Days and EPs, with eight years' uniformed experience behind him. Eight years that have altered him considerably, but there's no job he'd rather do.

After two years at a college on a business studies course, I was in retail for two years – a bit constricting. I was in the right age bracket for the police, the money looked tempting – which is quite amusing when you reflect now!* – and I thought it'd be a total change. Scared stiff, of course, at the thought of it.

When I joined, my beat at Birkenhead was as rough as any of the areas around St Anne Street, and everybody knew me. I made an effort to know everyone, and you'd say, 'Well, So-and-so, what's yer lad doin' tonight?' You'd laff and joke about it, and you'd be digestin' all the time. That is the way, in my opinion, to do police work.

But over here you've no longer got the bobbies on the streets because there're not enough policemen to do the job, or you're driving past situations and haven't the time to get involved in them. Y'know, you haven't the time to go round and visit Mrs Jones, who lives on her own and has to carry her coal up to her top flat every day. You should have the time, because that to me is just as much part of police work as going out arresting thieves. (*Smiles*) One day Mrs Jones will see something over the

*He had been working for almost three weeks without a break in order to boost his monthly take-home pay to around £200. His basic was £212.55 a month plus a rent allowance of £55 (on which there was an annual tax rebate). One child; wife doing secretarial work at home.

216

balcony of her flat and tell you about it; that'll start up a chain reaction and you'll get an arrest out of it.

And now they say bobbies are frightened to walk around Soho Street, the Four Squares. I can understand that. They're young. Their tutor cons have been young, and they've said, 'Ooo-ooooo, it's dangerous over there!' It's this, that and the other! I suppose it is quite dangerous – I've had all sorts thrown at me – but the innocent people who live there, who are the greater majority, won't be receiving proper police attention.

The problem with this job now, getting right down to basics, is the fact that every month people of my experience – five years and more – are leaving. My tutor con had seventeen years in. If you get a tutor con like that, and he's got a bit upstairs, he might be a bit unorthodox, but he'll teach you the job. A recruit can't – a recruit doesn't know it!

Yet you get tutor cons with three months' experience, and a lot think they're superior to the people. Now, not all people who walk round in denim jackets and jeans are idiots, y'know. Some of 'em are, but not all of them. I spend a lot of time in Soho Street and the community centre and this type of thing, where you get to know them. They talk to you – not freely by any means, but they get to know you – and they know me by my Christian name. Which to a lot of fellas would be 'Oh, that's a bit of an embarrassment!' – but I can walk down the street and people say, 'Hello, Tommy', y'know. I suppose I really should have joined the job about 1954, because I've got an old-time bobby's attitude, and there're very few left with that attitude. (*Laughs*) With others it's come to work, eight hours, go out and fight the animals, come in and go home, basically!

But, going back a bit, I wouldn't say I don't get frightened, because that would be ludicrous. I've been assaulted on numerous occasions, although never anything particularly serious. I mean I had me hand broken earlier on this year, and I've laughed about that since – I've got me criminal [injuries] compensation claim in. Y'know, get some of me overdraft paid off! In fact, I probably get more frightened than most in situations, and the reason I've got a reputation for goin' in is, basically, I wouldn't want to lose face in front of my colleagues. I think the majority of the fellas would say that, that they don't want to lose face. Secondly, we're here to do the job – that's what we're bein' paid for – and if you're not prepared to do it, then you shouldn't be doing it. (*Shrugs, loses some of his ebullience.*)

I've seen some atrocious sudden deaths. I dealt with two that were blown up in a boiler – there was a big *im*plosion, actually, and they were blown to pieces. I mean, there were arms and legs and everything – it was just *frightening*. Well, who else is goin' to do it, if the police don't do it? So we were baggin' 'em off into which bit we thought belonged to who.... (*Laughs, shakes head*) I laff at it now, which must sound terribly callous. I've seen people go off the top of high-rise flats and I've laffed about that. I got to one and someone said, 'Are there any witnesses?' So I said, 'There's a fella on the eighth floor who saw this woman goin' past sayin' "What's the name of that Red Indian?"' A terribly callous thing to say – there's this girl and there isn't a bone in her body not broken – and I said it because I'm tryin' to cheer him up, and I'm feeling pretty sick. This other guy got on top of Haig Heights, tied a washing machine to his leg, threw it over and followed it down. My mate said something like, 'I *think* he's dead' – and I'm cryin' with laughter, and I had to go and sit in the car. Some poor old fella who must've had a terrible life – it turned out he was a right vagrant, everything had gone wrong for him – and there he is, a terrible tragic death, and me laffin'. I'm not laughing *at* him; it's like a nervous thing.

But I've been very fortunate. I've only had one incident involving kids – a terrible incident. A TA where a van goes on its side and was on fire, and there's four kids in the back. I got there when the kids were still screaming, and I couldn't get near the van it was so hot – if I could've, I would've done. And I waited for the screams to stop and the smell of pork and – that, that was pretty bad.

Makes me put a big mushroom round my lad, y'know, knowing all the social evils there are, the ones the average man in the street doesn't know about. My missus shouts at me for that, but I rough-and-tumble and lark about with him and everything, and he loves it – he's one. She says he's going to grow up into a right hard case, but I reckon that by the time he's twenty he's going to need to be a hard case to survive in this world, y'know. You've got a moral responsibility, I think, if you bring a child into this world, to bring him up as best as you can – it's like the nuclear thing. Y'know, you have all sorts of contingency plans, and certain people are rated higher than other people, must be protected at all costs.

But about sudden deaths, one I've gone in and treated as a death – it was in the middle of winter last year, off Scotland Road. I was all ready to start the ball rolling when she moved

218

and I nearly jumped out of me skin! She looked for all the world as if she was dead, but she was just completely dehydrated; there was nothing left of her. And the state of the place was really bad; it was filthy. She'd kept the house as well as she could, but she'd lost all control, couldn't go to the toilet, and it was ending up in the middle of the ruddy bedroom, the kitchen, everywhere – and she was going sort of loopy, didn't realise what was happening. The stench was absolutely unbearable! Neighbours both sides – nobody had taken any notice.

I'm not a great social reformer, but, sitting here now, just think of all the people who could be in sheer distress or dyin' – or, in fact, those having just died – that nobody knows about. I'd hate to think that I was goin' to die on me own. That I was just goin' to be there and clock out – it's a terrible thing, y'know, a wicked thing. That to me is police work. I'd rather do that than go and pinch Joe Soap over there for pinching a packet of fags because – well, there's an end product to it. He'll come again some day, but she won't. She'll be dead tomorrow.

3

Midnight. A new day begins, but the ball is far from over. Church Street teems with high-spirited extras like the sound stage of a musical just before the big downtown number. Seated in his car up at the top end, Inspector South watches the loving couples huddle by, the gangs of lads strut and swagger, the newly permed wives arm in arm and their husbands following two paces behind them. There's zip, there's zing, there's swirl and squeal and laughter. There's a message on the radio to say that a bomb has been planted in a club just around the corner.

The white Escort moves off on a surge of adrenalin into streets jittery with jaywalkers hell bent on becoming the bomb's first victims. Perhaps its only victims, because the chances are the bomb doesn't exist anyway – outside the sick imagination of an anonymous caller. Mindful of this, and reassured by Alpha Control that the public has been cleared from the threatened premises, Inspector South makes his way with-

219

out spectacular haste towards Victoria Street, passing by almost unnoticed.

He has an impeccable Edwardian moustache which, taken in conjunction with his stature, upright bearing and patrician features, evokes a sepia portrait of a Guards officer on the eve of 1914. His manner, tempered by a working-class background, is quietly self-assured without a hint of arrogance, and he speaks with a throwaway bluntness. His interests are very varied. Shortly before coming on duty at 11.30 p.m., he took part in the weekly inter-divisional quiz contest at St Anne Street – *Question:* What is a ryot? *Answer:* A Hindu peasant – and shared in the victory over 'E' Division. If the bomb should turn out to be a real one after all, exploding just as he reaches it, then it will first be remembered he was thirty-five, married to a nurse, and the father of a young family.

Inspector South noses the Escort down a narrow twisting lane to stop short, his path blocked by a horde of punk rockers, many evacuated with drinks still in their hands. The important thing, however, is that they're now all safely out of any danger.

'Oh fok, will yer look at this!' someone yells. '*Another* fokkin' pig! Jesus!'

And the mob turns to boo and blow raspberries as Inspector South gets out, locks his car and is greeted by one of his patrol officers. The youngster, flushed and apparently agitated by the reception afforded his superior, quickly briefs him on the position. With a nod, Inspector South starts across the cobbles.

'Shit face!'

'Oink! Oink!'

'Pig!' 'He's fokkin' deaf and all this one!'

'Wanker!' 'Let us in, will yer?'

'Bastids!' 'Shit face!' 'PIG! PIG! PIIIIIG!'

'Can't yer smile?' chides a giggly grotesque, as she moves aside to allow him through. 'C'mon, let's see yer smile! Smile f' me!'

Inspector South carries straight on into the crush, which parts and then closes up again behind him and his colleague like a devouring amoeba. The mob senses its power. There are jeers from the timid-faced, more mocking obscenities, mis-

220

directed streams of spittle, leers, groans, grimaces, whistles, and the usual outraged demands to know what right the police have to interfere with the freedom of people to enjoy themselves. Every step of the way, Inspector South is eagerly scrutinised for signs of shock or fear perhaps, but remains totally preoccupied.

Nobody inside Eric's really believes in the bomb, either, but a bomb hunt is a bomb hunt, whatever its probable outcome, and nothing suspends disbelief more readily than being in the immediate vicinity of something that might yet go off at any second. Expressions are strained, voices lower than usual, and sweaty palms are wiped in surreptitious gestures. Inspector South seems to command respect very easily, even from strangers. He takes over, establishes that the ground floor is safe, and descends to make a thorough search of the cellar, assisted by members of his group and by some of the club staff.

At the foot of the stairs, doubt begins to fizz like a fuse, and every nook and cranny looks lethal. There is also, however, that fatalistic feeling of committal, familiar to nervous passengers once their airliner has left the ground, which can quieten anxieties in an instant.

Quickly and purposefully, the search party disperses into the smoky haze between the squat columns, while Inspector South concentrates on the more confined spaces such as lavatories. A paper bag hidden in a female cubicle turns out to contain nothing more than a change of conventional clothes – and a possible insight into one young punk rocker's relationship with her parents. It's surprising how many bits and pieces are tucked away here and there, each bringing a breathless moment before being discarded as a wicked waste of precious seconds. Then the tension reaches its apogee and declines. Attitudes alter and false alarms are welcomed as further confirmation of what everyone has believed all along: there is no bomb.

But Inspector South, upon whose judgement alone the lives of around two hundred young people depend, makes one final check. It is impossible ever to be completely certain about a thing like this, of course, so the best anyone can do is arrive at a firmly held opinion based on experience, training and a measure of plain intuition. He decides the call must have been a hoax, shrugs off the management's thanks and leaves to a sardonic cheer from the press of impatient punk rockers outside. Nobody spits this time, but several faces turn to him in gleeful anticipation.

This alerts him. He checks and finds his off-side rear tyre is flat, deflated by a matchstick still stuck in the valve. He gets into the car and reverses out of the lane, thwarting the mob's plan to ridicule his progress through its midst. He parks in Victoria Street, radios for a replacement, and settles back to watch the crowds go by, just as he was doing a while ago back at the top end of Church Street.

I joined the job at nineteen with all sorts of idealistic ideas – I've got more realistic since then. As far as I am concerned, this is the least objectionable way I know of making a living, so I'm not going to get uptight because someone's let my tyre down.

I work on a very slow fuse. If I see somebody committing a traffic offence and he says, 'I wasn't drivin' the car!' – when he blatantly was – I don't argue with him. I just say, 'You're going to be reported' – the hell with you, y'know – tell the magistrates. Or say I bring someone in on suspicion of committing a crime, and I bloody well *know* he's done it but I can't prove it without an admission, I'm not going to beat him. I'll try every method short of that within the law, and if I don't get it out of him I'll let him go. I'll feel exasperated after that, but I won't lose any sleep over it because he'll come again. Some bobbies, y'know, really get the bit between their teeth – the thrill of the chase, catching the thief is all important. I think this is where people go astray, they'll use any method, the planting of evidence and that. In the short term, it's to the benefit of the community, but obviously in the long term it can be highly dangerous, y'know.

Some things really irritate me. What really irritates me is when I'm doing my best for somebody and they don't appreciate it. But, as I say, I work on a very slow fuse. I've seen policemen go into a situation that was basically orderly and turn it into a bloody riot. I can imagine a certain policeman turning what happened to the tyre into a bloody riot, so I think a lot depends on the individual. I find I get more aggravation from the bosses

222

than the bucks, and I can switch off to the bucks because I know that's what I get paid for.

4

Over on the North Sub, the panda driver settles a quarrel between a man and his common-law wife with enough good humour to make them laugh at themselves, offer him a beer and promise not to trouble the police again – or, at least, not before his shift ends at 2 a.m. As he resumes patrol, he reports back to Alpha Control: 'That domestic you sent us to, I've advised the parties.' This provokes an amused snort – or it might have been static.

I dealt with a serious stabbing two years ago over there (*nods at tenement block*), and the ambulance's there, and this guy's lying on top of his bed. Pitch black, no light; the electric had been cut off months ago. There's blood everywhere and he's fully conscious. It turned out later he'd got twenty-eight stab wounds. He was in a *terrible* state – his missus had gone to town on him.

And all he could tell me to do was 'Fok off!' I said, 'I've come to help yer. Now will yer let— ?' 'Fok off out of me house! You've no right to be in me house! Fok off out of me house!' And I kept on tryin' and tryin', and he said, 'Fok off!' So I thought: Well, all right, I'll fok off. I got on the radio and said, 'That job you've just sent me to is a domestic dispute, and I've advised the parties.'

Now, I did the right thing, in my opinion. He didn't want me. P'raps he's got some sexual fetish about bein' stabbed – I don't know! It's like when an ambulance comes and there's a fella bleedin' to death in the street, and the blokes say, 'Come on, get in the ambulance', and he says, 'Don't want to get in the ambulance.' 'But you need hospital attention!' 'Don't want it.' 'OK,' they say, and they leave him. I was quite satisfied with what I'd done: If that's your attitude, mate, good night! I'm wastin' me time here. . . .

They got a second call, and the woman eventually got done for attempted murder or something. Somebody said to me, 'We 'ad a good laff about that,' he said, 'comin' away from there and sayin' it was duff! Bloody hell, you should've done this and

223

done that!' I said, 'You show me in the book where it says what I should do when a householder tells me to leave his house. As far as I'm concerned, an arrestable offence hasn't been committed, because he isn't complaining, and that's it. I'm leaving.'

5

The van arrives in Victoria Street with a spare wheel. While it's being fitted, Inspector South strolls over to assist a taxi driver into whose cab eight revellers are trying to wedge themselves in a frenzy of parsimony and fraternal feeling. A few quiet words amid all the shouting have much the same effect as a soft bark at a cat fight, and those ejected go off in high dudgeon, looking bewildered by their own acquiescence. As they reach the corner, a wide-eyed young probationer appears, clutching the strap of her shoulder-bag and gazing round her at the milling pavements. Perhaps she's also clinging to the rule of thumb passed on by her tutor con: 'It's D-and-I when they fall in the gutter, and D-and-D when they fall in shop windows.' If simple drunkenness were an arrestable offence, she'd not know where to begin. Inspector South passes a couple of minutes in conversation with her until his car is ready, then leaves her to patrol her beat while he responds to a radio message that someone has just attempted to murder two of his men.

I've never met a policeman yet who was ill-mannered enough to turn to a peewee and say, 'You're bloody useless', 'cos I don't think they're useless. In many ways, they can run rings round the male officers, intellectually at any rate. In fact, if you speak to the recruiting officer, he'll tell you that the standard of female recruits is a bloody sight higher than that for the average male recruit. So, if they were six feet tall, they're all potential chief superintendents! What I mean is, if they were male officers they'd be above average in many cases, and a real asset to the force. The only thing now, of course, is that you could go to a fight and put out a call for assistance, and it could be answered by two or three women. Now, they do their best, I've got a great deal of admiration for them, but there's no bloody substitute for muscle in a punch-up.

224

It surprises me that one of them hasn't been well and truly thumped or raped, quite honestly, although I think even the Liverpool buck is chivalrous about not thumping a girl, because we've had relatively few assaulted. He wouldn't think twice about thumping a six-foot policeman – or, more usually, a five-foot-eight weakling of a policeman. And when you get trouble the male officer will probably go charging in, y'know, because he's got his masculinity to think about, whereas a female can stand back and look helpless and call for assistance. If some of the bobbies had any sense, they'd do the same.

Back to Square One. At the top end of Church Street, Inspector South pulls into the kerb, where one of his Days and EPs constables is waiting for him in a state of shock. He is a big man and has to crouch low to speak through the car window.

'It was attempt murder, sir!' he says, the fright still visible in a face normally unexpressive. 'He tried to kill us, this fella!'

'Exactly what happened, Tom?' asks Inspector South, aware that this veteran of police duty in Northern Ireland, with a medal ribbon on his tunic, isn't a man who frightens easily. 'This was in Fleet Street?'

The officer nods, very angry indeed. He and a colleague had been walking along together when, quite without warning or provocation, a motorist had swung out of a parking-space and driven straight at them. They'd jumped aside and hadn't properly recovered from their surprise when the car charged at them a second time. Boxed in at that point, they'd literally had to dive for their lives, and had only just escaped being run down. The motorist had then made off, but they'd managed to get his registration number – from which they now knew he was a local man. And if the officer could catch up with him he'd like to. . . .

Inspector South's response is sympathetic but unemotional. He tells the officer that he'll have the Night CID or someone pick up the offender, and suggests he oughtn't to worry about that side of things. Gradually much of the steam goes out of the situation.

The big constable shrugs. 'I don't mind fighting a buck or a drunk,' he says, smiling wanly, 'but this was taking it a bit far.'

225

The Escort moves off again, turning in the direction of Copperas Hill where Inspector South will arrange for the arrest to be made. He started his police career in Manchester in 1961, and served in the Bermuda police from 1964 until 1967. 'My wife wasn't very happy there. I was completely indifferent really; if she'd said, "I want to stay here", it would have suited me. But as it happens I probably did better coming back.' It's his belief he benefited from the huge gap left by the post-war intake who are now retiring. 'In the last two years there has been a tremendous amount of promotion; you pass your exam and you get promoted – there's no doubt about it. I've got sixteen years' service in, but possibly somebody of my ability might not have made inspector for twenty years before. I've got eight sergeants on my group now, at least four of them, I think, with only five or six years in – y'know, they're barely experienced constables. But I suspect in five years' time you'll be waiting for dead men's shoes again.' Characteristically, perhaps, his regard for the police service is without sentiment.

I don't believe in the Golden Bobby Age. That it's a myth is a theory of mine, but I think I could substantiate it to a certain extent. I've spoken to old policemen who've told me that if anybody came into the police station to complain about a policeman he was looked at as if he'd gone mad. 'How dare you complain about a police officer! Get out – or I'll lock you up!' Y'know, hence fewer complaints. And, again, before the war people knew less about their rights and probably complained less. I've read this book, *Trenchard, Man of Vision*, which is his biography, and he was put in to sort the Metropolitan Police out before the war because the CID was bent, but that was all hushed up. Robert Mark sorted out the Metropolitan CID recently and that was blown up in the papers. If it's not publicised, nobody knows about it and then it's not a problem, is it? I don't think police are any worse now – in fact, I think they're better educated, better motivated, and I doubt if they're any more brutal. I don't think we've got a brutal police force really anyway. The thing is now when a policeman does get out of line he's more likely to get caught; and if he is caught it comes to notice, and if it comes to notice it tends to make things look worse than they are.

226

6

'They get excited about prisoners for terrorism, murder, this, that and the other,' says the inspector on Nights this week at the Main Bridewell, 'but it's the simple drunk that worries me. He's the one who's going to die, because as well as being drunk he's got something else wrong with him.'

The ground-floor corridor booms with the steady assaults of the 'kickers' against doors a fist thick, and there are groans and curses from the 'regulars' trying to get a bit of sleep. The inspector stops at the door of a safety cell.

'I won't accept unconscious drunks under any circumstances,' he says sternly. 'They'll go to hospital and I'll take them back when the doctor has said, "He's not sick; he's drunk." But you can't tell. The best doctor in the world can't really say with any certainty, until he's kept him under observation for a period and the alcohol's worn away. So you put them in a safety cell and keep checking them.' He looks through the judas hole. 'You expect a drunk to start surfacing after about three or four hours. There was one showing no improvement, and he was whizzed to the hospital; the poor devil died there two or three days later of a pulmonary embolism, I think it was. There was alcohol as well, so you get the package deal, you see – a combination of both.'

The inspector turns away from the door. 'Having said that, we have the meths drinker, the after-shave drinker, the mixture-of-milk-and-surgical-spirits drinker, and once they go under – like that one – they're dead to the world. You can get to six, seven, eight hours, and you've still got this fella in this terrible bloody state. Well, it can frighten you. It frightened me when I came here! How we escape ever having deaths in these cells I'll never know. . . .' He unlocks the door of the next safety cell along and goes in, breathing through his mouth.

The cell is about seven feet wide and twelve feet deep. The walls are painted black to about waist-height, and there is a lavatory pedestal behind a low wooden 'modesty board' in the far right-hand corner. A feeble bulb burns inside a robust fixture in the barrel-vaulted ceiling, surrounded by match-

227

soot graffiti, and above the prisoner's alarm push beside the door frame someone has printed, 'If you want cunt, then press bell and one will appear.' Three things make this a safety cell as distinct from an ordinary Main Bridewell cell, which is otherwise identical. There's unbreakable plastic in its small window. There's a large metal ring set into the wall, to which uncontrollably violent prisoners can be manacled. And finally, instead of the cell having sleeping-benches ranged down either side, the stone-flag floor is largely taken up by a sloping platform raised to about eight inches at one end.

A prisoner is lying semi-comatose on it with his head at the lower end, the idea being that when he vomits his spew will drain away and he won't choke to death on it. Judging by the puddles on the floor, and the condition of his matted clothing and rice-sticky face, his chances of anything like that happening have already been reduced considerably. Another virtue of the platform is that it's impossible for the prisoner to fall off it and injure himself.

'All right, lad?' asks the inspector, giving him a shake.

'Grundspleddy. . . .'

Satisfied by some sign of life being present, the inspector withdraws. 'It's a nonsense,' he grunts, turning the lock. 'I'd like to see drunk-and-incapable taken right out of the criminal justice system.'

The inspector is dark, bespectacled, 6 feet 3 inches tall, and tolerant yet very firm in manner. He isn't sure why he joined the police. His grandfather lost his job in the 1919 police strike in Liverpool, and never ceased lamenting the fact. But it was probably the publicity which went with the launching of the city's cadet scheme that acted as a catalyst for a grammar-school boy whose chances of going to university were slim because of his parents' circumstances. He began his probation in 'A' Division in 1954, when Rose Hill still stood in the shadow of three-storey artisans' dwellings, and moved to the Traffic Department about four years later. He came to the Main Bridewell after six years as a uniformed inspector in a division, liked it and said he'd be happy to stay on when the

228

usual twelve-month posting was over. That was four years ago. Since then he has been made a member of the executive committee of the Merseyside Council on Alcoholism.

Drunkenness is one of the main elements in the Main Bridewell, and I hadn't been here very long before I started thinking that D-and-I was futile. The revolving door, as it's referred to in other circles: the street, the police station, and then back again. So it goes on ad infinitum.

They're arrested for their own safety and they go to court. The court recognises the futility of it by sentencing them to one day – which effectively means they'll sit at the back until it's finished. Or the court will levy a five-pound fine, knowing they'll never pay it. When they've totted up a little bit, there's a warrant and they'll go inside for three or four weeks, maybe longer. They come out new men, because they've been on a solid diet and have been cleaned up and all the rest of it, and then the cycle starts all over again.

If you split off these drunks, the Skid Row types, what are you left with?

Well, with what I call the one-off drunk. The student who gets his exams off his back and goes out on a one-night blinder. Or the young man, married, first child comes along, goes out and wets the baby's head, gets stoned out of his mind, and finishes up in here, locked up for D-and-I. Because he's a one-off, he doesn't need the deterrent of going to court and being fined. The fact it's so strange to him – going through this place – and his family and friends probably knowing about it, that's enough to stop him coming back again. What the hell do you want to fine him for?

And you get the intermediates, who come in a few times a year. Borderline, if not actual, alcoholics who are perhaps having treatment through AA, and they'll slip now and again. Y'know, I've seen a fellow in here *cryin'* because he'd slipped – and court ain't going to help him. It's going to pile the agony on.

D-and-Ds are a different matter, because you've got Joe Public involved here. Invariably someone outside has been upset or somebody has been threatened with a fight or a car's been kicked. They tend to be young men with a whiff of the barmaid's apron, and they go over the top and just make a bloody nuisance of themselves. I think that offence should stay under the system because there is some deterrent. (*Shrugs and*

229

smiles) Although it seems to me that once someone comes in for D-and-D they'll come again. It's a pattern they seem to follow. Y'know, they've not had a good night out unless they've been involved in a punch-up with their mates, a screamin' match with their wives or girl friends – or they'll round on the bobby when he comes along. Violent crime in this city is drink-related – I think you'll find drunkenness behind most violent crimes from what I see in here; the fights in the clubs and pubs and even with football hooliganism to some extent, you'll find the worst offenders have been drinking.

In any case, the D-and-Ds tend not to be the Skid Rows, the regulars. They're always D-and-Is. They drink until they collapse and that's the end of it – they haven't got a fight left in 'em! I'm simply concerned with D-and-Is; I think it's high time something should be done about them.

The legislation exists now for detoxification centres,* whereby the police have the facility to take them straight there. Obviously the idea is to recover these people from alcoholism, but that's Cloud Cuckoo Land – they'd be lucky if three out of a hundred respond and reform. And it's another revolving door: it'll be the street, the detox, the street again. But at least it saves this pretence of going through court, and they'll be able to stay there for three days. They'll clean them up, give them decent clothing, get them on the start of a reasonable diet.

I did some reports on D-and-I – the first before talk of the detox centre came up – and there was general agreement. Oh, there were some hang-ups, particularly [with regard to] when we make an arrest, we've got to be prepared to take it to court. Taking them straight to the detox makes the police judge and jury, you see, but I had the reservation all the way through that people should be told on release, should they dispute the need for their arrest, they can take it to court. I don't really think people with any intelligence would suggest the police were getting up to any skulduggery here; they'd accept we were conscious of the problem and trying to do something about it. Organisations concerned with alcoholism tend not to be involved with the derelict because they recognise the obvious; he doesn't want to reform, and the chances of his reforming are so remote you can almost forget them. So this means there's no one left for the Skid Row type of alcoholic except us, the fuzz.

*Nothing had been done locally because of 'a shortage of funds'.

We're the only ones who pick these people up. For a young bobby, it's his introduction to the police service. He walks down Dale Street and he'll find one in the gutter. So he arrests him for his own safety – at the risk of being vomited on, spat on, urinated on, they're frequently jumping with fleas – and brings him in here.

It *is* a nonsense in normal terms. But in the derelicts' terms, equated with what they have, a lot of them come to regard this place as home – y'know, in a very extreme sense: it's where they go when there's nowhere else to go. We provide them with shelter overnight in a warm dry room, and something to eat in the morning – beans on toast, cuppa tea – which is better than they'll get outside, left to their own devices. We strike up a rapport with them, a sort of working relationship; we know them all, we laff and joke with them. We recognise they've got a problem and there's nothing going to change it, so we don't sort of say, 'This isn't good enough! What's the big idea?' We just accept them for what they are, and they respond to that. They never fall out with us, the regular drunks.

7

'Customers, boss!' the bridewell patrol announces, coming through into the small charge office at Copperas Hill from the enquiries counter. 'Dave and Ian in Mike Thirteen – got a sudden death to catch up on.'

'Bloody hell. . . . The key? Be with yer in a moment.'

It had to be a bridewell sergeant, they say, who wrote SELF-DESTRUCT in large letters under the general alarm button just across the passage. He or she is responsible not only for the bridewell itself, but also for the security of the entire building, its maintenance, cleanliness, equipment and supplies, right down to the paper-clips. To say nothing of the Telex room, the petty cash (bus fares and dog food, mainly), the armoury if there is one, and keeping a check on who is in the station at any given moment. And now, just as the last prisoner has been fingerprinted and put back in his cell until he behaves himself, the van is creaking to a halt outside again.

'Be with yer in a moment,' the bridewell patrol tells the crew of Mike Thirteen, collecting up the personal radios of the Days and EPs section that has just come off duty. 'This sudden death – what is it?'

8

The shift has had its moments. 'But generally you can gauge 'em, gauge whether they're going to fight or not,' says the Days and EPs constable who never thinks of 'them', likes talking to old ladies and once saw a councillor give two's-up to a Tory poster. 'The fella that stands like *that* – fists clenched, shoulders up – he's going to try and threaten and scare you by his actions. The fellow who's standing arms down, relaxed, he's the one to watch. There are the exceptions.' He shrugs an indifference and continues up the last flight of stairs, carrying a pint of milk in a carton.

About a dozen officers live on the top floor of St Anne Street divisional headquarters, cut off by a huge PRIVATE notice on the canteen landing. 'You never get troubled up here – y'know, people knocking, saying, "What's all this about?" If you can stand livin' so close to the job, it's reasonable accommodation. Basically a bedsitter, and the great advantage is the heating is paid for – no rent to pay, either, but of course you don't get the usual rent allowance.' The sort of place where, suddenly isolated from the hurly-burly after nine hours on a beat in the city centre, it's easy to feel somewhat at a loose end at this time of the morning.

I suppose I read a lot – too much for me own good! Anything going about; the book-swapping club in the residential block is phenomenal. I've even read Karl Marx – it was the most dull book I've ever read! It taught me nothin'. Mind you, I thought if I looked at it in a different light, but it was . . . orgh! Fantastic, y'know, Communism; it's a great thing. It is! In its pure form obviously, and the other thing it doesn't take account of is humanity's greed. (*Smiles*) Me dad's Lithuanian; possibly that's why I 'hate' Communists! I don't know. He was at Hamburg

232

University when the Russians marched into Lithuania. Eleven of the family were shot – can't say 'were shot'; *disappeared*, a much better word! – and he decided to join the German Army, which was recruiting, of course, at the time. Spent about four years on the Russian Front, was wounded and spent the rest of the war in hospital. Being Lithuanian, he was given the choice of where to go; came to Britain, met me mother and married her. I'm the black sheep of the family. I stayed at school until I was fifteen. Me eldest sister speaks about ten languages, me sister below me speaks about five, and me youngest sister – she's eleven, embarrasses me! – is fluent in German and French; my father can speak about seven or eight languages; me mother four or five. I'm the only one who can't speak more than English – and Lancashire, of course. We lived in a small town six miles south of Wigan. God knows what would happen if they had a murder or something like that there, y'know; a small fight in the streets makes headlines for weeks. When I joined the force; it made the local papers! I thought: Bloody hell. . . .

Tunic and boots off, he puts his feet up and relaxes with a hot drink and a paperback copy of *The Choirboys*, 'A' Division's 'book of the moment'. While four floors below a resentful suspect – released on bail – finds himself a half-brick and puts it through the traffic wardens' window.

9

The spare mortuary key, which has to be fetched from Copperas Hill after hours, has a small wooden coffin for a tag, complete in its painstaking detail down to a blank nameplate and minute handles. Slipped into an obscure door in an unlit cul-de-sac at the side of the Liverpool Royal Infirmary, it admits the young driver of Mike Thirteen and his section sergeant to a chill hallway, where not a second is lost in finding the light switch.

There's an enquiries office to the left, a waiting-room to the right, and ahead is a pair of doors marked *No Admittance*. They open into a deeper chill.

Once again the light switch is found quickly. The body lies

233

under a crumpled sheet on a trolley to the right, directly beneath a curtained window through which the bereaved can come to view the departed. In the blank wall opposite this window is the small dreary room's only fitting: a nail upon which can be suspended whatever form of religious symbol is appropriate to such an occasion.

Pulling on disposable plastic gloves, the officers glance through the next doorway into a dim cement-floored area, where a row of mortuary trolleys, each with its drip-bucket, has been left ready for the morning's post-mortems.

The sergeant draws the sheet back.

Mouth agape, dentures crooked, one green eye slightly open, the dead woman was in her late sixties, old enough to have been their grandmother. She died in a green dress, and her pink bloomers are still around her ankles, just as she was found in the lavatory in her flat. A lot of people die in the lavatory, they've learned; it's something to do with the bowels giving way before the rest does. It looks a natural death, even a peaceful one, but as she hadn't seen her doctor within the previous fourteen days the sudden-death procedure must be followed.

Grim-faced and remote, they begin stripping the body, finding the fastenings sometimes difficult to locate and undo, and then make sure there is no jewellery, other than the worn wedding-ring, to be removed for safe-keeping. So far their eyes would seem to have seen nothing, but now they must look carefully for any signs of possible injury. They pause, caps tipped back, well wrapped up against the cold, robust and vital, presenting a decided contrast to the inert flesh lying naked and past caring before them. The skin is the colour of mild cheese, the form ungainly rather than ugly, and if there is a smell, as there must be, then it is lost in the mortuary's own odour, disagreeable but hardly offensive.

For a dead thing, however, it is unpleasantly warm to the touch still. There are few wrinkles except at the extremities. There are no marks on the front. They roll it on its left side and hurriedly examine the back. No post-mortem lividity; it's too soon for that. Awkwardly, trying to be gentle with jointed weights that pivot and flop, they raise the body into a sitting

234

position, ignoring the soft unladylike belch. The head lolls forward, pressing a cheek against the quick rise and fall of the constable's chest, while the sergeant ruffles the hair at the nape of the neck, checking for hidden wounds or bruises. Just some dandruff.

It's over, the sheet goes back, the lights are switched off, and the lock turns, all in hasty succession. 'Paradise Street!' blurts the radio, breaking the silence outside that place of the dead. 'Two men fighting, using bottles – female informant.'

10

I've only done one informing of a sudden death. They weren't closely related, so it wasn't traumatic – but it was difficult to put over! They were Chinese.

Time for second refreshments south of the sub-dividing line. Several probationers in 'A' Division have parents in the Merseyside Police, including this tall personable young recruit with a reputation as a good footballer, whose father is a senior officer. He has been serving for almost a year now.

I used to find at first, when I first started on the job, that I'd spend more time bloody lookin' at meself in shop windows, to see if I looked the thing in the big hat, than I did lookin' round, y'know! I don't know whether you notice it yourself, but an awful lot of people tell me I've changed. I think it's definitely toughened me up a bit. I mean, me dad is a bit of a tough guy like, and the things you have to do as a policeman didn't particularly bother him, but me mother thought: Errrr . . . our Philip won't be able to do it, y'know. She saw me actually the other Friday – the first time ever in uniform.

She was walking in town with me dad, and I was on the third section for the day. I walked round with the two of them for a while, and she was made up – y'know, to see her little boy in his uniform! (*Smiles broadly*) I left 'em. Then there was a report of four drunks throwing bottles at each other by the Playhouse in Williamson's Square, and I coughed to that and went down. As it happens, there was a fruit-barrow there and me mum and me dad were there – about fifteen yards away, y'know. Two fellas

235

and a young fella, about twenty-eight, throwing bottles at another old fella and a woman, all drunks. I recognised one of the fellas as a lad locked up last week – I'd escorted him down to the Main, y'know, because he was a bit of a fighter.

So straight off I said to him, 'I know you; you've been locked up. You either behave yourself, or I'll lock yer up again.' They said, 'OK, officer, we'll take a walk, y'know' – and they finished off the bottles of cider, threw them in the bin and went off. And me mother afterwards said, 'Fancy having to deal with that type of people!' Apparently, the old barrow woman had been saying, 'Oh, those drunks are always causin' trouble. I feel sorry for those young bobbies' – and me mother was sayin', 'Oh, that's my son over there!' I was mad with her, y'know. (*Laughs*) Fancy makin' a show of yourself like that! But she was made up.

These people are often called 'the worst our society can offer', but I think some of them are great, y'know. The term everyone uses is 'a load of bucks' but, even so, some of them are good bucks – you can befriend some of them, people you've locked up. Like one lad came over and bought us a drink. Or you see them around and it's all 'Hello, hello, hello', y'know! I think every lock-up is an experience; I really enjoy it. And I love to be down in the city centre when it's absolutely thronging with people. Sometimes we'll walk down there just to look at the women – Saturdays can be fantastic, women everywhere! – and sometimes you'll talk to the characters you meet, the drunks and the vagrants. That's tremendous, y'know! There's the people on your beat – one night porter, he'll have you in the hotel for hours and hours if you'll let him, just so he can talk to yer. He just loves people and will talk about anything. Oh, there's loads of characters you meet. (*Laughs*) When I was a civilian, and obviously I was younger then, I used to regard town as somewhere to do your shopping and get out. I thought it was mad, y'know! I remember me dad saying 'As soon as you get out of that club, jump in a taxi and come home. We don't want any bobby snatching you off the streets!'

Oh, I enjoy talking and mixing with people. There are cons who don't, but I wouldn't put that at much higher than five per cent – I'm talking about my section. There's a bit of animosity on the other side; they think of everybody as gobshites, y'know. I'd hate to go and work on the North; perhaps that's the reason. I don't know. Perhaps it's a sort of defence mechanism: treat everybody that way till you know otherwise, y'know! I suppose

236

it's purely personal, isn't it? I don't think I just dive at anybody. (*Laughs*) It can depend on the mood I'm in!

And you start noticing an awful lot of things. This lad, my tutor con, used to annoy me. He was a brilliant bobby – in the OSD now – and he used to lock up regularly. We'd be going along and I used to think he was really rude, because he'd break off when you were talking to him, all of a sudden you'd realise he wasn't interested in you. What it was, he'd either seen something or was listening to an observation request over the radio. He was lookin' all the while, he was listenin' and doing his job, while I was sort of gaily walking along the streets, chattin' away, y'know.

You find you become a bit of a cynic in this job. I mean, I was thinking this tonight coming to work, driving down Great Homer Street. There was this car on the footpath by some shops, so I slowed down to see if I could hear an alarm bell ringing or something – y'know, whether they'd used this car to screw a shop! There was nothing in it, but if I hadn't been in this job I'd not have noticed that.

At first, when I joined the job, I was not in any way colour prejudiced. But I do find I resent black people in certain ways now, because I think an awful lot of them go round with a chip on their shoulder, y'know. I'm not in the slightest surprised there are so few on the job. I was up in Liverpool 8 the other month, and on one of the hoardings it's sprayed on: 'Liverpool police are racist.' This is the attitude they've got. Every time you have cause to have any contact with them at all, they just don't want to know yer – they're hostile to yer.

I blame the background an awful lot of the time. I've got a grandmother who lives in Bootle, and she thinks it isn't a particularly nice area. I say to her, 'You don't know where it is!' because she can go out and perhaps even leave the back door open and do her shoppin'. I try to impress on her that in Myrtle Gardens you just cannot go out of those flats unless one of the family is left in. You've only got to be out half an hour and some of these bucks'll notice it, and the bloody furniture's out – three-piece suite, telly, the lot! Everything. That's how bad it is up there.

And they're living that closely I think it would take an awfully demanding parent to make sure their child wasn't going round smashin' windows and that. When you walk up there and see some of the black kids, knee high, they don't stand a chance,

237

y'know. I've been stoned by kids this high! Three, four years of age, and they're all shoutin' 'Pig! Pig! Pig!' (*Shrugs*) OK, you can make a fool of yourself and chase after them, get hold of them and say you'll take them to their mother or somethin' like that but, meself, I don't bother. Sometimes they're great. Sometimes I've walked up there and you've got little kids wantin' to hold your hand – and you've got kids hangin' all over you! (*Laughs*) That's great.

People say to you, 'Where do you work?' And you say, 'City centre.' 'Hoooo, you must be a hero!' And you've just got to say to them, 'It's not really like that; it's not really that bad.' I think, in all, I've been in three or four situations when my heart's started to pump, when the adrenalin starts goin'; y'know, something really exciting. There's a lot of scope in this job; I'd like to try a few things. I definitely don't want to be a con walkin' the streets for the rest of me life.

II

Black is the night, blacker the Mersey. Distantly, in the deepest shadows of the Pier Head, a wraithlike figure moves eagerly forward. Round behind the Berni Inn, toes curled on the brink of existence, she stares down into the wet lapping darkness. The station keeper makes his approach nonchalantly.

He strolls up and says, in a butter-rich Irish brogue, 'Hey, girl, what're you doing here?'

'The water's talkin' to me, officer.'

'Oh aye? What's it sayin'?'

She looks down again, turning her head slightly, listening. 'Jump in . . . ,' she echoes tenderly. 'Jump in, luv. . . .'

'It's too bloody cold in there, girl.'

He leads her back to the tiny enquiry office, closing its glass door behind them.

She tries to walk through it.

'Sit down, luv, and tell us yer name.'

She can't or won't. She can't or won't give her home address, either. 'What am I doin' here?' she asks vaguely.

'I'm just tryin' to help you, luv.'

238

'Don't need help. The water's me friend. He's talkin' to me. . . .'

'I know but—'

'I'm goin' to me friend. . . .'

She bumps into the glass door again.

While transport is on its way, she bumps into the glass door repeatedly. 'She's not been boozin',' the station keeper remarks to a couple of passing colleagues. 'She's either on drugs or some other bloody disease.' Up the girl gets again.

'Listen, luv, *just sit down*, take it easy.'

She sits. He stands over her, arms akimbo.

'I haven't insulted you, have I?'

'No.'

'I haven't done anything wrong?'

'No.'

'But you see, luv, if you jump in the water, I'll have to go in after – and it's too bloody cold for me.'

'Oh, I see,' she says, looking up at him. 'All right, then.'

12

With his personal radio almost silent now on the desk beside him, Inspector South is reasonably content as he works his way through a basket of reports. The bomb-scare club closed its doors without further incident, and an arrest has been made in connection with the affair in Fleet Street.

Guy's been charged with attempt to do grievous bodily harm. That to my mind is all that needs to happen. (*Shrugs*) If that bobby had caught up with him within a short space of time, it would not have been inexcusable – in my opinion – for that bobby to thump him one, considering the fright he's been put to. It could have been loss of life, y'know! And for what? The fella probably had a few drinks. But, of course, having thumped him, the bobby has committed a criminal offence and, no matter what happened to the driver, the bobby would lose his job, y'know.

Gratuitous violence is just non-existent. When I say that, I mean completely and utterly unprovoked violence. Policemen

239

don't just say, 'Well, we'll have him tonight' – and go and beat hell out of him for laffs. Or, when there are prisoners in the cells, go in and kick somebody around for a bit of a giggle, y'know. Most of the violence that has occurred has been the result of action from outside. Completely inexcusable, obviously, but nevertheless provoked.

If a male officer often gets assaulted, I expect it of him because he's either very impetuous or a bolshy sod who upsets people readily because he's not very diplomatic. It's always been the case. I've seen some really arrogant buggers – there's not a lot of them, but it doesn't take a lot, does it? Y'know, if you've got a couple of arrogant sods on your division, they can sow more harm and cause more trouble than can be rectified by all the good the rest do. It's too easy to say you should weed the fellas out like that. He may well have been weeded out, but the damage is done, isn't it?

No, I've been a police officer for sixteen years and I've never been assaulted. There are two reasons for that. One is luck, and the other one is I don't fly off the handle before I jump in. I've never made a habit of moving in where angels fear to tread. I don't think it's cowardice; I've never run away from a job yet.

But I'll radio in and say, 'I'm going to talk to a crowd of yobs who look as if they're going to cause trouble. Could I have a back-up?' And if you get a back-up you can deal with a situation. You get so many male officers who will go in and stir things up: 'Come on, get off home!' 'Who're yer talkin' to, pal?' Bang. Another assaulted police officer. I always give people the benefit of the doubt, and speak to them properly first. Well, if that doesn't work, then it's anybody's guess. And I think that's another reason why female officers haven't been assaulted so readily: they're not so stroppy and aggressive. And, even when they are aggressive, it's perhaps more difficult to take seriously when you're being bollocked by a five-foot-four girl, isn't it? (*Smiles, and puts his pipe down.*)

13

The three police officers loom large over the small labourer standing with his back to them in a quiet corner of the Main Bridewell.

240

'You've only got five minutes, son,' warns the inspector.

The labourer nods, and tries again to urinate into the jug he holds in front of him. About ninety minutes ago, he rode up to a red light on his motorcycle, stopped, put his feet down and, too drunk to stand, fell over. Having failed to provide a blood specimen – he has a horror of needles – his alternative was to supply two urine specimens within an hour, the first of which is disregarded. That hour is nearly up, and the tension in the fingerprinting-room is contagious.

'Four minutes. . . .'

The arresting officer fidgets with the sterile sample-bottle. 'What's the pill in the bottom for ?' he asks.

'A poisonous preservative,' explains the inspector.

'To discourage 'em from destroyin' the evidence, y'see,' quips one of the bridewell patrols. 'Any luck, lad ?'

The labourer shakes his head. His unsteadiness would indicate that the whole procedure is somewhat academic, but it's his right to be given a sporting chance of survival.

'Three minutes,' says the inspector. 'Do you want the tap on ? Will it help you ?' He turns on the tap at the nearest sink.

Nothing happens. The tap at the other sink is turned on. A pair of feet shuffle.

'Two minutes. . . .'

They try whistling. A chorus of soft suggestive trills that ends in laughter.

'Don't leave it too long,' says the inspector, 'or we'll all want one!' He switches the taps off.

Smiles fade.

The inspector checks his watch. 'Try and relax, young man,' he urges. 'You'll block everything else if you start straining! I'll give you another half-minute. . . .'

Boom, boom, boom, someone's kicking their cell door.

'Sorry,' mumbles the labourer, holding out the empty jug – and, in effect, surrendering his driving licence. 'Don't know why.'

'You're putting your licence on the line because you're afraid of a bloody needle! If you like, the doctor's still here. . . .'

The labourer nods; the inspector looks pleased with him.

241

Back to the medical room, when the senior police surgeon receives the necessary consent, and applies the black cuff of a sphygmomanometer to the upper arm. He pumps the cuff tight, watches the veins engorge, makes a check with his stethoscope, and takes up a syringe.

'No!' gasps the labourer. 'I can't! I'm sorry, but I can't!' He looks up at the inspector. 'I can't take needles. I'm sorry.'

'It's your problem, lad. Don't apologise to me!' retorts the inspector. 'Come, you can have your ciggies now.'

The senior police surgeon puts away his sphygmomanometer. 'I use this because it's not like a hospital where a doctor can go along and try six times. You can't muck about; you've got to get it the first time. A driver could say, "I've offered you blood and, if you can't get it the first or second time, that's your hard luck, mate!" – and you can't do much about it.' Urine samples are no concern of his, being a police responsibility, and anyway there the boot is, so to speak, on the other foot.

Although he has a number of deputies, the senior police surgeon chooses to do much of the work himself. 'I see well over a thousand cases a year, which is four times the average for Great Britain. It's like a fireman's job: you can be doing nothing, then get five, six, seven jobs at once. I couldn't do it every night – it would kill me off!' His evening began with a suspicious death.

A body was brought into Walton Hospital with a hole in his head, and the doctor refused to do anything further about it before calling the police. I went along and I was satisfied he died of natural causes – subject to post-mortem, of course. But it's important that we make decisions *now*, rather than get hundreds of men out on a possible murder hunt. I'm sort of the hinge of a whole force that could be set in motion. I don't do p.m.'s – I'm not qualified to do them, because that is another field altogether. The forensic pathologist may meet me at the scene, we'll discuss evidence on equal terms, and then he will go off and do the post-mortem, and I'll carry on with all the suspects as well.

The living fascinate him as much as the dead, which is why he prefers to be a police surgeon. He jumped at the chance to

242

become one half a lifetime ago – he's fifty-six now. 'I was in the Army, and I found when I came out that I missed the comradeship. It's not like television, y'know, where one man does the whole lot! It's one big family. This is teamwork. More often than not, the police are with me and help me by picking out items that I don't see. We're all working in the dark, and everyone's helping each other.'

He delights in being helpful. He has designed and had printed a simple pro forma that guides arresting officers almost effortlessly through the obscure pitfalls of the 'drunk driver' procedure. He assists understanding among police officers and juries alike by never using a word like 'contusion' when 'bruise' will do. 'I use baby language! In fact, if you read my reports, you'd think I didn't know medicine at all – no jargon!' And he has introduced a printed diagram of the human form that not only helps juries to grasp easily the distribution of injuries marked on it, but is also admissible as evidence, which often spares him the trouble of appearing in court personally. An outline representing the inspector on Nights is in his jacket pocket at this moment, showing where a female prisoner kicked the officer on the leg and bit him on the forearm. 'I gave him an injection of long-acting penicillin in case of any transmitted infection from the mouth – I was thinking of VD, to be quite honest with you.' And, perhaps because his civilian status offers him no immunity to the hazards of police work, he also tends to say 'we' a lot.

We had a murder job only last week, and I dealt with the husband. Now, he was a psychopath and, although he was quite quiet while I was dealing with him, I was very wary of him. It wouldn't take much for him to pick up something and stick it in me. I was frightened of him, but I had people around me. They do it in a second; it can be very dangerous. I've been assaulted several times. In fact, very often I have to make an opinion without touching them, and there you need great experience. You don't dare examine them – you'd get murdered! (*Laughs*) And I have to make sure in my own mind. Are they ill? Are they just drunk? I'm not just a police surgeon, y'see; prisoners are also patients, let's not kid ourselves. The GP side of it keeps me balanced; I think it's a good thing. I examine ordinary people,

243

everyday people, the children, the mothers, the husbands; having been a GP for thirty-four years, I've seen everything, delivered babies at home and so on. I think that gives you a good background, and it also helps with insight into some of these crimes, especially domestic disturbances – and psychiatric cases. We see an awful lot of psychiatric cases in criminal work, and I can't say they're criminals half the time – they don't know what they're doing. But what else can we do with them? They're the psychopathic types – the mental hospitals don't want them.

He chuckles as he puts away the last of his things, closing the cupboard door which has a picture of his wife pasted behind it. 'When I've had a whole night of forensic like this, and I'm really getting tired, I get very humorous, cracking jokes and everything, teasing people. This prisoner came in and I was deciding which arm to take blood from. He said to me, "Are you having trouble, doctor?" "No, there's no problem," I said. "I'm just looking to see which arm. If I have any problem, I'll cut your throat if necessary." He just collapsed on the floor – and I got the fright of my life!'

14

There's a limit to the number of times anyone can wander round the bridewell at St Anne Street at four o'clock in the morning, seeking some diversion other than the notice which growls, *Do NOT put stray dogs in the kennels used for police dogs.* The bridewell patrol gathers up four paperbacks left lying about, and retires into the easy chair against the yard wall. *Fahrenheit 451*, *The Eagle Has Landed*, *The Erection Set*, *Winged Escort* – he chooses the Douglas Reeman. A minute later he tosses it aside, yawns, and nods to two colleagues who have come drifting in to get some reports done. One sticks his head into the wireless room and is informed, by way of a grunt, that the division is as dead as a doornail. The other asks whether there might be a pot of tea brewing. The bridewell sergeant stares at the calendar and wonders aloud when his next 'staff appraisal' is due. This annual ordeal in the life of

244

every police officer, regardless of rank, seldom fails to get a conversation going.

'Don't fancy it – y'know, me next one,' says the bridewell patrol, who has yet to adjust to working under the eye of his superiors.

An older constable shrugs. 'I've a thing, y'know, about bosses,' he volunteers, 'about how to treat 'em.'

'Yuh?'

'Aye, my theory is that if a boss comes in and you say, "All correct, suh!" and he says, "What's doin'?" and you say, "Very quiet, sir" – then he'll say, "What's that cup doing there? Look! There's *another* cup there! Look at that! This place is. . . . Sergeant? Will you have a word?" And that's when yer drop in the shit. But, if when a boss comes in, and you say, "All correct, suh!" and he says, "What's happenin'?" and you say, "Oh Christ, sir, I'm glad yer here! I'm goin' fokkin' mad!" – then he's off, gone, doesn't want to know!'

Laughter, and a grunt from the wireless room; the radio operator is missing half the fun, not being able to see the deadpan delivery.

'We had this superintendent, a good fella,' murmurs the poker-faced constable, seating himself on a corner of the sergeant's desk. 'He was pissed.'

Joyous snorts and sniggers.

'He'd been to this do, y'see, and he was waitin' for this mate of 'is to come and drive 'im home. Then who does he sort of catch sight of, just on me way out? "How long", he said, "since yer last appraisal?" "Well, sir. . . ." "Come along," he said. "This won't take a minute!" So I'm up in his office and he's sittin' behind his desk, and he said, "Hey, lad," he says, "you haven't signed it!" "But there's no line to say where to sign it, sir, and I haven't—" "Just sign it," he said. "Go on! Yer wastin' me time 'ere!" His mate hadn't come yet, yer see.'

Grins widen.

' "Anyway," he said, "you've had a good report off your inspector. There's last year's – and here's this year's. Anythin' you want to discuss?"

245

' "There is really," I said. "I suppose you know in me off-duty periods I am a medium ? A spiritual medium ?" '

The finely conveyed shudder provokes hoots of delight.

'So he said, "Well, no. . . . I didn't know that," he said.

' "Yes," I said, "and I've wanted to discuss somethin' with you for some time. We have a group of mediums who—"

' "Actually," he said, "I don't want to have anything to do with that."

' "Well," I said, "it's just", I said, "about a month ago at one of our sessions, I went into a deep trance," I said. "I Went Over. I Went Over Onto The Other Plane, and—"

' "No," he said, "I don't even like talkin' about it! When I was a lad", he said, "I used to live in the Dingle, and me mother and me granny", he said, "used to go to 'em. I was always *terrified*," he said.

'So I knew—' The hilarity has to die down first. 'So I knew he had a soft spot, y'see. He was another fella who 'ated ghosts – it's surprisin' the fellas, y'know, who are terrified of ghosts. So I said, "Well, I have—"

' "Oh, no no no!" he said, and he puts up his arms like this, sort of shieldin' himself. "I don't know why, lad," he said. "I don't want to talk about it!"

'I said, "But I have this message," I said, "and I've got to give it to yer."

' "No !" he said. "No, I'd rather, er. . . ."

' "You see, I saw you, sir," I said, "in Another Life. You have always been a leader of men. I saw you", I said, "at the head of a Roman legion."

'He looked up a bit then, y'know. And he said, "Did yer ?"

' "Oh yes," I said. "You had one of these helmets on – with all the stuff going down the back – and you had yer breast-plates, yer short leather skirt – you know how they were designed – and yer short sword in yer hand. It was you," I said, "there was no mistaking. There are some of us", I said, "that are just here to serve," I said, "and there are others of us who are leaders of men. I would like you," I said, "if you could spare the time, to come and join our group one Sunday evenin'," I said. "You could sit in, and perhaps together we can Go Through The Ether and—"

246

' "Ah, no!" he said.

'And he got real horrified! He kept sayin' "Me mother and me granny used to go to that when I was a kid" – and he kept on about the Dingle, y'know! Horrified, he was! If I'd said to him, "And the Spirit said to tell yer I'm to go in the CID", I'd 'ave been in the next mornin'!'

15

CONTENTED BOBBY: Fortunately, as a con, they can't put me any further down the ladder than I am – unless they put me back in the cadets, and they can't do that! It's a nice position to be in. You haven't got to watch your p's and q's everywhere. Y'know, if you think there's something wrong with the job, you can turn round and tell the boss exactly what you think of it. Obviously he can turn round and bollock you, but he can't sack you. With a promotion candidate, he's got to watch his p's and q's.

16

In the cold light of dawn, a very new recruit meets up with the probationer on the adjoining beat, who has about nine months' service behind him.

'There was this big club-owner, y'know, and he was fightin' – y'know, a really big fella,' says the novice. 'I found 'im fightin'.'

'Last night, yer mean?'

'I'd been talkin' to this fella, y'know, I was quite pally with 'im, and he ran away, y'know. I ran after him and I got him, y'know, and I told him, "You're locked up for D-and-D." This fella said, "Listen, if yer lock me up, I know so many people in this city you'll have to look behind yer every second step." '

'Oh aye? Who was he?'

The novice tells him. 'So I never locked him up. I said, "On yer bike", y'know. I'm not goin' round with anythin' like that

247

on me shoulders, y'know, because he's the sort who'll carry his threat out!'

'Tell me, was Steve on rest day yesterday?'

The conversation digresses to this and that. One of the first Ribble buses rumbles by. They stand a moment in silence.

'You should really have locked that fella up, y'know – you shouldn't have let him go.'

'I know. Yeah. But there were two Traffic fellas there, and they said to let him go. So then. . . .'

'Oh.'

Constant threats are one of the first small shocks to the system of the city-centre recruit. 'We'll find out where yer live!' is a favourite cry of those arrested. The threat offered in this instance was made not by the club-owner who frowns at the Plain Clothes, but by another who receives them most cordially.

17

Breakfasts are being served at St Anne Street, and the canteen talk is a mix of different worlds, all of them sited on 'A' Division. The uniformed officers speak chiefly of incidents, and the CID of individuals. 'Them' to one side are the 'bucks', while the other seems to regard the 'briefs' as their major opposition, Goliaths sent out by the Philistine 'villains'. But the basic difference between their spheres of activity would appear to be the degree of control over events that is available to them.

A detective sergeant who has been up and about since a little after dawn, although his day doesn't really begin until nine, looks over a list of property he's just recovered and stirs his coffee.

The CID has very few assaults because you go prepared. If you're going with your mate to lock somebody up, and you look up his form and see he's got a couple for wounding and a couple for assault police, you then say to two other mates, 'Come along.'

248

A brave man will have a go at four! You make sure you know about the person you're going to.

And you don't go at ridiculous times. You don't go at ten o'clock at night into a pub where he's been drinking since half-past six, and has consumed about nine pints of ale and is ready to take on the world! (*Laughs*) If it was a very, very serious offence you'd go, obviously, but mob-handed. Which doesn't mean there wouldn't be any trouble. But with most fellows the ideal time is seven o'clock in the morning. They're half-asleep, they're in their bare feet, they're not going to be running away – and, at that time of the morning, having consumed nine pints of ale the night before, he's in no mood to be in a mêlée.

The detective sergeant is twenty-nine, sturdily built and has a lilting Welsh accent. He used to play a lot of rugby, and qualified for a trial in the England under-nineteen team while a police cadet in Liverpool. 'I didn't get into the selected fifteen but, when you think of it, it was just as well – we were playing Wales at Cardiff!'

When I was at school, I was in two minds as to what to do. Either to join the police force or to become a teacher of music, because I'd been taking piano examinations with the Royal Academy in London for a couple of years. I was in the first year of the sixth form, and roughly eighteen, when I decided I didn't fancy having a job inside all day. I still play – I bought a piano a couple of years ago – and I'm hoping to go to the Welsh National Opera, which is on at the Empire. But the only thing is, of course, finding the time.

I came to Liverpool because it was a city force. I lived in Snowdonia and thought there'd be far greater opportunities and the variation would be also much greater. I think the biggest problem was understanding people's speech; there were odd words that, if you were given them out of context, you wouldn't know what they were on about!

The thing that I've found that assists me greatly in interviewing people in this city is the common denominator: football. Obviously, you wouldn't dream of speaking about football to somebody in charge in one of the departmental stores. You'd start off saying 'And how does VAT affect you?' – especially if it's someone in accounts. But usually, if somebody won't give you the time of day, then if you start on about football – either

249

team – you'll find he and you are on the same wavelength. Once you get somebody on the same wavelength, they realise you are just the same as them: you go to football matches – although you may be in the police; they go to football matches – although they screw shops. And so there is something you both do.

That's why there isn't a lecture in the CID course on interviewing. As a CID officer, you can't generalise at all; you've got to treat everybody as an individual. I think you mellow a lot. I'm not saying I couldn't care less what happens in court, but, providing I know I've done all I could have, and that we've presented the strongest evidence we possibly could, the fact that a fella is given a verdict of not guilty has very little to do with us. We've done what we've been asked to do; it's the court that has said there is insufficient evidence to convict. They're not saying he didn't do it.

Some of them are most likeable, and I get on with most of them very, very well. Some treat it as a game: there's them, there's us, and sometimes they lose and sometimes they win. You lock somebody up and you do his house over, and you get lots of property back and he shouts at you. Nobody likes getting caught, do they? Let's be fair about it. He shouts at you, 'The next time I see you, I'll kick your brains in!' – words to that effect. All right, he may have form as long as your arm, but you see him seven or eight weeks later in a pub, and you say to him, 'What're you having?' He'll accept and that'll be the end of it. Obviously there *are* other people who are vicious, but they don't have to take it out on you directly. They know the car you're driving, so all they've got to do is come round the back of this police station – as they've done over the last few weeks – and slash a couple of tyres. That will cause you far more inconvenience, for the simple reason you couldn't prove who has done that – whereas, if he had a go at you, you would know him.

It's very nice to be involved in a job (*touches list*), to do a lot of enquiries and to conclude it satisfactorily – and I don't just mean locking up. Say a shop's been broken into, you do the enquiries, lock up the fella and he gets fined or sent away. *That's* not finishing the job satisfactorily. That's neither use nor ornament to the shop manager. What he's interested in is getting his property back. If you get their property back for them, even if you haven't got a prisoner, they are more satisfied than if you get the prisoner and no property. I have thoroughly enjoyed the ten, eleven years I've been in Liverpool. I can't recall one instance when I've said to myself: I wish I was back there.

250

(He glances out of the windows behind the serving-counter. Far, far off in the hazy distance and wreathed in cloud are the mountain peaks of Snowdonia; dreamlike reminders of a boyhood so different from any spent on the grey slope in the foreground.)

18

Contrition is sobering, even mildly shocking in a bridewell.

'It's disgustin',' sobs the boy, as he's led into St Anne Street charge office. 'Disgustin'! Me mam will put us in a 'ome!'

The constable called to arrest him looks ill at ease as he relates the circumstances. This eleven-year-old was on the way to his grandmother's flat, it appears, when he slipped a *Dandy* and a *Beano* into the *Rover* he was buying at a newsagent's.

'It's wrong, y'know,' mutters a casual onlooker. 'It's wrong we've got to bring that kid in. Know what I mean?' And he mimes a quick clip round the ear.

'Aye, when I joined,' agrees a colleague, 'I'd have took 'im round his granny's house. "Look, luv, are yer goin' to smack 'is bottom for this, or am I?" ' He shakes his head. 'That lad's in a terrible state. . . .'

'But yer can't any more, can yer? Get a complaint against yer.'

Once the boy's name and other details have been extracted between outbursts of bitter sobbing, he is placed in the juvenile detention room while his grandmother is contacted. He tries to take control of himself but in vain, and attracts a number of curious faces to the glass panel in the door.

The sergeant with the tan goes in and crouches down beside him. 'What's all this, son?'

'Uh-uh-uh. . . . I were goin' to me nan's – me mam'll put us in a 'ome! – she'll—'

'Can't be as bad as that!'

'She *will*! She doesn't care since me dad died. She—'

'Oh? Yer dad's dead, is he?'

'He were killed inna car down by the, down by the – he were wrapped round a tree. She'll be *disgusted* with me! She said, "Where did yer get that?" It were only two days after me

251

birthday – one of the presents I got, see. She said, "Where did yer get that? You ever go thievin'," she said, "and I'll put yer in a 'ome! Promise I will!" She doesn't care any more, me mam. She doesn't. . . .'

On the contrary, as he continues his disclosures, it becomes more and more obvious that the young widow cares a great deal about him. Her threats are plainly intended to safeguard him while she's out earning their living, particularly as most of his playmates regard shoplifting as an everyday means to an end. In fact, she'd sent him to his grandmother's for the day to escape their influence, and the final irony is that he now admits he'd never have tried the same trick in the area where he was known.

'What comics were they?' asks the sergeant.

'B-B-Beano and a Dandy, s-sair.'

'A Dandy? Desperate Dan still eatin' his cow-pies, is he? Y'know, those massive pies with the horns and the tail stickin' out?'

'Aye!' says the boy, surprised into a smile. Then his face crumples again, but he cries more quietly.

19

'Shoplifting's a very, very funny offence,' says one of the two detective constables who work with the Welsh detective sergeant. 'You either get the big teams and the real baddies, these people who just get a kick out of it, or the people who are a little bit ill, who need treatment or something.

'I think menopause and periods can have a big effect on some – I really do. And in places like supermarkets and Boot's, they're *asking* people to make a mistake. I did it once at Tesco's. I put something in me shopping-bag I hadn't paid for. Now that girl never said to me, "I haven't taken for those yet!" – which I feel she should've done, rather than wait for this girl detective to grab me outside. Luckily, I was still at the till when I realised what I was doing – but you wonder how many people can do this.

'You feel very, very sorry for the old folk who take some-

252

thing because they actually need it. But now the new system's come in where they treat them exactly the same as the juveniles and caution them, which I think is a smashing idea. I used to get heartbroken with some of the old ladies that would come in. There are so many people who come in and you think they shouldn't go to court, really they shouldn't – they need somebody to help them. I think the caution should be extended more widely at the police officer's discretion because, unless you can put yourself over in a report, it's very, very difficult to explain how you feel when you've dealt with someone, perhaps talked to them for a couple of hours. All they see in a report is the bare facts: somebody went into a shop and took something without paying.

'But then again, the police have to be very careful because the shops start causing trouble. It's happened before. Shops have gone straight to the Chief Constable because somebody has decided not to take a shoplifter from them, and they've caused trouble that's come bouncing back here.'

She is twenty-nine, attractively chic in well-chosen clothes, and worked in a bank after grammar school and commercial college. 'A small office with a lot of bitchiness in it. I seemed to be doing nothing all day. I walked into the recruiting-tent at the Liverpool Show, and this policeman said, "Oh, *you* look tall enough!" Before I knew it, I was in. My parents were very pleased. I'm a twin and it meant one of us – my sister's a secretary – was doing something different, had a career.' That was ten years ago. After her probation, she was a driver in the Traffic Department for almost five years, and thoroughly enjoyed it – especially a 100-mph chase up the East Lancs road. She didn't want to switch to CID work but four months as an aide changed all that. 'It was great! I really enjoyed the idea of just going out and people often not knowing who you were, and of getting to know people in a sort of different world, a different class to you. I've made some smashing friends I'd never have come in contact with, unless I was in a job like this.' Her chief interests outside work at the moment are building up a new flat, now her marriage to a police officer has ended, and home winemaking.

She initials the 'spike' and returns to her desk to work out

253

her priorities. Two hours later, she's having to revise the list again.

When I've an awful lot on from the night before – like today – then perhaps I take just an easy theft: I took a theft of a cassette from a hairdresser's. I've got a burglary from last night, a break-in at the Electricity Board and three prisoners on that, locked up by Uniform. There are also the two lads two policewomen locked up last week for burglary of a shop next door to here. They're denying it, so there's all sorts of forensic stuff to take from them. I've got a conspiracy case on the go with my DS – it's like a nightmare! I've got a few burglaries that I haven't got prisoners for – fingerprints but very few names, shoplifters and what have you.

These three lads from last night have sort of admitted it, but what they'll say when they get to court I don't know, because they change their minds as easy as wink! This lad of thirteen had done so many he doesn't care. First of all he was very hard and his face was set – they all have this expression, an old look – but when you get down and talk to him he's such a lovely little lad. Really and truly, deep down they're nice kids, but they just don't stand an earthly. But the time they're adults they're as hard as nails. It must have taken the first half-hour to convince them I was going to help them as much as a 'detective' would! (*Laughs*)

Some people are a bit funny, but other people will talk to you more because you are female – I find that as well, especially around this area. You deal with a job and the next thing they'll ring you up and want to come and have a chat with you about this, that and the other. You know that six-year-old who was sexually assaulted? All I did was take a statement from the mother – that's all I really had to do with the job. But the mother came in three days later, because she'd got to such a pitch not being able to talk to anybody, and she just wanted the release really. And so she came in and was chatting to me for an hour, and that's all my purpose was really – to talk to her, because she felt I knew all about it and could talk to her.

I think if your whole idea was just prosecution all the time you wouldn't get through your day. You'd become very bitter, I suppose, towards life – towards everything! I don't think you can do that, because I hate people not to like me.

My very first experience of someone not liking me was with the very first fella I ever did. It was for an excise licence – when I was at Belle Vale – and he went to court and was found

254

guilty. About a fortnight or so later, I was walking down the Belle Vale Road and he was coming the other way, and he purposefully crossed over the road. He walked down the other side and crossed back, so he wouldn't have to walk on the same pavement as me. I was so hurt, so *terribly* hurt he'd done this to me! (*Laughs*) But you get out of that with experience.

Occasionally I get depressed by my job. When I'm on duty I'm not so bad, but I've gone home and been sick; gone home and cried my eyes out over various things. You can do it because you've got to do it at work – you cope. And then you go home and be sick. But I don't find things so depressing in the CID. You don't come across so much pain all the time really, and you're dealing with so many different things. Plus the fact that in the CID, before you go home, you generally have a drink in the last half-hour – I think that helps you to wind down. I can never go home and go to bed. I've never done it yet. You have to read something first. I read all sorts of things, adventure stories mainly – I must go through three books a week.

You get people that you take to court and they cry out for help. There was this girl, she was sixteen and knocking round with this older fella, and she was caught shoplifting and she assaulted the store detective. She was a cracking little girl. I got her back here and she got a caution, but a week after she was back again. In the meantime, her boyfriend had gone to Borstal, so she wanted to go to Borstal. Now she's done everything – right down to robberies; she's done that many jobs it's incredible. She's twenty now and in open prison. She was a disappointment to me, because I got quite well in with the family, and I used to go up and see her, but now everybody wants her for something. She wanted to go to prison because her boyfriend was in prison – that's as far as she could think.

But I feel what we're doing is achieving something. Otherwise you wouldn't go on, because it'd get you so down. You get quite a few 'cautions' that you see in town, and they call to you, 'Sally!' Come and chat to you, and call you Sally.

20

A businessman in a hurry, briefcase swinging and one shoe-lace coming undone, swerves off course and hastens down the steps of the public lavatory in Victoria Street.

255

Clamping the briefcase between his calves, he stands in front of one of the stalls and undoes his flies. He glances at the man who steps up to the stall beside him. Then he looks again.

It's the same man who had been standing at the foot of the steps, as though about to leave.

The man is looking at him intently.

The businessman glances over his other shoulder. There are two well-dressed, professional-looking types standing in curious juxtaposition at the far end of the ten-stall urinal. Then it becomes obvious that one is masturbating the other.

And now the man beside him is toying with himself, smiling a very friendly smile.

The businessman colours. He looks down, willing his bladder to void itself quickly. Not a drop.

He zips up his trousers, grabs his briefcase and hurries out, not pausing to tie his shoe-lace until he reaches the street again.

'There's only a very limited number of the section who will go into the toilets,' says the fundamentalist sergeant. 'It must be the lousiest job we've got. Because – '

'They're frightened to try it in case they like it!' jokes the other Plain Clothes sergeant, then barks a laugh.

' – because you've got to go and stand there, y'know, for twenty, twenty-five minutes before you're accepted by the fraternity. And you're not to laff! After about ten minutes, the cons just boil up inside and they've got to rush out, go down a back-street and Ha, ha, ha! Get it out of their system and then go back in, y'know.'

'We have some well-known city characters, solicitors and various dignitaries who frequent these places,' murmurs the inspector. 'I think it becomes a fetish after a while, because they don't have to these days – they could go to a club at any time of the day, as it were. They've probably got used to it; it could be the toilets that turns them on, y'know.'

A car carrying Plain Clothes constables passes through Victoria Street, and the new one among them mutters something.

'The queers, y'mean? Oh, they're terrible down there! Y'know, all noddin' and winkin'.'

256

'Wankin'!'

'You look to see how many feet you can see! There was this one a few weeks ago, down on his hands and knees, gobbling.'

'We've been told not to bother any more, because you're agents provocateurs.'

'It's importuning, too, y'see.'

'I've done a few with Rich, because it's an easy lock-up.'

'I don't know so much! Some of them are bloody violent! Once they realise they're being locked up – boom! Bloody hell, what when me friends hear about this, y'know?'

'Aye, yer show 'em yer warrant card and they go bloody mad!'

As the car leaves Victoria Street, a woman laden with shopping sends her small son down to spend a penny.

21

'I'm tryin' to trace me 'usband and me dog,' the little woman in the head-scarf explains, confronted by yet another officer at the Main Bridewell counter. ' 'E got locked up for bein' drunk last Wednesday, and I've not seen 'im since.'

The officer studies the details already recorded by his colleague. 'Doesn't ring a bell, luv,' he says, and cross-checks with the prisoners' list.

'The thing is,' she adds, 'me 'usband 'ad this four-month-old puppy with 'im.'

'Yuh, you said. Hang on a minute.'

The officer retires into the vast records section. Another five minutes drag by before both officers return.

'Are you sure he was locked up?' the first officer says, scratching the side of his head with a ballpoint. 'To be honest with yer, luv, we can't find any trace of him.'

'I'm not bothered about *'im*, sair – it's the puppy I want!'

'Oh well,' says the second officer, 'that's all right, then. He got bail, the puppy, luv.'

22

The one that tickles me more than anything else is the Liverpool artisan you find from time to time here on the mortuary slab who's got a list of convictions as long as your arm, and on his left forearm you'll see 'Death Before Dishonour'! And he's got convictions for beating his wife up, and on his other arm there's 'I Love Jane'.

Every two or three days, one of the two sergeants working for the Coroner's Officer – a chief inspector – makes the rounds of the hospital mortuaries, collecting up samples for the City Analyst. As he waits for the mortuary technician to find a free moment, the sergeant glances through into the duck-boarded post-mortem room, where a hospital pathologist, appointed by the Coroner, has just opened out the widow who died in her lavatory.

The first thing people say when you get posted is that you'll be watching post-mortems, and post-mortems can be harrowing. But, for instance, a medical student or a doctor might find them very interesting, and I find them absorbing now – I'm accumulating a little knowledge anyway. Indeed, much to the annoyance – shall we say! – of senior officers, when you're talking to a very friendly pathologist like our Home Office pathologist you can ask him all sorts of questions that aren't really relevant to that particular case.

Taking down a pathologist's notes during a post-mortem is the start of this learning process for most newcomers, who grab for the section's much-thumbed medical dictionary when confronted by words such as 'petechiae' or 'glottidis'; and it's inevitable that, having found how to spell a word, they take an interest in its definition. The sergeant also imparts knowledge by giving lectures to recruits on the functions of the Coroner's Office.

When I joined, I saw the typical example of a coroner's officer – y'know, built like a brick toilet, with a bald head, a stern face and a droning voice! (*Laughs*) So I tell them straight away: 'I apologise for my sense of humour; it's merely a *deflection* because

258

the subject is rather gruesome.' I also go to great lengths to remind them that we are all going to die, and we would like to think that somebody will come along and deal with it compassionately. I never say 'post-mortem' – it's always 'an examination'.

As a probationer in 'A' Division himself thirty years ago, the sergeant's first three sudden deaths were all 'floaters' – bodies found drowned in the Mersey. Death was, however, something with which he was already perhaps more familiar than most recruits.

Well, I'd been in the meat trade – wholesale meat, not retail – and I was quite used to going along to see the ritual slaughter of sheep for Mohammedans or something, and that didn't distress me at all very much. I'd been in the Royal Air Force police, and [in Germany] I was the investigating officer where a head had come completely detached from the rest of the body, and I had to carry him by his hair. It didn't affect me very much. I found a girl who'd drowned herself, and I also came across fellows who'd shot themselves accidentally, blown themselves up. I wasn't particularly bothered about it. Then came the day [in Liverpool] when I was allegedly going into the CID and, on what they called a Criminal Investigation Probationary Detective Course, they asked me to watch a post-mortem. Naturally, you've got to view post-mortems in the CID, and you've got to attend murders and things like that, so it's pointless having a clown who's going to fall over at the sight of a body. What they did was get a frightful mess of a body, as gruesome as possible and usually one that had been dead for a few days, and get all the people round the table, viewing this dreadful mess, and then proceed with the post-mortem. But I refused because this clashed with – I thought – my Christian beliefs. I said it served no useful purpose for me, only curiosity and nothing else, you see. 'Look,' I said, 'it doesn't mean anything to me. I *object* to this. That person is a *person*, and I think it's undignified.' I resented the fact that someone was being displayed, if you like. That is what really annoyed me.

His father joined the Liverpool police in 1904. 'He had five boys and four of them joined the police – and one of them is a minister, which I think goes to prove either cops and robbers

259

or insanity runs in the family!' He might be mistaken for a progressive nonconformist minister himself, his 'big bobby' build notwithstanding. His voice is warm and pleasantly modulated, his face open and alert, his person well groomed, and the stone in his gold ring matches the lilac stripes in his dazzlingly white shirt.

You get posted to this after you've indicated a willingness – you apply for a position when it becomes vacant. Of course, you have to put up with jokes. There's a fellow who comes up to me in the police club from time to time, and he says, 'Hello, Bob! How are you?' – while he's measuring me with this imaginary tape measure!

The mortuary technician has several containers of stomach contents and some blood samples for him, together with a few other odd bits and pieces. They talk shop for a few minutes. An old woman has died in hospital after a fall, which means the Coroner's Office will have to go out and take a look at where it happened. As for the multi-coloured widow on the stainless-steel table, it has already been established that she died from natural causes. Two undertakers arrive, so the sergeant takes his leave and heads for Walton General.

Dealing with death all the time has made me very conscious, very *aware* of being alive. It may sound a stupid thing to say, but I push this down the throat of the recruits. You're conscious of people being alive one minute – especially with colleagues – and *very* dead the next.

When a person is dead, he is dead. I resent the poorer people paying a lot of money out to go into a ritual which is going to bloody bankrupt them for the sake of saying, 'Oh, he's had a good funeral!' As far as I'm concerned, there's nothing wrong with a cotton shroud and a heave down the pit, y'know. You see people buying huge caskets and hiring dozens of cars, and you're saying to yourself: He's only dead. That's it. Finished.

I'm upset, frankly, by things which everyone else in the office would not be upset by. For example, some time ago an old fellow came in on his own, a little old man, and I just caught sight of him going down the corridor. (*Laughs*) This is pure melo-drama and gross sentimentality, of course! Anyway, he was on his own, and I said, 'Anybody looking after you?' 'No.' So I said, 'OK, what are you here for?' and he said, 'I've come for documents for me wife.' As I'm taking the brief details from him, I said, 'You're here on your own?' and he said, 'Oh, yes.' So I looked at his wife's age, and I said, 'How long have you been married?' 'Oh, sixty-one years.' I said, 'Have you really? How many children have you got?' He said, 'I haven't any.' 'Oh, so you're all on your own?' 'Yes,' he said. 'There was only the two of us.' I said, 'I'll get you a taxi, pop; see you on to it.' 'No,' he said, 'I've got me bus pass.' 'And you're all right for a couple of bob?' 'No, no,' he said, 'I'm all right.' Now that upset me for a long time afterwards. There was only the two of us. . . .

23

'Patrols Alpha and Bravo, patrols Alpha and Bravo, a stolen vehicle, Rotunda junction, children on board. A purple Marina being driven at this moment by children. Stand by. . . .'

'Not another lot!' exclaims Inspector South on Mornings, already in pursuit of a Morris Minor taken from the city centre.

He sees an OSD car sweep into a gap between two derelict warehouses, and follows it through. The Morris Minor is there all right, one of the kind that have been cherished for years, probably by a pensioner who dusts and polishes it each day. Its windows are smashed, its bodywork is battered by brick-bats, and its tyres are slashed. It must have happened in seconds.

Whooping and jeering, prancing about on huge blocks of concrete not fifty yards away, is a group of children on their summer holidays. They jerk two-finger gestures at the police, confident that any attempt to catch them will be about as successful as a deep-sea diver trying to lay hold of a colony of Barbary apes. Yet they seem disappointed when nobody moves to make a game of it.

24

A BOBBY: Mind you, it's the worst job under the sun for gossip, y'know. It really is. It's in their nature to collect information and share it.

261

The gossip at noon centres on the antics of two Metropolitan detectives last night, who frightened the wits out of a night porter after discovering something wrong with their hotel room. Although the porter had set matters right in a trice, they'd made it clear they were not to be appeased without a complimentary bottle of Scotch. Unable to oblige, he had given them several large Scotches on a tray, paid for out of his own pocket. 'Jacks from the Met' are not infrequently the subject of stories told with a mixture of awe, shock and amusement.

A DETECTIVE: A lot of the blokes down there, if they weren't detectives they could well be sort of car salesmen – they'd go down to clubs anyway. They definitely have a certain dialogue between themselves and the people [professional criminals] they're dealing with. There are very, very few of that kind in the CID here, and in that respect we're less sophisticated. I went down there on a training course, and I was amazed that I could find so few men I could equate with the men I work with. And yet I've been to other places and you could imagine the detectives there coming to work in Liverpool. Everybody worked the same, everybody went out for a few pints at night – they were basically the same type of bloke. It's as if you get various people coming on the job, and when they get to the CID, their personalities level out to a level you recognise. Whereas down in London, the blokes I met, their personalities had been established long before they came in the CID. Y'know, big handsome lads in eighty-guinea suits, and sometimes you get the feeling they're better suited to deal with them. But, by the same token, that's where you get the danger of stepping over the mark, bribery and corruption and everything. I think there's very little likelihood of anyone in our office getting involved in that kind of situation.

25

Just as every dog has its day, some days have their dogs. The first entry in the wireless log sheet this morning concerned a 'ferocious dog' that was preventing an old lady from leaving her house to do her shopping, and was answered with some trepidation by a young policewoman. Then at midday comes another call.

'Alpha, go ahead.'

'Y'know that D-and-D you just sent us to?' asks another policewoman. 'It could be a D-and-I, 'cos the fella's a cripple, but the thing is he's got this dog with him, and it goes mad if you just go near him! Could I have some assistance?'

The last call – hopefully things happen in threes – comes just before lunchtime, and the radio operator looks sickened as he puts it out.

'Roger, well, if you could make Paradise Street car-park. We've a report of a dog thrown from a considerable height.'

A constable overhears this on his own set out in the bride-well office. 'Bloody hell, not again! Those fokkin' bucks must be sick, y'know! Doin' that to an animal – imagine!'

'Makes yer wish yer were armed, a job like that,' someone murmurs. 'Y'know, if it's not dead and that, and you've got to stand by while its guts is hangin' out and it's screamin' and twistin' and everything. Can't put it out of its misery with yer staff, can yer?'

26

Being the summer holidays, the red-and-white scarves of young Liverpool supporters are already in evidence in the city centre, although the mid-week match against a London team doesn't kick off until this evening. One runs across in front of the Operators Inspector for 'A' Division, who is out checking the route that the visiting fans will take from Lime Street station, up past St Anne Street and on into 'B' Division. All seems in order, with the exception of a large metal skip filled with rubble that lies almost opposite the station entrance. He will have to ask for this 'ammunition dump' to be removed – or see that the necessary precautions are taken. It's his responsibility to supervise all large gatherings in the division, and this area was the scene of his severest test after the European Cup win.

263

For the civic reception for Liverpool, we had 600 police officers and a crowd that was estimated at 100,000 in front of the library. You couldn't move for people; it was just one swaying, heaving mass. Hysterical, some of them were. I was up at the front with my sector and they were passing out like flies from the pressure of the crowd. The first-aid people reckon they treated about 1200, and about 900 of them had to be physically lifted over that barrier by my policemen – and by quite a lot of policewomen, who are young girls, remember. Some of them quite small and petite; they were exhausted. You've got to keep looking and saying, 'Look, you've had ten minutes there; you're knackered. Better go and have a cup of tea.' It's difficult for the youngers, I suppose, but when you've done it a few times, crowd control's just another job. The only excitement is the booze-up afterwards, and then gettin' home late to your wife and sayin', 'I'm sorry I'm late, but *by God* we were busy!' Then making sure that you take the paper before she gets up in the morning, so she doesn't have a chance to read that only five turned up.

27

A quick rap of knuckles on the half-open door.

The detective inspector in charge of Copperas Hill CID looks up from his meat pie. His appearance is as crisp as a new bank note. He wears a dark suit, has a full unlined face, and favours a distinct parting in short black hair combed with a quiff. At thirty-one, he is junior in years to his five sergeants and several of his DCs, but his manner makes him decidedly the boss. It's brisk, blunt, businesslike and very self-contained.

'Excuse me, sir,' says a tall lean detective sergeant with craggy features and a particular fondness for Maigret novels, coming a pace into the room, 'there are two down below in the cells, one's a juvenile. Dey're from Doblin, soir.'

'Oh yes, soir?'

'They came on the boat this morning, and they've been shoplifting as well.'

'As well as what?'

'As well as buying. They've got two pairs of shoes, and we

264

checked – they did buy them. One's fourteen, the other's eighteen. We're going to stick 'em before the court this afternoon.'

'Great.'

'And we're going to try and fix up a child welfare to be at the court—'

' – in case they're remanded in custody. Have they admitted the job ?'

'Oh yes, sir. We're having a word with the Garda at the moment, to check them out and see if they've got any form.'

'Why are they over here ?'

'They say to come shopping. They've quite a bit of money on them, y'know. Irish money and English money.'

'That's the most expedient way of dealing with them. They may be wanted over there.'

'They say they've never been in trouble before, but they lied to start off with – said they'd never taken the stuff.'

'Well, we're not going to extradite from Ireland on a shoplifting job!'

'I'll go!' suggests the detective sergeant on his way out.

A lot of my crime is shoplifting. Coupled with cars, thefts of and from, I would say it's sixty per cent of the crime. Fortunately for me, shoplifting's a detected offence. If they can be detectives in a sub-division like this – and don't go under – they're doing bloody well. Each deals with about 450 jobs a year and, of course, the number recommended by the Home Office is 150. It's ludicrous.

As a detective inspector, paperwork and administrative duties occupy most of his time, except when anything of any magnitude occurs. 'The city cathedral was definitely my job – the value was £13,000. Rapes are sergeants' jobs. Buggery, sergeants' jobs usually – proper buggery, not just gross indecency. We haven't had a bank job in the eighteen months I've been here, and we haven't had a shotgun fired.' On his desk is a bulging file concerning a fifty-six-year-old man found dead with an injury to his forehead at the foot of some stairs in a nightclub. Any death in clubland is always the subject of an intensive enquiry. After 1488 interviews and 111 statements had

265

been taken, it was concluded that the man had died of natural causes, and had picked up 'carpet burns' in his fall. 'We were completely satisfied there was no foul play, but that took me and a lot of men ten days to do.'

Although clubs are responsible directly and indirectly for much of the CID workload on the South Sub, the detective inspector believes that he is spared one menace usually associated with them.

Protection rackets don't exist in Liverpool. I think this is because of the stand of the club-owners some time ago. I wasn't here then, but I understand that the Krays and the Richardsons came here from the Smoke – and to Manchester – and were knocked back by the club-owners of the day. They had certain gangs in this town then who were being paid protection money, and it was with the assistance of these in receipt that they were knocked back. I think the club-owners realised that, if you could get rid of the likes of them, you could get rid of the fellas who were local. I've never yet had a club-owner coming to me and saying, 'I'm having the squeeze put on me.'

This spirit of independence may not be unrelated to another aspect of club life that does prove troublesome.

We regularly have problems with bouncers because they think they're a law unto themselves and, if they're pulling someone out, can use whatever they want to paralyse. They go a little bit too far, and occasionally it's necessary for me to go and see the management and say, 'Hey, quieten down – or somebody's going to be in trouble.' Only last year I had a manslaughter: a bouncer smacked a lad and he fell back on the pavement, hit his head and he died. It's as simple as that. It can happen. I don't give any leeway at all to a bouncer, but identification is a problem. It's pointless charging people if I know it's going to be thrown out on their first appearance in court. And if people won't make a statement we've got no complaint, we've got no job.

There is also the decided effect that certain clubs can have on the crime rate where property is concerned.

You'll get a situation where you perhaps have a bawdy club or a badly run club, as we had in —— Street up to a few months ago.

266

As they're coming out at three, four, five in the morning, these people are right in town and welly, in goes the window. We had one particular shop that was going once a week certainly, and sometimes more than that. But we were lucky; we locked up on consecutive occasions, and that seemed to stop it. The badly run clubs are meeting-places for villains. That is a matter for the magistrates to decide. I wasn't present at the hearing when —— was granted a licence, but I know he had the licence personally at ——, whereas he can use front men on other occasions. How he ever got that licence, I don't know. The police either slipped up or were overruled by the magistrates, because he should never be in possession of a justices' licence, that man. So once you've got a villain at the helm, you're going to have a crew of villains following him, aren't you? I think there should be statutory grounds under which you will not obtain a licence. (*Shrugs*) But let's not be naïve; you'll always get your front men going in, so how do you get over that situation?

The detective sergeant pops his head back into the office. 'This Irish saga, sir. . . .'

'Oh yes?'

'We're not going to put them before the court until to-morrow. They've got quite a bit of money in their possession, so I had a word with the Port Unit, and they say there's eighty-odd gone from the purser's office on the ship.'

28

UNIFORMED OFFICER: The law regarding licensed clubs is almost enough in itself to deter anybody, even the most determined, from applying it. Essentially, after 10.30 p.m., dancing, music, entertainment and proper meals must be the primary reason for the club still being open on a special-hours certificate.

PLAIN CLOTHES OFFICER: We can apply for a revocation of the special-hours certificate only after three months [have elapsed]. So at the end of three months he can close his club down completely and he never comes to the notice of the police again. And then he can apply to have it back, and it's not always certain we're going to win. Very often he does get it back, and then he sets it up again and we start again.

As only the worst sort of club has its licence revoked, it often shows no hesitation in having a final fling during the three-month grace period. By continuing to sell liquor behind closed doors until around six in the morning it can make good any legal costs and build up capital for its grand reopening under a different name in another building. And as such a club also tends to have the worst clientele, these extended drinking bouts lead inevitably to an increase in the city centre's crime rate. Yet it would appear that little would be gained by further raids during this period, because they would only prolong the legal processes involved.

29

The afternoon sky turns as grey and cold as the photographs being shown to a class of recruits by the sergeant from the Coroner's Office. He has a whole pile of them.

A steep flight of carpeted stairs and then the body of a fifty-six-year-old man found dead at the foot of them. Two points to remember here. First, that all club deaths are automatically deemed suspicious. Secondly, that in every case of sudden death it is the police – and not the GP, hospital doctor or police surgeon – who must decide whether it should be treated as suspicious.

A touch of colour. A battered pensioner sits strangled on his sofa, with drops of his blood, in a separate enlargement, making big red exclamation marks on the wallpaper.

Grey again. A grey morning. Another scene of sudden death that looked at first like a murder. The buxom corpse in the photograph is sprawled on its back in a jigger, with its legs wide open to the camera and its skirt thrown back, exposing the genital area. 'No bruises, no nothing. Fit as a butcher's dog, this kid. Thirty-six, prostitute, etcetera etcetera. No tablets, a little booze. It came out it was vagal inhibition, caused by sexual excitement.'

268

30

The droll sergeant's group is on Afternoons this week, and standing by for the influx of London football fans due to arrive en masse any minute now at Lime Street station.

Before they started running these specials, the supporters used to come off the trains and the first thing they'd do was ask the nearest person where the grounds were. They'd be directed over towards Gerard Gardens or somewhere by the cowboys waiting for these fellas, and we used to have them trooping into St Anne Street without their coats, their boots, their shoes, and their money had been taken off them and everything.

The skip is still there, but a constable has been posted beside it. Not a great number of other officers are in evidence, and the sergeant himself is seated at the open door of a vanload of 'back-up' men, keeping a low profile. He is dark, balding and has large baleful eyes, all the better to hide his sense of humour behind. He was a pay-roll clerk, looking after the wages of 1200 workers, when he decided to join the police. 'I think the main attraction was that training was provided on the job. I was twenty-two then, and now I'm thirty-eight. In fact there's a lot more emphasis on training than there used to be. The changes have been remarkable. It was still a strictly disciplined organisation. The inspector was very remote, and the chief super was God as far as we were concerned. Now there's far more contact, and the CID isn't a world on its own.' One change he regrets, like so many of his colleagues, is the loss of the Land-Rovers. 'You get a jeep with a couple of bobbies aboard, and they're worth six bobbies on foot, because they're split up over an area. Things have got time to escalate now. A jeep could deal with ten minor incidents in a night, which could be ten fairly major incidents otherwise. We're getting examples of this all the time.' The station exit suddenly fills with the vanguard of 2000 supporters, looking as any new arrivals in a strange city usually look, slightly dazed and unsure of themselves.

'Turn to yer right, lads,' says the first Liverpool policeman they set eyes on. 'Turn to yer right, keep goin'. You've got a long way to go, y'know, so don't waste yer—'

269

'How far is it, then?'

'Two mile – but don't let that bother yer. Keep goin'!' He grins and adds, 'Lambs to the slaughter!'

That gets a big laugh, and a forecast of Liverpool's imminent fate in terms cheerfully scatological. Lambs they may not be, but they seem willing, even gratefully eager, to be shepherded along Lime Street in a wide column, keeping up the exchange of good-natured banter.

Funnily enough, we've always had a very good reputation for handling football crowds in Liverpool.* People from other places are amazed that the bobbies walk up and down, laughing with the crowd. I don't know why. These other places they go to should be experienced. But everyone says the same thing: the attitude of the bobby isn't the same. And in Liverpool we move them far quicker. The biggest trouble is when they start getting impatient. You push them along, but you keep it light-hearted.

Then the sergeant's van moves ahead of the marchers to check the route once again for any pockets of ambushers that may be lurking. The sweep up round the back of St Anne Street is too exposed to present a problem, but Great Homer Street, with a defensive wall of shops within a stone's throw of the road, is another matter.

31

'Yes?' snaps the bridewell patrol.

A shabby youth tries to make out which of the officers through the hatchlike enquiries-counter at St Anne Street has addressed him. 'They said to come down at half-six like. CID.'

'Been warned in?'

The youth shrugs.

'Name?'

The youth gives his particulars and is instructed to sit on one of the four stacking chairs provided for the public almost

*Continental police forces have sent observers to Liverpool to see what can be learned by example, and they have reported 'astonishment'.

270

in the centre of the large entrance hall. He fidgets uneasily as people come and go around him. The chairs are positioned in this way so that passing officers – particularly recruits – can familiarise themselves with customers past, present and to come.

'Yes ?' snaps the bridewell patrol.

A stocky Roman Catholic priest edges up to the bright rectangle of light as he might approach a tank of turtles in an aquarium, and peers in cautiously.

'Well ?'

'It's just I've had this message, officer, to come down, you see,' says the priest, who proclaims an affinity with his flock by wearing a flat cap made in black clerical cloth with a high shine to it.

The detective constable waiting upstairs for the youth's arrival is the other DC who works under the Welsh detective sergeant's supervision. He is twenty-three, stands 5 feet $11\frac{1}{2}$ inches, has been married a year, and has the broad-shouldered clean-cut vitality of a swimmer, playing water polo for the Merseyside Police team.

I think you've got to have a certain amount of fitness – especially out on the beat. It's not so bad in the CID; it's very seldom you actually come across something, say in the middle of the night, when you've got to run after somebody.

Yes, people usually come in when you send for them. It's very surprising actually! (*Laughs*) Most of them will because, y'see, if they don't come in, it's only a matter of going to their houses in the early hours of the morning, and they don't want police cars rolling up outside. We usually try to make it a station near their house – say, Belle Vale – and they'd rather come in.

I don't mind the bucks personally. They're the same as us – just the other side of the fence, aren't they ? That's all it amounts to. A lot of fellas will treat them as 'You're walkin' down there; you're nothing.' They may be nothing, but. . . . Well, I think with a lot of them, when they get out there in uniform, the power goes to their heads. I've always felt it anyway. I've always found the small fellows, the ones who aren't very fit, a bit weedy; they tend to play on the uniform a bit – which I personally don't

271

think is right, y'know. (*Shrugs*) I think the public's more at ease with yer in the CID.

I don't think it's putting a different face on, but because you're in plain clothes. I think the uniform frightens a lot of them – y'know, if you see a uniformed policeman [at your door], it's always bad news. My beat was Upper Parliament Street, Myrtle Street, Myrtle Gardens, all very dilapidated. You quite often had to go and give a message when somebody died or whatever. You didn't know who you were going to meet, or how she was going to take it. I'd imagine that's about the worst job we've got really.

No, I don't see myself as Starsky and Hutch now – I haven't got the car anyway! (*Laughs*) That's good to watch. Could never happen in real life but, if it could, it'd be great! I've had one complaint against me; they must have *fifty*. There was some money that went from an office in town, and you have to interview the staff, and obviously some people take offence to this. Two girls complained; obviously one said, 'Well, if you complain, I'll complain.' The letters were identical, word perfect, and both arrived the same day. The boss sent a letter out saying he'd seen the three officers and it wasn't going any further, but it was time-consuming. With a report like that, you've got to answer every little detail. And Kojak! Some of the things he does – incredible. They all must be very tolerant people over there, or the bosses don't bother.

Time. You just haven't got the time in the CID. If you could get one job – like the Pier Head. There's loads of jobs down there, and if you had the time you could collate all the others coming in, and just deal with them yourself. Nobody's got the time to do that. A shame, really, but just one of those things.

Before going down to fetch up his suspect, he has a quick word with his sergeant about an evening out they have planned. 'Both our wives only see us at midnight every other day and often not at weekends,' says the DS, 'so I think it's a good idea they know each other. They can ring one another up. It's not as if they're on their own.'

A distraught young woman bursts into Copperas Hill from the Bullring, startling two suspects seated on a bench beside the doors. 'I've got a bit of a problem,' she gasps, trying to catch her breath.

272

'Haven't we all, my love?' sighs the bridewell patrol, looking up from his copy of the *Sun*.

'I've been assaulted!'

'Do you know him?'

'Yes!'

'Then,' says the bridewell patrol, putting his paper to one side, 'there's no sweat, is there?'

Much of the spirit of old Rose Hill seems to live on in this overcrowded police station, set firm in the community opposite the Bullring. 'We had this bobby that never liked to go in there without his mate, y'know, and we had this nickname for him. Oh, the people all knew it. They'd come in the bridewell and say, "Aye, aye, and where's the Reluctant Matador tonight, then?"'

32

'I feel it's one thing we fall down on in the service,' remarks a Plain Clothes constable and former paratrooper, 'the fact that there isn't much insistence on physical fitness. A good three-quarters of them couldn't run a hundred yards, carrying somebody on their back, without being absolutely out of breath and shattered. When violence does flare up, these are the people who get seriously injured: policemen who can't look after themselves because they just can't cope with it. The number of prisoners I've caught after a good chase, y'know, is a satisfaction to me. They respect you for it and they remember you for it: "He was the busy who caught me."'

DETECTIVE SERGEANT: The detention centre still seems to be a short sharp lesson from what I can see. Up first thing in the morning, do some PE or a run; back in, scrubbing out, cleanin'; breakfast, a morning's work, lunch; lay off then maybe a walk or another run, back to work again. They seem to be put through the hoop for the three or six months. (*Laughs at an afterthought*) Of course, when they come out, they're that fit they can run like hell when they've done a job!

33

Two thousand London football supporters have reached Anfield without a single arrest being made. Last Saturday, the number escorted to neighbouring Goodison Park, to watch their team play Everton, was 10,000 – and none of them was arrested, either. The narrow road running between the high stadium wall and the row of two-storey red-brick shops is carpeted in fish-and-chip papers left scattered by Liverpool supporters already on the terraces and on the famous Kop – another of those Afrikaans words. The mounted police are here, and so are officers from the OSD, as well as men from 'A' and 'B' Divisions, all in their kept-for-best uniforms. The Chief Constable has made it an order that everyone should be at their smartest on these occasions, as this will encourage respect, and not in their rally jacket 'battle fatigues'. The sun decides to shine; there is dust, excitement, a feeling of wellbeing and the thrill of anticipation. When the visitors emerge again, darkness will have fallen on 'A' Division.

The biggest trouble is they're complete strangers. If they stay in a crowd, they'll be far better off and we can handle them easily. The trouble is that they start breaking up into little groups, and this is when the fights start. This is what they're looking for, these local buckos – so-called supporters, but we don't recognise them as such.

And as the droll sergeant crosses back into the North Subdivision, which is littered with rubble or what the locals call 'the debris', an expression dating back to the war years and the bombing, he regards his surroundings with something of a strategist's eye.

I think it might have been a good idea for these so-called city planners to have consulted us. Look at Scotland Road. You can join it at the traffic lights below St Anne Street, but it's more than a mile before you can turn off again! Blocks, cul de sacs, railings all over the place. I don't see, quite honestly, why so many railings are needed. Oh, quite a few of our problems are caused by planning. Take the way they lay out these new estates – it's ridiculous, there's no rhyme or reason to the

274

numbering. In the old days, you could go to the road and say to yourself: Right, that end's nearest the town hall, so that's where it starts numbering; odds on your left, evens on the right. But not now. If you get a serious call, an emergency call, and you haven't worked that area a lot, you're stumbling around in the dark looking for numbers all over the place.

34

Hazards and emotional stresses are not what the detective inspector at Copperas Hill talks about when asked what pressures his staff work under.

Occasionally we'll find a younger detective going under because of his paper. I can see it happening and – generally when he's not there – I'll go through his desk. It has a twofold effect, this. The other lads there – and the ones who come in in the morning – all know that their boss was there the night before, going through somebody's stuff, and so they all get their bloody rubbish out of the way then, because they may be next. (*Laughs*) I'll have him in and say, 'Why is this like this?' 'Listen, boss,' he says, 'I've that much bloody stuff I couldn't do it.' 'Why didn't you come and knock on the door?' And he says, 'Ah, I didn't want to be a failure.' Of course he doesn't want to be a failure, but it's no good going on and on until it's too late, and he's thinking: Christ, I'm going to have a big hat on me head after this lot! I don't bollock him, not on the first occasion. I impress on him he can come in at any time, and I say, 'Sit at your desk for two days. I know what you've got to do. Get it done, and we'll start from Square One again. I'll forget all about it.' So from time to time they do get in a stress situation, but sickness is not a bad thing in this office. If it was a worrying situation, they might end up with ulcers, I don't know! But no, until I drop on them, they're not worrying, and it's instantaneously dealt with the next morning.

He has just been on such a sortie down into the almost deserted detective constables' office, and has a heap of crime report booklets before him. But his attention is on a report, filed by a detective sergeant, that is a model of its kind.

It's nice to have a file in front of you that anyone else could pick up, knowing nothing about the case, and be able to read it and know what has gone on. You see, we get detected offences three or four years hence, and that particular bobby who dealt with the offence may have retired, resigned, transferred to another force, or just isn't available. Other officers may have a more slapdash method, I don't know – but I ask for a particular standard, and I get it.

His original ambition was to have been a chemical engineer – because that was his best subject at grammar school – but he anticipated failing his O-levels, and left to join the police cadets.

I'm not going to come the guff of the humanitarian who wanted to look after the public and all this. I was looking for a job, and I got into the cadets very easily. I thought it was smashing. It gave me an insight into the public, and what we did with them, and the sort of people we lived alongside – in inverted commas. I was put into a CID office and I took to it like a duck to water. I thought it was the bee's knees! Not because of Agatha Christie novels or anything like that, but it was a very good happy office. The fellas in there accepted me as well. [Instead of three months, he stayed for six.] It got to the stage when I could sit at the type-writer and do their routine reports, and I'd knock all these out for the lads – only simple things – while they were out.

He also read a good deal about police work, and was top student on his training course at Bruche, becoming a sergeant four years later. Now he has few interests outside the police force, other than helping with a Cub Scout pack to which one of his sons belongs.

The pleasure I get from the job is assisting people who have been offended. There are times when I get pleasure from assisting the offender if it's a genuine, remorseful situation where he's done something wrong – or a series of things – which he would not normally do, and this is the only time he's going to do it. Now, that's a hard thing to detect, and sometimes you wonder. I used to do this with kids particularly. I've not got a soft spot for kids, but I've got two boys – aged six and nine – and I can see the problems. I live on a reasonable estate and it's got its problems. But these kids out here have got next to no bloody chance, and

276

if I can help them in any way I do do. But if they're out-and-out villains I cast them from me mind: It's hard luck; you're just going to be that way the rest of your life, sonny. You're just going to have to put up with us being the pigs and you being the villain, and it's a case of who's going to win. So I'm human in that way – or like to think I am. (*Laughs*) Of course, I don't see much of them now I'm a DI, because I'm not locking up that type of person. If I'm involved in a job, the fellow has gone beyond it, and you're never going to get him to be a good citizen again. It's a game of cops and robbers, and if I can pit my wits against the villains, all very well. If they win, it doesn't mean I dislike them – they're just a little bit cleverer than I am on this occasion. I'm not the ace detective, but somebody here may have a better idea – and they'll come eventually.

35

Darkness has fallen. The big fella steps smartly aside for a young policewoman leaving the radio-room. 'Hi, Liz! Comin' to the do after?'

She walks right on, not noticing him.

'What's 'er problem?' he asks the relief radio operator. 'Pretend yer me best friend, and let's hear the worst, son.'

'Got a sudden death to do, just come for the details.'

'A sudden?'

'Fatal, a TA up at Carlisle, young lad of sixteen. Got to tell the parents.'

'Bloody hell,' says the big fella, his face falling.

'Aye.'

The enormous fan buzzes and hums.

'Ever tell yer', chuckles the big fella, whacking his thigh with his torch, 'about the night old man Dell died? Oh, what a wicked, *evil* bastid 'e was! He croaked and it came over the phone. I was putting it out over the air, and there was a great roar of "Ooray!" from all over the division. Can't remember who the bobby was who went there, but he knocked on the door and as his missus opened the door she started effin' and blindin' at 'im, accusin' 'im of this, that and the other, y'know.'

277

'Oh aye.'

'So he just stood there and looked at 'er – and there's loads of kids around, and they're all spillin' out and spittin' and throwin' things at the bobby. And when she shuts up eventually he just said, "Yer ol' fella's dead!" – ran, jumped in 'is car and shot off!'

'He never!'

'He did! Now, if that'd been me, I'd have done it different, been a bit more subtle. Soon as that door opened, "*Are you the Widow Dell?*" '

36

The night is filled with promise, to judge by the brisk shuffle of a slight figure in grey trousers, a black jacket and very shiny shoes, who is making his way up a side-street off Islington with a laden Burton's shopping-bag. A white Escort with an illuminated POLICE sign draws up beside him, and Inspector North on Afternoons gets out. He is a broad urbane man in his mid-thirties whose uniform and signalling-stick seem incidental, for his voice and his manner are rather those of a successful family doctor.

'Sorry to trouble you,' he says in a detached breezy sort of way, 'but what have you in that bag, please?' Anyone can be stopped and searched in the city, under the provisions of a local bye-law.

The man looks guilt-stricken. 'Er, I've got six Guinness, sair,' he says, and holds open the bag for inspection.

'Six Guinness?'

'Yes, sair....'

'Oh, I thought you'd been to Burton's for a new suit!'

'No, sair....' He laughs immoderately.

'Oh well,' says Inspector North, sizing him up, 'enjoy them, then!'

'Thank you very much, sair....'

'Good night. Thank you!'

'Cheerio....'

With his thoughts seeming to trail like his sentences, the man continues on his way, turning twice to look back. Perhaps he's been the subject of a stop-and-search before, and expected, 'What's in the bag, pop? Crown jewels? That all? OK, on yer way – and see yer behave yerself!' Inspector North has a style all of his own, being a trifle intolerant of what might be termed the 'mystique' of his chosen profession.

What makes the job so much fun for me is that you're continually in situations which aren't unique, perhaps, but very, very unusual: you see, I could speak to thirty or forty people in a watch, whereas most members of the public speak to a policeman once in a year maybe. And so I'm very conscious of the fact that, while this may be routine for me, it could be earth-shattering for someone else. Because of that, people react very strangely when spoken to by a policeman, and you've got to make allowance for that. If you don't, you could be in dead trouble. This is what I'm always trying to get across to young bobbies. I say to them, 'You're just finding your feet; you're doing your best to be blasé when dealing with members of the public, and that's the worst possible thing you can do – because for them this is their special incident of nineteen-whatever and they'll remember it. For God's sake, do it properly!' It's hard to convince them maybe. (*Laughs*) Still....

Although a Liverpudlian, Inspector North's atypical rounded speech is no affectation. 'I went out to Mombasa when I was three, and spent most of my childhood out there. My father was on the ill-fated groundnuts scheme, and then he got a job in Nigeria. It was a case of extended visits and coming back for schooling, so I'm an adopted Scouser maybe, rather than the real McCoy.' When he wishes, however, Inspector North can be a superb mimic, and not only are his young family aware of this.

That's the funny thing about this job: accents. If you were to walk into a situation in a really rough area and speak with an Oxford accent, you'd probably – rather than have the mickey taken out of you – be treated with deference. They wouldn't be too sure about you. They'd think: Well, if he speaks like that, he may be more intelligent than I am, and so, for the time being, I'll be careful what I say. Whereas, if a bobby goes in: 'A'rice zere, cock!' – well, he's the same as me, no better than me, etcetera etcetera. So it can be very valuable, and I've tried it once or twice.

I love doing this. I like approaching people in different ways and just watching their reaction. I must confess I've done this in the Main Bridewell, where I was a sergeant for a while. Someone would come in, drunk and fighting, and I'd say (*Oxford accent*): 'Good evening, my man! What seems to be the trouble?' '*Huh*? Well, er, dese fellas 'ave, er, locked us up like – y'know.' 'Oh, *have* they? Officer, will you tell me the circumstances under which you arrested this individual?' And the bobby, looking at me a little strange, goes through all this, relates the circs. I say, 'Oh? Have you heard and understood what this officer said, my man?' 'Er, yes like.' 'Well, is there *anything* you want to say about it?' 'Er. . . .' 'Oh, it's all right, then? You were drunk and you have been disorderly?' 'Well, er, I s'pose I've 'ad a few bevvies like. I'm not *really* drunk, but er . . . I was shoutin' a bit, y'know.'

It's surprising how it can work! I must confess this wasn't an original idea of mine. We've got this very seasoned constable in this division – Liverpool born and bred – who speaks to every member of the public in this beautiful American accent, and he's perfectly polite, never has any trouble. He used to bring prisoners in to me at the Main Bridewell, and he'd say, 'Good eva-ning to you, Sergeant! Ah hay-iv ay-rested thee-is may-un [*laughs*] for the obstruction of the highway in Church Street, and the circumstances of this grand capture are, I wuz on uniformed foot patrol' – he'd go on like this! And the bucks would *look* at him, but they didn't want to react just in case he was an American over here, and they offended him in some way.

37

Stop-and-search pays regular dividends, and almost anyone carrying a bag after dark is liable to be stopped because of this.

I've often bumped into things. This fellow had a load of things in a sack and a carrier bag. 'Where did yer get your stuff from?' He hesitated, then said, 'I had a bit of a row at home, and I've taken them from the wife.' There was lots of pewter tankards and that, all engraved. 'What's all this?' I said. 'Oh, I don't know,' he said. 'But surely, if they're in your house, you should know what's written on them? I'm not satisfied with that – you're locked up.' We got him back to St Anne Street, and he's going to be charged with stealing the property of someone unknown, because we haven't got a complainant for these things. But he also had a typewriter, and in it was a piece of paper he'd been messing about with, practising. It was all little nursery rhymes and everything, and fourteen names and addresses in Birkenhead. CID checked them out – he'd burgled them all!

38

Kkkk-kik
   'CH – Alpha.'
   'Alpha.'
   'Thank you, Alpha. Reference this crowd of football supporters. We've got them surrounded – or near enough – at the Rotunda junction. Requesting further assistance, Bravo coming through at the moment. Can you have your mobiles make up there, please?'
   Nine-thirty and it's happened. The London supporters, who came out of Lime Street station like toothpaste from a tube, have broken up in the general surge leaving Anfield, and now one of their groups has come under attack just as it crosses back into 'A' Division.
   Kkkk-kik
   'Five-one-two-three.'
   'Five-one-two-three.'
   'It's a vehicle check, please.'
   But the computer terminal is out of order, so the regular night man, who has this minute taken over the wireless-room, rings through to CH for assistance.
   'CH? "A" Division Communications, Serious Radio Operator. Hello, my luv, how are yer?'

The Serious Radio Operator points out that as there is already a Serious Crime Squad, a Serious Incident Unit and a Serious

281

goodness knows what else besides, he's merely doing what he can on a personal basis to counteract the rising tide of undue frivolity in the police service.

'Me? I'm well, my luv, sittin' 'ere in me wet suit and me helmet. Will yer do a motorists' check, please?'

He has twenty years' service as a constable, and must be one of the most highly regarded, best loved officers in the division. His appearance is very much in keeping with his first choice of career.

I went straight from school to the Adelphi Hotel on Lime Street to train as a chef. I served a seven-year apprenticeship there, includin' me two years in the Army doin' me National Service, and I came out and I got fokkin' sick of it. They used to advertise on the bus then – y'know, 'Join the Police'. We did split shifts at the Adelphi: you went on at half-past nine and you worked till half-past two, you went back at half-past five and you worked till nine. So I thought: I've got to get out of this job, workin' in kitchens and that – and I thought I'd join a *man's* job. (*Dismally*) I was in about a week and I realised it wasn't much fokkin' different to the Adelphi, y'know!

Big and broad, balding, with clean-shaven pink cheeks and an expression of offended innocence, veering close to cherubic at times, he bends the plastic clip on his ballpoint at a right angle, rolling it incessantly between finger and thumb. And as the pen glitters round and round, his fund of stories is endless.

Willie came from Birkenhead 'cos he wasn't doin' very good – they all come 'ere if they're not doin' very good. It's in the early hours of a Sunday mornin', and there's a shop been screwed in Soho Street, and there's no one to go and stand by. So I said, 'Hey, Willie, go to these premises in Soho Street and stand by.' We get in touch with the keyholder – he can't come out, but he wants the place boarded up. So we get on to Expo [security firm run by ex-policemen] and they said they'd board it up. About two hours later Willie's sergeant comes on the radio, 'Position o' Willie?' – and I'm shoutin', 'Willie!' No answer, y'see. Last known position is Soho Street. So they go along there, and it's all boarded up. Then Willie comes on – he's inside the fokkin' shop! So we had to get Expo out again, so we could have Willie back, and they boarded it up. When he gets back, his

282

sergeant says, 'As yer goin' on yer 'olidays on Mondays, where's yer book?' It's inside the fokkin' shop.

Laughter is one of the first things most officers associate with him; another is an expertise that allows them to patrol the night, confident they could not be in better hands.

I do nights all the time because I have problems domesticwise; my wife's an invalid and has been hospitalised for long periods, y'know, and there's the family to see to. I've got a daughter that's sixteen, I've got a lad that's fourteen, and I've got a little fella that's four. I wage war with consultants, y'know – that's a thing that annoys me. If people want to complain about the police – it can be anything: some policeman doesn't please you the way he acts – you just come in a police station and you say, 'I wish to complain against a police officer.' And we give you a pamphlet, tellin' you how to do it. You try and complain about any other service – doctors, nurses, Electricity Board, Gas Board – they won't even tell yer their name! Who you're talkin' to! I work every night except Sundays and, added to that, I come in early three nights a week, working half-past nine to half-past seven in the morning. If they suddenly said there was no overtime, I couldn't manage – and that's after twenty years! (*Laughs*) I'd be better off on the dole, y'know.*

A Days and EPs man sticks his head into the radio-room. 'Did yer see that buck that's just waltzed out? The one with the little yellow jacket on? He's lobbin' bricks over Lime Street and there's a bobby standin' about two feet away from him. He just grabs him and frog-marches 'im into the panda. Didn't know what 'it 'im!'

Another man at his shoulder laughs and says, 'There was one in Lime Street, got over the fence – he was goin' to fight 'em all! – then realised I was right behind him, and apologised!'

Other officers are milling about waiting for checks to be made on whether their prisoners are wanted on warrant – they arrested theirs up near the Rotunda junction. Just enough time has elapsed for them to take stock of what they've been

*His take-home pay was about £260 a month, of which £48 went on travelling expenses and canteen meals. The revised pay structure in 1977 should have added roughly £43 to his basic wage before tax.

through; agitated, visibly shaken and above all relieved to have escaped injuries, they laugh a lot and brim with righteous indignation. It was a close-run thing that the London supporters reached Lime Street without any serious casualties.

'They were walkin' down the east side, hidin' behind the police cars – we've got five vehicles there – and there wasn't very many, about two hundred.'

'Two hundred and fifty, yeah.'

'Possibly three hundred.'

'And there's about seven to eight hundred Liverpool bucks on the west side, average age fifteen, and they're chantin'. Next thing, they're on the debris and they're pickin' bricks up, and next thing a bottle come.'

'It hit the Vauxhall Viva, didn't it?'

'No, just in front of us. I looked in the rear-view mirror, and there's this contingent crossing the dual carriage-way at them – a proper bloody mauling!'

An older constable shrugs. 'Still, it's all in a day's work, isn't it? But what I don't like is bein' right in the middle, sittin' in that panda with all that glass and whatever, and havin' the bricks comin' in.'

'Yeah, I remember Alec standing with his hand on the car – next thing, his hand broke. Brick hit his hand and of course it was on the vehicle, smashed his fingers up.'

'A glass winda isn't goin' to stop anythin'!'

'Look at my old helmet – an air-rifle hole through it!'

'It's ludicrous.'

'How often do they read the Riot Act? If we had a proper riot situation, y'know, we could control it! But the problem is that if the chief officer reads the Riot Act he's got to pay for all the damage done – so they don't do it, just because it's uneconomical. But the Riot Act!'

'So many powers – crikey.'

'You can just lock up anything that moves – you don't even have to give evidence. The fact they were there is enough.'

'I don't like bein' in the middle!'

'Aye, and it could've been a proper bloody mauling!' one of the Lime Street officers is told once again.

284

'There was no point in sayin', "Now stop this, go away – that's bein' a bit naughty," because they'd just 'ave laffed at yer. So we go in, show a bit of force, and bloody whack out.'

A driver nudges his companion. 'His MO is he batters them round the legs with his baton.' Everyone laughs.

'Yuh.'

A big fella grins and says, 'I just pick 'em up by the hair and *remove* them!'

'Well, I haven't got the size to remove the big fellas, so I've got to 'it them on the knees. I've been on the job now for five and a half years, and that's the first time I've ever used my baton on anyone. It doesn't hurt them.'

'It does! They get a bloody bruise.'

'Well, it doesn't do the same damage as if you hit them on the bloody head.'

'This Riot Act—'

'If I was the Home Secretary, I'd make the football club responsible and make them pay for any damage.'

'I say that all people under eighteen must be accompanied by an adult.'

'Make it X-certificate, yer mean?'

A big laugh.

'No, listen. You go over to America, y'know, and at the ice hockey there you can't get in without your parent or a guardian.'

Someone nods. 'Yuh, y'know, they can't go into the films unless they're a responsible adult, so they're not responsible to be walkin' round the streets on their own.'

'They're all half young cut-throats.'

'They're not *'uman.*'

'But it was never like this before, was it? I couldn't take my lad to a football match now.'

'Right! I saw Dave over here before, and his lad was goin' to this match and he was worried sick, y'know. "I hope he's all right," he said. What a bloody state of affairs when he's worried because his lad's gone to a bloody football match!'

'And you go to court with one of these' – he nods at a smirk of young prisoners out in the charge office – 'and it's you that's on trial! Not the little animal you've locked up.'

'Oh no, you're the bloody villain.'

'I'm fed up with it.'

'They've had a gate of what? Forty? Fifty thousand? And how many of them are about the town, causin' damage?'

'About a thousand – two thousand.'

'So you're talkin' in terms of—'

'When's it goin' to stop? It can only grow worse, and so they will bring back birchin' or somethin'.'

'Well, what is goin' to stop it? A thousand-pound fine won't do it – they'll have a whip-round or somethin'!'

That gets a big laugh, too, releasing the tension.

39

The South Sub inspector on Afternoons has been taken ill, so Inspector North is now covering the entire division for the remainder of the watch. Turning left instead of right at the foot of London Road, he passes the Adelphi, Liverpool's grandest hotel, and sweeps on up Mount Pleasant. Near the crest of the rise, he bears left again, going round Paddy's Wigwam – the conical, very modern Roman Catholic cathedral counter-balancing the Anglican megalith at the far end of Hope Street – and makes his way through the area occupied by Liverpool University.

It is very noticeable that students as such are hardly ever mentioned in casual conversations on the South Sub, except where they happen to be the complainants in a case – or when generalisations are being made about attitudes toward the police. Like the sub-division's large Chinese community, they seem to be regarded simply as a benign presence, colourful but of no particular consequence. 'Well, they're no problem, are they?' says one Copperas Hill constable in a typical response. 'It's nonsense they're all into drugs and things like that. The only time I ever think of 'em, to be honest with yer, is when they have this rag-day march or whatever once a year – and that isn't too bad, y'know. The women on that are great!' In fact, words like 'student', 'university' and 'graduate' appear to

286

provoke a strong reaction only when used within the context of the police service itself.

Most officers in 'A' Division left school as soon as the law allowed, and many tend to the belief that anyone with higher qualifications is lacking a proportional amount of sound common sense. At its most rational, this view is apparently based on the conundrum: With decent qualifications, what reasonable man would *want* to be a bobby? And so graduate recruits have been subject to considerable suspicion in the past, and often to forthright prejudice – as this tale about the gruff inspector and a twice-bitten newcomer to St Anne Street would suggest.

Having sent for the new recruit to make his acquaintance, the inspector said, 'Got a degree, I hear, son?'

'Um, well,' the recruit mumbled reluctantly, 'er, yes. . . .'

'Me sister's at the university.'

'Is she, sir?' said the recruit, brightening immediately.

'Aye,' replied the inspector, raising a forefinger and thumb held about two inches apart, 'in a fokkin' bottle *that* big.'

But while this anecdote may typify an attitude, it could also serve as its epitaph, for ever-increasing numbers of serving officers have begun degree courses in recent years, and there is a growing interest in further education generally.

Part of the reason for this, especially among those engaged on completing high school levels of attainment, is an awareness that as many police officers retire relatively early they will need some sort of paper qualifications to compete in tomorrow's job market.

Then again, the police service is in itself an educative process, inasmuch as people become, willy nilly, close observers of man and his condition, while it also introduces them to all manner of 'new worlds' and thought-provoking situations. This can lead to a desire to know more, to compare knowledge, to structure it, and to apply it more effectively – all of which is now possible with the establishment of the Open University, and the police authority helps with some of the costs involved.

The Merseyside force has, moreover, a scheme whereby it sends five officers to Liverpool University each year on full pay, allowing them to take any three-year course that they like, provided it has some relevance to police work. On top of which, officers selected for the Special Course at Bramshill, the National Police College, are able to win scholarships to universities all over Great Britain.

Among the most popular choices of subject are modern history, the social sciences, politics and, of course, law. Having once made a start on further education, many officers find that study becomes such an enjoyable part of their lives that they persist far beyond the limits of their original target. One uniformed sergeant, for instance, is now also a barrister.

40

The campus is quiet. Inspector North continues towards Myrtle Gardens, and is passed by a green Capri going like a rocket with a 'jam butty' Traffic car hard on its tail.

That's exciting – gets the adrenalin going! Man against man, and machine against machine! (*Laughs*) But if you do it too much, if you're constantly at it all the time, even the excitement becomes routine; it no longer stimulates you the way it used to. I imagine an analogy is taking drugs. It's euphoric at first, but once you're hooked you don't even enjoy it when you do have a fix.

The Capri and its pursuer vanish. Myrtle Gardens is quiet, but here the hush has a different quality, a brooding, smouldering twitchiness. Inspector North returns the waved greeting of a security guard, set to protect some repair work being carried out by the council, and stops for a word with the constable on that beat. Then on again to check the Social Services building on the corner of Upper Parliament Street and Grove Street, which is frequently raided by people who have apparently 'cased the joint' while seeking assistance there. Despite the sophistication of the alarm system, they always seem to know exactly what they're after and the quickest way to get it out. By coincidence, another green Capri appears, nosing out of Falkner Square into Grove Street. Inspector North

288

follows it, but it's just completing the fourth side of the square, and returns beneath the avenue of trees again. About half a dozen prostitutes are out, and there's a minder parked near the telephone-box.

Self-respecting cows – as they're colloquially known! – seldom have intercourse. Their primary objective is to get their client to achieve orgasm before that ever takes place. Y'know, a very convenient way of making your money. . . .

The driver of the green Capri slows down and stops, smiling in supercilious delight at the police vehicle as it passes him. Or perhaps his smile signifies more than that, making the flesh creep ever so slightly, because, as every Plain Clothes officer soon learns, a police presence can be enormously titillating for some members of the public. In fact, the threat of arrest is probably a major reason why the 'Victoria Street queers' prefer a public place to a private one, and adds a 'forbidden fruit' piquancy to late-night drinking in clubs that should be closed. There are, of course, other dangers lurking in an area like this.

Mugging of clients goes on, but it's not wholesale. It's not one of those things which has presented itself as a problem at the moment that we've got to deal with. We had a terrific increase in the number of robberies a few years ago, so we formed a robbery squad and next year the percentage went down.

That's one of my criticisms of the police force. When a problem presents itself, we form a squad to deal with it – and it does deal with it, because it can afford to. You deal with *a* problem, you develop this *esprit de corps*, and you're not given other stuff to do, so all our squads have been very, very successful.

But if you're a [Uniform] policeman, you've got an awful lot of responsibilities – emergency calls, summonsing motorists, disturbances, burglaries – and you tend to get bogged down in routine of one sort or another. We give first aid to everything. We go to a domestic dispute and we say, 'Now look, don't do it again. If there's a breach of the peace, we'll have to arrest you.' If we do arrest them and take them to court, we're still giving first aid – we're not attacking the problem at its root. Perhaps that's not our function, but the point is that nobody else is, so the problem recurs. To my mind, although squadding fulfils a useful function, if we had a lot of those personnel in these squads

289

on the beat, to patrol and deal with incidents the way every other policeman does, then we'd be far more in a position to tell whether we were in control or not. The *real* problem is that different policemen doing different jobs experience different problems.

I believe we're grossly undermanned. Statisticians tell us we have more policemen per head of population on Merseyside than other places do – it's something like four-point-something a thousand. But it doesn't matter what statisticians say; we're having a certain volume of crime, and it should relate to that. In other words, you want a good job study on what each policeman's got to do, and only then can you perhaps start making predictions about what we should be directing our attention to.

And one of the disadvantages of forming policemen into special squads, special departments – like the CID – is that it becomes a form of reward. People going into plain clothes get a lot of autonomy. They can go into public houses and drink without asking the permission of a senior officer – that's just one example of the sort of freedom they have. It's a kind of concession: 'Look, we're giving you a good job – and you've got to prove you're good at it, if you want to stay there.' So the penalty they pay for that freedom is to work efficiently and very, very hard; harder, perhaps, than their uniformed colleagues do. And you get him trying to show that, despite the slings and arrows of outrageous fortune, etcetera etcetera, he's really very efficient.

There are pros and cons to it. I'm conscious that from one point of view mine's a very formal, structured argument, and there is a heavy demand on the police to detect offenders. But what I'm saying is that we shouldn't let that dissuade us from our primary responsibility: i.e. *preventing* crime – and I don't just mean the bars-and-bolts side of it.

Inspector North tries to pick out what is being said over his personal radio, but it's 'breaking' badly and he makes for the open space beside the Anglican cathedral at the end of Canning Street.

That's fine in theory! (*Laughs*) But in practice we measure our efficiency by how good we are at *detecting* crime, and we shouldn't do. For example, the Chief Constable commends police officers more often than not for their good work in detecting crime. There are several phrases that appear time and time again in

290

Chief Constable's Orders, like 'zeal and assiduity', and they always describe how many thieves or burglars a policeman has arrested within a given time which is, perhaps, better than average. Now, far be it for me to decry people who work hard getting a reward – I've enough faith in psychology to believe behavourism really works! (*Laughs*) But at the same time there are lots of policemen walking round who know who every thief is on their beats, who know where to be at the right time to prevent trouble breaking out, and these people never get rewards, never get patted on the back – except for their endeavours to *detect* crime. There's no encouragement for them to fulfil their primary function. (*It is suggested that a police officer, knowing a crime is about to take place, does his career more good by allowing it to happen – and then making the arrest – than if he prevented it occurring.*) Taking it to that extreme, he's legally wrong to do that. (*Smiles*) But a lot of people would argue that there's far more to be gained from catching a guy who's determined to become a criminal than by preventing him from doing it! Because only then, once you've caught him, can you take him before the appropriate authority and have him treated, rehabilitated, punished – whatever you happen to believe in.

'Alpha to all patrols – theft from the person, Hardman Street! Youth wearing black leather jacket, blue denim jeans, running *kkkkkkk*.'

Inspector North corners hard into Rodney Street.

There was this professor in America who picked a town that was very similar to Edinburgh. He found that in Edinburgh there were about three murders in the year – speaking figuratively – about forty-seven robberies, thirteen or fourteen rapes etcetera etcetera; and in the same year in the American town there were forty-six murders – twelve of which were on policemen – God knows how many rapes, God knows how many robberies. Then he went on to compare the police forces. (*Smiles*) He found that the police in the States were far more efficient. They had far more equipment, which they knew how to use far better than we did; they had their beat system arranged far better; and they had computers – which our police had never heard of then. He found the British police to be very, very inefficient, and so he concluded that the police have very little to do with the level of crime: it depends on how orderly the community is. It may sound like stating the obvious, but I think it's a very valuable point to make. I put down the reason for the low level of crime in this country to the fact there's far more general consensus as to what the law of the land should be, and what is moral and what is immoral, what's criminal and not criminal, sinful or not sinful, depending on what terms of reference you use.

'That's the one, sir!' confirms a constable, panting up.

'I done nothin'!' protests the writhing boy, trying to break Inspector North's grip on his arm. 'They said to me, "Run!" '

'Who said to you, "Run" ?'

'All the lads! They said the coppers were comin', so I started runnin'.'

'What lads?' In a deserted street, it's an obvious if awkward question. 'You're not obliged to say anything unless you wish to do so, and anything you say will be taken down in writing and may be used in evidence. I'm arresting you for a theft from the person in Hardman Street a short time ago. Anything you want to say to me about it ?'

'I've told yer – I done nothin'.'

'Thank you!'

Inspector North makes for Copperas Hill with an air of some satisfaction, even though this arrest, made shortly before the end of his watch, will mean his getting home two or three hours later than expected. As a graduate twice over – his first arts degree was awarded by the Open University, and he has just returned from getting a Bachelor of Arts degree in sociology at Liverpool University, under the force's own scheme – he likes to feel he's still very much a 'street bobby'.

41

Weariness pervades the dimly lit saloon bar. The shutters are up, the ash-trays emptied; the last customer was turned out of the pub more than an hour ago. The landlord and a few friends linger on, slowly unwinding at the end of another long day.

292

'Romans,' murmurs the barmaid, as she peers with one eye at the world through a glass of mild and bitter. 'I go back to them days – I fantasize like. They were wonderful, them Romans, weren't they?' A gentle silence. 'I mean I read all about them Romans, and me mam says I'm daft.'

'No,' grunts a gallant old regular, 'better edgy-cated, Tilly.'

'D'yer fancy them Romans?' she asks the young man in a blue shirt beneath a cheap windcheater. 'Well, do yer?' The bobby shrugs, too tired to think of an answer, just happy to be there.

THREE

1

Sunday night and a small car comes to a stop beside a tree in Falkner Square.

'Doin' business, luv?' asks the driver, grinning at the prostitute sheltering there from the light drizzle.

Her smile becomes real as she acknowledges the irony of being addressed in the exact words she herself uses on the kerb-crawlers. 'I've been stood 'ere that long', she says, 'that a dog's been up twice to piss on me leg.'

'Aye, very quiet,' he agrees, looking round and seeing no one else out. 'Well, luv, don't do anythin' I wouldn't do.' And he's away again. The Plain Clothes check on the square becomes very much a matter of habit after a time; he's actually on his way to parade at a secret rendezvous outside the division.

2

'Hurry up, officer!' urges a well-meaning citizen, bursting into the Pier Head enquiry office. 'There's an old fella down there' – she points in the direction of the all-night coffee-stall – 'and he's havin' a fit! He's goin' berserk!'

'What's he look like?'

'Well, he's got a hump on 'is back, and his one eye's lookin' at yer and the other eye's lookin' for yer, y'know – and he's flat on 'is back!'

'OK, luv, be with you in a minute.'

The station keeper retires into his improvised office, collects his jacket, helmet and radio, locks the glass door and strolls down toward a circle of revellers all agog.

The first time I saw Angus doing this, I got the ambulance straight away, y'know! He was kickin' and goin' and mouthin' away, and I thought: Oh Christ, get an ambulance! The am-

294

bulance fellow says, 'Oh Jesus, not Angus again!' Now Angus'll throw a – it's not a fit, it's a self-induced thing – and I'll go and prop him up and say, 'Angus! You're a drunken spastic! Now, bloody shut up and don't annoy me any more tonight!' 'A'right, Jock!' And he'll come right out of it; all it is, is someone to buy him a cuppa tea, get the ambulance, and the ambulance take him home.

The gawping circle parts to allow the station keeper through, then tightens a pace or two, feeling less apprehensive of the writhing, gabbling figure drumming worn heels on the concrete. The policeman props him up and has a quiet word. 'A'right, Jock!' says the little Scotsman and, with disappointing suddenness, the show is over. The station keeper saunters on, and decides – now he is out – to make his first check of the observation deck overlooking the landing-stages.

Angus knows I'm Irish – he knows the lads call me Pat – but he calls me Jock. I don't mind, he's harmless. So's Molly the Cat – she's Irish, been here many years. She wears a red paddy hat like Bill and Ben on the kiddies' programme, and she jabbers away like them as well. I'm Irish, but I need a bloody interpreter when she starts! She'll come along and say, 'Ah, f-f-f-fuckin' hell, f-f-f-fuckin' hell! Dey're callin' me names, mister!' 'What are they callin' you?' 'Stutterin' Annie!' 'You don't stammer, do you?' 'Ah-ah-ah-ah, *no*!' They all know her down here, and try to take the mickey – extract the Michael. She doesn't like this, y'see, and comes in about twenty times a night. 'Are they at it again, Molly?' 'Ah-be-dah-be-dah!' 'Right, be with you in a minute.' You put on your jacket and you go out, and just for Molly's benefit you say, 'Hey, lads, pack it in!' 'A'right, boss! A'right, chief. . . .' And she says, 'You're a goo-goo-goo-good lad.' 'OK!' And off she'll pop. (*Laughs*) She enjoys all that really; she's happy; it's someone to talk to. The bucks take the mickey, but they're very good-natured with her, not nasty with her. You know, you get some of the hardest bastards around here, but if anyone goes too far with the divvies the bucks'll take their part regardless.

The station keeper steps into a glass shelter and gives a nudge to a 'divvy' sleeping there out of the drizzle.
    'Fok aff!'

'A'right, John?'

'Fok aff!'

The observation deck is otherwise deserted, and so the station keeper makes his way down the steps and back to the enquiry office.

You know, he doesn't mean 'fok aff' nastily, the way some people use it. To them, 'fuck off' means 'I'm all right, Jack – I'm fine, y'know.' Some bobbies go along, wake them up. The only reason I do that occasionally is to see if they're all right, that they haven't snuffed it. They don't bother anybody. They don't beg. The only nuisance they make is they lie around. They're happy with their existence – if you can call it that – down here.

A gaunt wild-eyed woman in a red bonnet, with a black kitten peering out from between the lapels of her soiled fawn raincoat, is waiting for him at the glass door.

'Blood suck!' she declares. 'B-b-blood suck! He's a b-b-blood suck! There!' She points a crooked finger back at a group of grinning youngsters at the food-hatch. 'A blood suck, m-m-mister!'

'A'right, Molly – be down in a minute.'

But she turns and flurries away into the night, hugging her kitten close to her and whispering love in its ear.

3

Half a dozen or so Plain Clothes officers are now in the dimly lit canteen of a neighbouring division's headquarters, waiting to go on a club raid. Some of them, who left home halfway through *Soldier Blue*, are seated in front of the colour set in the corner; the others gathered round a vinyl-topped table with the head of the section. He is a thirty-nine-year-old inspector who smokes a pipe, wears his hair short, dresses conservatively, and conducts himself with a quiet twinkling inscrutability. Straight as an arrow, his subordinates say, but you never know what he's bloody thinking – not about you anyway.

Nobody at the table, other than the inspector, knows more than 'there's a job on', which gives the occasion an edge of

296

pleasurable suspense, as they gossip over cups of tea and coffee. 'I said, "Are yer doin' business, luv?" And old Mary said, "I've been stood 'ere that long a—" '

The telephone shrills on the wall above the trays trolley, and the inspector crosses over to answer it. 'All quiet,' he reports back to the table. 'Shutters down, not a soul in the place.'

'Where was it, sir?'

He names a flashy club that has been ignoring the closing-time regulations, and in particular the earlier deadline of 12.30 a.m. on Mondays. The sergeant, dispatched some time ago to the South Sub, will now try another club that's been suggested to him.

'Trust old Mary to be out,' remarks one of the group, demonstrating a police officer's facility to carry on a conversation despite any number of interruptions. 'The young cows are giving her that much competition. She said what, then?'

4

It's coming up to one o'clock. The Pier Head can be an extremely unpredictable place in the small hours of the morning.

They come down from the clubs – they're let out at all hours – and they come down and wait for the first bus, which is at six, six-thirtyish. Bucks and buckesses; you see lassies gettin' on the first bus who've been out all night. Occasionally you go and pick the mouthpiece, and you talk to him in his kind of language. (*Laughs*) To use normal language, or the language I'd use in my home, is a waste of time. You go up to the fella and say, 'Listen, Roger Bollocks, any more noise out of you, and I'll bloody throw yer in the river with a stone around yer neck!' You don't mean it, wouldn't dream of doin' it – I'd like to sometimes, mind you! – but that they understand. I had a fellow a couple of weeks back who was tryin' to get four lads to fight with him. He was pissed, so I told him to go home and behave himself. He started swearin' and shoutin' at me. I said, 'Look, get a bus, go home; there's no point in a hassle.' No way. Next thing, his hand went down and he had a knife half out of its sheath. So I grabbed his arm and

297

took the knife off him, locked him up for an offensive weapon. But I've never been attacked as such.

Unlike most uniformed constables in 'A' Division, the station keeper appears barely conscious of the dangers that he faces on duty, and has to be prompted before he'll talk of them. The warmth of his personality – plus his self-assurance, born of considerable experience – might suffice to explain why his attitude is markedly different. Then he'll let slip something like: 'The first time a car backfired in Dale Street, I dived into a doorway. That was just a natural reaction, y'know. People passed by and they said, "H'mmm".'

5

The canteen telephone rings yet again. So far the Plain Clothes sergeant has had no success with a list of probables over on the South Sub, and it looks as though, somehow or other, word of a raid has leaked out.

'It's on,' says the inspector.

6

The station keeper on Nights this week at the Pier Head, which is regarded by many as a posting to 'Siberia', asked to be sent there. He has sturdy Celtic good looks, curling brown hair, and an infectious laugh. He is on the PTA committee at his son's school, helps with a handicapped group, and spends quite a bit of time improving the police house he's buying.

I'm twenty-eight now. I left school at fifteen – thirty-bob-a-week job in a shop, y'know. Chucked that, no chance for advancement, worked on the factory floor, went from that to storekeeper, stock controller. Saved them a couple of thousand in the first year I was there, petty pilfering – asked for a rise, nothing doing. I knew most of the policemen in my home town of Armagh, and a couple of them said, 'Well, why not join us?' Why not? I thought. 'But', I said, 'there's only one problem: I'm a Catholic.

298

Will I be accepted?' They said, 'Yeah, no reason why not.' (*Smiles*) So after losing me exam papers a couple of times – I don't know why! – I eventually got in and went straight to Belfast.*

After trainin' in the school, I went to the Ardoyne. There were some happy times in Belfast; there were some bloody lousy times as well. I got injured in a bomb blast planted by the IRA. The flat was attacked three times [his police flat was in a Protestant area], and my wife had a miscarriage after the second one. That's also when they began to boycott my wife because she was a Catholic; she might have to wait half an hour to be served in a shop with only one or two people in it – that sort of thing. I almost shot the kiddie one night. I was watchin' television and the gun's at the side of me as usual, and I heard nothing till I saw the door move. Picked the gun up and cocked it – I don't know what stopped me, but it was my kiddie, climbed over the side of his cot. That scared me. Don't really like guns, y'know. I was one of the first bobbies into the Ardoyne [after it had been a no-go area], and I went in unarmed. I don't like carryin' them, but it was a necessity. Once, only once, I could have killed someone. Two friends of mine, both off duty, unarmed, went into the back room of an off-licence for a drink, because you couldn't go into a pub openly the way you do here. Two fellows walked in and shot them through the head. One [of the dead] was a Catholic with five kids; the other fellow was a Protestant who was due to go on leave that day, and he had about sixteen years in. When you went out in the jeep to deal with a domestic dispute, you had a driver, an observer and a rear gunner; the driver had a pistol, the other two had pistols and submachine-guns. The rear gunner jumped out and took up a position in somebody's garden to cover you, and the driver did the same thing – that was the way you went to do a call. Policing as the typical British bobby is almost non-existent.

The federation over there tried to get a pound-a-day danger money – the pay was exactly the same as here. It was bloody hilarious, y'know! (*Laughs*) We were told the danger factor was no different to here. I could have argued about that, but didn't bother. It was one of those situations where you adapted as best you could, or you got out. Quite a few of the bobbies left the job for physical reasons; there were quite a few with ulcer jobs

*He sat the examination three times.

through the strain. But the wives were under the biggest strain, and I think in many cases they were the driving factor for the bobbies to leave. I stuck it for what? Two years and ten months. The wife was on the verge of a breakdown, and the kiddie wasn't being helped the way he was. [Desperate to move his family, he applied to three North Country forces simultaneously. One turned him down flat, possibly as a matter of unwritten policy in support of the depleted RUC; one was so offended by being 'one of the list' that it didn't trouble to reply formally; and the Liverpool force arranged an interview.] Within ten minutes of the interview, although they said in their letter they could only give me single quarters, I got the offer of a police house. We came over in '73.

In Northern Ireland, your role was basically security. As I see it here, I think basically a bobby should be trusted by the public. He should help the public. I don't say he should bow down to them and pander to their bloody every whim: he's basically a peace keeper. And by keeping the peace I don't mean you thump somebody because he shouts at you! (*Laughs*) Basically, I try and find out why he shouts at me. I won't lock someone up if I can get through to them that what they're doing is wrong, and they understand it's wrong and go about their business in a proper fashion. It's like in here with the divvies. If I'm too busy, I'll tell them to 'fok aff'. They know me and they accept it. Because the next time they'll come in and I'm not busy I'll sit and talk to them for half an hour – they're lonely, y'know. What can you do with them? They've been in contact with the Social Services dozens of times, and they don't want to know. Plus they'll tell you things, which is another part of my job.

I'd like very much to go somewhere, a little village where it's quiet and peaceful, later on in my service, but not now. I prefer to be where there's something happening. I don't want to be bored, that's all. It can be a little bit boring down here [the Pier Head]; sometimes everything happens at once. It's all right. I came down initially to study [for his sergeants' exam], but my studies haven't gone very well because I've got so many pressing problems at home. My wife's had another miscarriage; she's very depressed – it's her third 'miss', y'know. I've got problems with my lad.

His seven-year-old is a bright sensible boy with a reading ability three or four years ahead of his age. He has, however,

300

developed an acute phobia for anything related to medicine or dentistry, and this is felt to be a form of transferred anxiety. 'It's the only thing I can put it down to. For a year after we came here, he was, y'know, like a cat, curling up in the corner of his cot. Then he seemed to get over it. Still a bit nervy, y'know – if you walk towards him, he jumps. That has always been a throwback to Northern Ireland.' Obviously nobody in the family was left unscathed. 'Any fella who tells yer – a bobby or a soldier – they weren't scared, he's a bloody liar. Either that, or they're mad! Because you must feel fear at some time – I know I certainly did. If I'd been single? I would have stayed there; there's no doubt about that. It's my home. Sounds Irish that!'

7

The game is on. Just one slip, one instant of bad luck, and it could all turn very nasty. The Plain Clothes officers park their cars in a side-street some twenty yards short of a dilapidated Victorian town-house, and the sergeant comes over to confirm that further customers have been admitted to the club in the basement since his telephone call to the canteen. All that remains now is for the last-minute back-up of uniformed officers to arrive.

The night air is invigorating after the long wait indoors, and people move restlessly, keeping their voices low. Part of this restlessness is excitement, and part is a degree of apprehension, for every officer present has seen at least one hideous wounding, and almost without exception it has been associated with club life. There has been such a succession of woundings in this particular club, as it happens, that a judge has recently made informal enquiries about when it was last raided. In a minute or two they'll be down those steps and surrounded by resentful drunken people, all within easy reach of a bottle or glass, and a great deal will depend on denying the moment any of the melodrama suggested by the Harry Lime setting: wet

301

paving-stones, deep shadows, peeling paintwork thrown into sharp relief by a solitary lamp-post.

The uniformed constables arrive. 'Right, lad, I want you down the side here, in case some try to come out the back, and you, lass, on the door,' says the inspector, giving the nod to two 'bucks' who will set the ball rolling.

They set off for the basement steps, while the rest of the small party waits hard in against the street wall. The radio mutters softly, and the inspector cautions, 'Turn it off, lass.' Not only might it alert the doormen, but the sound could also heighten the tension once they're inside the club, just as the sight of a truncheon might.

The bearded 'buck' raps on the black door. It opens very slightly and a youth looks out – a youth he recognises instantly, having arrested him while in Uniform. But there's not a flicker of recognition in return.

'We a'right f'pints ?'

'Er, I'll 'ave to 'ave a word with the boss, like.'

The door closes. Seconds become minutes. Dealing with people who aren't necessarily cold sober can also have advantages at times, and yet. . . . The chief bouncer opens up and takes a look. 'Well, lads, just checkin' yer not the busies,' he says, winking. 'A'right, let 'em come in.'

The bearded 'buck' taps him on his retreating shoulder. 'By the way,' he says gleefully, holding out his warrant card, 'you were right the first time.'

'Fokkin' hell! If you want the boss, he's just gone through there. . . .'

The manager is at the bar, frantically tugging on the metal grille which should be down in front of the beer pumps. 'Bar's closed!' he calls out. 'Bar's closed!'

And the signal is given to those waiting outside. Down the steps they go, along the short passage and into a smoke-filled pungent room that is, in the words of an observer, 'bloody heavin' with bucks and buckesses pissed outa their minds'. The initial reaction of this dense crowd is mixed; several seem unaware that a raid is in progress, some stand mildly bemused, others jeer and laugh at the sight of so many sports jackets, while

302

looks of surprise are reserved chiefly for a young blonde with her hair in bunches, who could be mistaken for an infant teacher abroad long after her bedtime.

'Piss off,' someone hisses.

'Fok aff, will yer? Jesus Christ!'

A few try to leave, but the uniformed policewoman turns them back from the front passageway. The rest of the officers make for the bar, taking care not to jostle anyone as they move through the crush, and ignoring everything said to them. A glass breaks.

'Are you the licensee or the manager?' the inspector asks the man at the grille, his tone politely casual.

'Manager,' he replies, coughing.

'Is the boss in the club now? Is he present?'

'He gone now. He was here, but he gone.'

'Well, nobody will be leaving now, so you stick by that, do you?'

A cough and a nod. 'I locked up at twelve,' says the manager, with no attempt to sound convincing.

'We've seen people coming in,' murmurs a constable with an unmistakably military bearing who is already examining the till. 'Have you any books?'

'Members' books?' adds the inspector.

While the manager fetches them, a long-haired man of about twenty-six, with a scar down one cheek, lurches over to the sergeant. 'I've done three years for the likes of youse twats!' he slurs, rocking slightly, arms hanging limp. 'Fokkin' twats! Tha's all youse are. . . .'

The sergeant's face reddens but his voice stays low and neutral. 'You're entitled to your opinion, pal.'

'Three fokkin' years!'

'We'll not keep yer long if yer behave yerself.'

A crony sidles over to make peace, but is shaken off. 'Know what I think o' yer?' sneers the man with the scar. The sergeant remains silent, his knuckles very white.

303

8

'I'll tell yer a better story,' says the poker-faced constable, and pauses while the relief radio operator walks through the bridewell to go and have his refreshments. 'Me vasectomy.'

Whoops of delight. Nothing can be more boring than hanging about after midnight on a wet Monday morning, convinced that nothing is going to happen in the entire division until 7.30 a.m., and half-wishing it were Saturday night again.

'Have you had a vasectomy?' the constable begins mournfully. 'Some rotten bastid said to me, "It's easier than havin' a tooth out". Well, y'know, you read all about it, and it sounds such a simple thing.'

Guffaws, and someone says, 'Shhhhh!'

'I got there about half-past eight – funny how it always happens in the cold light of morning – and I said to this nurse I found there, "I'm Mr ——, I'm havin' an operation." "Oh yes, a vasectomy. Just sit down there," she said, "and I'll take a few details. Next of kin?" Bloody hell. . . .' His gloom deepens. 'Then she said, "The first thing we do is remove yer fur coat, y'know." I didn't think it was funny at first.

'Next thing, an old male nurse comes along and we go down to the ward. I'm naked, lyin' on the bed, he's shavin' all me hair off, and I'm thinkin': What've I let meself in for? Then they give you one of these dressing-gowns that don't quite fit – they're specially made, y'know – and I'm sittin' there until ten to bloody ten. They come and they take this dressing-gown off me, and they put on this white thing. They're bent, nurses are – they took me teeth out. I *told* them I wasn't going to eat anything.'

'Shhhh!' The laughter goes back on simmer again.

'And they wheel me to this big green door – just like on the telly, y'know.' A long sigh. 'All the walls painted white, lights, the operatin'-table.' Brightens momentarily. 'Nice nurse there!' The bleak look returns. 'They put up a cage with a green sheet so you can't see what they're doin', and then came

304

the entry of the fokkin' gladiators. This doctor came in; he was one of the weak who 'ated the strong, y'know – you could tell that. Took an instant dislike to me. He's standin' up and he can *just* see over the operatin'-table; two eyes and a green beret.'

A great big belly laugh.

'Anyway, Hiram Holiday got goin' – he looked about fourteen; I was probably the first live corpse he'd ever operated on. He wasn't older than sixteen. I said, "Excuse me, doctor" – they don't like yer to talk to them – "but when I come here with the wife, like, we saw the consultant. I assumed, er, he'd be doin' this." "Naw," he said, "this is just like varicose veins." "No," I said, "it's a vasectomy." "Yeah, but it's like a varicose vein or gettin' a wart removed, y'know." '

'Sounds like GBH!'

The dead-pan nod. 'Now, this rotten bastid who put us up to this, he'd said to me, "It'll only be five minutes"! About twenty minutes later, I'm still lyin' there. It doesn't hurt, more a pullin' round – when they pull on the strings, you sit up, y'know.' Agonised groans of empathy, more guffaws. 'This nurse is chattin' to me. She said, "You're a policeman, aren't yer?" "Oh aye." "You're all dirty bastids, aren't yer?" she said. "I go to a lot of parties," she said, "and all the bobbies there have this done to them. Do you know what they shout out?" I said, "Well, I don't feel like bein' humorous this mornin', luv." Now, this bastid said they took this much tube off, about an inch, he said – and Hiram's got hold of somethin' like a Biro refill. I said, "Is that mine, luv?" "Oh yes," she said. "He's finished the one side," she said.'

When the laughter subsides, there's still no sound from the radio room.

'Anyhow, *forty* minutes it took, and then they lifted me back on the trolley. I had a look. You know this fella with his head stitched? Frankenstein? All black threads hangin' out? So they very gently give me me teeth back, and wheeled me back to the ward. Embarrassin', isn't it, when you've never been in hospital before?'

305

9

Now that all but the most befuddled have realised they're not going to be arrested for being in the club after hours, the level of overt hostility has eased a little. The raiding party never comes off guard, however, knowing that this could be tantamount to dropping a grenade after pulling the pin. Outnumbered at least four to one, there is no saying what might happen before help arrives, even though the inspector is confident 'they can all handle themselves well, including young Susie'. The manager and his staff seem particularly aware of the delicate balance being maintained, and make it plain that they are more than familiar with the sudden ferocious violence of which their clientele is capable.

'They're running me,' sighs the manager.

The inspector nods, keeping an eye on his young officers as they move about the room, making people fill in pro formas detailing their membership status, if any, and what they have had – or intended to have – in the way of food and drink. After completing the forms, they are being allowed to leave.

'They're not fokkin' 'uman, are dey?' a voice growls. 'I mean, wot's wrong in 'avin' a bevvy? Load o' perverts!' Girls snigger, and an acned youth turns to stare scornfully at the bar, his face frozen in a mug shot.

Gets the adrenalin goin'! Y'know, you notice little details; they're brighter, sharper sort of. Also, you're relyin' on yer mates not to lose their bottle, and knowin' you can rely on 'em is part of this good feeling, too. Do somethin' stupid and there's nothin' down for yer.

After name, date of birth, occupation and all the rest of it, the last line on the pro forma reads: *Reply when told the facts would be reported.* 'Youse are fokkin' cases,' replies the man with the scar. The officer writes this down using phonetics, signs the form and jerks a thumb at the exit. 'Right, and the next. ...'

Gradually the club empties. Six customers have had samples of their drinks taken, but are unlikely to hear anything further.

306

The kitchen – a vital area for evidence, as 'special hours' certificates are issued expressly for the late-night provision of food and drink – proves to be a dusty neglected room with a small stove and empty refrigerator.

Then a wizened man of about thirty-five, lolling back in his seat, becomes the centre of attention. When the low table in front of him is moved aside, four bright yellow discs of Macleod tartan appear where the legs had stood, showing the original colour of the grime-grey carpet. His friends, the last group to fill in their pro formas, crowd anxiously around.

'You will observe', says the bearded 'buck', striking a conjuror's pose, 'that I have nothin' in me hands! Nothin' up me sleeves, neither!' And he shoots back his imaginary cuffs with such panache that not only his delighted colleagues see the funny side of it. 'I'm goin' to search yer, mate – a'right?'

'Huh?'

'And what', the officer says a moment later, holding up a tiny brown-paper packet for everyone to see, 'have we here?' He opens it with a flourish. 'A *twist* of *vegetable* matter!'

Laughter.

'Naw, I—'

'Listen, man, I showed you my hands for that reason! Yer locked up, Joe, suspected possession of cannabis.'

'Ah, let the poor fella—'

'On yer way, luv,' says the uniformed policewoman, 'and the rest of yer, come on, on yer bike.'

The prisoner's friends shuffle out into the night. Without further protest, he allows himself to be led over to the exit where, despite his predicament, he waits with a silly grin, exuding euphoria. But, while he may still be savouring a heady intensity of sound, scent and colour, this wretched hole in the ground, with its stained furnishings, gimcrack decorations and urea-sharp fug, is fast becoming oppressively sordid and dull.

And so the inspector has a final quick word with the manager. 'That's right, we want you and the boss across at St Anne Street at six tonight. We'll be on our way now.'

Then a double-edged irony makes it the turn of the raiding party to regard the basement as a tolerable refuge from life's

307

harsher realities. Just in the nick of time, the relief radio operator comes through with a warning that their bluff has been called, and that an angry crowd, which had presumably expected to find the street alive with big hairy bobbies, is now waiting for them outside.

'Won't be disappointed for long,' someone murmurs. 'Not if our lads in the mobiles. . . .' And the prisoner, possibly sensing a quickening and a sudden warmth of comradeship in their midst, smiles more broadly than anyone.

10

Like a bugle call in Apache territory, the request for a further back-up outside the raided club is answered by assorted cavalry galloping in from all directions. A panda, a dog van, another panda, a supervision vehicle and an OSD mini-bus arrive almost simultaneously, as eager to dispel tedium as they are to disperse the mob. This swift response is self-defeating, however, inasmuch as the street empties as fast as their headlights can fill it, leaving only a handful of sozzled squaws and bellicose young bucks to provide the briefest of diversions.

Inspector South on Nights this week continues his rounds. He is a broad-shouldered youthful man of forty-five, with a small mouth and a wide smile. When he isn't smiling, he very possibly reminds people of the gunfighter in *Shane*, having much the same set to his strong, faintly Slavonic features. The drizzle's stopped; the night has become fine and clear, if a trifle chilly. A green Capri noses out of a side-street, tags along for a while, then turns off behind the Anglican cathedral. A young coloured man and a white girl are crouched at the door of a Georgian terrace house in Canning Street.

'What's the problem?' asks Inspector South, drawing up beside them.

'Our key – it's broke in the lock,' replies the young man.

'Has it? Let's have a look, then. . . .' Twenty minutes later, he's on his way again, having broken the monotony by trying his hand at a forcible entry.

308

'Hullo, sir,' says a very new probationer, who has at least two inches of windcheater showing beneath the hem of his tunic.

'Hullo, young William! You all right?'

'Yes, sir.'

'I've just done your staff appraisal, by the way. I'll tell you something: get yourself a big pullover instead of that; it's showin'. You look like a washerwoman. OK?'

'OK, sir.'

'It's not that cold,' murmurs Inspector South, moving off to give his last 'peg'. 'If he gets in a fight, he'll boil in that.'

I reckon the CID have a very soft job compared with us, because it takes half the stress off you, being out in civilian clothes. You're just an ordinary member of the public, and nobody hardly gives a damn what you do – unless you run along without your pants on or something! (*Laughs*) Really the uniform's like an advert – it's carryin' a big lamp on your head. Everybody sees you, sees what you're doing, so it's up to us to be really aware of ourselves, and that puts a strain on you. You go about for eight hours very aware of yourself. Any man wanting to join the police and knowing the dangers – because it is a dangerous job – has got to be a bit of an adventurist type, a *male* type, if you know what I mean. (*Laughs*) A chauvinist type! And he has got to be proud of himself – or should be. I always walk straight and my shoulders back, and I go back on my heels a bit, y'know. Therefore it behoves him to walk around upright, to have his hands out of his pockets, his hair a reasonable length, and not to go leaning on walls. And they're aware of this, and it is a strain.

The smartness of his own appearance is much enhanced by the very fine old signalling-stick on the seat behind him. It is made of a darker, much heavier wood than those issued today, and the quality of its wrist-cord and brass ferrule is far superior. He calls it 'an anachronism', and says of batons, 'I don't think the situation's ever been resolved as to what we should have, or what weight it should be, or what length it should be. But we do have a system whereby, if the constables draw their staffs, they're supposed to put in a report to say why they found it necessary, and if they use them they're supposed to.

We live in Cloud Cuckoo Land! We're accountable right down the line to everybody and to every bloody thing, and at the same time we're told we're special.'

Inspector South was born in a narrow three-storey Victorian terrace house over on the other side of Upper Parliament Street in the next division.

I lived in the commoner part of the Dingle. My parents spoke a little better than the neighbours, and the family was one of the few 'special' families – not all that special, but the steps were always clean, the curtains were always clean, and we watched our 'p's and q's'. Others weren't quite so good, and there were a few families of known thieves and everyone looked down their noses at them. The vast majority, though, were good law-abiding people who, if they didn't respect the bobby, feared him. They paid attention to the values of 'poor but honest', and they knew what shame was. If I got caught doing things, I cried to the bobbies not to take me home. I'd *willingly* take a smack off a bobby, rather than be taken home; Mother had a bad heart, and I knew she'd be ashamed of me.*

My father was a postman; he'd been in the Scots Guards. A nice solid fellow, about six-foot-three, but not over-bright, y'know – a bit dogmatic! My mother was a very little woman – five-foot-one, very intelligent, and like a lot of working-class people who wanted to better themselves. I lived in seven different houses before I was eighteen. I was bright as a lad. My parents taught me to read before I went to school – I taught all mine to read before they went to school. Anyway, I was bright enough, I've got to say that for myself – you won't find any unnatural modesty in me! (*Laughs*)

I've got a name for being aggressive unfortunately – and I can't deny it. I am aggressive. I react very quickly to slights, or to anybody slighting the uniform. In fact, I'm too aggressive, I know I am – but, anyway, my name was Noel and I lived in this working-class district, and sections of it were rough, and my mother insisted I went to Sunday school. There was this big tin hut called the Seamen's Mission, and this little madman used to take the services. We'd give him money, and he'd ring the bloody

---

*His chief delinquency was climbing up the drainpipes of a four-storey school building to play cards on the roof.

310

bell all the time, shoutin' and bangin', y'know! The Toxteth Street gang used to go for a laff, but I *had* to go, me brother and sister with me, and on the way home we had to cross a debris. Having the name Noel, and being the very nice clean lad with my hair cut properly, the Toxteth Street lads would want to fight me. To be fair to them, they didn't all want to set on me at once, like they do these days. One would fight me and, if I won, good-oh! I fought one fellow three weeks on the run, won every time, and eventually Noel became, apart from being posh and what have you, a bit respected. And, of course, the neighbours' kids objected to me because I hadn't stayed in Liverpool throughout the war. I had to fight to get [back] my place in the gang. I became a bit of a hard knock and proud of it.

Then when I was twelve I went along to this boys' club – what an effect it had on me, it really had. There was this flight sergeant, an ex-PTI, a beautifully built man, could do anything, a real hero for a lad; a nice man, well spoken, flashing white teeth, handsome, only about average in size, and he really dragged that club up. He taught us gymnastics, weight-lifting, and how to defend ourselves – very crudely, but very efficiently. None of these fancy arts! You don't need them; you need to be direct and positive. I'm direct and positive when I'm in trouble! I often say that's why I'm so good-looking still. (*Laughs*) When I came out of the club, I'd knock round with the lads on the corner – God knows what they'd been up to all evening! – and the bobbies would come along and tell us to go away. What you knew about policemen was they were people who chased you off the bloody corners, seemingly for no reason at all – though at the back of my mind I knew there was some reason. And they did tricks too, these bobbies. They'd have one little bobby come up and tell you to clear off, about ten of yer, and you'd start givin' lip. Next minute there'd be a bloody vanload there, battin' hell outa yer! (*Laughs*) But I'd always gone by then. The lads called me soft, even though I could beat them physically, but I went out of fear and respect for my parents.

The war disrupted Inspector South's education and, although he'd won a place in a grammar school, he ended up on the 'crafts' side of a makeshift educational experiment in Liverpool. He left at fifteen and started work at a big garage in the city. 'I was going to be apprenticed at sixteen to be a Rolls-Royce mechanic, which was something a bit special, y'see.

311

Anyway, it never came off, because of an oil crisis or something, and all the people who weren't [already] indentured were laid off. I then decided I'd become a furrier – it's a specialist craft, y'know, being a furrier. We all worked for buttons, but there were some pretty girls there, and the job was soft enough. It had some posh thing to it.' His apprenticeship was interrupted by National Service. He turned down a chance of aircrew training, because this would have meant signing on for longer, and had almost finished his eighteen months when National Service was extended to two years. After serving this, he went to a manufacturing furrier to complete his apprenticeship. Artificial furs appeared, the market fell, and a policeman's weekly wage of £14 – compared with a national average of £12, and his own of £5 – suddenly seemed attractive, especially as he had just met his future wife.

I went to Bruche and fell in love with the job; I accepted all the ideas about what we were about. I had a very happy time as a bobby. There was no opportunity, as far as I was concerned; you could have ten or twelve years' in before anyone thought of promoting you. I was coming up to twelve years when things changed, and somebody said to me, 'You're a fool. You been an acting sergeant for the past eighteen months, but you've not passed your exams.' So I did six weeks' hard study from then on, came top of the mock exam, third out of the whole area, and I had enough marks to have a chance of going to the selection boards for the Special Course to sergeant [then inspector]. But I didn't get the opportunity, because I was promoted to sergeant two weeks later. The chap who came top is a superintendent now, and has been for some time. So things altogether haven't worked out for me, as for timing and education, but I'm not cribbing.

II

The radio blurts its warning to all patrols of a 'silent alarm' now ringing in a record shop on the North Sub. An OSD inspector's car U-turns like a pinball coming off a flipper, and zips back down the deserted street. He has only seconds to get

312

there before the alarm becomes audible in the shop, and the intruders – if this isn't another 'fault in system' – know their presence has been detected.

'Ideally,' says the Crime Prevention sergeant, 'we'd like a five-minute delay. The old adage, "We can get anywhere in the city in three minutes!" is gone now, mainly because of the one-way system – it's bad, the build-up in traffic, and a lot of roads being blocked off, especially on the North Sub. But you'll find a lot of insurance companies won't have that, y'see. They're not interested in catching the criminal; they're interested in savin' their stuff from being stolen.'

Thus a drop in the detection rate does not necessarily mean less zealous policing or cleverer thieves, but it can reflect the increasingly materialistic and 'I'm all right, Jack' values of society as a whole. And like alcohol, that other great comfort in times of misfortune, insurance probably plays a far larger part in crime than is generally realised. Not only is it often 'on the side' of the criminal, inasmuch as it gives him a head start and an opportunity to repeat his activities elsewhere, but it can also assuage his conscience. 'They were insured, weren't they?' an intelligent young vandal is said to have asked.

The OSD inspector is the first to arrive on the scene, but stops a few yards short to look at a red-haired youth of nineteen, who walks by with a friendly nod.

'Just a minute, son,' says the inspector, getting out of his car as two mobiles stop outside the shop. 'Can I see your shoes?'

'Wot's this, boss? Somethin' op?'

An odd question when the night is already migraine shrill with the clamour of a 'silent alarm', silent no longer, and there are splinters of glass all over the pavement further down.

'There's glass in the front of yer boot.'

The youth laughs. 'Walked over that lot, didn't I? I mean, that's obvious – didn't yer see me?' He stands quite casually, beer on his breath, and could be much drunker than he appears.

'Where've yer come from?' asks the inspector.

313

'Me mate's 'ouse.'

'Where's that?'

'Gerard Gardens, boss. Look, I didn't do nothin', know what I mean? I mean, I were—'

'OK, son, but just sit in the car for a minute, come on.' The youth obliges, claiming bewilderment in a good-humoured sort of way, and someone is left to sit with him. 'What's goin' on?' he asks.

The larger pieces of plate-glass have been stacked neatly to one side of the shop window, to allow for a swift withdrawal. But proximity – the x factor in all this – has given the police the advantage this time, and they soon unearth an intruder who hasn't had a chance to escape. Caught 'bang to rights', he says he broke in alone and on impulse.

Leaving the panda crews to remove the prisoner to St Anne Street, the OSD inspector returns to his own vehicle and asks if the youth has been behaving himself. He has indeed, having asked very politely if he could have the car windows open a little, as confined spaces make his nose bleed. And then, when his nose succumbed anyway, he had politely asked to borrow a handkerchief. The inspector glances at him suspiciously, then frowns.

'Right, open 'em up!' he snaps, grasping the youth's hands and shaking the blood-soaked tissue from them. 'What are those?'

Several long, shallow cuts – just the sort that could so easily happen to someone stacking large fragments of shattered glass.

12

The green Capri is circling Falkner Square, and three drab, weary-looking girls have come out to stand on the corner near the telephone box, just as Inspector South passes through.

On his return to Copperas Hill, he hands over the keys of the Escort to one of his section sergeants, and then gets down to a stack of reports and an appraisal he has to finish.

My brother's a big-looking fellow – y'know, like Garth. He'd been a dog handler in the Air Force, but they wouldn't let him in

314

the police years ago, because his spelling wasn't up to scratch. Nowadays he'd lose most of the kids I get who have got O-levels in English, and he'd have been a better and bigger man than most of them.

Needless to say, perhaps, Inspector South does not approve of the abolition of the Women's Section, and looks forward to a return to the status quo. He feels his young policemen have enough on their plate without having to provide 'cover' in situations where they themselves, being far more robust, could cope on their own.

The public don't know what the police are about, and consequently young fellas joining the police don't know what the police are about. A lot of them fall in love with the idealism of it, the necessity for it, and they come out thinking that something like ninety-five per cent of the public are good guys, and are going to help us, actively support us. They don't know! They don't know what we know! They learn that ninety-five per cent aren't going to actively support us, and when directly involved they're going to be anti. There are about eighty per cent of them who'll say, 'Yes, we're pro-police, definitely' – and that's all right until they come up against the police or their sons do, and then they've always had a bad deal off the police. 'Me and mine never do wrong – it has to be the bobby!' (*Laughs*) It's just a fact of human nature. A victim will help you – unless he's been a victim twice, and has learned how difficult it is to get justice [or] because of all the inconvenience they're subject to. A lot of them cut their losses and say, 'I never saw anything! I don't *know* anything!' So really we don't win by respect; we do win by fear. We used to have a better result when we had the public frightened of us, in ignorance of us and what we were about. Now they're all educated, it has relieved them of their fear of us, and the respect we get is minimal – and the assistance we get is minimal. Yet, by our history, we're a group of men that they selected to do their job for them and, if we didn't do it, the public would have to do it on a rota basis, as they used to do.

13

A long-haired man with a scar on his cheek is led up the corridor in the Main Bridewell to a cell, passing the open door

315

of the surgery. There the senior police surgeon is waiting for an 'alleged rape' to come down from the hospital, where she was taken to be treated for shock, after being found wandering on the North Sub. Her story is somewhat confused, but it seems the attack in the car-park could have occurred a little after midnight.

They're always difficult, rape injuries. Here you need an awful lot of experience. They go to the hospital in a state of shock, but if I possibly can I have them removed here. First of all, I've good facilities here, all my equipment is here, and a hospital is not geared to forensic work. It *is* a little different from going to hospital, but I find from my experience the really genuine rape jobs can't do enough to assist you – there's no doubt about that. The ones who are awkward are probably going to be no job at all. To use police jargon, if we're going to crack this job, I'm going to do it here – and I'm not going to do it at the hospital. There they may misunderstand my intentions. I've got to say, 'Do you realise the seriousness of this? That you have got to go to Crown Court and give evidence?' 'Oh, I don't want to give evidence!' they say. 'That somebody's going to be arrested?' If I talk like that in front of a nurse at the hospital, they're going to think I'm unduly biased or I'm not interested in the job. On the other hand, the chaps here know that, if she's going to withstand my request for consent to examine her, it may well be a good job. When an alleged rape comes in, I haven't got time – as I'd like to have available to me – for [laboratory] information about sperm being present and so on and so on. I have to make a decision at the time as to whether the police have a job or they haven't. And we all wait with bated breath to say, 'What did you find, Doc?' 'Right, if you've got a body, go and arrest him.' If I say, 'It's rubbish, nothing,' everyone goes off, has a coffee, writes a few statements, and that's it. It hinges on that point. By the way, the Metropolitan police surgeons, as I understand, do not do these – they get female doctors to examine females – so their experience is limited. It's all wrong, in my opinion. Here we do them, it doesn't matter what sex. It gives you more balanced experience. I take swabs, blood, saliva, any scrapings that are important. Then, if we get any accused males in, I do a similar thing with them. I think an awful lot of alleged rapes are genuine, and yet the evidence isn't there. I can't *make* it there.

316

You know, where a girl goes back to her flat with someone she's met at a dance-hall, doesn't intend to have sex, just coffee and so on, but the boy thinks he's on, and then rape happens. You've got to prove to a jury that she didn't go back with the same intentions. It's very difficult. On average, I see about one alleged rape a week.

14

Rape, incest, indecent assault and other offences against women and children were once the speciality of the Women's Section, the members of which were not recognised as police officers *per se* in Britain until 1946. About a dozen of those who went through the further transition of becoming 'fully operational' are now serving in 'A' Division.

Briskly capable, warm, with bonny brown eyes, rosy cheeks and a pair of dainty hands, perfect for laying on a fevered brow, this Days and EPs constable could as easily be the sister in charge of a hospital ward where the patients all smile and say they're doing fine. But for one thing.

When I was in the cadets, I had a bit of an urge to do nursing. You're allowed to go on courses, so I worked as an assistant to a nurse at Birkenhead every Sunday and all me holidays for twelve months. I got an insight into nursing, and thought I'd rather have the police. In nursing you meet people at the lowest point you can get them at, and obviously that's emotionally different from the police. The public can all be irate with you, and you can cope with that, but when you see someone who's totally down, lost control over themselves, and they could be a reasonable age – twenty-eight, y'know – I think that hurts more than anything. I just don't like it.

She is twenty-four, and can still vividly remember, 'When I first started, it was terrible! I used to give a jump every time the radio went.'

I was patrolling on my own when I was in the WP section – it isn't a new thing in 'A' Division. On Afternoons, after scoff, you used to walk round together, but during Days you walked round

317

on your own. It's all this walking round together that's a new thing; they used to go mad, you'd be disciplined! I wouldn't call for the assistance of a male officer then – I'd have thought it out for myself or left it, y'know. I always had this complex that the bobbies didn't want to know you anyway, because you were just a policewoman. So far as I was concerned, rather than, say, ask for a lift to another division, I would walk.

I was personally pleased with the change from the WP section, but a lot of policewomen were dead against it. They didn't want to know! – mainly because you did seven and a half hours, you had an hour's refreshment [as against forty-five minutes], your own policewomen's room, policewomen bosses and your own beats. Quite honestly, the training I had as a policewoman now proves an advantage. My paperwork – my indecency statements – are a lot better than the girls do now, because they haven't got the sergeant saying, 'This is wrong,' and, 'Put that right.'

But bobbies get on better with policewomen now, especially the younger ones. When I first joined, the older bobbies were still out in the streets, y'see, and they were getting the young lads and telling them that the policewomen were rubbish, y'know, have nothing to do with them. But now the younger bobbies are being taught by younger bobbies, so this aggro against the policewomen has lifted an awful lot. They watch their language; if they do swear, they'll usually apologise to you. You should expect that from your colleagues – I mean, I don't accept it from a buck. If a buck tells me to eff off, then I'll say, 'Hey, who do you think you're talkin' to?' There was this sergeant here, and he said, 'You're on effing equal money and doing the same effing work, so you can take the same effing type of language' – so I 'it 'im! (*Laughs*) This will always be a man's job, and the women are just intruding on it.

Not being tall and physically daunting, she's asked for permission to carry a baton, thereby inadvertently earning herself a name as a militant. 'There are occasions when you really need one. At ten to eight one morning there was a scramble. Two bobbies had stopped two bucks – a stop-and-search, they were loaded down with stuff – and a big fight started. It was in the tenements and all the families had come out, and the bobbies were gettin' hammered. I turn up – but what can I do?' The only time she has been assaulted was when, while

318

still in the WP section, she tried to defend a policeman who had been knocked down. 'He pleaded guilty to hitting the bobby, but not guilty to me, because the sentence would've been harder! You get other police girls who get wellied quite often – how they go about it, I don't know.' There are times, however, when policewomen come into their own by undertaking hazardous duties that male officers are incapable of performing. A short while ago, she was in the Plain Clothes Section.

There was a girl up there [Falkner Square] of only fourteen, and the prostitutes themselves warned her off. The youngest one I've come across is ten. The mother was a prostitute and as deaf as a post, and the father was daft and deaf, and she started off at the Pier Head. But what amazes me with these prostitutes is the fact they're not on the Pill – they just use Durex. All it boils down to is laziness, not ignorance; they just can't be bothered to go to Family Planning, which is on their beat anyway. At one stage, I was put out on the streets meself, literally! I laff at it now, but it wasn't so funny then. It wasn't frightening – I knew there was a bobby nearby – but I literally had to solicit, get picked up [as part of a murder enquiry]. There were all sorts of funny people! And once I was in their car, I'd say, 'Look at this,' like – and show me warrant card. I had these pro formas stuck up me jumper; it was winter, mind you, and I had this heavy coat on. This fella kept comin' round, and every time I went near the car he'd put his foot down. Well, obviously he didn't fancy me, y'know! In the end, he stopped for me and I get in and take a look at him. He's got black shoes on, black socks, black trousers and a white shirt. Oh my God, I've got a bobby here – *and a boss*! I flashed my warrant card – this fella goes white then. On the pro forma was, 'What's your name?' What were you doing on these dates?' I just said, 'What're you doin' round here?' 'Oh, I'm just doing some work for my church' – he was a clergyman! And he's off. (*Laughs*) It was like that all the time. Some were nasty; they'd drive off as soon as you were getting in the car, and you'd end up on your bum. I didn't mind during the day, but at night it was a bit sticky, because the bobby would be on the other corner sometimes.

She's quite content to be back in uniform, even though the weather is beginning to close in and winter will soon be here.

I've often wondered what I like about my job because, y'know, when you're walking round for hours, lookin' for jobs, getting wet, you think to yourself: What am I doin' here? The job's exciting at times. I think that's why I do it. At one stage, *nothing* happened – and I missed that feeling of fear. If anyone says, 'Oh, I'm not frightened of anything!' I think that's a lot of rubbish. Y'know, you go to a fight and you feel scared. Sometimes, when I don't go to fights – or when I was in Plain Clothes and not on beat work – you feel you miss an awful lot because the fear isn't there. But fear, it keeps me going. I don't know why – I just like it. It makes you feel very alive.

15

The Main Bridewell buzzer sounds. The inspection panel slides aside for a moment. The broad steel door swings inwards. Faces turn. Blue shirts left, ragged overcoats right. Boom, the outer door closes. 'This way, luv.' Strange-shaped pillars, glass-fronted offices, no light in them, reflections. Full-length reflection: detectives, policemen, policewomen, bedraggled figure. 'Left, luv.' Door to corridor. 'Left again.' Moans, groans, thudding, cursing, weeping. Cell doors. Real cell doors. 'No, luv, you turn right here.' Long dim passage, big black bars, barred gate, beyond a man calling for mummy. 'No, it's here, luv. It's this door – mind the step.' Bright white light. Inside an igloo. Surgery. Sink, swabs, couch. 'Mummy, mummy, mummy.'

16

The Days and EPs constable purses her lips for a moment, as she thinks back over the past five years. In that time, she has seen virtually a little of everything, and some the stuff of nightmares.

The things that have affected me are rapes. I've been involved in about five, and it takes me two or three weeks to settle down again.

320

It's a difficult subject really. I've felt sick for the woman over the way the CID man has questioned her and gone at her, because you've got to be very cold – he doesn't like doing it, but you've got to get the truth.

And, if you actually get the truth, you'll often find that she's been with him that evening, led him on so far, and then said, 'No.' But I've been at others where it was a case of he's just grabbed her and raped her. She can't help that. She reacted very strangely, though. Whatever you asked her, she'd give you a straight answer, really sort of calmly and coldly. She didn't sort of break down herself at all. It's amazing how people react under strain.

Really, I think the police deal with it in a very good way. I know it's rough on the girl, but it's even rougher on the guy if he hasn't actually done something. The stigma's there for the rest of his life, especially if he lives in the same place, so you've got to get down to the truth – and the only way of getting down to the truth is being hard and callous about it.

I've never been to the Main Bridewell yet. All the jobs I've assisted with were in 'E' Division, and that was in the doctor's room in the police station.

17

'Who was that that's just come in?' asks the bridewell sergeant at St Anne Street, looking up from his very early morning paper.

'Fists of Steel, boss.'

'*Wings* of Steel,' corrects the radio operator. 'Haven't yer heard he's gone on to mobiles?' And when a new recruit laughs hard at that he adds, 'Had a fella once we called the Olympic Torch.'

'Why was that?'

'Well, he never bloody went out, did he?'

Showing due sensitivity, the recruit dons his helmet, turns up his radio and leaves. His place at the counter is taken by one of the mobile crew.

'Locked up?'

'Naw. Coulda done, if we'd had a fokkin' ladder. There were

these three bucks in these shop premises in Howard Street, sort of an engineerin' shop, only we needed this ladder to get in, see? And by the time we gets one from this pub across the road, well. . . .'

'Aye, bring back the jeeps.' His face brightens. 'We had a lad on our section wanted to drive a jeep. So we said, "Have you done the ladder course?" He said, "No – what's that?" "Oh, on top of the jeep, there's a small ladder, so if you pull up by a building the ladder goes up and you're up on the wall, y'see. You have to have a special course." "Oh," he said, "I didn't know." "It's only a day course," we said. "Put a report in." So he types out a one-o-four: "I wish to be considered for a ladder course to enable me to drive a Land-Rover." So the report goes through to the sergeant, who submits it to the inspector, who's fully aware of what's going on. It comes back: "Has this lad any previous experience of ladders?" So he types another one-o-four, "Well, I've done the outside of the house," and all this sort of thing. It was about an inch thick in the end!'

18

Over at Copperas Hill, the supervision Escort swings into the vehicle-yard, stops, and a section sergeant gets out. She is very slim, just on nine stone and 5 feet $6\frac{1}{2}$ inches tall, although her fashionable 'golden dandelion' hair-style adds at least an inch to that. A model agency would possibly file her picture under everything from 'jeans, outdoors, etc.' to 'yachts, la dolce vita' and undoubtedly give a miss to 'uniforms, for the use of'. Vivacious, emancipated and very self-possessed, she and her husband live in 'a third of an acre of jungle with two German boxers, brindle and white'. Her family were 'very opposed' to the idea of her becoming a police officer, but after joining the cadets in Manchester about ten years ago she just 'sort of drifted' into the Women's Section.

I certainly wouldn't go back to the old system now, but the one thing the new system's lost is that the policewomen are no longer

322

trained by a policewoman. You don't *need* to be hefty. The standard of recruits they're taking is far superior amongst the women from an intellectual point of view, and from a maturity point of view, too. Women are always more mature: a nineteen-year-old woman is as mature as any twenty-five-year-old man – and, as far as bobbies are concerned, women are more mature at thirteen years old! (*Laughs*) I was taken round by a policewoman with four or five years' service in, and we'd get into a fix and she'd say, 'Now, this is how we get out of it.' They now go out with a young constable, get into the same fix, and he says, 'Now, this is how we get out of it' – and that's all right for him to start blundering his way through, but you can't do it.

It's a matter of feminine guile and a little bit of tact – y'know, the female of the species is far more deadly than the male under most circumstances! I've been in a club when somebody's been going mad with a knife, and I'd say that I handled the situation far better, being a woman alone, than if you'd put five or ten bobbies in there. I went up to him and said, 'Will you buy me a drink?' – and he did, y'know. We had a drink and we talked, and during the course of the evening he put his knife down, and that's when I got it. I suppose policemen could adopt our tactics to a certain extent, but on the whole they're not renowned for their tactfulness! They're too direct, they'll storm into a problem, whereas a woman – because of her weaknesses – will wait and think about it first. I think if they could do that they'd probably get the same results.

I've no particular skills like judo or anything – I've got a vicious left knee, which has always stood me in good stead! And I don't fight fair. I'd rather fight a man than a woman any day – *any* day! And a man would say the same. With a man, you can more or less judge what he's going to do, but when women are fighting they lose all sense of reason and just go hysterical. It's a frightening thing – it frightens me.

With the girls of my section I get on very well. I've got the same interests as they have; I socialise with them; so as far as I'm concerned, it's first-name terms if they want – when there are no bosses around or anything like that. Then they call me 'sarge' or 'boss'. (*Laughs*) I never have any problems. I imagine it's easier for me to handle women, because I know how they work. A male sergeant will sort of pull a girl up for something, and she'll immediately burst into tears. Next thing, arms round the shoulder, 'Never mind, luv, it's all right' – and she's quite

323

happy sitting there thinking: I've *got* this one. It's so obvious to another woman, y'know, and off she goes into the ladies to wipe her eyes! (*Laughs*) It's what every woman does; it's your first line of defence. But in my section it doesn't wash, y'know! They just get laffed at, so they don't give it a try.

I don't trust women; I'd rather place my faith in a gang of lads than any woman. (*Laughs*) I've found with my section it's a bit of a novelty that their boss happens to be a woman. It's painful at times, the over-protectiveness of bobbies. You go into a pub, and you're getting all the comments from the people, and it's 'Shut up! Don't talk that way to the sergeant!' But I'm quite happy for it to carry on: you can have a chat with the locals, and with me being a woman there's a far more relaxed attitude. There's no threat there, as there is sometimes with a male officer. Only you can't turn round to them and say, 'Calm down, lay off – I can handle this myself.' It's nice in some ways – y'know, 'manners maketh man' – and socially I'd probably expect it, but out on the streets you must allow people to react to you exactly the same way as they would to a male sergeant. So what the hell can you do? (*Laughs and shrugs*) It's a problem.

I went on a three-weeks sergeants' course [she was promoted just as she turned twenty-five], and of that three weeks you spend two days on man-management. At the end of the two days I can quite honestly say that practically nothing of what had been said has any bearing on the way I do my job. The superintendent turned round and said, 'Well, how do you go about manipulating your men?' I turned round and said, 'Well, Number One, I use my sex.' The *shock* on his face, y'know! You're not allowed to do it that way; you've got to do it according to the book – all this psychology, and nothing's actually said about sex, y'know. But it works, and they're happy, and I'm happy. Of course, it's only now that you're getting policewomen sergeants in charge of men, and these bosses down at Bramshill, studying these things, have so far only understood the relationship between a male sergeant and a male con. This they *don't* understand, even though it's so obvious!

I don't so much make allowances for menstruation, but you recognise that for four days out of every twenty-eight a woman does not function at her peak – she's falling below par. All the men recognise is that for one or two days during the month you walk round holding your front and going 'Oooorgh.' And that's all they'll recognise – nothing else with it, no psychology or

324

anything. The inspectors moan if she's off one day. They're just unable to perform their duties because they're *physically* unwell. (*Laughs*) You get more sensitive towards things that women normally get upset about, and I find girls in the toilets crying over things. You say, 'What's up?' 'Oh, it's nothing – I don't know.' I just allow them to carry on with their duties, and if they feel they don't want to do something like a sudden death I expect them to come and tell me. Very few policemen realise that the reason they're a bit niggly the week before, or they're not doing their job properly, has any association with that. Because with that sort of thing bobbies as a breed – well, the blinkers are on. You could no more sit a group of sergeants down and start talking to them about this than – they'd just be up, y'know, walk out: 'If they can't do the job, they shouldn't bloody well be here!'

And the police force is now finding out that it's got the same sort of problems that offices have, and every other situation where you've got men and women working together. (*Smiles*) I've always found it's best to let them carry on unless it interferes with the job; if you worry about it, you can cause a hell of a lot of problems. I have two on my section who are deeply in love, but when you're nineteen that is the only important thing in life, y'know. I used to find them on Nights, patrolling together holding hands. Some of the other sergeants pounce on them, shouting and that. I just move them to another beat.

The reason I'll get on in this job, above and beyond my own capabilities, is the fact I'm a woman, and I don't think that is a disadvantage. I'm also a young, very inexperienced sergeant and I quite readily admit things I don't know.

The sergeant returns the keys of the Escort to Inspector South, exchanges some good-humoured banter, and goes into the sergeants' office next door to see what reports have been submitted. Apart from having removed the giant who bends beer-pumps from some licensed premises, her night has been very quiet as well. Then her section begins to drift in, it's soon 7.30 a.m. and she's on her way home out of Liverpool.

It never occurred to me in Manchester that if I walked down the street at night on my own anybody would have a go at me! When I came to Liverpool, my first experience was in Kent Gardens: half a brick came off the fourth floor and knocked the front of my cap. Now, another three or four inches and that brick would

325

have killed me. This was a little lad, nine or ten. That's the way they are here. I remember once chasing a shoplifter out of a shop on Smithdown Road, and the two of us were rolling around on the pavement, and the one memory I have of that, apart from a very sore neck, was that people were stepping into the road to walk past. When people do that, you lose an awful lot of respect for the general public – they just won't come to your assistance. These were full-grown heavy dockers. You're not here for their protection, you're here to cause them trouble, and to put obstacles in the way of them doing what they want to – that's the attitude in Liverpool. I've been assaulted, but never what I would call seriously. I recall sort of twice, and I've had a couple of black eyes and very sore hips – but only since I've been in Liverpool. It's not the level of violence among the police here that's higher than anywhere else, it's the level of violence amongst the *populace* that's higher than anywhere else!

The things that don't surprise me now are the things that concern me. You don't get involved – y'know, it's a strange feeling. I can go to a sudden death and it just doesn't occur to me to think: Well, somebody's lying there and they're dead. The minute I go out, I've forgotten about it; whereas before I could get emotional about it, I can't now. Sort of child batterings I can take quite coldly, because I've dealt with so many of them. It's a reflex, I think: if you allowed yourself to get involved, tied up in knots, you'd be. . . . I worry that I'm getting hard and bitter. You get cynical, very cynical, until with the people round here you get so [cynical] not only don't you care about them, but you can't even see their point of view. You just go out and you deal with them.

I think the problem we've got is that you arrest somebody for an offence, you put them before the court, and nine times out of ten they're found guilty, they're dealt with, but they've 'got away with it'. They come out of court and they laugh at you. Some buck coming out of court, and you've put a hell of a lot of work in, and he'll say, 'I told yer I'd get off!' And they've been found guilty! (*Shakes head*) I'll wait, you think. You'll come again.

Normally, having ended her week on Nights, the sergeant would have to be back at Copperas Hill in less than eight hours to begin a week of Afternoons. But it's her rest day and, provided her husband's work as a surgeon doesn't have him called out, they'll be able to spend the evening together for

326

once. About three times a year they treat themselves to a week-end and to two plays at Stratford-upon-Avon. She discovered an avid interest in Shakespeare six or seven years ago, when she helped a friend take a school party to the theatre, and reads a fair bit, too, being in the middle of *The Christians* by Bamber Gascoigne.

19

A BOBBY: The worst part of being a police officer is that you're only human – it interferes with your work no end. It should interfere with it beneficially, so that you can see other people's point of view, but actually a lot of the time it's negative. Say you get a call to a domestic: what happens often depends on what side of the bed the bobby got out of – that's my major problem! – or what sort of marriage he's got. Having said that, I must con-fess the guy I most admired at domestics was a fellow who used to walk in where someone had bashed the wife, take him by the throat and say, 'Next time you punch your wife, I'll break your nose.' He was very good, y'know, very effective – although, as far as social needs were concerned, I suppose he was a bit lack-ing. But there again, you're only human yourself, and you look at some relationships and you think: *This* will have to stop.

20

Remote from the hubbub of the change-over taking place at St Anne Street at 3.30 p.m., two constables in the Car Squad maintain their watch on a multi-level open-sided car-park, and try not to grow drowsy in the afternoon sun. The one with the binoculars suddenly reacts as though soused by a pail of cold water.

'Bloody hell! Level four and they're bang at it! Bang at it! In broad bloody daylight!'

'How many?' asks his partner, snatching up their radio.

'How many d'yer think? Christ, take a look!' And he passes over the binoculars. 'Yellow Cortina, about the middle.'

327

The focus has to be adjusted. 'Yellow Cortina. . . .' A laughing woman is sprawled over the front wing of the car, her skirt hitched up and her legs locked round her lover. '. . . *bloody hell !*'

And, perched on a precarious vantage-point, the two constables nearly kill themselves laughing.

While up in the shadow of the Anglican cathedral, keeping an eye on the cluster of tourists' vehicles, are two other members of the Car Squad, whose afternoon has so far proved uneventful. One of them is a sturdy brown-haired 'buck' with a strong chin, a courteous manner and no trace of a Scouse accent in his softly spoken clear-as-a-bell diction.

My ambition was always to become a doctor, but the grades I got for my four A-levels weren't good enough for me to go to the Faculty of Medicine. I don't know why I chose the police; it was something that had always been latent since grammar school, but the system didn't really allow you to think of a career without going to university. It's very hard to say. . . .

I'm certainly interested in people; crime fascinates me, and the infra-structure of the working class has always fascinated me, because it's never really been part of my existence. So that's always interested me, as far as the police goes – it's a good opportunity to study it. My own background is essentially lower-middle-class; my father's an executive with Littlewoods. It actually started when – I was always short of cash – I took a Saturday job at Littlewoods; nearly everyone at the store was working-class – y'know, their outlook was so totally different to mine, and I wondered why. I suppose I've also a strong sense of morality, although I'm an agnostic really, and I saw it as a vocation, as giving a service. (*Smiles*) But apart from that there was a certain amount of self-interest in it: for instance, I knew I would be well qualified for the police, and I hoped I'd do well because of the qualifications I'd got.

I foolishly joined the cadets when I was eighteen and a half, which was a really silly thing to do – my personal opinion is that the cadet corps is a total waste of money. Then I went to Bruche, which I didn't enjoy very much – I don't like any form of regimented life. I came straight to 'A' Division after that, and my first beat was Dale Street and the Pier Head. I really enjoyed

328

that, because it was busy and I was never bored. As for violence, I was quite surprised and quite shocked as to what went on in the big city, so to speak.* But after a while you tend to treat it as normal – which is the trouble, of course, because it *isn't* – and get a bit blasé.

The most upsetting thing for me was the total lack of remorse on the part of some of these people responsible for the serious assaults – it didn't seem to sink in, the seriousness of what they'd done. I don't know why. I think with a lot of them the blame lies with the parents. With a lot of the juveniles, they just have no sense of responsibility, whether moral or religious, no idea how they should behave. If they see a car with stuff in it they want, they'll just put the windows in and plunder it. They have no regard as to the thoughts of the guy who left the car. None.

I think the police service is better than I expected – I've got more satisfaction out of it than I thought I would, let's put it that way. When I first joined, there was a lot of animosity. They wanted to know why a guy with eight O-levels and four A-levels had decided to enter the police service.† They didn't understand me at all. I realise now that the friends I did make in the police eventually were *good* friends for the simple reason they understood me and respected me for my views. I think I've won the others over since then, because I've shown them I can do the job as well as they can, and for that reason they respect me – even if they're still slightly suspicious of me. Some people's behaviour would alter when I was around, others' wouldn't; they'd go out of their way to antagonise me, and probably to shock me. (*Smiles*) They were obviously wondering how I'd react. Well, I'd never remonstrate with them. In a job like the police, I don't think you can be a Lone Ranger; you must be able to work with your colleagues. A lot of the heavy-handedness could well lie with the way people have been brought up originally – to fight is probably the way they've solved their own problems, and perhaps they haven't changed their attitudes. Most of it's force meeting force, but generally the treatment of prisoners is dispassionate, and most of the violence takes place out on the streets, where it should do. I think it's cowardly to treat a

*He had lived in a number of different places, but went to grammar school on the Wirral, where he and his young bride were then living.

†An applicant must have either four O-levels or sit a special test.

prisoner violently once he has come to the station, and a lot of people feel like that as well.

Probably what puts off so many people of my background from joining the police is walking the beat with the big hat on. (*Laughs*) I don't think they appreciate the opportunities for advancement. You are eligible to take the sergeants' exam two years after your date of appointment, and I started working for the exam as soon as I got to 'A' Division. The exam's very hard, probably because most of it is rote memory work, and there's no opportunity for discussion, which I think is very bad. But it seems to achieve its object, as only about four per cent actually pass it. I was determined to pass first time round, because I knew I wanted to go to Bramshill on the Special Course, which only takes a maximum of about forty-five people out of the country. The course – a year on full pay – is for constables and sergeants under thirty, and you're promoted to sergeant before you go on it. When I come back, I'll remain a sergeant for twelve months, and then I'll be an inspector at twenty-four. As I was the youngest candidate for the course, that'll mean in fact – God willing – I'll be the youngest inspector in the country.

Outside the police service, cinema is my particular interest – I liked *Taxi Driver* immensely, thought it a brilliant film. I also read quite widely – I like Colin Wilson – and I still maintain my old interests, so I read a lot of biology and bio-chemistry material. I think I've changed a lot. One thing about the police is that it does make you grow up quickly. Overnight almost.

21

The mood changes at St Anne Street. It's a little too much to expect the new shift to bustle about, fresh-faced and eager, because its members have been away from the station for barely seven hours, and by the time they get home again they'll have worked at least sixteen hours in the last twenty-four. None the less, this group seems to have an esprit de corps that gives them an edge on their circumstances, and even the grumblers try to sound amusing. Radios are issued, a mobile crew discover they're going to be on foot after all, as their car won't start, and several constables remain behind to catch up

330

on a backlog of reports left over from a week on night duty. Another goes back down the passage to the open door of the inspector's office.

'Er, all right if I have a word, boss?'

'Come in, lad,' says Inspector North on Afternoons this week, as chipper as always, moving a couple of borrowed LPs from his desk to the small table beside him. 'Country and Western – you're a Jacqui and Bridie fanatic, aren't you?'

'Oh aye, got the lot of 'em now. What I was – well, it's just, y'know, I'm havin' a bit of a domestic with me fiancée. . . .'

Inspector North nods. He is forty-eight but nobody seems particularly conscious of this, least of all himself. Dapper, pragmatic, with a shrewd engaging face, he stands 5 feet $8\frac{1}{2}$ inches, has an average build, and gives the impression he could have been any number of things other than a policeman, each with an equal degree of success. As such, his professionalism is of the deceptively effortless sort.

These young ones I've got are very keen and they're very good – far better than when I joined. Obviously, you've got to keep your eye on them, keep them on the straight and narrow, but I don't really have many problems with my cons – when you do, it's silly things like straying from their beats, or not answering their radios. To discipline them, you find out what they don't like, and then give them it to do – there's the radio or BP, or you make them stand by broken windows until the keyholder arrives – and they soon learn to toe the line. (*Laughs*) But I've got a lot of good bobbies on my two sections. It's difficult to define a good bobby, because they're all different. —— ——, she's a good bobby. I suppose a good bobby keeps his or her eyes open, asks questions and doesn't get put off by answers that smell wrong. Some will immediately accept a story; others will dig into it. Yuh, a good bobby is nosy, and they must have confidence in themselves. I've always said that you can make a policeman parade on time, make him smart, make him get his hair cut, make him make a point every half-hour, but in between you can't make him look for jobs. The only way you're going to do that is by creating a happy section. An inspector's got to know the sections, and you've got to have them working together, not as individuals. He's also got to be a father confessor. I think it's the most important job in the force actually; an inspector is the only officer in close touch with the lads and the girls on the ground. They've got to be able to come to you for advice, both about the police and their own domestic circumstances, and they've got to be able to confide in you, otherwise you get discontent and disillusionment. They can always knock on my door and come in and talk to me about anything at all. Mind you, they can with the chief inspector and the super, but they don't know them as well, so they're not likely to. Surprisingly, they don't get many colds, considering they're soaking wet very often and how the temperature varies, coming in and out of hot stations. Ulcers are a problem; I've got an ulcer, and I'm sure it's through shift work, what with the unusual hours, meals at different times, the different shifts. Even on Mornings, you'll be on refreshments at half-ten one morning, half-eleven the next, or if you get involved in a job you might not eat until after one, so you're not eating like a normal person with four hours in between. Oh, a lot of them have bad stomach upsets, and then there are the occupational hazards like assaults. We had a girl assaulted last night when she stopped a vehicle, but she's on again tonight. We usually have one off every week with injuries – this week we've got nobody sick, but two off with assaults. (*Smiles*) If you came to work thinking about the things that could happen to yer, you'd never sleep. You'd be a nervous wreck! As I always say, you've got to be slightly mad to be a police officer – or it certainly helps.

As the device on Inspector North's right tunic-sleeve shows, he has twice been awarded the coveted 'merit badge'; on both occasions, he arrested an armed man while unarmed himself.

22

The Copperas Hill detective constable with a farming background has to bring in for questioning someone accused of criminal damage and a serious assault. He finishes his tea, asks a CID aide to accompany him, and warns that their man has a formidable reputation for violence. The aide fishes a baton out of his desk drawer, and they go down to the vehicle yard.

332

If I know I'm goin' somewhere I'm likely to need me stick, I'll put it in the inside pocket of me coat. (*Grins*) I had an insurance policy with the Prudential when I first joined, and then the silly Home Office put out a thing saying Liverpool had the highest rate of assault on the police, and that every officer could expect to be assaulted three times, one puttin' him in hospital. My premium went from one pound to twenty in a matter of days, so I cancelled it and left it at that. It's always the same, whenever I leave for work: 'Be careful!' And the answer is: 'I'm *always* careful.' (*Laughs*)

The aide is twenty-four, married to a former nursery nurse, and has a daughter of just over two. 'The cows say, "Ooooo, look, it's Michael Caine!" ' – and the resemblance is undeniable, although he's too animated for the impression to last. Tall, talkative, bubbling over with amiability, dashing in a fawn leather jacket, the aide was a terrible one for straying from his beat as a probationer.

I joined the police eight years ago today, straight from grammar school – got conned into it by a mate. Neither of us had any idea of what to do, so he sort of said, 'Our kid's in the police cadets, y'know – it's a good life', and all this. I get in by the skin of me teeth, then he goes and fails the medical – I'm on about five pound a week, and he's on eighteen as a porter in Mulgrove Hospital, y'know! (*Laughs*) I was suddenly the black sheep in the area where I lived, mind you. It's about as old as I am: an overspill from Great Homer Street. At first, a lovely area in a green belt, and the woods used to be open to the public. Then it starts, the vandalism, and the woods were cordoned off. At thirteen, it was gang warfare in the streets – always the same gang, always the same clique, tryin' to show what hard knocks they were. When I was a paper lad, they used to hang around, kickin' their steel-capped boots against these steel poles, and one would say, 'What about a coupla bob?' The inference was, if you didn't hand over the cash, you'd be on the receivin' end, and they'd done it to countless lads. I know for a fact there were a lot of us who were frightened to go out after dark; we just wouldn't go over the doorstep, unless it was round to a friend's house. If I went down to the chippie, I took our boxer dog with me! (*Laughs*) He was a belter. I'd trained 'im and, before I got to them, I'd already have said 'Fetch!', so he'd be snarlin' and

333

they all backed off, y'know. They were terrified of him! Then they started disappearing off the streets; they were being sent away for burglary, theft and all that. Mind you, in these families there's always about six of 'em – they go down like a step-ladder – and the next moment, the next ones are up! I was told if ever I went on the beat down there I'd get me head kicked in. [He was put on that beat and survived unscathed. What upset him, however, were threats of bricks being thrown through the front windows of the house where his mother and father – a postman – lived.] Durin' the day, I was always off my beat. I couldn't really do fellas – who'd known me since I was knee-high to a grass-hopper – for no tax on their car, and then come down the next weekend and natter to 'em in the pub with me dad. So I used to do a mutual swap with this bobby on the next beat: he used to do the people on my beat, and I would on his. (*Laughs*) I was very insecure then.

He began working as a CID aide two months ago, after being in the OSD. 'In the first three weeks here, I was all set to put in a report to go back! I just couldn't take it; everythin' was movin' too fast! The responsibility's more yours, too – the sergeant's got his own jobs to do.' But, although feeling rather unsure of himself again, his enthusiasm is unbounded, and violent confrontations are something he has learned to handle with a fair bit of confidence.

The CID Cortina stops outside a block of council flats as un-lovely as a grey shoebox left out in the rain. The DC and the aide cross the litter-strewn forecourt and climb the foetid flight of bare concrete stairs to a cramped landing, where they pause for a moment to prepare themselves.

The DC knocks twice, quite lightly. 'Hello, luv,' he says, with his customary politeness, as the door opens. 'Jimmy in?'

'Aye, Jimmy's—'

'My name's —— ——. I'm a detective from Copperas Hill. I'd just like a word with him.'

'I'll just go and—' The work-flushed woman stops to collect her thoughts, and wipes her wet arms on a cloth while three small boys peer round her. 'Just go and tell 'im you're—'

'Don't you bother, luv,' says the DC, stepping through the doorway. 'Where is he? Down in the back room?'

334

She hesitates, returns their smiles, and leads the way down a humid passage filled with sharp smells of laundering. 'You'll 'ave to excuse,' she apologises, stepping over a hosepipe that crosses into her steamy kitchen. 'I'm helpin' me neighbour out, y'see, and yer—'

'Should see ours!'

The woman smiles again; a careworn, once comely girl in a shapeless dress that sparkles with soap suds. 'Won't be a minute,' she murmurs, leaving them in the living-room.

The aide glances at his mentor. That was neatly done. Whereas many a citizen will defend his threshold like the portals of a besieged castle, however humble, the chances are he will be less likely to think of doing battle in the bosom of his family, to to speak. They look around them. The living-room is completely bare, save for an old television set in confrontation with a lumpy sofa set beneath a shadeless light-fixture. There is not an ornament, not a toy nor even a newspaper to mitigate the soul-searing bleakness of these arrangements, and all life seems to lie beyond the flickering screen in the corner. Then the three close-cropped small boys begin to dart in and out of the room, grinning and grimacing in a high state of excitement, to be followed shortly afterwards by their father.

He is a tiny shaggy-haired ancient in his mid-thirties, as lined about the face as an old paper bag, and yet very sharp, very alert and very tightly wound. He grins as the DC introduces himself, grimaces scornfully at the allegations made against him, and agrees to go across to Copperas Hill, quite confident his innocence will be quickly established.

'Yer goin'?' his wife asks, coming out of the kitchen.

'Aye – not f'long. Got money for some ciggies? I'm out.'

She finds him a screwed-up pound note in a corner of her purse, and the whole family comes out on to the landing to see him leave. In fact everything passes off so naturally it doesn't seem significant that she hasn't asked why exactly the CID have called.

335

23

The owner and the manager of the club raided last night are due any minute now at St Anne Street.

'There was nothing to it,' remarks the Plain Clothes constable who's 'dealing', as they say. 'It can get a lot more awkward – you can get two hundred and fifty people in a place like that, and it can be chaotic. If one policeman steps out of line, says something or has a go at somebody, then whoop – it goes up in smoke. I was a little bit shaky myself. I don't like going to anybody's front door or searching somebody's house. It's alien to me. But it's part of your job, and you've got to face up to it.'

He was in the Parachute Regiment until joining the police about four years ago, and served for a while in County Armagh, Northern Ireland.

'I've found I've had emotions on this job I thought I'd never have – I was talking about this to my parents today, actually. As a soldier, I spent six years in the Army, and thought I knew a little about life, but I've learned a tremendous amount since then.'

The constable is twenty-nine, stands 5 feet $11\frac{1}{2}$ inches and weighs a trim 12 stone. He keeps himself in first-class physical condition, which undoubtedly contributes to a mild reserved manner that nobody could mistake for anything other than steadfastness and self-discipline.

In the Army, it's all been thought out many, many years ago – even centuries ago, in fact, because some of the customs do go that far back – and it was thought out for a particular reason: your safety and wellbeing. This is why I thought in the police force there'd be a right way to do things and a wrong way. But it's not black and white as it was in the Army, y'see. You've got the whole of society to deal with, and you've got to use a little bit of flexibility.

I wasn't very happy when I first started. For two years I was merely patrolling a beat in the dock area [Love Lane] and that was very, very tiring – mentally and physically tiring, because

336

there was virtually nothing doing there. It's a real test of character. (*Smiles*) You're on Nights and you're walkin' round there, a rat jumps out in front of yer, and you look at your watch and you've another three, four hours. . . . One of the worst things was the loneliness of it all. Maybe it's hard to appreciate, but I used to think: I wish somebody would talk to me, say 'Hello!' or 'Would you like a cup of tea?' or something. It was just walkin' round hour after hour with just my radio to listen to – who wants to do that for a living? That's why they get them leaving, hand over fist. I don't think there's many of the [senior] officers who had to go through that kind of experience. In the old days – this is what they'll tell yer – the sergeant used to say, 'I'll meet you at Dale Street and Great Crosshall Street at one o'clock' – and you had to be there, or you were on a charge. But at least you had something to move towards, somebody to be with, even if he may have been your sergeant. That was proper pegging.

People say you should make work – stop motorists, this sort of thing. I'm a motorist and, in my opinion, unless I've got a reason to be suspicious of someone, I've no right to stop them, so I never made work in that respect. You can go to a domestic dispute between families – cups of tea here, cups of tea there, explain to each faction their rivals' particular views, so they end up lovin' each other and shakin' hands! – and come away exhausted after an hour, but I found the job doesn't thank you for that. When you're a probationer, it's pressure to put things on paper – statistics, arrests, summonses, this type of thing.

I know I can't talk with authority, but I think the best quality men should be out on the streets, out in the pandas, because they're the people who have to make the quick decisions. The impression you create as a Uniform man goes a long way; it often decides whether people have confidence in the police. And this is why I feel strongly about them sending nineteen-year-olds out on the streets – they're not sending anybody really experienced with them, and that's why they're getting assaulted. There's this tendency for people who're 'going places' to do the two years in Uniform and then get drafted into other departments – which is fair enough, I suppose, but the man who's out in the streets bears the brunt of it.

Who wants to go out, though? (*Smiles*) I'm on four to midnight. I'll skive off later for half an hour to take my wife to night school, and then I'll come back and I've loads of paperwork to

337

do, and then I'll drive up to Falkner Square. Now, I'll be in no way inconvenienced – I won't be out walkin' round these places or anything like that. I won't be gettin' bottles or sticks hurled at me. Nobody will be giving me abuse!

I'd never done this type of job before, and there's a tendency to think, Cor, y'know, I'm gettin' in on the real nitty gritty part of it! But. . . . (Shrugs) You see, I can only look at these prostitutes as the people they are, and think to myself: What would I do if I was in their place? If I'd been brought up in their environment? They're mostly all from broken homes. I know the answer lies not in locking them up like we do. If you say to them, 'Have you ever worked, luv?' they'll say, 'Well, I used to work in —— Bakery, but I was workin' shifts and didn't like it.' Or they'll say, 'I left 'ome and I came to Liverpool, and somebody told me I could earn a few quid if I came down 'ere.' They charge three, four pounds for masturbation; or five, six pounds for full sex – some of 'em do it, some of 'em don't. We've an awful lot of motorists coming round wanting oral sex, but the only ones who'll do it are the real old hags who can't get anybody otherwise – it's a terrible thing, it's a *pitiful* thing really. It's all very sad, I think.

And you say to them, 'Well, what did it feel like the first time you went with one of these folk?' and most of them say 'Terrible!' Even the hard ones says, 'Oh, it was bloody terrible – I was terrified.' And you say, 'Why do you do it?' 'Well,' they say, 'it's like everythin' – you get used to it, y'know; you get confidence, and the money's easy.' (Smiles) Some of them will say, 'Oh, come on and lock me up, then I'm free for the rest of the night.' They're not technically free, but you don't lock them up [again] because, y'know, when they go before the court in the morning we'll be accused of harassment. Some I talk to and try and reason with them, and sometimes, when you look through your record of work, you think: I've never seen her again – just that. Well, maybe I have done some good there, but it's no big deal. I bring my wife to work by way of Myrtle Street and Myrtle Gardens in the morning, because it's better traffic-wise, and a few of them see me in the car, y'know. My wife says, 'Look, they're looking at you!' and I say, 'Yeah, I know; I happened to lock them up last night.' And my wife says, 'Ooo, don't they look terrible?' – and they do. It takes a toll on them. In fact, y'know, sometimes I've a little bit of sneaky admiration for them. They come out, night after night, and they stand there

338

in the freezing cold, hour upon hour – well, I wouldn't do that. (*Smiles*) Even when I was on the beat, walkin' round, I knew I could come back here for three-quarters of an hour, have a bite to eat and put my feet up.

Then the telephone rings. Two men at the bridewell counter with an appointment for six.

24

'Let's forget about the assault for the moment.'

'I've told yer. I never hit that—'

'I know you didn't,' says the DC, in the improvised interview-room at Copperas Hill. 'And you can thank your lucky stars you didn't! Now, what about this criminal damage to the sign?'

'I've told yer.'

So he has, several times over, and it would seem that the lesser allegation was also malicious and unfounded. The DC exchanges glances with the CID aide, then looks back at the likeable little man perched on a chair on the other side of the desk to him.

'There's something else. This fella said you did it because they'd banned you out of there.'

'Me? This boozer, yer mean?'

'This pub we've been talking about.'

'I know the barmaid there very well – so does me judy – and I've never been banned out of there in me life!'

'You're quite sure, Jimmy?' asks the aide.

'Ask 'em. Go on, ask 'em. They'll tell yer.'

The detectives keep a steady gaze on him. Quite unconcerned by this, he takes a stray paper-clip from the desk-top, straightens it out, and twists a hanging-noose at one end of it.

'All right,' says the DC, with a note of finality, 'what form have you got?'

'Mine's all violence.'

'Any criminal damage?'

339

'*Never,*' says Jimmy.

And with that, it's all over, bar the formalities. The aide slips out to fetch a form, and the DC puts through the routine-check call to Mercro.

'I'll just do this and you can go, Jimmy.'

'OK.'

The stub of the one cigarette the detectives have managed to scrounge for him – they're both non-smokers – fits neatly into the noose. He's getting very fidgety, and obviously dying for a smoke again. Out comes the pound note, and it's carefully unfolded and smoothed flat over one threadbare knee, ready to be tendered at the first tobacconist's he comes across on his way back home.

'Sorry – could you give me the number of that ?' asks the DC.

And the small man opposite him begins to smile a thin tight smile as he eavesdrops on the conversation. He pokes at the pound note with the paper-clip, blinding the Queen in one eye and then in the other.

'What's up ?' asks the aide, the moment he returns.

The DC puts the receiver down. 'Mercro. There's a commitment warrant out for him – failure to pay a fifty-pound fine.'

Somebody passes the door whistling.

'You're in the shit, aren't you, Jimmy ?'

'I know it,' he mutters, poking a hole in the Queen's ear.

'How much have you paid ?'

'One pound.'

'Shit.'

'Ah, well,' says Jimmy, looking up with grim perkiness, 'I suppose an arrest's as good as a change.'

The DC's smile fades. 'Does your wife know about this warrant ?'

'I didn't know about the warrant – you told me.'

'I know. Well, it looks as if you'll be staying with us. I'll find you a seat downstairs until I can get a van.'

'I'm sorry I come up now! Somebody'll have to tell me wife.'

'Oh, I will.'

The whistler goes back down the passage the other way.

'Me ciggies – is there any chance . . . ?' He holds out the perforated pound note.

340

'Got some change on you?'

'No, but she give me this.'

'It's only our ciggie machine's got to have change, y'see.'

'Oh, that *bastid*,' says Jimmy, with a bitter, bitter smile. 'I'll kill him for this. . . .'

25

'It breaks your heart sometimes,' murmurs the gravel-voiced sergeant in charge of the general enquiry office in Hope Street, as he waits with the telephone receiver to his ear. 'These three Italian ladies out there – the only clothing they've got left is what they've got on. Just finishing a three-week holiday in England, parked by the —— Hotel, right in the centre of the city, and all the suitcases have been taken out of their car. They're in a pitiful state.'

No answer.

'You feel deeply sorry for these people. I think they're bending over backwards to please the criminals for some strange reason – I don't understand it at all. I had a couple in when I first came on, an old couple who live in north Wales, and their car had been taken yesterday. What about all the inconvenience they've had over the last twenty-four hours – is that not to be considered? Is it just hard luck on their part?'

Still no answer.

Being situated almost exactly between the two cathedrals, he spends a good deal of his time trying to assist the victims of thefts of and from vehicles. 'After mass on Sunday, cars gone, radios gone. . . . These thefts are really vicious.'

He tries another number, and this time has some success.

'I've got a kind lady at the YWCA to put you up for the night,' he tells the three distraught women, 'and then in the morning—'

'Santo Cielo! Che cosa faciamo addesso?'

'Yuh, I know, luv, but there's no answer from the consulate.'

Eventually the enquiry office is quiet again, and he can spare a few minutes for an old dear who pops in fairly regularly, bearing the strangest of tidings.

341

It's another disease of our times, if you like, that a lot of people only get talked to when they go to a hospital, an unemployment bureau or a police station. And they'll come in and just say anythin', just for the sake of talking. You must listen to them, thank them very much and tell them you'll do something about it – and they'll go on their merry way quite happy about it, and come back again in a few weeks. The public's great – I love 'em. You get your elements everywhere, but I'd say about ninety per cent of the people who come in here are nice people. Their car's been done, they've got problems with the house – anything's to do with police work, as far as I'm concerned. I know this attitude is changing now but, you see, I was educated at Rose Hill, where if the people needed a plumber, the electricity was off, or they'd lost their keys and couldn't get into the house, they'd come for a bobby. In that respect, they don't rely on us much nowadays; you've got a lot more social work going on, and there's the residents' organisations to help them.

The sergeant is built like a great bear, comes of Irish extraction, and was twenty-nine when he joined the Liverpool City Police nineteen years ago after being at sea. In many ways, he personifies the most reassuring type of traditional 'British bobby', but says with a shrug, 'The job isn't geared any more to the fellow walkin' round the streets with the big hat on – it just isn't. I've got another two years to do. The job's been pretty good to me, I can't dispute that. Oh, I've struggled at times – I'm struggling now. I've got six children, y'know, one's working and I'm keeping five – the youngest is eight. I've just taken them for a week's holiday, and I had to go into my savings for that. I did have a car; I got rid of it five years ago, when the petrol went up. I'm picking up about two-fifty a month, and I live in a police house. But there are a lot of people worse off, a *lot* worse off.' An echo, perhaps, of that sense of affinity.

The constable working with him was injured while making an arrest in a club, took a transatlantic flight during his sick leave, and will soon be a Canadian police officer. 'In Toronto, they issue the equipment you need,' he says. 'They make sure the money comes from somewhere. And you're not in the bottom eight per cent of wage-earners; you're in the top eight. You're respected because of your job.' And, whereas the most he and

342

his wife would hope for on Merseyside would be a pre-war semi-detached house, they will soon have a modern bungalow, 'his' and 'her' cars, and perhaps even a swimming-pool. Professionally, he will have to start from scratch again, as he's found that the training is very much more intensive, but this doesn't dismay him. 'I like the job I do – it's one of the few jobs I've ever liked doing. But here the Government just isn't behind yer.'

A lull. The sergeant sits alone at the counter, staring out through the glass entrance of force headquarters at his small patch of Hope Street. In his locker is a letter from the head of a Catholic secondary school in Northern Ireland.

Dear Sir,

On behalf of the teachers and pupils of this school, I would like to thank you and all your police officers at General Enquiries HQ for all your kindness and generosity to both the children and myself while stranded in Liverpool last weekend. I know that you kept reiterating that what you were doing was your job, but I have never, nor have the children, experienced such an execution of one's duties with so much warmth, sincerity and genuine understanding.

We flew from Manchester Airport on Sunday evening, and arrived here safely on Sunday night, and far from our experience in Liverpool diminishing or being forgotten about, it stands out in everybody's mind as the most memorable, valuable and educational part of our whole trip. Living in Northern Ireland as we do, with so much bitterness, hate and suspicion, our children do not have much opportunity to witness this kind of unselfish concern for other people's welfare, and believe me, it is most edifying and will go a long way to restoring hope and faith in people, regardless of nationality, creed or colour.

Once again, words cannot express our gratitude, and a special 'thank you' to Cecilia of the Headquarters Bar for the party that she brought up to the children on Saturday night.

Yours sincerely....

These pupils and their head teacher would not have been told, of course, that this particular patch of pavement and roadway has a special significance for the sergeant who helped them.

343

A car had been stopped right across the street from here. I went out to see what was happening and everything seemed in order – these three men were out of the car, which had been stopped for driving through the set of traffic lights back there. Then I went out again, and this character was across the street with a pistol aimed at me [he was a member of the Provisional IRA, as it turned out]. I got the main part of the bullet here, in my thigh; a piece in my eyebrow; a piece in my chin; a few splinters in my hand; and some in my chest. I was only off for five weeks. I personally feel he hit the deck in front of me and it [a .38 slug] ricochetted up. We were lucky. Had the officer got him into this office, as he'd intended to, we'd have been three dead policemen – there's no doubt about it. (*Shrugs*) It was a one-off. Being shot hasn't altered my opinion in any way: I would still not like to see the day the police in this country carried firearms.

26

Inspector North is scarcely more expansive when he comes to talk about the experiences that gained him his two 'merit badges'.

'Oh, it was about five o'clock in the morning with nothing happening. A call went out: "A shooting at the Harvey Hotel, Nelson Street – two men have just left in a white Mini, and have driven off towards London Road, one dressed in a red shirt." It was good how we picked them up. Before the call went out, —— —— had already seen a white Mini come round the corner from London Road at a fast speed, and he was chasing it – he's in the CID now. "I'm behind a white Mini now", he said, "with two men in it and one's got a red coat on." The chase went on for quite a while, and the bobby lost them for a minute or so, so we thought they'd got rid of the gun – a .45 Webley service revolver – because they'd had chances to. We followed the Mini for a couple of miles, way out into "E" Division, and then we arrested them. When I got to the car, he put his hand in his waistband to pull the gun out, and I didn't wait to ask questions. I just hit him, and the gun fell on the floor and his mate tried to kick it under the seat. I dragged

344

them both out and made them put their hands on the roof and searched them properly. Even when I saw the gun, it didn't bother me very much – you don't think of things at the time. Afterwards, when I picked the gun up and saw the five live rounds in it, then I started to twitch a little bit.'

He makes even less of the other incident, in which he and a colleague (also awarded a 'merit badge') came perilously close to being the inadvertent victims of a fish and chip shop proprietor in Soho Street, who was besieged by hooligans trying to set fire to his premises. 'I was just about to go up-stairs when I heard a footstep behind me and I turn round. It's the husband coming down with his double-barrelled shotgun – he's very excitable, as Greeks are – and it's pointing at us. It was a quick bang up to the ceiling, I got one arm and the bobby the other arm, and he's flat on his back, y'know, with me sittin' on him.'

Then Inspector North begins to smile. 'In both cases, when I went to court, the barrister said, "Didn't you ask what he was doing?" I said, "When a fella's got a gun pointin' at you, you don't ask him *anything*. You either get out of the way, or you hit him." He said, "But you could've—" I said, "You try it some time. It's when you say, 'What are you going to do with that?' that it's too late. You're gone!" ' And he chuckles, as though savouring some splendid absurdity.

27

Rap-rap on the door, lightly. It swings open to frame a rococo madonna caught up in plump billows of steam and encircled by a cling of close-cropped cherubim, short and wiry. Before a word can be uttered, a soft sigh and a smile of total resigna-tion.

'Mmmm, mmm,' she murmurs, as the DC from Copperas Hill explains about the warrant committing her husband to jail for defaulting on payment. 'Mmmm – well, I. . . .'

'We didn't know, luv – or we would've said. Didn't know till Mercro came back with it.'

345

'Mmmm.'

Perhaps she had presumed there was a warrant out, but had said nothing for the sake of the children; her husband has, after all, indicated that had he known about it he might not have been as co-operative.

'Anyway, Jimmy said to tell you to go and have a word with some woman who – Ellen, was it?'

'With Ellen.'

'Get her to fix you up with the money, then he can—'

'Aye, I know, thanks. Where is he?'

'Well, down at the Main Bridewell for tonight, so if—'

'I'll go now, now this minute. Soon as I get someone in to mind these for me.'

And the children look up with fresh excitement at the big man on their doorstep, whose own young – another world away – tend to growl when he's out working Lates like this.

Years ago I arrested two men for gross indecency. Now I'll always remember that case: two dirty bastids – at it – in a public place. You don't think. Gross indecency, and they're locked up. Both men of reasonable backgrounds; one happened to be a councillor. Job goes to court, trial finishes. Then you realise there's innocent people also being put on the rack, and they'll stay on the rack – their immediate family. And sometimes you think back: Well, I could have turned a blind eye – or I could have said, 'On yer way! Get off home, or go somewhere it's private.' Would that have done more good than arresting them? Sometimes you do feel like that. If you have any conscience or any mind at all, you *must* feel like that. It has another side to it. With people who are prepared to use anything to steal – who perpetrate violence on other people – to me, they're beyond the pale. I'll pull out all stops to get them if I can, and I'll have a pleasure in seeing them convicted.

The DC's next call is reasonably diverting. In search of a statement, he is ushered into the living-room of a former lady of the night, now respectably married to a coloured Liverpudlian. There is a spear on one wall and the only light comes from a red bulb in the ceiling.

346

28

Two unjaded blondes of pleasing appearance, one short, one tall, in light-coloured raincoats, have just been picked up by a kerb-crawler in Falkner Square, despite having already been cautioned by the Plain Clothes constable and his companion. The officers stop the car and recognise the driver as a young security guard from the city centre.

'I'm not doin' anythin' wrong!'

'Maybe you haven't anything to fear from the law, but are you married?'

'Yeah.'

'Say one of these women was badly beaten up around here or even murdered? And we came round to see you at your home address? What would your wife think?'

A pause. 'I hadn't thought about it that way before.'

The two girls are highly indignant when arrested, and deny that they were in the square for immoral purposes. A weary look crosses the constable's face.

One of the emotions is frustration, sheer frustration. Now, we've got to comply with the law, we're the servants of the law, and our job is gathering evidence to prosecute somebody who's done something wrong. You do the job to the best of your ability, and you place it before the court and. . . . (*Shrugs*) Often you'll find a prostitute will go to trial at the magistrate's court, and you spend the whole afternoon there with your colleague, and you spend a couple of hours in the witness-box, giving your evidence. The defending solicitor or whoever he may be will pull you to pieces. To me, it seems grossly unfair, that type of thing. I'd say most of the bobbies were decent honest fellas, and we're not of a higher education to be able to deal with these chaps, the barristers or solicitors. I mean, they're there day after day, they know the tricks of the court room, and you're there and you're criticised. I've come out of there with a sore stomach – I've done this quite often, especially early on in service. I can feel my ears going red and the lot, and I've come home mentally and physically shattered. Once. . . . [While off duty, he noticed three juveniles behaving suspiciously, kept them under observation for some time – thereby missing an appointment – and subse-

347

quently arrested them for attempting to steal a car radio.] I'm the lone prosecution witness. I must have spent forty-five minutes in the box, while this barrister called me everything – she more or less called me a liar to my face. Now, this is in front of people I don't know, in front of magistrates, and this is when you feel a natural reaction of really deep frustration. The magistrates believed me, and the case was proved – and those lads have since committed dozens. You see, I go home after something like that, and I just sit down and the wife says, 'What's wrong?' And you try and explain.

The girls have less than 10p between them. They also have a large knife – presumably for protection – and a number of condoms – presumably for customers. They persist in protesting their innocence, are processed and bailed.

Back to the square again, up through the swinging city centre. 'I'm rather glad of the fact we're not supposed to go into the clubs, quite honestly – it's all small talk and it's pathetic really, I think. But then again, you get information sometimes from these people about bigger things. I'd close about ninety per cent of them, if I had my way – that's purely my personal opinion.'

The green Capri makes its appearance and begins to circle.

Now, that chap who came up tonight, the coloured chap from the club, he said, 'Three year ago,' he said, 'I shoot, protecting my property, so I get two year in prison.' Apparently he shot three bucks who were tearing the place apart; he killed a fella and badly wounded two others. 'No way,' he said, '*no way* am I going back to prison. Last month – ninth of last month, check if you don't believe me – look at this. . . .' (*Bows head*) He didn't have much hair on the top of his head. 'Fifteen stitches,' he said. 'What happens? I'm in the club, three men attacked me – boomp, boomp, boomp – me on the floor, two hundred pound from my till – boomp, boomp, boomp – they're away. What happens? They haven't been caught. I've tried to make a living.' He's about fifty-two, a coloured man, not a very good education, he's been in that place about eight or ten years, but he says he's selling it now. Because, he says, you tell people to get out when time's up, and they just call you a black bastid – which I know they do. They tell him to eff off and all the rest of it, he says, 'and

348

I'm trying to make a living'. I said to him, 'I sympathise with you. Some people say to me, "Well, I wouldn't have your job!" but I wouldn't have *your* job, not for a big clock.' And I've been thinking about it, and I've thought: Well, if he sells that place, what's he going to do? He wouldn't get another job. Or he might get a job as a security guard somewhere, getting 20p an hour – but what's he got to look forward to? It's a terrifying thought, really. He only lives in a terraced house in Liverpool 8, so he hasn't made a lot of money. You don't know, you see. Maybe it's the involvement – the fact that he knows he's working – that gives him a little bit of pride. He might have a wife and family, and he leaves every night to go work, y'know, and that might be his pride. His wife might worry, but he knows – or thinks he knows – he's doing a worthwhile job.

The green Capri is slowing down and stopping. It must be amateur night: the fresh young face looks terrified.

29

Like a galleon under full canvas entering a yacht basin, the big detective sergeant in a weathered mackintosh bursts into the studied calm of the CID office at St Anne Street, forges the length of the room between pink and yellow spinnakers, and heaves to alongside a pair of desks in the far corner.

'All right, blue?' he rumbles, digging into the bag of apples he originally bought for his lunch.

'Aye. Give us a few minutes and I'll be with yer,' replies his partner, the light-hearted detective constable who chose the wrong moment to become a hippy in France. 'The Post Office job?'

'Well, we could try a few clubs.'

'Great, only make it half-past. OK?'

Munching on an apple, the DS sheds his mackintosh and commandeers a typewriter, having a little of his own paper-work to finish off. The machine just fits into a relatively clear space on his desk, which is stacked with reports, files, folders and a mass of other documents in that state of creative con-

349

fusion often preferred by lively-minded people, knowing they can put their hand on anything they require within seconds. He starts on the last page of some 'verbals'. Most statements of this sort are largely in indirect speech, and read something like this: 'Asked what he was doing in the premises on that occasion, he said he had heard the alarm ringing and had come to investigate.' The page emerging from the typewriter looks something like this:

DS ——: Now stop acting bloody soft. You were in that shop.
JOE BLOGGS: I heard the alarm, didn't I?
DS ——: Meaning what?
JOE BLOGGS: I heard it go, so I come down to see what the matter was, see? Same as anybody would.

And so it continues, very neatly and with many shades of nuance, right down to the very last words exchanged:

JOE BLOGGS: All right, I'll have a think about it. You won't forget?
DS ——: The ciggies?
JOE BLOGGS: And me paper, like you said.
DS ——: The Sun?
JOE BLOGGS: Mirror. Cheers.

You take any file off my desk, and you'll find every file of mine is LIFE. If what I said to him was, 'Listen, Joe Bloggs, you're a bloody clown', then I put that down, 'Listen, Joe Bloggs, you're a bloody clown'! That's what I said to Joe Bloggs. It's a fact. This didn't use to happen much, but you look at any file of mine: they're all straight up, and they're in the first person. There's no barrister who can get up in court and say to me, 'I don't like this.' He can just go and jump in a lake.

Irreverent, vital, no larger than life but packed full of it, the DS – who is in his greying forties – has the energy of men half his age, and seems to consume it at twice the rate, being seldom still for a moment. Once a 'County bobby' on a motorcycle up in Southport, he has twenty-one years' service altogether, over a third of which has been spent as a detective – including a

350

spell on the Serious Crime Squad, dealing with the really professional criminal. He has a very expressive, round bucolic face, large eyes that might be soulful save for the gleam in them, and a rollicking, buccaneering manner that masks a high degree of sensitivity, astuteness and 'bottle', as his partner calls it. While a schoolboy, he raided wasp nests for their grubs, reckoning that a few dozen stings were worth the pennies it earned him from anglers who coveted this form of bait. But the first and lasting impression he makes is of a wry worldly man who laughs a great deal, has an air of whacky unpredictability, and goes about his work with a sort of despairing zest. It is also difficult to imagine him as anything other than a detective.

This is the one (*extracts file from bottom of a heap*), this is the one! They did this armed robbery and off they pop, and a little while later the night-safe bags are found washed up on the shore at Speke. They'd been slashed and they were crammed full of all sorts of bloody rubbish – we found out later they'd been thrown down a sewage thing, and heavy rainfall had washed them out to sea, and the sea had very kindly washed them back again. And when we came to root through these soggy dirty things – they were obviously from this job; full of bank-note wrappers and bank bags – inside one of them is this piece of paper that somebody's left a message on. It says, 'Johnny, gone to the shops wonte' – with an 'e' – 'be long, Vera.' This paper has folds in it, and we look at it, and when we fold it up we find it becomes piece of a bloody envelope. Looking at it, it just says 'General', there's a 'one' stamped on it, and there's part of another stamp which makes it look as though it's 'Regis—', then it stops. So we sit down and think about this, and I said, 'This is going to be from a registrar of something, and that's going to be Sefton General bloody Hospital. Let's bloody well go to Sefton General!' 'No chance; they'll send thousands of—' 'No,' I said, 'let's bloody go!' So we all go over, and we see this registrar of births. 'Oh aye,' he says, 'I remember that one.' 'You *what* ?' 'I remember that,' he said. 'I sent it to a fella at Speke, because him and the woman he's living with have had this child, and they've failed to register the child within the statutory period. If they fail to register the child, I can do nothing else but take procedures against them. I stamped it with everything

351

in the bloody office! See that "one"? I never use that stamp. Here, that's where it's gone' – and he gave us the address. He must be jokin'! So we go up there and we turn this place over good style – in there, lobbo! We knew we were on the right track. . . . Would you believe there was *another* note there? This one. Look at that: who spells 'won't' with an 'e'? She does all the time! She had nothing to do with it – she didn't know he'd done the job. Obviously, going out to do the job, Johnny had put the note in his pocket, and he'd crammed it in with the wrappers and everything. We only found cash in the house, but we worked out it was his share of the money, less what he'd gambled. I think he's doing ten. And that's all we had to go on – that envelope – but it turned up an armed robbery. That's the sort of thing you could write a television script off! You really could! That's a model: follow it up and see what ye shall find.

Not that the DS has much enthusiasm for television crime stories as a general rule.

Oh Christ, television does its bit! Oh, they really watch these programmes, because a lot of 'em give them ideas. 'Z Cars' was the worst for that. A bloody good programme – but was it a good programme to policemen? We used to cringe. Ow, thanks for this! Put it on 'Z Cars', and the week after you're getting it real and live. It taught them how to break in using the brace-and-bit method – bloody hell, what a pain in the arse that gave us! I could set fire to that bloody television programme, I could honestly. They didn't half cause us some work. Don't forget, these are loons, aren't they? 'The Sweeney' shows a lot of MOs, but half of the dingbats don't have the intelligence to carry 'em out – it's too big for them. You lock 'em up; the first thing is they're unemployed, and the second bloody well illiterate. Now all my income tax has been stuffed up their noses to teach them to read and write, and they go to school for the best part of twelve, thirteen years, and they come out illiterate. (*Laughs*) Are they going to become some kind of big-time criminal?

Half-past and time to make a quick sortie into the city centre. As the DS and his partner go down the stairs they pass the Welsh detective sergeant on his way in, having just clinched the matter of the alleged rape who was examined at the Main Bridewell early this morning. She has admitted that, in the

352

hope of escaping her father's wrath for being out late, she had opted to 'cry wolf' and be taken home in a sorry state in a police car. A surprising number of Cinderellas attempt this deception as the lesser of two evils.

30

'If they've got nothin' else in the house, they'll always have a telly. . . .'

Television is mentioned again and again in various contexts in 'A' Division, but seldom if ever in relation to its possible effect on violent behaviour. 'Oh aye, you see that in the papers,' grunts one officer. 'Y'know, how it gives them the idea to go round smackin' people. But they won't see anythin' on the telly they haven't seen or haven't heard about where they live, you must remember – even in their own homes in many cases. If you ask me, the telly's a very non-violent thing to them, the kind who'd do that. It's when they stop watchin', go in the kitchen and start askin' their mam what's this and what's that, that they get belted. "Go on, get back there, yer little bleeder! Can't yer see I'm busy?" So violence is something they tend to grow up with, whereas the middle-class type of person – they're the ones that are always on about this, aren't they? – only ever comes across violence when it's on the telly, and it must come as a bit of a shock at times. It must do. They're the ones who get ideas.' More succinctly dismissive is the officer who murmurs, 'Do I see any connection between it and physical violence? Not really. Once had a TV set come off the top landin' that just missed us.'

The hardware side of television should not be overlooked, of course. Perhaps the medium's most decided influence on crime patterns has been that a burglar can now break into almost any dwelling, however unpromising from the outside, and be reasonably sure of finding at least one portable item of considerable value.

To return to the 'message', the police do not exempt themselves from some of the imitative dangers is presents. As the Chief Constable has dryly observed in the *Liverpool Daily*

353

Post: '. . . almost every night I get reports of two or three police cars that have been involved in smashes. Could it be that a young PC thinks he is Starsky and Hutch belting down, say, Allerton Road?'

But it has its beneficial side-effects as well. The number of 'breaks' in 'A' Division is said to plummet during the live broadcast of an important football match, and there is a measurable drop in 999 calls – which reach force headquarters at the rate of one every ninety seconds or so during peak periods – whenever 'there's something special on the box'.

Perhaps those seeking to establish the relationship between television and crime should look farther than programme content, for there is another aspect of viewing that might have an even greater effect on behaviour – especially in deprived areas like 'A' Division. 'If they've got nothin' else in the house, they'll always have a telly . . .', and that telly, as any observer will soon learn, is almost invariably tuned to a commercial network. This means that for upwards of ten minutes in every hour the viewer is subjected to advertising material which has the sole aim of making everyone feel a 'have not', let alone those least able legitimately to change their quality of life on impulse. In wretched circumstances, given the subliminal impact of so much advertising and the cumulative effect of yearnings built up over the years, it can't take much to see a shop window as a sort of large television screen with one vital difference: it can be broken and plundered.

31

The detective sergeant's car is expressive of his partner's general philosophy. 'All you want is something to get you from A to B – it doesn't matter what sort of car it is, does it? I don't know, but I have far more fun with a banger than a new car, and the same goes for people as well. People who're basic and down-to-earth are the only ones I can take to – I can't do with posers.'

354

But getting from the A of St Anne Street to the B of club-land is beginning to seem beyond its capabilities, and the DS has to speak very firmly to the engine before, with an uneven roar, it comes to life, shudders, and sighs its way out of the impromptu car-park. The car is the best he can afford for his personal use.

It's ridiculous, when you come to think about it. (*Laughs*) These blokes are professionals – I'm talkin' about somebody who does a decent bloody job – and they're far better organised than what the bloody police are. They've a better intelligence service than we have, and they've got better equipment for a start. Even the bucks aren't out catchin' buses when they're on jobs! But there's not enough over – after you've paid 'em to get all their equipment and to keep them high-rise flats from fallin' on the bloody ground – to pay a proper police force. Oh, *what* a state of affairs. . . .

If all the world's a stage, then the DS seems to see himself caught up in a black comedy on the banks of the Mersey, where he faces three classes of villain.

There are no criminals that are good lads, but there are the big-time fellas you admire for not being cryin', cringin', screamin' belly-achers. I can't do with those lesser mortals of crime who, once they're locked up, start screaming and kickin'. They're the children of crime, they're the babies – the ones you've taken the dummy off.

With the professional criminals, there's no aggravation. They don't come all the rubbish, because they know the score. When you interview the dingbats, the first thing they say is, 'Where's me brief?' But a good-class fella doesn't act soft like that – it's a pleasure to deal with 'em. And in proper good-class criminal circles they have a code. The first crime is interfering with children – bad news. There's nothing down for you if you go inside for that; the first thing that's going to happen to you is you're goin' to fall off the [prison] landing. The second crime is sexual attacks against women. Anything like that, and you're in for a leatherin'. Even the hard knocks will come across – they wouldn't tell me who had done this Post Office job, but they would tell me who'd attacked a woman or beat up the old lady. They *abhor* that, they do.

355

Well, what have you got in the middle? one asks. The violence merchants. There's very few good-class criminals that go in for violence – they don't need it, 'cos they use that (*taps temple*). So you get some idiot who lives in that pile of garbage over there, who'd crush the back of yer skull for thirty bob. He would! Because he's of such low intellect that would be the only way he could get the thirty bob. These professionals abhor that, they really do; they think they're the lowest animals of the low – they'll agree with yer. The violence merchants have got to be dealt with, but they're just no-marks. They're there through circumstances, they can't help theirselves, and the only way they can sort of express themselves is by smacking some poor old bird. They'll almost get the accolades of the gods for this, y'know, some of their mates are so thick! From starters, I shouldn't touch 'em at all. They should be allowed to do this, 'cos they're the have-nots and they're entitled to take from the haves. They genuinely think they're entitled to. . . . The unfortunate thing is the whole system is geared up for them. From the word 'go', all the money that can be accumulated is poured over 'em, but they don't appreciate this. So they thieve from the persons who have provided them with this shelter, food, education – and what happens then? These people still have to pay for their bloody defence at *vast* cost. It's a ridiculous state of affairs. (*Laughs*)

The other extreme is the dingbat who gets bevvied in some club and throws his mate through a window and pinches a stereo. *They're* the ones who give you the aggravation. I can immediately tell a good-class criminal from the minute I knock on his door. You go and turn one of the bucks over, and you get all the mouth in creation, y'know! They shout and scream and all sorts of nonsense. You just play him on, play him on, and at the end of it his little brain will go bang, because he's got himself into such a bloody tiswas. It's mind over *him* – there's nothin' you can learn about interviewing; you're either a good actor or you're not, you either have the gift of the gab or you haven't. It's the dingbats that get up my nose, and it's ninety-eight per cent dingbats – fortunately! Otherwise this country would sink beneath the waves, wouldn't it?

Be-dee, be-doo, pah pah. Down into the city centre with an upbeat number on the car radio lending soundtrack excitement to the familiar streets, façades, faces, while the talk ranges widely, skips from the Post Office job to next weekend when

356

the DS is going fell-walking, getting away from it all, and the DC and his wife – There's that fella who did the serious wounding by the Playhouse – are going to a barn dance – Wonder where he got that motor from? – there had to be someone on the inside – Barn dances, I love 'em – only stands to reason – They're a bloody good laff, because everybody's makin' a fool of themselves – there's a dingbat nicely bevvied – Try the club round the corner first – and why not?

Two men purposeful on the wide pavement, nobody else walking their workaday walk; gaits change when darkness falls, ease off, slow down, meander, stumble, shuffle, people enjoying themselves, succumbing to the ale; two men purposeful on the wide pavement, swinging strides, compact, moving towards a doorway from which comes a punch of stunning sound. Not a bad club this one, quite classy in fact – a very different proposition to the ——— where the DC had that nasty moment last week.

It was a den of iniquity, it was a dive – all the villains go in there. When I say 'villains', not the big villains, just the divvies; y'know, the ones you see in court every week – the ones who're always caught. It's very dark inside there and all smoky, and George's way over there, talkin' to somebody, and I was just swallowed up by these bucks. This big fat fella gripped me by the arm and he was bevvied – you know how their eyes go when they're well away? 'You!' he said. I was petrified; I was expecting the boot to come in, because when they're bevvied they will – you could have your head put in, anything! (Laughs) But I just talked me way out of that one, y'know, and next day I saw him in town actually. I was fuming about it, because I'd been that petrified, but I said, 'Oh, you were bevvied' – to sort of excuse it. 'Ah, sorry about that, boss! Felt bad about that after. Owe you a bevvy next time I see yer!' I said, 'OK.'

The brace of bouncers part, instant recognition in their eyes but their movements lazy enough to convey a mild insolence – or perhaps they're simply musclebound. Beyond them, people packed like a cocktail party in an elevator, and the only way through them is sideways, keeping close together. An effusive welcome from the club-owner, his wife, a cousin, a business

357

associate; everyone old friends; everyone miles apart, shouting to overcome this and the noise of the disco. A very brief exchange, then on past the floor-lit dance-area, where the young move suggestively in a world of their own, to a quiet bar at the back that serves the pool players and their hangers-on. In the midst of so much sound, silence. Only the detectives speak to each other, while the players pause, cues raised, mouths shut. The DC smiles across at them.

The tension always goes up when you go into places. The thing is, you see, they *know* you know them. And even if you don't know them you make out you know them. I'll say to George, 'Ah, there's that fella you were talkin' about the other day. . . .'

The DS orders a couple of drinks and grumbles at the prices being charged. Detectives each get 50p a week 'informants money' – just enough for two half-pints and a bag of crisps – to cover their incidental expenses, and the rest of what they spend on gathering information comes out of their own pockets. Occasionally, when enquiries lead to an arrest, some of this can be reclaimed, but it could be months afterwards.

'There's a fella back there who looks like he fancies a word with you,' murmurs the DS, flicking a glance toward the main bar. 'Do you know him?'

'Oh aye – it could be somethin'.'

Left alone at the bar, the DS turns to confront the display of hostility around the pool tables. Given any excuse – by the look of them – the scowl of players would leap forward and batter him to pieces.

Our job's as hazardous as you make it. I've run into trouble lots of times – I've nearly been pushed off the top of a four-storey buildin' and all this rubbish – and they've all been through bloody pig-headedness. But if you work out what you're doin' first, then it's not hazardous. Of course, you can't *always* think it out first – you get your loons – and I've never confronted a guy with a shooter; but it doesn't bother me not bein' armed, because I don't think about it. I don't even expect to use me fists, but me mouth. It's very, very seldom I've had to use actual physical violence – I don't think it should be used. There are times when, in desperation or out of frustration, one thinks: Christ, I could

358

smack 'im! (*Shrugs*) Force is used against society, but I seriously think that when society starts to use force back, it lowers itself to the level of the goons, the yobs and the clout-heads. The anarchists – the extreme Left and Right – are all violent people.

The tension increases. The DS responds to the glares with gleeful satisfaction, well pleased that his presence as a police officer cannot be regarded with indifference. If this is the way they want to play the game, so be it – although it's often more fun when the opposition tries something less unsubtle.

You can get compromised quite easily. If you start playin' away with a bird – and you're dealing with a big-time villain – forget it. He's got you bang to rights, and straight off he'll bloody have yer! I've been into guys, into company directors, who've paid private detectives to follow me round twenty-four hours a day. Mind you, I've sussed 'em, and I haven't 'alf cost 'em some money playing the bloody goat with these fellas. (*Laughs*) By Christ, it's cost him some money! I've led them right back to his bloody house, and then I've taken the mickey out of him! But what would you do if you had a few bob, and you stood to lose your company, you stood to lose your bloody marriage and your bloody freedom, all through one little man? Because that's all you are as a detective constable or a detective sergeant – you're a little man: (*a*) you don't have the social standing, and (*b*) you don't have the monetary standing. Christ, they know what our wages are – they're published – so he's lookin' down on you for starters, isn't he? You're a no-mark in their eyes. No matter what anyone says, you are judged by how much money you can pull. There's no point in being an ace detective on forty pound a week when a dustbin man's pullin' sixty, because you're the divvy. You *must* be the divvy for doin' it! (*Laughs*) It's common sense, isn't it? Ab-so-lute common sense.

32

The skinny wild-eyed woman whips open her imitation fur coat in the glass-walled side-office and looks archly at the Main Bridewell inspector. She is stark naked save for a pair of soiled tights.

359

'Ugh,' says the inspector. 'I've seen it all before, luv – honest. Don't do that or you'll catch a cold.'

'I want a judge!'

'Listen, what you want is medical attention for that arm. If you don't get it, you'll get gangrene and your arm will fall off. Will you wait in here quietly until the doctor can take you?'

He leaves her and goes through to the surgery, where the senior police surgeon is examining a breathalyser case.

'Nystagmus,' murmurs the police surgeon, moving his finger across the prisoner's line of vision, and the two glassy eyes follow it in a series of sharp jerks. 'You've got another of these for me?'

'Yes, but first there's this common-law wife that's been evicted by her old man – should see her arm, makes you sick. Twenty minutes, do you reckon?'

'About that.'

Back at the counter a young drunk extracts his money from the hip pocket of his skin-tight jeans and lays it on the counter.

'I'll be glad when the fashion changes and you get back into proper trousers, you young fellows,' mutters the bridewell patrol, as he teases the notes apart to count them. 'You're ruinin' the Queen's currency.'

The youth signs the charge sheet and is led away.

'Right,' says the inspector, pointing at a fat untidy-looking man in a brown overcoat, accompanied by a very short, greasy-haired type in a leather jacket, 'you two are next – let's have yer!'

There is a moment's suppressed hilarity, while the bridewell patrol explains in a whisper that the pair are the military escort who've arrived to take away a deserter arrested by Plain Clothes.

'Right,' says the inspector, pointing to a vague-looking young man in blue-lensed glasses, 'then let's have you, son. Breathalyser?'

'Yuh, yuh.'

Every breath-test prisoner is invited to take another test on arrival at the Main Bridewell. 'If it's still over the top, you'll be asked for a sample; if it's still under, we go no farther with it.

360

If you decline, you'll be asked for a sample anyway. Do you want to take this breath test?'

'Yuh.'

'You fully inflate it – like a balloon. Take a deep breath before you start, and don't stop blowin' till I tell you. If you do anything other than what I've just told you, I will treat it as a failure to provide a breath sample. Do you understand all that?'

'Yuh.'

'Now take a deep breath and blow away.'

Like the onlookers in a parlour game, almost the entire bench of waiting prisoners cranes forward to watch the bag expand.

'Keep going!' urges the inspector. 'I want all those creases out! Just a touch more. . . .' Cheeks puff out empathically in the background. 'OK, that's fine.'

Rather proudly, the prisoner hands back the bag, and watches while another is produced for comparison.

'There's an unused tube. What colour are those crystals?'

'Gree—' After some thought, the prisoner raises his glasses. 'Yellow.'

'And there's yours. What colour are they?'

'Green.'

'That's right, so you're over the line.'

The prisoner replaces his glasses, stares at the tubes and looks puzzled. 'But they both—'

A sudden, savage sound comes from the side-street outside, followed almost instantly by a 'con requires assistance' call on the radio. 'Large-scale disturbance in *kkkkk*!'

'Will yer sit quiet?' one of the arresting officers asks his prisoner. 'There's a fight outside and—'

'You go, chief! Don't worry, chief!'

And the other prisoners offer similar assurances as the room empties of policemen, hurriedly putting on their helmets. The bridewell patrol waits at the door, and everyone listens hard, trying to make out what's happening. Sixty seconds later a lesser uproar reaches the porch outside, the buzzer is pressed, and five prisoners are brought in, fighting every inch until the big door booms shut behind them.

361

'What's all this ?'

'The usual. Bobby was bringin' this fella in, and all his mates decided to have a go. Had his 'ands full, you could say.'

The inspector grins and is about to go back to the breath-test youth when a very indignant new arrival comes up to the counter.

'They left me wife!' he bellows. 'They left me wife outside!'

'Well,' replies the inspector, with sweet reason in his voice, 'they couldn't arrest her as well, y'know.'

The man blinks. 'Aye, that's fair enough,' he concedes, and shuffles off to join the end of the queue.

'Funny old night for a Monday,' murmurs one of the bride-well patrols. 'Just don't know what you're goin' to get next, do yer ?'

33

Inspector North delights in the feel of a busy night with a buzz to it. His Escort worries at the warehouses down Love Lane like a terrier at a warren, exploring every alley-way at the canal end, and checking every potential weak point. Many of the doors and gratings have been attacked so often it takes a sharp eye to detect any fresh damage, but there is none. He relies a great deal on his hearing as well, and drives with the window down. Up one side-street and down another, back and forth in an unpredictable pattern, the Escort cruises quietly with just its parking-lights on, working slowly towards the southern boundary of his territory. Although tonight seems to hold a certain promise, his patrols are generally as active as they are reactive, and the sub-division becomes a hunting-ground.

He is nearing the city centre when the radio goes again: 'CH – Alpha. We have a report from a taxi driver that there's a man in Exchange Street in a bad way. Apparently he's been beaten up.'

Taxi drivers frequently alert the police to matters requiring their attention, just as the old Scotland Road buses once flashed their headlights. 'They're great,' in the opinion of one

362

young constable on the South Sub, 'especially the older fellas. But with any of them really – say, you're runnin' to a scramble call – you can just hop on the first one you see, tell him, "Bold Street!" and you're away, no bother.'

The prostrate man bears no sign of injury when Inspector North bends over him to check for dilated pupils. The eyelids flutter, then open very wide.

'Hello, mate – what yer doin' ?'

'Aaah.'

'On yer way home ? Where've yer been ?'

The man sits up, shudders then scrambles to his feet. 'I've bin to the She.' He stands with barely a waver.

'And you're all right ?'

'I'm a'rice.'

'We thought you were dead! Got your wallet ?'

A fumble and nod. 'I'm a'rice.'

'All right, then.'

'Cheers, boss!' And he's off.

'Thanks very much,' says Inspector North to the cabbie, who has been waiting with his fares on the far side of the street. 'Could've been rolled quite easily.'

'Just gettin' his head down, was he ? He's all right ? Bloody hell!'

Inspector North laughs. 'Quite often the uniform has a sobering effect on them. You see someone staggerin' and you think they're rotten; you jump out and – as soon as they see you – they can walk straight again!' They watch the retreating figure for a few seconds longer. 'Oh well, he's walking well now.'

By coincidence – although this isn't immediately obvious – a scramble call comes through at that moment. 'Scramble! Violent drunk at the Royal Infirmary!' And the cabbie and his fares are treated to the sight of a lightning take-off.

Few things ever disturb Inspector North's equanimity, other than a vicious attack on one of his colleagues, or the thought of a police officer who sees life in terms of black and white with no greys in between.

363

Two of us were after a couple of bucks [for a minor street offence] and I'd caught mine, when this bobby – he was a bit further on than me – caught his foot on a kerbstone and went a terrible bang on his face. The lad he was chasin' was about thirty yards away and heard the bang, stopped, and went back, picked him up, dusted him down and said, 'Are you a'right?' You know what? He said, 'Yes – and you're locked up.' I said to him, 'You *creep*. That fella could've just *walked* away and you'd never have had him! No wonder the public doesn't think much of the police.'

In a broader context, Inspector North would undoubtedly want to qualify that remark, because he shows no indications of having a strong sense of 'them and us'. To a colleague who complains, 'Bein' a policeman is not an accepted profession, They still look down on yer,' his reply is, 'Oh, I don't know – it depends where you live.' He lives with his wife and two teenagers in a community about sixteen miles north of Liverpool, and has been elected this year's chairman of the local Royal British Legion branch. He spends a fair bit of his spare time at the Legion's clubhouse, enjoying the company and playing match-level snooker, but it forms only one of his many extra-mural interests. Music is his 'first love', ornithology runs it a close second, after which comes reading, browsing through encyclopaedias (he's another member of the quiz team), motoring, puzzles of any sort, tropical fish, sport – and virtually anything else that can enhance his very evident enjoyment of life. Coming a full circle, this would include being a police officer, for he 'loves the job' and has been chosen by his colleagues as a Police Federation representative. Perhaps it is significant that he didn't become a policeman until relatively late.

I had an uncle, a chief inspector in the CID, and he'd say, 'Join the police, lad! I'll get you made sergeant or made inspector.' I didn't want to join under those conditions. When I did, he'd just gone on pension, and he died within four months.

But I'd never had any ambitions as a lad of being a policeman. None at all. When I left technical school, I went to serve my time as an electrician. We used to go round all the public houses – they'd a contract with two breweries – renewing flexes and

364

puttin' new plugs in. I did that until I joined the Army at eighteen, and didn't want to go back to it. A neighbour of mine, who had his own decorating business, said: 'Come in with me' – he was gettin' on – 'and when I retire take over the business.' So I served my time, took over the business and got married. Then one particular winter – the winter of fifty-four – it was very cold and there was a lot of frost and snow. I'd plenty of work, but people didn't want you goin' in, particularly around Christmas and New Year, and you couldn't work on the outside. I had six weeks without working, a lot of bills outstanding, and we were relying on my wife's wages to live, sort of thing. I just went out one day, just walked into a police station, got the papers and applied to Liverpool City – straight out of the blue. When my wife got home, she was *most* surprised. (*Laughs*) When I told me mum, she just didn't believe me. 'You're far too quiet,' she said. 'You'll never make a policeman! They'll drive you off the job! They'll make you all bitter!'

And that's how I became a policeman, out of necessity – and I found I liked it. People used to say my beat at Westminster Road [a desolate area just over the boundary in 'B' Division] was a punishment beat, but I did two and a half years on it, and it was a great beat once you got to know it. There were all sorts of people to go and see, interesting things to do. I had no ambitions about promotion and that. I was in the First Aid Team – I've got loads of things I've won at home, y'know, shields and cups and things – but I was really after Traffic, and I got into Traffic after about nine years. I loved it. Then I saw fellows gettin' promoted who were – puttin' it mildly – idiots, and I saw the error of me ways. I was twenty-six when I joined, so I was thirty-odd before I sat the exam, and I had a bit of a struggle at first. The first year I failed; the second I passed and got made within six weeks. I sat for inspector and passed again, then waited seven years to be made. I've always been in uniform except for four months' attachment to the CID as a sergeant passed for inspector. I realised it would have suited me, and I was a bit sorry I hadn't joined before, but I like uniformed work. It's just I think three shifts for thirty years is a killer.

There are already two panda cars outside the outpatients' entrance to the Royal Infirmary when Inspector North arrives and jumps out, and the small waiting-area inside is alive with police officers.

'He had a bayonet, sir!'

'Where is it?'

The grim-faced sister brings it to him, and nods towards the nearest side ward where several officers and nurses can be seen standing round a lank youth seated on a bed. Inspector North walks into the ward and the youth takes one glance at him before rising to come rigidly to attention.

It must be the braided cap and shoulder pips. 'Carry on,' murmurs Inspector North, in the nonchalant manner of an army officer inspecting a barrackroom, and brings his signalling-stick up under one arm like a cane.

The 'violent drunk' immediately sets about making his bed ready for inspection with pathetic attention to detail, and then, still in the belief he is in the presence of a superior officer, submits to his arrest without any further trouble. Even as he does so, a very red-faced constable comes pounding through the entrance, having run a good half-mile to the 'scramble', and earns a nurse's smile for his trouble; both know only too well what having a dangerous job means.

Inspector North returns to his car somewhat saddened. As he had supposed, the young man with the bayonet was a soldier sent over from Northern Ireland for 'rest and recreation', but his nightmares had travelled with him to be released by the first pub crawl he'd known in months of unrelenting tension.

'Fancy a lift?' he asks one of his section sergeants, as he turns out of the infirmary gates.

'Thanks, boss!' replies the sergeant, jumping in.

I could do with a supervision vehicle – I think it's something drastically lacking. Very frequently I'll cover four foot sections – which is ten beats, plus the men inside – like on Nights last week, when there were only two sergeants and we had nineteen men. I can't get round all my men to say, 'Right, how're you doing?' Usually it's too late when they come to me, and I like to show them how to do things on the spot. The ideal would be to have fifteen men on my section, plus a vehicle. Quite often you have the situation when everyone's off the streets, and the Days and EPs and the pandas are left to cover. You can have twelve calls

366

outstanding, which is rather unfortunate, but that's the way it goes.

The sergeant is twenty-seven, heavily built, fresh-complexioned, and has a moustache every bit as serious as his nature. He was a 'county bobby' once, and had a panda beat to himself as large as all of 'A' Division in which middle-class householders were well represented. 'You're not a policeman here,' he says, 'going round talking to people; you're more of an arresting officer.'

'Over there,' says Inspector North, suddenly accelerating down London Road, having caught a glimpse of movement in the deep shadow of a narrow alley.

Braking to a halt, he gets out and confronts a couple on their hands and knees, giggling in the dark. The woman gets up and turns a broad simple face to him.

'We've seen a rat on the corner, so he says, "I'll get it", y'know! So we ran down there and I 'appened to drop my cigarettes and me matches. So anyhow, we were lookin' for my ciggies and—'

'OK, luv.'

'That's true, boss! There was this rat, see? This rat, and she dropped her ciggies and her matches and—'

'OK, that's OK. G'night, then.'

'OK!' says the woman, excitedly. 'OK, OK, OK!'

'OK!' says the man.

And they entwine arms and go off down the pavement, leaning on one another for support, still giggling, misshapen, dishevelled, bare ankles showing above ill-fitting shoes.

Inspector North very rarely reflects aloud, but he settles back behind the wheel and sighs, 'Unlawful sexual intercourse with an imbecile. . . . And they'll have children, and what chance have those poor children got?'

The sergeant nods. He is about to become a father and this has brought a painful conflict of feeling within him.

I must admit that if my wife had said to me, 'Let's not have any; it's a terrible world', then I'd have said, 'OK.' It comes from being a policeman. You see the worst, don't you? I would *like* a

367

child but. . . . Well, I can only think that sixteen years from now, if a bobby came knockin' at me door to say, 'We've got your lad down at the nick' – that would break me. I'm going to try and bring my child up as best as possible. (*Shrugs*) Nowadays I'm gettin' to listen to the news less and less. I don't want the world's problems – got enough in 'A' Division on me own. I enjoy coming to work, but you never forget you're a policeman, and your wife gets it when you get home. You've nothing else to talk about. But it's a married man's job, isn't it? As a single man, I had a very good time, but I was very lonely – a lot of lonely hours.

Down London Road, round into Islington, up on to Everton Brow, down towards St Anne Street, along Soho Street and into a cul-de-sac to take a look at the warehouse door that was attacked on Nights last week. Three or four youngsters had chipped away at the brickwork surrounding it, watched by a bank of flat-dwellers who were still there at their windows when the alarm went off and the police arrived to loud cheers and raised beer-cans. The doorway has been bricked up.

The radio clicks and announces, 'Large-scale disturbance at the —— Club. Ambulance is on its way.'

And, within seconds, so is the Escort.

The Harry Lime setting, deep shadows, peeling paintwork, the single street-light and a soft rain falling on a pair of panda cars parked outside. No sign of a large-scale disturbance, but a grey-haired woman is standing half-slumped against the railings beside the club entrance, being assisted by a panda man.

'My mother's dyin'!' wails a gigantic drunk, hovering over her ineffectually. 'Me mother's havin' a heart attack!' He turns and sees Inspector North following the sergeant down into the club. 'Will yer get the wife out?'

'Certainly. What's the name?'

The scene in the club below is enough to give most elderly women a heart attack. It isn't just that a coloured patron has been hideously wounded, but that his blood seems everywhere.

'That's me,' says a woman, when her name is called out.

'Your husband wants yer, luv, because his mother's not very well. They're just at the top of—'

'Oh, I'm enjoyin' meself 'ere – I'm stayin'.'

368

'*My mother's dyin'!*'

The panda man is trying to get the old woman's handbag open, but is being hindered by having to support her and by her son's agitated tuggings.

'Well, c'mon, yer bloody git!' bawls the drunk. 'Me mother's dyin'! You're not doin' nothin' for me bloody mother! She's dyin', y'know!' With that, he snatches the handbag away.

'Don't be stupid! If she's havin' a heart attack, let's get those tablets out!'

The drunk flails him across the face with the handbag, and fumbles at the catch. She recoils from him, rolls her eyes and groans, slides a little farther down the railings.

'Give here!' snaps the panda man, grabbing the handbag back.

And as the drunk lunges forward in rage Inspector North – a good head shorter and half the weight – catches hold of him. 'It's all right; there's an ambulance comin' and your mother'll—'

'My mother's dyin'!' the drunk screams in her face, exploding into violence and kicking out behind him. 'My mother's—'

In a twinkling, he's flat on his back on the wet pavement several yards away, with his great head locked between Inspector North's calves. His right arm is pinned down by the sergeant's boot, and his legs are being held in the air by reinforcements, incapacitating him like an upturned beetle. Rule One, when dealing with a violent prisoner in Liverpool, is to contain him in such a way as to leave your hands free to ward off the almost inevitable rescue party. Rule Two, when outside a club filled with other drunks, is to radio for a van without a moment's delay.

'My mother's dyin'!' bellows the drunk, then turns bitterly ironic. 'Let my mother die and lock me up! I'm askin' for a favour!'

'Shut up,' says the sergeant, rather absently, more interested in seeing whether the panda man has had any success in finding the tablets.

'Let me up now, will yer?' wheedles the drunk.

The tablets have been found and the ambulance has arrived.

'Let me up. . . .'

369

The ambulance crew go down into the club, and emerge with their patient, bringing in their wake a bustle of women who gather round the old woman, who has apparently declined any further medical assistance.

'I was givin' me mother a fokkin' tablet and he fokkin' knocked me on the floor!' bawls the drunk with quavering bathos. 'I was givin' me mother *a fokkin' tablet!*'

The women swing round. 'Don't yer take him in!' they screech, surging over in high indignation. 'Don't yer take him in, yer bastids! He's done nothin'!'

While they pummel at the police officers, the drunk tries to struggle free, but a little extra pressure on that boot keeps his grasping arm pinned down until he relaxes again. 'Don't yer fokkin' do that again, yer coont!'

'Sorry, never heard anythin' then,' the sergeant replies airily, preserving an undramatic calm in the midst of so much intoxicated melodrama, and enjoying the comic effect.

'Harry!'

'Go on, you go home, luv. We'll look after him.'

'*That's my mother!*'

'All right, all right – we've all got one.'

'Yer shower of coonts!' shrieks a tubby woman. 'Yer shower of bastids!' The others take up the chant. 'Yer shower of coonts, yer shower of bastids, yer shower of—'

'Get this fella's number!' the drunk roars into the seat of Inspector North's trousers. 'All I was doin' was givin' my mother a tablet! These fokkin' bastid coppers!' He starts sobbing.

'Harry!'

'I was givin' yer a tablet and they didn't want to know!'

'Haven't yer got a number?' demands one of the women now hopping up and down around Inspector North, trying to see the number on his epaulettes – as a ranking officer, he doesn't display one. 'Haven't yer got a number? Where's yer number? Oh, yer bastid!'

The sergeant grins, not being averse to a touch of slapstick, either, then finds himself the butt of the joke when the women switch their attention to his own broad shoulders, hopping up and down and shouting out the number to each other.

370

'Harry!'

'Just get his fokkin' number, will yer?'

'We'll look after him, luv,' urges the sergeant. 'Off you go now!'

'*Get his fokkin' number!*'

The drunken roaring and shrill protests reach a crescendo as the van arrives, and the prisoner is carried over to it like something large captured on safari. Supine he is just manageable; if allowed to stand upright, it could well be the start of another large-scale disturbance.

'Let 'im walk!' the womenfolk shriek, tugging and jostling. 'Let 'im walk, yer bleedin' coonts! Yer shower of bleedin' gits! Let the poor fella walk!'

The van doors bang shut and the drunk immediately sets about trying to kick his way out, and is still rocking the vehicle as it lurches off.

'What's 'e being done for? Tell us that! What?'

'D-and-D, luv – drunk and disorderly.'

'But 'e was only tryin' to give his mother a fokkin' tablet!'

And off the women go, the mother and all the rest of them, hot foot for the Main Bridewell, where things have been unusually lively tonight and may – before the shift ends – become even livelier.

'Bloody hell, boss, you got me in it again, hey?' laughs the sergeant, getting back into the Escort. 'No numbers!'

'Oh, definitely a complaint against police there,' says Inspector North with a chuckle, starting up.

'If I'd known your bloody number, I'd have given it to them!'

Another good laugh, heightened by the effects of the adrenalin still coursing through them – for even the commonplace has its critical moments – and then up towards the north-western corner of the sub-division, where the sergeant wants to do some pegging.

'Con requires assistance!' barks the radio, half-way along Scotland Road. 'Great Homer Street! Scramble!'

'Oh no . . . ,' groans Inspector North, trapped in the road system and unable to cut up one of the sealed-off side-streets.

They drive hard, go the long way round, the only way round, cursing every second lost, and enter the broad bleak stretch of

371

asphalt from the northern end, slowing down as they spot a group of officers gathered round a crumpled figure at the kerb. In the sudden silence, it's a shock to hear a young girl weeping – another shock to see she's the same young girl who was assaulted on her last shift.

'Oh, sir. . . . Oh, *sir*,' she sobs, dazed and bleeding from a head wound. 'Oh, sir . . .,' she keeps repeating.

And fists are clenched in fury as her tale is told. She had stopped a car to make the driver take a breath test, and when he'd attempted to restart his engine, she had reached through the window for his keys. He had closed his hand over hers, forced it to turn the key in the ignition switch, and then had driven off without letting go. She had been dragged for over a hundred yards before he'd finally released his grip, leaving her to go sprawling backwards into the roadway.

'Oh, sir. . . . Oh, sir,' she says.

The intensity of feeling surrounding her is almost choking. This is no part of the game, the bloody great game with a few variations; this callous, craven, despicable act is an outrage, and the cloth lies defiled with blood on it.

'Right, what's the vehicle's number?'

'All we know is it's a yellow Cortina and one of the females is wearing a white jumper.'

'A yellow one passed us a bit back,' recalls the sergeant.

Into 'B' Division, up one street, down another, headlights blazing, radio going, cars converging, keep on trying, keep on trying, the futility of it all. . . . Back into 'A' Division.

There, in a side-ward at the Royal Infirmary, the probationer sits hunched in a blanket, bedraggled and tear-stained. By some minor miracle, apart from grazes and bruises, her only injury is a laceration at the back of the head, which has already been treated. Inspector North leaves her side, and comes out into the waiting-area of the outpatients' department looking rather drawn.

'Her father's not very well,' he tells the sergeant, 'and she's a bit worried about what he'll say when she gets home. I offered to go and have a word with him, but she said it'll be all right. You don't want to impose on their private lives too much.'

372

'Aye, boss,' says the sergeant, falling in step with him as they make for the exit.

Then Inspector North brightens, and the spring returns to his step. 'She's talking about court cases and reports she hasn't done, so she's still talking like a bobby, y'know!'

The game is on again.

PART THREE: PERSPECTIVES

I

Old Chalky's cronies on the Wirral know better than to press a point when they see him all spruced up for a crossing.

'Fancy another jar, Chalky?'

'Er, not today, lads – got a bit o' business to attend to.'

And they daren't draw any ribald conclusions from that, leastways until his back is turned.

When, with a twirl of his brass-tipped walking-stick, and a step as brisk as his parting nod, he sets off for the ferry, boards it with his usual thirty seconds to spare, and finds himself a good speck to leeward. Cutting things so fine has left him a little breathless, but he likes, he says, to get the adrenalin going. Just as he enjoys the thought that, with the change-over coming up at half-three, bobbies in civvies are converging on Spike Island* from all points of the compass.

The ferry casts off and turns ponderously towards Liverpool, bringing into view a spectacular waterfront dominated by the strange mythical creatures atop the twin cupolas of the Royal Liver Building at the Pier Head. Tirelessly vigilant, those Liver Birds, for he has heard it said that they flap their bronze wings whenever a Liverpool virgin chances to pass beneath them.

'Crackin' day!' enthuses Chalky to the old dear at his side, and waves his stick at the flawless blue backdrop.

'Yer blowin' fer tugs,' the old dear remarks sympathetically. 'Goin' up the chest clinic, are yer?'

'Got a bit o' business to attend to,' says Chalky.

The sergeant's car is almost driving itself and making excellent time before the tide of traffic turns. Formby, Crosby, place-names like top billing on Palladium posters, and then into 'B' Division where the property steadily deteriorates. 'I live at

---

*Derived from 'spike', the name given to workhouses, casual wards and similar institutions, many of which had iron spikes along their walls.

Southport. It's like a big cloud that lifts off me as I'm driving home, y'know. I think that's why the majority of bobbies buy outside the city, purely so they can get away from it all and relax – for a change of climate! But as you come in this cloud sort of creeps up on you, and – well, you couldn't call it depressing, but your spirits do tend to sag a bit.' So saying, he crosses that invisible shoreline.

Jauntily, glorying in the perfect weather, Chalky makes his way up to Castle Street, where he spies a constable in the Dog Section on patrol outside the banks. A good fella, this dog man, with a merit badge – awarded for some incident involving a Greek and a shotgun – sewn to the right sleeve of his tunic. But before they can meet the radio intervenes and the dog man, his dog and their van vanish. A pity, that; Chalky had wanted to ask him if the bucks still spread occasional confusion in the ranks by introducing a bitch in season to the crime scene. His quick eye for something unusual picks out a disturbance outside Blackburn Chambers, but it's only a bereaved and somewhat drunken family being sent on their way by a sergeant from the Coroner's Office.

2

'That's one thing that *does* make you cynical when you come to work in the Coroner's Office,' says the sergeant who has a chuckle over some tattoos, 'and that's to see the pettiness in families over cash. Y'know, they come down here, and they're practically fighting over the funeral arrangements and the property of course. "I'm the eldest!" "But you never done nothin' for her!" Oh, we see some very touching things. There was a man who lived on the south end of the city, a man with a lot of money, and when I said to him, "Well, your mother's going to be taken by Thompson's down to the city mortuary for examination", he said, "Oh yes, um, who – who will pay for that?" I said, "The State pays for that." "And will she remain overnight?" I said, "Yes." "Who – who pays for that?" I said, "The State pays for that." "Ah, I see." So I said, "I'll

378

just phone Thompson's" – and he *hesitated* before he allowed me to use his phone! "If you prefer," I said, "I'll go along to the nearest police station." "No, but we want to take the children away on Monday for their holidays. Do you think we could have the funeral on Friday?" But then a fellow as black as the ace of spades came in here and said, "You called for Mrs Smith of such-and-such an address?" I said, "Yes – do you know her?" "Oh yes," he said, "she's been a neighbour of mine for five or six years. Her children, kin, they don't want to know her." So I said, "Well, who's going to look after the funeral arrangements?" and he said, "I am." She was white and he was prepared to— "Now, look here," I said, "this is going to cost you over a hundred pounds." He said, "I'll find it from somewhere." I was really impressed.'

The sergeant works in a set of cheerless offices adjacent to the Coroner's Court, which is itself just a corner of one floor in a dull block of offices largely occupied by the legal profession. The functional furniture, brown woodwork and off-white walls compound the impression that here dwells bureaucracy at its most basic, yet that isn't necessarily the way it feels.

You could civilianise the job, but you wouldn't be saving anything and the only sufferer would be the general public. I maintain that once the seven of us were moved out they'd send fourteen people to take our place – that's not conceit that, just basic fact. Fourteen people all tending to be like local government officials – there'd be no compassion. Sometimes, y'know, we have to prop these people up, talk to them, and really go out of our way – you wouldn't get that with local government. The people would just get: (*low groan*) 'Neigh-mmmmmm? Aaaaaaay-j? Yes, I'm sorry – go to Brougham Terrace, talk to them.' (*Laughs*) Now that's very true! But a policeman's been doing this all his life, you see, so he's got that little bit more. He's been used to going round the other end and there's *nothing* worse – I've done this, too, many times – than to knock on somebody's front door and, as she opens it, to see the colour draining out of her face. She bloody knows! 'Are you Mrs Smith?' 'Yes— Oh, it's *not* . . .!' And you say, 'You'd better come in, luv.' The funny part about it, reverse the situation so the fella opens the door, and do you know what's he's thinking about? His bloody motor car! That's a cruel thing to say, but it's true.

379

What complicates things is that a lot of the people dealt with by the section have been drinking. One man, who overturned tables, threw chairs about and threatened to assault the staff in a maudlin passion, has filed a complaint for having been forcibly evicted, but his remains a unique case. 'The things you put up with in here', says the Coroner's Officer, with a trace of lingering surprise, 'you wouldn't put up with as a policeman in the streets.' Then he shrugs. 'They're bereaved, they're under the influence – you accept it.'

Chief inspectors do not volunteer for the job: it's a posting. 'I was in "A" Division for about six years, and on promotion about eighteen months ago I came down here. I'd never had anything to do with the Coroner's Office, so I came down full of apprehension, and I must say those first few p.m.'s I went to – well, I couldn't eat me meal afterwards, y'know.'

In his late thirties, he has a broad pleasant face, a diffident manner stiffened by authority, and would probably be much happier in uniform. When asked what impact the job has had on him, his immediate reply is: 'My life has altered inasmuch as the rental for my phone is now paid for by the police; you see, when I get home, there's people ringing me up, and I'm always on call.'

Plainly, he's a pragmatist, and quite unlike one of his predecessors who became so obsessed with the post that he insisted on being informed of every single death in his area, suspicious or otherwise, whatever the hour – and deaths in the area total some 3000 a year.* 'I don't think', he says, 'that seeing so much death has an accumulative effect on me. But I'm more inclined now to get the book and look at the ages of the people who have died. He was only forty! They tell me I've become cynical on certain matters, but you can't feel it yourself.' Perhaps some of that cynicism is what one of his two sergeants would call 'deflection'. 'I don't know how these mortuary technicians put up with it every day,' he says. 'I wouldn't have their job for a big clock.' And he owns to having

*3372 deaths were reported in the area in 1977 (it excludes Sefton, Knowsley and St Helens; and the Wirral); there were 2015 post-mortems and 463 inquests.

remarked to one of them, with a nod towards a mortuary refrigerator: ' "She'll be happy now." He said, "Why?" I said, "Y'know – a prostitute, and she's got two men on top of her!" ' Another element of that so-called cynicism could be that he has adjusted to the grotesque sights and sounds of a post-mortem room.

When you first come in, you think of it as being a human being on the slab, then that changes and it's just a carcase after that, just a piece of meat that's being examined. The only thing that I still don't enjoy seeing is kiddies being examined – and smell is something I'll never beat. I've got to steel myself, especially if they've been in the water a long time. Policemen who smoke are lucky! I don't, you see, and initially, when I first came down here, I used to put after-shave on me handkerchief – and I'd go in like this! (*Laughs, and covers the lower half of his face*) I think it's a question of blanking your mind out.

And he does seem to have the wistful air of a man suspended in limbo. 'In fact, a lot of policemen don't know us. I look in St Anne Street, and they say, "What are you doin' here?" I say, "I'm toutin' for business!" ' But the 'blanking out' can only be partial, because he has become very interested in forensic pathology – having got over the 'double Dutch' stage – and, on reflection, has found that his mind has been stimulated in other ways.

One thing did strike me the other Saturday, while I was waiting for the photographer to come to the mortuary. I went to the fridges and was just gazing at the names, when I suddenly realised that families might be upset if they knew, for instance, there were C of Es mixed with RCs mixed with Jews, y'know – these values that we have in life are gone. (*Shrugs*) This is purely individual, but I still can't believe – having been there – that it all ends on that slab. I just cannot believe it. I think the body's dead, but there's something that goes on afterwards. I started thinking more about it, actually, when I came into this job. I think it's the shock of the job – there's no other way to put it – the *shock* of the job. It hasn't changed me.

3

With his pace having dwindled to the purposeful dawdle of a bobby on his beat, Chalky makes his way up Dale Street, noting this and noting that, pausing for a few words with well-remembered faces, and then pressing on once more.

'Got a bit o' business to attend to,' says Chalky.

Cheapside is a temptation; it's been a while since he was last in the Main Bridewell, just a few paces up the side-street, but at this time of the day they can be pretty tied up with court work.

'A'right, Chalky?'

It's a con in the Plain Clothes Section, basking against the entrance to the magistrates' courts, looking bored.

'Fit, lad, very fit. Keepin' yer busy?'

'Waitin' for the Herdsman.'

'Oh aye?'

'Fella all the cows get to act for 'em.'

'Bloody hell,' chuckles Chalky, who locked up his last prostitute long before legal aid could put a twinkle in her eye. 'Seen anythin' of Fat Lizzie lately?'

'Pensioned off!' quips the con, too quick with the repartee to avoid some embarrassment.

Pleased with the way his playful punch connected, Chalky strolls on, spinning out the pleasures of familiar surroundings for as long as possible, and muttering about such innovations as free representation and personal radios.

4

'In the old Liverpool force', grunts the teetotal chief inspector in charge of the Main Bridewell, 'we didn't have this blight on the police, the personal radio. I was a long time making up my mind about the personal radio, and now I'd throw the whole bloody lot away. A whistle is good enough. I once tried to blow my whistle, and there was half a Woodbine stuck down it.' He grins and then adds, 'Sometimes we needed assistance we

382

couldn't get in the old days, but equally we didn't overreact to a situation.'

Lean, tall and angular, the chief inspector is fifty-three and has the face of a desert-hawk, being as easy to picture on an Arabian stallion as on a palomino amid cacti and tumbleweed. He is, however, far from laconic, but a renowned raconteur and, at times, a shamelessly outspoken reactionary with a gift for comic hyperbole. People can make terrible fools of themselves by taking his every utterance too literally.

The main thing is the preservation of law and order, and the prevention of crime. The rest could, I think, very usefully be left to some other agency. You could take all your sub-standard policemen – the little fellas, the partially sighted, the morally deaf – you could put them in the CID! CID work is the sort of work any good Prudential insurance man could do, but the work that's hardest is the copper on his own, making his own decisions.

I'll try to illustrate that. You get a young man acting sergeant for the first time, and he finds he has a situation where there are five school crossings, the crossing patrols are off sick, and he has three men to cover them. Now, there's no way of doing it, other than *he* decides which two crossings won't be covered. Everybody thinks that's a trivial decision. It's not. It's an important decision, and he could have to live with it for the rest of his life. This was brought home to me because – well, that's just what happened to me. I covered the crossings I thought were the dangerous ones, and a kid was killed on one I'd assessed as less dangerous.

But the CID man is away before he's reached that stage, and all *his* decisions are arrived at by consensus after due consideration.

With his profound sense of personal responsibility goes his intense antipathy for recent developments in uniformed policing, such as the defunct Task Force or London's Special Patrol Group.

If you give people sort of special names, two things will happen. First, they'll behave as though they're special and, secondly, the newspapers will start referring to them as something special. Immediately you get a situation where it's no longer the police force, it's the Special Patrol Group. It's *not* the Special Patrol Group!

383

Now, as soon as you bring men into that sort of group, and you use them as teams, they get their courage from each other and not from themselves – which is a bad thing – and the lowest common denominator tends to set the pace.

In the old Liverpool force, the bobby would try to get his ability and his courage recognised by the superintendent. Once your ability and courage was beginning to be recognised – and this is one factor you can't measure: courage, which is the most important thing that a policeman's got – you stood a chance of being put on Days and EPs. Our Days and EPs men then were looked up to by other bobbies, because they'd proved their worth. There's no doubt we were the heavy mob, we were the snatch crowd, but because nobody gave us a special title we never became a target. No newspaper ever said: 'Ah! *Days and EPs!* What are they?' The answer was so banal: they worked day and evening patrols. And the lowest common denominator didn't set the pace, because we acted as individuals.

The chief inspector became a policeman in 1952.

My record is different from most people in that I was twenty-eight when I came on the force. I was an Air Force officer; I was in trainee business administration; I was an assistant manager for Littlewood's chain stores all over the country; I'd done progress chasing – I was a grown man, and I'd already formed most of my opinions.

Accommodation got me in, funnily enough. We were living with my father-in-law at Chester, and I'd put down for a council house in Huyton – where I've lived nearly all my life – and for one in Chester. The house in Huyton became available, so I needed a job. (*Laughs*) It's surprising the things that influence you! I'd had contact with a couple of ex-policemen who were security officers, and one of them always had a full packet of twenty cigarettes. Now I'd been brought up in a time when for a working man to have five Woodbines – well, he was going to try and make them last several days, y'know. A big fat packet of cigarettes was at least comfort and respectability, and I thought that maybe in the police force I'd have that. I was wrong about that. I also thought it was going to be boring, and I was wrong about that, too. It's the most fascinating job – there's isn't a more fascinating job anywhere!

He has been a lecturer at Bruche, and has prosecuted in the magistrates' courts – 'usually a CID corner' – but has never

384

been a detective, despite rumours to that effect which cause him some wry amusement. And now, as Governor of the Main Bridewell, he takes an obvious delight in his honorary title, and in the palpable sense of tradition which surrounds him.

Some rusting leg-irons and a brittle 'birch' or two, discovered in the attic during renovations, lie in a corner of the converted cell that serves as his office, but what he is particularly partial to are the huge leather-bound charge-books he keeps wrapped in a sheet of brown paper. His forefinger runs down a column of copperplate entries, and stops at one recorded on Monday, 22 November 1880. '*Sober* and assaulting the police constable in Cockspur Street,' he reads out with a chuckle, 'Catherine Heart, aged sixteen, twenty shillings costs and fourteen days!' And on another page is an assault on a police officer that took place within the Main Bridewell itself.

I had a superintendent in whose wife is a barrister, and he was saying a solicitor friend of theirs had been telling them about the 'ham sandwich' we have here. We put a mattress on the floor, we put a man on the mattress, we put another mattress on top, and we jump on him. (*Laughs*) And obviously this friend believed implicitly it went on. I would think that the *only* people who *don't* believe that violence is commonplace here are: One, policemen who work here; and, Two, people who get locked up here – the regulars know it's a myth. In fact, the amount of violence in here was always slight, and it's even less now I've adopted a particular policy against violence that may strike one as a right cack-handed way of doing it, but it works!

I've always found the key to everything is the man at the top, and if the man at the top is weak the people below him don't know how to behave. You'd think that if the man at the top 'sanctioned' violence that would then cause violence throughout – and yet the reverse is true. You get a lot of violence in —— where the —— is weak, one of these do-gooders, and so the staff assume they know better than him, and keep him out of it. We've had weak governors here, and if somebody stepped out of line the bobbies would wait till he was out of the way, and then they'd bend this fellow. I've made it clear from the outset that if somebody needs violence applied to them, then I'll do it – personally.

And I've done it, when it's been necessary. A lot of prisoners are very, very violent – 'Don't touch me! Don't search me!' They've got to be searched. A lot of them are looking for a hiding to prove a point – to prove they've been wrongfully arrested, y'know, because their only way out of some of the things they've done is to be violent in here. I mean, we get a lot of people who *want* to be knocked about, and we oblige them by refusing to. But occasionally you really do have to apply force, and I'll bring 'em into line.

Now, having established that point, I don't need to use violence, because the policemen subconsciously will be driven to say, 'Look, for Christ's sake don't behave like that! – he's a fokkin' madman!' (*Laughs*) And the other side of the coin is this: they say, 'If there's any violence needed, he can do it himself – he's well capable of it, he's shown us himself, there's no need for us to do it.' [And so risk a complaint being made.]

5

The incline has become noticeably steeper, and Chalky has had to halt several times for a breather, less interested now in his surroundings than in reaching his destination. But the sight of Gerard Gardens – a sort of second cousin to the Bullring – restores his flagging energy, and he turns the corner to look on what was once 'D' Division. Nothing to see, really. The public library still stands there, like the last battered book on a dusty shelf, doing business behind boarded-up windows, and one street-sign has been preserved, as though for cruise-ship trippers with an archaeological bent, on metal struts in the undergrowth. At the foot of the last bleak climb of his journey, where the sun-bleached sky makes him blink and the going is hard and uneven away from the path, Chalky decides on a short detour over to the left a bit. He picks his way through the weeds, crosses cobbles and overgrown kerbstones, and arrives at a half-hidden rectangle of debris, where he pauses for a ruminative moment. Then, glad of his stick, he covers the remaining hundred yards or so, and takes the steps up into St Anne Street.

386

6

Older bobbies never die; they move indoors and make themselves useful. There's a pair of greying constables, with offices on either side of the main entrance, who think no longer in terms of a beat but of the entire division – each from a very different standpoint.

The stocky, gentle-faced officer behind the door on the right has been a policeman for two decades, and was a soldier for six years before that. He has a cheery disposition and an air of great resourcefulness.

For my first nine years I was on foot patrol on the beat. I was as happy as Harry – I was bloody made up. I didn't have a radio; I didn't have a car. I had me own little beat and I used to work it diligently. I used to lock up far more interesting jobs than you do now – they're only hand-over jobs, there's no glory in them. I used to take a pride in the fact I'd patrol me beat on me own. I'd see somebody breakin' into a shop, I'd arrest him, I'd march him to the nearest police station, I'd charge him, and I'd take him to court. I'd feel I'd done something really useful. I've got six commends for crime detection, y'know – each for between fifteen and twenty jobs – and that was all before we had radio and bloody cars. Let's face it, you're drivin' – well, you're watchin' the bloody road, aren't you? And you've got the radio blarin' next to you. What does a policeman rely on? His senses. What are they? There's yer sight, hearing, sense of smell. I was in Korea, and a few minutes before I get involved in anything I always get this prickly feelin' – it's uncanny. Perhaps it's something I hear. By watching the antics of a cat one night, I got myself two shopbreakers.

And without conscious irony he goes on to say: 'My main concern in this job are the radios. They're worth about two hundred each, and I've got to see they're kept in working order. After radios, it's vehicles – quite a headache, believe me. The fellows are always complaining.'

He is now the divisional equipment officer, which means he's part quarter-master, part flag-master (flags are flown only on special occasions) and part caretaker. The nearest he comes to

387

dealing with crime is when a locker gets broken into, and he has to see that the catch is repaired – or when, for example, he has to measure up the traffic wardens' window for a new pane of glass. As for his senses, he keeps an ear cocked for the sound of young police officers slapping fresh batteries into their radios. They like to pretend, he says, that they're loading magazines into automatic pistols, and the jolt can snap a vital connection.

Tidy and snug, stocked with everything from new helmets to signalling-sticks and floor polish, his small office reflects the pride he takes in whatever job he's given. 'Well, it's like the Army – it's what you make of it. If I was content to sit here all day, I'd be bored in no time. When I've finished this report, I'll go through all my lockers again, because bobbies are greedy buggers, y'know! Even though there's a shortage, they'll have one here and then, when they get posted to Copperas Hill, they'll have one there, too. So I've got to keep goin' round, crackin' me whip, keep chasin' them out of bloody lockers so there'll be some for when the recruits come.' On the shelf to his right is the dictionary he received as one of those six commendation awards.* It seems – just as he does – somewhat out of place among order forms, inventories and simply worded vehicle reports.

The Mini is all right for getting from A to B, but it's not a policeman's car. I used to be a jeep driver, then one night my Land-Rover was off the road, and I went up to this call off London Road – a shop window had been done – in a Mini. There were policemen all over the place. No sign of this fellow, although he was allegedly seen walking away with this model [shop dummy] with the goods on it. All the fellows gradually drifted away, but – being an older bobby – I knew he'd gone to ground and, if I waited long enough, I'd bloody find him. I waited up a side-street for half an hour, just listenin', then I started to cruise round slowly – it was my scoff time. There was a stack of boxes in a doorway, and I saw a *foot* stickin' out of it! So I said, 'Tally-ho!' – and jumped out and fell flat on me bloody face, didn't I? Bloody seat-belt wrapped round me bloody legs! (*Laughs*) Well, the fellow had started to scarper by then. I got up, started to run after him, tripped on the kerb and hit the wall

*Commendation awards are no longer books but gift vouchers.

388

with me shoulder! I was off for a fortnight. You drive a little car round for three or four hours, and then get out and expect to run – you don't stand a chance. These bucks are walkin' round all the time, and they can just lose yer.

So there isn't much that muttering panda drivers can teach him about the literal shortcomings of their patrol vehicles. In fact, the equipment officer could probably teach them a thing or two about thief-taking, if he didn't have those recruits' lockers to see to.

The panda car was originally intended as no more than a means of getting an 'area beat' constable from A to B, where he would get out, lock it up, and make a patrol on foot, thus combining the advantages of old and new methods of policing. The benefits of the scheme were felt by police and public alike, but the manpower shortage is said to have led to its collapse, as each constable took on greater and greater areas until it became impossible to maintain a useful degree of neighbour-hood contact.

The spry, slightly built and personable older constable in the office on the left of the main entrance was once an area-beat bobby, and also served in Traffic when it still involved itself in everything from road accidents to domestics. 'I'm not running down the service,' he says, 'but the policemen that are made today aren't as good as the ones made years ago. There's too much specialisation.' He is now something of a specialist himself, but in his case the resources of an experienced officer are being more fully exploited.

I was on Great Homer Street when the area cons were on, and I got to know quite a lot of them up there. I'd go round the youth clubs, have a game of table tennis with them, y'know, and they knew you. They used to call me by my first name, the kids around there. I think it was a good system actually. I sometimes go down there, and they still remember you. You used to get a lot of information that way, too. The information isn't coming in like it used to when the man was on the same beat all the time.

As collator for the division, information is now his stock in trade, and has been for the past four years. It comes in over the

389

telephone, on scraps of paper, as a snippet mentioned in passing, and sometimes from other divisional collators' bulletins. They all seem to have the same mild grumble to make about an obvious source of data.

You do get information from the CID, but they tend to keep it to themselves. This has always been the thing in the police force, that the CID treat themselves as another part of the thing altogether. (*Smiles*) They like coming in and using the system, but they take out more than they put in.

'The CID have the viewpoint', says one senior officer with a wry grin, 'that knowledge is power – that's why they're not too keen to share it!' Looking at this trait from within the CID itself, one detective observes, 'It's bloody awful. I know there are blokes in the office who won't speak to others for fear some of their information is going to be of help to someone somewhere else – a feather in an opponent's cap really.'

The collator's office is open from nine to five (he can also be called out when occasion demands it) and the day begins with a breakdown of the last twenty-four hours' crime. There is bulletin material to prepare, intelligence to be funnelled to Mercro, and a stream of queries to be answered. Although a divisional collator doesn't pretend to compete with the sophisticated service offered by the central index system at force headquarters, he or she can often prove the quickest source of certain information.

There's the Vehicle Index, which is cross-indexed on makes and colours, and notes who is currently using them.

There's the Street Index, a collection of blue and white cards which have the date, the offence, the *modus operandi* and what was stolen – when applicable – on the back of them.

'They're not very imaginative with their MOs,' remarks the collator. 'They don't even try to remove the alarm bells. The blue cards are for shops, warehouses, anything like that. A chemist's, burglary, BP – bodily pressure – on the front door; twenty-seven break-ins in seven years. Or look at the likes of this one, where they have a policy of not putting guards on their windows.'

390

Ninety-nine breaks in seven years.

'I'd hate to see their insurance!' says his assistant, a big easy-going constable with a length of service to match that period. 'Those windows must cost – well, over a hundred?'

It isn't part of the collator's duties to estimate what these ninety-nine breaks – one of which involved the equipment officer's man with a dummy – have cost in police man-hours so far. The shop, one of a chain advertising its wares on television, would of course pay the same rates as a business less determined to appear so enticing.

'The white cards are dwellings,' explains the collator. 'They've either been broken into, or there's a criminal we know of living there. I don't think we've got any privately owned residences, except on the south around Catherine Street and a few university people. And we keep domestic disputes now – they've gone quiet lately. "Dispute with son over drinking. . . . Hit her husband on legs when he had cramp. . . . Argument with husband returning from work drunk, no injuries, advice given." They're the hardest things to deal with.' And, as domestic disputes tend to recur, it's a great help to have even these brief details of previous encounters; but whether this information is ever actually used is another matter.

There's the Active Criminal Index. 'Three thousand-odd cards, and that's only in this small division!' says the collator. 'If we haven't heard from them in two years, they go down to the non-active file.' He flips through a few hundred names, addresses and barest essentials. 'We don't go in for descriptions in the sense of finding the card to fit the description. You can get that from Mercro.'

His assistant gives an amused snort as he enters the year's 229th piece of information in the book. It's a new and astonishing nickname, which will now go into the special index kept for that purpose, and be cross-indexed with the active file. Cross-indexing is kept to a minimum, because two men and one typewriter have enough to do without duplicating the work of the Central Intelligence Section.

Chancing her arm a bit, a policewoman looks in and asks,

391

'Do you know who this fella is that's going round with his hair coming out?'

'Alopecia?' says the collator, raising his brows. 'Just a minute. . . .'

In seconds he finds the card to fit the description and hands it to her, faster than a computer.

Somebody can come in here and it will *click*, and you can go back two or three years. Things like that stick. Not only have you written it out into the information book, you've typed it out, and you've sent it out.

But whether a civilian doing his job would develop the same high level of interest and retention by these modestly expressed means is debatable. 'I can put a face to a lot of the cards here,' he says, closing the drawer of the active file, 'especially from the area I was on, y'know.' And plainly the sense of continuity gives him a good deal of quiet pleasure.

7

One-armed bandits are something Chalky never expected to see robbing bobbies blind in a police station, so he still tends to boggle a bit when confronted by two of the buggers on the third-floor landing. Miraculous machines, though, he's been told, raking in a small fortune in exchange for an occasional £40 jackpot – or, if you like, the equivalent of a con's weekly wage-packet. This means that the social club can afford some superior amenities, as anyone can tell by simply looking at the fine pair of elegant doors set in the institutional gloss-painted wall opposite the lift shaft.

The past and present secretaries of the social committee are two seasoned sergeants in the divisional administration office on the floor below. When they look up from their desks, they see 'A' Division as a large board covered in small hooks on the wall. From these hooks hang coloured discs bearing each officer's number; there are blue tags for lads, pink tags for

392

lasses, green tags for drivers, and sergeants are a jaundiced yellow.

'The bar is the aspect of the social club everybody sees,' says the secretary, a dark-haired gregarious Liverpudlian with seventeen years' service. 'Tomorrow night there's a traffic wardens' disco. But there is also the welfare side of it. If a fellow's off for anything over a fortnight, he gets a basket of fruit, bottle of scotch, cigarettes – something like that. There's funerals – we always send flowers if a wife or a member dies, and one or two of us will go. We also look after the sporting side; we finance the football team, cricket team, the annual competitions for golf, snooker, darts, squash, badminton, bowls. Up to eleven, the kids go to the Christmas party; up to sixteen, they get a two-pound gift voucher. Pensioners' parties.'

Pensioners are associate members of the club, and so is every civilian employee in 'A' Division. Honorary membership is extended to any police officer from outside, and to members of the prison service and armed forces. The latter are most commonly seen in the bar after attending a bomb scare.

The 'A' Division General Purposes Fund was the basis of the operation. 'It came into being', says the past secretary, a tall white-haired man with a donnish look, 'during the war when the GP fund used to do like knitting socks and scarves and that, sending them off to the lads abroad, y'know – a bit of baccy.'

'I think we had about sixty pound in the bank', says his successor, 'when this building was opened in 1972 and we found we had a bar in it. We started off very tentatively, hoping for a couple of hours a week, and talking about twenty- and thirty-pound takings. It snowballed. The gaming machines run at a fifteen- to seventeen-thousand-pound profit. All we want from the bar is that it pays for itself – it's open half-two to half-ten. We lost one per cent on the bar last year, which is as near as you'll get to the ideal.'

Although some of the old school question the propriety of having 'licensed premises' in a police station, the clubroom's effect on morale cannot be questioned – nor is this just a matter of having somewhere to unwind.

393

'I think this bar has done something else,' says the secretary. 'At five o'clock, when we go for a pint, the boss can be there – or his deputy – and you can stand there and have a chat with him. They'll talk to young bobbies; this never happened before. The bar has two sides to it – one side goes into the officers' dining-room, and that was to be an officers' mess – but the chief at the time was very good. He said, "If any of my officers want a drink, they can go in with the troops and have it with them." '

'And it would be lawful, you see,' murmurs his colleague. 'In a registered members' club, the law says everyone shall be equal – that was another thing.'

Slightly daunted to discover he is almost three times the age of anyone else in the room, Chalky hangs back, hoping to catch the club steward's eye. Almost the entire counter is taken up by a group on Mornings letting off steam, and the gaps are filled by young jacks he doesn't know from Adam – probably members of the Regional Crime Squad who, like the OSD and the Drugs Squad, are really 'lodgers' in the building, not being part of 'A' Division.

'Yer usual, Chalky?'

'Oh aye – Chevas Regal.'

Not that he usually drinks fine whisky, far from it. But even pensioners can be choosers at these rock-bottom prices: 22p for a pint, and most spirits a new penny cheaper, knocking at least a fifth off the cost in his local.

'And yer change.'

'Cheers, Bert!' A good fella, Bert; always cheerful, if a touch on the quiet side, and keeps the place spotless. 'Old Eddie comin' across, then?'

The question is rhetorical. Chalky's visits to St Anne Street are timed to coincide with Eddie's spell on Mornings at Copperas, but he likes to establish he isn't there just to get legless.

'Could do,' replies Bert, 'unless he's on rest day.'

Chalky waits near the door, where he can keep one eye on the lift while he scrutinises 'Rose Hill', the first in a series of pen-

394

and-ink sketches of old police stations that encircles the wood-veneered walls. The piped pop music begins to make him edgy, and then, badly shaken by the sight of a pregnant detective, nice girl as she is, making for the canteen, he cuts across the lounge area and goes into the spacious if spartan games room beyond. There, gathered round two full-sized billiard-tables, blue-shirted bobbies are playin' crash, all yellin' and screamin'.

8

Nostalgia is not a marked trait in the constable who feels like a dinosaur after twenty-six years in the division. And, although change is something of which he has grown very wary, it is also something he strives for.

I suppose I could say I spend most of my time building bridges, only for the bridges to be blown down by some incident that occurs. Quite often the incident is correct and – I'll give you an illustration. Two years ago in Latimer Street, two detectives saw a youth – who they know is on the run – and he's in a stolen car. They gave chase and he crashed that car and killed an old lady at the corner of Sylvester Street and Latimer Street. The detectives arrested the boy, and they were attacked with stones and hammers! The boy was released from police custody. And when the parish priest came to the rescue of the two detectives *he* was stoned. They turned on him, and that's a ninety-nine-point-nine-per-cent Catholic community.

The constable is the North Sub's assistant community liaison officer, and a large handsome man with a deep resonant voice that he uses with the inflections of a BBC announcer. The word 'public' seldom passes his lips; it's always 'people'. He may well have always seen the division in this light, going right back to when folk came in with dog bites or for a gas shillin'.

'We've a sort of open-door policy with people who write in wanting to look round,' he says, having just returned to his office after escorting members of a youth club through the building. 'I think it's a good thing to let them come in and see

395

us as we are.' Then he smiles. 'Do you know the story about the teacher asking the children to write about the police? One lad wrote: "The police are bastards." She was so upset by this that she talked to the local bobby, and he arranged a visit for him. They showed him everything – motorbikes, dogs, horses – they gave him pop. And when he went back to school she set him the same exercise. He wrote: "The police are *cunning* bastards." Sometimes that joke comes to mind, there's no doubt about it!'

The idea of community liaison officers was raked from the ashes of the unit beat system. 'I believe it was one of the finest ways of policing ever devised – a super idea; the bobbies did a great job and earned a lot of respect from the people. Just one thing about it: we didn't have the manpower, and so it slowly disintegrated. The situation became so bad the Chief Constable said, "We'll revert to the three-shift system so I'll have the maximum number of men available all the time" – and because he was concerned about the deterioration in the relationship between police and public he made each sub-divisional commander a community liaison officer. Then as a stroke of genius – not because I'm one of them, but for sheer practical reasons! – instead of appointing an inspector or a sergeant as the assistant, he appointed an ordinary constable with no chain of command. The bobby's job is to go out and meet people, talk to people, visit all the community associations, Age Concern, youth clubs, schools – and because my feedback is direct to the superintendent I can get things done far faster than almost anybody.'

He has also been calling at a 'neighbourhood' Borstal near Wigan to talk to some young offenders from 'A' Division.

The idea was for them to meet a policeman for the first time in a non-confrontation situation – there was a probation officer and a prison officer there as well. (*Laughs*) They have started off with a great deal of aggro when we go in: 'All police are bastards!' 'They're all bent!' 'We all get beaten up!' I mean, those lads will never ever get to like me at all, because I represent the police, which isn't a nice thing to them. But they found it quite incredible that I could admit some policemen are bent and that

396

sometimes people do get beaten up. And they agreed that these alleged beatings they'd received mightn't have been beatings, but being grabbed by the scruff of the neck and thrown in the back of a jeep, things like that. One admitted he'd never been beaten by the police, although he'd been arrested a number of times – you can imagine, to go to Borstal these days you have to appear pretty often. After a little while, we start talking about something constructive – about their ideas on crime, for instance. They have no compunction about stealing from shops or what-not, but the majority of them say that people who attack old folk should be locked up. Strange, isn't it ? And one lad came to me when he got out and said he'd done a number of jobs before going to Borstal, and he'd like them taken into consideration. I'm not the 'good-doer', incidentally, I am a *police*-man, but I believe some of those boys in Borstal are so socially inadequate there should be other places of treatment for them.

These kids get the hell beaten out of them for *all* the wrong reasons at home. Never because they've done something wrong, something socially unacceptable; they get beaten purely because they've aroused the anger of their parents in some minor way. And the parents here don't talk to their children, never have conversations. You know how mothers chat to their children when they're tiny ? Here, no; no concept. I'm not saying they don't care for their children, because they're more fiercely pro-tective against outsiders than wild animals, these mothers, but they have a totally different attitude towards them. And what about the wife who does something wrong ? If her husband just says, 'Don't do it again' – well, he's no man around here, he's a bit of a queer. He's got to knock her back into line, oh yes – and she'll love him for it! I mean, there are more children born here as a result of masochism. . . . Back from the pub, Saturday night, the wrong word, bang-bang knock her about, chuck her into bed, make love to her, another child.

Of course, there are the exceptions. There are people round here who are the salt of the earth. You couldn't meet nicer people, no matter how well educated they might be, however much money they might have. Because people who don't fall by the wayside here are really first-class people – as you can imagine, they have to be. I would *not* like to bring my kids up in an area like this, because I don't know what chance they'd stand. So these people have to be admired. (*Shakes head*) They're so strong they make me feel like a weakling.

397

I think the people around here feel more hopeless than they ever did. I won't even try and say I have a solution to crime and vandalism, but it does seem to me the more liberal we become – please don't immediately say I'm a fascist and a beater of children! – that the more we allow our standards to be eroded, the more we seem to be encouraging this kind of behaviour. You see, this is a very, very high crime area, but there are kids here who never come to the notice of the police, who never get into trouble, who work hard at school, and they have no reward whatsoever. There's no reward for positive good any more, which I think is wrong. But I don't know how you redress that.

The liaison officer's main interest outside police work is his family. 'I've a large family – actually, it's not so large now, because two of them are married and my daughter's expecting a child. We do fell-walking as a family, and just a little bit of rock-scrambling. I have to be careful of television, because I'm the type of person who can be mesmerised by it. I like reading, mostly history – I suppose I'm a political animal. Not actively political, but I do see a lot of things in political terms, and I think politicians are responsible for an awful lot of the mess we have now. The funny thing about them is they seem to have no accountability except to the voter, and the voter can't do much about that because he votes for the Machine today. You could put a monkey in and call it Harry Bloggs, and if it was a socialist area Harry Bloggs would be elected; and if it was a stockbrokers' area Harry Bloggs would be elected. It's a pity, that.'

On his desk is a message about the five-a-side football tournament run by the Youth and Community Branch. 'One year one of the teams who won were baddies, but we weren't really concerned whether they were children with previous convictions. Our concern is to get them off the streets in the summer holidays, and I think in that we've succeeded. We've had teams from everywhere – street-corner teams, mixed teams, girls' teams – but this year we have had to register with the FA, and they won't allow mixed teams. The final was to be played at Anfield – it was at Goodison last year – but unless the teams are registered they'll deny us the use of the ground. If

398

you have a bureaucratic mind, I suppose this tends to happen. It's a bit of a heart-ache.' It also makes the job of encouraging young people to respect authority all that much harder.

'The job's very frustrating, very rewarding, very exciting,' he says, 'and I enjoy doing it, but I can't say I've had any conspicuous success. It's a very nebulous thing; I'd *think* that we do a good job but, then, it's my job! What I can say is there's probably quite a lot of people now, dotted round the division, who think the police are not too bad after all. They might not *like* us really, but they might have a little bit more respect for us and may appreciate some of the problems we have. With the community associations, it's like speaking to the converted – they're the people who care, otherwise they wouldn't be there. The strange thing is the majority of them want *more* police, which unfortunately we cannot give them.'

Then it's back to thinking up ways of building bridges of understanding between St Anne Street and the 'unconverted' who dominate most of the shop talk between probationers in the social club.

I've some idea why the people round here are so anti-police. We're inheriting the mistakes made fifty, sixty, seventy years ago, where you got a set of people and treated them like animals. Most of the people around here worked on the docks, and they'd put men into pens and they'd choose them at seven o'clock in the morning, and at half-twelve they'd have to go back into the pens and hope to be chosen for another half-day's pay. So imagine the power wielded by the people who did this! Imagine the corruption! The men willing to pay part of their wages to that man so he'd choose them – and their housing conditions were appalling, their schools were atrocious. Now, just think about that going on for generations! Just imagine the terrible unemployment – just imagine people thieving, stealing to *eat*. You see, we forget these things. But this went on until the late 1930s, and of course it's still in the people's memory. These people *hate* authority in *any* shape or form. It's been bred into them to hate authority. It's like socialists saying, 'Remember Tonypandy!' Who can remember Tonypandy? (*Laughs softly, and glances out through his window*) But it's a rallying cry, a reaction to appalling conditions.

399

9

No sign of Eddie – it must be his rest day after all – but Chalky is quite happy in his corner of the lounge, now that a nine-to-five veteran has joined him in a heated debate with some youngsters over how 'A' Division should be policed.

'Now, take all these assaults . . .,' says Chalky, beginning a new tack, having demolished the personal radio.

'It's a fact', the cynic interrupts, 'that at the turn of the century, unquote, common assault in Liverpool was six and half times more, and there were *fifty* times the aggravated jobs! *Liverpool Echo.*' And he sits back smugly.

'So? I'm not talkin' about before the war even!'

'Things have still changed since then,' murmurs the quiet fella, who has a stubborn look to him. 'Y'know, we're more of a fire brigade really, not havin' the men, and so we need the radios just so we know where all hell's breakin'—'

'Assaults,' says Chalky, very firmly. 'That's what I'm on about – and I'm talkin' about all these assault police, not what the bucks fokkin' do to each other!'

'Bloody hell . . .,' mutters the quiet fella.

'I think', says the veteran officer, setting down his beer-mug and speaking for the first time, 'there could be a bit o' truth in what Old Chalky's been sayin'.'

'Correct, Sarge, only he doesn't allow for the way the attitude of the people – y'know, the complaints system – and—'

'He's just sayin' we're not a load of hard-knocks same as—'

'Just listen a moment. I hear they've been lookin' into all these assault police in Discipline, and they've got this theory it could be the radio gettin' yer to the incident too soon.'

'Huh?'

'Well, you remember what it was like, don't yer, Chalky? A summons in the old days would bring the sergeant and the con just meanderin' down. "No need to 'urry, son. Give 'em a chance to sort it out like, and then we'll pick up the pieces." '

Even the cynic laughs, while Chalky looks momentarily disconcerted.

'Oh aye,' he agrees. 'Now what happens? Yer make the street and all the neighbours are out, watchin' and shoutin',

400

made up with the battle, and the busies come and – y'know, when the adrenalin's going, Round One, and you – well, it's *askin'* for trouble, isn't it?'

'It's also a fact', adds the veteran, 'that a bobby with a radio can feel a lot braver – he can call in assistance very quickly should his lack of tact result in an uproar.'

'True,' says the cynic. 'Same again, Chalky? Dave? You, Mick?'

But Dave and the others take this opportunity to slip away, having enjoyed the Rabelaisian stories – especially the one about the glue-drops on the bridewell floor – but not much of the talk now going round in the same old circles.

'I don't know,' sighs Chalky, while the drinks are being fetched. 'They're good lads, but some of 'em seem, y'know, sort of on a different wavelength somehow.'

10

'Nobody has to steal to eat on the North Sub if they are reasonably au fait with the Welfare State,' says a section sergeant, enjoying his pint in another corner of the social club, 'but in terms of psychological needs it's another matter. I'm not really qualified to say how much of the crime is need, but those needs could be as real as hunger, and you've got to refer it back to the conditions in which they live. It's airy-fairy referring everything back, but that's what you got to do. You could say breaking windows is a form of release, really, or taking cars. In terms of physical need, I'd say: Nil – unless you say having a stereo set is a physical need, and that could be argued!' And he laughs.

Quizzical, idiosyncratic, an incorrigible realist with the appearance of a Saxon gladiator turned centurion, he looks at the world from a height of 5 feet 11 inches and seems to see there a good deal to amuse him. At his most serious, he is never quite serious, but prefers to keep things in wry proportion.

I don't think there are any particular physical risks in the job. We get smacked in the mouth and stuff, but you'd get smacked in the mouth if you were there and you weren't in the police.

401

Furthermore, you'd stand a good chance of being locked up for being involved in the situation where you got smacked in the mouth – or, at the very least, you wouldn't have about three hundred mates piling out of Land-Rovers to back you up. I mean, I feel safer in the police than I do out of the police! If I go out for a Saturday night, I feel terrified. (*Laughs*) But when I'm out in uniform there's nothing to worry about, is there?

I enjoy violent confrontations quite a lot, and so do a lot of policemen, because it's back to Cowboys and Indians – you're like a television policeman again, y'know! There's your man and away you go! (*Laughs*) And I like catching good thieves – I don't get much chance to do it now – but that's quite rewarding in the actual feeling of the collar. What happens in court makes a mockery of it, but you still have that little warm glow – the almost sensual feeling of catching him. Because it's back to huntin'. We're the last of the great white hunters – in this country anyhow – and it's man we hunt because all the animals have gone! (*Laughs*) It's like working with a game licence, where you can't shoot certain rare and treasured animals – elephants and leopards – and we can't shoot prostitutes, clubs and councillors!

A lot of people have an absolute belief in catching thieves; it is a hunting instinct really. The best thief-catchers, the best policemen – that's in inverted commas! – fall into that category. The guys who receive the most credit are the ones with this absolute belief, and they're probably the happiest ones, y'know. They get the most notches on their gun, and they can believe in the notches.

Of himself he says, 'I enjoy the job – I've severe misgivings about a lot of it, but I get a lot out of it.' And, perhaps to make sure being a policeman doesn't sound too special, he adds with a grin, 'I don't know what I'd do otherwise, y'see, and that's what it comes down to: not what you're doing, but what you'd do if you *weren't* doing it.' The sergeant is twenty-six, married and comes of a working-class background.

When I was twenty, I'd tried two clerical jobs – one at the Giro and the other at the university library – and I'd reached the stage when I didn't feel cut out to be a clerk or something. I thought in terms of the Army, but I didn't have Maths O-level, which you need to enter as an officer. So I put in for the police to my

402

own and most people's surprise really. I was going in in a sort of a vacuum. None of my family were in the police – they were all about five foot eight – and, apart from that, I don't think by background or anything they were inclined to join the police, so it was a bit of a shock. I only did it on the nothing ventured, nothing gained basis – I suppose you get conditioned by TV programmes unconsciously, but I tried to go in with an open mind and see what it was like.

The major thing that hit me was that I had me hair cut before I went, which I thought was a great sacrifice – it was the shortest I'd had it in years. Then, when the fellow at Stores was helping me on with a helmet, he couldn't get one to fit, and the other fellow said, 'Oh, that one'll fit after he's had his hair cut' – which terrified me, y'know! I expected an army-type regime at Bruche, which it was really compared to what I'd been into before. After about five weeks, it got past the joke and novelty stage; you go in and you think, OK, I'll knuckle down and polish me boots, but the appeal of the masochism starts wearing off, because you think it's going to be like that when you go back on the streets. I thought very seriously about packin' it in, and I had a word with my instructress. She never actually said, 'Don't pack it in' – but after the interview she mellowed a bit. I did boxing, so I got excused for that. That side of it, the sports side of it, was easy and you could get away with a lot of things through being into sport, which is the police all over, y'know. (*Laughs*) I hadn't had any bouts before I went in, but my uncle owns a boxing gym and it was a bit of a family tradition.

My first division was exactly opposite to this division, where they put everybody young on three shifts and the older fellas on Days and EPs. I did Days and EPs for about eighteen months; it was superb, y'know, great camaraderie, a great help. Our sergeant used to throw us all in the back of a Land-Rover, and it was a question of 'Arrest that man!' We'd all jump out and arrest him, then ask what we were going to charge him with. Which was OK, because the sergeant was there and presumably had some inkling of what was to follow – sometimes anyway! (*Laughs*) Then I went into the divisional office for a bit, I went on three-shifts on foot, and I went in the CID aides with two years exactly, which is basically the minimum. The first thing the superintendent said to me was 'Are you a driver?' 'No.' 'So what are you doing here?' And that was *it* really. After that, I went on the driving course, did reliefs like the wireless, went

403

back into the divisional office when they were short, drove a panda, passed the sergeants' exam, did acting sergeant and stuff like that. Then I went into Juvenile Liaison, put in for the Special Course and got through to the last stages of it. I didn't get it, so I put in for it again.

The idea of CID work still appeals to him, but he has little hope of ever becoming a detective. Having won a place on the Special Course, and having got through it with flying colours, he will be an inspector three months from now – and, in a sense, too highly qualified to be a beginner. In the meantime, he is an 'extra' sergeant on three shifts at St Anne Street, helping those at the very bottom of the ladder. 'Probationers have the problems of late adolescence, if you like, and the pressures of the job,' he says. 'The two combined make it a very precarious existence.'

My family had a saying which was quoted to me after I joined: 'Once a policeman, never a man.' Very hurtful! (*Laughs*) But there was something to it, y'know, which is why there's something hurtful to it, I suppose.

As a disciplined uniformed body you have to present a uniform front to the world because the police have different standards to the world. The public have like a dual morality; criminals have an anti- or *non*-morality; and policemen as a bloc have their own morality. The police have to take a defensive stance against criminals – that's accepted, but also against the public, because the police are going about doing their job differently to what the public wants at times, whether the public realises it or not. Police morality differs in, say, motoring – that's the classic. Nobody *ever* thinks they deserve to be done for parking on double yellow lines or for no tax or no insurance – or for beatin' the wife or whatever! But the policeman works for a system which says they should be done, they believe they should be done, and they do them.

Immediately, as soon as they start enforcing this type of thing, they're at loggerheads with society – or, rather, with the individual with whom they're dealing. There's also things like 'theft as employee', stuff like that. Unions will fight against that; they'll go on strike if you do stop-checks outside a factory. And the firm will say they don't want you to do it – you've read about

404

firms sackin' security guards for searching people – because they can write it off as a tax loss. As soon as the police start doing that type of thing, then they're anti-social. What's the term? Dysfunctional! (*Laughs*) It's what I say about corruption: frogs can only breed in swampy ground. It's the same with the Commercial Branch's customers: they can only operate because society basically allows them to do it. It's like income tax evasion, which is regarded as a smart trick and something quite clever, whereas it's just straightforward theft, in my opinion. But that's society. . . .

People look upon crime like a pyramid with working-class crime forming the base, and it decreases as you go up the classes. But actually it's a sort of square block, if you take the money involved – possibly it's even an inverted pyramid. I don't know about the geometry of the thing, but it certainly ain't no pyramid. (*Laughs*) Pharaoh wouldn't recognise it! The police perpetuate the system really. Just imagine them saying, 'This month we'll have an all-out campaign on the middle-class', or 'This month we'll go for a few top-liners'! It just doesn't work like that. They just keep it going as it is – and, the way it is, it happens to be the working-class people get the hammer. Who cares when there's a conspiracy to bankrupt a man? But wounding and violence is a working-class characteristic, so who cares? We do, because it's a working-class crime, and down we go! (*Laughs*) You could put a completely different emphasis on it – I can't picture how.

But I'm quite sure if this was a different society you could have begun at the top of this building, and that you'd be more successful – *if* people wanted you to be. The breathalyser – now, that was a binge on the middle class. The mayhem there's been over it, the protests, the negative and confusing case-law, the procedural mucking about . . .! A breathalyser file ties a bobby up good-style like a commercial file; it's a complicated file and, the farther up the class scale you go, the more complicated it becomes. The present file is an improvement – when they first started, you couldn't understand them – but they're still very difficult, and it isn't being used to its full potential. We could all go out and get one each tonight with no bother at all and quite legitimately, but it doesn't happen. And it's all because of the pressures – plus maybe policemen are a bit aspirational to the middle class themselves! (*Laughs*)

I don't lose any sleep over all this because I'm part of the

405

system, and you go with the times, y'know. I've gone through all the processes and I'm a policeman basically, whether I like it or not. Theoretically, if you like, it's irksome – but, practically, I'll go out tonight and look for a couple of lead-thieves. The system makes it hard for me, y'know; I could hardly go out and look through somebody's accounts on night duty!

Like it or not, his promotion will involve more than swapping his stripes for two pips, and he himself has said, 'As the police go up in the ranks, I suppose they could do some quite startling social changes. The social mobility must be tremendous, and adapting to it must be the hardest part, y'know. You go from being a buck, fightin' with people in the gutter, to having dinner with the Lord Mayor! Tremendously difficult to cope with.' Anyone with his undoubted ability must stand a very good chance of being at least a chief inspector in time. What then? 'The huntin' 's finished,' he says, smiling broadly. 'They take me bow and arrow off me.'

II

The detective chief inspector in charge of the fingerprint, scenes of crime and photographic department, known traditionally on Merseyside as 'the Studio', spent much of yesterday in a forest, stalking wild birds with a camera.

'I'm something of a loner,' he admits readily. 'There is quite a social life in the police if you so desire it – a lot of policemen are very, very gregarious people by nature, and there are always functions and whatnot. But I'd much sooner be off wandering in the woods, miles away from anywhere and anybody. I'm not terribly successful – bird photography needs specialised equipment – but it's a hobby and always has been.'

Chess has also always been an interest of this self-styled 'armchair detective' – a neat dark-haired man in his late forties with heavy eyebrows, who favours plain cigarettes and plain speaking. But as he very rarely has to match wits against 'them', in the same way as other CID officers do, it's really his naturalist's eye for minutiae which has its everyday uses. Not that he seems conscious of this; it just keeps cropping up in conversation.

406

The fingerprint bureau has twenty-seven civilians to help with its main collection of 200,000-odd fingerprints at force headquarters in Hope Street.* 'We don't have an aptitude test for our searchers – we just take people on six months' probation. Not many fail, and I think it's quite simple really: observation depends on whether you're interested. Most of the policemen in "A" Division can recognise their senior officers by their cars. I can't. I've no idea what the car-number of any member of this department is, simply because cars do not interest me; they're a means of getting from A to B. If I was walking along the road and there was a blue tit or even a bullfinch, I'd notice it, where somebody else would think, It's a bird, and it wouldn't register. I can only remember my *own* car's number because of my wife's initials! And yet I've remembered a fingerprint that was seven years old.'

He has his wife's fingerprints, his own and those of his children, too, in a filing-cabinet in his pleasantly near-Edwardian office, which is hung about with wooden-framed photographic displays of a mildly grisly nature. 'Having worked with fingerprints so long,' he says, and his experience goes back over twenty-three years, 'one realises that *nothing* is the same. It teaches you that every person – right down to a single cell in their body – is different, and every leaf on a tree is different. But I've got my obsession – it's nothing to do with police work. It's my belief it's possible to prove paternity by means of fingerprints. Now this isn't my personal theory or idea; evidence of this kind is accepted in Bulgaria – whether supported or not, I'm not sure. But I've done two tests under clinical conditions, and I was able to select the father from several putative fathers.' He takes out his family prints. 'There, you can see what I mean. Features, for want of a better word, are observable in the fingerprint, and they can come from both the father and mother. They're not *identical*, but there are characteristics – like when people say, "That baby's got his father's nose!" '

Heredity has an almost Darwinian fascination for him.

*The bureau also serves north Wales. During 1977 a total of 7910 cases were dealt with, of which 6560 came from Merseyside – the number of local identifications was 1337.

'There are people looking at the occurrence of particular inherited illnesses as they relate to fingerprints. In mongols one finds pecularities which can occur, I suppose, on non-mongol people, but there's a tendency in mongols to radial sloping patterns on the ring and little fingers, for example. If you find these features in a normal person, there's every reason to believe that they should seek advice from these chromosome counsellors. They could be a mosaic mongol with the extra cell on the twenty-first pair which leads to this condition.' Yet he is equally widely read in the forensic field, touching on such things as lip-prints and even ear-prints. 'I think it was a Swiss case, where the offender was seen leaning against a window, listening.'

His police career began in 'E' Division, followed by two 'soul-destroying' spells on the docks, and then a posting to the relatively rural area of Fazakerley. He was enjoying being a street bobby, and felt he was good at it, when the prospect of a return to the docks loomed once again. 'I didn't even know this department existed, to tell the truth. I think I'd have applied for the Mounted, I was so keen on not going back to the docks! However, I saw a vacancy advertised in Chief Constable's Orders, and I applied – little thinking I'd get it.' And, having found his feet, he decided it suited him perfectly – even better than the streets, in fact.

There are no 'fingerprint men' as such in the Merseyside force. His Scenes of Crime officers – there are thirteen of them for the five city divisions, and seventeen cover the rest – do all the 'lifts', take all the photographs, and see to finding and preserving other forms of physical evidence. Nothing is stinted in the provision of their equipment, from colour-processing machines down to vehicles; some of it is 'home-made', but only as a matter of expedience. Each SOC officer carries in his car a tripod and a camera-case containing a Mamiya C330 $2\frac{1}{4}$-square double-lensed reflex, a normal and wide-angle lens, ten black-and-white films, and five colour films with which injuries are recorded. He also has with him a rather awkward wooden box that opens out sideways to reveal squat glass bottles of chalk, carbon and other dusting agents. The wide

408

roll of Sellotape 'lifts' the fingerprint, which is then stuck to a 'foil' or sheet of clear plastic measuring five inches by four. The rest of the kit includes a magnifying glass, an ink pad for elimination prints, a pen-light torch, plastic bags, chalk for marking off areas, forms, adhesive labels, scissors and four very soft brushes, one with a rubber bulb. And then, tucked away in a small storeroom, is the 'murder bag' – something closer to two secondhand suitcases – around which rubber boots stand at the ready, kept company by limp white overalls. Although this part of their equipment plays a major role in Liverpool's proud boast of self-sufficiency in matters of mayhem, SOC officers invest it with no more glamour than a district midwife might confer on her collection of essentials. 'Oh, gloves, plastic bags, swabbing kit,' one of them murmurs, casting a practical eye over the contents. 'Red tape and all sorts, nothing special.' The intention seems to be, not so much to debunk a myth, as not to start one.

Very often, the SOC officer is the first on the scene after the initial response by uniformed officers. This is something for which, their chief feels, they must also be properly equipped. 'My officers have to have exceptionally wide shoulders and a change of clothing daily,' he says, with a quiet smile, 'because most victims of crime want a shoulder to cry on. Uniform officers provide it to a degree, but somehow somebody in civilian clothes seems to attract it. My own personal view is that there's no need for a detective to visit the scene of crime, but it's part of the PRO. Because anything that a detective will note at the scene – apart from fingerprints, that is – will probably have been noted already by Scenes of Crime, that the offender has defecated or whatever.

'Some of the things we find are unexpected. On one occasion, we came across an employment card – unbelievable, but true! – with the name and address of the offender on it. And several years ago, when I was out in the field, the offender had defecated on the premises, and wiped himself with a piece of paper. On examining the paper – it wasn't very pleasant – we found a very nice thumbprint actually *in* the body waste. This fella was a reasonably professional offender and he wouldn't

409

admit the offence at all. Until I told him there was a fingerprint in shit and he'd be a laughing-stock in court – he coughed immediately!'*

Television is something else he enjoys. 'I like the TV cops,' he says, 'but you've got to appreciate they're so far removed from real life it's simply amusement. Occasionally, on a programme like "Tomorrow's World", they'll use a fingerprint as a backdrop, and the damn thing's *upside down*.' From time to time, his evenings are interrupted by a call to the mortuary.

'PM's don't affect me much. You're actually working, so your attention's focused on that, and not so much on what the pathologist is doing. It's just a piece of meat. I've never really believed in the after-life, so I've never – I'll tell you this much: I'd sooner be present at a post-mortem where somebody has been hacked to shreds than be in the presence of someone who is alive and suffering – or an animal. Generally, it's rather smell than sight that affects me personally – the floaters, the smelly ones that have been in premises for a long time. It also affects my wife. She always knows when I've been in a mortuary; she can smell it on my clothes. Then it's "Get into the bath! Hang your clothes out on the line!" ' A gentle affectionate chuckle. 'I don't notice it myself sometimes, but you go home at four o'clock in the morning, and your wife looks up and – bingo! – you're *out*.'

Leaving a mortuary at dawn is possibly less depressing for him than for many people. 'Even in the Dingle', he remarks, 'you'll hear blackbirds and song thrushes in the early hours of the morning.'

Just after the early evening news, a Scenes of Crime officer finds the right door in 'A' Division and raps twice. He is a thin-lipped rangy detective constable in his thirties, with a blond quiff, high cheekbones and a laconic cauterising wit.

---

*'Some of them think it's a joke,' says a CID officer. 'With others, it's nerves – they're literally shit-scared, y'see, and crap themselves. Or it's the excitement. From our point of view, it's a useful MO. If they're inclined that way, they usually repeat it.'

410

He stands 6 feet 4 inches and is almost twice the height of the drawn-faced woman who opens up to him.

'Don't take no notice,' she says, kicking slippered heels at a yammering mongrel, keeping it behind her, 'he's *useless*, 'e is. Yer from the police, then?'

'Aye, luv – Fingerprints. All right if I come in?'

The air in the overheated flat is stifling and as sour as an old roller towel. A surly youth slinks away, leaving the woman to lead the DC into the living-room. The walls have been papered to look like walnut panelling, but it's peeling; the worn carpeting clashes colours with the furnishings, flaunting its cigarette scars; Mediterranean sunlight pours out of a huge colour set, bronzing a sultry girl sipping Martini in a bikini. Opposite her, a middle-aged man, lying fully dressed on a grimy sofa, quickly pulls a crocheted shawl over his head.

'Me 'usband,' explains the woman. 'He's not feelin' very well, y'know.'

The man remains hooded and silent while the plundered canister on top of the television set is examined. There isn't a clear impression on it anywhere, so the DC goes through into the kitchen to inspect the window that was forced. On the ceiling is a dirty smear left by the intruder as he steadied himself before jumping down from the greasy draining-board.

'I'll mairder the bastids,' sighs the tiny woman, 'God forgive me. I've bin like this for hours.' She holds out a shaking hand.

'Aye, I know how it is, luv.'

'That were me money for the electric they took – and me rent money, y'know. It isn't right, is it? It isn't *right*. I mean, I'm the only one that's wairkin' – know what I mean?'

The DC nods and asks her about her job, and they chat for a few minutes. 'Well, I'm not goin' to get any prints tonight,' he says. 'It's all this condensation, see? Maybe if you left that top window open for a bit. Will somebody be in in the mornin'?'

She nods towards the living-room, and then wonders aloud where she'll get the strength to go on. The mongrel keeps protectively close to her ankles all the way back to the front door.

'Tell yer husband', says the DC, with a hint of conspiracy in his voice, 'to keep that thing over his head so that I'll recognise him.'

411

Just for a moment, her face lights up. 'Thanks very much for comin', luv,' she says, smiling.

On average, for every thirty calls the DC makes, he finds prints at five or six, and only one of these will be identifiable. 'A lot of the yobs now are wearing gloves,' he says, getting back into X-ray 13. 'They see it on television and they aren't bloody soft. Your only hope is that at some stage they take their gloves off to open something – or to look at something.'

The DC was a probationer in 'A' Division, and went on to work in Days and EPs, Plain Clothes and the CID. But he has also seen service where he had to familiarise himself with the Suppression of Witchcraft Act, as a police officer in Rhodesia. 'I found coloured people quite different out there. The African is more respectful – I don't mean subservient – in his attitude to other blacks, and to whites.' After three years of uniformed duty in a rural area, he was transferred into the CID in Salisbury, where he worked with black partners in the townships. 'I got on very well with them – excellent. But I think the black's his own worst enemy: that country won't go black, it'll go red.' And so he returned to Liverpool and put in for a three-month course as a Scenes of Crime officer.

'You do about a week in the fingerprint office: general searching, filing, the classifying and the comparisons – only at a very elementary level at that stage. You do two weeks in the Studio, learning photography; you're inside for about five days, then they let you loose with a camera and say, "Go out and photograph what you feel like." We went to the tower at the Pier Head, and to Sefton Park to do close-ups of flowers.'

Since then the close-ups he's been taking have been very different. 'I'm turned up to a certain extent by some of my job; I don't think anyone's immune to the horrors you can come across. After seeing the injuries or death of a child – not so much murder, but natural causes – it's very difficult to get out of your mind you've got kids the same, you know kids the same, and it does seem such a waste of life at that stage.' He has a daughter of eleven, and a son of seven. 'I go home and look at mine, y'know, and you think. . . . I try not to be a strict father, but because I see so much of it you say: "The Green

Cross Code – for God's sake use it! That's what it's there for." '

But nothing has ever put him off enjoying a light meal in the canteen at Hope Street, when he returns for his break and to see what new jobs have come in.

'You're the poached eggs?' asks a very harassed young helper behind the counter, using her free hand to brush a damp strand of blonde hair from her face.

'Too true, O Flower of the Orient.'

She hands over his plate and is about to turn to her next customer when she sees him pause, staring down at it. 'I'll take for them later – or's somethin' the matter?'

'No, it would've died anyway; it's eyes are too far apart.'

'*Honestly!*' she giggles, brightening.

The technical side of his work holds no particular interest for him beyond being a means to an end. The job appeals to him because, in his utterly unsentimental way, he likes people. 'All coppers are bastids – you see it on walls – until something happens to their little girl, the house gets burgled or their car gets done, and then it's a case of "God bless yer, luv, yer some mother's son! Come in and have a cuppa tea!" And you're a copper's bastid the next week, when it's all sorted out, y'know.' He gives a lopsided grin. 'But there's that many laffs – especially with the people round here. Once you're in with them, they're as good as gold.' He also likes having a minimal amount of paperwork to do, the satisfaction of having a definite list of 'results' at the end of a shift, and the diversity of demands made upon him.

The mood in the Scenes of Crime office is in fact very unlike that in a CID section, even though three of the four shifts last for twelve hours and everyone works just as hard. There is simply less stress involved: priorities are self-evident, encounters with the public are fairly brief, and 'confrontation situations' are the exception, for an SOC officer is a detective in a very literal, unloaded sense of the word. It also makes a difference having not one but several divisions to roam over.

After refreshments, the DC goes out to 'C' Division and to a semi-detached house in a keyhole-shaped crescent. What the living-room lacks in taste is offset by the variety of sumptuous

413

furnishings that have turned it into the warmest of nests for a close-knit family. But the focal point of these arrangements is missing.

'They're fools really,' laughs the wife. 'The colour hasn't been right for weeks – has it, Bert? I hope they're getting a bad picture!'

'Yes, let's hope so!' laughs her husband.

'At least they left me cassette player!' laughs the daughter. 'They were upstairs, too – or shouldn't we tell him?'

All three laugh and troop up to the main bedroom. The dressing-table in the bow window is a mess of spilled cosmetics, and the bed is strewn with torn wrappings and various small items, jumbled up with the family snapshots.

'Those are the presents I bought me mam for her last birthday,' says the wife, 'but she passed on, y'see, poor love, and I've not been able to take them down from the wardrobe – I don't know why. Now, will you look at them. . . .' Her voice catches.

The DC dusts a little powder here and there to no avail.

On the doorstep, the wife puts on a brave face again and asks, 'Is there any point in sending for Starsky and Hutch, then?'

'Not unless you fancy them, luv!'

And the laughter is very real this time; it's the most he can do for them.

'CH – X-ray 13, we have a fatal TA. . . .'

12

Old Chalky excuses himself and slips out into the passage, having had a warning nudge in the ribs from his duodenal ulcer. He skirts the two gaming machines, has the canteen door held open for him by a pretty policewoman with a nice smile, and walks a gauntlet of curious young eyes up the length of the long room to the stainless-steel counter, which appears unmanned at the moment.

'What you want?' enquires a disembodied voice.

414

Then he spots her at waist-level: a tiny, foreign-looking lady looking out at him through the second shelf of the self-service display unit. 'Er, a drop of milk, luv.'

'You want it from machine – or you want carton ?'

'Best make it a pint, I reckon!'

'Oh aye, goin' to be one of those nights, is it, Chalky ?' sighs a middle-service bobby, sliding his tray up and winking slyly.

'Medicinal,' says Chalky. 'Got a bit o' stomach—'

'Well, you will have by the morning! Fancy a bite of somethin' while yer . . . ?'

Chalky sees the sense in that, and it isn't often he can enjoy a heaped plate of roast beef, roast potatoes, sprouts, carrots, green beans and lashings of thick gravy, with apple pie to follow, at these rock-bottom prices. So he joins young Charlie, a good fella, for a bit of scoff over by the window, and notes that the hands on the clock tower over the way, above the Rushmore Organ Company, haven't budged an inch in four months.

'Time it were wound,' quips Charlie. 'Oh dear, hark at that. . . .' And he laughs fondly.

A bumptious young constable has just met his match in the minute canteen lady, and is in full retreat back to the comfortable corner where the colour television set is surrounded by screens and easy chairs – provided by the social club.

'I treat them as my own,' says Lucia, who is fifty-seven and has twelve children and eighteen grandchildren. 'I treat them as the family, I tell them – I shout at them! They are contrary. If you have roast potatoes, they want the chips; if you have the boiled, they don't want it – if you haven't got it, they want it. On Mondays, it's always roast, but during the week it's always chips after that. Sausage is a must, some kind of cold meat, then we have curry, ham and pork – or you have beef, pork and sometimes corned beef. My youngest is eighteen years and nine months, he's the baby.' Little wonder, perhaps, that her last customer failed to impress her.

'I'm from Malta – I was there about five weeks ago. I used to sit next to Mr Mintoff at school. He lives by us – my sisters know him well, my uncle was his bodyguard – but I don't know

415

him; we were only infants then. Thirty-three years I have been here.'

For ten of those years, which began at Rose Hill just after Chalky's time, she has been working shifts in the canteen – except for when 'I broke my service' because of domestic problems.

Lucia moves down to the far end of the serving-area and looks into the officers' canteen, thinking she heard someone coming in through the other door. The narrow, simply appointed room, with its single dining-table and half a dozen or so lounge chairs, is empty. On the yellow wall at the head of the table a portrait of the Queen smiles down with quiet confidence, but there is little other decoration. The table itself is bare; only at lunch-time is it set with shiny cutlery, napkins and sparkling glassware, soon to be joined by a huge teapot.

'I've seen them as ordinary policemen go to inspectors,' she says, 'and there was one, John ——, and I used to say, "When you be inspector, I'll say, 'What do you want, sir?' – *not*, 'What do you want, John?' " ' Then she adds proudly, 'Now he is well up.'

'What about this Ivy?' enquires Chalky, addressing himself to his second slice of beef.

'We posted her to Copperas, y'see – d'yer know who I mean?'

Chalky's mouth is full; he wiggles his eyebrows.

'Oh, she's this old dear,' chuckles Charlie, 'this divvy who thinks she's a peewee. It's a shame really. Somebody made up this notebook for her, and she'd come in the Pier Head, come on duty, and get us to sign her book for her. She was bloody made up! But it got a bit – well, y'know. So she came in and we said, "What you doin' here, luv?" "Huh?" "Y'know, you've been posted to Copperas Hill" – we sign her book, and off she pops. From what I hear, they must've got a bit fed up like with her comin' in the bridewell, so they posted her again, y'see.'

'Here? To Sas?'

'How she bloody did it, I don't know! Next thing there's this bobby on the phone from West End Central. "Er, we think

416

we've got one of yer policewomen down 'ere. Can somebody come down to London and fetch her?" "One of *ours*?" "That's correct; it's your stamp in her book and all. Goes by the name of Ivy." '

'Bloody hell!' chortles Chalky, nearly choking.

13

Often it's not at all difficult to spot two detectives standing at the bar of a club. Even disregarding their ties, their habit of keeping their backs towards walls, their roving gaze and the fact that they often have drinks pressed on them the moment they enter, their feet give them away. No matter how insistent the beat, those feet seldom if ever tap in time to the music that blares out around them, coaxing responses from others. It's a different story behind the door of the manager's office, where even a uniformed sergeant's size twelves have been seen to jiggle, and a different story entirely in the social club.

'I like hard rock,' says a CID aide seated near the disco floor, enjoying an informal 'do' being held to wet a baby's head. 'I like Tchaikovsky – I like music.' If told he were a musician, people might stereotype him as a violinist: he's a spare sensitive-looking man of thirty-five with an outsider's view of 'A' Division, having started his police career in Birmingham.

I went to a commercial college for two years, and then I had these three interviews – two commercial apprenticeships and one for the police – and the police one came up before the other two. Dad was a sales manager and he advised me dead against selling anyway. I was a bloody fool: I joined the cadets and wasted two years. OK, it was interesting, but with hindsight I think I could have put those years to better use. I was posted to the outskirts of Birmingham for three years – it was just like county policing. There was none of this bloody stuff here! (*Laughs*) In fact, I put only one person on the books for crime and that was by summons – a larceny by finding. After my probation, you could try for the departments. The first thing

417

that came up was applicants for the Mounted. I thought: This is great! I'll have a month, I'll learn to ride properly, and they'll pay me for it. The only thing I'd ever ridden in me life was a donkey! I passed with flying colours, and a vacancy arose – if I'd refused, I'd never have got on the Mounted again. So for the next seven years I was a mounted man. We patrolled like a man on the beat, so I knew all Birmingham like the back of me hand. I'd got nine and a half years in then, and I'd never had a crime arrest. Then I had a fortnight's holiday – you know how you feel when you come back to work – and we were in north Wales and this hotel was for sale. That was it. We had the hotel for about three years; a harrowing experience. Runnin' a hotel is a touch of the Ted Heath smile in the lounge. (*Laughs*) You have to see they go away at the end of their fortnight sayin', '*Wasn't* that a nice young couple?' It's not good enough for the bed to be comfortable and the food to be good. [His first experience of Liverpool came when he trained in the city to be a McVitie's cake salesman; the hotel trade proved too seasonal, and he had to work very long hours on the road to keep his family afloat.] So I thought: Well, what about joining the police force again? At least the money's there every week.

I had a very rude awakening coming to 'A' Division, as you can imagine. I'd never met crime and violence like this in me life! And I hadn't made a crime arrest in my life. I was posted here on three shifts in September '74, and the first night I was out we had a burglar. Well, I dragged him out of this bloody pub window, together with the guy showing me round, and I didn't know whether I was punched, bored or riveted when I got him to the bridewell. You see, I'd spent three and a half years out of the job, and seven years on Mounted, and I hadn't even learned the new Theft Act, which came into being in '68. But I've found nothing but friendship in this force, and they helped me to pick things up strand by bloody strand. After twelve months' probation, I went on to Days and EPs on the South – which I enjoyed very much – and got posted to the Car Squad for fourteen months. Touch wood, I've never come across anyone really violent – not towards me anyway. I try to keep cool with them. Of course, a lot of these fights involve bucks anyway, so they've forgotten about it the next week. But they can have a big psychological effect on the innocent bystander; some of them won't come into town – they've been frightened off. I wouldn't bring my wife into this city to a club, *no way*.

418

I suppose I'm a policeman because I have the power to do something I wouldn't normally be able to do: to help society. If I can put these violence bastids behind bars, then I'll gladly do it – but I wouldn't be able to if I worked in a bloody bank, would I? I'd like to see this society a peaceful society, but at the rate we're going we're not going to get it. This is the frustrating part of the job. If, havin' locked 'em up, I could stop them doing it in the future, I'd be more than satisfied. Say, if they could change them – not punish them or anything like that – and they came back ordinary people, that'd be great, fantastic! Why *can't* we all be friends? It's ridiculous – isn't it?

He isn't too sure if he enjoys the role of a detective, though, and may try for something like Juvenile Liaison. Perhaps being in the CID is a little too like what his father warned him against.

14

On the wall by the door in the Juvenile Liaison Officers' room at St Anne Street is a sheet of paper with this typed on it:

What kind of peace may grow between the hammer and the anvil?
T. S. ELIOT

And the paper has yellowed a little since it was first pasted up there.

At a desk near by sits a big burly constable, who has two youngsters of his own and must be somewhere in his late thirties. 'I have always been in "A" Division – vice squad, Days and EPs, docks, collator and, before I came here, traffic accident enquiries. I'd worked in most departments, and thought this was one aspect I'd never looked at. It's quite interesting – I think I'll stick with it.'

Across the way from him is a slender pleasant-faced constable in her twenties, who isn't too sure what made her join the police. 'It was probably watching "Z Cars" and that; I didn't want to work in an office, and I didn't get the qualifications at school to go into teaching. It was on my training course when a JLO came to speak to the class, and it sounded really interesting; I just harped on about it for so long that I think they put me in here just to shut me up!' Before this posting, she was in the Task Force. 'That twelve months was unbelievable – you really *live* all the time you're there, y'know. But I don't miss that sort of thing now, and I haven't got anything in mind that I would rather do. At least you always get an end result, not like the CID where they can be plodding on for months and still come up with nothing.'

Both JLOs dress quietly, conduct themselves quietly, and would not seem out of place in a corner of a staff common room.

Liverpool had the country's first juvenile liaison scheme. It was started in 1951 by the then Chief Constable, Sir Charles Martin, after a visit to New York, and it comes under the Youth and Community Branch. As well as combining forces with the assistant CLO when their interests overlap – visits to police stations, and summer sports programmes – JLOs have a special responsibility to the sub-divisional commander in his role as CLO. 'A juvenile is somebody over nine and under seventeen. When they get into trouble, they're not charged in the bridewell but sent home with their parents – what we call "discharged for further consultation". The file finds it way to us, and we then have to have a look at the background of the child, the home circumstances, school reports and so on. After this, we make a recommendation – generally, we recommend a caution.'

Cautions, which can apply only when an offence is admitted, are given by a JLO in most cases, with the superintendent taking over when an offender errs more than once or does something that warrants a 'high-level bollocking', as one bridewell officer puts it.

'When you caution them,' remarks Richard, 'you know that a high percentage of the ones taking no notice will come again. But with the others, well, you reduce them to tears sometimes – I know I've felt *that* big – but you've got to do it. That way you know they're responding to you, and that they're thinking about it. I try and instil in them that they'll only get one

420

chance, and this is *it*. After that, it's up to them – not their parents, nobody else, just themselves.'

'And quite often you can tell they won't do it again,' says Jennifer. 'They're really sorry, they're frightened, and all the rest of it.'

'I'd say most of them are impressed by the caution.'

'Especially the girls.'

The background checks have given both these officers a view of the North Sub at variance with that held by many of their colleagues.

RICHARD: 'Surprisingly, the majority of the children around here are very well cared for. It's only a handful that exist from charity – or school clothing, as we call it, where the schools keep clothing and dish it out to needy families.'

JENNIFER: 'Most of the home conditions are very good, especially for the area. Some of them are palaces, really, y'know – colour television, with fitted carpets and everything.'

RICHARD: 'I've been in about three I couldn't get out of fast enough.'

JENNIFER: 'That was amazing, that house, wasn't it? It was a *horrible* house. It smelled and everything, y'know, and the kids obviously didn't have anything to wear except what they had on. And the mother was out doing community work, wasn't she? We were amazed – we thought they should send her round to her place.'

RICHARD: 'Sometimes it doesn't matter how good the home is.'

JENNIFER: 'You'll go to a house and the mother will say, "Well, I've got six lads and they were never in trouble with the police!" And there's their daughter, picked up for shoplifting. It's horrifying for the mother – especially it being her daughter, y'know – but she's got mixed up with people outside the home circumstances.'

RICHARD: 'It's hard for people to bring their children up properly in this area, but it happens – it happens more often than you'd think. It's parental control, basically.'

JENNIFER: 'You go over the other side of Scotty Road there, it's like a ghost town. The Bomb's fallen and everyone's been evacuated. It's just so *totally dreary* you just wonder how anybody could possibly live there – and you're not surprised they're apathetic, that they've given up. But you get parents that care and really try, y'know.'

RICHARD: 'If the parents care, you usually find that the teachers know the parents care, and they'll carry this on at school.'

The JLOs clearly identify themselves with this same process. 'We get excellent responses from schools,' says Richard. 'They're of the same opinion as us. They know the kids, they work with the kids, and a lot of them have taught the parents.'

This is plainly a great help with those who simply stray from the straight and narrow, and have to be brought back again, but the real problems are presented by an incorrigible minority whose parents have more often than not been in trouble with the police themselves.

'I went to a house a couple of weeks ago about a girl,' says Jennifer with a smile, 'and the father said, "It's no good talkin' to me! I was locked up last night – I don't want to know." You can't sort of be a juvenile liaison officer in these circumstances!' She laughs and adds, 'You can't get through to them at all.'

If an offence is denied, cautioning fails or something serious is involved, like taking and driving away a motor vehicle, then the matter goes before a juvenile court.

RICHARD: 'Usually it's a conditional discharge; a small fine and possibly attendance centre; or a supervision order – if they go on, they eventually get a care order, organised by the Social Services.'

JENNIFER: 'Before the '69 Act, the JLOs used to do the caution and then carry on supervision. Now you'll very often ask for supervision by the Social Services, but they just can't do it, y'know. They haven't got the people and they're struggling to cope with the court orders.'

RICHARD: 'They have old people, mental cases, everything – whole families where they practically have to run the home.'

JENNIFER: 'And the court will make a care order, and then have nowhere to send them. The kids go to court, go home and see

422

the same social worker, so nothing's happened as far as they're concerned. They've got away with it really!'

RICHARD: 'Whereas before you'd send them from court to an approved school. It's a mark of respect, isn't it, with some kids? The fact you've been to court.'

JENNIFER: 'They relate the whole case to their mates; they think they're great – and they're laughing up their sleeve at the social workers. Especially if they get a young social worker who is trying to relate to them; they don't stand much chance at all, y'know. You've got to discipline them, not be a friend to them, because it just doesn't work.'

RICHARD: 'They look to adults for this discipline, rather than the "I'm one of the boys" sort of thing.'

Getting through to some social workers is often a problem, these officers find, although their objectives are nominally the same.

JENNIFER: 'I know I dealt with a couple who were very, very anti-police, and it was very difficult to have a working relationship with them. They have these fixed ideas about the police, and nothing you say alters these views at all. You'd say, "That's not true!" but they wouldn't believe you. If you aren't going to believe a police officer, then who are you going to believe?'

RICHARD: 'The younger ones have a preconceived idea of what happens.'

JENNIFER: 'And they pick up the views of the area. (*Laughs*) You know, this business about a police officer getting a day off if he arrests somebody. So obviously we're all out arresting people to get days off, y'know! People around here think like that, and there are social workers who *believe* that! And it's no good saying, "No, we don't!"'

RICHARD: 'Eventually the penny drops, and they realise they've been taken for a ride by the kids they're dealing with. They're so disillusioned that they either leave or get transferred somewhere else.'

JENNIFER: 'They're coming and going all the time. But the older social workers, who have been here for years, stay for years. They're usually very good.'

RICHARD: 'I'd say the longer they're here, the more their

423

views coincide with ours. They're in the area, working the area, and that's the only way they can find out.'

JENNIFER: 'The police probationer is out there on three shifts, including nights, and he sees what's going on. The social worker tends to be *told* what's going on, and doesn't actually see it happening.'

RICHARD: 'Also, he doesn't make his own decisions the same way. Probationer or not, a policeman confronted by a situation must make a decision. The social worker won't – that isn't the way they do things. They have case meetings every Friday and decide what to do – and this involves everybody, including the seniors.'

JENNIFER: 'We think they should be police officers first. They go to school, then to university, and then they go out into the world to sort all the problems out, y'know. They're just not qualified, I don't think.'

And one thing about being a JLO that Richard feels very strongly is: 'If you become too involved in their problems, you're useless – you might as well not do the job. I feel very sorry for them, but I won't get involved to the extent it affects me outside what I'll recommend.'

Both would like the parents of persistent offenders to be penalised by the courts. 'For something to be taken off them,' suggests Jennifer, 'to bring it home to them what their kids are doing, because they really don't think anything of it.'

'I'm all in favour of corporal punishment for violence,' says Richard. 'Most of them are cowards really, and commit their violence in a group against one individual, when they know there's no chance of them getting hurt.'

'Especially with an old lady, y'know.'

'I know someone who's had the birch on the Isle of Man. I also know he's classed as a hard case, but he won't go back there because it "hairt 'im".'

Speaking more generally, Jennifer's view is: 'I like the idea Willie Whitelaw came up with, a glasshouse type of place, y'know; sharp discipline for a short length of time. They don't get any *caring* discipline for a start – they might get a crack off their father, but it just means *he's* irritated, nothing to do with *them.*'

424

Then again, neither officer pretends to have a solution to the problem of juvenile delinquency, and they joke wistfully about banging their heads against a brick wall for much of the time.

'They don't want to be children round here,' remarks Jennifer. 'They want to be grown-ups. I think that's the main problem really. They want to be big in a world that doesn't take much notice of them. I've dealt with one girl who does shoplifting purely and simply for attention. The school goes up in arms, her father goes mad, and when she's down at the police station everybody's talking about her.'

But it's a 'grown-up' world on their own terms, in Richard's experience. He says: 'I think they're totally indifferent to adults, in that they don't believe adults have any right at all to tell them how they should live. They just think we don't know anything about their world, so how could we possibly tell them what to do. You get dumb insolence, don't you? They just look at you sort of quizzically, as if to say, 'What do *you* know?' Then he picks up the file of an eleven-year-old who has been caught taking cars more than twenty times, and goes out to see how he can help him.

And Jennifer says quietly, 'You think you're doing some good in this job – even if it means you've just made a kid stop and think a bit.' Then she smiles. 'It's like the Salvation Army selling the *War Cry*, y'know: if one actually reads it, it's worth while.'

15

'You walk ahead of the procession and keep your eye on the crowds – you *never* march in step with the band, bloody hell, no!' laughs the Operations Inspector, who has been making arrangements for next Sunday's Orange Lodge parade through part of 'A' Division. 'You daren't do that, dare you? You've got to be completely impartial. I never listen to the music generally; I'm on the radio most of the time saying, "Will so-and-so at that junction stop the traffic now?" Your mind is always about a hundred yards ahead. Some of the marchers are absolutely paralytic – they can hardly stand to play their instruments in that dull monotone – and it only needs somebody to yell, "Fak aff, yer bastids!" and it's been known for them to stop playin', down instruments and chase this poor bugger!'

The two Orange Lodge parades each year – the big one is on 12 July – go along the eastern edge of the North Sub, come down London Road and then go into the magnificent St George's Hall, almost opposite Lime Street station. They are very unpolished if heartfelt affairs; each lodge has a tatty banner and usually a very inexpert band, William of Orange is represented by a young girl in platform shoes wearing a piece of bright satin as a cloak, and their general appearance is of a jumble sale on the move – whether this is due to poverty or a paucity of imagination may be a moot point, but the amount of drink so obviously consumed must have cost something. For the duration of the march, however, an Orange Lodge parade is very nearly a law unto itself, and demonstrates police discretion at its most discreet. Besides the fact that, taken singly, many of the marchers would qualify as a D-and-I, there is the constant threat of them turning D-and-D should anyone have the temerity to cross the street through their midst. The lodges provide special marshals to police occasional gaps through which the general public may scurry from one kerb to the other, but it's still touch-and-go every yard of the way, and the subdivisional commander makes an appearance in uniform just in case his superior authority is urgently needed. The marchers are so sensitive to any intrusion on their somewhat joyless progress, in fact, that the Operations Inspector will have to take very great care they do not catch sight of the thin ranks of the Battle of Britain parade taking place at roughly the same time.

But his responsibilities are not limited to processions, celebrity appearances, civic receptions, polling stations, industrial disputes and other foci of potential public disorder. A daily preoccupation is the problems associated with being in charge of the Traffic Warden Department, which is nine understrength at thirty-one in the meter zone, and down to ten instead of twenty-one at St Anne Street. 'We're minus six school-crossing patrols, which places an unrealistic burden on

426

this section up here,' he says, 'and we're inundated with letters of complaint because parking regs aren't being adhered to. It's the economic state of the country and government restrictions on recruiting.'

These letters of complaint will have been from traders whose loading-bays have been blocked, or from others with a vested interest in keeping areas empty. He also takes the brunt of the culprits' indignation, and his vision of 'A' Division is largely one of asphalt, yellow lines, parking-signs and roadworks.

Whenever someone says to me, 'It's a pity you haven't got somethin' better to do, like go out and catch a burglar or a murderer!' I always say, 'Yes, but the motorist is in charge of a lethal weapon, something far more dangerous than the average thief has in his immediate grasp. And, if your child was killed running out from behind a car parked where it shouldn't be, you'd be the first one to sit down and write a letter.'

Now, which is worse? In the case of burglary, it's more often than not the aggrieved person's fault because he's been careless with his belongings – more careless than ever today, in my opinion, because he's insured half the time. But you can't replace a life or make up for serious injury. And, of course, there's another way of looking at it. You get one vehicle parked where it shouldn't be, and a whole row of vehicles will follow suit unless something is done about the initial offender. If it isn't, the road network very quickly becomes choked and that has two effects. Delay has an economic effect, hasn't it? It's delaying a person's valuable time, which could be better employed in other directions. There's also the wastage of fuel, which must be considerable. And the other effect is that the old adrenalin begins to rise, and the motorists accelerate off at x miles an hour and they—! I always mention these points when people come in fuming and pulling their hair out. My attitude is the double yellow line is known internationally, and if they park there and get done it's their own bloody fault.

I think we've got eighty or ninety different parking defects in the city at the moment – to be lawful, a yellow line has to have an accompanying sign on a wall or a post just adjacent to it. (*Smiles*) I think it's motorists more than vandals: they get up the posts and take down the signs. That's eighty or ninety *streets*, because one street might have twenty defects itself, and it's a

427

constant battle with the local authority to get them put right. Oh, well, it's the economic climate again – or the unions won't allow it. All these local-authority workers seem to be on bonuses, you see, so if somebody comes along and digs a hole and leaves twenty feet of yellow line missing it's more difficult to get them to reinstate it than to do the whole thing again, because they don't get a bonus for twenty feet. Similarly, they'll put up a hundred plates, but they won't go up and put the odd one on. Surprise, surprise, a contractor comes along one Sunday and *he* does it. Then a traffic warden says, 'You know where there used to be a single yellow line?' You say, 'Yes.' 'Well, there's a double yellow line there now!' I spend an amazing amount of time going out and looking at things like that. They're supposed to ring us up and tell us about any major roadworks, but often they're quite naughty and that's why you can't sit in this building and plan one of the big events. The Orange Lodge parade in July was on a Tuesday – lo and behold, on the Monday the Gas Board had had some contractors in who'd dug up a bloody great slice of London Road! (*Laughs*) It was opposite the Bullring, which is notoriously Catholic, and the Orange Lodge is Protestant, of course. Very fortunately, we haven't had that much trouble in recent years, but you don't leave any ammunition lying round if you can possibly help it – plus the fact they couldn't have walked down there. I had to rush round and say, 'Will you fill it in?' You don't have the power to do a lot of things you do do, but you persuade them.

The Operations Inspector, who shares the three-shift inspectors' office at St Anne Street, is a compact, very alert man of thirty-two with a sharp edge and no trace of sentimentality. He lives seventy yards from the sea on the Wirral, goes sailing with his wife and 'two budding criminals' (aged two and four), and has been a police officer for thirteen years, after what he jokingly refers to as a 'meteoric' start.

My mother wanted me to be an accountant because we've got a family tradition of being either accountants or farmers – with one exception: my brother, who's a police inspector in Manchester. I wanted to be a Royal Marine officer, but you had to have your parents' permission and my father said, 'You're never going to do that.' He served for six and a half years, fought the

428

Japanese, and thought the armed forces were still like they were previous to 1940. I went and did four years of accountancy. I took Part A of the Final and passed that, took Part B and failed it. I said, 'Oh, sod it – I don't want to be an accountant.' It was a bore, terribly mundane; it was *agonising*. I joined the police force because I couldn't think of anything better to do. (*Laughs*) In Cheshire. Two years on the beat, CID for eighteen months, the force crime squad, was promoted and for three months went as training sergeant, then I went to the police college on the Special Course. Came back, was a uniformed sergeant for eight months on the street, then I was promoted inspector.

Unlike a lot of people, I don't think I'll stay in the police force after thirty years' service, whatever rank I've attained. You've done what you set out to achieve and, if I stayed on a day after thirty years, I'd only be holding up the promotion prospects of a lot of younger people who might have better ideas. I haven't got the idea that, if I go tomorrow, the job'll fall down, and I don't think I'd mind giving up the power that some people. . . . Well, they're *somebody*, aren't they? They're a 'sir' whilst they're a boss here, whereas you're just a 'Mr' the next day. Anyway, apart from that, there's the financial aspect; I think you're a fool to continue. I've moved house six times in six years and I keep putting a little money away each time. I'm saving up to buy a small-holding in another seventeen years, so many months. That's what I want to do. I don't want to die a policeman. I want to go out and get some fresh air in a different environment.

Making the arrangements for an Orange Lodge parade always takes a bit of time, especially the liaison necessary for getting together several hundred officers, backed up by the Special Constabulary, and there are many little details to be attended to – a certain Days and EPs constable, for instance, had better be kept well away and put on the Battle of Britain list.

Not only is it roadworks you've got to be aware of, but you've got to have a lot of local knowledge. (*Smiles*) The 'wearing of the green' is enough to incite them – you've got to watch for anyone with green on. There's an old dear in the Bullring who used to come down every year when the Orange Lodge marched past, bend over with her bottom towards the parade, and lift her skirt to show her big green knickers. You know, 'Knickers to you lot!'

16

'Talk about addicted,' says a detective sergeant in the Drugs Squad, which has its offices directly beneath the social club, 'I'm addicted to creosote. If you're painting a fence, I'll come and stand by your shoulder the whole day long.'

Now in his forties, his retirement plans are already made, too: he's off to California where a job awaits him as a security officer at the Walt Disney Studios. 'I love California; not New York – I think they're very abrupt and ignorant.' When he retired as a petty officer after nine years in the Royal Navy, he wanted to go to sea again but his new bride objected. 'I didn't have a trade and I thought the police would be a good job. I've no regrets. I play golf and socialise a lot.' He has been in the CID for eighteen years, eight of them as a sergeant, and moved into the Drugs Squad from 'A' Division, having also been in the Regional Crime Squad.

The Drugs Squad, backed up by divisional Plain Clothes section which concentrate on users rather than suppliers, is run by a detective chief inspector with a staff of ten: an inspector, four sergeants and five detective constables, one of whom is a woman. 'We're more or less the drugs intelligence for the whole of Merseyside,' explains the ex-petty officer, a big bluff matter-of-fact man in a collar and tie.

We do very well without going under cover – you get informants to do your work for you. You can get some impressionable policemen and, if they did go under cover, well. . . . (Laughs) How true this is – things do get embellished – I don't know, but in ———— they had a few fellas underground, working with these hippies, and the ———— drugs squad did a raid and found these two fellas smokin' pot. Well, you can imagine that if you're mixing with the scene and you didn't smoke yourself people would think, 'There's something going on here!' And, if you go to a party on the scene, people have had LSD slipped into their drink.

These informants are largely people involved in drug-taking, but the squad has other sources of help. 'Where a thief will never tell you about stolen goods, a lot of them frown on drug-taking, and they will tell you things.'

430

Liverpool being a seaport, we deal more in cannabis than anything. It seems to be localised. Liverpool is cannabis and LSD; you'll most probably find St Helens and the Manchester area deal in barbiturates and amphetamines; Leeds is more or less similar to Liverpool; and then in London it's cocaine, heroin. The Chinese don't do many deals in Liverpool – they'd be more likely to make the deal on Crewe railway station, well away from his own locality. I think the barbiturates is just as dangerous as the hard drugs.

I don't know whether doctors or chemists are overworked or what, but sometimes I'd rather go to a vet – the only trouble is I don't like where he puts his thermometer! (*Laughs*) You go there and you get a load of tablets and it's: 'Well, come back in a week's time – if they're not any good, we'll give you another course.' What generally happens is that you get about ninety-four tablets, go home, feel better in three days, and put them in the medicine cabinet, where they stay for three or four years. We're finding that youngsters are getting hold of these. I think soccer hooligans are taking barbits with drink, which makes them very aggressive. They're actually selling ones they've taken from their own homes in parts of Liverpool, and selling them for 30p a tablet. Y'know, with the price of beer being so expensive, they buy one of these barbiturates and away they go! They'll fight anyone. We also find that a lot of drug addicts will go to a doctor's surgery for the first time and get themselves put on the books; a lot of doctors don't bother to check their medical history, never bother to examine them, and just give them thirty Diconal tablets. In the meantime, while the receptionist's attention is on something else, a handful of these prescriptions will go into their pocket, and then they'll travel, say, from the north end of the city to the south end. By the pharmaceutical law, a chemist is supposed to be familiar with every doctor's signature in his vicinity, and, if he comes across a dangerous drug like this Diconal and isn't familiar with that signature, he's supposed to ring the doctor and ask, 'Is this prescription right?' But so many times they haven't bothered. We have sixty-three registered drug addicts in Liverpool, by the way.

The squad has two full-time 'chemist officers', a detective sergeant and a detective constable, who do nothing but run checks on drug transactions and break-ins.

Not long ago we did a dawn swoop on a load of squatters. We

431

found five drug addicts there that'd broken into a chemist shop the night before – barbiturates, amphetamines. One of the drug addicts had two children – one was three and a half, the other twelve months – and these children, by the way, were born suffering the signs of withdrawal effects from heroin and so straight away had to be given a complete blood transfusion. We searched and recovered approximately forty thousand barbiturates and a load of other tablets. They were all brought down here and charged with the burglary of the chemist shop, and then the mother was allowed bail to go and look after the children. At the time, the chemist more or less said there were about forty thousand stolen, and we thought we'd searched thoroughly and recovered the lot – except for the amount they'd taken themselves with glasses of wine. But the children recovered the remainder of the tablets two days later, and now the three-year-old is dead and the other one is in hospital with severe brain damage.

They're a pitiful sight, these drug addicts – I feel very sorry for them myself. I know they've brought it on themselves, but the whole mind and body gets dependent on it. They always seem to have dogs about and don't bother to take them for walks, and the excreta is generally all over the floor. Many times we've rushed into a place and there's been a couple lyin' there, amongst the excreta, with the syringe still stuck in their arm and blood everywhere. Y'know, this girl with the two children? We broke into her house one day – she hadn't a dose and was in the act of putting water and coffee into her veins. I feel very strongly when I see intelligent people abusing the drug so much they're – let's be very straight about it – no good to man or beast. They can't work, can't look after themselves, suffer from malnutrition; I feel very, very sorry for them. With the craving, a lot turn to petty crime; not sophisticated work, just a brick through the rear window of a car to get a brolly or something like that. Desperate acts.

To enliven the talks he gives to various groups, such as nurses and pharmacists, the detective sergeant has a number of 'visual aids' in his office, plus assorted paraphernalia of the drugs world. 'Those are joss sticks – they usually have joss sticks in these places to take the smell of the cannabis away. Here are some letters – it's amazing, y'know, these people all write letters to each other, and we get a lot of information that way

432

when we find them. LSD tablets. We have a nickname for them in the office: LSD Airlines – you're always finding people trying to fly with it; we've got two fellas going round paralysed in wheelchairs at the moment. LSD tablets change colour every month as they deteriorate. If you're on the scene, you'd know September could be green, October could be blue. Some of the songs the Beatles wrote were names for it: "Lucy in the Sky", "Yellow Submarine" . . . .'

Heroin, cocaine, mescalin, different varieties of cannabis – most far stronger than the marijuana of Mexico. Blocks of cannabis resin, phials of hashish oil; the former is often eaten on an empty stomach, and the latter is spread on cigarette papers that are sold for 50p each. 'A fellow on the scene was telling me the other day that he puts a bit of cannabis resin on his finger – he's a bit gay – and puts it up his rectum, touches his sensory system and gets an erection, ejaculates with it. But it burns pretty quickly, you see, so he's having to do this quite a lot! Those are cannabis seeds. It's not an offence to have them, but once they start to germinate you can get done.' A bottle of crushed cannabis leaves and another of mint, looking very much alike.

Whilst I was in America, the head of medical research at the University of California said he'd been doing experiments with cannabis and he found it didn't do you any harm. His opposite number of Chicago said, 'I've done the same experiments and I think it affects your brain cells.' When you get two eminent men in research arguing amongst themselves, who are we – as laymen – to argue? All I know is that we keep a dossier, and we ask these lads when they come in, 'What made you go on the hard stuff?' And they all say, 'Well, I started by smoking cannabis, then someone gave me this and you go on a bigger trip altogether.' (*Shrugs*) What I think the governments are doing now is to see nobody gets the opportunity to make cannabis legal. Alcohol – like smoking – has been with us for such a long time that we can't say, 'That's it, the end, you're not going to get any more.' They proved that in America with Prohibition, and look what that did to their crime. (*Smiles*) We have a lot of rip-offs in Liverpool. We got a tip-off that this fella had bought a load of cannabis, and we went on a raid at his house. One of our lads brought out this

433

bag, and the fella said, 'Yessir, I paid five hundred pound for it.' The lad looked at me, I looked at him; we smelt it and pulled a bit out. The lad said, 'I think you've been done here.' 'Oh no, that's good stuff, that, sir!' So we sent it away to be analysed and the report came back: parsley and cabbage leaves. There was nothing *we* could do about it! So you have yer laffs as well.

17

'What it costs the ratepayer, I don't like to think,' says Charlie, grumbling on about having to turn out for the Orange Lodge parade on his rest day. 'Not that I'm saying "no" to the overtime, mind! But it'll be what – a couple of hundred bobbies? Plus the OSD.'

'And the Specials,' adds Chalky punctiliously.

Charlie makes a face. 'Yuh, all doin' it for their bus fare. Reminds me – anyone tell yer there's a bit of a do in the Specials' room? Old Fred's been made up, y'know.'

'Old Fred? Never! Well, I must. . . .'

'Got to get back, so off yer go, lad – and behave yourself! Down the back stairs, next floor down, it's on the corner.'

'Cheers,' says Chalky.

The Specials' parade room is packed with happy sound and so many off-duty officers that it almost overflows, giving Chalky cause to pause on the threshold while the fella in the centre of the group, blocking the way, caps a colleague's funny story, aided and abetted by his audience.

'Johnny and Mary have a typical Saturday night fight, y'see –'

'Oh aye!' comes the chorus.

'– where Johnny arrives home pissed, urinates in the fire, throws his dinner out the window, and Mary's sister comes runnin' to the bridewell. "Sir! Sir! Mary's fella's been on the ale again!" '

A deeply appreciative laugh.

'And Mary drags all her kids to her sister's flat, and says, "Fifteen years I've slaved for that bastid! I'll get me separation in the mornin'!" '

434

'Bet she fokkin' doesn't!'

'The usual stuff,' says the storyteller, beaming. 'Anyway, Mary hits Johnny with a milk-bottle, y'see, and a few minutes later Johnny collapses and dies. He's laid out, and all the scruffy dirty Mary Ellens are kneelin', sayin' the litany of the dyin' – '

'You're talkin' about the women I love!'

He gets his laugh, too.

' – are kneelin', saying the litany of the dyin', and waitin' for the insurance money to come. So, anyway, comes the mornin' of the funeral, and Mary and all the scruffy Mary Ellens, half-pissed, back teeth floatin' with the Guinness, and – '

'Backbone of the wairld!'

' – and Mary arrives at the funeral, and Johnny's family are all there. Well, as the coffin is lowered into the grave, Mary – with typical buckess self-dramatising – bursts forth from the clutchin' Mary Ellens – '

' – to throw herself on the – '

' – and she runs towards the coffin, sayin', "I'll miss yer, Johnny! I'll miss yer, Johnny!" And one of Johnny's family shouts, "Yer didn't miss 'im with the fokkin' milk-bottle, did yer?" '

A roar of laughter.

'Quite true,' insists the storyteller.

'It *is* true,' seconds his back-up man. 'Superb.'

'Chalky! What'll it be, son – Scotch?'

Chalky raises a thumb to Old Fred, who's grinning at him over the other heads, and sidles into a gap behind the inspector's desk.

'Be with yer in a second.'

Now the storyteller's voice is lost in the hubbub and clink of glasses, so Chalky glances round behind him for a moment's diversion until a drink in his hand will make him feel one of the party – as always these days, there are so many new faces. He glances at a copy of the 'A' Division contribution to the *Specials' Gazette* of last year, taking particular note of the arrests made in a period of six months.

435

D & D – 26; D & I – 15; attempted burglary – 7; disorderly behaviour – 1; criminal damage – 7; assault on police (Specials) 8 (including actual bodily harm & wounding, including a broken nose, black eyes, lost teeth, split lip, damaged hands and legs, etc.); theft – 4; wounding – 2; attempted theft of motor vehicle – 4; suspected persons loitering – 9; illegal immigrant – 1; fatal traffic accident – 1 (first aid given by Special Cons to no avail). TOTAL – 90 arrests & charges. . . . The Court results for all the above jobs range from a fine of a few pounds to fines of several hundred pounds, and also prison sentences which range from one day to nine months. . . . As far as the social side of the Special Constabulary is concerned, I am afraid 'A' Divn does not shine, but I believe the above résumé of our work proves our value.

'The Acts of Parliament covering the Special Constabulary go way back before the regular force was formed – "All's well!" and all that,' says the special inspector seated at the desk of the parade room one Saturday at eight. 'In fact, we always boast we were the original police force. But we've been an *effective* police reserve, I think, since the war, when we were brought out into the War Reserve, and they realised that any form of reserve had to be trained to a reasonable level. It developed then into a regular practice where the parade system began of Specials reporting to police stations as often as they could, to do foot patrols and not just back up the regular force in all forms of emergencies or big occasions. Each division has its own Special Constabulary back-up – there are two special inspectors, two special sergeants and thirty-five special constables in 'A' Division; we're under strength by over a hundred. Each division has its parade nights; you might get one where it's Wednesday night, here it's Fridays and Saturdays. The Saturday parades are very poor – it's a dead parade, Saturday, usually. But on a Friday you've got an average of six, seven men, a sergeant and an inspector.'

Special inspectors and sergeants work a roster, but constables are under no more than a moral obligation to attend at least twelve parades a year. Once the special inspector knows his 'parade strength', he reports to Inspector North, who may

436

request specific assistance or leave it to him to decide their beats, depending upon circumstances.

'As soon as I walked in,' remarks the special inspector, 'the sergeant said, "We're going to be very lucky if we get anyone here tonight, what with the holidays and this IPA thing in Edinburgh." '

One special constable does turn up, and an informal parade is held round the desk. Ask a policeman why he joined up, and half the time he's hard put to find an answer – it was an accident, an alternative to boredom, an outdoor job, a steady wage in hard times. Ask a Special, and more often than not he'll say right away he always wanted to be a policeman.

'I believe in natural calls,' says the special inspector, a slightly built, rather aesthetic-looking education welfare officer of forty-seven, with twenty-seven years' service in the corps. 'When we're babies – well, for some deep-rooted reason, fellas have wanted to be a doctor or a nurse or a fireman or an engine driver or a policeman, and it sticks with you. My left eye dropped me – in those days, you had to be six-six in each eye. I was heart-broken.'

'And you had to be six-six when I wanted to join,' says the special sergeant, 'which I was – and still am – but it didn't do *me* any good, because me eyes weren't high enough off the ground!' He is thirty, broad-shouldered, jolly and volatile, and works as an administrator in telecommunications. Ironically, after repeated attempts to get into the Liverpool police, he finally grew 'that extra inch', but was loath to halve his income by then. 'I'm happy now,' he says, 'and I've got rid of this police thing.' Everyone laughs.

'It all stems back years ago,' says the special constable, a quiet unassuming electrician of twenty, built like an oak and above the minimum height of 5 feet 6 inches required for male Specials. 'I think as a child you see the policeman as the Man – it's always something you wanted to do. I tried for the regular force – no good, me eyesight let me down – so the next best thing was the Specials. It was frightening at first because you don't know what to expect, what you're going to meet, if you're going to be able to handle a situation.'

437

'By Christ,' laughs the special sergeant, 'you learn quick enough – or you die!'

'I suppose we're a lot of police failures in many ways really,' says the special inspector, with a smile. 'I think in every Special there has always been this inner desire to *police*.' When he was young, he had the option of emigrating to a country where his eyesight would not have stopped him becoming a police officer. 'It was often suggested to me, but I've got a rather slushy idea about the British bobby. I know it's a bit romantic, a bit sad, really, but I like the traditional policeman with his helmet on – the young, crisp, bright police officer – and the British attitude towards the police. Whatever help is needed, "Quick, get the bobby!" '

'Oh, I'm far too insular,' says the special sergeant. 'I've only been to the Isle of Man! I've no desire to travel. There's only one police force as far as I'm concerned: Merseyside. But if I *had* to leave here, I'd have to go to the hardest toughest police force – New York. I'd have to prove myself.'

'I've never really thought of it,' says the special constable.

Their dual roles bring a share of conflict. 'Your wives get no reward from it,' the special inspector points out. 'My wife's sitting at home now worryin'.'

'One wife took the fella's duty trousers so he couldn't come out!' laughs the special sergeant.

'They get a lot of pressure from the wives to pack it in.'

Then the special constable makes one of his quiet observations: 'When they found out I was a Special where I was working, they just wouldn't speak to me. They moved me to another site where they know, but they don't do anything.'

'And yet', says the special sergeant, 'these are the very people who, if they have an argument or anything, come running to the police. These sort of lower – it's difficult to describe them really – lower-educated types of people are brought up to hate the police, I think. A lot of people hate the police because they think they should, rather than they've got any actual grievance against them. Their father supports Liverpool, so they support Liverpool; he hates the police, so they hate the police. But, if you ask them why, they can't tell you. "Oh, I

438

don't like the police!" "Why not?" "Well, er, they're a shower of rubbish, the police!" "What have they done?" "Er, dey're fascist bastids!" '

'It's like the conflict between black and white,' murmurs the special constable, 'isn't it? "Why do you hate them?" " 'Cos they're black." '

There's a silence.

'I work with social workers closely,' says the special inspector, 'and social workers are not very happy about policemen. So when I go to case conferences I get it in a different way. They expect me to come up every time with a sort of fascist decision. I'm prejudged. I'm an anti-violence person; violence makes me ill. I'm very opposed to capital punishment, for instance. I get very offended when these social workers label me, just because I'm a part-time policeman, as a vicious stupid bastard.'

His colleagues nod.

'You've got to ask yourself: Why *am* I a Special?' he goes on. 'I think most special constables have had a natural call. I honestly don't believe it's power-seeking. There might be a certain amount of uniform queening in it, because most men like to wear a uniform, but—'

'You soon forget your power as you're walking round, don't yer?' cuts in the special sergeant. 'In the first week!'

'Yes, it soon wears off! I also think that the men of twenty-five upwards really do regard it as a very valuable part-time contribution. We've had men who've committed offences, just as there have been regulars discharged for dishonourable action, but I've never been able to put my finger on anyone about whom I can say, "I know *he* joined the Specials for the advantages of the uniform." '

'We can spot bullies.'

'A nasty class of person, a bully – he wouldn't last. It's something we're very wary of.'

A recruit to the corps attends thirteen weekly lectures before being sent to a division, and further lectures are given at intervals during his service, but these three officers would like very much more instruction. 'Specials have the harder job, not

439

being as well trained as the regulars,' says the special sergeant.

Soon, they believe, things are going to get even tougher for them when, instead of the 'S' on their epaulettes (where St Anne Street officers have an 'A'), they will wear a shoulder-flash spelling out their status: *Special Constabulary*.

The special inspector shakes his head. 'There's an awful lot of people that'll come up with: "Oh, you're *only* a Special." Now this is very, very embarrassing – very bloody annoying! If you have the same authority, same responsibilities, then it's not fair that someone should say to you, "Go away, you're only a Special". A Special will lock you up just as sodding fast – *and* faster probably – than some of the regular policemen will lock you up, and they're just as tough and hard as some of them as well. You see, you shouldn't be put in the position of looking like a second-class policeman – that's dangerous. You're giving the thug a psychological advantage.'

'I was down at a wine lodge,' says the special sergeant with a grin, 'and they were having one of their brawls – y'know, you open the doors and it's like a scene from the Wild West! Chairs and glasses and bottles and people! Just this mêlée, and you try to go in there and do something about it. The first fellow I saw looked at me, looked down a considerable way, and then he said, "Aaaaah! A fokkin' Special!" – and gave me such a smack on the nose – whoomp! – me eyes watered for a fortnight. Now, I've never been able to work out whether, if I'd come in there as a bobby, as a regular policeman, he'd have done that.'

Everyone laughs, then the special inspector returns to the point he was making. 'The regular force obviously feel: We're paid professionals, we're highly trained, and here we get some hobby bobby wearing the same glorious uniform that we strove to get through training and passing exams and so on. I understand that. But in practice this distinction in uniform isn't a practical thing to do. We all feel weakened, terribly weakened by this. We quite agree that there should be a distinction for administrative purposes, but the "S" is enough – we all feel very strongly because we have to try twice as bloody hard to get the same result.'

440

The matter of distinctions can be a vexed one. 'One of the things that annoys me', adds the special inspector, 'is that you constantly have young lads joining the Specials who do the duties, they arrest and go to the Crown Court, win their cases, get smashing comments from the Chief Constable for their fine jobs, and can't get in for some minor technical reason. Of course, they always come up with the old expression, "Well, you must draw the line somewhere." '

'Usually it's he might not be good at paperwork,' explains the special sergeant. 'He can get by, but as a regular it wouldn't work the same.'

Again and again the 'regulars' are mentioned in tones of the greatest respect. 'You get a young policeman of nineteen,' says the special inspector, 'and he's called to a violent pub scene. We expect him to go in there like bloody stupid Dixon of Dock Green, and say, "Come along, now – would you mind coming out ?" At the same time, we expect him to be a bloody all-in wrestler, with the physical fitness of Superman; we expect him to be intellectual enough to go into court and cross bloody swords with barristers; we expect him to keep his cool in the middle of a serious smash-up – we don't half expect a lot from him, you know! And we pay him in bloody buttons.'

Special Constabulary officers receive no more than bus fares and other modest out-of-pocket expenses for their pains, which are not infrequently quite real ones in 'A' Division.

The special sergeant shrugs and laughs. 'You go home, you have a bath – say, on the Sunday after – and you can see on yourself about five or six big blue bruises, and you can't remember getting them. You know, you're kicked, you're spat at, people are sick all over yer, they thump you – sometimes not sufficiently for you to make it an assault if they're drunk. Oh, I would think I've been *seriously* thumped at least ten times in ten years. Once a year!' He points to a scar over his eye. 'I think I had eight stitches in that – a drunken steel worker, a little fellow with an eighteen-and-a-half-inch collar! – for which, incidentally, I got a hundred and fifty quid from the Criminal Injuries Compensation Board. But, as for thumps and bumps and bites and scratches and ankles twisted,

441

they just don't get logged – you'd get a sore finger through writin' 'em! If you're prepared to get stuck in, this is what happens. We had one fellow this year who was actually killed on duty – it's not as bad as it sounds: he's alive now.'

'It was a general big scrap going on—'

'There was a gang of youths kicking an Arab, of all things – a full flowing-robed Arab, a visitor to the city! – kicking him down the stairs in Williamson's Square.'

The special inspector nods. 'Two Specials went over to try and stop it. It became a bloody big mêlée, and our lad got knocked to the ground and kicked, and the other had his testicles kicked up into his groin, his kidneys bruised, lost a couple of teeth—'

'Start at the top,' suggests the special sergeant. 'He got bangs on the head, nothing bad; bloody nose; teeth missing; both kidneys badly damaged – I think they stopped functioning; his heart stopped three times in the hospital; his testicles were bad for months – I don't think they're right yet; his leg was broken – that's still in a bad way, and they may have to remove his knee-cap.'

'And while he's hanging on to a fellow on the ground,' adds the special inspector, 'being booted, a woman comes up and she's smacking him with her handbag, saying she's going to report him for police brutality! And that is *true*! He's waiting for her to report it, then he's going to lock her up for assault!'*

The special inspector was in a similar mêlée in Williamson's Square a few Saturdays ago while off-duty and trying to assist a friend in the force with some football rowdies. 'I once arrested a bloke who was actually charged with murder,' he says. 'The man was next to dead and I ran half-way across the bloody city and caught the fella, took him back to the Main Bridewell. They said, "Just hold on to your prisoner" – the jacks had gone to the hospital – and I did; he was cold sober and a big lad. The two CID men walked in. "Who locked up the fella in St John's Lane?" "I did." So they came over – I can see that look now! – and said, "A Special? Hey, lad, you've got a good job here, y'know! This is going to be a murder job, straight up.

*The offenders in this case were jailed for nine months.

442

He's not going to last the night, accordin' to the doctors." I thought: Whooo-hoo! About six in the morning, they came back and said, "He's going to live" – so it was reduced to grievous bodily harm.'

'What he's not going to tell you', the special sergeant remarks, 'is that he got an illuminated commendation on vellum.'

The night awaits them. The special constable, who has had three D-and-I arrests in his five months' service, puts on his cap, and the special sergeant picks up his signalling-stick. Specials patrol the city centre in pairs after dark – it's an official ruling – and more often than not, like tonight, without personal radios.

'We take radios if they're available,' says the special inspector, 'but they're in very short supply.'

The cheerful hubbub is still as noisy in the Specials' parade room, although the crush has thinned a little and Chalky is able to drift from group to group, saying how fit he is and joining in the joke-telling.

'It's ale, ale, ale – in the streets, everywhere!' begins the wit near the door, waving his pint about. 'Get in there, lads! – y'know.'

'Oh aye!' comes the chorus.

'A weddin' in Myrtle Gardens and all the bucks are pissed, jazzin' round. A typical bloody weddin': vomit in the lobby, back door full of Guinness bottles. The bobby's there – and he's pissed. Anyway, about half-way through the weddin', the bridegroom appears and says, "The do's off! The do's off! You can all fak aff!" So they say, "Wot's the marrer?" "Never yer mind," he says. "Youse can all fak aff!" "But dere must be *somethin*' the matter?" So he says, "Some dairty bastid's raped the bride!"''

'Oh aye?'

'So they all walk out into Myrtle Gardens, very disconsolately, y'see, and as they're half-way through Myrtle Gardens the bridegroom leans over the landin'. "It's all right," he shouts to 'em. "The do's on again – the gentleman's apologised."''

443

A great roar of laughter. 'Typical buck weddin', that!' says Chalky. 'I've been to a few and all, I can tell yer.'

18

Lucia puts down the cup of coffee and leaves the officers' canteen to the OSD chief inspector, who is at the window watching darkness fall over 'A' Division. He is thirty-four and joined the police as soon as he could – right on his nineteenth birthday.

'I'm one of those classical things', he says with a smile, 'that recruiting officers are always looking for: the boy who always wanted to be a policeman.'

In another age, he might have been taken for a Spartan: tall, well built, athletic, with keenly intelligent eyes set in a face that gives nothing away it hasn't decided to. His features are clear-cut, his fair hair trimmed short, and he wears a dark-green leather jacket with a cream shirt and narrow tie.

Obviously I can't analyse my thought-mechanism, but in the street where I lived there used to be a policeman who was a nice fella, a popular fella, and he took an interest in the kids. At some impressionable age, some of the things he must have said stuck, and it grew into an ambition. I didn't think of becoming a cadet. In those days, the cadet was just the office boy in the building, and I was pretty sport mad at the time, playing rugby for the school's first team. I had very narrow horizons then! When I joined Wallasey Borough it was only two-hundred-and-eight or -ten strong, and it only had about six cadets. Like everybody else, I did my two years' probation, and then I was posted as relief cycle patrol – and people stopped talking to me over that. (*Laughs*) If you were relief cyclist, you were somebody; they all thought I was too young and must have a silver spoon in my mouth.

He went on to spend three years in the CID, during which time he took his sergeants' exam and came in the top 400 out of about 10,000 candidates in the country. This led to his going on the Special Course and he won a scholarship to Oxford,

444

where he later read Modern History at Pembroke and played rugby for the University's first fifteen. On his return to Merseyside, he spent about four years as a uniformed inspector at Birkenhead, before becoming staff officer to the Assistant Chief Constable (Crime Operations) at force headquarters in 1976. He was promoted to chief inspector about four months ago, and took over as second-in-command of the Operational Support Division, which was formed at the very beginning of the year.

I'm in a very fortunate position now, because I've got the best chief inspector's job in the force, and I think this division is the best division in the force – and I don't say that pompously or anything like that. This is sharp-end policing and it suits me. We can demand from our men a higher level of dedication and determination than one would find in general, and that should be right because we select them. At the moment, we've over fifty applications for sixteen places. Everyone is a volunteer – he knows it's a difficult job and, like all difficult jobs, it's rewarding. Anyone who has a drink while he's on duty in our division is *out*, and anyone who comes to work smelling of drink is *out*, because we hold the major firearms responsibility for the [entire Merseyside] area. Otherwise he could play in a cricket match, have a couple of pints, come on duty and five minutes later have a gun in his hand. We're looking for enthusiasm, people who'll work hard, who're energetic, because if you have the zeal and enthusiasm to start with, you can mould it.

The chief inspector admits to a 'fetish' about drinking on duty. 'I like to drink. I drink at home, I drink at the rugby club, the golf club, in the pubs, but I never *ever* drink when I come to work. I wouldn't dream of having a drink here. I've never been in the club room since I've been here. I never will do.' During his three years in the CID, however, he wasn't able to be strong-willed enough to stick to soft drinks, but reached a working compromise. 'I used to drink bottles of Guinness,' he says, smiling, 'because I can't *stand* Guinness. There was no way I could drink more than two in a night!'

He enjoyed his time at Oxford, but speaks of it without nostalgia. 'We lived outside in the village of Wheatley,' he says

445

(he has two young daughters), 'and it was just like going to work: I went in at eight and came back at seven. We had a good social life in the village – mainly people connected with the motor industry – and it was just like having a job.' Whether it changed him or not, he cannot say, because everyone changes all the time wherever they are. 'The one thing about Oxford is that it teaches you there is always more than one side to everything. I think that's of value, because it helps you to keep your perspective in the police service where obviously one sees a lot of things one could get very upset about.' As a police officer, he believes in doing everything by the book. 'The service – perhaps that's what is attractive to me – has so many definitive terms that, if you accept its rules, accept its objectives, and accept its shortcomings, it's a very structured way to be – and I like to be structured, and I like to be organised, and it suits me. That's not to say you can't change the rules! If you don't like them, then you do your best to get them changed.'

As the OSD has a force-wide responsibility, 'A' Division forms only part of the police map he carries in his head, but it is undisputedly the most troublesome area. In his opinion, having probationers there 'is not the best way of training young police officers', but they should begin somewhere that has a relatively static mixed population and a variety of activities; somewhere they can get to know people. The OSD has patrols permanently deployed in the division, which he regards with some foreboding.

The city centre is out of hand to the extent that I wouldn't *dream* of coming for a night out in town with my wife. First of all, I wouldn't dream of leaving my car parked – it's been pinched once there already, or it might get damaged. And, secondly, there are, you know, certain dangers just walking round the streets at night. But, having said that, there are certain 'acceptable' levels of violence unfortunately, and our horizons are always being broadened. I mean, in 1946 there were 450,000 crimes in this country, and last year there were 2,150,000 or something like that. If you'd said to them in 1946 there'll be a million crimes a year by now, that would have been totally unacceptable, yet 2,000,000 today don't even rate a headline in the newspapers. People always say it's going to reach a plateau – they've been

446

saying that for the fifteen years I've been in the police! (*Laughs*) If you look at the situation in major conurbations in America, then the centre of Liverpool is *paradise*, absolute paradise. But the hackneyed phrase is, 'What happens in the States, happens in Britain in ten years' time.' Well, unless we're very careful, we could have an American conurbation problem in this country before long.

The light is fading fast, and the details of the slope below St Anne Street are now lost in the gloaming.

With a small 'c', most policemen are very conservative, in that they tend to harken back to some former golden era – and that is often how they see the ideal society. But, of course, such an era never existed. We can all remember a golden era. Some of us think it was when we were at school – oh, when I was at college, that was superb. . . . When I first got a job, and I wasn't married – that was superb. . . . (*Smiles*) We can all ride the horse looking to the back, but we tend to fall off.

19

'There we are, sittin' in the back of this jeep – radio: "Man with a knife, gone berserk, Clancy Gardens." "Let's fokkin' go!" So we go.'

And the stalwarts of Fred's party, the last of the drink in their glasses, grin in anticipation as the new storyteller wets his whistle before carrying on.

'And there's no proper address and it's all fokkin' A, B, C, D – y'know. We meet an old dear and she said, "I know where you mean, officer! Second door along." There's the fokkin' door with a light in it. What shall we do? A light but fok all else, y'see, and this bastid's goin' berserk with a fokkin' knife – you know what I mean? So we put the fokkin' door right off its fokkin' hinges, and there's this poor old bastard sat in an armchair with a dot in the fokkin' telly, y'know.'

Chalky leads the laughter.

'So out we go, and she said, "No, sair – the next fokkin' one op!" Upstairs, door's open, in we fokkin' go! There's blood

447

and snot everywhere, fokkin' crockery smashed to smithereens, and this soft twat, standin' by the sink, wavin' a carvin'-knife, y'see. We take the fokkin' thing off him, lock him up, shove him in the back of the jeep, and that's the fokkin' end of it. Then we think: That poor old bastid upstairs. . . . So we go back up again and we walk in. "Thank God you've arrived, sir!" he said. "Christ, I could've been killed! *Three big fellas*," he said. "I could be fokkin' dead! The fokkin' door came off its hinges!" So we rang 'em up and they came and put his door on within twenty fokkin' minutes, and I was the finest fokkin' bobby that ever walked the fokkin' streets, y'know!'

A huge laugh, gasps and wheezes. 'Aye, those were the days!' says Chalky. 'Anybody fancy a last glass in the club, then?'

The club room is crowded almost to the doors, for the new father's celebration has been joined by a group disco, and some visiting detectives from the South are being treated to true Northern hospitality. But Chalky manages to find space enough for the three of them to stand under 'Westminster Road', and is lucky enough to catch Bert's eye within seconds.

'A'right, Chalky?'

'Crackin'!' says Chalky, and gives his order.

There's a small party of Days and EPs cons at the circle of seats nearest to him. The auburn-haired lass, in the shawl and brown patterned dress, is obviously popular and she's being treated as an equal by the lads, which he finds unusual.

The auburn-haired constable will not be at the Orange Lodge parade on Sunday. 'I got a whole pipe band locked up on the twelfth,' she discloses, 'kilts and everythin'. The superintendent said, "Turn your back on the road and face the crowd." So there's this fella comin' at me with the big bass drum, and I said, "Will you move behind?" He said, "*You* move!" – and hit me with the drum. I got hold of him and the whole lot piled on me, rotten drunk. I can't walk along there now because there's an Orange Lodge club there, and it was their band I got arrested!'

She is twenty-three, has two and a half years' service, and a reputation for being dependable in any situation; she was the

448

policewoman who guarded the club exit during the raid, and it was she, incidentally, who stopped the burglar with a type-written list of his recent conquests. 'You can't hope to have a good relationship with a bloke when you're on shifts,' she says. 'I've been engaged three times and gave it up as a bad job!' But otherwise she hasn't a great many grumbles, although she would like policewomen to be allowed batons and to do duty at football matches. And then there is the matter of children. . . .

It was strange how the equality thing came out. On the Sunday I was on Afternoons and you weren't allowed in the dark on your own, and on Monday I was on the dock road, doin' Nights all on me own! You get more freedom now, and you're treated like a human being. They're not sticklers, getting reports back all the time; they don't have such high standards. You will get lumbered with missing-from-home, children and that, which you shouldn't. I personally can't stand children – I've no time for them. I've seen fellas cope with them far better than policewomen – y'know, blokes that are married with a couple of kids. Any kids I've caught, they never speak to me; they always go to the bobby with the big hat on! (*Laughs*) Once you get them in your confidence, though, you can get anything out of them – they're smashin'.

I was a telephonist in the GPO after school. It was really depressing; you never saw the daylight or anything. Me mum and dad were both in the police, and they'd been goin' on at me since I left school – I think it's because they tried to get me in that I wouldn't. I like the freedom more than anything. Some of the girls say, 'Oh, I wouldn't walk down there, down a dark alley!' If I thought like that, I'd probably frighten myself so much I wouldn't do it. They should know what to expect: it's not all roses.

One fella wound the car window up on me arm and dragged me up the road. Somebody tried to run me down in Dale Street, and I've been attacked a couple of times – once was here in the yard. Somebody brought in a guest, and they'd got a bit stroppy, and I was given the job of hurlin' her out. I got bitten to *bits*. (*Laughs*) I'll tackle any bloke at all, but women are just so-and-so's.

When I first joined, I was sent to a pub in Dale Street to throw this bloke out. 'C'mon, gel,' he said, 'we're going to the Main Bridewell' – and he had his arm round me and everything.

449

I walked him there and everyone went, '*How* did you get him in here?' 'Why?' '*Don't* you know who he is?' 'No.' 'Well, he used to go in pubs and grab the pump-handles and bend them over....' (*Laughs*) I went to another bar last week and there were fourteen bobbies there. 'Hello, gel!' he said. The worst thing you can do is touch him; he goes berserk – bobbies have split their staffs on his head and all kinds. He's hard. The only person he's frightened of is his mum. You threaten him with his mum, and he'll go quietly.

I'm quite lucky really: I've only ever had one sudden death. We got there and Social Service had been tryin' to get in. There were net curtains with a little space, and you could see him laying on the bed. I had a cadet with me. We tried to knock the door down, then we put in the window. The police doctor came to certify he was dead and said, 'He's still warm. How long have you been here?' I said, 'About an hour and a quarter.' 'How did you get in?' I said we'd put the window in. 'Well,' he said, 'it's probably the shock that killed him.' I couldn't *wai* for the Coroner's report! I was thinking: Oh, crumbs, what have I done now? I supposed that's his warped sense of humour, though. He'd do something like that. He's great.

Now if I go out – I don't like going to clubs because there's always trouble. We went to the ——— the week before last, and the amount of villains in there! As we were comin' out, a fella sort of moved forward in his car. I said, 'Watch where you're going!' He said, 'You remember me, don't yer?' 'No.' 'You should do!' 'Well, I don't, so who are you?' 'On the tenth of April. . . .' 'Yeah?' 'You breathalysed me outside the Adelphi, yer cow!' (*Laughs*) You always get somebody who recognises you.

Recognition of a different sort is being accorded her this evening in the social club, where she sits as the latest Mallet Award winner. 'Some time ago,' explains the Days and EPs panda driver who would hate to die on his own unheeded, 'I came up with this word for describing silly people – "Oh, he's a *mallet*." So I decided, with us being such a close section, that I would supply the mallet – it's a real wooden mallet – and it would be awarded each week to the person who'd done the most ridiculous thing. I've won it myself for thinking my mock promotion exam was on a Wednesday night, when in fact it had been the Tuesday!' After almost a month without a break, he becomes a little vague about dates.

450

'And I was waiting for the bus after working all night,' she says with a grin, 'and going straight to court at nine o'clock in the morning. I was standin' over there like a zombie, waitin' for the bus, and I thought: It's not going to stop. . . . So I put me hand out and it *screeches* to a stop. The bus driver said, "It's a good thing I saw your uniform!" I said, "What's up with you?" "Well," he said, "I don't *usually* stop at lamp-posts." '

20

'The worry of the job', says Superintendent North, 'is that things will go wrong through people being too involved in the job. They work an awful lot of their rest days here, and that's a nag at the back of your mind: worrying whether somebody's going to blow up.'

Nobody could appear less likely to have a nervous breakdown than the superintendent himself, despite the pressures he works under. His placid manner is utterly unaffected, warm, and rooted in the tranquillity of a man who seems to be very fond of the human race, without wanting to make a fuss about it. He is forty-six, has sandy colouring, a friendly face, three grown-up children, and a pool with a miniature cascade in his immaculate back garden, beside which he likes to laze, listening to the water and watching the goldfish. His small office in the characterless divisional headquarters building is rather like a study, combining the elements of both efficiency and comfort; a coffee-making machine stands on a small table next to the easy chair where he peruses long reports, and in the bookcase by the door *Stone's Justice's Manual* and *The Criminal Law Review 1977* rub shoulders with works on sociology, Wordsworth, Blake and Beethoven.

I was an apprentice bricklayer and played the clarinet. When I finished me apprenticeship I joined the Army in the hope of getting into a military band, but I wasn't good enough, so I served in the Royal Horse Artillery for two years, and I went to Egypt. By the time I came out of the Army, I was married and I went back to bricklaying. We had a particularly severe winter

451

which meant, although I wanted to work, I couldn't work – we had enough money to manage with, but that really put me off the building trade. The first job we did was at a railway station. My father had been a railwayman, and I showed an interest – I'd always been interested in trains and railways. The station-master's son was in the Essex police, and he came home from time to time and chatted, and I got very interested in the police. The stationmaster said, 'Well, I know the superintendent of the Norwich railway police – why don't you join them?' I did three and a half years with the railway police, working on the Plain Clothes, Special Branch and CID, and then I thought I might as well go to a different force.

I joined the Lancashire police with no formal qualifications whatsoever, and I was very happy to be accepted as a police constable and had no ambitions as such at all. Then you find the job grows on you, and you begin to think you could do the job your sergeants are doing. In those days you had to do educational exams as well. So I got down and did a postal course in my educational exam to sergeant, and then my police duty exam. [Two further examinations to inspector followed, and he joined the Liverpool and Bootle force in 1967.] This got me in the way of adult studying, I suppose – the family had got used to me studying! – and in 1970 I went to Bruche as an instructor. While I was there, I took up the Open University. That opened the door to me. Since then I went on a special course for graduates at the Liverpool Polytechnic, and I obtained a Certificate in Municipal Administration, which I was very pleased to get.

The superintendent's Bachelor of Arts degree was in the social sciences, and the highlight of his course was the obligatory summer school. 'I had a week at Bath [University] and that made me regret I'd never gone to a conventional university – when I say "made me regret", not to the extent of worrying about it.' Although he plans to do his honours degree as well, he is taking a break to catch up on household improvements and on seeing more of his family.

I can't give a specific example of how this has helped. It's just a general broadening of the mind – I know this is a bit hackneyed – but I think before I was going through life with the blinkers on. For one thing, I've learned to analyse – not to accept something on its face value. I used to say to myself, Well, they're all volun-

452

teers, and now I've come to the view that they're the product of their environment which, to a certain extent, is true of all of us. What it did teach me was how different attitudes and cultures affect what happens. We as police officers deal with people who – if we don't understand their culture – well, we can very easily put value judgements on them: unless they conform to our values, our standards, then they're wrong. And what it taught me to think was: What do *they* think is right? And how can we reconcile the two? Regarding the race situation, this is probably what we need to do: to understand different cultures. But I'm not sure we ought to make provision for separate cultures to the extent it stops them from becoming fully integrated in a British society – meaning all kinds of cultures, getting a general mix-up together.

With this background, the superintendent takes an intense interest in his role of Community Liaison Officer but, like everything else, it has to be squeezed into what time he has available after seeing to the stack of complaint files on his desk. 'You've got to constantly organise your day around these enquiries,' he says. 'For two or three days at a time, you cannot do anything other than the complaints enquiries. I think I've got six at the moment – concerning officers in other divisions, of course.'

These are not internal disciplinary investigations, but complaints made by the public. He has never had one alleging corruption; his most serious so far has been an allegation of perjury. 'In the main, they are complaints of assault, usually at the time of an arrest, or complaints of abuse that resulted from searching people's houses, following the arrest of a member of that household.'

I believe that, as a professional body, we follow up the enquiries as impartially as we possibly can. I know a lot of people outside the job wonder how we do, but we do. I'd be failing not only my duty but myself if I didn't investigate them as I would a crime. I think it's important that, if police officers are abusing their authority, they should get pulled up about it. I'm not always sure it's necessary for them to go to court – unless it's a serious offence, of course. But the vast majority. . . .

I've got one now where an officer is supposed to have shown

453

a picture of a deserter in a launderette. The thing was that the cancellation of this warrant [issued by a branch of the services] didn't reach the division; but here we've got the situation where a mother's sat at home, knowing her son went absent without leave and has given himself up, and the next thing she hears is that a policeman is going round the launderette, showing all the neighbours this lad's photograph. I think she's genuinely aggrieved – it's not a malicious complaint. Some people will complain just because they've been arrested, and that'll come out in evidence. They feel the bobby acted wrongly, and immediately they say, 'It's not *me* I'm worried about – I just don't want him to do it to others.' (*Smiles*) It does take a lot of time. I sometimes feel you're not able to stamp your personality as much as you'd like on the sub-division because of this commitment to investigations – I'd like to see a different system evolved.

There is a map of the division, broken down into beats, on the wall above his desk, and a brightly inked line runs round the North Sub. Domestics, art treasures worth millions, bonded warehouses, difficult housing conditions, traffic problems. . . .

When I come in, I look at the night report, the circulation, see what's gone on in the city and the division. I have a look in the bridewell, see if there are any prisoners, and go through the books, just to check there's nothing untoward which requires my immediate attention. Then I go through the paperwork with my deputy, and he will generally remove the vast bulk of it and pass on to me what I should see. A lot of my paperwork is to do with welfare, a most important part of my job. It touches on duties, first of all; I try to see they're working the most amenable duties commensurate with my responsibility for providing adequate cover for my area. Mr ——— [the other subdivisional commander] and I aren't too happy with the three shifts; we'd like to lessen the incidence of night duty, and get away from the quick change-over. Then I've got progress reports and appraisals. There's training. You don't make people into policemen in the classroom, you do it by on-the-job training, but this is made more difficult because most of them are probationers. I know if I want an experienced person to put in a fairly responsible job I've got to look long and hard; most of them are either driving or in the bridewell. But this loosely ties in with welfare, of course: if they're happy in their job. . . . Well, I purposefully try to develop

454

a casual easy esprit de corps, so when they come here they know they belong to a team. This is what policing is today – the day of the 'individual' police service, I think, has gone. Everybody has to work now.

It's how often they work that places him and the other sub-divisional commander in a constant dilemma.

'The other worry of the job', says Superintendent North, 'is that a situation will arise when we haven't enough men. Fortunately, with public order, the warning is usually there, and we're able to build up a good reserve of manpower. And, drawing from the force as a whole, we'd probably be able to manage if a jumbo jet, for instance, landed on those blocks of flats out there. But what I'm thinking of particularly is if something happened when the clubs were turning out, and we haven't sufficient men on the ground to get there very, very quickly – it would end up with some officer being very, very seriously injured. It'd be no guarantee, of course, that he wouldn't be, but it would be nice if you could turn out ten or twelve foot-men and four cars doubly manned. Actually, we need twenty-six to cover the beats, and sometimes I get a little concerned when I find we've only got four foot-men out there [on the North Sub].'

21

'Kids on this job now go in fear of bein' complained about, y'know,' mutters a burly constable with considerable service. 'They are worried sick they'll get a discipline form in front of them. It affects their attitude to the public, and it's wrong.'

The new complaints procedure – still in its infancy* – is a major preoccupation among officers at all levels in 'A' Division. Whereas complaints were once handled locally, and frequently informally when the complaint was not of a serious nature, now

*The Police Complaints Board was set up in June 1977. Complaints on Merseyside rose by 33 per cent during the first six months – and the number of complaints withdrawn increased from 20 to 30 per cent when compared with the previous year.

455

every complaint is recorded and fully investigated. These investigations are carried out by officers with the rank of superintendent or above, and their findings are sent to the Police Complaints Board at the Home Office. The Board, which has a staff of thirty, three full-time members and sixteen part-time members, can order further investigations or confirm the findings as they stand.

'It's not just every job's a major enquiry now,' says the constable, 'but we even supply these pamphlets tellin' 'em how to have a go at us. The pamphlets also warn that *we* can have a go if the complaint is libellous or defamatory, but it's the position it puts you in.'

Another experienced officer remarks: 'I'd say the complaints system has certainly affected behaviour, not necessarily moderated it. Where there might have been a slight scuffle in the past, and the bobby's gone in and given a few backhanders, he'd be more likely to make an arrest now.'

What concerns many officers is the inhibiting effect that all this can have on the 'good' achieved by a bobby who is a 'little bit naughty' at times. The teetotal chief inspector who said he didn't mind telling a lie, having 'learned the psychology of the crowd', is a case in point. Would a young constable, they ask, dare to place himself at the crowd's mercy today? Would he admit to a thirst – and to the notion of supping a quick pint after hours? Now that the slightest sign of human frailty in a 'pig' has become grist to the complaint-maker's mill, it would be far less risky for him to call for assistance, thereby escalating the incident out of all proportion – and probably sparking off a violent confrontation.

'I still administer a clip round the ear,' admits an officer of the old school, 'and I stick me neck out – hell, because that's the way it's done! If all bobbies were perfect, we'd have a funny situation. If everything was done perfectly to the letter of the law, I reckon the non-detected crime rate would increase by thirty per cent.'

Many simply treat the new procedure as a 'vote of no confidence', and point out what this could do to morale. 'There's a very thin blue line – in some ways, it's an imaginary line – of fear and respect between us and the people who ride roughshod

456

over authority and the establishment. When it sort of boils over, they don't give a damn who's around – they'll attack each other with any weapon they can lay hands on. And once they've lost that fear and respect, well, I think the public doesn't realise how easily this line can be broken. Because if police officers came on duty with an attitude of "Oh, the hell with 'em! Let's do our hours, get paid and go home", it would have a definite marked effect. In a busy division, men can easily justify their existence by simply dealing with incidents as they come up, but it takes an extra thing to go looking beyond that. And it's the ones who go beyond that keep the line standing.'

Another sore point is that people object to the investigations being 'kept in the family', but dissidents do exist.

'I'm not really bothered by the new complaints procedure, but what I'd like them to do now is to say senior police officers will no longer be the investigating officers. Let's have civilians – solicitors, for example. A solicitor can't turn round to a probationer and say, "Now, I'm a superintendent and you're in your probationary period, and I hope you realise we can get shot of you within those first two years and there's nothing you can do about it. All I want from you is a statement putting the bobby in it." A solicitor could just say to you, "Would you make a statement?" "No – er, is there anything else you want to know?" And superintendents don't come and see you: you're given an order and you go and see them. You can't turn round and say, "On yer bike! I don't want to speak to yer!" Of course, it's not too bad with a bit of service; you just sit there and you don't say anything.'

Whatever else this may suggest, it makes abundantly plain that 'keeping it in the family' can be far less convivial than the public may suppose. At best, a superintendent from another division is something of a distant relation; an elder whose concern for the reputation of a lesser member can hardly match the interest he takes in his own reputation or, indeed, in the 'family name'. Moreover, it would be presumptuous to imagine that what follows is a mere formality conducted at a cosy domestic level. By all accounts, it is a time when the 'family's' patriarchal structure is most acutely felt.

'Eight months after the incident,' recalls a doughty young

457

officer, completing a tale told in a different context, 'I'm in front of the Chief Con. It was the most terrifyin' experience on this job I've ever had. I'll never forget it. I'm stood to attention – like this – then in you go. The prosecutor's on yer left, me defence is on my right, and there's a fella at the back with a tape. I can feel me helmet shakin' on me head – which shows how much *I'm* shakin', y'know! The Chief Con reads the charges out. Not guilty to the first; not guilty to the second; guilty third and fourth. The prosecutor's up – "We're going to withdraw the charges he pleads 'not guilty' to" – and I'm told to sit down. I don't salute. I don't do anythin'. I felt like cryin' or bein' sick – I didn't know what to do. My defence reels off, and suddenly starts talking about "not giving this officer the sack". I thought to myself: Christ, I didn't realise it was like that! I didn't realise I was on the brink of it! I can't remember what the Chief Con said to me. I was on the brink of collapse. Anyway, he gave me a caution on both counts, which can be scrubbed from my records, if I so wish, in three years' time. God, what an experience! Never again.'

22

Back in the billiard-room, rather hoping he'll be invited to join a game of crash, Chalky nurses his last pint of the evening – he's promised his ulcer that – and pretends an interest in the view on the St Anne Street side, while he does a bit of eaves-dropping.

'And there's children trapped upstairs and the fire engine's been sent for. The hall was ablaze, so I tied this thing round my face, started crawling down the pitch-black hall – I can hear the fire engines. Next thing, *whooosh!* It was a jet of water that comes up the hall, catches me in the backside and washes me into the flames – I'm screamin' at the top of me voice, "For God's sake, turn it off!" And I came out, wringin' wet, covered in black from head to foot, and they'd been rescued through the back window by neighbours!'

Chalky's reflection grins back at him, while out of the corner

458

of one eye he spots a great big fella in a grey suit come out into the yard, carrying a personal radio.

'It's almost a can-opener job to get me in and out of one of those,' remarks Chief Inspector North, as he passes a panda car outside the prisoners' door to the bridewell. 'I'm six foot three and seventeen stone – you'll appreciate there are many as tall as me and as broad!'

Even so, the deputy sub-divisional commander is an uncommonly imposing figure and his sense of humour is proportional, giving him an informal unflappable manner, all very low-key. It seems only fitting, then, that the portrait displayed in his office should be an excellent caricature, which allows his full, rather whimsical face to dominate the foreshortened uniform. 'When I joined, you decided whether you were going to be a CID man or a uniformed man – in those days they were virtually two separate and distinct forces.' He was a chief inspector at thirty-six and is now forty-one.

I'm a fairly ambitious sort of man or I don't think I would have come away out of Wales in the first place, would I? I'd possibly have been chasing donkeys up and down the sands at Rhyl now – or in a high-street bank, if my mother had had her way. She was determined I should do something, well, legitimate – and this kiddie was saying, 'No way.' (*Laughs*) I got interested in the police while I was still at school in Rhyl. The Met sort of go off to Scotland and catch them with nets, don't they? This was a more subtle move on the part of the Liverpool City Police, as it was then: they simply sent down some literature on the cadet corps. It's difficult to know what the appeal was. I wanted an outdoor life – I was, er, a very different physical character to the one you see today. I was so thin people used to *worry* about me. Out of the blue came this literature, and I said, 'That's what I want to do.' Relatives and everybody pooh-poohed it, and said the only thing going for me was perhaps my height, and that I'd be a constable at fifty and all this sort of thing. I think they thought I couldn't take it because I was pretty shy in those days – I still am to a certain extent. I don't start speaking until I'm invited to, then it's my opinion they get, and not what I feel I ought to tell them. I've been described in a staff appraisal as

459

blunt and forthright, which either means this individual is bloody rude or speaks his mind – I'm not sure which yet. Anyway, I left grammar school at sixteen with five O-levels and came to Liverpool, did two years in the cadet corps and then National Service. I served a whole two weeks in the Royal Artillery, transhipped to the Royal Military Police, trained for about sixteen weeks, and then went to Austria. You may have seen my film, *Four in a Jeep*? I came on the force here in July of 1956. I wanted to work; I'd come on this job to do well. Some of the old sergeants just wanted a quiet life, and if you came in with too much in your notebook they'd threaten to send you out without a pencil or something. There were none of these booklets then, which you just hand to a typist, and the sergeants had to type the stuff out, y'see. So when it came to a toss-up between him sitting in front of the fire, toasting his toes, and just taking a short constitutional, and him sitting up in the wee small hours, typing furiously because of one of his recruits. . . . (*Laughs*) In those days, of course, before we had radios, it was much more leisurely. And if you found a kid in somebody's back garden with his pockets full of apples you could safely dispatch him with a clout across the back of his head. He'd go home and he wouldn't dare tell anyone he'd been in the orchard, and he wouldn't *dare* tell anyone he'd been clouted. Now, you can rest assured, he'd repeat that fact, and they'd be down with their offspring to complain about *you*. (*Laughs*)

He opens the door to his six-year-old car and gets in. 'There is no supervision vehicle for me to go patrolling in – in point of fact, I rarely go out on Days. A week for me comprises three, possibly four Day duties, and two split duties; the split works from nine until one, and from about seven-thirty until midnight, and you're covering the whole division.' He starts up, listens for a moment, then noses out of the exit. 'It's crying out for a new exhaust.' The lights on to St Anne Street are red. 'I get the princely sum of 48p for a split duty, which is the return bus fare from here to my home – quite how they expect me to get home on a bus after midnight, nobody makes clear! Anyway, I use my own vehicle – usually on the way in – and I call on the other stations in the division to sign the book.' The green shows, and he turns towards Copperas Hill.

'Phil and I do almost the same sort of job, except he's got

460

his complaints – in fact, I do more of Phil's job than Phil does, for the simple reason that, by virtue of this complaints system that has sprung up over the past four or more years, so much of his time is taken up investigating complaints I am left to run this sub-division. There are certain things that are special to me, like firearms and police support-unit training. Paperwork is paperwork. There isn't a lot to it – it's just you do it over and over again!

'I think our job is getting more and more difficult. I feel the status of the police is being continually eroded, particularly in the light of this recent complaints procedure. It appears quite wrong to me that if some other public servant is rude to me I can write to his employer and possibly not get the courtesy of a reply, whereas if somebody makes a complaint about me, however trivial. . . .' He slows down to catch the lights at the Islington intersection. 'Doubtless you've heard about the case – not in this police area – where a policeman was reported because he had a garden bonfire to his neighbour's annoyance? And the set-up is such it had to be proceeded with.'

I think adult prisoners tend to get what they ask for. If a prisoner is co-operative, he's just put in the vehicle and brought back. But, if he cuts up rough, I don't think the ratepayers are paying my wages to see me knocked to the ground by somebody I've put under arrest. You start with a reasonable approach but, if somebody takes a swing at me, he'll be restrained with what is termed a 'lawful hold' – a hammer lock and bar or whatever – and he'll be advised by me that, if he continues his activities, then *he* – not I – will bring about a break in his arm or something. I've now got twenty-one years' service in, and I've been assaulted once – that was in the first six or eight months of my service. Admittedly, size and weight are on my side, but I think I learned something from it. (*Smiles*) I don't see myself as a particularly aggressive character. If you make the right sort of noises, it often *works perfectly*.

During those twenty-one years, Chief Inspector North has had a very varied career. 'After about two and half years, I had a twelve-month Plain Clothes attachment, and then I went on Vespas and mine had a *radio* on the back – I was in the big

461

time, sort of thing.' He came second in a CID course but, wanting his promotion to sergeant, he opted to stay in uniform. He was a sergeant at seven years' service, which was relatively 'young' in those days, and went into the Prosecutions Department after serving in the city and the docks – 'I was appearing twice daily before the worships for three and a half years.' He became an inspector at twelve years' service, took an instructors' course – 'We had drama specialists, speech therapists. Oh, they took it seriously, y'know' – and went to Bruche for two years. And then, after a spell in the football-ground division – 'Where I got to thinking there *must* be more to police duty than minding Liverpool one week and Everton the next!' – he was seconded to a training school in the Midlands, and while there rose to chief inspector. If he has any regrets, then it's having missed any proper CID experience, which could be a disadvantage in the promotion stakes to superintendent.

And there, on the left, is Copperas Hill. He takes his car round the back and drives into the vehicle-yard. Not all that long ago, he was using it to take his family – he has a son aged two and a daughter of five – to a caravan camp in Brittany for a fortnight. It rained for eleven days and they came home on the twelfth.

I wouldn't be unhappy if my young son wanted to follow in my footsteps, but I would like to think he could do better for himself than that. I'm not ashamed of being a police officer, but I certainly don't go around broadcasting the fact. I'm not unhappy in my own company, and I'm just thinking now whether it's time I changed pubs. I've been going for some years to a little pub up in Walton, some distance from where I live, but now they have got to know me, and I'm getting involved, y'know. I'm quite happy to sit with a pint and cigar – I'm toying with the idea of moving along. If I go away on holiday, I prefer to remain incognito, as it were, because, if ever it does become apparent you're a police officer, some will go immediately off you. Others will *insist* upon telling you how bloody unfortunate they were to have been done for speeding at 41 m.p.h. in a 40-m.p.h. zone, while others will want to talk about the job until you're ready to *scream.* (*Smiles*) I say I'm in an office, just an office job in Liverpool – which isn't telling lies exactly.

462

Up the three steps, along past the bright bridewell windows, and into the Cottage, where a relief BP is seated at the desk behind the front counter, surrounded by a faint but fragrant perfume, and listening to the night on a spare personal radio. Chief Inspector South is, of course, off tonight, having worked his split shift yesterday; he is a former 'county bobby' of considerable experience, and enjoys a reputation among his colleagues for knowing a great deal about the law, being immersed in both the spirit and the letter of it.

23

Three months to the day after first walking out into 'A' Division as a police officer, the young constable squares his shoulders, checks his tie and then knocks on the deputy subdivisional commander's door.

'Come in!'

He enters the office and stands to attention in front of the desk, raps out his force number and waits.

Chief Inspector South is a tall spare man with large expressive eyes, a narrow face and a head of greying hair; his manner is quick, lively and edged with authority. Having looked the probationer over, checking on his smartness, he invites him to stand easy and take a seat. He glances at the progress reports on his desk, submitted by a sergeant and the inspector, and then tells the probationer where he stands, noting with particular satisfaction that a good mark has been given for 'manner with the public'.

Chief Inspector South is particularly keen on probationers getting their priorities straight, and quotes the official definition of a constable: 'A constable is a citizen locally appointed, but having authority under the Crown, for the protection of life and property, the maintenance of order, the prevention and detection of crime, and the prosecution of offenders against the peace.' Here he pauses for a moment. 'It has a lot of substance. It's very carefully worded if you have a look at it – although, at first sight, you might not think so. "A constable

463

is a citizen" – and he is nothing more than that. He's a citizen that has basically no more powers than a normal citizen, apart from the odd one written in by law. He's "locally appointed" – that means he's recruited locally and he's a Crown servant – *not* the servant of the local authority. That's very important. So his first job is the protection of life – that's the ultimate. The next thing is the protection of property. Then we have the "maintenance of order", the wellbeing of the community, and his next priority is the prevention of crime. After that, it's to detect crime, and lastly the prosecution of offenders.'

The probationer confines himself to saying 'Yes, sir' and 'No, sir', but the chief inspector's earnest avuncular approach is clearly calculated to make the ordeal as friendly and helpful as possible. It must also be gratifying to be told by a senior officer that he can see in the probationer the makings of a good policeman. Attached to the back of the report is a list of eleven arrests – mainly for shoplifting and drunkenness – and seventeen summonses, mainly for motoring offences.

And that's it. After a short homily and some other words of advice, the constable comes to attention again and is dismissed. Outside in the corridor, he beams with relief.

But, despite the efforts of senior officers to make these occasions beneficial, the negative effect of the 'progress report' is clearly far greater in the minds of most probationers.

Sometimes this is caused by things that shouldn't happen. 'I had mine two days ago, and I got a B-minus for "manner with the public". Since I've been on this station, not one of the sergeants has spent a minute walking round with me, and has never seen me with the public.' Another probationer has doubts for a different reason. 'My inspector calls me every other name except my own name; there's nothing so depressing than when someone doesn't even know your name yet – and then does a progress on you.' With a crooked smile, a third observes, 'On my progress was written, "This officer gets too many shoplifters" – and a week later I was put on the shoplifting squad!'

The pressure to make up a respectable list of arrests and summonses also causes a great deal of dissatisfaction. 'You get

464

probationers coming in here,' says one sergeant, 'wanting to know, "How do I go about summonsing a guy for working ten feet up a ladder without a safety harness?" What the guy up the ladder must think, I don't know! But people are becoming a bit more aware of this, I think, and they're saying, "Well, he's only a young policeman who did me" – as if he didn't know any better. It works in a negative way, because you get through two years of this intensively pressurised work, and you say, "Fok this!" – and you don't do anything. They go to great lengths not to summons people, they get completely out of hand. They have a revulsion for it, and see summonsing somebody as an admission of defeat. And, as a probationer, you've got to go to the boss every three months and say, "I've got that many arrests and that many summonses" – so that's your discretion out the window.' In defence of the scheme, one of the most convincing apologetics offered is that 'You've got to see what arrests and summonses they have, because that's the only way we've got of testing their *resolution*. Nobody likes giving a summons – it's a horrible thing to do when you first begin.'

But even those who are content to have their resolution tested in this way, and have no complaints about the assessments made of them, are far from reconciled to the idea that the scheme is actually good for them. 'I'm at my happiest getting results,' says one probationer with an exceptional record, 'and that isn't necessarily locking somebody up. This is it, you see; this is what annoys us as well with regard to our progress reports: the fact only the jobs that have *got* results are there for the boss to see. You might have a period of a week when you've done absolutely nothing – but that week might have been Mornings when you're running round like a blue-arsed fly, helping people stranded from home and all this. I enjoy that, y'know, but that isn't there to show people.'

'It's back to the old definition of a good policeman, isn't it?' ponders an older officer. 'In terms of that sort of "good", there's nothing down for the young bobby with this system; there's no reward. I think it makes some of them very, very disillusioned. It makes them think like Specials, y'know – Specials don't really talk about anything except the fellas they

465

lock up. Well, they're not in the same sort of social role, are they?'

And, talking of definitions, the progress-report system does seem at variance with the given order of priorities, should any probationer reflect on this.

By the very nature of police work, and by virtue of the fact it is carried out by people as susceptible as any to human behaviour that captures the imagination, priorities are bound to cause some confusion at times. Here a senior officer turns a critical eye on the problem.

I always feel that undue emphasis is placed on murder enquiries by the CID, basically because they treat every murder as a major enquiry. Even if it's a name-and-address murder – a domestic – the whole gamut turns out, and the enquiry will be conducted by a senior officer. By the other token, you get deaths where motor vehicles have been used, and this is allocated to a uniformed constable. For instance, there was a motorist who knocked down two elderly people on a crossing, killed both of them, carried them several hundred yards on the bonnet of his car, and then disappeared into the night. These enquiries were allocated to a uniformed constable – far more complicated enquiries than you'd get at a name-and-address murder, involving all sorts of forensic evidence. The funny part of it is that the uniformed constables usually do such a good job on it, and the finished job usually involves far more work than the average murder case, so far as reporting is concerned. Of course, he'll get assistance from his sergeant and his inspector, but he nevertheless remains in charge of the case. It's just this idea that one form of offence is paramount – and this attitude applies to all crime really.

There's a large section of the police force that thinks Crime is King, and this is the only thing we should be worried about. I've always found the opposite is true. The average member of the public isn't really very concerned about crime, big crime. The average person living on the Northern Sub-division couldn't care less whether the warehouses on the docks are broken into every weekend – that doesn't affect their personal lives. They're more concerned about things happening in the street. There are more sort of heart attacks or nervous breakdowns caused by

466

street nuisances: hooliganism, vandalism, even such things as football. These cause people real and serious problems, and can lead to even more serious offences when they go out and clout a kid, driven to the end of their tether. We had a case where a man actually discharged a firearm at some gang of youths who had been pestering the life out of him for months – just minor offences, like kicking at his front door, this sort of thing. He was driven to the end of his tether – and indicted for murder.

These are the sort of things that police forces in general don't seem to pay much attention to. One of the reasons for this is, of course, when they're asked to measure their effectiveness, they've got very few things to measure it by. It's an historical fact that they've always turned to the crime figures – or the detection rate – and a chief super can, in fact, deploy his men solely on the basis of last month's figures. So, if he's got a high area of a particular crime with a low detection rate, he can draw men off Uniform patrol duty and put them into plain clothes to deal with that particular crime, because that's the only thing he's going to be measured on at headquarters at some later date.

I'd like to see some sort of other measurement devised, and we've got to take the community into account in this respect. We've been rather arrogant in the police force since time immemorial. We've set our own objectives, we've decided how best to police an area, and we've allowed no interference from outside. There has been some feedback from councillors and this sort of thing, but the people living in that area should have a voice. We've had a recent example of this, of course, where people up in Liverpool 8 are fed up with kerb-crawlers. Now, policemen don't see that as a particular *police* problem while nobody is making a song and dance about it, so they're content to leave it fallow – they just make a token effort to contain prostitution, so that they're sort of beyond criticism, as it were. It takes the residents to come up to the Chief Constable and say, 'Why don't you do something about this *evil* in our district?'

No doubt the CID must be in the forefront of those who believe that 'Crime is King'. The irony would seem to be, however, that the CID, through the intimacy of its contacts in the community, is actually more aware of the people's needs and sufferings than any other branch of the service.

467

24

Chief Inspector North is on his way again. From Copperas Hill, he'll call in at the enquiry office at Hope Street, carry on down to the Pier Head, and perhaps put his nose in at the Main Bridewell, before returning to St Anne Street.

The relief bridewell patrol goes back to her desk behind the counter. She is a slim, almost fragile twenty-three-year-old with a dark pony tail and the delicate bone structure of Nefertiti; her laugh is soft, her manner imperturbable, and her carefully applied make-up completes the impression of crisp elegance. 'I don't know what it is about make-up really – some of the girls can't be bothered, y'know, working shifts. But I feel better; it's like a man having a shave. Normally, when I'm out on foot patrol, I put me hair in a bun, but I have it like this in the bridewell – it's still above me collar, and that's the rule. Sometimes I wear perfume, not always. I suppose it helps – you get a few comments from people you're locking up sometimes: "You can arrest me any time, officer!" ' She reaches out to the counter-top. 'Touch wood, I've never come unstuck with any prisoners so far.'

And that is after being in the force for two years and eight months, having started off in the Women's Section in the city centre, arresting mainly shoplifters and drunks. 'Integration's worked for the better mostly,' she says. 'There are some snags, but not many. I must admit I hate being on my own on Nights. I'm not frightened; it's the sheer boredom of it.' Before getting a woman sergeant on her section, she got ticked off a couple of times for the amount of make-up she used; perhaps it was thought to make her seem frivolous. Her attitudes would appear, however, to be those of a 'citizen locally appointed', who has no fear of being herself nor of viewing her workaday world from her own perspective.

I was twenty when I joined. I'd been a lab technician in a boys' school. I'd worked in an office; I'd had part-time jobs as well, as a hair-dresser, in a cake shop – I'd done everything really! (*Laughs*) I left the lab, didn't know what I wanted to do, so I took that office job, y'know, filling in for a while. I just noticed

468

an advert for the police in the paper one day. I've got no relatives in the police – mine are more the other side, I think – but I just thought it looked interesting. I've not changed at all since I joined; I think people who change were a bit naïve. Woman of the world! (*Laughs*) I've been in 'A' Division all the time, and I used to work here before that, so I knew the city pretty well – in fact, I've locked up a few of the boys I used to work with. I live not far from the city centre, and it's not as if I've come from Southport and I'm amazed, y'know; I know the people pretty well and it hasn't changed at all really. I think the public view of us is mainly good. The local residents don't on the whole, I think, like the police unfortunately. The abuse doesn't bother me. Perhaps, having worked with kids – I mean, you can imagine being a female lab technician in a boys' school! Occasionally you'd be left in the classroom with the whole class of boys, helping with the equipment and that when the teacher went out, and I probably got used to it then. I think that we are better at dealing with the kids. The men tend to be a bit abrupt with them, and can't differentiate between the little kids and the big ones who should know better. I feel sorry for the kids – I do, I sympathise; it's usually their parents' fault or their big brother's fault, y'know. I find a lot of policemen – not all of them – are very cynical towards people in general, because some of them join as cadets and don't know anything else. All they know is the criminal side and the good side; they don't know the in-betweens. You must have heard the expression 'buck'. I'd never heard it before I joined. Bucks and buckesses! (*Laughs*) That's a good police phrase all right – they use it on virtually everyone. They say 'a good buck district', y'know. You could say where I live is a buck district, but I know there's good people amongst the bad even though they're not well-off enough to live over the water at Crosby or somewhere. I think the joining age is too young. I mean, you can get a mature nineteen-year-old, but you can get some as immature as a fifteen-year-old. (*Smiles*) They soon put them right around here. Honestly, the people have no respect for you – they probably take more notice of a girl – and they take no notice of these young lads. And they do have this terrible attitude, some of the young lads; they think they know it all, and they come unstuck. (*Shrugs*) I'd like to make a career out of it. I find there's excitement in the job – no, it's not excitement; it's just variety more than anything, I think. Even when I'm sitting here, I'm listening to the radio, listening to what's going on outside, I'm sort of interested.

469

She may not have changed – she doesn't want to carry a baton, and has never needed handcuffs – but becoming a police officer has none the less had its effects. 'Working shifts tends to interfere with your social life and, although I try to keep my friends outside the job, I've lost friends through it. I lost a close friend I'd had since I was twelve or thirteen; it was a bit upsetting. One day her husband's brother got locked up, and next thing she was on the phone: "My husband says can you and your boyfriend not come round any more – he's gone very anti-police, y'know." I said, "That's a bit silly, isn't it? It wasn't us who locked him up." She said, "I'll phone you next week" – and she hasn't phoned since.' And so, like it or not, she has become part of a minority group subject to indiscriminate bigotry in some quarters, and this must jar someone with a fairly cosmopolitan outlook. 'I love cooking, foreign cooking – Italian, Chinese. Half of it goes in the bin, mind you!'

There's only one half-caste girl in the force that I know of, and very few coloured policemen as well. I think it would help to have more but, then again, I'm not prejudiced. I did a lot of voluntary social work while I was at this school; I used to take a lot of kids out from the Liverpool 8 area, and they were mainly coloured kids. I think prejudice is ignorance really – it's like in this job, where the only black people policemen lock up are black criminals, y'know; they don't think of the thousands they don't lock up, who live perfectly innocent lives. It's just ignorance – and it's not just policemen – but I think it's better in Liverpool than some other places. I haven't ever been to an incident caused by race, nothing like that at all. I've not had any complaints about it, either, and I work up in that area, Myrtle Street. That's my beat now. I don't think it's a problem at all. (*Shrugs*) Even this can get a bit routine. I'm hoping to get into the CID – I applied only last night, to be honest. One girl's just left to have a baby. I could use my brain more, whereas the Uniform side of the job's more physical.

'You've got quite a lot of social work to do,' says the detective inspector in the Drug Squad. 'Many a time, when you go into the home, you're the answer to their prayers really, because they know there's a problem but they haven't a clue what it is.

470

'But, then, once the problem has been identified, the mother immediately turns round and blames the father, the father blames the mother, and the son goes in the corner and thinks: Fokkin' hell, they're at it again. . . . And they're not solving the problem. You've got a bloody big domestic on your hands!

'We've got to educate them, advise them on how to look after their son, how to help him. Because, if it's taken him six months to get here, it's going to take him six or nine months to get off it – and he's going to fall a few times, if he's that way inclined. But they don't see that. They only say, "Well, I'm not going to court because I'm at work", and the wife says, "Well, *I'm* not going to court because *I'm* at work, too!" Nobody wants to go to court and help him out, and you begin to see how he got into it in the first place.

'With youngsters you can often find a definite reason for why they're gone that way. Again, you get others that go that way because their friends take it, and they fall in line. I think this is the worst part about the drug world: they're always drawing somebody else into it. If they kept it to themselves, it might be a different thing.'

The detective inspector is a big bland man of thirty-seven with an easy nonchalant manner, who started out as a trainee salesman in the corn and seed trade, then decided at twenty-one that his prospects might be far better in the police. Being a policeman offered him not only greater security as a married man, but also a share of excitement and a healthy outdoor life. 'I play nearly every sport: league cricket in the summer, a bit of tennis, golf, squash and badminton – I play badminton in the British police team, and I've won a few national titles.' His wife plays badminton as well, and they have four children between the ages of thirteen and two. He has spent nearly all his sixteen years' service in the CID, but was a uniformed sergeant, toying with the idea of being an instructor, when asked if he would form a drug squad on the Wirral – although, up until then, he'd never given drugs much thought.

There is never any heat in his words when talking about drug abusers, neither does he associate them with particularly anti-social acts. 'We don't get any violent crime from addicts,'

471

he says, 'but if you start talking about dealers, then the violence will come into it. We in this department, now – it's rather difficult really – we are going toward the supplier all the time. If we can prevent the quantities from getting out on the street – well, we're preventing more and more people from being able to try it for the first time.'

He makes no apology about his views on cannabis. 'All the heroin and morphine users that I know – irrespective of what anybody says – have all started off on cannabis and have progressed, wanting to know what this could do to them, and what that could do to them. Cannabis is not just used by students – in fact, to categorise them as users would be very, very wrong. It's no respecter of society. But the majority of smokers we deal with are – shall we say? – from the upper working class – y'know, fairly good backgrounds. Liverpool itself might be slightly different, but if you go out into the Wirral or to Southport you're not going to find the real buck element dabbling in cannabis – they're more interested in committing crime to have the money to go out birding it and boozing it. We like to think we're at grips with both scenes, the cannabis as well as the morphine.'

The trouble is that Diconal has become a substitute 'hard drug' in the city. 'You can get it by forging scripts, plus there are a fair number of doctors with addicts on their books and they treat 'em with Diconal. It's generally prescribed for people in severe pain, a lot of cancer patients and people like that, and it's meant to be taken orally. There are addicts who will inject themselves with it – they say it's just like having a sexual orgasm through the top of your head – but there are certain parts of the tablet that will never dissolve, and so they inject themselves with particles as well. We've had a couple of deaths as a result of this.'

Even so, it is also something with which the squad can come to grips, and he goes back to saying, 'Your hardest problem sometimes is educating parents. They haven't a clue about drugs *or* what their kids are doing. It's a sad part of life really.'

I remember outside Liverpool Stadium one night we picked up two lads. Morphine, LSD, cannabis – oh, they had quite a bit

472

of stuff on them – and we whistled them off here. They were juveniles, so we were duty bound to have the parents here when we interviewed them. This lad told me he was from Crosby, so I rang his mother up. 'My son's with friends in Maghull,' she said. 'You've got the wrong person.' *Would* she believe me? In the end, I had to put the lad on the phone. And when the parents came down they didn't recognise their lad in the bridewell. They said, 'But when you were home this evening you had your school blazer, your white shirt, your school tie, grey slacks and black shoes!' And here he was in dirty off-white pumps, blue denim jeans that had been bleached, a tacky old shirt, and the usual proverbial dirty old duffle coat! What these lads used to do was tell the parents they were going to see each other – the parents never checked – and get on the train to Lime Street, where they had all this gear in a left-luggage locker.

'I'd hate to think my kids were going out and I didn't know where they were going,' he says. 'To be quite honest, I'd check – I wouldn't let them know I was checking. Equally, I'd take a look through their belongings when they were at school or what have you. It may be nosiness, but it's a way of ensuring – if they do go astray – that I get in on an early part of it.'

He would also hate it if anyone took him for 'a white knight in shining armour, trying to charge through the city to keep everybody clean'.

I'm just one of the old fuddy-duddies, I suppose, that thinks drugs are for making unwell people well, and not for making well people unwell. It's one of the sad things today that we live in a pill-orientated world; if anything isn't quite right, everybody searches for a bottle or a tablet which is going to ease that situation for them. It could be through sheer hard work you get a headache, but immediately people think: Christ, I must have an aspirin! A Disprin! Whereas if they just put the books down and went home and had a good night's sleep they'd probably be all right in the morning. The problem is, I suppose, everybody's busy, everybody's *rushing*. If doctors had a little bit of time to listen to people, listen to their problems, they wouldn't need half this stuff they get. (*Shrugs*) I suppose society's got a hell of a lot to answer for in itself really. But I don't believe that – just because of the personal whims of a few people – we should just open the floodgates until proper research has been done to prove conclusively whether or not cannabis does you any harm. I always think that these so-called do-gooders don't look at the picture as a whole with regard to the whole of the community. They identify themselves with just that particular body of people, and say there's no harm in this, that or the other – a lot of bloody bullshit, as far as I'm concerned. They get so wrapped up in one thing it's laughable really. I remember I locked a lad up, and I took him home and saw his parents. His father said, 'That's *it*. Here's me, a marriage guidance counsellor,' he said, 'and you've – I'm packin' it in now! Drugs!' And then it came out that his daughter had been divorced twelve months earlier. He didn't count that as a failure on his part but, because his lad was on *drugs*, he couldn't be a marriage counsellor. And I thought to myself: how the bloody hell do you equate that?

25

Earlier on today in the bridewell at Copperas Hill, a young Chinese boy was brought in for shoplifting a toy and caused a small stir. When the bridewell patrol crouched in front of him, and asked him to raise his arms to be searched, the movement of the boy's jacket exposed a loaded cap-pistol in a plastic shoulder-holster. That brought small smiles all round, but it was the fact he was Chinese that made the occasion memorable.

I've never seen a Chinese locked up. In ten years on the job, I've locked up one Jew – I don't know anybody else who has. One Jew, and that was for taking stolen gear which is, y'know, fair enough. I've found that full-bloods – Somalis, Jamaicans, Nigerians – you never get *them* locked up. Well, nearly all the blacks that have been brought in this bridewell, since I've been here, have all been half-castes.

I don't mind the coloureds. I've got some good mates among 'em. It's in a mass they frighten me. If you come across a bad white, he's bad; if you come across a bad black, he's bad; if you come across a bad half-caste, he's *evil*. I know some half-castes, great guys, but they always carry a weapon for some reason, or they'll use anything to hand.

We deal with a lot of coloured youths in the CID. They usually get involved in the robberies or the very good break-ins to clubs

474

and places like that – particularly the half-castes. They're the ones who run amuck, but usually accompanied by white lads as well. You see, the problem with the half-caste is that he's got this big chip on his shoulder; you don't know whether you come from A or B, so you find your own level with the villains. Their choice of identification is wrong; that's where they're falling down. It would be better if they went to a club where all the kids liked to do sport or whatever – but would you like to bring your kids up there? What chance have they got really?

Each of these statements is the result of a direct question about race. The fact of the matter is that 'A' Division's police officers seldom mention the coloured community in the ordinary course of events, and coloured people are not always designated as such when, for example, incidents are being recounted in the canteen. These sentiments, expressed by a former 'woolly back', may shed some light on why this should be.

I don't like the coloureds around here as a race. I'm not talking about blacks in general – I'm talking about Liverpool blacks. I've got lots of friends who are black, doctors and that, black as the hobs of Hell, but the ones you're dealing with around here are not so much different to ordinary Liverpudlians.

Some of the true blacks that come over, I can accept. But some of the young half-caste blacks are nasty – you can't win with them, so it's just a matter of trying to maintain the status quo. This afternoon, down in St John's precinct, it's full of young half-caste kids who go there for the sole purpose of causing trouble. They know that the bobby's going to be down there, and that's what they're waiting for. Probably two or three of them are going to be locked up, and they'll start crying 'Yer only pickin' on me 'cos I'm black!'

A buck's a buck – no matter what bloody colour he is – in Liverpool. I think most bobbies draw that line: a buck's a buck, and it's the first thing you notice about him. You can spot one a hundred yards off, even before he turns round and speaks to you. It's the way they behave – and that stands out more than colour.

And here is one of those canteen stories. 'Do you remember that buck I locked up in Fine Fare, London Road? He pulls four hundred quid out of the till, and I go there and asked for a description. He's a coon wearing a yellow T-shirt with a big number 77 in red on the back. I mean, it just shows the intelligence! He was locked up in two minutes – he couldn't go wrong really!'

Then there is the reverse side of the same coin. 'I suppose I just accept them like I accept any of the people living round here; some have got bigger chips on their shoulders, but I treat everyone on his own merits – if he'll let me, y'know. I say "coon" and "cooness" sometimes, and sometimes I say "coloured fella", but "nigger" is a word I hate. It's got something nasty to it.'

So, one way or another, it would appear that the coloured community is not regarded as special enough to be a common topic for discussion, whether by those with an all-embracing prejudice or by those who prefer to make their own individual assessments. The latter see no reason for complacency, however, when it comes to actual encounters on the streets.

I can understand the frustrations of people living in a depressed area, and it doesn't help when you've got young lads, who're supposed to be the guardians of society, leaning out and saying 'Hey, nigger! Come 'ere!' I cringe. Not only because he's denigrating that person, but because he's denigrating himself, too. I don't know where the younger people in particular get these entrenched attitudes.

The Youth and Community Branch cringes, too.

We get very frustrated. We have quite a big programme, we talk to all recruits about race relations, we try to give them a balanced outlook, but it seems that as soon as they hit the streets they start picking up all sorts of traditional attitudes from other people. A lot of the attitudes are formed before they come into the police anyway, of course, so they're only mirroring the attitudes of people outside. But it's frustrating because you get the other end of it then: policemen *already* tend to stereotype – y'know, they stereotype all low-income white people as bucks. But they tend to stereotype blacks even worse.

I had a black lad in only the other day, a respectable black lad, brought in by his employer. He's got a stomach ulcer and one thing and another because every time he goes out in his car – he has a fairly decent car – he can guarantee that at least three times

476

a week he'll be stopped by the police. I tried to explain it as best I could to him. 'You've got to look at it the other way,' I said. 'A lot of black youths commit a lot of crime, and there are policemen who say, '"If that's a black youth and he's in a good car, then he's stolen it."' This is no consolation to *him*, but at least it explains some of the motives. But he counters that by saying, 'Yes, it wouldn't be so bad if they came up to me and said, "Look, we think you've stolen this car" – but at least half of them are abusive when they speak to me. "Get out, sunshine!" – this sort of thing.' And if he's got a girl with him, 'Is she on the game?' So it's a really bad stereotype.

'What are you?' asks a probationer. 'You're a racialist pig. You're a fascist. You're a fully paid-up member of the National Front. You hate the sight of anythin' that isn't lily white. And that's before you've even said *one word* to them, and you're getting this in your face. I had coloured mates and all sorts before I came on the job, and now I find I'm getting very bitter, y'know, very, very cynical. It's frightening how many people say the same.'

But back to the Youth and Community Branch for a moment.

I heard a very good story about stereotyping that happened in London. A couple of fellas in a panda car see a coloured youth going along at half past eleven at night with a sports bag in his hand. They stopped the car and shouted to him, 'Come 'ere, sunshine!' So he goes over to them. 'Where've you been?' they say to him. 'As a matter of fact,' he says, 'I'm just going home after afternoon duty' – and he had his helmet and stuff in the bag.

This could be the nub of the matter. 'Do you know,' one police officer remarks, 'I reckon we've got more *bucks* in this job than coloured bobbies.' Seen from this point of view, the coloured community must very easily appear to have aligned itself with the only other section of society that finds joining the police quite unthinkable, namely that of the 'born-and-bred' villain. 'I mean,' says another officer, 'you've got to think of them as Them, don't yer? What choice have you got? In my book, it's actions that count louder than words.'

'Basically, they feel they're Uncle Toms if they join the police,' says an inspector in the Youth and Community Branch.

477

'They just don't want to be bothered because we're part of the establishment, and joining the establishment is just *not* the thing to do. I've thrown challenges out, done all kinds of things to try and get them to come along and join us. After a year's work, we might be partially responsible for two recruits, an Asian and a half-black – other than that, it's a non-starter. I don't think they'll take on anything where they might be taunted. As bobbies already get taunted, add to that the fact he's black, and he might be getting "Sambo" and other things said to him. The black lad we do get in the police is a fellow who has played a lot of sport, he's mixed in a school team that's mostly whites, he's travelled around, broken out of his natural environment, and he doesn't feel threatened. He's used to taking a bit of stick and giving it back – or just ignoring it. Those sort of lads can join us and they don't have any bother, y'know.'

There seems little doubt that a coloured probationer can expect to be judged by most officers on the basis of his or her character. The last black probationer in 'A' Division is re-membered as a 'crackin' lad' by many officers, including at least one who, incidentally, can recall often being called a 'big black bastid' at closing-time on Scotland Road. And one sergeant tells this story. 'There was this large-scale disturb-ance, and when I get there there's this crowd of coloureds lookin' very nasty, so I said to the recruit with me, "Listen, luv, you'd best stay in the car." Then I said, "Hell, but this lot are *yours*, aren't they?" You forget completely.' The real bother will come out on the streets, and will take considerable courage and strength of character to overcome – virtues that will not pass unnoticed by his or her colleagues. Perhaps the coloured community does itself a grave injustice by not actively seeking out young people of the right calibre and giving them every encouragement to share in the work of keeping the Queen's peace. There is, however, a third stereotype involved that undoubtedly confuses the issue.

At a recent conference on race relations in the Caribbean Centre on Upper Parliament Street the West Indians were saying that they feel the schools, the police and the courts are far too lenient

478

– and that's why their children get into trouble. They would prefer the police to be abrupt, stern in manner; that they should be thought of in terms of 'My God, here's a policeman!' They don't want a friendly bobby – they want a hard strong approach that will deter their boys. The dads are used to this in the West Indies, apparently. We pointed out that this was at variance with our policy of the friendly bobby, that it's no longer the way things are done in society, and that it would be wrong to treat them any different.

'It's going to be difficult,' says the superintendent in charge of the Youth and Community Branch, 'and it's going to take time, but we really do need more coloured people on the force, because it's only contact with the good sort that's going to straighten their minds out on this, you see.'

26

Superintendent South nods at his telephone. 'What I like about the police service', he remarks, 'is that it's five past eight, and there's nobody who can tell us what will happen at six minutes past – in fact, I think the youngsters love this more than anything.'

Time is where he places his emphasis in most things to do with the sub-division, and this means, for example, that he considers age of greater significance than colour. 'West Indians have a tremendous tendency to come back at you,' he says, 'and I think it's due to it being a young bobby that's dealing with them. If you got an older bobby – one of the six-foot, ex-military style policemen we had in the service a few years ago – I think he'd cope quite well with them, and they'd respect him more. First of all, he'd be quite humorous to them; and, secondly, he would take no nonsense. He wouldn't hit them or anything like that, but they'd know he was the boss on the ground. Now you've got a nineteen-year-old telling a bunch of lads in their twenties what to do, and it's just youth against youth to a certain extent.'

The superintendent is a humorous no-nonsense man him-

479

self, with a forceful personality, a strong physical presence, and a handsome distinguished face. Now in his mid-fifties, he can't have changed much over the years, but remains a trim strapping figure capable of making his civilian clothes look like a uniform.

I had a grandfather who had two farms, and it was the intention that I should learn butchering and we would do wholesaling by picking the cattle up in Wales, fattening them up, and retailing them through butcher shops. I went to train as a butcher and then I joined the Navy when I was seventeen. When I came out, my grandfather had died, the farms had gone, and I then had the alternative of either butchering for someone else, rather than my own business, or seeking some other career. My friend, who had been in the Irish Guards, had joined the police; I spoke to him and he liked it and I thought I would try it. So that's how I came to join the Lancashire Constabulary, more or less after leaving the armed services during the war – I was about twenty-two then. I was posted three miles from Manchester city centre, and served four years on foot and cycle beats. I then went on to crime cars, passed further advanced driving courses and went on to Traffic cars. I've never been in the CID at all, never had any wish to – I never fancied the CID hours; it must be a vocation, the CID. I would probably have come up through Traffic if I hadn't volunteered to go to Cyprus in 1958 as a temporary sergeant with the United Kingdom Police Unit at the time of the struggle for independence. I thoroughly enjoyed it, and when I came back in 1958 I was promoted sergeant. [After working in Lancaster, then a mining area, and in Manchester again, he became an inspector.] I came over to Seaforth, the dock area adjacent to Liverpool City force, and I did prosecuting, community relations and operational policing there. I was then a twenty-four-hour inspector in better-class commuter-class districts, promoted chief inspector and went to a larger sub-division, and then promoted superintendent and came down here to this city centre division in December '66. I married later on in life. I met my wife in Cyprus – she was the daughter of the Civil Commissioner there – and we've two children, both at independent schools. My wife is a part-time librarian at Knowsley Hall; we own our own house; we get on all right. (*Laughs*) Contrary to a lot of people around this part of the world!

480

He shows a marked sense of identity with the area, a liking for its inhabitants, and is quick to point out that Liverpool has taken a 'hell of a hammering' in terms of lack of money and of bad planning. 'Don't you think that it's reflected in the outlook of the people ? There's this determination they won't be put on again. They're a very determined people at bottom, and they're a very witty people at bottom, the true Scousers – very much like a Cockney. What I'd like to see round here now is more money pumped in, and let's see some of this rebuilding taking place. What we need here are small factories to employ people close to their homes. It's vitally necessary to put life back into this city.' Then he adds with partisan feeling, 'There's life in this city, but it's life that is brought in by people living outside.'

Crimewise, I have peaks. I have an awful lot of petty crime done by a certain percentage of inadequates and also by greedy people. That we can cope with under normal circumstances. As it's a city centre, we have a tremendous number of theft of – or from – cars, and so we have to extract men from patrol and put them on specialised duties to cope with it. On top of that, there is a big increase this year of really vicious crime – the robberies we now call muggings, and things like that. That worries me. I don't think I'm winning on violence, although I think that percentage-wise we're locking up more.

Society seems to want – or accept, if it comes to that – nothing should happen to them. I'm convinced that you've got to remove from society some people who are basically bad, and that society deserves to be protected. But that's the old copper coming out, isn't it ? (*Laughs*) That's not really the modern way of thinking! It's a small minority; there's nothing much wrong with a lot of youngsters today, but there's a small element that need putting away. They're getting away with it, and that's disheartening for a policeman. You bring a person in, you charge him, you bail him, and within a week he's back again and he's laffin' at you. And this goes on for a long, long time before the magistrates finally put him away.

It's the 'care society'. It's in the process of transition from the old society to the new one, and I think we're suffering as much as anyone while it is in transition. Whether it will swing back, I don't know – I'd like to swing back a little bit, not right back.

481

There is a case, for instance, for juvenile cautions; I like to see youngsters being given first chances, because if I lived in, say, Myrtle Gardens I'm not sure I would be straight and honest and all the rest of it. Equally, there are people who get away with bankruptcy, and that's a damned sight worse than [a pensioner] nicking five quid's worth of groceries in Marks & Spencer's. But I think it's gone just that little bit too far now, and the really hard youngster now *knows* he's getting away with it. If I could take out the juvenile crime, I could take out a lot of crime, of course.

As for the clubs and the trouble arising from them, Superintendent South would like to see some changes in the licensing laws. 'I think that restricting the hours of food with drink is quite ridiculous; it should be allowed any time on specialised premises, twenty-four hours a day. I don't see it presenting any difficulties to us – cash would control it. But I don't know if I'd like to see twenty-four-hour licensing as it is in France, though. I think there needs to be a restriction on public houses to take care of the people who can't, in a way, take care of themselves – y'know, if they get money, they have to drink it.'

Another change he would like to see concerns policewomen. 'I think they're very good, I don't doubt their courage at all, but there's a physical limitation on what they can do. We're reaching the stage where they need to see if there should be government legislation to control the number that can be in the police service.'

And the one change he wouldn't want to see is a different policy on firearms. 'I have access any time I want to firearms, but I would issue them only after very considerable thought – I'd be very, very reluctant indeed to use them. I'd personally *hate* to serve in a police service where we had to start wearing firearms like they do in the States. This is because I believe myself that the police service in England is based on *the best of what one can get from the community*, and it's got to be that way if we want it to carry on the basic functions as originated in 1829.'

Part of the sub-division is a poor residential area. It has a high crime rate but, to be fair, it has the highest unemployment rate

482

in Merseyside, and with that you're bound to have problems, aren't you? I think it's quite remarkable that we don't get more problems than we do. The colour problem gets no more importance attached to it than any other problems of Liverpool 8, which is a good district that has run down and, I think, is now on its way up again. I want to put band concerts on for them next year on a Sunday afternoon, if I can do it, and get the dog vans in – give them a display of the dogs and things like this.

There's colour prejudice with some of the officers – y'know, you can't cater for the odd individual, can you? I try to project this – and I'm sure the vast majority of the officers I've got follow this line – that you treat people as they are. So they're not unduly bothered whether they're black, white or Chinese, as long as they're a decent sort of people. If they're troublemakers, they'll get what's coming to them – it's as simple as that. I don't hear them saying things like: 'We're going to sort them out just because they're coloured.' They invariably say, 'We're going to sort these bucks out.' If they're coloured, they're coloured; if they were Chelsea or Millwall, they'd be sorted out just the same. Because, let's face it, in Liverpool we're different: we've very few Muslims, Hindus, Pakistanis; the coloured people we've got here – the vast majority of them anyway – were weaned here; they're just black Scousers, and most people here are the same as everybody else.

Having such young people on the streets is, I would think, one of the greatest difficulties of the police service. Not in quality – I think we're dealing with an increasingly higher-educated strata – but the sheer immaturity and lack of experience. What I say to them is this, 'Go out there and say "good morning" to people. The first day, anything could happen! [*Laughs*] The second day, they might turn their back on you. But, if you keep at it, one of these days they will say "good morning" back – they're no longer afraid of you, and that's when you must strike up a relationship.' It must be a cordial, firm relationship, and I hope a helpful relationship, because I think that's what we want now in the police. I'd like to keep them up there longer, but we're a young force and as soon as they qualify they can opt for a specialist department. And so I don't have a community constable up in that area, as I might have done a few years ago. I think this is sad, because I'd like to have a constable on each of those beats who builds up a wonderful knowledge of the people. More than likely, a man might do less than two years there [at

483

the moment]. You've also got to be fair to the man himself; they all like to be down in the city centre where it's swinging – they all want to be down there.

I think it's a pity that a lot of retired constables couldn't be redeployed when they leave the job, and brought back between 8 a.m. and 10 p.m. inside the police stations. I think a lot of them would be delighted. Then you would have a mature police officer meeting the public when they come in – and that's an awful lot of it, that first impression. The first person I saw when I came in from the forces was a reserve sergeant; it was fantastic the things he taught me. If I could have two long-service constables on each shift, what a difference that would make! But for some reason – I don't know what it is – they don't seem to want to do this any more.

I firmly believe there is still a tremendous amount of goodwill towards the police. One can even go into bad houses, and a sense of humour and a cup of tea can produce a result even at that level. But you've got to have an experienced bobby to go in and talk that way, y'know. A good bobby is a damned good social worker. He has a damned good knowledge of human behaviour, he's a worldly person, and I think he makes strong decisions.

Superintendent South is thinking of becoming a school bursar when he leaves the force, but nothing has been decided yet. 'I can retire next year,' he says, 'or I can carry on until I'm sixty.'

27

In a sudden shower of driving rain, St Anne Street divisional headquarters rears up ahead like a battle cruiser high on a vast dark wave, picked out in a glitter of lights against the black sky. Chief Inspector North parks his car and makes a run for it, arriving in the entrance hall none the worse for wear. He tells the bridewell staff he is back, glances at an old fellow with a stick, who is dithering about near the doors, and goes down the passage to his office.

From the cons' room across the way comes the tick-tack, slow tick-tick and tack of a probationer typing out a report.

*

'A précis is quite a difficult thing to do anyway, as an exercise in English,' says one of the section sergeants, 'and they're not doing a précis from a set work, they are doing one from a set of hectic circumstances. Certain things have to be in to prove the job – which they don't know; certain things have not to be in, because they weaken the job; and other things are frowned upon, because you have professional phrases for certain events and a report has to be in that idiom. So basically they're hopeless at them. But, having said that, they are difficult things to do, because you're writing something that a barrister, solicitor or at least a senior police officer is going to read verbatim to a full court, and it's got to be a fairly skilled document.'

'Fellas come on this job who've never used a typewriter in their lives,' grumbles a Days and EPs constable, 'and so (*a*) it takes them ten times as long as a decent typist; and (*b*) the mistakes are just unbelievable. Certainly when I was at Bruche you never even *looked* at a typewriter; nobody's trained to use one, although it's really one of our basic skills, if you like. You see them typing with one finger – I've done it myself – and it's terribly time-consuming, that. A ludicrous situation.'

'I think we should get shorthand and typing,' says Detective Inspector North, who is working late tonight. 'To me, the job's not locking up, it's the paperwork afterwards. Anyone can lock up, see a buck putting a brick through a window – he gets the credit, but it's the jack who has the problems to solve.'

He was a fitter fourteen years ago, and is a giant of a man with a face from much the same mould as Henry Cooper, although the marks it bears come from playing rugby football. 'I was at the atomic energy factory at Windscale – it was dead borin', y'know, and I could see me getting nowhere in that.' His probation was spent in a rural division, and he went on to work in the Task Force and with a special squad 'with a roving commission', as well as the CID. He finds 'A' Division a very decided contrast. 'At St Anne Street you get a hundred and eighty jobs a week – y'know, compared to at Newton le Willow, where you might get twenty, if that. They're great people to work with – not like the fellas down here. I never used a

485

warrant until I came to Liverpool, because people let you in the house. " 'Ere, lad, wot yer bin doin' ?" And they'd give him a slap before they knew what was doin'. Of course, there were the odd ones out, but on the whole that's what they were like. Here they're a bit sharper; they've been made wise by briefs and that; they more or less know their rights. That's the first thing they ask, y'see: "Where's yer warrant ?"

'There you could manage the jobs at the time. If you got a bona fide wounding, you'd drop everything else. I think I did about three bad woundings in three years on my old division – with a startin'-handle, something like that. The rest were all fist jobs. You could always catch up, but here I don't think you'd be likely to catch up, there's that many piling in every day. The detectives do crack up, y'know. The first year I came, there were twenty thousand jobs on the division.

'I don't think we're holding it down; everything is snarled up in the courts, y'know. What makes it harder here as well is that ninety per cent of these plead not guilty; in the county, you've a good seventy-five per cent that plead guilty, which minimises the paperwork we've got to do.'

Tick-tack, tick-tick-tick-*cling*.

'Chalky, old son! What are yer, comin' or goin' ?'

'Eddie, yer bastid!' says Chalky, turning in delight from a brass plaque on the wall.

'In memory of comrades who died in the Great War ?' queries Eddie, glancing at the inscription. 'A bit before your time even, isn't it ?'

'If I should die,' recites Chalky, 'think only this of me: that there's some corner of a foreign field that is forever England.'

'Bloody hell,' chuckles Eddie.

And Chalky, whose much-thumbed volume of Rupert Brooke's verse was an early commendation award, grins happily. That's what friends are for, he says, they're people you don't have to explain things to and, as anybody can see for themselves, Eddie is one hell of a good fella.

'Well, like I said, which is it ? You're on your way or what ? I got held up at the Crown Court, y'see; missed Fred's do an all.'

486

'Never catch a bus in this rain,' decides Chalky.

And they share the lift part of the way with an urbane well-dressed man in a suit who is carrying a briefcase and has, in a very quiet way, 'boss' written all over him.

28

The superintendent in charge of the Operational Support Division goes down to the far end of the corridor and into his corner office, where he drops his briefcase on a large uncluttered desk. The whole room has a very businesslike, restrained look to it, and is dominated by a map of the entire force area. If the OSD is sharp-end policing, then this is the bridge, and he has, besides his deputy, three inspectors, fifteen sergeants and 106 constables – six of them women – under his command.

My ambition was to be an architect. If circumstances were as they are at present, then I'd probably have done that. I went along, got an interview with an architect here in Rodney Street, and was accepted to be articled with him, but it was such an expensive business the family couldn't afford it. I left Liverpool Grammar School at about sixteen and a half and went into a big firm that used to design specifications for people who submitted tenders for paint. I was to be a designer and adviser on paint schemes and things like that. After two years there, I was drafted into the Army, National Service, did two years in the Royal Signals as a lance-corporal, and found I didn't like the idea of going back to an inside job again. At that time, I met my wife, and we decided we'd make a clean break from both families and move down to London – the Met police were advertising quite widely, and the advert caught my imagination. Although, looking back now, we certainly had a police tradition because my grandfather was a policeman, and after I joined my brother joined.

London was also, to my mind, an interesting place to police, and I wanted to go somewhere with plenty of work to do. I've got two children and we lived there until, with all the families well away, we found we were marooned to a certain extent. I think it reached the point where my wife said, 'You either leave the police or we go nearer to one of the families.' I started off at

487

Westminster Road as a uniformed bobby, was promoted sergeant in charge of mobiles, then into the vice squad for two years, was attached to the CID for three months, did another three months – at that time, I was set on a CID career. I was promoted inspector and was at Copperas Hill for about a year before going into the police college, then I came to St Anne Street as Plain Clothes inspector. After that, I became the recruiting officer – he's called the appointments and careers officer since the amalgamation, and the job was upgraded to chief inspector. I did about three years in it; a very interesting job. Then in December '76 I was promoted superintendent and came here in charge of the Task Force, as it was then.

I still paint now: landscapes, seascapes, oils and scraperboard, a little bit of watercolour, but there isn't an awful lot of time and I've a full schedule. I'm mixed up in the police table tennis, and play for one of the teams. And, as I've moved house recently, my big interest at the moment is digging gardens. (*Laughs*) I like constructing gardens – my wife likes moving. Once I accept the fact we're going to move, I quite look forward to getting a bit of rough ground, as it's always a new house we move into. A bit of rough ground and starting from scratch and building, landscaping a garden.

His time in London has given him a yardstick against which he measures most of his observations about 'A' Division.

I think the whole of the violence in Liverpool city centre seems to revolve around licensed premises. If you look at the division and the number of licensed premises it contains in that very small area, you'll see it might be a powder-keg to some extent. I'd say it was safer than central London. I think there's always a tendency to dramatise these things. After twelve years in London, and seeing the type of villain down in London, and coming down here and seeing the people who are causing the trouble.... (*Shrugs*) Many of them are drunks. I think in London there is certainly a greater amount of viciousness – it may well be it is on the increase here. I wouldn't be particularly worried about bringing my wife into the city centre, although I wouldn't want to be out at one o'clock in the morning. But to go to a theatre or a restaurant, I wouldn't hesitate; the thing that would worry me would be parking my car. One of the problems is, of course, you're always torn between the fact you're a policeman and

488

that you're with your wife. If something happens, then you're under some sort of obligation to get involved in it, and, of course, if you leave your wife standing there, there *are* dangers. And if you go into clubs. . . .

Clubs are self-evidently another matter altogether. Of more immediate concern to the superintendent is the effect that policing 'A' Division can have on potential recruits to the OSD. 'I really do think that for a young bobby to be suddenly thrown into the middle of Liverpool, with the amount of training they get, he must be quaking a little. And quite often the attitudes of young bobbies are being formed by young bobbies, because they're being trained by them – by that I mean informal training, and where attitudes are really set: in canteens and that, listening to other people. It's such a problem that when we do an OSD induction course we devote practically half a day to police–public relations and attitudes and things. We try to encourage them to be polite to people when they stop them in the street, because this immediate aggressiveness and offensiveness is an overreaction, born from lack of confidence. I hope my lads get confidence from their divisional status – this, in itself, can give a sort of professionalism.'

Land-Rovers are still, of course, very much part of canteen lamentations. 'The decision to remove the jeeps was the Chief Constable's,' says the superintendent, 'and once again it was a matter of public relations, because jeeps present a sort of para-military image. I know it gives a policeman confidence to be in a jeep – it's the same as being six foot six, isn't it? But I consider jeeps unprofessional myself. I've policed the city centre, Scotland Road, London, and I've never policed in a jeep. I'm a policeman and I do the job; I don't need the image of the jeep to do the job.'

Neither had he any need for a special-sounding title when he took command of the new mobile reserve, known by the ir-reverent as the Odds and Sods Department.

It was my idea to change the name. I think this 'Task Force' was an emotive name really, and it was an unfair description of the organisation which replaced it.

The history of the Task Force went back to the Commando Squad, which was formed because crime was rampant in the city centre. They did a very effective job and crime was brought within limits. The next thing that came along was hooliganism in the city centre, and a lot of drunkenness, which develops into disorder. The Task Force was formed under the chief super of 'A' Division to get to grips with all this. They did a very good job, there's no doubt about it, and then, to some extent, the particular task they had been formed for was no longer there. This was recognised in February last year, and new terms of reference came out. It had broadened itself completely and, of course, we had to change attitudes, because we weren't dealing just with city-centre disorder, but with all sorts of different jobs. Whenever a chief super on a division hadn't enough men to deal with something, whether it was disorder or whether it was crime, he was encouraged to turn to us and ask for extra men. But trying to convince chief superintendents out at St Helens, out at Knowsley or over the water that Task Force could help them was a losing battle, because they knew it had its traditions in policing the city centre. Policing an urban area is, of course, rather different to policing a small town or something like that; in the city you're policing people you'll never meet again, and you'll never get the same relationship. Changing the name was to convince them we were able to deal with their jobs as well.

We concentrate on areas subject to a high level of crime and [/or] disorder. This is done in two ways: either high crime figures are brought to my attention by divisional commanders, or through monitoring the force crime figures, which we do. If we see patterns develop with high crime rates, then it's a diplomatic job and I ring the chief super and say, 'You've got problems, so-and-so, would you like us to come and take a look at it?' There was a bit of resistance at first, because support policing is a new concept, and the first thing a chief super has to acknowledge, in calling us in, is that he can't handle it himself. Of course, some of the older chief supers were very reluctant to do this, yet it's an intelligent idea as crime isn't static nowadays – criminals move about. You can't set up an establishment for a division and say, 'Right, that'll deal with the problems' – and you can't post extra men. But now there is no hesitation anywhere in the force. Now when you ring them it's 'Yes, certainly!' That is our first commitment.

We also provide the main police commitment at major events

490

occurring within the force area; things like the Grand National and the royal visits. We assist the CID with major enquiries, do the house-to-house enquiries, the follow-up enquiries, and we're called in to assist by Serious Crime Squad and Regional Crime Squad. We do high-security escorts – bullion, IRA prisoners – and also deal with disasters and with bombs. We're very similar to the Special Patrol Group in London, but our equipment is not as sophisticated.

I think that support policing is something which will develop in police forces everywhere. In fact, it's the style of policing that could become very important over the next ten years, and I'm thinking of things like disturbances and public-order problems.

The superintendent sits down behind his desk and opens his briefcase to take out some papers, which are sharing the space with a stray unit from his Open University course for a BA degree. He is doing the social sciences at foundation level this year – 'I've found it a bit woolly really, having been used to right-and-wrong legal stuff, but I can see it's to get you in a way of thinking' – and next year he's going to tackle 'Decision-making in Britain'. By then his garden should be finished and, because he doesn't like gardening, his wife will have taken it over.

29

'There,' grunts Eddie, handing Chalky a pint of best bitter. 'Fill yer boots, lad!'

'Cheers, Eddie.'

'And what was it I was sayin'?'

'About this fella that mixes his words up like.'

'Oh aye, doesn't he just! There was this other time he locked this buck up, caught 'im bang at it, and this brief says to him in the box, "Exactly what did you see, officer?" So he says, "I saw him come runnin' out the place with a bungle of notes."'

Chalky can't top that one, and so he just sits there with a happy smile on his face, watching the youngsters enjoying themselves. When he glances back, Eddie has gone all morose again.

491

'Nine months,' says Eddie, shaking his head. 'Still can't believe – not after what he did to that fella. Nine *years* is me minimum for that kind of job! Do yer think nine years from now that poor old sod'll have forgotten?'

'Oh, he won't last nine – not now, not after that happenin' to him. He wouldn't want to.'

'And when yer think of the Great Train Robbers. . . .'

'Disgraceful.'

'And that jury had us sweatin'!'

'Musta done. Six hours they were out, y'said?'

'Near enough. Well, get that down yer! I'm about ready for another – I'm that shattered, y'know – and it's you that's buyin'.'

'Ah,' says Chalky, raising his untouched tankard and spilling a drop or two.

A considerable number of officers admit to finding their court appearances an emotional ordeal. 'I can be more scared, standing up in court and giving evidence,' says one Days and EPs constable, 'than I could going into a fight. Honestly! I get me words mixed up – I've gone to pieces in court, my mind's gone blank, just lost the whole thing, although I've known it off by heart. My bottle goes! It's amazing.' One of the more blasé has concluded, 'Well, it's stage-fright, isn't it? It's not what you'd call a *real* situation; it's more of an act, a game, if you like, and it's a closed shop.'

One of the most unreal things about courts, most people agree, is the punishment meted out to those who commit assaults.

Unless they do something about sentencing, I think we're going to lose the battle. People are screamin' for laws to be improved – they don't need improving. The laws are there already; it's the sentencing. There is no justice, to my mind, when you've got a fellow coming up before the court on a motoring offence and being fined a hundred pound, and you get someone fined fifteen pound for a serious assault.

I was always told when I joined the CID, 'Don't bother about the punishment – you've only got to get him there.' But you get

492

frustrated at times, after you've worked on a job and everything, and some brief puts some explanation which you know isn't true, and he gets off with probation. You see, the jury doesn't see the victims at the time. They're seeing them months later when their stitches have healed and, unless you can take a close look, you don't see the scars.

Take the Great Train Robbers – look at the sentences they got for that! Thirty years and all the rest of it! All right, the guard's going to be a cabbage for the rest of his life, but why doesn't a young fella who knocks an old woman down – and gives her a good hidin' – get ten years? It's the same offence, still robbery, but he doesn't get ten years – might get three months. And, if we get a conviction and the fella gets three months, we're made up about that!

My argument is, if they don't do something about vicious assaults, then two things'll happen. Some bobbies are goin' to start to take their own action, and the bobbies that wouldn't ever want to do that, they're going to leave. I mean there's not a lot of job satisfaction in being a bobby when you do all you can for some innocent person, and you want this *animal* taught a lesson, and he walks out of the court laffin' at yer. Waste of time really.

I think what the public doesn't realise is that when they read in the paper that this lot that scarred her for life have got four years, that it isn't four years at all, not if they behave themselves. Those buggers will be out in eighteen months! With any sentence over three years, once you've done a third you're eligible for parole. So what's eighteen months? Nothin' at all. Seven, and they'd have done at least – it's a cynical way of lookin' at it – two and a half.

Two reasons are usually advanced for 'light' sentencing. One is that there is 'political pressure' – some call it 'economic pressure' – to keep down the number of prisoners in Britain's jails, because the Government cannot afford to build new institutions or to staff them. The other is that the judiciary takes far too much notice of what 'do-gooders' have to say. 'What we want', one officer claims, 'is more working-class magistrates, people whose own personal lives are affected by things in the street, y'know – not fellas livin' outside the city

493

who go to parties where people'll criticise them for not havin' enough psychological understanding and all that load of rubbish.' The group of 'do-gooders' that seems to attract the heaviest fire is the National Council for Civil Liberties. 'Don't get me wrong, I believe in some of the things they're always on about – my liberty's important to me too, y'know,' says one of their more moderate critics, 'but, honestly, they're a laff. To my way of thinking, an old dear down in Vauxhall Gardens should have the liberty – that's freedom, isn't it ? – to go round the shops, or for her pension, without bein' terrified some yob's goin' to smack her one, or do her house when she's out. There's old women who never come out, y'know! There's one I know of has to have the electric light on all day because her windows are all boarded up. Anyway, say she does get smacked, say this yob gets locked up, you tell me whose civil bloody liberties they'll be worryin' about.'

Legal aid is another topic that brings heated responses. Nobody seems to question the principle involved – 'I mean, how many bobbies could afford to pay a brief themselves out of what we get ?' – but most subscribe to the belief that it is not administered properly.

One would hate to think a person suffered injustice because they couldn't afford to pay for legal advice. But the old rule still applies, y'know: you still get the best legal advice *if* you can pay for it. I don't think lawyers try their best on legal aid. There are many cases today when there are totally unnecessary remands – and elections to go for trial – just so the lawyer can make money out of the legal aid system.

You get people who *want* to plead guilty, and the solicitor says, 'Plead not guilty, and I'll go for another remand.' He gets paid for every appearance he makes, you see. Then he says, 'Look, at the second appearance, ask for trial at the Crown Court' – and now a barrister gets brought in, and he also gets his fees paid, all out of public funds. And in the end they get this man before the Crown, and he pleads guilty. It's just a bloody racket.

A change of plea to guilty means that the depositions laboriously gathered for the 'paper committal' at the magistrates' court are suddenly rendered redundant, and so frustration may

494

exaggerate the number of times this sort of thing really happens. What nobody ever mentions is that, provided the accused is prepared to risk the stiffer penalties the Crown Court can impose, and if he or she has no intention of pleading guilty at any stage, then election for trial by jury has decided advantages. Instead of 'flying blind' in the magistrates' court, the defence is furnished with all the prosecution's depositions, so it knows exactly the case it has to answer, and juries are generally believed to be more likely to plump for an acquittal where any shadow of doubt still remains. But, to return to plea-changing, there is another side to it that seldom gets an airing.

I locked a fella up for possession of an offensive weapon. He turned out to be quite a good fella actually – said to me in the cell, 'Don't worry, Dave. I'll plead guilty at the Crown. I'll plead not guilty on the way up and then, as soon as it gets to the Crown, I'll plead guilty.' I said, 'That's going to cost thousands of pounds, y'know!' Not that it means anything to him, because he's on legal aid anyway. But the reason he gives for pleading not guilty is that he'll be sent to Risley on remand for five to six weeks, and he'll enjoy all the privileges of being on remand. He'll be separate from the other prisoners, allowed cigarettes, television, extra free time, extra writing materials – all sorts of things. But if he pleads guilty at the magistrates' they'll send him for sentence to the Crown anyway, which would again take five or six weeks, but as a [convicted] prisoner he wouldn't get the privileges!

Most of the criticism is based on the effect legal aid has on the quality of the defence, which should not surprise those barristers who say things like: 'Well, the police are often very critical of one; funnily enough, this never seems to be the case when one's appearing for the Crown.' But there is a body of opinion that claims prosecutions are being affected as well – and for that very reason: the dual role.

Barristers are overpaid; they're *far* overpaid for what they do. They're making so much money and having so many briefs, they can't be bothered reading the briefs. So, when you lock a fella up, you have to ask them the questions the barristers should

495

be asking them in court – *used* to ask them in court – because you know a lot of them haven't got the nous. We're getting to resent this. You're doin' their job for them, as well as lockin' the fella up.

There are those who say they're coming to the end of their tether over the way they feel things have changed.

The whole system is rubbish – and I'm not speaking as one, I'm speaking as many. The whole system is geared up to making the police look idiots and the guilty look innocent. Sir Robert Mark knows what's going on, I know what's going on, the whole world knows what's going on! Who was it who turned round to me today and called him 'that over-promoted policeman'? It was that barrister. (*Laughs*) I wonder why. . . . I just wonder why. We – the public – are the ones being taken for a ride, and we've had enough. We locked a team up for about thirty grand – they'd stolen this, stolen that, a total of a hundred and thirty offences all round. Now this great, brilliant, stupid, idiotic government – I wouldn't kick them in the Mersey! Wouldn't waste me shoe leather! – has decided, *if* you don't mind, that I can't steal off you more than once. Now, if I steal off you forty times, that's once – as far as they're concerned. What a load of rubbish! This team had done a hundred and thirty offences, and it came down to about six in the end. One hundred and twenty-four jobs down the drain, and I've worked me bollocks off! For what? So they can sit back in their little offices in London and say, 'We've got the crime down.'

Others take things very much in their stride, although they feel that the aims of justice are often thwarted.

You try and get somebody to appear as a witness. Quite often they won't come, they never saw nothing – they know the courts can't protect them, y'see, so we have to rely on other evidence. That's why our forensic laboratory at Chorley is overworked; we have to rely on forensic a lot more these days. Once upon a time, a policeman's word was accepted – not now and, to a certain extent, rightfully so. But I think you've got to strike a happy medium, and I think it's gone too far the other way.

Up at the bar, crowded two and three deep now last rounds are being ordered, Chalky waits his turn very contentedly, warmed by a sense of belonging, of good companionship, and by the

496

lively vital talk going on all around him. Earlier in the evening, he would have listened to the man on his right without letting on, but now he turns and beams at him. Nobody seems to mind and, anyway, they're too intent themselves on the yarn he's telling.

'We go into this house, a young woman, about twenty-eight or thirty, attractive, see-thru blouse, big knockers, one of these three-quarter-cut bras, y'know. The place's been screwed, she's got about three kids there, and we say, "Well, the winda's still a bit vulnerable, luv. Get yer husband to secure it." She says, "Oh, I haven't got a husband." "OK, luv, fetch the Corporation and they can do it." So we leave her place, go out and go into the shops for a packet of cigarettes. The shopkeeper says, "You're the police, aren't yer?" "Yuh." "You've just been to that flat over there?" "Yuh." "There's a cove been hangin' round outside in a mackintosh, you see – he's about twenty-six, twenty-seven. I don't know what he's up to, but he's been hangin' round, lookin' at that flat." "Yuh? We'll go and have a word with him. Thanks very much." We get back into the car and go round to where he was. "Can we have a word with yer?" He takes off, y'see! Like a startled fawn, he's away down a back jigger, y'see! So my mate's off like shit off a shovel, round the corner the other way, and up the back, and we nobbled him in the jigger, y'see. "OK, what's the score?" "Oh, I don't want to tell you, boy-o!" Real Welsh Wales, he was – from Bangor. "Well, you're going to have to tell us, sort it out here – or tell us at the police station." "Oh no, I *couldn't* tell you!" So we put him in the back of the car, and we're going to the police station. "All right," he says, "I'll tell you, boy-o. I've had her recommended to me," he says, "fifteen pound for an hour." She's on the bloody batter, y'see!'

'Superb!' applauds Chalky, amid the laughter.

'And he's been hangin' round, waitin' for us to leave, so he can pay his fifteen pound, have a jump and go back to Wales – he'd come all the way from Wales, the soft git! I said, "Are yer gettin' short of sheep down there or what?" "Oh no, boy-o, no." We had a bit of a laff and let him loose, y'know.'

497

Then Chalky becomes aware that Bert's looking at him across the bar with an odd sort of look in his eye, and he quickly thrusts the empty glasses forward.

'All right, Chalky?'

'Very fit! Oh aye, never better!'

'You're sure?' asks the steward, showing concern.

Chalky steadies himself against the edge of the counter and nods brightly. 'Have one yerself, Bert! *Anythin'* – a Chevas Regal?' And the jacks beside him start on another tale that'll go down a right treat with his cronies at the local.

30

'I've often said to my husband, "When my days of bringing up children are over, I'm going to open a home for little old men," ' says the detective constable now on maternity leave. 'I feel very much towards these little geriatrics! I was down at the Pier Head, relieving the bridewell patrol one night, and I'm sitting in me little desk, quakin'. I heard this bottle being banged against the glass door. I went out – very brave! – and it's Joseph with this white-wine bottle. He's Polish and you couldn't get across to him the fact you wanted him to go away. A crowd gathered and in desperation I pulled him inside – and once he was inside he gave me his bottle and sat there and was delighted. All he wanted was a bed for the night in the Main Bridewell. Ever since then, if he sees me in town, he'll wave his stick and shout in Polish – then he'll dive across the road, and he always kisses my hand. The only way I can get him to go away is by giving him money. It used to be very embarrassing, y'know, this policewoman in full uniform getting her purse out and payin' him to clear off! Oh, he's a lovely man.'

Her baby is due in December, and she's been away for almost three weeks now, although some afternoons – like today – she pops into St Anne Street to have tea in the canteen with her husband, a detective constable in the Regional Crime Squad.

A lot of policemen either marry policewomen or nurses; I think a lot of it has to do with the shift work. Before I was married,

498

if I went out with a civilian – that sounds *terrible*! – and they were on a nine-to-five job, well, I had to work two weeks out of three of an evening. And of course, if you met a boy at a dance and he asked you what you did for a living, and you said, 'I'm a policewoman,' you couldn't see them for dust! (*Laughs*) My girlfriends and me often used to go to dances, and on the way there we'd say, 'Well, what shall we be tonight?' We might be anything from assistants at Woolworth's to yer actual air hostesses, depending on how sort of gullible the fellas looked.

The police force don't put themselves out to accommodate you and your husband, I did find that. I mean, I don't expect people to fall over backwards accommodating my wishes, but half the time they weren't even considered. When we first got married, Tom was on five shifts in Traffic and I was on three. It was a case of us leaving each other notes, as we didn't have a telephone at that stage. When it got to bedtime, I'd leave him this lovely little note about how I was missing him and all this sort of thing, and then, when I got up in the morning, he'd be still in bed and there'd be a lovely little note from him. (*Laughs*) And in the end we sat down and said, 'This is ridiculous!' The notes were then more something like, 'If the milkman calls, pay him the bill.' Something basic!

I shall miss a lot really. I shall miss dealing with the public. I'm missing them already – when I go out shopping, I want to talk to everybody, y'know, and, whereas before I had my sort of reason for doing it, now I haven't. The people out our way keep themselves to themselves, but if anybody speaks to me in a shop – albeit it might just be 'Isn't it a lovely day?' – I take them up on that! (*Laughs*) I'll miss. . . . When I started with Peter [her former detective sergeant at Copperas Hill], he would say, 'I've got to go to such-and-such a place' – and more often than not it was to the home of someone he had locked up in earlier days. Although he had locked up a member of the family, he was still very much accepted by the rest of them as a person, and they'd ring him up over a little problem, nothing at all to do with the police – income tax forms or their dole, something like that. So it can be done; you can lock people up and stay friendly with them later on. I'll miss that. I had an old lady, she'd been the victim of a mugging, and I went to see her in hospital, and I went to see her when she came out to get statements off her. Then I went to see her a couple of weeks later, to say we hadn't locked anybody up, and I carried on those visits. Not on a

499

weekly basis or anything like that, but if I passed her house I'd call in and have a coffee with her. She wasn't a police informant or anything like that – she was seventy-two years of age (*laughs*) and only saw what went on within her four walls normally – so to a certain extent it was a waste of time; I mean, really it wasn't even boosting police–public relations, because the foundations were already cemented. But whenever I left the house I felt elated, felt as if I'd done something really worthwhile. And I've found this with juveniles' parents, too; I sort of go and have a cup of tea with them, or speak to them in the street – it isn't all this anti-police stuff.

And I'll miss my old friends and colleagues. If any child of mine wants to, I wouldn't stop them becoming a police officer. The day you don't look forward to coming to work in the police force, is the day you really should pack up. I still think there are a lot of bobbies doing the job regardless of the money and the aggro. There are bad policemen, and bad policewomen, but there is a good majority – I *know* this is going to sound soppy! – who do have the interests of the community at heart. That's another thing. If a bobby is so bad – I don't mean bent, but 'bad' because of his attitude to the public and this sort of thing – then he loses the respect of his colleagues and, quite rightly, the bobbies will turn against their own. I found this in the Task Force, where everybody had the reputation of snatching anything that walked, but only two or three bobbies really deserved this reputation, and they weren't liked by their colleagues. It got to the stage that if they had a good arrest, a decent crime job, and they wanted one of the other crew to go second jockey for evidence purposes, nobody would do it – even though they knew *this* job was good and it was straight. They didn't want to be involved in anything Mr X did.

It annoys me when one bad apple spoils a whole barrel. It's like the good people and the bad people – I don't think automatically people divide into criminals and non-criminals, but I'm not that naïve I think everybody's nice. Sadly, everybody gets tarred by the same brush, everybody gets the same bad name. In all honesty, the good people in that area* aren't living there by choice. A lot of their living conditions are very poor, and a lot of them make and mend, so to speak, try hard to make the best of a bad thing; the majority are salt-of-the-earth types, they're

*Liverpool 8, her beat seven years ago.

500

just rough and ready – very outspoken, but as good as gold. The coloured community I always found were very friendly – I wouldn't say pro-police, but very friendly and outwardly pleasant to me. While I was at Copperas Hill [in the CID], if I did come across any of them, it was usually by way of them being complainants – the few coloured arrests I've had, I had absolutely no trouble with. There is a minority of bad bobbies, and sadly it's their actions which are always remembered and everyone gets this bad name. If I'm dealing with somebody who tells me they've been badly treated by police prior to then, I often say: 'Well, you've never met me before, you've never heard of me or anything like that, so give me a chance to prove I'm not going to give you a bad deal.'

She is almost twenty-seven now, and joined the cadets straight from school at sixteen, after considering a variety of clerical jobs and the idea of being a dental receptionist. She saw a film at a careers convention and just signed up. 'I don't know why; it was something I did on the spur of the moment. My first arrest was criminal damage and assault police – how about that?' And she laughs. 'Technically it was an assault, because I had a chap come at me with a bayonet after he'd smashed up a sweetshop. It was very sort of dramatic; hysteria and everything from the wife, and she was trying to push herself between him and me, and I was trying to get out the door! To cut a very long story short, we reasoned with him and eventually he agreed to walk to the police station with us – he wouldn't get in the car. He was imprisoned for six months for a first offence, which was *terrible*. When he came out and, without a word of exaggeration, up until about eighteen months ago, I was still getting threatening messages from him by way of other police officers, acting as go-between.'

Buoyant, warm, with dark hair cut simply, a winsome face and a womanly figure, she has a reputation as a detective to match her popularity. 'I like to think I'm a good judge of character,' she says, when asked how she used to go about her work, 'so if I thought I was on a winner I'd chase it all the way. And if there was anything I was doubtful about I'd get somebody to assist me – especially when I was working with Peter. We had a lovely little system going, where he was the baddie who shouted, and I was the goodie who reminded them of their wife, their daughter, their girlfriend or what have you!'

Peter was once a ship's purser. 'I left after a domestic squabble within the company, and I was looking for a secure job with prospects – it wasn't the attraction of going out and locking people up or fighting crime or upholding justice. I've never regretted it, although I must admit there have been times when I've sat there thinking how nice it would be to be back on a bloody ship in the middle of the ocean, with no pressure to get this committal ready for tomorrow or that committal for next week – just phases that pass over. The best rank in the force is the one I've got: DS. There's no doubt about that: you've got the little bit of authority you might want; you're on bloody good money – the year before last, I earned as much gross as my CID superintendent. As he said, "There's only one difference, lad: you're putting the bloody hours in and I'm not" – which is fair enough.' He has been on the Liverpool police for twelve of his thirty-two years, mainly in CID work of one kind or another, and came to Copperas Hill on promotion three years ago after being in the Regional Crime Squad. 'The trouble with this place', he says, 'is the lack of interviewing facilities.'

You've got to have a crackin' relationship with the person you're working with – it's an uncanny relationship, because you've got to be able to read each other's minds, and to know when to kick in while your mate's recharging his batteries. Quite often you'll get fellows taking turns: 'You be the hard fella, I'll be the nice fella.' You can start with some crack to find out which [football] side he supports. Then, if there are two Liverpudlians interviewing an Evertonian, one of you does a quick swap to support his side, and he becomes the soft man. It's a very handy little thing. But if you've got a good team working together you'll find the hard fella's always the same because, if you don't, you can slip into the soft fella or vice versa. I can only interview for two or three hours on my own, but with a mate much longer. We had an armed robbery in '75 and there were only two of us on. We pulled in six coloured lads at four o'clock, who we found in this house with the cash-box and the gun, and we didn't know

502

which ones were which, so it was a talking job. We nailed it down to the three older ones in the end, and we carried on talking to them until two in the morning, when they admitted it – not a finger was laid on anyone. We take them to the Crown Court, and they'd been belted off every wall, the lot! (*Shakes head*) The majority of people we deal with are slow plodders; you quite often have to repeat things. They're not unintelligent – in fact, in some aspects of life, they're far more intelligent than you and I, and what they lack in common sense they make up for in animal cunning. There are some you'll never con; there are also some who'll never con a detective; and so, in the end, it'll balance out eventually.

He climbs the stairs to the CID a little wearily, having spent the last two hours taking a statement beneath the beady eyes of a stuffed cobra out in 'D' Division. It was touch and go all the way in that small, exotically decorated front room, where the complainant in a case of attempted murder, still in considerable pain, kept flinching as he coaxed her to remember every moment of a night in town she's doing her best to forget. There were moments when, like a fly fisherman using a line of low breaking strain, only his skill and sensitivity kept her from fleeing the room in tears, and he seemed to find this other side of interviewing very gratifying. For her part, the complainant appeared to find the ordeal cathartic, and she was very much calmer, almost cheerful, as she and the children showed him out again.

After a pause on the landing, where he decides against any further experiments tonight with his length of knotted string, he carries on along to the detective sergeants' office and dumps himself in his chair, just inside the door. He glances through the statement. Here and there, the complainant has adopted the phrasing of his questions, and has added impersonal quasi-forensic touches of her own, as though seeking a buffer between herself and too much reality. He tries to set up buffers as well, by being very wary of becoming emotionally involved in his work, but it isn't always easy.

This job we had last week, two fellas who threw a petrol bomb into a Chinese restaurant. They were charged with arson and attempt to endanger life, which carries a maximum of life imprisonment. Two got four years, and the fella driving the car got two years – you can get four years for doing a straight bloody robbery, a good housebreaking! Possibly I got a bit involved in this one, but the girl's children wouldn't go near her – her hands were covered from here to here in scabs, both hands, which had to be scraped off every two weeks. Her face was a big blotch of burning, right down to her throat, and she's got red marks – like when you sit too near the fire – on her hands, her face and her chest, and she'll have them permanently. Her kids now, two of the eldest will go near her without any trouble at all; the other two are very, very wary still. And from my own personal experience with her – she's a nurse, so she knows what treatment she's going to go through – she's been mentally scarred, I'd say, for the rest of her life. To my mind, they should have got seven years for throwing that.

He tosses the attempted-murder file into a basket, and finds a note to say that one of his former 'lock-ups' would appreciate a word with him about 'a bit of a problem'. Outwardly, he could still pass as a ship's purser on shore leave, being a big phlegmatic personable man, well used to handling people, and his experience as such is also reflected in the competent way he manages his paperwork. 'I suppose you've got to classify it as a clerical occupation,' he says, 'because there's no doubt about it, I spend most of my time these days bloody typing – or assisting the lads to type.' Inwardly, he recognises some changes although, temperamentally, he and his work seem ideally suited. 'I thrive on stress, if I'm honest about it,' he admits, 'from the point of view that phone could ring now, and you wouldn't know what the hell's on the other end – it could be someone to say, "Look, we've got a body". CID-wise, it's a good life. There's a saying that all detectives are nasty bloody suspicious people anyway, and that you can't get away from the job. To a degree, that's very true. Subconsciously, you're always aware of what's going on around you in the street, and even when I'm off duty and having a drink I suppose my mind is still at work – I like to know who is around me. Crime-wise, I think things are going to get a bloody sight worse before they get better. I'm very hopeful that in the next ten years we're going to go a full circle from a society point of view. I certainly

504

bloody hope so, because I'd hate my kids to live in this society as it's going at the moment.'

He and his wife – who nurses part-time so they can afford an annual holiday – have a daughter aged fourteen and a son of six. Tom and Liz, now about to start their own family, are among their closest friends, so he won't be losing touch with her, but there will doubtless be odd moments when he'll miss her professionally.

The classic one with Liz was when we had this arson case in a hotel last year. We interviewed the whole staff, but we know who it was the moment we walked in there. Liz said nothing the first two or three times we interviewed him; she just sat there, taking notes. He'd admit nothing. On the third day we went there, I started to shout at him – which he didn't like – and all of a sudden, he jumps up and starts to lean across the desk. I said, 'Be careful now! I reckon I could knock you ten bloody chairs back with one push.' So he sits down and starts to cry and weep a bit, and I went out – to see one of the security staff, I think it was. I came back ten minutes later, and Liz said, 'Can I have a word with you?' So we go out and she says, 'Well, he's admitted setting fire to the storeroom.' We went back in and, as soon as I walked in, he went and sat next to her – and it was just like mother and son. He wouldn't speak to me, either, so in the end Liz had to take the statement from him. I'd never seen anything like it before; it was incredible.

31

The detective superintendent who heads the CID in 'A' Division may not log the same hours as his subordinates but, then again, there is never any minute of the day or night that he can call entirely his own. Should there be a murder or any other major crime, then he has to be contacted without delay, often to take over the investigation. Dealing with offenders is, however, only part of his work, and his skills as 'an old and cunning detective' would appear to play as great a role in his capacity of administrator.

'My detectives tell me they're very hard-worked,' he re-

505

marks with an amused gleam in his eye, 'but you've got to be careful what detectives say – you have to measure it against what you believe with animal cunning.'

We're subsidising the job out of our own pockets. I would agree that there is a certain amount of supplementing of the local authority in that they use their own vehicles on occasions and can only claim at public transport rates. Really, the local authority is getting the job done quicker; I mean, if they had to travel by bus and wait for buses or whatever, it would take them far longer, and obviously they can't walk when they're bringing a prisoner back and things like that. You have to make do. We've got five vehicles but we never have five vehicles at any one time, because if they break down or get stoned we're without them until they get repaired. If we had those five all the time, we'd probably have enough. But, nevertheless, in a division like this – which is ideally compact – legs have not gone out of fashion, and you can meet a lot more people walking than you can riding. I walk, I walk regularly, because I meet a lot of people that way. *Our expenses are ludicrous.* They get a detective duty allowance of around four pound a month which they never talk about because it comes in the pay. What they're talking about is this 50p a week incidental money – it's never been changed for years, and it's peculiar to Liverpool really, because you don't get this fixed amount in, say, West Midlands. But what are we talking about? Does it mean, if I go out with an informant to have a drink, that I would expect the firm to pay for my and his drink? Because that's the way some of them do it: expenses are not just what they've spent on the informant, but the total amount they've incurred. An argument they regularly put forward is that they're drinking only because they're dealing with an informant, but nobody *makes* them drink. And if you get down to the nitty-gritty of it – let's be honest about it – in social activity we spend money on drink. I could say that in the course of my duty I smoke a lot of cigarettes and that I give a lot of cigarettes away to people with whom I'm dealing. I don't expect the firm to pay for that! I've always found this force to be particularly good on expenses, and they can always put in an extra sheet if they want – whether it'll be paid is another matter. Quite honestly, if a man can say he's out of pocket, he will be paid.
Our caseloads are out of this world. We deal with on average 22,000 crimes a year, and that sort of rate is greater than the whole of

506

the county of Lincolnshire, for example, and greater than many other small counties as well. Having said that, *I* know precisely what the caseload per man is, but I'll lay you a five-pound note to a pint of beer that – apart from my chief inspector and my inspectors – nobody on my staff can tell you accurately what their caseload is. They're certainly harder worked than ever I was as a young detective, but I've compared the figure with a division where I worked two years previously, and that division had a higher caseload per man than this division. Figures can cloud the issue anyway; a large amount of our crime is thefts of and from vehicles.

The detective superintendent is, in short, not a man who would like anyone to think they could pull the wool over his eyes, but at the same time there is little doubt about whose side he's on. 'There are two ways of running a division,' he says. 'You can shut yourself off, examine their work, and give them a shellacking every time they do something wrong. Or you can look round, see what they're doing and take an interest in it, try to bring them on slowly – that's the way I do it. Some people might say, "You're soft". Well, maybe I am soft, but if anybody has a better method of working my team, and can get better results than I do, then they're welcome at any time to sit in this chair. I keep a personal interest in all my officers because, based on my experience as a young man, you never let down the fella who is looking after you.' He sees them as divided broadly into two groups. 'There is the extrovert who makes a detective virtually in spite of himself, because he makes such an impression on people they just cannot avoid talking to him. He's the mixer, the go-getter, the manhunter, the pointer – very often, when he's got you, he doesn't know what to do with you. But the plodder does, and he's the man who comes in with an eye for detail, the man who painstakingly fits the thing together, and he's the man you normally shackle with the extrovert. You'll see this in CID offices all over the country.'

Now approaching fifty, the detective superintendent would seem to embody both sides of the CID coin, as well as retaining the looks of a 'crisp bright young bobby' with wavy blond hair,

507

a slightly chubby face and determined chin. He has a grown-up son and daughter.

I didn't start till I was twenty-four. I was in the joinery trade and working very close to the Traffic headquarters of the Birmingham police. During the lunch times, when we had a walk around, we'd see these motorcars going out and these officers all smartly shined and buttoned, and I thought to myself: That looks an interesting job; I wonder if it really is interesting? It's tedious at times, but I think I can say, after twenty-five years, it's certainly proved interesting. When I joined in 1952, the fellow showing me round had two months more service in than I had – it's always been the same. I went into the CID after my probation, and I've been in ever since because I changed forces. I was with the Birmingham City Police until 1967, when Liverpool advertised for inspectors. I certainly intend to do thirty years, but I don't know what to do about the void which comes when you leave the job. Over the last twelve years, every October a pal of mine and I take the families on the Norfolk Broads; I suppose I'd like to live there and carry on the fishing. I'm a fisherman, a coarse fisherman; I do quite a lot of gardening and greenhouse work; I read a lot, usually in the early hours of the morning because I don't get any time other than that. I suppose I've read all of C. S. Forester's books; I've a fascination, if you like, for a writer's style rather than the events he's writing about. I read quite a lot of crime fiction; most of J. J. Marric's books, most of Proctor's – who's an ex-policeman, and very good they are, too – and I like Dick Francis. I've also read Jack Dash's book, *Good Morning, Brothers*, and I thought it very, very interesting indeed.

One of the frustrations he experiences today is the continual drain of manpower back into uniformed posts. 'It's always with the promise that one day they'll return as detective sergeants,' he says, 'but, nevertheless, I've trained them and I've lost them. The replacement might be a good fellow, but it takes a long time to train him because of the terrible amount of procedure involved that you have to learn the hard way.' Not only have procedures to be absorbed, but attitudes as well.

I would never like to think that any of our jobs were written off because we hadn't a hope of getting anywhere with them. My

508

view of complainants – and I say this at our meeting every month – is that they are the best sources of information. You deal with them right, and it matters not to a complainant whether you clear the crime or not, and at least you get to know another person in your area. And you can get a lot of information from them because, when they start to talk, they're very often knitting facts together about people with whom they work, with whom they associate, and they are very valuable to us. There *is* a proportion of jobs that are unclearable. If you take the insurance claims [months after the theft] and the goods [lost] in transit – which is really bad accounting – there is at least fifteen per cent of crime which you can never detect before you start, so you're only working toward an eighty-five-per-cent detection rate really.

Violence is also something about which he holds strong views.

It's no use saying that never ever in the investigation of crime is there no use of a fist. If somebody pokes me in the ear with his fist, I'm going to make sure that he gets a poke in the ear with *my* fist. But, having said that, in twenty-five years of police work I have never ever been assaulted. And I say this – and I mean it – that any of my detectives who physically assaults a prisoner to get him to admit a job wouldn't stay with me two minutes after I found out about it. To me, anyway, a detective trades on his personality and his integrity and his cunning, and if you can't beat a man by facts, then you oughtn't to be a detective. . . .

He is equally vigilant about alcohol.

There are people who will say that, as a detective, you've got to be able to drink fifteen pints a night, and I keep a very close eye – and so do my inspectors – on the amount of drink that is being consumed. My limit of an evening is four halves – I never drink in pints – and then I go on to lemonades. I always think that I could be rung up at any time during the night and be asked a question that concern's somebody's liberty or some detective's future, and so you cannot go home befuddled by drink. I keep this very close eye because if a man is drinking, and he's drinking heavily, he may have a problem. I can't think of any one of my staff who's gone off with a drink problem, a mental problem or an ulcer, although the whole basis of life as a detective would seem to push you that way.

509

The detective superintendent has what appears to be a singularly sanguine disposition, a canny, imperturbable air, and a profound regard for the police service. 'It's the only job I know', he points out, 'that will take a man – even today – without any qualifications at all, and, if he's any good, he can get to the top merely by doing his job and doing it efficiently.'

You can't be a detective unless you're an optimist. A pessimist would not last two years because you'd say that everybody who you locked up would never do any good. Now, I'm not boasting, but I must have locked up hundreds of people, none of whom – on my side – have ever fallen out with me. I can go out now and meet people I've taken before the courts, and have a civil word and a drink with them. I've helped people to get jobs, and some of them now have good businesses. That is to me detective work. So, as an optimist, I wouldn't like to predict a rise in crime, and I would like to think we will stamp out this violence and get back to the more stable society I served in in 1952. The gentleman housebreaker – although you could never excuse him – at least was a gentleman about it. If he was ever disturbed, the first thing he wanted to do was to get away – he never hurt anybody. That's gone now; there's more avarice, more jealousy and more viciousness than there ever was before. And certainly, over the last few years, crime has been increasing. Whether this is because of the society in which we live, I don't know, but more people now seem to be acquiring more possessions and, of course, the more you've got, the more there is to be stolen. So there'll always be work for thieves – and essentially, thank goodness, there'll always be work for policemen! (*Smiles*) But I wouldn't like to say which way it'll go. Everybody sort of says, 'Well, what America does we'll be doing five years from now.' I don't believe that. Our style of policing is entirely different: it's unique in that without the public we would never do our job – it's just not possible, because of the powers we've got. A lot of people think a policeman has tremendous powers; he hasn't. In fact, he has very few more powers than the average citizen has got – if he used them – and long may it continue.

510

32

'Me stick,' says Chalky, feeling at the side of his chair and then looking under the drinks-table. 'I've lost me flamin' stick.'

'You're sure?' murmurs Eddie.

'Or else some bugger's nicked it,' growls Chalky, trying to fix his focus on the circle of young bobbies nearest to him.

'No need to panic. The jack who's giving us the drop isn't goin' for a minute yet, and it could've been in the canteen you left it.'

'Ah,' says Chalky, 'yer could have somethin' there.'

'No, you stay put. I want a packet out the ciggie machine anyway.'

'Cheers, Eddie.'

Chalky watches Eddie, one helluva good fella, amble out of the club room, and then turns a benevolent eye on the rapidly thinning crowd. The new father is recumbent now, as helpless as his firstborn, smiling and making small contented noises, while arrangements are made to carry him out to a car. The music has stopped, the grille has been lowered in front of the bar, and Bert is starting to collect up the empty glasses, helped by one of the social club committee and a couple of the lads.

'A'right, Chalky?'

'Smashin',' he says, handing over his glass. 'Got a minute? There's a story I never told yer.'

The youngster perches on the arm of Eddie's chair, and Chalky relates the tale of the Welshman and the lass with the big knockers, making it sound very much his own – as it might have been, given the same set of circumstances.

'Oh aye?' laughs the youngster. 'What about the Welsh fella Traffic stopped last week? They said, "Can you make a U-turn?" And he said, "Give me a pair o' wellies, boy-o, and I'll make its eyes water!" '

'*Su-perb*,' wheezes Chalky, after an ecstatic fit of coughing. 'What do yer think of the new boss, then?' he adds quickly, like a man who doesn't want to sit alone.

'The chief super?'

'Crackin' fella!'

511

'Oh, so you—'

'Now, there's a fella with bottle, no doubt about that. There were these two Yank soldiers once – you know about it?'

A shake of the head, and a glance at his watch.

'These two Yanks, y'see, military police I suppose they were, come up here and they say there's this deserter with a gun and all, and he's with this lass, see, in this house they've got the address of. It was somethin' like that. Anyway, could they have some co-operation? "Let's take a look at the place," he says, so he drives them round there in his car and, yes, the neighbours've seen this lad. So the Yanks, these MPs, they say, "Well, we'd better get some armed men here. Are you armed?" they say. "No," he says, "but I tell you what. I'll just go and see what's what in there." "Are you *crazy*?" they say. "This guy's gotta gun! This guy's gonna start shootin'!" "Just hang on," he says, and he leaves them in the car and they're wettin' themselves. He goes up to this door and he knocks on it. The lass opens it, a nice lass, and he says, "I'm from the police, luv. Can I come in and have a word with yer?" So he tells her what the position is, and he asks her to get the young fella's gun for him, and to tell him there's no point in doing' somethin' stupid, because he's going to get locked up whatever happens. So she gets the gun, she talks to the lad, and five minutes later out he comes without even any cuffs on or anything. These two in the car – I mean, they're just *peerin'* over the windows like, and they can't believe it. All the way back, they just can't believe it! And you know what? Six, seven months later, this lad's back to thank him for not letting his girl get involved in any trouble.'

'Aye, well, that's really the difference, isn't it? You fixed for a drop? Me mate's going soon, and he lives over the water.'

'I'm fine, thanks very much,' says Chalky, noticing Eddie approaching with his walking-stick. 'Canteen, was it?'

'Specials' room. Ready for the off?'

'Oh aye,' says Chalky, standing up and sitting down.

Bert and the others call out their good nights, and then look discreetly away again as Chalky is helped out by Eddie on one side and a very nice young jack, who looks a bit like a violin

512

player, on the other. Not that Chalky needs the help, as he keeps explaining, but he doesn't want to be awkward, he says, doesn't want to give the wrong impression.

33

A message from New Scotland Yard lies on a corner of the divisional commander's desk. One just like it has arrived every year on or about the same date for almost a decade, following him from job to job, reminding him of one of his most intriguing cases.

'At the time, I was a detective chief inspector on the docks, and Mr Jones was an assistant Scout commissioner on the Isle of Man. He brought a troop of Scouts over for the Scout Show at Port Sunlight, left them there and went to a friend's house in Birkenhead. Then, as the show wasn't until the evening, he decided to come back to Liverpool and do some shopping. This was the last time he was ever seen by any friends of his. The next morning his car was found at the extreme north end of the landing-stage at the Pier Head, which was a bit different then to what it is today. There was a bloodstained handkerchief, the seats were bloodstained, so was the steering-wheel, and there was no sign of Mr Jones. . . .'

Large capable hands take the message and square it up on the blotter of his desk.

The chief superintendent in over-all command of 'A' Division is a thickset wide-shouldered man in his late fifties; a man's man with a military haircut and craggy warrior-like features. His manner is wholly self-assured, courteous and open, his speech gently modulated, and his eyes have a warmth to counterpoint their astuteness.

I served in the Royal Navy during the war, came back, was dissatisfied with working in a factory – I was an electrician by trade – and looked around. I had a chum in the Birkenhead Borough Police; he packed it up in the end, but was instrumental in me joining them in 1950. It wasn't a case of a duck taking to water.

513

(*Smiles*) At the end of the first six–nine months I was most dissatisfied. I'd had a beating-up by a man called Selby, who was an ex-Commando. I didn't know Selby, Selby meant nothing to me, but within quarter of an hour I *knew* Selby. (*Laughs*) Because it was one hell of a fight – ex-Commando against ex-Navy man. Blimey! That had some effect. The weather was foul, I wasn't sleeping very well during the day, everything was getting on top of me, and I was ready to pack up and go back to my trade, y'see. My tutor constable, a man with about twenty years, talked to me like a Dutch uncle for a couple of days, and I seemed to get over it. I adjusted to the life. Then I went into the CID and I could see that I could build up some sort of career. I remained in the CID from 1954 until 1962, when I was promoted to Uniform sergeant. I did eighteen months, went back as a DS, and then I was transferred to Bootle Borough in 1965 as a patrol inspector. I stayed a patrol inspector for only two months, became a detective inspector, and then – through luck, call it what you will, being in the right place at the right time! – I was promoted DCI only ten months later. In 1969 I took over the role of DCI on the docks, and in 1971 I was promoted superintendent and took charge of Task Force, as it then was, working mainly in 'A' Division. I stayed here until May 1974, when I was transferred to Wallasey as second-in-command there. On the first of September 1975 I was appointed divisional commander back where I'd started at Birkenhead, and now I'm back here two years later.

After so many years in the CID, I like to spend as much of my free time with my wife as possible – when I was a young detective, it was quite common for me to come out of a morning and go home the next morning. But in an average week there's probably not a great deal of time when you can say, 'Right, I'm at home tonight, feet up, switch the telephone off the hook.' In fact, you can't switch the telephone off the hook – you can never go anywhere without saying where you are. And as chief superintendent we get invited to all sorts of functions – there's one here, you see, to an Oriental evening. I'm also chairman of the Birkenhead centre of the St John Ambulance Association, and I was chairman of the Wallasey Sea Cadets; these are the sort of things one gets involved in through the police service, and it's an opportunity, if you like, to further police–public relations. When I'm at home I like to sit with a good book, light fiction, adventure – Forester, I've probably read most of his books. I come here and read law reports, so fiction is my therapy! (*Laughs*) There's also

514

do-it-yourself around the house obviously, in this day and age. Our children are our life. My son is head of the classics department at Rock Ferry School. My daughter also went to university; she took a degree in Spanish and is married to a Spaniard, an air controller in Palma, where she teaches *English* at King's College, a private school for all the moneyed people to send their kids to! Americans, Brazilians, Spanish, Dutch and Swiss – she has quite a problem.

And so has her father, who took over 'A' Division only a few weeks ago, and sees it first and foremost as 'a vast garage from eight o'clock in the morning until – a conservative guess – four o'clock in the morning', when the last clubgoers leave for home beyond its boundaries.

'I'm always optimistic,' he says, 'but that doesn't mean I'm a super-optimist. This division is a problem. I look upon it as a challenge. I think one of the first things I've got to tackle is an improvement in the relationship between us and the residents. That is of paramount importance.'

There is this attitude in 'A' Division: The bucks! They're not all bucks. There are a lot of bucks – nobody's going to deny that – but really this division's no different in that sense to many others in this force area, which have their fair share of bucks too. The youngsters come in, and they see only the seamy side. They haven't got the time to deal with the decent working-class type of person who is predominantly in this division. They haven't got the time to go walking round the streets and talking to them. So their experience is all too often a form of confrontation.

Is it right that probationers should start off in the city centre? The answer to that is Yes. I can't think of a better place to gain experience as a police officer – *provided* that experience is gained under the supervision of somebody with a little more kokum than they themselves have started with. All too often, they're straight from school, straight from university, without a *clue* as to how to deal with the public. There again, there's a problem: today officers are being promoted to the rank of sergeant and inspector far younger than was the case a decade ago. They themselves haven't always got the experience necessary to guide a youngster, and so, to use a favourite expression of mine, it's often a case of 'the blind leading the blind'. That escalates, comes up the line until it sits on this landing, and it's something a

515

senior officer is always conscious of: Is the supervision on the streets adequate ? At times I suspect No.

It seems likely, then, that you would share the reservations so many other police officers have about the cadet corps.

One of the basic requirements of a successful police officer is a knowledge of human nature. You get a cadet coming in straight from school, at the ripe old age of sixteen years, and he does develop a police mind, it's inevitable. So he doesn't get that knowledge of human nature until a few years later – if ever – because he doesn't understand the other person's problems. He's never been *part* of those problems, never worked in industry or commerce or whatever. I personally don't like the cadet system – I admit it, and I accept that. Having said that, there are some very good police officers who were cadets, and that tends to negate my argument. They could be exceptions to the rule! Be that as it may, the better laddie or lass usually is one who's knocked about a bit outside, and has learned a little about life. On balance they're more mature, more sensible.

Would it help to have the probationers spend only part of their time in 'A' Division ?

It's well worth considering rotating the probationers, so that they serve in an outside division as well. The difficulty is, of course, the mechanics of initiating that sort of a scheme at this time. When you look round the whole force area, you have difficulty finding experienced bobbies.

The 'progress report' is often blamed for creating negative attitudes.

They seem to have it in their minds that it's some kind of league table. Again, that's human nature. We try to point out that it isn't a league table, but we take note of your volume of work. Now, there's a very sound reason for that: when you take away the various courses and attachments they go on, we've got eighteen, twenty months in which to decide. Are they going to make efficient police officers ? When you stop and think about it, that isn't very long. One of the requirements of a police officer is an ability to enforce the law, and it's my experience that a lot of them have not, nor ever will have, the ability to enforce the law, because they allow their hearts to rule their brains – and this comes over loud and clear. I've had them throughout my service, where they want to go out and carry the uniform. You've seen them, lording it down Church Street, Lord Street, Dale Street, resplendent in a nice uniform, and that's all they want. That's not what *I* want! Nor what the Chief Constable wants!

516

Nor the public – it's not what they're paid for. One of the ways we *have* to judge them is by saying, 'Now get out and deal with the public – you're not persecuting the public, you're enforcing the law. You'll be learning how to deal with the public, and you'll be learning how to submit reports – the two most important things in a policeman's life, his bread and butter.'

None the less, probationers still feel it should take account of the 'good' they may do outside the context of law enforcement.

I suppose there are many things that they do we don't see on the appraisal. I'll quote you an example from my last division. One old lady lost her handbag, old widow, pensioner, lost everything she had, and one of my bobbies gave her a fiver. That never came out in any official report, but it came to me through the back door. The laddie or lassie who goes out of their way to help the public is noted. They may not think so, but in my experience it comes out in reports on that individual, or in a phone call to me – that quite often happens. It isn't always noted each time it happens, but this is a trait in that lad or lassie, and if they'll do it once they'll do it again. This is the lad we want, isn't it? The lad who is willing to help the public. (*Smiles*) When I say 'lad', I'm using it loosely, of course! I should say lads *and* lassies!

How do you view the integration of male and female officers?

One tries, since the Sex Discrimination Act and all the rest of it, to forget they are women – but you can't. In my last division, I saw the night parade one night, sent them out on the streets, and I looked at them. Every one was a youngster, and there was near enough fifty per cent of them girls. Now, one doesn't like this, but you've got to accept it. We tell them what's expected of them: we don't want them to go into a fight, they're to stand off and call for help, and nobody's going to think any the worse of them. There is a risk, and an unfair risk. Unfair to us as senior officers that they should be there, exposed to this. Many of the girls, in my experience, are better academically than the lads, but they're obviously not physically equipped to do the rough stuff on the streets. When I look around this division, there's not really anywhere you can say, 'That's quiet' – and send them there. I don't like it. I'm sure that somewhere, some day, some girl is going to be badly attacked by some idiot.

Talking of attacks, how do you view the Special Constabulary?

I know with a lot of police officers the Specials are considered to be the people who take the bread and butter out of their mouths.

I don't accept it. I like to look on the Specials as a body of responsible members of the public who are willing to assist the police in the discharge of their duties. That might sound trite, but it's the only way to start off. When you reflect on what they do, they are to be admired. They give up their own free time, they expose themselves to the same volume of assaults as a regular officer does – in fact, they get assaulted more often because they're fair game. Y'know, that Special flash or whatever, the difference in dress that the local bucks notice straight away. We'd be struggling without them. In my last division I tended, where possible, to mix them a bit; perhaps the regular officers were more amenable over there – I don't know. Quite often I'd put a Special with a regular, and I think they gained from that. It's something I'm going to check on.

This 'volume of assaults' you mentioned. . . .

I think a group having at least one officer off sick through assault or injury is only to be expected because of the nature of this division. The majority of these assaults are always of an evening or during the early hours of the morning, when the beer is in and the wit is out. And the vast majority of police officers assaulted are youngsters, who lack the experience in how to deal with a drunken person. It's a job with a high degree of risk. Without being emotional, a laddie or lassie can go out of this building at any time of the day, turn the corner and not know what's going to face them. I'm just stating a fact. You look at these lads and girls – they're only kids, aren't they? In every meaning of the word, they're kids. But they're going in and having a go! They're not sitting back and pleading youthfulness. They're doing the job they're paid for.

What do you feel about their pay?

We have spoken about the dangers – if you like – of having so many young people. But it has been my experience that the vast majority of them are full of enthusiasm for the job, they're willing to work extremely hard, and it's most rewarding and pleasant to see what effort they bring to it. The quality is certainly getting better – it may be because of the situation outside now in unemployment – and I'm quite happy with them by and large. They work damned hard; they also take an awful lot of chances; and when you think of their working conditions throughout the twenty-four hours, the weather, and what they come away with, compared to what people outside are earning, it is *ridiculous*.

Many officers feel the courts do not support them as they should. . . .

518

Sometimes the punishment is farcical in relation to the severity of the offence that was committed, and they naturally get a little uptight about that. You can only say, 'All right, again remember what you were taught; the punishment's got nothing to do with you' – but, y'know, that's very much tongue in cheek! We are only human when all is said and done.

And the new complaints system would appear to be having a very negative effect on their morale.

They're very exposed, they're very vulnerable and, again, they're very human. It's all well and good at the end of the day, when there's been an enquiry, for the chief superintendent to say to this laddie or lassie: 'No further action will be taken.' That laddie or lassie has been the subject of an enquiry, and has certainly been a very worried young person for a few weeks; I don't care what anybody says, that can have an effect on their minds and can affect them when dealing with the public in future. I'm a hardened hairy old policeman, so I could probably brush it off better than they would, but I never suffered from *this*. In my younger days, there was a complaints system, and even in those days you didn't like it, you were worried, even if you'd only been doing your job and had nothing to worry about. A complaint is just like an allegation of rape: it's easy to make, but quite often very hard to disprove.

Perhaps the greatest threat to morale lies in the quantity and quality of the equipment such as vehicles and so forth.

The number of vehicles we've got now is insufficient to actively efficiently cover this division. (*Smiles*) I *hate* to see police officers in police cars without their caps. It's not a good thing; it reflects adversely, and it suggests a lack of discipline. But all too often it's just because the bloody things are too small for a tall man! I feel sorry for the Chief because he knows the problem, but money is. . . . 'First aid' has become quite the general accepted level of policing, and that's wrong, just 'first aiding' something. But you take the average vehicle: it never stops; it just goes from one thing to another. What else can you do but 'first aid'?

'More men is the answer to my problems in a division like this,' says the chief superintendent, 'which contains every problem I would want to think about.' He doesn't think that increasing the civilian staff would necessarily be the answer – 'They'd be lost trying to do the collator's job, for example' – but is happy to entertain the thought of being helped by retired constables

519

and others, many of whom would be of his own generation. 'If the First Police Reserve were brought back, they'd probably be an asset to the operational force,' he says. 'They served a useful purpose in that they did many of the office jobs that require experience.'

'Experience' is another of his favourite expressions. 'I believe in interchange between CID and Uniform. When I was down at Scotland Yard on a course a few years ago, there were many who argued very strongly against it. But it gives a man a better understanding of another department's problems, and you get a better-balanced individual. I enjoyed CID work. I miss it. My wife doesn't! Let me say, as a practical man, it wasn't all work. Obviously quite a lot of it was you'd go round the pubs drinking and you'd be enjoying yourself. It was still part of your job, but essentially a pleasurable couple of hours, and a part of your day. Now, of course, they're paid for over-time and have to be a little more accountable. My purely personal view is it was a bad move – the detective duty allow-ance should have been increased instead, to compensate for working long hours. If there wasn't this overtime available, some of them today would not be working. You can see it in their attitude. Being a detective is a way of life. Even today, in this rank, I still get telephone calls from my informants, and I haven't been in the CID since 1969!'

The very year he was a chief inspector on the docks, and Mr Jones, an assistant Scout commissioner from the Isle of Man, made his mystifying disappearance.

The message is smoothed out on the blotter.

'Mr Jones is still recorded as a missing person at New Scotland Yard, you see,' says the chief superintendent, 'and every twelve months he's resurrected. After the car was found, the baby became mine and was investigated as a suspect mur-der. I got some information from an approved school, some-thing about a boy changing money, and I went there. I can't remember why, but the information was sufficient for me to say, 'Yes, this money belonged to Mr Jones.' I interviewed this boy and he named another boy. After a very, very long inter-

520

view, this other boy admitted that he had, with two others, attacked Jones in a toilet at the bottom of Brunswick Street. The other two were whipped in and, in the event, they coughed and all three were charged with robbery with violence. They pleaded guilty; they said they'd attacked him; they said they'd left him in the toilet – and, as far as they were concerned, that was the end of it. It's probably a fatal thing to say, but I was reasonably satisfied that was the truth. We searched every building and bomb site within a half-mile radius of the Pier Head – never found Mr Jones. Enquiries went on; we had sightings from all over Merseyside, all over the country – never found Mr Jones. What Scotland Yard want to know is: Are there any grounds for cancelling this circulation? There are none. I'm no further on than I was in 1969.' Then the chief superintendent sets the message aside with a slight smile and a twinkle in his eye. 'Oh, I *suspect* I know where he is. . . . There's a particular point of the story that's never been exposed.'

But it's plain that, like dead men, hardened hairy old detectives tell no tales, not when they haven't a single piece of hard evidence to support an otherwise immaculate hypothesis.

34

Old Chalky stirs on the back seat of the car, opens one eye and takes a look at the night sky, which is all he can see from that position.

'Mousehole?' he says.

'Oh, we're well past that,' chuckles the young jack at the wheel. 'We're on the Wirral, Chalky. Have yer home in no time.'

'Oh dear, oh dear,' sighs Chalky.

Eddie looks round at him. 'A'right? Like a window open?'

'Which is it now?' the young jack interrupts. 'Do I take the next left or what?'

'Aye, that's the one,' says Eddie.

'Stands the clock at five to three?'

'What's that, Chalky?'

Chalky closes his eyes again and laughs softly, clutching his stick to him. 'Stands the clock at five to three? And are there chip butties still for tea?'

Eddie and the driver exchange grins.

'Eddie, you're a helluva good fella.'

'Don't mention it, old son.'

'OK, now which house is it?' asks the driver.

'You,' says Chalky, 'you're a helluva good fella, too. Two hell'va good fellas. Both.'

Eddie touches the driver's arm. 'Right here, Mick. Just stop by the Morris Minor, and—'

'Good fellas,' slurs Chalky. 'Only thing is, yer haven't a fokkin' *clue* what I've been sayin', have yer? Not a—'

'Steady, old son, you're back now,' says Eddie, helping him out. 'Don't want to wake the missus, do you?'

'Oh, a terrible thing, that, terrible. You, you know how it is, Eddie, a fine, fine woman till 'er bottle goes. Shhhh!'

The driver nods and takes his other arm, and they start up the short path.

'Not a fokkin' clue,' sighs Chalky.

'Rupert Brooke,' says Eddie, winking at Mick. 'It always is, when our mate here's well away. No lights on, so you stand a fair chance, Chalky.' And they stop on the doormat.

'Fellas,' mumbles Chalky, turning to them, 'much obliged. Crackin' little evenin'.' Then he stares at them with great solemnity. 'If I should ever die,' he says, 'think only this of me, that there's some corner of a foreign field—'

Eddie laughs softly. 'C'mon, Chalky lad, get yer key out.'

And Chalky, after patting one pocket and then another, sighs his deepest sigh and says, 'Oh dear, oh dear. . . .'

35

Not five miles away, in a leafy suburban street of neat houses, Doug and Sue have been spending a quiet evening with Sue's brother, Paul, who has a farm in north Wales. Sue brings through the after-dinner coffee – for once, the meal was a marvellously leisurely affair – and picks up one or two things left lying about by the children. It is a very pleasant room, furnished in the best of taste, yet essentially a family room, warm and relaxed.

'I don't really think I bring the job home,' says Doug, a spare sensitive-looking man in his mid-thirties, who works as a detective in 'A' Division. 'Really I don't.'

The subject had been dropped at the dinner-table.

'You do,' says Sue, 'of course you do!' And she hands her brother his cup.

Doug frowns stubbornly. 'I don't think I do.'

'You've got this aura round you sometimes. You come in and I think: God! He's *evil* tonight! I can sense you've been with somebody hateful.'

'You're probably not aware of it,' says Paul, smiling across at him.

'The set of your mouth,' says Sue. 'The look in your eyes.'

Doug laughs.

Sue turns to her brother. 'He's perpetually frustrated here in the CID, in 'A' Division.'

'I wouldn't mind a smaller place in the CID,' concedes Doug, totally without conviction, 'where you could get your teeth into things. But if I thought I was going to be slung back on the beat, walking the streets of Gloucester or something, nice place as it is, I'd—'

'He needs a bad city,' Sue cuts across, smiling ruefully.

'Well, I need somewhere where there's work, yeah.'

'But do you know, Doug, what I fear most of all? That a lot of your attitude will rub off on our children.'

'My attitude is—'

'I've done night duty on my own in a great big barn of a place,' says Sue, handing him his cup, 'and I was never afraid to walk through it. But now I wouldn't like to walk through Liverpool on my own. You've instilled this awful fear in me. I loved the city when we lived in Cheshire!' Her laugh gets tangled.

'That's Cloud Cuckoo Land,' scoffs Doug.

'But it's lovely, isn't it? Don't you think a child's mind ought to be – I don't know what the word is....'

'Yes, it's lovely to be like that. But in eight years' time Wendy

523

will want to go to Liverpool to do some shopping, and she's walking up Church Street with a bag, and someone comes and belts her across the mouth and takes the bag. That's not very nice, is it?'

Paul glances at his sister.

'I know,' she says. 'But we're teaching them too much the opposite way. We're teaching them not to trust people until we know it's safe to trust them, and—'

'Well, didn't your father and mother teach you that?'

'No. Judge people on their own merit. You were right about that neighbour we once had, but that was instinct. Don't you think we should leave the children their instinct? You're giving them the bad side of people all the time.'

Doug shakes his head. 'I say, "Don't talk to men you don't know. Don't stop when you go to the post office." But I don't say to them, "Your Daddy's in court today because one man knocked another man down, so he's just sittin' there like a vegetable"!'

'The ideal', murmurs Paul, 'is to bring them up in such a place where it isn't absolutely essential for them to know these things at an early age.'

'Precisely,' agrees Sue. 'You know, I've become a cynic, haven't I? And I *hate* it, because it's contrary to my normal nature.'

Paul drains his cup.

'But, y'know, I'm not as bad as a lot of policemen,' Doug says defensively. 'I mean, I do take people at their face value in the main. You can get a lot more out of these baddies if you try and be friendly with them. I don't go out of my way to be abrasive with them, unless they're abrasive with me.'

'It's the environment again,' remarks Paul lightly. 'It's abrasive – they're abrasive.'

'OK, I tend to be a bit fascist about these bastids,' says Doug, 'but honestly. . . . OK, you can argue it's their environment, but you can't go on doing what they do, as far as I'm concerned. Thump someone by all means – if you've got to. But when it comes to stickin' a glass in someone's face, *they shouldn't breathe God's air*, as far as I'm concerned! That's not

524

a very nice thing to say, but I'm afraid that that's how I feel, because I've seen so many of the victims. Sue shouts at me when I go on like this but, I'm sorry, that's how I feel.'

Sue helps her brother to another cup.

'I can go a long way before I snap and start talking like this,' continues Doug, biting on his thumbnail. 'But it sickens me to see innocent victims, and I tend to place myself in their shoes. If I can lock these bastids up, great! I don't place myself in the bucks' shoes; perhaps that's wrong – perhaps that's my upbringing. Because, if I was in their bloody shoes, I'd get away from the bloody place! They go to sea – why can't they go down to Warwickshire or Worcester and get a job?'

'Do you know,' says Sue, 'you make absolutely no allowance – *this* is why I get so mad with you – you make no allowances at all for human failing. You think: All right, I'm not a university graduate, but I make a decent living and support my family. You make no allowance for the fella who didn't learn to read and write, who has no confidence in himself whatsoever, except when he's being violent.'

'Huh!'

Paul nods. 'It's completely different for us, isn't it? We've had proper education; we've not had to live in a filthy house in a filthy area and—'

'But what would *you* do if you lived in a filthy house in a filthy area?' challenges Doug, bristling.

'Well, a lot would depend on the way I'd been brought—'

'I'd go out and get a job!'

'You *think* you would,' says Sue, 'but take our life together. We've only got what we've got because we strove together. Because when I flagged you said, "We can't give up!" and when you wanted to give up I said, "I'm making the effort. Why can't you?" ' She laughs fondly. 'It's true, you know!'

Doug just shrugs.

'I mean, I looked after children in a residential nursery who'd been burnt by cigarette butts because they cried when their mother was makin' love to some fella for five pounds, and one little child was kept in a pram until she was four and her legs were all twisted up, and when she was hungry her mother

525

threw her a milk-bottle. They found the pram littered with milk-bottles and sodden papers. Now, you can't tell me that child stood a chance in life; it wasn't born like you, in a silver cage!' She pauses to join in the laughter. 'You were special. Your parents always protected you. With these it was always a smack round the ear and—'

'This lad,' says Doug, 'this lad I had, who was off doing Giro cheques down in Worcestershire, he said to me, "Oh, it's lovely down there!" He said what you've just said – "I'm sure it's the environment," he said. So I said, "Why don't you bugger off down to Worcester, then? Get yourself a job!" But they don't see it that way.'

Sue smiles. 'That's like putting you in a desert, and you think: Oh God, there's no cold-water tap! Where am I gonna get water from? Yet a Bedouin wouldn't think twice about being put in a desert, and he'd be frightened in a city, wouldn't he?'

'That's the same with me really,' remarks Paul, 'although I'm not such an extreme case.'

'But what you've got to think of', says Doug, 'is that these lads aren't idiots, y'know. They're very friendly sort of people, Liverpool people; it's just they've got this. . . .' He stops and stares down at the carpet, his expression pained, bewildered.

Sue turns to her brother. 'You see, I'd very much like Doug to move to either Devon or Cornwall and be a village policeman – a policeman in a nice environment. Y'know, he's done his time in Liverpool; if he does ten years in Liverpool, it'll knock half the best out of him.' She looks at Doug. 'And, before you get too much of a cynic, for God's sake *move*. Because the whole of the thirty-odd years you've got left on this world – '

'Oh God!'

' – will be coloured by what you've worked in. Every morning you go into another world.'

'That's why I prefer to live this side of the water.'

'But do you know, Paul, the children wanted to go to the pictures, and Doug said, "Oh, do you *really* want to go?" "Yes, Daddy, we've got to – we love *The Sound of Music*! We've got to go!" And they kept on harping about it. "Oh, all right, I'll

526

take you. . . ." So I said, "Why don't you enjoy taking the children out?" And he said, "Because it reminds me of work." We never go into Liverpool without him saying, "Oh God, it reminds me of work." You're depressed and miserable from the moment you enter that tunnel – I mean, I sense it, because I'm married to you.'

'Y'know, honestly . . .,' Doug begins, then turns his attention to Paul. 'You could go into Liverpool tonight for a nice little night out, and you could go into a club and get a glass in your face because you looked at someone the wrong way. Do you think he should walk free? That fella? Because I certainly don't!'

'But, then again,' Paul says mildly, 'I'm not likely to frequent that sort of nightclub.'

'You might do! You don't know Liverpool *at all*!'

Sue picks up some mending. 'I'm too much of a realist,' she says, turning a small pair of jeans inside out, 'and it's this awful realism that's killing my sense of enjoyment of life. It's dreadful.' Then she concentrates on threading her needle.

36

'I think some people,' remarks the Plain Clothes inspector, leaning against his car outside St Anne Street, and tamping down the tobacco in his pipe, 'that some people, whether they know it or not, feel bruised at the end of a day's duty here. You come up against a lot of violence – and not necessarily just physical violence all the time.'

The sudden flare of a match lights up those reputedly inscrutable features. 'Physical violence isn't nice. I've been in situations with hostile crowds, been in a few fights, and I can't stand violence meself, y'know, but you find you just sort of react according to the circumstances. I don't think there are many heroes in the police here, but very few have been done for cowardice!' The match-flame dips into the pipe-bowl. 'I don't like the idea of people round here beating the police up, but at least they fight back, if you know what I mean – they're

527

not a cowed subject people. They've got some spirit, generally speaking, and I find it extremely healthy and refreshing, really I do. I'm not sort of condoning – I mean, I'm the first one to conduct reprisals if a bobby gets badly beaten up, and I'll see the fellows concerned are as quickly rounded up as can be arranged – but at the same time it's an indication of the anti-police state that operates here. In that respect, I find it refreshing; people aren't afraid to give the policeman a bit of lip.' He smiles, and a second match gets the pipe drawing properly.

'But there's violence all around you, wherever you look, y'know. Look at the Piggeries up there. Look at the vandalism, the graffiti. Or look', and he points his pipe stem the other way, 'at that industrial complex over that waste ground like a blasted heath – y'know, the modern version of a blasted heath; an allegedly smokeless zone, and it's pumping out filth all day. Look in the faces of the people.' A glimmer of amusement returns. 'Y'know, these allegedly work-shy people, I think the phrase is, according to the capitalist press – although I'm not a particularly avid socialist. When you read about work-shy people and then look around here, at the places where these work-shy people live, they're pouring out of their houses at five and six in the morning, coughing and spluttering in bus queues. And when you look at the kids around here. . . .' A twist of tobacco smoke uncurls lazily to hang tranquil and fragrant in the still night air. 'Well, it's been the same here for years. Most other places have had an improvement in environment, if you like, but here time has stood still since late-Victorian times – other than in material things like colour telly. Virtually everyone with a colour telly! But you can't blame them, can you? It lifts them out of their world.'

He feels for his car keys. 'So a certain amount of alienation creeps in because of the nature of your work really – the violence and one thing and another attached to it. It's a tendency in big-city forces; you'll find the same thing in London, and it's virtually the exact opposite to the way county police officers have felt about the job. I think it's best described as the Eight-Hour Syndrome. Once you've done your eight, ten hours or whatever, you just want to forget about the job in

528

the main. You want to go home and be a normal member of society.' Then he smiles again, just enough to mark his awareness of a basic irony.

The thirty-nine-year-old inspector, Liverpool born and bred, but now living thirteen miles away at Formby, joined the police twenty years ago after three years as a cadet. 'Bit of a waste of time really, but very enjoyable. Then I started off on foot patrol and had a few rubs up against supervisory officers. I couldn't quite make the big jump from being a civilian, a normal member of society, to being a police officer, and I found it difficult to detect offences – if I saw a car going along with a torn wing, it was just a car going along the road, y'know. But eventually I made the jump, and that was *it*.'

The shattering time is those first twelve months of your service. This is when personalities alter – you can see them. I always remember a chap who came on a section I was in charge of, and he was a barber and what a smashing fellow. You know what barbers are like! 'Good morning, sir! You all right, sir? What can I do for you?' – and all the business. A really pleasant man, and I watched him change and he grew a bit more bitter, a bit harder. (*Laughs*) He was *believing* things people told him, y'know. If he stopped somebody with a car, and they said it was theirs, he'd sort of believe them. Now he doesn't believe people any more, which is sad in a way, because that fellow will never be the same again.

But it's necessary you do suspect people – that's the very nature of the job. What you've got to do after that is to put back the bit that was there before you came into the police – y'know, the bit when you didn't suspect everyone. The kids coming on have to find this out for themselves. All you can do is leave a little avenue open to allow them to find it out a bit sooner than they might have done, y'know. I never tire of telling them that the people around here aren't all like the ones who get involved in fights and this, that and the other; that they're smashing people, if you actually go into their houses. Some police officers, of course, a few – but a significant few – never find it out, but are convinced that everybody's a buck, everybody's a thief. (*Smiles*) Of course, they always agree with you – they *have* to agree with you! You're their sergeant or whatever, their inspector.

529

There are various milestones when you look back over your life – and you actually knew at the time they were significant, which is the amazing thing. After my probation, I went into Plain Clothes in a division that came pretty near the city centre, and it gave me my first taste of not being strictly supervised from outside.

'It also gave me my first insight into how we work really,' he says, 'my first lesson in that you can get more out of people by allowing them their head to a degree, and that they generally show more self-discipline and work harder by the very fact they're given more freedom.' He was posted again and again into Plain Clothes, alternating with uniformed street-patrolling, until he was promoted sergeant and went into Traffic, where he rode a motor-cycle for two years. 'But I found after a relatively short period that the only people you were dealing with were your constables. Occasionally, to relieve the boredom, if you like, you'd do people for speeding – other nasty things like that! – but it really became significant to me that I was missing out somewhere along the line. It wasn't at all like it had been – in Uniform or in Plain Clothes, you're dealing with people, literally communicating all the time.' So he applied to join the CID, an almost unprecedented move by a 'Traffic man' and a sergeant at that, but was finally accepted on probation. 'I got stuck in, working fourteen, sixteen hours of the day, doing what was most important in my opinion – and still is: dealing with crime. I did reasonably well, got commended and that, and eventually got posted as a detective sergeant.'

There was another milestone when I was in the CID that I knew was significant to me. We were doing what we called a 'duck', which was a search warrant under the local Corporation Act, and so it had a Liver bird at the top of it. (*Laughs*) They were always known as ducks: 'We've got a duck out on this, that or the other.' This duck was on this sort of mean working-class terraced house, a hovel that stank literally – almost a gas-mask job, but you get used to it. (*Smiles*) It's almost like ozone to you! And we went in.

Mum and Dad were out, and there were all these silly kids milling about: the lad we were after and – in descending order

530

of about an inch – the rest of the tribe. But it was all right, because the lad who'd been doing all these screwings, house-breakings and shopbreakings in the area was eighteen, y'see, and so we went hunting round for radios and gas-meter cash, loads of shillings. Typical for a very dirty house, the beds weren't made. There's always like a mattress on the floor, which is sort of stinking, and the sheets are always grey in colour and coiled like a snake. When they get into them at night, of course, they uncoil them and wrap them round themselves, and then, when they get up, it sort of coils down! (*Laughs*) And, as we were going round, one of the lads was going round before us.

He must have been about eleven or twelve, about fifth in line; he'd a raggy old grammar-school blazer on – we still had grammar schools then – and you could see there was a spark of intelligence in him. He was going round before us – not trying to hide anything, but trying to tidy the rooms up. He was ashamed, y'know, and things like that hit you. It was very sad in more ways than one. I always remember being very glad at the time that I wasn't a social worker, because what chance did that kid have? He *might* have made it out of those surroundings, but I'd be frightened to go and find out if he ever did.

The next turning-point came when he left the CID in 1969. 'I hardly saw my wife and kids as a detective – my wife brought up two of the lads through toddler stage virtually on her own, y'know. It eventually began to seep through to me, in no uncertain manner, that I was going to have to change my life-style!' And he gives an affectionate chuckle. 'We've three sons, actually: one nearly fifteen, another fellow of eleven, and a young lad who's just six.' He moved to 'B' Division as a uniformed inspector, and then to 'A' Division where, as Operations Inspector, he helped to organise the Queen's Jubilee Year visit to the city, before entering the Plain Clothes Section once again.

My wife was a nurse. They sort of work shifts, as we do, and by calling into Casualty you get to know the do's that are going. They have the same, very similar outlook – there's a great affinity there, inasmuch as we're both probably seeing much the same side of human nature, the bit under the surface. We tend to develop a sort of personality shorthand, as it were, and a bit of a shell. I mean, sometimes you've got to be abrupt and curt with people, otherwise you'd get *nowhere*, y'know! (*Laughs*) You've got to develop your social skills in a certain direction, and this leaves its stamp on you – more so than many other occupations. In fact, one thing you realise after a few years as a policeman is that most other people, generally speaking, don't know much about their fellow man. We've had to find out pretty quick to sort of survive in a place like this! It's an accelerated course in living. The effect it has depends on what your make-up is really, on how you tackle it personally. These kids seem to get the idea that everybody who isn't a policeman – or isn't obviously upper-class – is a buck. (*Smiles*) Which is a very dangerous frame of mind to get yourself into, because that means we're all bucks when the eight hours are over.

The Plain Clothes inspector starts up his car and noses out of the car-park. He enjoys game fishing in his spare time, and ties his own lures. He also reads a great deal and, chiefly to give his reading some direction, has started an Open University course, concentrating on the social sciences and computers.

'This is one of the most advanced cities, believe it or not, for council housing,' he says, turning towards the city centre. 'The flats over there, Gerard Gardens, with the statue of the worker with the helmet on, were modelled on the Viennese workers' flats. In fact, they're mentioned in *The Road to Wigan Pier* by George Orwell.'

The next change-over is coming up fairly soon now, but his night has really only just begun. Heading his list of clubs due for a visit is one where, rumour has it, under-age drinking is becoming the accepted thing, juveniles are being used in lewd acts, and pot-smoking isn't uncommon.

There's a very powerful lobby that's growing that says cannabis is less harmful than drink – and there's a lot of truth in that, y'know. I've read a few books myself on various experiments, and there's little doubt that, in the hands of anyone who possesses any character at all, they could control the habit. But you still get examples like this latest one with Piers Shore, who started off with cannabis when he was fifteen or sixteen, and now he's dead after a morphine injection, self-administered. You're always going to get people like that, and it's for people

532

like that – who're in their adolescent experimental stage, who haven't developed characterwise – that the sort of work we're doing is all about. Juveniles are our main concern. (*Shrugs*) There's a sense of futility in the work, in the sense that you know it's always going to go on. There'll always be prostitutes, there'll always be various other vices, because these are human things. But when you look at it in the long term – that is, longer than your own lifetime, if you like – then you've got to have some force like the police to suppress the more natural vices, before they can lead to even more serious incidents and wrongdoings.

The smoke from his pipe uncurls lazily to be buffeted, whipped away in a flurry. Out of habit, perhaps, the Plain Clothes inspector, in his dark suit, neat collar and tie, is driving with the window down.

37

'A' Division has a curious feel to it tonight; a buzz, an edginess, a hint of wild wicked things yet to come, and already blood lies spilled, dribbled, splashed down twenty-seven feet of a pavement on the South Sub. Lino knives, they say, did the damage, slashed lattice patterns into fleeing backs, filled the narrow street with screaming. A young couple caught up in it, they say, a young couple with kiddies, trapped between the doormen and an explosion of savagery in a nightclub, turned to run, turned away their strangers' faces.

'Funny old night for a Monday,' murmurs a bridewell patrol down in the Main Bridewell. 'Just don't know what you're goin' to get next, do yer?'

And the game goes on, the bloody great game with umpteen variations, and they're all out there – Jimmy the Beast, Nick the Blade and the Graduate – playing it within those invisible shorelines. A dark island of the mind with its neon-scribble, bare-bulb, fluorescent lights all a-twinkle, and slowly the game gathers momentum.

'Get this fella's number!' the drunken son roars into the seat of Inspector North's trousers.

ABOUT THE AUTHOR

James McClure was born in Johannesburg, South Africa, and grew up in Pietermaritzburg, the capital of Natal, where he worked as a commercial photographer and taught art, history, and English at his former preparatory school. Later, while working for three major newspapers in Natal, he became a specialist in crime and court stories. After emigrating to Great Britain he worked at the *Scottish Daily Mail.* In 1965 he became deputy editor of the Oxford Times Group of weekly papers, a post he held until 1974 when he resigned to devote more time to writing.

James McClure is most familiar to American readers for his novels, of which he has written six. He won the Crime Writers' Association's Silver Dagger Award for *Rogue Eagle,* and their Golden Dagger Award for *The Steam Pig.* His most recent novel is *The Sunday Hangman.*

Mr. McClure is now at work on a study of an American police precinct, which will parallel this book.